SO-AIN-062

◆

# When Football
# Was Football

◆

*by*
*Joe Ziemba*

**TRIUMPH**
**B O O K S**
CHICAGO

This book is available in quantity at special discounts for your group or organization. For further information, contact:

Triumph Books
601 South LaSalle Street
Chicago, Illinois 60605
(312) 939-3330
Fax (312) 663-3557

Printed in the United States of America

ISBN 1-57243-317-5

Jacket photos courtesy of the author

Book design and typesetting by Sue Knopf
Cover design by Eileen Wagner

# Contents

# *Acknowledgements*

As usual with a research effort of this type, there are many people to thank. Perhaps we should start with my father, a draft choice of the Chicago Cardinals in 1940. A knee injury in training camp that year curtailed his football career, but didn't stop him from inspiring and directing thousands of kids as a teacher and a coach over the next three decades. His brief flirtation with pro football after an All-American collegiate career prompted this endeavor and hopefully this work will be a fitting testimony to his inspiration, encouragement, and guidance. He deserves it.

The driving force behind this project (although he will never admit it) has been Mike Coffeen of Indianapolis, who has endured double-duty most of his life as both my cousin and friend. Mike has been the impetus—whether offering sound advice or providing encouragement, he was always there when needed.

But there are many more to thank as well. Pete Fierle of the Pro Football Hall of Fame in Canton, Ohio, was helpful from the start and was most cooperative in continually providing information and guidance on obscure early NFL topics; Greg Gladysiewski, Paul Jensen, and owner William Bidwill of the current Arizona Cardinals were very generous with their personal time and recollections; Pat O'Connor of the Green Bay Packers Hall of Fame; Bob Carroll and other fellow members of the Professional Football Researchers Association (PFRA), who shared a mountain of documents, addresses, etc. about the early days of professional football; many friends such as Tom Bresnahan, Mike Rizzutto, John Maher, Dick Reyburn, Bret Kelsey, Roger Plechaty, Tim Coffeen, John Fitzgerald, and Larry Fitzgerald, who provided information and encouragement. A special note of appreciation for his technical assistance must go to Dominic Pacyga, Chicago historian and author, Jeffry D. Wert, noted author of the Civil War and the American West, Ron Tomczak for his interpretations of some forgotten NFL offensive formations, Phil Bouzeous (formerly of the Cardinals' organization) for his many contacts and insights, and to Peter Willis of NFL Films, who uncovered and provided us with early Cardinals' game films.

Still, with all of the above resources, the key to unlocking the history of the Chicago Cardinals was pretty much unknown at the start of this project. Little was available on the Cardinals before 1920, including verification of when the team actually came into existence. For this information, which served to definitely establish the Cardinals as pro football's oldest team (dating to 1899), I relied heavily on the resources of the following institutions: the aforementioned Pro Football Hall of Fame; the Library of Congress; the Chicago Historical Society; the Special Collections Department of the Harold Washington Library in Chicago; the National Archives; the Office of the Illinois Secretary of State; the Cook County Circuit Court; the Governor's State University Library in University Park, Illinois; the Newberry Library in Chicago; the Chicago Board of Education Archives; the library at the University of Illinois at Chicago; the Hammond and Michigan City, Indiana public libraries; the public libraries in Coldwater, Michigan; Frankfort, Woodstock, Joliet, Decatur, Moline, Oak Lawn, Maywood, and Rock Island, Illinois; La Crosse, Wisconsin, and Lock Haven, Connecticut—all of which helped to sort out very specific details in the history of the Cardinals. We also must acknowledge the many former Cardinals players who cheerfully shared their experiences and thoughts—especially the two players who were both there at the start of the Cardinals' renaissance in 1940: Motts Tonelli and Marshall Goldberg. Both were invaluable in providing extensive insight and materials for this project. Thanks also to the inimitable Chet Bulger for a million laughs.

Aside from the players, there were wives, sons, and daughters of former Cardinals who kindly volunteered their help. In particular, Mrs. Phyllis Davidson, the widow of former Racine

Cardinal Donald Davidson, shared a warm spring afternoon in her home with some strangers from Chicago. Special insight was provided by Carol Judge and Patricia Needham, granddaughters of original Cardinals owner Chris O'Brien.

Special thanks to friends and colleagues such as Art Klawans, a former Chicago Cardinals season ticket holder; Molly Hinshaw, for her valuable editing skills; and especially to my children Joe and Angela Kim for patiently "living" with the Cardinals for the past several years. And there are others who offered encouragement, hope, and help. For this, I thank Inez Milsap, Jennifer Zimmerman, Michelle Dunbar, Mike Maloney, Tony Tubacki, Amanda Lyons, Patti Wilson, Florence Guhl, Geri Moore, Marion Doyle, Helen Such, Larry and Shirley Groskopf, and Marjorie Ziemba. Two special friends, the energetic Mary Geismann and Kristin Doll, did it all, from analyzing the focus of the project to compiling decades of team records. Hog farms in Ohio are celebrating.

Appreciation is extended to a former gridder named Dan Grant, who came upon this project and personally ensured that we would have a record of every single game the Cardinals have ever played.

Once the data was collected, the book itself became a reality because of the guidance of old friends Chuck Bennett, Phil Bianco, John Brazill, and George Folsolm. Near the completion of this work, the reading and editing services of Marge and Bill Schaaf and Rosemary Coffeen need to be acknowledged. However, none of this would be possible without the energetic and talented staff of Mitch Rogatz and Triumph Books, including the ever-patient Laura Moeller, Anne Schlitt, Heidi Hill, Karyn Viverito, and others. Noted football historian Richard Whittingham did a magnificent job of editing the manuscript for technical and historical accuracy.

Then there is a special note of thanks to Dick Dystrup, formerly the Mayor of Lockport, Illinois, who once gave a kid a chance. Sometimes, a crack in the door can provide a world of opportunity . . . and that opportunity is never forgotten.

Finally, there is my best friend, wife, and partner, Carol Lynn. Plucked out of a high school cafeteria in Evergreen Park, Illinois, too many years ago to remember, she nonetheless has withstood an unending barrage of basketball games, football research, and wacky publication ideas to so deservedly attain the sainthood status my father predicted for her many years ago. To her, I can only say "Thanks" . . . this is for you.

Joe Ziemba
August, 1999

# Foreword

## By Marshall Goldberg

When I heard that someone was writing a book about the history of the Chicago Cardinals, I thought, "It's about time!" Finally, the story of this historic team is being documented. For too long, the Chicago Cardinals were considered the "other" team in Chicago—until one cold day in 1947, when the Cardinals claimed the NFL championship and Chicago learned it had another championship pro football team.

The title of Joe Ziemba's *When Football Was Football* is extremely accurate. The game was different, the pay was different, and life was different. My journey with the Cardinals began in 1939 after my graduation from the University of Pittsburgh, and I was able to ride with the Cardinals as they made the trip from the bottom to the top of the NFL in just a few short years. That ride was a joy to take part in, and I shared it with my fine teammates, many of whom you will meet in the following pages.

Back in 1939, our last game at Pitt was history, I was graduating, and I didn't have any firm plans for employment. We had lived though a depression, but opportunities for employment were still scarce. I wondered what I would do for a living if I was forced to move back home to Elkins, West Virginia. Our teams at Pitt had been the talk of the college football world. We were national champs in 1936 and 1937 and won the Rose Bowl. I was fortunate to be named an All-American twice and finished as the runner-up for the Heisman Trophy in 1938. Under Coach Jock Sutherland, we felt we were on top of the world. We played in front of 70,000 loyal fans and the entire program was first-class.

After graduating from Pitt, the only job offer I received initially was to be a traveling weekly wrestler. That was not for me. Then one day, one of my fraternity brothers burst into the room and said, "Hey, Biggie . . . you've been drafted by the Chicago Cardinals of the National Football League!"

I replied, "I've never heard of them. Who are the Chicago Cardinals?" That was my introduction to the Chicago Cardinals and the NFL!

I finally received a call from Arch Wolfe, the business manager of the Cardinals. He invited me to visit the team in Chicago and I accepted. I drove to Chicago in the summer and soon learned it was a very noisy city! As we drove down Wabash Avenue looking for the Cardinals' headquarters, the infamous "el" train rumbled by overhead and scared the heck out of me.

The team shared office space with owner Charles Bidwill's other businesses, and I found myself comparing this cluttered situation with the "big time" atmosphere at Pitt. However, once I met Mr.Charles Bidwill, I was immediately impressed with his easygoing, pleasant personality. There was never a nicer man than Charlie Bidwill. He did everything for me and I cherished his friendship. After talking to Charlie, I decided to sign with the Cardinals and stay in Chicago. I played for the Cardinals from 1939 to 1948, except for two years in the military service.

While the NFL at the time might have been considered "small time" in relation to Pitt football, Charlie Bidwill was always "big time" in my eyes. He supported the NFL and helped both the Cardinals and the Bears survive some rough times. Football was not a business to him—he had other more profitable businesses to worry about. He was visible, but never interfered with the coaches, and he took a genuine interest in all of his players.

This book covers the Charlie Bidwills, the Paddy Driscolls, the Jim Thorpes, and the other pioneers of pro football who sacrificed and persevered so that the NFL could survive and blossom. When you think of the multi-million-dollar contracts of today, remember that we received $2 per day for meal money and that a contract worth $6,000 per year was considered exceptional. There were long train rides and difficult playing conditions, but we didn't mind . . . we wanted to be out there, playing both ways and rarely getting off the field!

*When Football Was Football* finally presents the opportunity to recognize the teams, characters, and personalities of the early NFL and the Chicago Cardinals, the NFL's oldest team. Those days may be gone, but with the arrival of this book, they will not be forgotten!

# Introduction
## By Pat Summerall

I was told when I was at training camp at the Chicago All-Star game that I'd been traded to the Cardinals, that they needed a kicker. I came on board, and we were working out at the University of Chicago before the season started. I noticed that the deserted stands looked strange, because they were covered in tar paper, and I realized—that's where they had begun the research for the development of the atomic bomb. And I thought, this can't be a very good start.

My impressions at the time, having played at a major college, were that the equipment the Cardinals were playing with was not necessarily of the latest issue. Things were not very well organized, but there were some good guys on the team: Johnny Olszewski was the fullback, a really friendly guy; Jim Root was the quarterback; Jack Jennings; Jack Simmons—just a bunch of great guys.

They had put us up in this hotel, the Blackstone Hotel down on the South Side. I'll never forget the South Side then—it was like a bunch of little neighborhoods. You walked down the street and everybody knew you, everybody walked their kids to school at the same time, shopped at the same grocery store—it was like a little community. But playing in Comiskey Park was different—it was a very depressed atmosphere. The biggest crowd we ever saw was, I'm sure, no bigger than fifteen or sixteen thousand. It was not how you'd visualize the NFL.

Our record that first year, in 1953, was 1-10-1; our only win was over the Bears at Wrigley Field. The rivalry between the Bears and the Cardinals was still very fierce at the time—we hated them. I had a friend who played for the Bears, Fred Williams, who I had known in college and had maintained a friendship with. But we were almost outcasts, because we were friends and we wore different jerseys.

The player limit was thirty-three, and then they cut it down to twenty-eight. You had to play everything—you had to play offense, you had to play defense, you had to be on the punting team, the extra point team. I was the kicker, so of course I had to kick the extra point field goal. You had to do everything if you wanted to keep your job.

I had second thoughts about even coming back to play after that first season, but we did get a little better the second year, and by 1955, Ollie Matson was back from the service, we had picked up a guy named Dave Mann, we had two good receivers, Don Stonesifer and Gern Nagler, who we acquired from the Browns, and our quarterback was McCann. So by 1955, we were respectable, and by 1956 we were actually pretty good. We were winning, we were getting better.

Then 1957 was a down year. A lot of us at that time began to feel we were in for a shake-up, that a lot of us wouldn't be back for the next season. They had hired Pop Ivy as head coach. In the off-season, after the change of coaches, I called Pop Ivy and asked him how I fit into the Cardinals' plan. He said I was a big part of it, that they had big plans for me. So I thought I'd have a job. Then the next thing I knew, I picked up a paper and read that I had been traded to the Giants.

I left before the 1958 season with a bitter taste, because I felt I had been lied to. But it turned out to be a great break.

I learned to appreciate the good things I didn't have when I was with the Cardinals, and it made me appreciate what pro football was going to be and was becoming. The thing I miss about those years were the outstanding players. Charley Trippi was still there when I came on; he was the last of the championship team. Ray Ramsey was there, too, but pretty much everyone else from the early years and the "Dream Team" was gone. Players like Matson, Olszewski, Jennings—they were great individual players.

Any time you're in a situation like that, when you all live together, you develop friendships that never vanish. Some of the greatest friendships I've ever had have been with the guys I played with, and some of us are still in contact. The years of football were pretty dismal, but the friendships were invaluable.

# ◆ Part One ◆

# ◆ 1 ◆

## In the Beginning:
## 1899 – 1902

*"It didn't matter if we made money.*
*We just wanted to play football!"*

CHRIS O'BRIEN,
ORIGINAL OWNER OF THE CHICAGO CARDINALS

### 52nd and Morgan Streets, Chicago
### October 15, 1899

No one seemed to notice the small man as he shuffled toward the vacant lot. His bright blue eyes blazed in the warm autumn sun as he gazed across the plain patch of land known as "The Woods" on Chicago's South Side. He was much like any other man in this neighborhood; a working man who took the hours when available in the Union Stockyards or searched for other means to make a living, whether it be digging ditches or helping construct one of the many new buildings in the area. He was a laborer by trade, and if he was not happy with that description, at least he was proud of it.

Some were afraid of him; some said that he was ill-tempered and stubborn. Others feared his tenacity and his might. But on this bright October morning, he was just another guy, a guy who had decided to watch his sons play some wacky new game called football.

At least "The Woods" offered some solace and respite from the noise and congestion of its huge stockyards neighbor a few blocks north. With his hands folded across his chest, the man tried to listen as a group of boys argued over something he couldn't distinguish, and then began to point in one direction and then another. The disagreement continued until one boy, now holding a rounded ball of some kind, emphatically pointed at a lonely tree nearby. He then turned quickly in the other direction and the others followed the movement of his arm as he singled out another tree at the opposite end of the lot. The decision was final, and the other boys nodded their heads in agreement and broke off into two different groups. One group kept the funny-looking ball and moved together, while the other turned and walked away. When the latter group reached its destination, the two clumps of young men suddenly spread out, and faced each other as if on cue.

The man watched as his older son dropped the ball from up around his hip and kicked the ball toward the other group of boys. The ball soared to the sky, then caromed off the earth once, and bounced over to one of the boys furthest behind the others. He protected it with his arms, moved ahead a few steps, and waited as his teammates retreated, then gathered around him. He scooted in behind a wall of boys, grabbed the belt loop of the *fellow in front of him, and the whole mass locked together and surged forward. By this time, the team that had kicked the ball was swarming downfield, searching for the boy lugging the ball. The first to reach the pile carefully measured his steps and then attempted to dive over the wall.*

*His body was rejected by those in the mass and quickly tossed aside. But others were now throwing their bodies at the wall, using their legs and shoulders to tangle the opposition. Despite the ferocious attack, none of the participants wore any equipment to protect their heads, or for that matter, any other part of their bodies. The front of the moving wall staggered, then fell. The attackers clamored over their crumpled foes and stampeded towards the youth still holding the ball. He looked wildly for a place to turn, but was blocked in by his own companions. Suddenly he was hit simultaneously from two sides and struggled to keep his feet as another member of the enemy crawled through the debris to pin his legs together. As his motion slowed, he began to falter and reached out with one arm to break the fall. Surprisingly, once he hit the earth, he managed to wiggle free and inched forward on the ground.*

*Big mistake . . . Another invader noted the slight movement, flew through the air, elbows first, and landed squarely on the shoulder blades of the ball carrier. He winced, gasped, and shouted, "Down!" At that precise moment, two older men quickly moved in, separated all involved parties, and placed the ball on the ground where the carrier's progress had ceased. The game was on.*

*Still, no one noticed the quiet man on the corner as he viewed the game with interest. "So this is football," he thought to himself and shrugged. He rubbed the crevice on his otherwise handsome face and laughed as his youngest son, Chris, just a week or so past his eighteenth birthday, once again attempted to throw his slight body over the top of the pile. It didn't appear that his skinny son would be long for the physical aspects of this new sport. Patrick, on the other hand and two years older, seemed to enjoy knocking people down and kicking the ball.*

*The wind floating in from Lake Michigan shifted suddenly and brought a wrinkle to the man's face. The slight breeze now carried with it the reminder that the stockyard pens were just a few blocks away. The sticky aroma quickly engulfed the area, but failed to stop the action. They were accustomed to it; the stench was just a part of life as were the sun and the moon. You would just hope that on particularly bad days, the wind would push this annoying reminder in another direction.*

*By now a handful of people had gathered on 52nd Street. A few cheered on their team of choice, whether it be the Shermans from over on Racine Avenue, or the Morgans, who named themselves after their home street. The Morgans, paced by brothers Chris and Pat O'Brien, were excited about playing in their first game of the new season and it soon became apparent that they would have too much size, speed, and stamina for the neighboring Shermans . . .*

*A brief cheer erupted as Pat O'Brien crossed the imaginary boundary extending from a tree that had served valiantly as the goal line for this game. His father smiled.*

• • •

Perhaps the rare photos from 1899 tell the story best . . . Odd, eerie images of young men with wild eyes . . . and ears, noses, and chins stretching out in every different direction except the one in which God originally intended. They were football players, back *when football was football.*

They were young, fearless warriors and probably just a little bit crazy. They embraced a game that was only slightly less dangerous than war itself and eagerly raced to defend the honor of their streets, neighborhoods, and nationalities on the gridiron. With woeful medical attention, weary equipment, and little common sense, they pioneered the professional game of football in the Chicago area over one hundred years ago. Each Sunday afternoon, a local football game could easily be found on almost any vacant lot in the city of Chicago. "Prairie football" (named for the usual location of the competition) had suddenly won a unique popularity in Chicago, and although it was horribly disorganized, fans were attracted to this strange competition, in which rules were minimal and legal violence was rampant. There was enough of an attraction to draw some complaints from the locals on Sunday mornings, according to the *Chicago South Side Daily Sun* (hereafter known as the *Sun*) on October 2, 1897:

> *Complaint was lodged with the Englewood police regarding the Sunday ball games on a prairie near 61st and Centre. The enthusiasm of the crowd of 500 or more interferes greatly with religious worship. The police promised to apply corrective measures.*

"Prairie football," wrote Rocky Wolfe in 1932 in the *Chicago Visitor,* "played before the national league was organized, corresponded to the roughneck days of baseball, which was before any particular distinction was made between the sports classified today as pugilism, larceny, manslaughter, incitation with intent to riot, and lynching. All came under the prairie football heading."

Backed by the vocal support of neighbors who followed their heroes to each game on horse-drawn wagons, the players engaged their rivals in deadly combat—often on a field surrounded by a sturdy rope in order to keep the more vociferous fans away from the players themselves. With the passing game yet to be discovered, football as played in 1899 emphasized violent line "plunges," sneaky end runs, and an occasional off-tackle effort. The players' heads were unprotected by helmets. Thin padding, torn jerseys, and a rare nose guard device were the only items protecting the athletes a century ago.

It was a tough, dirty, dangerous game.

Football in the late nineteenth century was completely different from the polished and spectator-friendly entertainment package that it is today. The rules were different . . . the scoring was different . . . and the ball itself was different.

Games on the streets of Chicago were played between swiftly organized teams which rallied around the spirit of their individual neighborhoods, clubs, or nationalities. The competition was generally scheduled in a haphazard fashion, often with just a few days notice before the game was to be played. Because of the then stringent rules limiting blocking by the offense, and with the passing game just a rumor because of a bulky, round ball, high-scoring results were usually out of the question.

The game of football itself was scorned by educators, criticized by physicians, and feared by parents. But most importantly, without the protection of adequate equipment or free substitutions, the game itself was downright nasty.

Each play began with a violent crashing of human body upon body. Heads, arms, and elbows were the weapons of necessity. Injuries were frequent, medical care was inadequate, and even death was a regular, if unwelcome, visitor from injuries which would not be considered life-threatening today. On-field disputes frequently became shoving and punching matches. If the referee was drawn into such a fracas, it was not unusual for him to begin throwing punches as well, in order to maintain order. It was a wild game in the 1890s——one that would not suit to alter itself until some massive rules changes were initiated in 1905.

Football in Chicago in the early 1890s was most visibly represented by the University of Chicago and the Chicago Athletic Association (C.A.A.). Both teams played what might be considered a "major college" schedule with the C.A.A. roaming the land to battle the likes of Harvard and Yale—both among the nation's elite teams at the time. The University of Chicago, under legendary coach Amos Alonzo Stagg, was feared nationally, with a record of 9-2 in 1898 and 12-0-2 in 1899.

Current powers Notre Dame and Northwestern also fielded squads, but played a less difficult schedule. For example, both universities played Chicago's Englewood High School during the 1899 season, with Northwestern prevailing 29-0 and the Irish losing by the score of 29-5.

## *No Throttling, Hacking, Or Striking*

A major difference in the game nearly one hundred years ago was in the scoring. A touchdown was worth just five points, but the extra point could be added for one more score. A dropkick (field goal) was also worth five points in 1899, although as *Spalding's Official Foot Ball Guide* noted in 1899: "A drop kick, if successful, counts 5 points, but is, of course, even if attempted, by no means sure of resulting successfully." A safety counted for two points.

The rules of the game have changed dramatically since that time and have certainly unlocked the grand offensive schemes which have fortified the sport's popularity. But in 1899, coaching was prohibited and passing was only allowed behind the line of scrimmage. If it was "thrown, passed or batted towards the opponent's goal," according to the *Spalding's Guide,* the ball was immediately awarded to the opposition at the place of the infraction. While a team only needed to gain five yards for a first down, the offense was given just three downs to achieve those five yards. In addition, blockers were allowed to obstruct the defense with their bodies only; the use of hands or arms for blocking purposes was forbidden. Finally, once the ball was snapped, the first back to receive the snap could not run with it unless "he has regained it after it has been passed to and has touched another player."

So, picture if you will, a game of football without forward passing and often confined by the awkward placement of the ball at the exact spot of the tackle. If the ball was down five yards from the sideline, then that was precisely where the referee would initiate the next offensive play. It was not until years later that the game absorbed the sensible addition of hashmarks.

The offense ran the ball on every play, and if acceptable advances were not ensured, the team would likely punt or "quick kick" on the first or second down in order to place its opponent in a more difficult offensive predicament. The plodding ground game rarely generated any excitement except when the aptly named "Wedge" attack was used, especially on kick returns (kickoffs were not part of the game until 1894). In this formation, the offensive players would form a "V" by latching on to the trousers of the teammates in front and then rumbling down the field, with the ball carrier protected within the "V" as the formation smashed and rolled over the opposition. The defense needed to be equally as creative in order to stop this rugged pile driver.

Another unusual twist was that the receiver on the kickoff could elect to either return the ball or punt it right back to the opposition as part of the play. The best offense in those days was, indeed, a good defense. The skimpy offensive arsenal simply seemed designed to patiently plow ahead for any minimal advantage that could result from the numerous field position exchanges throughout the contest. It was better, it seemed, to wait for that one key error by the opposition in an era when more than one touchdown by a team in a game might be considered an offensive explosion. Along this vein, football critic Harry Beecher advised football teams in 1898 to pursue field position:

> *If your opponents are steadily coming down in your territory, rally your forces and get the ball if possible, and then kick it out of danger. It saves your men and discourages your opponents, and interests the spectators.*

If the offense was extremely nervous about handing the ball over too near its own goal line, another option was available, according to the *Spalding's Official Foot Ball Guide:*

> *Of course they will naturally endeavor, by running or kicking, to, if possible, free themselves from the unpleasant situation that menaces them. Sometimes, however, this becomes impossible, and there is a provision in the rules which gives them an opportunity of relief, at a sacrifice it is true, but scoring less against them than if their opponents should regain possession of the ball and make a touchdown or a (field) goal. A player may at any time kick, pass or carry the ball across his own goal line, and there touch it down for a safety. This, while it scores two points for his opponents, gives his side the privilege of bringing the ball out to the twenty-five yard line . . . and then taking a kick-out, performed like kick-off or any other free kick, but it can be a drop kick, a place kick or a punt.*

Playing on an elongated field (330 feet by 160 feet) enclosed by a rope or fence, there was plenty of room for the offense to operate. Unfortunately, with the rules hindering both blocking and passing, it was extremely difficult to move the ball (which resembled a leather pumpkin) anyway.

The ball would be put into play by snapping it back with either the hand or the foot. Typically, there would be seven men on the line, including the snapper, a quarterback who stood just behind the line, two halfbacks who were placed several yards behind the quarterback, and a fullback (sometimes called a goal-tend) who was at least a dozen yards behind the halfbacks. This stretched-out formation promoted the use of numerous lateral tosses between the backs as they approached the line; but, with the defense charging in virtually unscathed due to the blocking rules, it was often more sensible for the runner to punt the ball away rather than risk a huge loss or possible fumble.

Although referees were careful to police piling on, the runner who was tackled on each play was encouraged to shout out "Down!" so that the referee could officially conclude the play. Despite the rigorous and tiring action, the rules warned that a player who had been replaced once by a substitute could not return to the game. The rules also stated that there "should be no unnecessary roughness, throttling, hacking or striking with a closed fist." Tripping or tackling below the knees was also prohibited.

## *Whisky Jug Carried By The Chicago Team*

The types of teams varied widely near the close of the nineteenth century in Chicago. The metropolitan newspapers gushed over the feats of the distant major collegiate teams such as Harvard, Yale, and Princeton, while not quite neglecting the local grid power at the University of Chicago on the South Side. As noted, the Chicago Athletic Association (C.A.A.) also fielded a rugged club, but endured constant whispers about its alleged use of "professionals" who were apparently provided "expense" money when playing football for the associations. In fact, the man generally recognized as the game's first professional, William "Pudge" Heffelfinger, quit his railroad job in Omaha to play for the C.A.A. for "expenses" in 1892. Heffelfinger, a native of Minnesota, was an All-American guard at Yale from 1889 to 1891. His fearless, manic style of play was a favorite of early fans who enjoyed watching him fly through the air to batter the opponent's wedge with his own body. As such, a dominant player like Heffelfinger would be a prized addition to any local club that might wish to increase its gate as well as its odds in any side wagers with its opponent.

While on a six-game tour with the C.A.A., Heffelfinger was approached about playing in a game for the Allegheny Athletic Association in Pennsylvania on November 12. He agreed to take the field against the Pittsburgh Athletic Club for a princely sum of $500, the first documented "play for pay" football contract, according to the Pro Football Hall of Fame. Although the rules of the Amateur Athletic Union (A.A.U.) at the time allowed expense reimbursement, that still did not dissuade some universities from refusing to play any such association team. Heffelfinger, of course, received much more than expense money from his newfound team.

The C.A.A. openly courted postgraduate players in an effort to sustain a strong football team. With dues per member at a staggering $180 per year in 1894 alone, the C.A.A. generated a substantial amount of income for that time, although the construction of a new headquarters building in 1895 left the organization with a financial challenge in order to retire the debt.

In 1898, the C.A.A. roster included former Wesleyan player J. Weibly (Class of '95) and University of Pennsylvania grad Jake Camp. As it prepared for its big game against Harvard, the C.A.A. scheduled local games against the unfortunate Chicago Manual prep team and the Commercial Athletic Club of South Bend, Indiana. Still, the distrust for anything even remotely "professional" lingered, or as the *New York Sun* speculated: "It is reported that the crack Chicago Athletic Association eleven will have several salaried stars this fall who will figure on the eastern tour of the eleven." Although Harvard belted the C.A.A. 39-0, the reputation of the club team was stung when the *Chicago Tribune* implied that the C.A.A. players did a little "belting" of a different kind during that game:

*The one thing if anything in the game today that will go down in history is the whisky jug carried by the Chicago team. After each play the men were revived by means of this mysterious affair, and each time the crowd howled with delight. It was said upon investigation that the jug contained nothing but pure water, but the pleased expression on the face of the (player) as he allowed the fluid to guzzle down his throat makes most Harvard men think that the Chicago training rules are not quite as strict as those in old Cambridge.*

The University of Illinois went so far as to issue a press release detailing why its team would not schedule games against athletic club opponents:

*Our efforts for the purification of college athletics would be seriously interfered with if games with athletic clubs were permitted again. Moreover, there is no need for such games for purposes of practice. Athletic games are valuable only so far as they have an educational effect. Games with athletic clubs, over which the authorities have no control, would be likely to cause a degeneration in athletic ethics.*

In 1898, Northwestern earned the ire of other universities by scheduling a game against the Chicago Athletic Association. In order to deflect anticipated criticism or the possibility of being ostracized, Northwestern played the game in secrecy, so staunch was the prevalent distrust of any type of postgraduate football at the time. Even future President Theodore Roosevelt chimed in with his opinions about the perceived professional in an article he penned for *Harper's Weekly* in 1893:

*It should be distinctly understood among the academies and the colleges that no team will have anything to do with another team upon which professionals are employed.*

To suggest that professional football was treated with utter disdain by certain segments of the academic population would not be inaccurate. In Chicago, the Rush Medical College abruptly canceled its game with the Physicians and Surgeons team when the Rush Faculty Committee on Student Organization and Athletics surmised in the *Chicago Daily News* that "The P. and S. team cannot be considered in the ranks of amateurs."

## *Football Is A Boy-Killing, Gladiatorial Sport*

High school competition was also expanding in Chicago with results being noted by the press as early as 1885. However, the limited number of teams often forced the youths to play against older competition. In 1889, four Chicago high schools banded together to form the Cook County Football League. Despite growing opposition to the sport by faculty and administrators, the Cook County League quickly added several more schools, with the Englewood and Hyde Park High Schools dominating the competition over the next decade. Typical of the adult anti-football frenzy in Chicago was this comment attributed to Shaile Matthewsey, Director of the Chicago School of Divinity:

*Football is a social obsession. It is a boy-killing, education prostituting, gladiatorial sport . . . requiring the services of a physician, the maintenance of a hospital, and the celebration of funerals.*

By the fall of 1898, the Spanish American War was winding down, and the growth of local football was escalating in Chicago. Once again, Englewood and Hyde Park were the elite teams of the high school circles. When both undefeated teams met in October (Englewood won 27-0), extensive coverage was given by the local media and a near riot broke out in the stands.

In October of 1898, the faculty of Evanston High School disbanded its football team on the premise that "the scholarship of the team was far lower than it ought to be." While there was clearly a growing interest in football, there was still a dominant opposition to it regarding football's proper locale in educational institutions.

In Chicago, club teams such as the Garfield Athletic Club, the Young Men's Lyceums, the Schleys, and Eggleston battled, while a team called the Yales claimed the state 135-pound championship by defeating the St. Charles Athletic Club 12-0, ignoring the fact that there was no championship criteria in place. Early non-academic football teams usually advertised to play other teams with a similar "average weight" (e.g. 135 lbs.) per player. There were no formal criteria in place governing the accuracy of the "average" weight per player, but common sense apparently played a prominent role in scheduling opponents during this rugged era.

Business and industry also joined in the fun by sponsoring teams representing meat packers and railroads, among others. Both the Sears Roebuck and Marshall Field retailers sponsored teams in order to provide leisure activity for their employees. However, care was taken so that games and practices would not overly interfere with the attendance and job performance of the worker-player. This made for some interesting game pairings. For example, in 1899, the Marshall Field & Co. team defeated the Chicago Manual High School team 11-0.

Perhaps the most popular, if not the most unsung, type of football team was the neighborhood—or "prairie"—team. These teams, composed of youths from a certain street, block, or section of the city, would align themselves in impromptu games against other neighborhood forces. They would represent not only their own street or neighborhood, but often a specific nationality. This was important in the local culture, which often judged individuals by the sound of their surname rather than their character, as noted in this classified ad which appeared in the *Chicago Daily News* in 1899: "Butcher wanted. Scandinavian or German preferred."

However, for the "prairie" teams, whether they were representing their neighborhood, their occupation, or their nationality, it was not uncommon to borrow the name of a certain street as the team name. Hence, teams with names like the Peorias, the Princetons, the Wallaces, and the Morgans, all of which adopted the name of a street on the South Side of Chicago. As one leaves the current White Sox Park on 35th Street in Chicago and travels west, the name of just about every street from Wallace to Ashland was once used as a football team name at some time in the distant past.

## Chicago's Oldest Professional Team

From the chaotic conditions on the South Side rose the Chicago (then St. Louis, now Arizona) Cardinals, the oldest team in professional football. There has always been some confusion as to when the Cardinals actually began playing. This is due primarily to the lack of extant records from the team's historical early days. As such, the surviving paper trail has become quite meager.

For example, the *Arizona Cardinals Media Guide* traces the team's beginnings to 1898, as does the Pro Football Hall of Fame. According to the Cardinals' yearly *Media Guide,* the team follows its roots to 1898:

> *Founded in 1898, the team began as a neighborhood group which gathered to play football in a predominantly Irish area of Chicago's south side, playing under the name Morgan Athletic Club.*

*The History of Professional Football* by Harold Claassen claims that 1899 was the year of the football birth, while *Sport Magazine* agreed with the 1899 date in its January, 1955, issue that speculated on the history of pro football. One of the earliest local mentions in Chicago regarding the inauguration of the team appeared in the 1937 edition of *The Chicago Recreation Survey,* which noted:

> *Records indicate that the first football games regarded as professional were played by the Racine Cardinals of 1899. This team has survived throughout a varied career, and exists today as the Chicago Cardinals . . .*

In 1960, the *Chicago Tribune* published a series delineating the history of the NFL, but the articles ignored the very early history of the club by stating:

> *The Cardinals were Chicago's oldest professional football team, if not its most successful. Their history dates back from 1916, when Chris O'Brien, a 34 year old south side plumber, organized a semi-pro team to play in the vicinity of 61st Street and Racine Avenue. Because of its neighborhood affiliation, O'Brien's team became the Racine Cardinals.*

Still another book, *The Story of Pro Football,* favored 1899 as follows:

> *The Chicago Cardinals haven't enjoyed too many moments in the spotlight, but in the matter of longevity no team in professional football can compare with them. They had their inception back in 1899 and have been active continuously ever since. Chris O'Brien and his brother Pat organized them as a neighborhood team on Chicago's southwest side and they first were known as Morgan A.C.*

While the exact birth date of the Cardinals is not known, in reality, the great grand-daddy of today's Arizona Cardinals was a team simply called the Morgan Athletic Association. Initiated in 1899 by one Thomas Clancy, along with brothers Pat and Chris O'Brien, the Morgans organized themselves and began playing other neighborhood teams in the outskirts of the infamous Chicago stockyards. Composed almost entirely of players of Irish descent, the Morgan A.A. grabbed its name from Morgan

Street where the O'Brien brothers resided. Located just west of the current Dan Ryan Expressway, the street is named after nineteenth century Chicago landowner and developer Thomas Morgan. While the Morgan Athletic Association might have been called a "club" team, it was unlike the more auspicious Chicago Athletic Association, which boasted an impressive headquarters, elite members, and various athletic and social activities. The Morgan Athletic Association was simply a football team comprised of young men, but the more formal sounding "Athletic Association" tag provided the players with a little more respect, at least in their own minds.

These types of loosely structured organizations were common in the Chicago area at the time, according to author Steven Riess in his book *City Games: The Evolution of an Urban Society and the Rise of Sports*:

> *Social and athletic clubs first gained popularity around the turn of the century in predominantly Irish sections of cities like Chicago and were later copied by other ethnic groups. The initiative in organizing a club was usually taken by an outside agent, like a politician, saloon keeper or youth worker . . .*

When evaluating the history of the Cardinals, it is critical to establish the link between original Chicago Cardinals' team corporate owner Chris O'Brien and the earlier versions of the club. O'Brien was indeed part of the archetypal Morgan Athletic Association and then anchored several versions of the original squad until he ultimately sold the team—then known as the Chicago Cardinals—in 1929. O'Brien savored several roles with the team throughout the years, including player, coach, manager, owner, promoter, and NFL pioneer. Yet it all "officially" started for O'Brien and the Cardinals in 1899, when the eighteen-year-old athlete trotted onto the field on a warm October afternoon to battle the neighboring Shermans. The team would survive two world wars, an influenza epidemic, a depression, rival professional leagues, television squabbles, franchise movements, and even instant replay. The goal, however, on that sunny Sunday in 1899, was not only to triumph over the Shermans, but also to hope that the infamous aroma from the neighboring Union Stockyards would be drifting in the opposite direction.

## *Another Wave Of Fetid Odors Has Engulfed Them*

Every resident on Morgan Street lived on a daily basis with the aromatic intrusion of the nearby stockyards. In 1899, there were several significant outbreaks of the obnoxious odors which were even more annoying than usual. The *Chicago Daily News* reported:

> *Almost before the people of Chicago living north of the Stock-yards had recovered from the last visit of the Bridgeport stench another wave of fetid odors has engulfed them. It came early yesterday morning on the south wind. Some of the victims were awakened . . . shut their windows and tried, with ill-success, to sleep till day light. During all the day, indoors or out, they suffered from inhaling the nauseating smells. It was impossible to get away from them.*

In this environment just north of the stockyards, the O'Brien brothers resided with their parents, Patrick and Bridget Clarkin O'Brien, at 3150 South Morgan Street. Patrick had emigrated from the Parish of Bohermeen in the County of Meath in Ireland in 1882 and was naturalized on November 21, 1882. Bridget, born on May 18, 1847, was four years older than her husband, but apparently remained in Ireland with her three young sons while her husband sought employment in the United States. Patrick survived the Battle of Remolino in Mexico and served the Fourth Cavalry with valor until his discharge on August 10, 1876. He returned to Ireland and married Bridget on February 4, 1877.

While still in Ireland, Patrick and his bride began their family and welcomed three sons: Thomas (December 15, 1878), Patrick (December 4, 1879), and Christopher (October 3, 1881). Little did the elder O'Brien realize that his two youngest sons would be the cornerstone for the oldest team in today's National Football League and that Chris would be one of the founding fathers of the NFL itself in 1920. But back then, who cared about football?

## *The Game Was Very Monotonous*

The Morgans were not the first team in their part of town. One of the more ambitious teams was the Garfield Athletic Club, which hired a coach ("Henry of university fame" according to a local newspaper), and talked of traveling east for a series of games against unnamed opponents. The Garfields' roster included a sturdy young man at left guard by the name of Frank Ragen, who would later become a part of the early Morgans (albeit briefly) and one of the more infamous names on the South Side of Chicago. Ragen eventually climbed up the local political ladder and into the role of Cook County Commissioner, where his youthful followers became known as "Ragen's Colts." The Colts became an intimidating street gang that enforced its own type of ethics in the neighborhoods near the stockyards and certainly was most helpful in assisting Ragen achieve his political objectives. Other teams in the area went by the names of the Dearborns, Schleys, and Palmettos. It was an unusual collection of teams, since the rules at the time did not object to any limitations on weight or age. As such, untested teenagers might tangle with salty stockyard workers and students might clash with butchers.

Into this mix sprang the Morgan Athletic Association, which opened its 1899 season on Sunday, October 15, against the Shermans. This would be the first game traceable to the modern day Arizona Cardinals, and despite its unknown historical importance at the time, the Morgan A.A. showed no mercy on its opponents and walloped the Shermans 29-0. The following sports report appeared in the *Sun* and represents the first media coverage of a Morgans-Cardinals game:

> *The Morgan A.A. football team defeated the Shermans in a one-sided game by a score of 29-0. The game was very monotonous on account of the playing of the Shermans, who were unable to cope with the center rush or end runs of the Morgans. The features of this game were the punting of Green, the ground gaining of Kendrick, Ward, P. O'Brien and Kennedy of the Morgans and a phenomenal run of 15 yards by Corcoran of the Shermans.*

The teams battled through two twenty-five-minute halves in a game that was held at 52nd and Morgan. This vacant plot, known locally as "The Woods," became the team's home field for the first few years of its existence. Chris O'Brien, the man most closely associated with the first thirty years of the franchise, played the entire game at left end.

The lineup for the very first game played by the Morgans consisted of the following:

| | | | |
|---|---|---|---|
| LEC | O'Brien | REF | Kendrick |
| LTT | Clancy | LHW | Ward/R. Baker |
| LGK | Wimmerskirts | QBW | Daily |
| CP | O'Brien | RHC | Green |
| RGM | Breen | FBR | Kennedy |
| RTF | Tate | | |

Much of the above roster stayed together over the next few years of "prairie football." It is interesting to note that Pat O'Brien was entrenched as the center while his younger brother Chris was situated at the left end position. Later in their careers, both brothers would be in the backfield—although Chris would continue playing on sandlot teams, and would still be playing tackle almost twenty years later.

## If A Man Plays Low, He Never Needs A Nose Guard

The popularity of football also was catching on with local retailers. At the Fair Store on State and Adams, an interested player could purchase a pair of football pants for just 49¢—"made of 6 oz. Duck, strongly sewed and well-padded. Worth $1," extolled the Fair's advertisement. Fully quilted pants went for 98¢ while the new player could procure a football jacket for a mere 38¢. Around the corner at State and Jackson, The Hub department store utilized a large illustration of a football player with heavy, matted hair to entice readers to peruse its ad. The catalog house of A. G. Spalding & Bros. recognized the differences in skill and competition levels in the game and offered the "University," the "Club Special," and the "Amateur Special" types of football shoes. The "Amateurs" could be fitted for just $3 while the handmade "University" model, with three cleats on the heels and five cleats on the sole, went for $5.50 a pair. Spalding also offered optional equipment such as rubber mouthpieces (25¢), shin guards (90¢), football belts (60¢), and the "Bike Jockey Strap Suspensory" in three sizes for 75¢.

For the more visionary, and perhaps safety-minded of the players, the company marketed "Spalding's Special New Head Harness" for $4. The harness was not really a helmet, but more of a skull cap with ear muffs made of "heavy sole leather crown, filled with air holes and lined with lamb's wool padding. Ear protectors heavily padded with felt." An additional piece of equipment available was "Morrill's Nose Mask," a clumsy looking item that buckled around the forehead at the top and then was clenched in the teeth at the bottom so that both the nose and the mouth would be protected. How one would breathe with this contraption remains unanswered!

Still, all of this newfangled equipment didn't impress an old, unnamed football fan who told the *Chicago Daily News*:

*The nose guard, head gear . . . leather and rubber enough to start a shoe factory.
Every time the quarter gives a signal, out comes the nose guard . . . if a man plays
low, he never needs a nose guard back of the line or a headgear either if he has
a shock of hair!*

## Morgan Football Team Looking For Teams To Play

Meanwhile, Thomas Clancy began advertising for opponents for the Morgans in the
local newspapers, with such brief listings as the following that appeared in the *Chicago
Chronicle*:

> *Morgan football team looking for teams averaging 149 lbs. to play on Sunday.
> Contact Thomas Clancy, 948 53rd Street.*

One possible future opponent might have been the parish team from St. Gabriel's,
which knocked off the Ray School 11-0 in its opening game and publicly announced
that it would be interested in playing either the Morgans or the Schleys. While the
Morgans took the week of October 22 off from competition, the Schleys tied the
Brookline Cycling Club 6-6 ("One of the hardest prairie gridiron contests of the year,"
said the *Sun*) and the Dearborns edged the Mortons 4-0 on a pair of safeties.

Despite the relatively early stage of the season (prairie games usually started in early
October), the Schleys promptly announced that they would meet the Crescents, the
self-appointed West Side champions. If they defeated the Crescents, the Schleys reasoned, they would only need to overcome the Eagles and the Eurekas of the South
Side to claim the city championship. This coronation would be obvious, claimed the
Schleys, since they were so feared throughout the city that no team from the North
Side would dare face them! There being no East Side in Chicago (Lake Michigan has
ruled out that possibility), the Schleys would have conquered foes from all corners of
the city. The Crescents failed to show up for their game with the Schleys on October
29, providing further fuel for the oratory fire of the Schleys. Meanwhile, the Dearborns
slipped past the Morgans at 41st and Michigan by a score of 11-5 in a football game
that perhaps demonstrated the first use of both free agency and creative reporting. In
the Monday, October 30 edition of the *Sun*, the following brief game report was filed:

> *The Morgan A.A. was defeated by the Dearborns yesterday at the latter's grounds
> by a score of 11-5. The game was won on a fluke, the Morgans fumbling the ball
> on the Dearborns' 10 yard line, enabling the latter to make a touchdown, and
> by kicking goal, clinched the game. The Morgans is the first team that ever scored
> on the visitors (sic) and naturally feel highly elated . . . As a curtain-raiser in the
> big event the Dearborn scrubs defeated the Lafayette team 13-0.*

Yet, in an age when coverage of football was almost invisible, the *Sun* carried an
entirely different account of the same game in its October 31 edition. Instead of a
doubleheader with both the Dearborns and their "scrubs," the second version of the
doubleheader alluded to the fact that the invincible Dearborns played two separate
opponents on the same day:

*After 15 minutes rest, the Dearborns tackled the Morgan A.A. team and won*
*by a score of 11-5 through the famous guards back plays and the line bucking of*
*G. Braun.*

Why was there a change in the original game account? Why did the *Sun* bother to essentially retract its original story when it rarely posted football results anyway? To answer those queries, simply think of free agency before it ever existed. While the two game reports fail to shed any new light on the result, the lineups which accompanied each of the articles certainly reveal some insight. The starters for the Morgan A.A. vary strangely from the first report to the second:

|      | October 30th Article | October 31st Article |
|------|----------------------|----------------------|
| LE   | Ragen                | C. O'Brien           |
| LT   | Walsh                | Clancy               |
| LG   | Chaney               | Wimmerskirts         |
| C    | Corcoran             | P. O'Brien           |
| RG   | Breen                | Breen                |
| RTC  | O'Brien              | Tate                 |
| RE   | Kendrick             | Kendrick             |
| QB   | Daly                 | Daley                |
| LH   | Noonan               | Green                |
| RH   | Baker                | Ward                 |
| FB   | P. O'Brien           | Kennedy              |

The odd thing about this game is that the names listed on the initial report were not all on the original Morgan roster for the season-opening game. Ragen was a member of the Garfields and Corcoran was previously with the Shermans. Walsh, Chaney, and Noonan were either assumed names or "ringers" that the Morgans brought in for the game against the Dearborns. Possibly someone provided the *Sun* with incorrect names for its first report or perhaps the names were accurate, but the Morgans thought they would never be published. In either circumstance, it is clear that for whatever reason, a revised lineup was included with the second report on October 31. That in itself was unusual, since the local newspapers rarely reported on prairie games and printed the names of the players on even more remote occasions.

The Morgans bounced back on November 5 with a tough 6-0 win over the Palmetto Athletic Association reported by the *Sun*:

*The defense on both sides was something out of the ordinary, the Morgans at one*
*time holding the Palmettos for downs on the former's five yard line. The Morgans*
*center plays plunged through their opponents line for good gains every time . . . The*
*features of the game were the punting of P. O'Brien and the all-around work of*
*Baker.*

At this point in their history, the Morgans were exactly like every other "prairie" team in Chicago. They were constantly on the lookout for opponents and games were scheduled with little or no notice. While the teams were not professional in the same sense that they are today, there is evidence that the players would place wagers on the outcome of their game—sort of a "winner-take-all" mentality. Players did not receive expenses, à la the Chicago Athletic Association, but then again, they were not required to travel much further than a few blocks from their own neighborhood. Even when teams thought they had a game scheduled, there was no guarantee that the contest would ever take place.

For example, on Sunday, November 12, the Morgans waited patiently for their opposition, called the Garfield Juniors (also known as the Rough Riders). When the Rough Riders failed to show, the Morgans claimed a forfeit victory, and immediately began advertising for Sunday games through the rest of November as well as for Thanksgiving Day. Perhaps it would have been easier, and quicker, to pick up a phone and call other teams, but that luxury was many years away for the average household. With such communication handicaps, it is truly a wonder that the local teams were able to scare up any games at all. Most scheduling was done through the mail and any last minute changes in the schedule would be difficult to absorb.

## *The Morgans Had A Tough Proposition To Solve*

With the gift victory over the Rough Riders, the Morgan Athletic Association moved to 3-1 on the season, and then pulled off a real nifty trick on November 18. The team played probably its only true doubleheader in its history and knocked off both the Dearborns and the Kensington Tigers in the same afternoon.

The *Sun* reported on this unique twin-bill three days later:

> *The Morgan AA team defeated two crack teams, the Dearborn AA and the Kensington Tigers of Kensington, Illinois at the Morgans grounds, Saturday afternoon. The Dearborns came on the gridiron with a record of having never been defeated and the game was in doubt as to the winner until the Morgans pushed Green over the line for a touchdown. The features of this game were the . . . punting of O'Brien and end runs of Green, Noonan and Corcoran for the Morgans. Score, 6-0.*
>
> *After a short rest, the Morgans tackled the Kensingtons. These players are ex-college and ex-high school players and for a while, the Morgans had a tough proposition to solve, but when they solved it, they had things their own way . . . for the Morgans, Noonan made a sixty five yard run and Green, Corcoran and O'Brien were always found where the ball was. Score, 11-0.*

Pat O'Brien did most of the punting and dropkicking for the Morgans, but with the local news media choosing not to identify players by their first names, it is difficult to ascertain which O'Brien handled which chore for the Morgans. In this doubleheader, Chris O'Brien moved to right guard, a somewhat unconventional position for a 155-pound player. Apparently, the Morgans made it through both contests with just one substitute for the day and were well rested for another home game against the Englewoods on Sunday, November 26.

An anticipated game on Thanksgiving Day (which would become a staple of the Chicago Cardinals in the future) did not come to fruition, but the very thought of holding football games on this holiday was beginning to rankle the clergy. The Congressional

Ministers Association stated in the *Chicago Journal* that football on Thanksgiving is a "flagrant desecration of an institution conceived in the spirit of religion."

## Showing Their Country Friends

Aside from the forfeit win over the Rough Riders, the Englewood game proved to be the easiest game of the year for the Morgan A.A. The Englewoods had been organized in 1897 and claimed never to have been defeated since that time. However, the Morgans shattered that reputation by coasting to an easy 37-0 win. This game set up a season-ending duel with the Kensingtons, stationed around what is presently East 115th Street in Chicago. At that time, Kensington was not within the city limits of Chicago and so the team claimed the "championship" outside of Chicago. Whether this championship covered the south suburbs, the whole state, or the entire ecosystem, we'll never know.

Despite breezing to an 11-0 win over the Kensingtons in their remarkable doubleheader just two weeks earlier, the visiting Morgans were held to a 0-0 tie on December 3. Finishing the season with a 6-1-1 mark, the Morgans managed to be a success both on the field and at the gate. Typically, there would not be any bleachers available at the fields where the teams played, but spectators could gather around the ropes that draped the field after paying a flat fee to receive that privilege. As the team continued to win, word spread and the crowds increased as well. The coverage of the final game in the *Sun* on Wednesday, December 6, alludes to the financial importance of these early prairie games:

> The Morgans team played a tie game of football with the Kensington Tigers Sunday to an audience of 700. F. Breen had charge of the cheering forces. From the moment the game began until it ended, the boys from the interior showed their country friends that it would be useless to try and score. During the entire game, the Kensingtons only had the ball thrice in their possession. Twice the Morgans held them for downs and once they were forced to punt. At no stage of the game was the Morgans' goal in danger, the ball always being inside the Kensingtons' fifteen yard line, but still the Morgans could not score on account of the weight of their opponents, who average over 10 lbs. each heavier than the Morgans and the playing of two new men whom the Kensingtons hired for the occasion.
>
> From a financial standpoint, the game was a success, netting the club a snug sum of money. Among the many features of the game was the playing of the center trio, Wymerskirchs, Clancy, and D. Ward, while the playing of the tackles and ends, Ward, Gabriel, Welsh and Green, was the best ever seen on the Pullman Athletic Field. The Morgans backs Daily, O'Brien, Noonan and Corcoran, played the game of their life, always gaining whenever they had the ball. The punting of P. O'Brien was also of high order.
>
> For the Kensingtons, Padden, Warren, Mercier and a player whom the Kensingtons had hired, and whose name they would not tell, played a good game. Score, 0-0.
>
> This game ended the playing of the season for the Morgans and in the evening Coach Green gave a dinner to the members of the team at Kinsley's. W. Ward was toastmaster for the occasion.

This account of the game is significant for two reasons. It acknowledges that at least some of the players on the prairie teams (particularly the Kensingtons) were hired for some, or all, of their games, making them professionals in the true sense of the word. It also hints that with seven hundred paying customers, the Morgan Athletic Association would share in the gate receipts as the visiting team. Since the Morgan A. A. was not owned by any one individual and operated on an informal basis, it would seem logical that the players would thus share in any "after expenses" net receipts. That, in turn, could make the Morgans professionals as well. Like everything else, it all depended on how those "expenses" were distributed.

## *Growing Pains*

Following the inaugural 1899 season, the Morgans gathered for the 1900 campaign in hopes of duplicating the success of the previous season. The Garfields, headquartered at 5519 South Dearborn, were back as well, despite the raiding of some of their talent over the winter. The Garfield team went undefeated in fifteen games in 1899, but even more impressive, was not scored upon during the entire season. Elsewhere on the South Side, challenges were extended to other organized teams, such as the Ivys, the Clovers, and the Dearborns.

In those days, most of the teams attempted to select opponents with a similar "average" weight. For example, the Garfields averaged 128 pounds per man, but were "willing to play anyone," according to the team's Coach Kinally (newspapers at the turn of the century generally failed to mention first names in articles regarding sports teams). While the Garfields had been busy recruiting players from the previous year's Carter Athletic Club, other teams such as the Dearborns and the Scheys were organized with basically the same players who were teammates in 1899.

But for the game of football, it seemed as though the sport would never grab a foothold on its way to achieving more universal support and respect. Part of the reason could be attributed to the ever-present influx of injuries, woes, and generally poor public relations. This perception could not be traced to just one team or even to one level of play. In each category of play, there seemed to be reports of bizarre behavior, unfortunate deaths, or horrible injuries—all of which the press seemed to devour with glee.

One instance occurred in Crown Point, Indiana, where the boisterous fans of the host Athletics became disturbed with the aggressive tactics of their foes and chased the visiting Chicago Tigers back to their hotel, surrounding the place until the local police eventually decided to disperse the mob. The *Chicago Times Herald* reported that the Tigers were then locked in their room by "Sheriff Lawrence until they would pay their hotel bill and other expenses." On the South Side of Chicago, a game was ended between the Princeton Athletic Club and the South Side Academy when referee Fred Nichols (who was also the coach of South Side) was chased from the field by Princeton followers. As the *Sun* unabashedly reported: "His decisions were so one-sided that the Princetons objected and secured a new official out of the crowd." And then there was the increasingly familiar jab at non-educational teams: "The Princetons are composed of young men who work for a living and practice by moonlight." Even the lofty "academic" teams were not spared from unusual activity. Morgan Park Military Academy's

6-5 win over Lake Forest was marred by a fistfight between the opposing coaches. And who could blame Evanston High School principal Boltwood when he disbanded the football team in November of 1899 because the football players were "cigarette fiends!"

## Back To The Future: The Morgan Athletic Club, 1900

In the summer of 1900, the returning Morgan Athletic Association players joined forces with other local gentlemen in the "Stockyards" area, and the Morgan Athletic Club was founded. Athletic and social clubs at that time provided a welcome diversion for the youths and young men of the stockyards neighborhood. Baseball and football teams competed against other local clubs, with boxing matches and biking races also dotting the social calendar. Dances and receptions were held on a regular basis and tended to serve as a rallying point for neighborhood pride and recognition.

The Morgan Athletic Club was formed at a meeting on Friday, August 24, 1900, with the intention of providing an organization "for young men who reside in the vicinity of 53rd and Halsted" streets on the South Side of Chicago. The club quickly registered fifty members ("among whom are many well known local athletes") and promised to field teams to compete with other local clubs in various sports. Among its charter members were saloon owner Charles Kasdorf, shoe salesman S. F. Curtis, and real estate mogul John Traeger. It is interesting to note that the entire Morgan Athletic Association football team was absorbed by the Morgan Athletic Club (M.A.C.). "The Morgan football team, which is now a part of the above-named (M.A.C.) organization and which achieved much success in last season's work, is now making preparations to fill dates with some of the best amateur teams of the city," stated the *Sun*. "The team has been strengthened somewhat this season and expects to be equally as promising as it has been heretofore."

By the middle of September, the Morgan Athletic Club had secured and remodeled its first headquarters at 5256 South Halsted, including a gymnasium, along with areas suited for wrestling, handball, boxing, and fencing. Membership was up to 125 and already included several local notables and politicians, with its intent "to become the leading organization of its kind in the Town of Lake."

On Thursday, September 13, 1900, the Morgan Athletic Club announced additional plans for its new football team. The *Sun* reported that "the football team captained by Christy O'Brien, composed of last year's Morgans, are (sic) already in training under the guidance of Kirk Green of the University of Chicago. They are now open for a game with any 150 pound team. A game has already been arranged with the Delaware Athletic Club."

## Bestowing Much Laudation Upon The Club

The Morgan Athletic Club, the football team which would eventually evolve into today's Arizona Cardinals, took the field for the first time on October 10, 1900, against the Maplewoods (of Maplewood, Illinois). In what might be considered the first "official" game in the long history of the NFL's oldest team, the Morgan Athletic Club ambushed the Maplewoods 23-0 in a game played at the Morgans' home field at 52nd and Morgan. In the opener of this football doubleheader, the Morgans' second team thumped St. Gabriel 12-0. The teams played fifteen-minute halves and with the unusual rules still in existence, the losers only enjoyed two offensive possessions in the entire game. Chris and Pat O'Brien were in the backfield for the first time together, and Chris responded with a forty-yard scamper to set up the first touchdown.

While the basic group of Morgans had returned en masse as part of the Morgan Athletic Club team in 1900, it appeared that the team also recruited members from other area clubs as well, particularly the Garfields and the Shermans. Chris O'Brien, just a lad of nineteen, was selected as captain of this recruited aggregate. Frank Ragen was elected president of the club after being called back from Arkansas, where he had served as the gym instructor at the Hoxie Athletic Club. Ragen had played for the Garfields the year before and would join the line on O'Brien's team.

The first social event for the Morgan Athletic Club was held on Saturday, September 14, 1900, and provides some insight into what life was like without fast food, videos, television, and the World Wide Web:

> *During the progress of the program, those present were furnished with a club jug-gling exhibition by Mr. John Pickley, and a very well executed club swinging exhi-bition by Professor Ragen, late of the Hoxie, Arkansas A.A. Mr. Laurence Fitzsimmons responded to a request for a vocal solo, which was heartily endorsed. The committee on arrangements for the evening's affair were George Riker, William Donahue, Arthur McLaughlin, Christopher O'Brien and James Dolan . . . The affair started at 8 and continued until 12 o'clock when all left for their homes after bestowing much laudation upon the efforts of the club to become a leader among organizations of its kind on the South side.*

All in all, about seventy-five couples attended the festive "Ladies Night" event, and the young Morgan Athletic Club continued its impressive membership growth.

The second game of the season was set for Sunday, October 7, against the Hyde Park Columbias. Although considered a bigger, stronger team, the Morgans were knocked off by the Columbias 5-0 when they fumbled on their own twenty-five-yard line. The errant ball was picked up by Bakes of the Columbias and carried in for the game's only touchdown.

How would the Morgans explain this loss? By admitting that they had all thor-oughly enjoyed a "stag party" at their clubhouse the night before and stayed up way past their bedtimes. Never again in the history of professional football would a team use this excuse for a defeat.

No matter . . . a week later the Morgans defeated the Lakewoods 10-0 on two, forty-five-yard field goals by Pat O'Brien. Unlike most kickers, O'Brien did not use the dropkick; both of his long field goals (worth five points each) were held in place by the quarterback Daly. Next, Wabash fell to the Morgans 15-10 in a game marked by a ten-yard touchdown run by Pat O'Brien and a fifteen-yard scoring jaunt from Chris O'Brien. An impressive crowd of over two thousand roared its approval as the Morgans held on despite a seventy-yard fumble return for a score by Ed Ball of Wabash.

Now 3-1, the Morgans closed the October portion of the schedule with an easy 22-5 win over the Dearborns, thus avenging that sole defeat in 1899. Another pleased audience exceeding two thousand witnessed this contest, which the *Sun* said "demonstrated why they (the Morgans) are the champions of the city." The Morgans fell behind early as they lost another fumble for an opposing touchdown. The extra point failed and the score remained 5-0 until Chris O'Brien broke away for the tying score. With the game knotted at 5-5, Corcoran blasted away for an eighty-five-yard tally. Late in the game, with the Morgan Athletic Club safely ahead 16-5, young Hugo Bezdek, a student at Lake High School (now Tilden Tech) finished the scoring with a five-yard scoring run.

## *Accompanied By Two Hundred Rooters And Noisemakers*

With that 22-5 victory, the Morgans moved to 4-1 for the campaign and appeared to be getting stronger each game—at least when they played without hangovers! As the cold weather began to drift over Chicago, the M.A.C. searched for additional opponents to meet, and defeat, in order to lay claim to some sort of championship. Certainly the embarrassing loss to the unsung Columbias hurt, but there didn't appear to be any other dominant team among the heavier clubs in the city. In 1900, the Morgans averaged a scant 156 pounds, but the team was never hesitant to tangle with larger lineups. On Sunday, November 4, the Morgans entertained the much bigger Lyceums at 52nd and Morgan. Outweighed by about twenty-five pounds per man, the Morgans hung tough with the visitors but settled for a scoreless tie. Almost immediately, the club announced plans to travel out to distant Pullman (about six miles south) on the following Sunday (November 11) to challenge the undefeated Pullman eleven. The M.A.C. would be "accompanied by about two hundred rooters and noise makers," and it was announced that the team would depart from its clubhouse via a special car at 12:30 P.M. on the day of the game.

### Transportation

The role of transportation was a silent partner in the early years of football, especially at the intercollegiate level. While air travel between continents can now be measured in a matter of a few hours, the commuting times for football games was enormous in the latter stages of the nineteenth century. When the University of Pennsylvania journeyed west to take on the powerful University of Chicago in 1899, the team stayed at the Chicago Beach Hotel, just east of the UC campus. Following the game on Saturday, the team left the hotel at 6:45 A.M. Sunday morning in a large stagecoach-type wagon drawn by four white horses. The horse team then pulled the football squad about two miles west to Englewood, where the players boarded the 8:45 A.M. train. From Chicago, the train stopped at Buffalo before arriving in Philadelphia at 9:00 A.M. on Monday morning. In total, the team would spend about twenty-six hours each way in transit. The Wright brothers and their fancy experiments were still a few years away!

Although much less travel time was involved for the Morgans, the encounter with the Pullmans would prove to be a messy one, which wasn't all that unusual. With the Morgans leading 6-0 late in the game, the Pullmans inched their way down field before the Morgans' defense held on its own twenty. Instead of literally turning over the ball on downs, the Pullmans decided to ignore the rules and to continue on offense. When both the referee and umpire attempted to intercede, the Pullmans simply picked up the ball and left the field, forfeiting the game "amid the hisses and groans of the 1,000 spectators," according to the *Sun,* and "the rough methods of the Pullmans were always conspicuous to the spectators." The strange conclusion to this game pushed the Morgans' record to 5-1-1.

Next, the Morgan Athletic Club defeated the Grand Crossing Eagles to set up a city championship game with the Delawares on December 2. The Morgans had hoped to meet the Delawares earlier in the season but had been unable to complete the arrangements. Instead, an impromptu "playoff" agenda had been agreed upon, where the winner of the Morgans-Grand Crossing game would meet the survivor of the Delaware-Lyceum contest for the championship of the city of Chicago. While the Morgans were defeating Grand Crossing, the Delawares slipped past the Lyceums.

Heading into the championship game, the Delawares were undefeated (8-0) and had allowed just two points over the entire season. The game was given added importance when the old "Comiskey's Park" at 39th and Wentworth was leased for the big tilt. Holding the game at such a facility provided the teams, and the game itself, with a subtle type of respect, since it would be played at a recognized professional sporting facility. However, the city championship for 1900 eluded the Morgan Athletic Club when the Delawares' staunch defense paved the way for an 8-0 decision. Although this was by far the biggest game of the year in the area, none of the local newspapers provided anything more than the final score and the Morgans' lineup.

As the season concluded with a 6-2-1 mark, there was no doubt that the Morgan Athletic Club would be even stronger in 1901. With another year of training, more familiarity with each other, and perhaps a few new recruits, the Morgans could conceivably elevate themselves well above the rest of the competition on the South Side.

## *A Funny Thing Happened On The Way To The Morgans*

While existing historical football literature usually credits Chris O' Brien with being both the founder and owner of the Morgan Athletic Club, in reality, he was neither. Chris O'Brien played a key role in organizing the Morgan Athletic Association in 1899 and was the captain of the first Morgan Athletic Club football team in 1900. He was also one of the founding members of the Morgan Athletic Club, but it was a club where the members contributed as equally as possible in funding the club and its activities. There is no question, however, that he was the foundation of what is now the NFL's oldest team, the Arizona Cardinals.

As such, O'Brien became even more visible in 1901 when the name "Chicago Cardinals" was first used. Somewhere between the conclusion of the 1900 season and the beginning of the 1901 campaign, the O'Brien brothers and most of their teammates split from the Morgan Athletic Club and formed their own team called the Cardinals Social and Athletic Club. There could have been a disagreement with President Frank Ragen of the Morgan Athletic Club, who seemed to dominate the attention at any function presented by the M.A.C. After finishing the 1900 baseball season and then beginning the 1900 football schedule with the gridders, Ragen appeared to drop off the football team and concentrate more on social events. Perhaps there was a disagreement with Captain O'Brien over playing time, or maybe Ragen was forced to spend more time overseeing the rapidly expanding membership of the Morgan Athletic Club itself. He was probably the only "paid" staff member of the club, and thus it would seem that he would be developing a burgeoning power base in club politics, too.

The first public hint of the separation appeared in the *Sun* on September 18, 1901, with an article indicating that the Morgan Athletic Club football team had been reorganized:

> *The team, while not as heavy as last year, intends to make as good, if not a better, record.*

The Morgan Athletic Club asked that inquiries for games from 135-pound teams be sent to C. Goodman, captain, at 5252 South Halsted Street. A week later, the newspaper recounted the Morgans' 10-0 opening victory over the Blue Ribbon team, but now the team issued its challenges to teams in the 130-pound average range for future encounters.

The initial notice about the other half of the former M.A.C. appeared in the *Sun* on September 27, 1901, under the headline "Social and Athletic Club in Good Shape":

> *The Cardinals Club will open the season with an informal dance at Masonic Hall, 42nd and Halsted Streets, Friday evening, October 18. The Cardinals football team, which formerly played under the colors of the Morgan Athletic Club, has organized for the season with a line of about 160 pounds, and, aided by a competent coach, will endeavor to maintain its former reputation. Managers of teams averaging 140 pounds or more desiring games, are requested to send challenges to J. P. O'Brien, captain, 1038 53rd Place.*

The Cardinals would play their first game against the Garfields on Sunday, October 6. The encounter with the Garfields was a cheerless one, with neither team being able to score. Still, the *Sun* found a few things to highlight from the game:

> *In the last half, the Cardinals succeeded in carrying the ball to the (goal) yard line, but the crowd closed in so the Cardinals could not break though before time was called. Notable among the features of the contest was the brilliant work of the Cardinals halves, Bliss and O'Shea, who won the praise of all. Maloney, the center and Robinson and Palm at guard, were always in the game.*

## Origin Of The Cardinals Name

The "Cardinals" name first appeared in 1901 when the team left the Morgan Athletic Club and reorganized as the Cardinals Social and Athletic Club. Like its counterparts the Morgan Athletic Club, Dearborn Athletic Club, etc., the team members were routinely referred to by the plural of the team's proper name (i.e. the Cardinals, the Morgans, the Dearborns, etc.). There is a popular piece of lore that appears in several professional football history books and can be found in the Arizona Cardinals press guide as well which also traces the "Cardinals" nickname to 1901. At that time, Chris O'Brien was said to have purchased some used football jerseys from Amos Alonzo Stagg at the University of Chicago. The Chicago team was nick-named the "Maroons" and their jersey colors corresponded to that name. When O'Brien saw the faded jerseys, he is said to have exclaimed, "That's not maroon, it's Cardinal red!" and the use of the nickname evolved from that point. While that story may or may not be accurate, the first use of the "Cardinals" name did indeed occur in 1901. However, existing photos in the Chicago Historical Society from the turn of the century show members of the University of Chicago team in football jerseys which are significantly different from those worn by the 1902 Cardinals team.

## *Before The NFL, There Was . . .*

That would be the Cardinals' last football game for two weeks, but there was still a great deal going on between the two dueling athletic clubs. While the Cardinals Social and Athletic Club hosted its first dance at the Masonic Hall (42nd and Halsted) for 250 guests, the Morgan Athletic Club was busy moving into larger headquarters a few blocks south at 5403 South Halsted. But the biggest off-the-field news was the attempt of both groups to help forge an organization of all club football teams in the city. In a meeting held on October 11 at the Palmer House Hotel in Chicago, representatives of over thirty teams, including Pat O'Brien of the Cardinals, met and formed the "Associated Football Clubs." This organization was different from the "Association Football" circuit also in existence in Chicago at the same time, which was actually a soccer league.

The new football association apparently was formed to help protect the sport in the city of Chicago, since the game was already under siege from critics, parents, and academics who winced every time an injury or academic failure was attributed to foot-ball. The teams themselves, perhaps stung by the large number of forfeits or by the difficulties encountered in securing fields, decided that strength in numbers might be a sensible alternative for addressing future issues. The group also made a stab at sched-uling games among the members. The first weekly schedule for the association was set for Sunday, October 13, 1901, with the following lineup:

> *Garfields vs. Cornells, 55th & Indiana Avenue*
> *Montauk Indians vs. Tigers, Humboldt and Talman Avenues*
> *Wabash vs. Steinways, 50th & Michigan Avenue*
> *Morgans vs. Lehighs, 52nd & Morgan Streets*
> *Columbia Athletics vs. Maplewood, Maplewood Field*

Later in the twentieth century, the first edition of the NFL would be organized in similar fashion, with few set rules for controlling rosters and no firm procedure for determining the championship of the organization. The Associated Football Clubs orga-nization in Chicago really was no different, but it was the first attempt to bring some diplomacy, organization, and "professionalism" to the game in the city.

The newly elected board of directors seemed satisfied to arrange for some super-ficial scheduling rather than mess with more difficult matters, such as equitable com-petition, weight considerations, roster maintenance, and coupling teams within divi-sions according to ability. But it was a start.

## *Pink Tea And Football*

Another problem for the game was the focus of the media on the unfortunate number of injuries piling up nationwide on the gridiron. The *Chicago Tribune* kept a running tally of "Killed and Wounded" during the football season. By October 15, 1901, the *Tribune* had accumulated information on two deaths and thirty injuries attributed to football:

> *Although the football season scarcely has begun, the list of dead and injured has commenced to grow, and bids fair to be the most appalling in the history of the game if it continues at the present rate. Chicago seems to have been especially unfortunate, having furnished the first fatality of the year and its list of injured is believed to be larger than that of any other city.*

In a parallel situation, the Cook County High School League seemed to be going overboard in its attempt to govern activity on the gridiron. Rules were imposed which required players to maintain a certain grade average (seventy-five percent in every class) as well as to receive parental approval to play the game. The eligibility issue came into question when South Division High School was dropped from the league for using three ineligible players who "were below rank in their studies." On the North Side, Austin High School withdrew from the league because of the "parents' objection" rule, and other teams were expected to drop out for the same reason. It was conceivable that there simply wouldn't be enough eligible players remaining for some schools to field a team. As one member of the league's board told the *Tribune:* "It looks at present that the school which is not expelled from the league before the end of the season will win the championship."

The changes in the rules were seen by the participants as a lurid attempt to terminate football at the high school level. The prep academic requirements were more strict than those in use for athletes at the nearby and respected University of Chicago. But Superintendent of Schools Cooley would not be swayed. "I would rather see poor football teams than to make heroes out of poor students," he claimed. "While I am in favor of football in the schools, yet I also desire to bar out those players who are not students."

Another movement was proposed to the high school principals which would substitute a milder sport (soccer) for football. This proposal didn't fly, according to Principal James E. Armstrong of Englewood High School on the South Side:

> *Association football (soccer), where the ball is kicked and not carried, can no more be substituted for American football than pink tea can replace the ham and eggs of the working man. There seems to be little probability of change in the rules that are governing football. We can urge the playing of the game inside closed grounds that all players will get fair play without interference from spectators, and we may insist that the players in schools live up to the rules of the Illinois High School Athletic Association, which was formed last spring, but there appears little prospect of any radical change in the game for the present.*
>
> *In so far as the moral degeneracy is apt to result among students by reason of profanity on the athletic fields, and the betting by those who did not partake in the games, I do not see that pupils stand in any more danger from football than*

*they do in their society and fraternity life and in the college dances. It is unfair to call athletics to task when there are other things in student life which offer equal possibilities for bad effects.*

## *Fife And Drum And The Orphan Buffalo Club*

While this tidal wave of activity was pounding the game of football, the Cardinals quietly slipped over to 37th and Butler to take on the Dearborns on October 20. Before over one thousand spectators, the two teams tussled and muscled each other for nearly an hour before a victor was determined. Once again, the *Sun* was on the spot and provided the most extensive coverage to that date on a Cardinals football game:

> *The Cardinals kicked off to the Dearborns' 25 yard line; the Dearborns advanced to their 35. In the first scrimmage, the Dearborns skirted the opposition's end for 15 yards. They were then held for downs. The Cardinals then advanced the ball by hard bucking to the Dearborns' 10, where the Dearborns held them.*
>
> *The Dearborns then punted to their 50 yard line. O'Shea caught the ball and advanced 10 yards, there started the Cardinals' steady march for their first touchdown. O'Shea and O'Brien hit the lane for 5 and 10 yard gains then C. O'Brien went through tackle for the touchdown. O'Brien missed goal. 5-0.*
>
> *In the second half, the Cardinals scored again. The Dearborns gave way completely and every play netted big gains. Had it not been for the playing of the Dearborns' center and guard, Klaus and Braun, the score would have been larger. In this half, long gains were made by C. O'Brien and W. Ward. It took 10 minutes to score the second touchdown, made by C. O'Brien. P. O'Brien kicked goal. 11-0.*

This game account verifies one of the most common tactics used in football at the turn of the century. In the first half, when the Dearborns held the Cardinals at the ten on downs, the Dearborns elected to immediately punt out of danger, rather than initiating any type of offensive effort. With the 110-yard field being used at the time, the Dearborns booted the ball out to their own 50, and then took the chance that they could hold the Cardinals at that point and perhaps gain some additional positive field advantage.

Both the Cardinals and the Morgans were in action on Sunday, October 27, with the Morgans and the Garfields battling to a scoreless tie while the Cardinals blasted the Grand Crossing Eagles 23-5. The Morgans traveled two miles west to the Garfields' new field at 47th and Western. The team was followed by an energetic corps of neighborhood fans in what might have been the first time a Chicago post-collegiate club had a marching band. The Sun stated that "fully 500 Morgan supporters carrying club colors . . . assisted by fife and drum corps and members of the Orphan Buffalo Club paraded the streets arousing much enthusiasm for the team." Far from the noise and tumult, the Cardinals went to work and took apart the Eagles quite easily. However, with increasing numbers of teams vying for playing space, it was becoming difficult for the more recognizable clubs to secure fields, and the Cardinals game on November 3 with the Columbias was postponed when the teams were unable to find an open field. Teams such as the Morgans, the Carlisles, and the Monarchs were all using the same plot at 52nd and Morgan for games and practices.

After a week off, the Cardinals squeezed in a game with the Maplewoods and coasted to a 28-0 victory, and the game with the Columbias was finally scheduled on November 17. It was agreed that this contest would be for the "championship of the city" and would cap the 1901 season. Both teams were undefeated and the Cardinals (3-0-1) had only the early season tie with the Garfields to blemish their record.

The 1901 championship game was scheduled at the American League baseball grounds at 39th and Wentworth. Before a crowd of about two thousand, the Cardinals went to work quickly on a long run by Hugo Bezdek to the Columbias' fifty. From there, according to the *Sun,* "the ball was finally sent across Columbias' goal line by L. C. Bliss and O'Shea . . . P. O'Brien kicked a difficult goal from the side line at 25 yards." The Cardinals held on to win 14-5, with those points probably coming on a touchdown (five points), O'Brien's field goal (five points), and a pair of safeties (two points each). Although Bezdek's appearance was a surprise, the Cardinals finished the abbreviated 1901 season with basically the same players who had started the year with the scoreless tie against the Garfields.

As the 1901 season crept to a close, the Cardinals Social and Athletic Club enjoyed its first city championship and an undefeated record (4-0-1). Following the success of the 1900 Morgan Athletic Club (6-2-1) and the Morgan Athletic Association (6-1-1) in 1899, the teams with the O'Brien brothers had compiled a nifty 16-3-3 overall mark. With the core group still together of the O'Briens, Ward, Green, Daley, and Wymerskirts (whose poor name was spelled differently each time it appeared throughout his career!), the team could look forward to another strong campaign in 1902. But that season, like the three preceding it, would be marked by change and challenge as the world continued to grapple with the strange and intriguing game of football.

# ✦ 2 ✦

# The Emergence of Pro Football in the Chicago Area: 1902 – 1919

*"The Morgan Athletic Club is the largest of its kind in the city . . . its members are eagerly sought by heiresses and ladies of the nobility!"*

MEMBERSHIP PROMOTION
FOR THE MORGAN ATHLETIC CLUB, 1904

With the advent of the Cardinals Social and Athletic Club, one would have thought that a fierce rivalry with the Morgans would quickly develop.

It didn't.

For whatever reason, the two neighborhood clubs traveled north, south, east, and west for competition beginning in 1902, but never actually crossed paths on the football field that year. Oddly enough, there is some evidence that the two teams at times shared and borrowed players from each other. Despite the lack of head-to-head meetings between the Cards and the Morgans, football adversaries were readily available as even more athletic clubs with football teams emerged to compete in the prairies surrounding the stockyards.

In 1902, the Morgan Athletic Club and the Cardinals Athletic Club remained separate entities. As usual, the "amateur" season started later than the high school and college campaigns. The Morgans' first game was slated against the Glen Oaks on October 5. It appears that the club was content to play teams a notch below the caliber of competition from the previous season. Since the schism with the O'Brien brothers, the Morgans were unable to immediately attract the bulkier players in the area and so the team advertised for opponents in the 140-145 pound average range. Teams such as the Olympics, the Websters, the Vermonts, the Sheridans, and the Normal Athletic Club were among those challenged by the Morgans.

The 1902 season began with the Morgans whitewashing the Glen Oaks 11-0. Following this opening contest, the Morgans next scheduled a game with the Vernons on October 12 at 51st and Center, a new location for Sunday gridiron battles on the South Side. While the Morgans also won this game, the final score has been lost forever due to the local newspapers' annoying habit of neglecting to inform their readers of final scores of most games—if the result was posted at all. The game report a few days after the contest might have stated something like: "The Morgans celebrated their victory over the Vernons with a dance . . ." instead of "The Morgans crushed the Vernons 25-0 behind a grueling rushing attack . . ."

As such, it was difficult in 1902 to find much media attention on Chris O'Brien or his adversary, Frank Ragen. Coverage of the local "amateur" football games drifted solidly behind that of professional baseball, college football, bike races, high school football, boxing, and bowling. Still, the Cardinals inaugurated their second season on October 26 with a 6-0 shutout over the Cornells at the Cards' home field at 52nd and Morgan. Following the opener, O'Brien scheduled the next game against the town team from distant Elgin, Illinois. Elgin was viewed as a dangerous team after defeating the Chicago College of Physicians and Surgeons the preceding week by the score of 17-5.

The Cardinals made the long trip to Elgin and prevailed 10-0. The *Elgin Daily Courier* called the visitors "strong in their aggressive and firm in their defense" but stated that "their much boasted punter, P. O'Brien, failed to come near the goal." The *Elgin Daily News* was more resourceful:

*All things considered the Elgin town team did well to hold the Cardinals down to a score of 10-0. The latter has defeated all comers in Chicago outside the varsity teams and its average weight is 180 pounds, while Elgin's is 160.*

The Cardinals games were few and far between in 1902, but this club did stake a small claim in team history by scheduling its first out-of-state competition on November 16 in Michigan City, Indiana. The *Sun* predicted that the Cardinals Social and Athletic Club would encounter a tough foe over in Indiana:

*. . . against the crack town team. The Cardinals goal line has yet to be crossed this season, and the game is attracting a good deal of attention among the south side football fans.*

*O'Brien, the crack half, may not be able to play on account of injuries received in the Elgin game, which the Cardinals won. The position was filled last year by Bezdek, Chicago's crack half, and O'Brien is the only man that has thus far been able to hold it down as well as did the "Buzz Dog." McCarthy will take O'Brien's place if he is unable to start.*

Hugo Bezdek, who helped coach the Morgans in 1900 and then played with the Cardinals in 1901, is probably the most famous alumnus of the team from its early years. Born April 1, 1884, in Prague, Czechoslovakia, Bezdek attended Lake High School. Since that school did not have a football team at the time, Bezdek learned the game while playing with the Cardinals. He was then recruited by Amos Alonzo Stagg to play at the University of Chicago. While there, Bezdek enjoyed a stellar career, although he toiled in the shadow of the infamous Walter Eckersall. During his playing time with the Maroons (1902-1905), the team posted a marvelous slate of 38-4-2 and Bezdek was placed on All-American teams after his senior year.

But it was what he accomplished after graduation that earned him athletic accolades. Bezdek is the only person who managed a professional baseball team as well as coached a professional football team. He was the head football coach, and a very successful one, at the University of Oregon (1906, 1913-1917), the University of Arkansas (1908-1912), and Penn State (1918-1929).

In 1937, he was named the head coach of the new Cleveland Rams of the NFL. However, he failed to match the success he achieved in college coaching. He was able to win just one of fourteen games in the NFL before being "retired" in 1938. His last college coaching stint was at tiny Delaware Valley in 1949, where he concluded his collegiate career with an overall record of 127-57-14, including a Rose Bowl championship while with Oregon.

## Cardinals Scalp Will Be Dangling From Their Belt

While the Chicago newspapers did not cover the Cardinals' trek to Michigan City, the local papers pounced on the game as if it was the biggest event ever to hit the northern Indiana shores. Both the *Michigan City Evening Dispatch* and the *Michigan City Evening News* provided extensive pre- and postgame coverage and warned the locals of the impending dangers of the "Giant Cardinals." This was also the first time that the name, the "Chicago Cardinals," was used in reference to the football team long affiliated with the O'Brien brothers.

The Michigan City town squad was known as the I.A.C. team and earlier in the season it had experimented with other Chicago club teams, losing to the Kensingtons and defeating the Columbias. But the game with the Cardinal Athletic Club seemed to take on more immense attention because of the mistaken belief that the Cardinals were the champions of Cook County for five straight years and were also undefeated during that time. As noted previously, it was common practice for a team to claim the champion of something, but this was the wildest one to date concerning the Cardinals. Although the team's record was sensational from 1899 to 1902, there were a few smudges on its blotter. But, newspaper reporting of the era was great fun, and the reverent descriptions of the intruders no doubt helped to fill the stands.

This reputation also seemed to impress the local I.A.C. team, for it openly reached out and grabbed some recruits from the South Bend Athletic Club to help bolster its backfield. The media also hinted that the team might produce one or two college players from Chicago for the big match. But the biggest surprise to Cardinals' backers would have been the team's lineup, as published in both Michigan City papers prior to the game:

| | | | |
|----|---------|----|---------|
| LE | Corcoran | LT | Moeller |
| LG | Smit | C | Goodman |
| RG | Curtis | RT | Ross |
| RE | Collins | QB | Frazer |
| LH | Clancy | RH | Ragen |
| FB | Staeger | | |

Although a few of the above mentioned players (e.g. Clancy, Ragen, and Corcoran) had played with the O'Brien brothers in preceding years, this alignment appears to be that of the Morgan Athletic Club, rather than the Cardinal Athletic Club of 1902. Since it appeared in both newspapers, one might be inclined to consider that either the Cardinals were bowing out of the commitment and had asked the Morgans to play the game for them, or that the two teams would indeed be combining forces to play both this game and a game the Morgan Athletic Club had originally scheduled on this date (November 16) with Wabash. Still another newspaper report stated that the I.A.C. would be playing the "Chicago Maroons," another club team, on that day.

In any event, the I.A.C. team knew they would be playing someone from Chicago that weekend, it just was not certain who that would be.

The build-up for the game began early in the week in the *Evening News:*

> *The banner football game of the season will be played at the Lake Cities' grounds Sunday afternoon, when the strong Chicago Cardinals' eleven meets the I.A.C. team of this city. The Cardinals have the distinction of being the strongest athletic team in Chicago and for three years have been unbeaten. The team is the heaviest that will play on the local gridiron this season, the five linemen averaging 200 pounds even, the average for the entire team being 185 pounds. In view of the Cardinals' good record during the past three years and their weight, the local enthusiasts are in doubt as to the result of Sunday's game. Captain Herrick's followers however, are indulging in nightly practice and they feel confident that the Cardinals' scalp will be dangling from their belt after Sunday's game. Halfbacks Ben and Ed Koehler of the famous South Bend Athletic team will assist the local team in Sunday's game. The Koehler brothers are probably the only pair of twin brother halfbacks in the United States . . . The Cardinals have written manager Fedder that they are coming down to win and announce that they will be accompanied by a large party of rooters.*

## *Importing Halfbacks*

The "borrowing" of players was beginning to become a common practice at this level, but it was a bit unusual for it to be so blatantly announced in the newspaper. There was another football team in Michigan City at this time called the Yukon Athletic Club. Later in the season, when the Yukons were scheduled to meet I.A.C. for the city championship, the local press reported:

> *The Yukon club will back their team to the fullest extent, a fund having already been created for the purpose of importing a pair of halfbacks from a Chicago college to assist in the game . . . considerable money has already been wagered on the result of Sunday's game.*

It would seem that the idea of bringing in professional "assistance" for certain games was not much of a secret. However, it was a chilling reality for college coaches who feared the loss of their key players to injuries (or ineligibility) by playing in such contests. This theme would be a recurring one, and it would also prove to be one of the primary factors for conceiving the original version of the National Football League nearly two decades later.

The *Evening Dispatch* added to the Cardinals intrigue by commenting that "Reports from Chicago are to the effect that the coming players are giants in strength and size, who do not know what defeat is." With such glowing and fearsome attributes, it must have been quite a shock to the local residents that the mighty Cardinals proved to be rather easy prey for the Michigan City I.A.C. team, falling to their hosts by a score of 15-5. The team that showed up from Chicago was the Cardinal Athletic and Social Club, and both O'Brien brothers are mentioned in the lengthy game account which appeared in the *Evening Dispatch*. It is an interesting description and reprinted here in its entirety since it would be the most comprehensive report of a Cardinals game until the *Green Bay Gazette* and the *Rock Island Argus* provided extensive, play-by-play coverage in the early days of the NFL:

> *The giant Cardinals of Chicago, with their brilliant record of three seasons of playing without defeat, met the sturdy I.A.C. team on the local grounds yesterday afternoon, and the yellow and blacks came in for a big end of the money, the score being 15-5. The Chicagoans came just fourteen strong, after having written for tickets for nineteen men, and claimed that five of their players refused to come. In spite of this the visitors were represented by as formidable a set of gridiron artists as one would care to look upon. The contest, from a spectator's point of view, was one of the season's best. Brilliant runs, well mixed with fierce line bucking, were always in evidence, which kept the crowd cheering.*
>
> *Ed Koehler, the crack South Bend halfback, assisted the home team, and his work was a decided feature of the game. Ed looks every inch a player, and his assaults upon the opposing line helped to win the glory over to the home team, making two of the touchdowns himself. Wilson also got into the contest with good results. Art Reed, Boyd and Roose played their usual aggressive game. The exhibition of place-kicking and punting before the contest by P. O'Brien, the Cardinals fullback, was remarkable and deserved the applause given.*
>
> *Koehler kicked off at 2:45 to Johnson. Sadenwater broke through and spoiled the first play for the visitors. Koehler got the ball on the next attempt. Wilson was thrown for a loss, but Roose went over Palm for six yards. Boyd made a yard. Koehler four and Wilson two. Koehler went through left tackle and landed the pigskin within half a yard of the goal. On the next play he was pushed over for a touchdown. R. Reed missed goal. Score—Michigan City 5 Chicago 0.*
>
> *O'Brien kicked off to Koehler, who made ten yards. Wilson reeled off twenty-five yards around right end. Koehler added five. A. Reed four, while Birginski made twenty yards through left guard on two plays. Roose was thrown for a loss, but A. Reed hit the line for a yard and Boyd went around right end for twelve yards, placing the oval on the four-yard line. Koehler added two yards and Wilson went over for a touchdown. No goal. Score—Michigan City 10 Chicago 0.*
>
> *O'Brien kicked over the line and the ball was placed on the twenty-five yard line and Boyd punted. C. O'Brien made seven yards and P. O'Brien was equal to four. The latter made first down. The locals got the ball on a fumble. Roose made four yards, Koehler three, Wilson ten, Boyd one, Wilson four and Boyd two. The half ended as the ball went over to the visitors on downs on their own forty-yard line.*

Let's take a half-time break. This rare insight into a 1902 game of football illustrates another forgotten rule of the early game. If a team managed to score a touchdown, it also received the ensuing kickoff. Because of this rule—and aided perhaps by a running clock—the Cardinals were limited to just four offensive plays in the first half. However, if a team was lucky enough to have a kicker with a strong leg, that kicker might be able to kick the ball past the goal line. If this was the case (a modern "touchback"), the ball would be brought out to the twenty-five-yard line. Remember the field was 110 yards long back then, so an offense was looking at 85 yards of real estate to chew up for a score. If this task looked too difficult, the offense could immediately punt the ball right back to the other team and hope to gain a more advantageous field position in the inevitable exchange of punts over the course of the game. Michigan City used this stratagem following Pat O'Brien's touchback kick in the waning stages of the first half. Field goals, whether they be by drop kick or place kick, were also worth the same (five points) as a touchdown, so an accurate kicker could make his team a threat from fifty yards on in, especially with the goal posts being placed directly on the goal line.

Now, back to the action:

*Chicago kicked to A. Reed. Koehler, Boyd, and A. Reed made good, substantial gains, while Wilson got past right tackle for eighteen yards. Koehler carried the pigskin twenty-five yards through a broken field, and a moment later went over the line. No goal. Score—Michigan City 15 Chicago 0.*

*After the kick-off by Chicago, the locals lost the ball on downs. C. and Pat O'Brien carried the ball to the ten-yard line by straight bucks, from where Bliss carried it over. No goal. Score—Michigan City 15 Chicago 5.*

*Koehler kicked to C. O'Brien. The visiting backs advanced the ball to the center of the field, from where the fullback tried for a goal. The ball went wide of the posts and the game ended.*

*Personally, the Chicago boys were the most gentlemanly set of fellows that have been here this season, and they took their defeat in true sportsmanlike manner, although their heretofore unstained record was slightly disfigured.*

## Giants Are Beaten

The report in the *Michigan City Evening News* was focused less on detail and more on praise for the home team, but managed to provide more tall tales on the Cards' behalf under the headline "GIANTS ARE BEATEN":

*On the Lake Cities' gridiron Sunday afternoon the famous Chicago Cardinals, for the past five years champions of the gridiron game in Cook County, Illinois, outside of college teams, met the first defeat that they have suffered in that period at the hands of the eleven that plays under the colors of the I.A.C. of this city. The visitors went down before the local team in a game that abounded in spectacular end runs and line plunges. The final score was 15-5.*

Meanwhile, back in Chicago, the Morgans conquered Wabash 10-0 on the same day that the Cardinals were getting whipped quite easily in Michigan City. There is some evidence that the Cardinals were intending to bring a slightly different team to Indiana, with both the "alternate" lineup being released prior to the game and the fact that five tickets requested by the Cards had gone unused reportedly due to players refusing to play. If local custom was followed in this game, perhaps the Cardinals (or the Morgans) were planning on putting together an all-star team of local favorites in hopes of cashing in on a large side bet between the teams. Unfortunately, neither of the Michigan City newspapers published the lineups of the players who actually participated in the game, so it is impossible to determine if there were some "ringers" involved for the Cardinals. Even then, the use of assumed names could have obliterated any trail to the truth.

The Cardinals planned to renew their winning ways the following week against their old rivals, the Columbias, in a game to be played at 55th and Indiana. The Cardinals claimed a 6-0 forfeit victory when the Columbias failed to appear for the game. This set up another round of claims and challenges in the *Sun* on behalf of the Cardinal Athletic and Social Club:

> *The Columbias forfeited to the Cardinals by non-appearance Sunday . . . where the game was scheduled, thereby relinquishing their claim to the championship of Cook County, leaving that title to be fought between the Cardinals and the Woodstocks, at Woodstock, Illinois on Thanksgiving Day. As a strong rivalry exists between the two teams a good game is expected.*

Since the Associated Football League appears to have disappeared by 1902, the Cook County playoff between the Cardinals and the Woodstocks may have simply been contrived between the two teams. There had not been any evidence of a Cook County champion in 1901. But what about the Morgan Athletic Club which had been mowing down opponents each and every week during the 1902 campaign? The Morgans, it seems, would be vying for the "city" championship in its final game against the Garfields on November 30. Could there be some collusion between old teammates where an agreement was reached that the Morgans would claim the city title while the Cardinals would strive for the county championship? No one probably even noticed that Woodstock was nowhere near venerable Cook County.

## The Fearless Olivers

If you visit Woodstock, Illinois, today, it appears that the town in the north central portion of the state hasn't changed much since 1902. The downtown area, called the "Square" by local residents, houses an assortment of quaint shops and a unique red brick pavement, all placed in a square. The old jail is there. So is the courthouse and the railroad track, which is probably how the Cardinals arrived in this picturesque town nearly a century ago. Teams from towns such as Elgin, Dundee, and Woodstock met on crisp fall afternoons and defended the honor and dignity of their cities in the far north central region of Illinois. Woodstock was about sixty-two miles away from the South Side of Chicago, where teams represented their street or neighborhood, not their town. Still, the Cardinals set up their game with the Woodstock Olivers town team on Thanksgiving Day in 1902 (November 27) at the county fair grounds.

The game was front page news in the *Woodstock Sentinel* a full week before the kickoff:

> *As usual, the citizens of Woodstock will have the pleasure of viewing a good game of football at the Fair Grounds today. The game will be between the Cardinal Athletics, Chicago's cracked team, and the fearless Olivers, of this city. The Cardinals are a powerful team outweighing the Olivers from ten to fifteen pounds per man, but we have no fears for the outcome of the game as our home team has seldom, if ever, been found wanting when put to the test.*

The Cardinals eventually prevailed in this contest by a margin of 5-0, scoring the lone touchdown late in the second half. As typical of the type of game played during that era, the punter proved to be the most valuable player on both sides in the contest, as reported by the *Sentinel:*

> *Woodstock held for downs and by line bucks and end runs worked the oval to the Cardinals' 5-yard line, where the ball was lost on a fumble. The Cardinals then punted. Goodehue catching the punt and returning it 15 yards. Woodstock, by steady gains worked the ball back to the Cardinals 25-yard line, where they were held for downs. The Cardinals, immediately after receiving the ball, punted it back to the center of the field where it remained the balance of the first half.*

Despite the season-ending loss, the Olivers received the "gratitude of the citizens of Woodstock, for the able manner in which they have defended the football reputation of this city."

## *We Ran All Over The Princetons*

The Morgan Athletic Club rebounded from its recent lack of social activity by hosting its "3rd Annual Reception" on November 21, in which an astounding 542 couples participated. Two days later, the M.A.C. football team spanked the Princetons 11-0 to clear the way for the title match with the Garfields. The ever-present *Sun* avowed that the attendance at the game with the Princetons at Auburn Park was "the largest crowd ever seen in the park." The pro-Morgan followers then paraded around Auburn Park singing the praises of their football heroes:

> *Oh, how we ran!*
> *Oh, how we ran!*
> *We ran all over the Princetons . . .*
> *Oh, how we ran!*

The hype began to swell for the title tilt between the undefeated Garfields and the undefeated Morgans, which would be held on Sunday, November 30, at 79th and Wentworth. With wins over the teams representing Wabash, the Princetons, the Dearborns, and the West Sides, the Morgans were fairly confident going into the season finale. The *Sun* noted that both teams were undefeated on the eve of the title contest.

Unfortunately, the Garfields had agreed to meet the Princetons on Thanksgiving Day (November 27) and found that their impregnable defense wasn't all that foolproof. They fell to the Princetons 6-0, ending a four-year winning streak and threatening to take the luster off the title game with the Morgans.

Yet it didn't seem to matter as an estimated five thousand spectators showed up at Auburn Park to watch the Morgans defeat the Garfields 11-0 to claim the city championship. Ragen, Corcoran, Moeller, Curtis, and Ross, who all appeared on the Cardinals' preliminary roster for the Michigan City game, were standouts for the Morgans. After having gone undefeated for four years, the poor Garfields endured their second defeat in four days.

After returning from the conquering of Woodstock, the Cardinals scheduled still another game, this time for December 7 with the Kensingtons. For the third straight year, the O'Brien team would play its final game at the "American League Park," but this time it would be for the "State Championship." The *Sun* once again provided an insightful preview of this allegedly important contest:

> *The game will decide the championship of Illinois, as neither team has been defeated and between them they have defeated all of the claimants so a grand game is assured.*

Apparently, the Cardinals had neglected to spread the good news about their excursion to Michigan City when the above lines were written. It is accurate, however, that the Cardinals had not been defeated by any team in Illinois, which would justify the claim to a battle for the state title.

Although no record of that game exists, the team photo from 1902 does. This is the oldest relic from the erratic early history of the Cardinals and it suggests that the team did defeat the Kensingtons to capture the elusive state title. Due to fragmented records, it appears that the Cardinals Social and Athletic Club played just six games in 1902, winning five of them.

## *Everyone Went Home Happy*

As the 1902 season came to a close, the Morgan Athletic Club supplanted the Cardinals as the champions of the City of Chicago while the Cardinals claimed the championships of both Cook County and the State of Illinois. Everyone went home happy.

Club activity for 1902 concluded later in December when the Morgan Athletic Club feted its football team at a combined reception and "ladies night" at the Boulevard Hall at 55th and Halsted. As part of the festivities, the Morgans re-elected Frank Ragen as president of the organization. "We must again look to that man of wit, social and business principles to once more take the reins and guide us, as he has in the past to succeed," stated G. J. Martel, chairman of the Nominating Committee. In a related matter, T. J. Clancy, the original organizer of the Morgan Athletic Association, decided to step down as treasurer of the Morgan Athletic Club because of "stress of business."

Following the 1902 season, the Cardinals Social and Athletic Club disappeared from the local newspapers. While the Morgan Athletic Club continued to field a team, the former Cardinals likely became members of the Normal Athletic Association which had been active in both football and baseball on the club circuit. The Normals operated out of the neighborhood southeast of the stockyards area with a clubhouse at 68th and Lowe. Like the previous Cardinal Athletic and Social Club, the Normal A. A. used Boulevard Hall at 55th and Halsted as the site for its annual reception, which attracted two hundred members in October of 1903. Several new clubs also arose in this same vicinity including the Park Manors (73rd and Park Manor), the Yosemites (63rd and Halsted), and the reorganized Princetons (57th and Ashland). In addition, the revamped Gordan Athletic Club rented office space on 43rd Street, just off Halsted. The new Yosemites may also have claimed some of the former Cardinals, because the team quickly became very competitive in its brief existence.

## Their Yells And Songs Filled The House

The Morgan Athletic Club opened its 1903 season on October 25 with a 5-0 win over the Yosemites before "thousands of people," according to the *Sun*. The next week, the Morgans were scheduled to meet another new team, the Orioles, but ended up tying the Thistles 0-0 when the Orioles failed to show up for the game. Because of the increasing attendance, the Morgans promised to surround the field with a heavy cable to help keep the crowd safely away from the players at future games.

A massive street car strike immobilized the area in mid-November and forced the postponement of many events, including prairie football games and the annual Morgan Athletic Club reception. When play resumed, the Morgans tied the Yosemites 0-0 on November 29 at the Morgans' new home field at 58th and Halsted. This game was part of a doubleheader which featured the Royals versus the "All Stars," a team comprised of players from the various athletic clubs in the stockyards area. That evening, the *Sun* reported, "The Yosemites were banqueted and later a theater party went to the Avenue theater where their yells and songs filled the house!"

Another "All-Star" game of sorts took place when the Gordons and Crescents tied 5-5, also on November 29. After the conclusion of the contest, the Gordons were awarded the victory because "the Crescents had four 'ringers . . . two from the Royals and two from the Morgans," stated the *Sun*. "The Gordons would like to play the Crescents," added the newspaper, "not a picked team from all the clubs on the south side." As the season ended with the Morgans-Yosemites game, there was still not a mention of the O'Brien brothers—or their teammates—in any of the local media. When the brothers resurfaced again in 1904 (as the Normal Athletic Club team), the Yosemites were nowhere to be found. It is possible that an O'Brien-led team had masqueraded as the Yosemites for a season. A little further evidence might be discerned from an article in the *Sun* at the conclusion of the 1904 season. This note was in regard to an upcoming game between the Normals and the Morgans and implied that the two teams would be playing their "annual" season-ending contest. Since the Morgans definitely did not play the Normals in 1903, but rather ended that campaign with the Yosemites, there might be some connection in that reporter's mind between the Cardinals and Yosemites. This is pure speculation, however, since hard documentation, such as a roster for either the Yosemites or the Normals, does not exist from 1903.

While no championships were flaunted in 1903, the Morgans did claim that the football team had "never been defeated in three seasons."

## Post Office Fails To Deliver

The nation would elect a new president. The Morgan Athletic Club hired a football coach. And the post office failed to deliver.

These were the early season topics as the club teams on the South Side regrouped for the 1904 season. The O'Brien brothers returned in force with a familiar lineup, but were now representing the Normal Athletic Association football team. Hugo Bezdek, the fullback for the powerful University of Chicago team, agreed to coach the Morgans in his spare time.

As the collegiate football season ensued, Bezdek was briefly engulfed in a controversy when the University of Illinois protested his eligibility for allegedly participating in a professional boxing match. The allegations were later dismissed and Bezdek was able to continue his dual career of coaching the Morgans and playing fullback for the Maroons. Stagg's well-oiled machine would stroll through an 8-1-1 season in 1904, but UC would initiate that successful run by demolishing Englewood High School 67-0 in a practice game. Englewood may have been affected by the absence of lineman Albert "Yellow Peril" Donovan, who missed the game to attend the funeral of his great-grandfather in Milwaukee.

In November, Teddy Roosevelt was elected president of the United States, and within a year, this election would prove to have a dramatic effect on the game of football, including the demise of this early version of the Chicago Cardinals/Normals. But for now, the team was focused on the season ahead as a member of the very loosely organized Chicago Football League, which claimed an impressive total of 147 teams in 1904. The Normals played most of their games at Hand's Park (67th and Stony Island Avenue), just south of the University of Chicago, and at the new Normal Park (61st and Racine). One of the key matchups by mid-season was the contest between the Normal Athletic Club and Wabash. As usual, the *Sun* provided a preview of the encounter:

> *Two of the foremost teams in the city will meet and the result will go a long way in settling the championship as neither team has been defeated this year. The Normals have weight advantage, Wabash speed. Such stars as Morrissey, Jenks, Collins, Johnson, Maloney, Palm, Mulvihill, St. John, and the O'Brien brothers will be seen in the Normal line-up.*

Many of the same names, such as Morrissey, Mulvihill, Palm, and Maloney, had been with the O'Briens in previous seasons and still formed the basis of one of the top-flight teams in the city. This was an important element in the consistent success of this group of players. With the emergence of so many club and prairie teams, it was quite common for players to jump ship to another team on a regular basis. For whatever reason, the Morgans/Cardinals/Normals were able to keep the nucleus together each season.

While we cannot define these players as strictly professional, i.e. they did not play the game for a specific wage (or expense reimbursement), there were a few means for collecting funds through these contests. The team most closely identified with the O'Brien brothers through those early years appeared to be a step above other club teams. It wasn't anywhere near the wealthy organization affiliated with the elite Chicago Athletic Association club, but it was respected enough that it could request, and receive, a share of the gate at "away" games such as at Michigan City, Woodstock, and Elgin—areas that were not accessible via the usual Chicago streetcar system. More commonly, the managers of the athletic clubs sponsoring the teams, such as the Morgan Athletic Club, would encircle the field and then charge a flat admission fee to anyone wishing to attend the game. At many games, a hat or helmet would simply be passed among the gathered spectators and whatever money was collected would be used to pay the officials and then be divided among the players. Finally, teams (and their followers) usually participated in side bets with the opposition. This could be as low as $5 per side for prairie teams of high school age to well over $100 per team in the games involving the more recognizable teams such as the Morgans and the Normals.

The term "semi-pro" thus might be an accurate definition of the Normal Athletic Association football team in 1904. While the players did not receive a salary for each game, they likely received a share of the gate (or hat) receipts, as minimal as that might be. One payday which did not occur was on October 23, when a game scheduled with the neighborhood post office football team was postponed when that team failed to appear.

Meanwhile, the Chicago Football League established a thinly veiled schedule but once again failed to establish a criteria for securing the championship. Teams included the Eurekas, Whirlwinds, Sheridans, Mohawks, Royals, Mosleys, Hamiltons, and Primas. "Most of these social and athletic clubs were really outgrowths of gang activity," stated noted local historian and author Dominic Pacyga, "and all were tied in with local gambling."

While most game scores are not available, the highlight of the 1904 season was the Normals' season-ending tie with the Morgan Athletic Club. On November 22, the Normals rehearsed for the Morgans by slipping past the Maplewoods 12-0 and "clinched the championship of the city in the heavyweight division" behind "the play of C. O'Brien, P. O'Brien, St. John and Morrissey," according to the *Sun*. "The Normals will play their last game of the season next Sunday with the Morgan Athletic Club at American league park for $150 a side."

The huge amount of this wager, in addition to the large crowd anticipated at the ballpark, would mean a lucrative afternoon for the winning team. The *Sun* was excited in its pregame summations:

> *What promises to be one of the most exciting amateur games ever held in the city will be pulled off next Sunday at Comiskey's Park at 39th and Wentworth when the Normals and Morgans get together to decide the championship of Chicago. Both teams have practically cleaned the boards this year, having made remarkable records for prairie elevens. The two teams are bitter rivals and have trained conscientiously all season with this one game in prospect.*
>
> *The Normals and Morgans are practically evenly matched in every department, except in the backfield, where the Normals have the advantage in weight. The Morgan backfield expects to make up in speed what it lacks in weight and with this idea in view have acquired the services of Fagan, Henry and Cavanaugh. Fagan is the star halfback on the Englewood High School eleven; Henry has gained a wide reputation with the Woodlawn Country Club as an open field runner and Cavanaugh is noted for his wonderful line playing. The line-up of the Normals will be practically the same as in the Maplewood game last Sunday.*

This brief prospectus yields many insights into the complexion of football at the time. The quote of "bitter rivals" might be considered an understatement since many of the players from both sides had been united as the Morgan Athletic Club's first football team in 1900. Since that time, the O'Brien brothers and many of those teammates had achieved a significant run as one of the better teams in the Midwest, whether they were the Morgans, the Cardinals, the Yosemites, or the Normals. Their departure from the Morgan Athletic Club in 1901 must have resulted in some harsh feelings on both sides. The Morgans thought enough of this game to reach out and recruit some additional talent, including local phenom George Fagan.

Fagan, a junior halfback at nearby Englewood High School, had already experienced a busy week by the time this game rolled around on Sunday, November 27. On Thanksgiving (November 24), Fagan and his Englewood teammates traveled to Moline, Illinois, to play that town's high school. The team then hopped a train and returned home the next day in time to play a league game on November 26 in Chicago. His participation against the Normals on Sunday simply indicates that if someone wanted to play football, the opportunity was there.

## Hugo Bezdek

As a seventeen-year-old halfback, Hugo Bezdek was a star for the Cardinal Athletic Club in 1901 before moving on to the University of Chicago from 1902 to 1905. He later became a successful college coach and was the only man to ever coach an NFL football team as well as manage a Major League Baseball squad. While at Chicago, Bezdek was accused once of professionalism by the University of Illinois and his eligibility was threatened.

However, the fingers were not pointing at Hugo for his time with the Cardinals, but rather that he supposedly took part in a professional prize fight before he entered the university. While this controversy was well-documented in the Chicago press at the time, it was never really explained why Bezdek was exonerated, until George Strickler of the *Chicago Tribune* reported the facts in 1937. The following article coincided with Bezdek's first visit to the city as coach of the Cleveland Rams:

> It has been thirty-two years since Bezdek charged up and down old Marshall Field at the direction of the late Walter Eckersall for the glory of A. A. Stagg and old Chicago. The Maroons lost only four games and played a 6-6 tie with Illinois in forty-four starts during Bezdek's four year career.
>
> It was while he was at Chicago that Bezdek became involved in the first professional scandal in western conference football. Illinois protested him, saying Bezdek was a professional prize fighter who boxed under the name of Young Hugo. It all developed out of Bezdek's willingness to do some friends a favor.
>
> Hugo was a pretty rugged individual in those days and liked to fight. There was a toughie around Chicago named Buck Montgomery. Montgomery had whipped the Italian middleweight, Hugo Kelly, in ten rounds. Some of the boys around Frank Ragen's club in the stockyards district thought they would like to get Montgomery licked.
>
> They asked Hugo if he thought he could do it. Hugo, then only 16, said yes. The match was made and Ragen's boys scheduled it for a south side club. Not a dollar was exchanged between the promoters and Bezdek. They just asked him if he could lick Montgomery and he said he could, so he went ahead and did it.
>
> Illinois heard about it and someone, identified by Bezdek as an Illinois coach, sought out Montgomery, offering him $100 to make an affidavit that Bezdek had been paid. Montgomery made the affidavit, received the $100, and the protest was filed. But Montgomery immediately called all of his newspaper friends, arrayed them before the bar at Vogelsang's and

said: "What'll you have, mugs? Dis is on de University of Illinois."
Then he explained how he had come by the $100. The reporters, all friends of Bezdek's, drank up the $100 in champagne!

Bezdek would go on to coach football at places such as Oregon and Penn State and serve as manager of the Pittsburgh Pirates baseball team. Not bad for a kid who attended Lake High School (now Tilden Tech) in Chicago, which didn't even field a football team.

## Swept Off Their Feet By The Terrible Onslaught

The climactic game of the 1904 season was everything it promised to be, but when it ended, so did an era of innocence and perhaps sweetness in Chicago-area football. Outside forces were simmering and plotting to eliminate the game, while the related injuries due to the competition were mounting, adding further fuel to the opposition's fire. Change would arrive soon.

When the Morgans and Normals finally encountered each other on the football field, it proved to be a terrific struggle. It was a day of man vs. man, shoulder vs. shoulder, and sweaty, nasty pushing and shoving . . . and all for naught! Neither team was able to score, so the historic matchup between the Normal Athletic Club and the Morgan Athletic Club ended in a 0-0 tie. The lack of scoring did not lead to a similar lack of words from the beguiled *Sun,* however:

> *The Normal Athletic Club and the Morgan Athletic Club met yesterday afternoon at Comiskey's baseball park in their annual football match, the final game of the season. After playing for 35 minutes, the score was 0-0.*
>
> *The game was heavily attended and the rooters of the rivals made the atmosphere resound with their respective yells, as both sides were out to score a victory, and thereby win the amateur championship of Chicago.*
>
> *The Normals had much the better of the contest, through their ability to play well together, while the Morgan team, composed mostly of present and past college stars, found it utterly impossible to play in union, owing to a lack of practice.*
>
> *In the first half, the Normals kept the ball in the Morgan territory continually, at one time having it as far as the Morgan five yard line, only to lose it on downs.*
>
> *The second half was practically a repetition of the first, the Morgans being swept off their feet by the terrible onslaught of the Normal backfield. The Morgans, however, braced when in danger at being scored on and thus were fortunate enough to come out of the struggle with a tie.*
>
> *The features of the game were the playing of O'Brien, Morrissey, Collins, and St. John for the Normals and the work of Moloney, Hogan, Towle and Cavanaugh for the Morgans:*

| NORMAL ATHLETIC CLUB | | | MORGAN ATHLETIC CLUB |
|---|---|---|---|
| *Lambert* | *LE* | *LE* | *Gilfoyle* |
| *Mulvihill* | *RT* | *LT* | *Cavanaugh* |
| *?* | *RG* | *LG* | *Pember* |

| | | | |
|---|---|---|---|
| *Maloney* | *C* | *C* | *Rallou* |
| *Doyle* | *LG* | *RG* | *Carmody* |
| *Johnson* | *LT* | *RT* | *Brennan* |
| *St. John* | *LE* | *RE* | *Henry* |
| *Jenks* | *QB* | *QB* | *Towle* |
| *P. O'Brien* | *RH* | *LH* | *Moloney* |
| *Collins/Morrissey* | *LH* | *RH* | *Fagan* |
| *C. O'Brien* | *FB* | *FB* | *Hogan* |

The final score and the fact that the Normals lost the ball on downs probably indicates that the field was not fitted with goal posts. Otherwise, with a field goal still worth the same amount of points (five) as a touchdown, the Normals would have no doubt utilized the strong leg of Pat O'Brien from the five-yard line for the easy chip shot and the victory.

Once again, a team led by the O'Brien brothers could claim a championship, this time a share of the city championship with the Morgan Athletic Club. City champions, county champions, state champions . . . the O'Brien brothers continued to compile the most successful record of all the early grid teams in Chicago. Their success was even more significant since the majority of the team members were graduates of the prairie football school of hard knocks, not gaining playing experience or instruction at high schools and colleges. While the run was not yet over, the end was near.

## Bloody Shambles Of Football

By 1905, the game of football was feeling the pressure for reform. Injuries were well-publicized nationwide and the *Chicago Tribune* continued to compile an annual report on the dead and injured. At the conclusion of the season, the *Tribune* published its yearly football casualty list which totaled 19 deaths and 159 injuries during 1905. Most fatalities were due to head or spinal injuries. The *Tribune* was quite vocal in its call for reform but it was perhaps two separate incidents late in the season which ultimately prompted massive changes in the game.

The first incident occurred during the last week of October 1905 in Worcester, Massachusetts, when Teddy Roosevelt Jr., the son of the president, was injured in a football game between the Harvard freshmen and Worcester Academy. Then on Saturday, November 25, William Moore, the right halfback for Union College, was fatally injured in a game against New York University.

The first injury snared the attention of the president. The second situation earned the interest of his nation. The *Chicago Tribune,* in noting the loss of Moore, stated:

> *The death of Moore may have far reaching consequences. He may be the sacrificial victim on the altar of "sport" whose blood will cry aloud with so much insistence that even the deafest of college authorities must listen, and listening, act.*

Immediately, the *Tribune* dispatched a telegram to President Roosevelt, "to whom the safe and sane devotees of college sport are looking to lead the way out of the bloody shambles of football as played at present . . ." In the telegram, the newspaper doesn't demand the abolition of the sport, but strongly hints at significant reform:

*HON. THEODORE ROOSEVELT*
*WASHINGTON, D.C. NOV. 25*
  *The 1905 football season practically closed today with two dead on the field of battle. Today's fatalities bring the total of slain to 19 and the injured (record being made of accidents out of the ordinary) to 137.*
  *This year's record of deaths is more than double that of the yearly average for the last five years, the total for that period being forty-five. A significant fact is that the teams playing an open game have escaped with less than their usual quota of accidents.*

### THE CHICAGO TRIBUNE

Between the lines, the *Tribune* was exhorting the president to grab the lead in forcing any changes needed to reduce the significant number of injuries and deaths so well associated with the game. Clearly, the manly interaction and the thrill of the collisions between the teams transfixed the spectators and was a major part of the game's appeal. One Chicago minister, the Rev. W. A. Bartlett of the First Congregational Church, described it as such in the *Tribune:*

> *Not since the days of the Roman games in the Coliseum have such concourses of the leaders in society been gathered together . . . People will crowd to see these games as long as they are played. The terrific nature of the struggle and its risks are a matter of fascination. But for eighty-three of the finest sons of the country to be killed and wounded in three months makes a costly amusement, and just now comes the news that a preacher dropped dead from excitement in watching a Thanksgiving game. This may be considered the latest theological departure!*

The main argumentative theme seemed to focus not only on the need for changes to the game, but rather whether significant change would be enough or whether football should be abolished completely. Already some colleges and high schools were dismantling their football programs and the *Tribune* encouraged comments on this predicament from different institutions. Notre Dame favored the abolishment of the sport in high school "for the protection of immature boys" and "purified in colleges." Cornell University requested that "authorities immediately purge football of its evils and danger to life and limb," while the University of California called for the game to be "entirely made over as far as playing rules are concerned, or abolished." President C. L. Mees of Rose Polytechnic in Indiana found another sort of evil:

> *Professionalism in players with coaches must be absolutely done away with. Making a winning team a means of advertising an institution of learning should be branded as quack advertising.*

No matter what the opinion, change was in the air. In Chicago, the death of Oak Park High School's Vernon Wise during a game with Hyde Park prompted both schools to initiate proceedings to abolish the sport—even though the injury occurred in a reserve game. On November 28, 1905, President Roosevelt quickly released his "Football Reform Platform" encouraging uniform eligibility rules, reduction of brutal play, and greater accountability from each school regarding the enforcement of rules. Roosevelt went on to add:

*. . . it would be a real misfortune to lose so manly and vigorous a game as foot-*
*ball, and to avert such a possibility the college authorities in each college should*
*see to it that the game in that college is clean.*

While Roosevelt's suggestions were a start, they would not be enough. In early December, the football rules committee, including Stagg of Chicago, met in Philadelphia and proposed sweeping changes to the game. One of the biggest adjustments suggested was the yardage requirement for a first down being moved from five to ten yards (although this still needed to be accomplished in just three downs until another rules change for the fourth down came about in 1912). Forward passing was also allowed although it was accompanied by some wacky rules, such as that a pass needed to be thrown at least five yards to the left or right of where the ball was snapped back to that passer. An offensive team could lose possession on certain incomplete passes as well. Finally, a neutral zone was established, hurdling by runners was outlawed, the balls were physically streamlined, and games were reduced to a pair of thirty-minute halves (down from thirty-five).

The intent was to lessen brutality and to develop a more wide-open game. At the time, left guard Merrill Meigs of the University of Chicago (who now has a Chicago airport named after him) agreed with the new regulations:

*The ten yard suggestion . . . will mean the trying of many more experiments by*
*the team having possession of the ball. I believe it will tend to develop a kicking*
*game and a tendency to end running. It will develop stronger interference and*
*a speedier team all around. I regard the suggestion of having two umpires as excel-*
*lent. It will do away with much of the unnecessary dirty work.*

What did this have to do with the Morgans, Normals, etc.? Plenty!

## *Take Your Girl To The Circus*

The local season had started out in 1905 with a shocker when it was learned that the O'Brien brothers and their usual assortment of teammates would rejoin the Morgan Athletic Club team. Frank Ragen took over as coach of the football squad, promptly named Pat O'Brien as the team captain, and announced his plans for the season in the *Sun* on September 29:

*Coach Frank Ragen scrimmaged against the second team coached by assistant coach*
*Riker. "Eleven stars" reported to Ragen for work and the number included some*
*of the best men in the city. Coach Ragen hopes to open the season soon and has*
*been promised a game with one of the university teams.*

The Morgans in 1905 now more clearly resembled a local all-star team with this unique combination of the two best heavyweight teams in the city. The club itself also invested $1,000 when it took over the entire building at 5401 South Halsted in order to expand its headquarters.

The powerful Morgan Athletic Club football team captured one early season victory with a forfeit win over the Maplewood Indians. The Indians were unable to attend the fracas on the fresh field at Sherman Park, thus disappointing the Morgans' followers, according to the *Sun:*

> *Over 300 members marched in body to Sherman Park, led by the Morgan Fife and Drum Corps and had their pictures taken in a group after which they all returned to the clubhouse where a program had been arranged for their pleasure.*

A few days later (October 26), the newspaper reported that:

> *The Morgans, for four years champions in the football world and their strong competitors, the Kershaws will meet on the Morgans' grounds at 58th and Halsted to decide the long-claimed laurels ownership.*

While the Morgans easily defeated the Kershaws 27-0 on Sunday, October 29, they also snuck in a game against the visiting Rock Island Stars on the preceding day which resulted in a scoreless tie. For the first time, it appeared that the Morgan Athletic Club was seeking opponents a step above the old tried and true club adversaries on the South Side. Following the Rock Island contest, Ragen arranged for a game with a team from the Fort Sheridan military base on Sunday, November 5. Fort Sheridan actively competed against the foremost collegiate teams and this would be its first challenge against a non-academic football club. Most recently, it had lost a close 5-0 encounter to Northwestern University. The strength of the Morgan Athletic Club could now be compared with those of the leading Midwest universities which had played Fort Sheridan previously.

Ragen also coaxed Hugo Bezdek back to help coach the Morgans as the team increased its practice load to four nights per week in anticipation of the big game. In reality, the scheduling of the game with Fort Sheridan was probably both an economic and a social boost for the neighborhood. While the game itself was a unique attraction, Ragen planned a "military demonstration" of some kind before the kickoff and encouraged local members and merchants to rally around his team. For example, Miss Nora Breheny of 349 West 43rd Street hosted a Halloween party for the football team and decorated the house in the maroon and gold colors of the Morgan Athletic Club. Also on Halloween, a trio of sisters (Anna, Julia, and Rita Butler) held a reception for the Fort Sheridan soldiers. This was apparently big news for the *Sun,* as it reported the evening in great detail, including the entertainment:

> *Games such as the boys usually indulge in on occasions of this kind were the order of the evening, "post office" and "take your girl to the circus" were prevalent.*

Ragen added to the building expectations by announcing that the team would venture out to the hinterlands at Auburn Park (79th and Wentworth) for "secret" practices.

The Normal Athletic Association, as it was now known, continued to play football games in 1905 at its new park at 69th and Green. However, its difficulty with relatively minor opponents, such as a 6-6 tie with the Young Royals, demonstrated that the Normals football team had been sapped of its previous strength.

As the days and hours ticked down to the kickoff with Fort Sheridan, an extremely heavy band of thundershowers swept into the city and forced a postponement of the game. When the two teams finally met on November 12, the Morgans zipped out to an early lead and blanked the soldiers 27-0. The easy victory astounded the crowd and generated favorable comparisons with the undefeated University of Chicago powerhouse which finished a perfect 10-0 in 1905. Although UC did not play Fort Sheridan that year, the Maroons defeated Northwestern 32-0 and Illinois 44-0. Northwestern, on the other hand, had shut out Fort Sheridan 5-0 while the Morgan Athletic Club had dealt the soldiers a 27-0 defeat. Based solely on these comparative scores, the Morgans might have been at least the second-best team overall in Illinois that season.

The lineup of familiar names for the game with Fort Sheridan included the following: Gilfoy (LE), Johnson (LT), Myers (LG), Maloney, Palm/Pember (RG), Mulvihill (RT), Fagan (RE), O'Brien (QB), Collins (LH), and Morrissey (FB). The right halfback was not listed, but was probably Pat O'Brien, with Chris O'Brien handling the quarterbacking chores.

Although the Morgan Athletic Club never did play a university team in 1905, it did manage to close out its stellar season with a game against the Deering Maroons on November 13. As usual, the dependable *Sun* provided its readers with glowing information on the importance of this game, which would decide the heavyweight championship of the city:

> . . . these being the only heavyweight teams that have not lost a game, and the winner of Sunday's contest will decide who gets the banner which is being given by the Chicago Football League. The Deerings are considered by North siders to be the best team ever got together outside of a college. Most of the men have had high school training on the gridiron. Five of their men are old North division stars, two are from Northwestern. They are being coached by Leo De Trey and Wallie Steffen of Chicago University fame. The Morgans have Hugo Bezdek showing the team the fine points of the game, and as his time is up at Chicago, he will be in the Morgans' line-up Sunday. It was with the Morgans that he first learned the game. The rest of the Morgans line-up will be the same as usual. As this is the last game of the season, a record-breaking crowd is expected.

Yet despite the hype and anticipation of this final game of the illustrious 1905 season, none of the newspapers in the Chicago area mentioned the final score. If victorious, the Morgan Athletic Club and the O'Brien brothers would have grabbed still another city title in a remarkable seven-year skein of success. We do know that Bezdek returned to action and played right halfback while Chris O'Brien started at left end. However, by 1906 the well-publicized games of the Morgans, Cardinals, and Normals had all but disappeared.

## *Brutality Has Been Added To Football*

The wildly popular game of prairie football ("from 5,000 to 8,000 people watch these games every Sunday," stated the *Chicago Daily News*) finally met its match via a bureaucratic decision in Chicago that was prompted by the massive rules changes of late 1905. Grabbing on to the shirttails of the national football reform movement, Edward B. Degroot, athletic director of the Chicago South Park Commissioners, announced that he would immediately revise the rules governing local football. Mr. Degroot's objective was to eliminate injuries and brutality in all games played on the nine football fields in the city parks on Chicago's South Side. Primarily, the changes would include arranging all schedules for games played in the parks, supervising each game, and pitting teams of equal weight average against each other. Degroot told the *Chicago Tribune* (December 14):

> *The park commissioners have done well to recommend changes in the game as it is played in the parks, as there is much greater need for reform among these players than among properly coached college teams. It is unfortunate that the word "brutality" has been applied to football, as I do not believe there is any real brutality in the game. There is, however, a great need for improvement in the management of the games in the parks, aside from the changes in the rules. Crowds gather at the games and surge over the field, contributing much to the rowdy spirit and often causing disorder amounting almost to riots. With proper supervision, this will be eliminated.*

While the new football rules on the national level were almost universally praised, a "test" game between two small schools in Kansas (Washburn and Fairmount) was played on Christmas Day, 1905, using the revised procedures. While the game ended in a scoreless tie and no serious injuries were experienced, neither offense was able to get anywhere near the opponent's goal line. The main difficulty, surmised referee Dr. John Outland, was the new requirement of gaining ten yards for a first down. After the game he said:

> *It seems to me if ten yards is required in three downs it would almost eliminate touchdowns, except through fakes or flukes . . . I firmly believe the ten yard rule will open up the game, but the teams must be given four downs to make the distance.*

The rules changes, both nationally and locally, had a dual effect on teams such as the Morgans. Most importantly, teams would not be allowed to charge admission if they played in a public park. In order to benefit financially from these games, the semi-pro teams like the Morgans would need to scramble in order to find playing space at a privately owned facility, such as Normal Park, or an open space which could be converted into a football field. Also, if they did use the parks, the teams would be subject to the scheduling whims of the park commissioner which in itself could lead to a whole new arena of problems. But there were some available solutions, according to historian Dominic Pacyga, history professor at Columbia College in Chicago:

> *Since football teams were not allowed to charge admission if the games were played in a public park they would often hold "Tag Days." Gang members would stand outside and sell tags to anyone wanting to see the game and this money was then often used for gambling. Of course, this was totally illegal, but since police officers and park workers were members of the gangs, no one seemed to notice.*

The new rules would also have an impact on the prairie game. With the ten-yard gain for a first down rule in place, the games could become dreadfully boring, especially since many of the fields used at the time did not have goal posts. With the opportunity to kick field goals removed, the chances for scoring were reduced even more. Finally, one must also consider the competition factor at the time. The Morgan Athletic Club of 1905 had easily outgrown its competition and was now playing at a level well above the neighborhood club team.

For whatever reason—the lack of fields, the threat of boring football, or the perceived lack of quality competition—the Morgan Athletic Club football team apparently disappeared after the 1905 season. Later in 1906, the South Parks Commissioners would hinder local football even further by closing the parks to prairie football games unless the teams requested, and received, a permit to play on a certain field. All players were also required to take a physical and receive the approval of a physician in order to play in any game on a park field. This caused considerable consternation since many football followers mistook this as a threat to eliminate football. Not so, countered Degroot:

*I have never been in favor of abolishing football; for I once liked to play myself, and there is a fascination in the game for the youngsters.*

Superintendent Foster of the Parks Commission told *The Daily News* on November 6 that the rules were necessary to ensure the sanctity of the game:

*Our ruling is a necessary precaution for the lives of these hundreds of boys must be guarded, and the only way it can be done is to request permits and physicians' certificates. It is readily seen that it would be foolish to allow boys to play such a strenuous game in the public breathing spots if they carried with them weak hearts or lungs.*

The Normals played a few scattered games in 1906 at Normal Park as a member of the burgeoning Chicago Football League, said to include over 150 teams in several weight divisions. While the teams and players moaned over the new local mandates of the South Parks Commission, they were also frustrated by the evolution of the rules themselves, as reported by *The Daily News:*

*Teams playing in the Chicago Football league, the Prairie League, as it is called in some circles, complain that teams working with the new rules find themselves handicapped on the end-run plays by the crowd which gathers around both teams close to ends of the lines. The one crying need is a clear field for the players and this many teams seem unable to secure, except on the enclosed grounds.*

*The new rules, which call for ten yard gains, must be mixed up with forward passes and quarterback kicks and punts to be effective. A kick into the crowd is sure to drop to the ground and the man who gets there first has all the luck and the chance for a long run. With the forward pass there is little or no chance to get the play away successfully.*

The highlight of the season was an intriguing "professional" game played at Comiskey's Park. Over twenty-five hundred spectators watched the pro team from Massillon, Ohio, edge a group of college all-stars 9-4 on Thanksgiving Day in what was called the "First professional football game under college rules played in Chicago." The *Tribune* described the game as "excessively slow, old time football," and added:

*It is questionable whether the innovation scored a success sufficient to make friends of the college game fear for the effect of the professional encroachment.*

The local season concluded on December 16, when the Hurons captured the Chicago Football League championship by defeating the Spaldings 4-0 at the National League ballpark on the North Side.

Following the 1906 season, the history of the Cardinals/Morgans/Normals becomes foggy, sketchy, and somewhat invisible until 1916. While traces and clues of the team's existence during that "lost" decade are rarely evident, Chris O'Brien apparently did continue to field teams and managed to stay active as a player as well. Because these teams toiled in the obscurity of the "prairie leagues," their scores were rarely reported in the local media. While playing football, O'Brien also concentrated on his family and his career as a painter. He had married his wife Frieda (Benecke) on July 28, 1904, at Visitation Church and moved to 5150 South Halsted. Meanwhile, his brother Pat had become an electrician and now resided at 1038 West 53rd Place. By 1910, Chris had opened a paint shop at 5531 South Ashland and rented a house at 5640 South Centre. His only child, Edward A. O'Brien, was born that same year. The household also included Frieda's sister, Anna, who worked in the paintshop, as did her widowed mother, Sophia.

Football continued to be under the microscope, although the deadly injuries started to diminish. It wasn't until 1912 that additional rules were implemented which modernized the game as it is known today. The field was shortened to one hundred yards, the fourth down was added, and a touchdown was now worth six points (field goals had been reduced to three points in 1909). Some of the archaic passing rules were whipped into shape as well to make that aspect of the game more attractive. Previously, passes had been limited to twenty yards and any ball caught in the recently added end zone was now a touchdown, not a touchback.

## The Oldest Team In The NFL

During this time, the cheerful *Sun* went out of business (and eventually was absorbed by the *Englewood Times*), leaving football fans, both at that time and in the future, without a solid resource for extensive coverage of local football games. In its place were publications such as the *Englewood Times,* which largely ignored football.

By 1913, the Chicago Football League had reorganized and was pairing teams according to light and middleweight divisions, but the league was not without its difficulties. The *Chicago Tribune* reported on the result of a game on the far South Side:

*After the Thorns football team had run up 56 points against the South Chicagos at Bessemer Park yesterday the adherents of the losing team surged on the field. Timothy Murphy, the lone park policeman, plunged into the melee and both sides started for him. Murphy decided to take more time to investigate which side was in the wrong, and selected the field house as a first class place for his deliberations. The football players followed him all the way, but couldn't have caught him without wings to help them. When reserves arrived the crowd had vanished.*

Although there were few semi-pro and club teams in existence at the time, one interesting team was the Chicago Ripmores. This team played an eccentric schedule, traveling to Detroit to lose to the Heralds 19-0, while also staying home to play high school teams. By 1914, the North Ends proved to be the toast of Chicago by defeating the Cornell-Hamburgs 7-0 on November 1 at Comiskey's Park for the city championship. However, in a rematch (probably because there was no one else to play) on November 26, the Cornells won 20-15 at Northwestern University, prompting the victors to claim the Cook County Independent Football Championship.

Ragen's Colts (sponsored by now County Commissioner Frank Ragen) returned to prominence in local football circles in 1915 when the team reached the semi-finals of the heavyweight football division. However, it wasn't until the following year (1916) that Chris O'Brien resurfaced with his new team, the Racine Cardinals. In a word, this edition of the renewed club was "bad." O'Brien was so starved for gridders that he usually placed his own thirty-six-year-old body in the lineup. The Cardinals failed to win a game in 1916, but even worse, they were unable to score.

This appearance in 1916 verifies that the Arizona Cardinals are the oldest NFL club in terms of continuous operation. With Chris O'Brien as the "link" between the Morgan Athletic Association and the Racine/Chicago/St. Louis/Arizona Cardinals, the team can claim an unequaled heritage dating back to 1899.

Football seemed to explode in popularity in the Midwest in 1916, with professional and semi-pro teams prominent in Indiana, Ohio, Illinois, and Michigan. Knute Rockne was playing end for the Detroit Heralds while Jim Thorpe was active with the Canton (OH) team. In Chicago, the North Ends, Cornell-Hamburgs, Stayms, and Pullman Thorns emerged as the top teams, with the Cornells capturing the championship of the Cook County Heavyweight Football league with a 7-6 win over the North Ends on November 30. The largest crowd (ten thousand) ever to watch an "independent" game viewed the title tilt at Northwestern University in Evanston, Illinois.

One of the reasons for the renewed popularity of the game might be traced to the increased use of the forward pass as an effective offensive weapon. Scores were higher and the game was more wide open. Interaction with teams from other areas added to the interest. Often, the scoring was detrimental to the enjoyment of the game as in 1916 when Ohio State blasted Oberlin 128-0, St. Viator smashed Lane Tech College of Chicago 205-0, and Englewood High School eased past Morgan Park High School 77-0.

As for the Racine Cardinals, they were unable to do anything with the football, being shut out by the likes of the Cornell Athletic Club (6-0), the Iroquois Athletic Club (28-0), the Standards (41-0), and the Alpines (20-0). The Cardinals were not part of any formal league in 1916 and struggled to schedule games and fields. O'Brien preferred nearby Normal Park when it was available. By this time, O'Brien and his wife Frieda had moved to 5626 South Racine (four blocks from Normal Park). If local football custom held true, this is where Chris created the name Racine Cardinals; Racine from the street of his address and Cardinals presumably from his previous team of fifteen years earlier. Most early teams grabbed the name of the foremost street in the neighborhood to serve as the identity of that team. Since the team lacked games, O'Brien may have looked into joining the Chicago Independent Football League, which included the Cornells, North Shore, the Alpines, the Lexingtons, the Blue Bells, and the Wallaces if there were no other alternatives.

# *He Was So Fast . . . His Interference Got In His Way!*

If there was a central theme to broadly define football in 1917, it might be called "organization." In Chicago, the Chicago Football League was reorganized with the Cardinals among the many members. Spokesman and organizer Tom O'Conner described the CFL as the "biggest amateur association ever introduced into the city." Over in Indiana, teams from Hammond, Wabash, and Pine Village agreed to a three-team professional league with "home and away" contests scheduled between each of the three clubs. The Fort Wayne Friars were also invited to participate, but the Friars insisted on playing all home games and were promptly forgotten.

Hammond (IN) would prove to be the most ambitious team in the Chicago area. Manager Paul Parduhn took over a team previously known as the Clabbys and actively recruited players from major colleges and universities, despite the scarcity of available talent due to World War I. "Salary is not a question with him," wrote the *Hammond Times*, "it is only a matter of getting players for the backfield equally as good as his celebrated line . . ." The team had tremendous hometown support and was not hesitant to play any opponent in the Midwest. For the first three games, Hammond would go on the road to battle the Detroit Heralds and Davenport (Iowa) before returning home to face Racine, Wisconsin. This club was much more cosmopolitan than its counterparts in the Chicago area, with only three players on the roster actually being from the Hammond area by 1919.

Parduhn scored a coup just two games into the season when he signed Swede Hallstrom of Illinois and Northwestern All-American Paddy Driscoll to play for his team. Driscoll should have been a senior on the Northwestern team in 1917, but he played in thirteen games as a baseball player for the Chicago Cubs the previous summer and therefore lost his remaining collegiate athletic eligibility. Chicago sportswriter Leo Fischer actually put Parduhn and Driscoll in contact with each other. Fischer recommended that Driscoll be given a tryout and Parduhn agreed, later offering Driscoll $40 per game.

Paddy made an immediate impact in the game at Davenport by scoring all of the points in a 9-3 victory, including a sixty-five-yard run for a touchdown in the first quarter. Later he scored all of the points again in a 13-0 whitewash of Pine Village, only the second defeat in twelve years for that team. Driscoll was so fast, complained the local press, that "his interference got in his way."

Parduhn stated publicly that his payroll was already $450 per week and he hoped to increase that to $500 a week with another key acquisition or two. By the end of the season it had risen to $700. To offset his expenses, Parduhn offered reserved seating at home games for $1 each and non-reserved spots for 75¢. He made certain that those in the cheap seats didn't block the vision of those lofty $1 ticket holders! The team also arranged for train transportation if giddy fans desired to join the players on their trips to Davenport, Lafayette, etc. Hammond was a fan-friendly organization and was proud of it. But the entire city took umbrage on October 29, 1917, when the *Chicago Examiner* grouped the team's results in with the "Prairie Football" scores. The *Hammond Times* quickly retorted:

> *Where those birds get prairie football we don't know.*
> *With rows of machines (autos) making the league park look like the Indianapolis Speedway on Decoration Day, a grand-standed field enclosed by a barb-wire fence*

*to puncture little boys when they perch atop; visitors from a dozen cities near and far; Curley Kimball's hot-dogs; old Doc Young, the club saw-bones, running gaily out on the gridiron now and then to set a fractured collar bone . . . SAY, WHADDJA MEAN BO BY "PRAIRIE FOOTBALL?"*

Despite having Driscoll and Hallstrom in camp, Parduhn wanted more after accepting an offer from the Fort Wayne Friars to play for the professional championship of Indiana. He publicly offered Ohio State's talented young halfback Chick Harley the uncommon sum of $200 per game to play for Hammond after the collegiate season ended. When Harley politely refused in order to maintain his eligibility, Parduhn created an even more bizarre marketing ploy than usual (although he was fond of constantly being accused by other teams of "loading up" for certain games. He never seemed to deny these claims, but always replied with a "legitimate" excuse.) After several college luminaries turned down his offer to play for Hammond, Parduhn, for whatever reason, contacted film star Douglas Fairbanks. Parduhn offered Fairbanks a total of $1,000, plus ten percent of the gate receipts and expenses, to play with Hammond and add "pep" to the team for the big game with Fort Wayne. News of the offer was picked up by the United Press wire service and published all over the country, giving the Hammond team unprecedented national publicity. Of course, Fairbanks was unable to accept the offer but responded anyway with "I am very sorry but previous arrangements necessitate my declining your kind offer. Hope you have a great game."

## Bite 'um, Kick 'um, Slug 'um, Kill 'um

However, Hammond was able to add former Cornell halfback Johnny Barrett for the remainder of the season. Called the "most famous professional football player of them all" by the *Hammond Times,* Barrett had just completed his season as the manager/coach of the Youngstown, Ohio, team and stepped into the lineup for a Thanksgiving Day victory (15-0) over the Cornell-Hamburgs, defending champions of the Chicago Football League. The Cornells, noted for their liberal interpretation of the rules, were surprisingly timid against Parduhn's array of former collegiate stars, reported the *Hammond Times:*

> *All of the elements of football and a few of another game in which a referee's services are needed were visible to a holiday audience . . . the bite 'um, kick 'um, slug 'um, kill 'um tactics for which the Cornells are noted were used with little effect . . .*

The contingent of Hammond professionals then proceeded to wallop Fort Wayne on December 2 to capture the championship of Indiana. Parduhn decided to cash in on one more big payday and invited the Detroit Heralds with the legendary Jim Thorpe to play in Hammond on December 9th. With so many players enlisting in the military, it was felt that this would be the last professional football game in the area until the conclusion of the war. With the rugged Thorpe in Detroit's lineup, there was a great deal of excitement in the air for this final game. Although a combination of snow and ice prompted its cancellation, Hammond would prove to be a football power once again in the very near future.

For the Cardinals, success in the 1917 campaign did not come easily. During the off-season, O'Brien added some talent with players like Red Nelson, Ambrose McGurk, and Mac McInery and acquired a more reliable schedule for the year. Unlike other clubs, like Hammond, where "salary was not a problem," O'Brien needed to locate talented players and coax them into playing with a team where "salary was a problem."

Once again, the Cardinals started off very slowly and failed to score in the first two games, a 0-0 tie with the Mohawks and a 20-0 loss to the Hamlins. But "a 55 yard run by Smith of the Cardinals helped beat the Opals 13-7" on November 18, according to the *Chicago Evening Post.* By Thanksgiving, the Cardinals had improved to 2-2-3, but they were well behind the undefeated Logans and Thorns in the league standings. It didn't seem to matter to O'Brien, however; he was having too much fun. It had to be a thrill for him to open up the *Tribune* the day after a 25-6 loss to the Tornadoes early in the season and read "Chris O'Brien played a star defensive game for the losers." On Thanksgiving Day, the Cards stopped the Standards 19-6 to improve to 3-2-3. Overall, the league games were competitive, prompting the *Chicago Evening American* to write:

> *Interest is increasing in amateur football circles as the year gets well on its way. The rivalry displayed by the various clubs in the Chicago league has gone a long way in the staging of very interesting games. As a result, the fans of the city are being treated to a great brand of the gridiron sport.*

The players seemed to be earning some income due to the influx of fans to the games. The *Hammond Times* explained some of the "behind the scenes" financial negotiations between the East Chicago Gophers and the Pullman Thorns:

> *. . . the winner of the game will carry away sixty per cent of the net receipts, while the loser will grab off the remaining 40 per cent. Besides this, the contract calls for a $250 side bet which must be deposited with Harry Cohn, a well known East Chicago business man by Tuesday night.*

## We Wore Shimmels

One of O'Brien's key players that season was a 5'10", 163-pound end named Donald Davidson, who spent time with the Cardinals, the Pullman Thorns, and the Tornadoes. The story of Davidson (born in 1898) is a delightful one. After completing his football career, he spent twenty-seven years with the Pullman Company in Chicago manufacturing railroad cars. He then retired briefly, but returned to spend twelve more years as a manufacturer's representative for the Imperial Brass Company. Still he was not done. At the age of sixty, Davidson went back to school and earned a degree in Business Administration from the University of Chicago. But it was not until the age of ninety-one that he was "discovered."

Like many Chicagoans, Davidson retired from a lifetime of work in the Windy City and then migrated to Arizona. His wife Phyllis recalled that although her husband played for the Cardinals, "he always followed football, especially the Bears." When the couple moved from the Chicago area and eventually resided in Green Valley, Arizona (south of Tucson), Davidson quietly shared some of his faraway football experiences with his neighbor and friend Joe Grass. Afterwards, Grass made some inquiries and it was apparent that Davidson was one of the oldest surviving members of the Cardinals. Soon Davidson was featured in the local press as well as honored at a Cardinals game during the 1989 season.

While Davidson didn't quite grasp why he was the object of all of this attention, it was a long-overdue tribute to one of the early pioneers of pro football. Because of his "discovery," Mr. Davidson was able to provide information on the early days of the Cardinals which had previously been unknown. On November 5, 1989, Davidson was presented with a personalized Cardinals jersey and served as the honorary team captain for the pregame coin toss with the New York Giants. Although Mr. Davidson has since passed away, his legacy will live on through the numerous interviews he provided in 1989. Here are a few of his statements (courtesy of the Arizona Cardinals) as he reflected on his early playing days on the South Side of Chicago:

**On the game of football:** We called it prairie football in those days. We practiced at a public park and we would practice two nights a week after work. Then we would practice a little bit before the game on Sunday to go over our signals and so forth. We played sixty minutes. We didn't have an offensive team and a defensive team. We didn't have a huddle. There was very little forward passing. It was mostly all ground plays. And we had to buy our own uniforms. No one issued anything. Neighborhood doctors came to the games to help if anyone was injured.

**On football equipment:** We wore shimmels (shoulder pads) and leather helmets.

**On salary:** It was a weekend activity. There was no salary involved. You didn't get paid anything for a game. If there was any profit at the end of the season, maybe you got a couple hundred dollars out of it. You played for the love and the glory of the game and of the neighborhood that you represented. The competition was really between the neighborhoods. They had great pride in their football teams.

Davidson joined the Cardinals in 1917, but his playing career was interrupted by naval service in World War I. When he returned home, Chris O'Brien petitioned him to rejoin the team but to no avail. The decision wasn't about money or playing time, as Davidson told the ***Green Valley News and Sun,*** it was simply about travel—local travel. According to Mr. Davidson, the Cardinals "worked out at 45th and Racine. I had to get there by streetcar. The (Chicago) Tornadoes practiced at 115th Street and Halsted, which was a lot closer for me. O'Brien wanted me to play with the Cardinals. He was pretty mad. But I told him, 'What's the difference?'"

Davidson finished his postwar football career with the Pullman Thorns and later with the Tornadoes, but he'll always be remembered as a Cardinal.

Back in 1917, as the game was finally beginning to gain its footing and respect in the city, the not-so-subtle tugs of a world war were becoming apparent to players such as Davidson and the teams they represented. The United States had entered the First World War with a declaration of war against Germany on April 6, 1917. As a result, the government initiated a selective service system which mandated a draft registration for all men between the ages of twenty-one and thirty. As the war effort intensified from late fall of 1917 and into early 1918, many players like Davidson bravely heeded the call to serve their country.

There was no question that the war effort took precedence, but the movement of manpower into the trenches understandably left football teams at the postgraduate level searching for able bodies to fill the holes on the roster.

## Cigar Box Football

The 1917 season would prove to be the lengthiest in the Cardinals' history, brought about in part by an odd playoff system as well as the availability of an indoor field to finish things when the regular season refused to end. To bring this curious tale together, let's rejoin the Cardinals in November. As noted, on Thanksgiving Day, the Cardinals stopped the Standards 19-6 to improve their slate at 3-2-3. Nothing incredible, but a significant improvement from their 0-2-2 start a few weeks earlier. The *Chicago Herald* provided the following brief description of the victory:

> *Although outweighed, the Racine Cardinals trampled on the Standards at Normal Park yesterday, the final score being 19-6. Forward passes featuring Davidson, Irvine and Gibly decided the game.*

The following week (December 2), the Cards checked in with still another score-less tie (their fourth of the season) when they met the Logan Square club at DePaul University on the North Side. Despite a rather mediocre—and unusual—3-2-4 record, the Cardinals were included in a peculiar five-team playoff to determine the champion of the Chicago Football League. However, because of very brutal winter weather, the games were continually postponed until it was agreed that the contests would be played indoors at the Dexter Park Pavilion, now known as the International Amphitheater, at the Union Stockyards.

The Racine Cardinals were paired against the Tornadoes, while the Logan Squares would face the Mohawks as part of a football doubleheader on December 23. Following these opening games, the winners would square off for the opportunity to meet the Thorns for the overall city championship. The Thorns kept in shape by playing in an indoor charity game against the visiting Minneapolis Eagles on Christmas Day and raising the princely sum of $8,000 for the local Knights of Columbus Soldier Recreation Fund. Although a surprising 3-0 loss to the Eagles dropped the Thorns from the unbeaten ranks, it did not tarnish the Chicago League playoffs since this was considered an "exhibition" game.

The *Hammond Times* embraced this idea of playing football indoors:

> *As far as it is known, Chicago is the first city to attempt "cigar-box football," as some of the large dailies have termed it. There is no doubt, whatever, but that the indoor game has many advantages over the outdoor, especially at this season of the year.*
>
> *Football enthusiasts from South Chicago, East Chicago, Gary, Hammond, Hegewisch, Riverdale, Harvey, Blue Island, and Morgan Park are eager to take advantage of the increased facilities provided for the fans at Dexter Park Pavilion. There will be a seat for everyone with the thermometer at a comfortable temperature. Adieu frost-bitten feet, noses and ears. Just imagine sitting in a comfortable chair, with an unobstructed view of a gridiron almost as large as the regulation outdoor variety . . .*

On December 22, the day before the doubleheader was scheduled to take place at Dexter Pavilion, the *Chicago Daily News* announced a change in the matchups. The Tornadoes would now play the Mohawks and the Racine Cardinals would face the

Evanstons. Following the conclusion of his playing season with Hammond, Paddy Driscoll decided to play with Evanston and participate in this new indoor football experience."Each of the four contending elevens has a formidable line-up of former college and university stars and keen and interesting battles are looked for by the fans," stated the *Daily News.*

However, both games ended in ties, as reported by the *Evening Post:*

> *The Mohawks and Tornadoes played a 0-0 tie while Paddy Driscoll's Evanstons and the Racine Cardinals played a 0-0 tie at Dexter Park yesterday afternoon. A big crowd saw the indoor football performance.*

Since neither of these games helped ease the gridlock, another indoor doubleheader (against different opponents) was locked in place for Sunday, January 6, 1918. In this set of games, the Cardinals, with aging Chris O'Brien at halfback, tied the Tornadoes 3-3, and the Mohawks concluded their afternoon with the same score against Evanston. The *Chicago Daily News* provided some brief insight:

> *The first of the double bill was the Cardinals-Tornadoes tussle. The Racine lads scored in the first period on a field goal by McGurk. The advantage looked good until the final period, when Busch dropped back to the 35 yard-line and sent the oval between the uprights. It was anybody's game right up to the finish.*
>
> *The trusty toe of Paddy Driscoll, former Northwestern star, saved Evanston from defeat. Driscoll booted the pigskin over the bars from the 35 yard-line in the third quarter . . .*

Would this season ever end? League officials, puzzled by this rash of tie games and lack of offensive movement, plotted still another round of games. But this time, the rules would be changed in an effort to improve the offense as well as determine a winner. The initial attempt to reschedule was set for Tuesday, January 8, but the clubs requested an extension in order to practice under the altered rules. Meanwhile, a huge blizzard socked the Chicago area on January 12 and the games were moved to Sunday, January 20, again at the Dexter Pavilion. Finally, things were in place, according to the *Tribune* on that morning:

> *With the rules changed to allow more chance for scoring, another attempt will be made this afternoon to decide the Chicago Football League semi-final when Racine Cardinals and Tornadoes clash in Dexter Park Pavilion. Four tie games have been played thus far. Drop kicking will be eliminated and teams will have to gain only eight yards in four downs, instead of the regulation ten.*

With the relaxed rules, the Tornadoes proved to be tougher on offense and brushed aside the Cardinals with relative ease, 21-7. The following week, however, it was the Mohawks, not the Tornadoes, who challenged the Thorns for the championship. That game also ended in a scoreless tie. Out of frustration, officials allowed the teams to keep playing until somebody won. At the end of three hours, there was still no score, although the Thorns had a touchdown overturned by the referee following a protest by the Mohawks. After playing for three hours, the teams agreed to play ten more minutes in an effort to end the tie. When play resumed, the pushing and shoving between the two teams escalated and the Mohawks decided to call it a day. The players walked off the field and were content to settle for a share of the title . . . or so they thought. The referee, however, announced a forfeit by the Mohawks and awarded a 2-0 decision to the Thorns.

There was one more item of business for the Cardinals that winter. In an endeavor to aid the war effort, Chris O'Brien organized a reunion of his old buddies on February 1 at the Celtic Hall. Once again, the Cardinals encountered a bit of bad luck when the Celtic Club burned down the week before the reunion. The event was moved to White City Casino on South Park and even made the pages of the *Herald:*

> *A war benefit dance for the 57 members now at the front will be given by the Racine Cardinals at the White City Casino tonight. The Cardinals are one of the oldest and best known athletic clubs on the south side and close to 2,000 people are expected to attend.*
>
> *Some of the well known athletes the club has turned out in past years are Hugo Bezdek, present manager of the Pittsburgh club, and Nick Bruck, famous bowler. Frank Ragen, president of the Ragen Athletic Club, will also be present.*

The *Chicago Evening Post* added:

> *The club, now located at Fifty sixth street and Racine avenue, now has a membership of 300, but expects to increase this inside of the next six weeks . . . The Cardinals football team, finalists in the Chicago league, will be guests of honor, as will a majority of 1901 players, including Nick Bruck, nationally known bowler; Dan Ward, state pin champion, and Cook County Commissioner Frank Ragen. Hugo Bezdek, Pirate manager, who also played on the 1901 team, is in Chicago and will attend the dance.*

When the 1917-18 season was finally put to bed, the Racine Cardinals held an unofficial 3-3-5 record.

## *The Team Appears To Be Unbeatable*

As the war in Europe dragged on in 1918, football squads on the home front battled another fearful foe: a deadly outbreak of influenza, which threatened the entire nation. The Chicago area was hit especially hard. Public events, including football games, were postponed or canceled in an attempt to minimize exposure to this particular nasty virus. With the double whammy of an incredibly contagious strain of the flu combined with a wide-ranging draft to support the war effort, football teams at all levels were facing a season of uncertainty. In the Western Conference (now the Big Ten), coaches were scratching their heads and wondering how many players would actually be available once the season began. The "18-45" draft law definitely made an impact on the college game, forcing coaches to use unseasoned players in key positions.

So where did all of this talent go? As part of the campaign to maintain a positive public outlook during the deadly war, the military developed service "teams" in football, basketball, boxing, and baseball. The athletes on these teams frequently skirmished with the top collegiate teams as well as with each other.

Consequently, the best football team in the Chicago area in 1918 was the one representing the Great Lakes Naval Training Station north of Chicago. The Great Lakes lineup was rock solid with three future NFL Hall of Famers ready to be unleashed upon the opposition. Included on this historic team were none other than Chicago Bears icon George Halas, future Cardinals superstar Paddy Driscoll, and NFL pioneer and future Cardinals coach Jimmy Conzelman. All were young men who had enlisted in the service to defend their country but were not put out by the prospect of pursuing athletics while in the service. This collection of players prompted some observers to christen Great Lakes as the finest team in the nation, and their results did nothing to subtract from that equation.

With impressive victories over established teams such as Rutgers, Illinois, and Iowa, the Great Lakes team was clearly the best of the Midwest. Even with Conzelman hobbled by a broken collarbone early in the season, this "temporary" team was deep enough to sweep aside any and all opposition from the collegiate ranks. Legendary player/sportswriter Walter Eckersall noted in the *Chicago Tribune* that, "On paper, the team appears unbeatable, but it remains to be seen what it will do against a team of equal weight and experience. It has not been put to a test so far this season." Due to the draft ramifications on university rosters, it took only the first three weeks of the season for fans to notice a definite trend in the results: the service teams were just too powerful for their younger counterparts.

Eckersall explained it this way in the *Tribune:*

> The service football teams are too strong . . . for university and college elevens, now composed of young and inexperienced players . . . these service aggregations are composed mostly of players who have played three years of college football . . . the men know football and need little coaching to perfect team play and learn different formations. The strict naval or military life leaves them in the necessary physical condition to stand the wear and tear of hard struggles.

Back in Chicago, the leaders of the Chicago Football League met on Sunday, September 22, to organize the schedule for the upcoming season. Only seven teams were left in the circuit to vie for championship honors in 1918: the Racine Cardinals, Andy Sheahan's All-Stars, the Stewart Athletic Club, the Standard Athletic Club, the Logan Squares, the Silent Athletic Club, and the Thorns. Chris O'Brien was elected president of the league and he eventually coaxed five more teams to join, bringing the competitors up to twelve for the new season.

## There Might Be A Carrier Of The Disease At A Football Game

With World War I still raging, scheduling on the collegiate level was difficult early in the 1918 season due to a mandate from the government forbidding overnight travel until November 1 for college football games between any universities with army training units. In addition, the nation's bout with a roaring influenza epidemic affected all levels of football competition. Schedules changed daily and even last-minute diversions were not totally unexpected. For example, the Great Lakes team traveled all the way to Pennsylvania to tangle with the University of Pittsburgh for an eagerly awaited intersectional clash. Upon arrival, the visitors were told that the influenza outbreak was so intense that all public gatherings (including the football game) had been canceled. On the same day, Wisconsin's game with Beloit was lost for the same reason, while Minnesota and Illinois both scrambled to find opponents to replace South Dakota and Ames (Iowa State) respectively. In a wacky display of creative scheduling, Illinois played the Chanute Aviators, Minnesota logged in against a collection of local all-stars, and Wisconsin decided to host its second team. In Philadelphia, the rapid spread of the "Spanish" influenza forced the local Board of Health to close all schools, churches, theaters, and other public places.

Meanwhile, in Chicago, the epidemic arrived in force during the first week of October and visited forty-sixty thousand people according to the *Chicago Tribune*. In a six-day period ending on Friday, October 4, more than four hundred Chicagoans lost their lives due to the flu. Still, Dr. C. St. Clair Drake, the Director of the Illinois Department of Public Health, reported to the *Tribune* that despite the four hundred deaths and the possible sixty thousand cases of influenza, "The situation [is] not regarded alarming by local authorities."

Public announcements in the local press advised citizens about precautions to take in order to avoid the curse. Such recommendations were not entirely comforting. For example, a Dr. W. A. Evans offered the small consolation that, "If a person has a mild case, the chance is about 200 to 1 that he will not die from it. A disease that kills less than 1/200th of those it attacks is not one to get in a funk about." Instead, Dr. Evans provided the following advice for anyone who might exhibit any symptoms of influenza:

*Keep warm.*
*Use hot foot baths.*
*Do not permit constipation to continue.*

Of course, the best way to avoid influenza was simply to avoid crowds as well as contact with anyone with a cold, including "the breath or expelled secretions from people suffering from colds."

The severity of the flu outbreak brought football in Chicago to its knees. Following the lead of many other cities and states, the Illinois State Health Commission closed all "places of public amusement" on October 15, 1918, including football games. Once again, Dr. C. St. Clair Drake issued a statement outlining his views on the subject:

*The chances for catching influenza are less in the open air than within doors. There is no assurance, however, that one will not be infected outdoors. Everybody should keep away from crowds. There might be a carrier of the disease at a foot-ball game that may endanger every person there.*

With such sound encouragement, the 1918 football season in Chicago coughed, gasped, and slowly collapsed. All football games in Illinois were canceled by the State Board of Health on October 17. The only exception was for teams who might decide to play behind closed doors. In the case of semi-pro football teams in Chicago, it meant business as usual. As the *Hammond Times* stated:

*It is barely possible that some of the scheduled events will take place, even with the grand stand and bleachers vacant. The high school teams to the number of about two dozen are slated to engage in combat, and as these are not staged for financial gain, it will be possible to play behind closed gates. This is optional with the schools involved. A few independent "grid" teams also can perform, as they usually play in some open lot minus spectators.*

Despite the possibility of playing, albeit without fans, school officials in both Chicago and the suburban high school leagues also agreed to cancel all games on October 18 in order to abide with the decree from the State Health Department.

Since the Racine Cardinals didn't worry too much about crowds, the team's games continued as scheduled. As members of the Chicago Football League, the Cardinals opened their exhibition season on October 6 with a trip to Gary, Indiana, for an exhibition game against Gary Tech. In preseason prognostications, the Pullman Thorns, with former Illinois standout Len Charpier, and the Cornells appeared to be the class of the Chicago area.

As for the Racine Cardinals, only twelve men played in the opening contest in Gary, where the Cards and the Techs battled to a 0-0 tie. The *Hammond Times* filed the following game report:

> *The Racine Cardinals of Chicago and the Gary Techs fought to a nothing to nothing tie here. The Techs had the advantage in the first half, but the Cardinals evened things in the last period. A forward pass, Black to McGurk, netted the Cards thirty yards and put them out of danger.*

Chris O' Brien, in a career that seemed would never end, played the entire game at right tackle, perhaps buoyed by the fact that he celebrated his thirty-seventh birthday that same week. Hammond still had a team in 1918, although only three members remained from the championship team of 1917. In Hammond's first outing, it blasted the Chicago All-Stars 32-0, a group comprised of former Evanston North Ends and Cornell-Hamburg players. Up North, the team representing the Great Lakes Naval training station needed to overcome a protest by the University of Illinois early in the season. The Illini, it seems, were reluctant to play Great Lakes because of the former professional status of Paddy Driscoll, both in football and baseball. Since the naval station did not have any eligibility requirements except that a player must be an enlisted man, the protest was dropped. But the ban on most sporting events in mid-October engulfed most of the 1918 schedule. It wasn't until the weekend of November 9-10 that football resumed on most levels in the area. Great Lakes tied Notre Dame (with George Gipp and Curly Lambeau) 7-7, Englewood routed Austin 101-0 in prep action, and the Thorns edged the Cardinals 6-0 before a crowd of three thousand, with the only score resulting from a blocked punt. The game was played at 103rd and Corliss and the *Daily News* noted that "both teams were amply fortified with plenty of former college and high school talent."

## *Paddy Is A Dodger From Dodgerville*

On November 16, Driscoll once again was in the national spotlight as Great Lakes overcame a 14-0 deficit to rout Rutgers 54-14. Paddy scored six touchdowns and added five extra points for a total of forty-one points. "His long distance runs through broken fields, combined with snakelike twists and dodges, repeatedly thrilled the spectators," wrote the *Tribune*. The *New York Times* was even more impressed:

*Paddy is a dodger from Dodgerville, Dodge County. It is doubtful if there is a sheriff anywhere around here that would catch him. Sometimes he skins around like a fox trotter, and then again he is wiggling away from somebody with the graceful movements of an Egyptian dancer. Then again he just runs right along straight as if the Old Ned was after him.*

With the war officially ending in Europe and the flu epidemic under control, a wave of euphoria swept through the country in November of 1918. The Cardinals returned to action on November 10 with a 6-0 loss to the Pullman Thorns and then scheduled a November 17 game with the Logan Squares, as noted in the *Evening Post*:

*The Squares, under the name of Igorrotes, cut a wide swath in the ranks of independent elevens for a number of years. Last season, the Cardinals surprised the fans by holding them to a scoreless tie. Manager Chris O'Brien of the Cardinals has secured several of the best players on the South Side for the game. Manager Harley of the Squares promises to spring men who have made country-wide names for themselves with the pigskin.*

Despite the lavish buildup, no score from this game was reported. The Cardinals did surface on Thanksgiving Day (November 28) with a win over the East Chicago Gophers before losing to the Thorns once again, 20-0, on December 1. The Thorns (with Donald Davidson back in town) then claimed the local semi-pro championship by defeating the East Chicago Gophers 7-0 on December 8. The Cardinals finished off the season on a high note by edging the Igorrotes 6-0 at DePaul University before stopping the Gophers 13-0 in the final game on December 15.

Prior to the concluding game with the Gophers, the Herald Examiner recognized Chris O'Brien for his numerous contributions to football:

### Racine Cardinals Manager to Play in 168th Gridiron Game Today

*Twenty-one years of amateur and semi-pro football on the prairies and sand lot gridirons of Chicago!*

*That is the record of Chris O'Brien, coach, manager and tackle of the Racine Cardinals, of whose club, by the way, he is president. Chris will participate in his 168th football game this afternoon at Normal Park, where the Cardinals will stack up against the powerful East Chicago Gophers, whose lineup includes a half-dozen Indiana and Purdue collegians.*

*And for those 167 sand lot and prairie moleskin battles, requiring a brawny body and even stouter heart, Chris has emerged practically unscathed . . . Chris has seen independent football grow from a novelty to a highly developed pastime in which college stars of national reputation find themselves eclipsed by home grown performers.*

*Chris was a fleet halfback in the good old days, but after nearly 20 years of service had slowed him down, he went into the forward wall, and since then has been playing at guard and tackle. He is built more along the line of a halfback than a line man, yet, despite the fact that he yields weight to the ordinary run of opponents, Chris continues to shine. In a recent game he outplayed a husky tackle who a couple of years ago was heralded as a member of the Ohio State eleven.*

> *Chris . . . has no thought of giving up football. He has played few games this year because of his duties as coach and manager, but he says he will stick to the game until he has rounded out his 250th battle on the gridiron.*

From an historical perspective, this rare "feature" article indicates that O'Brien continued to play football even after the Cardinals/Morgans disappeared from the newspapers around 1906 until the Racine Cardinals appeared in 1916.

Following the win over the Gophers, O'Brien attempted to schedule one last game against a team from Melrose Park but was unable to finalize the contest. The Cardinals' fragmented 1918 season ended with a respectable 3-2-1 record.

## *Chris O'Brien Was Reelected President*

On Monday, December 23, the *Chicago American* reported that Chris O'Brien was again selected to head the Racine Cardinals Athletic Club:

> *Chris O'Brien was re-elected president of the Racine Cardinals at the annual meeting. Tom Dougherty was selected as vice president in place of Honan Crowley, who is in the army, while another new officer is Mike O'Hanlon . . . Joe Crowley and Larry Sullivan, the retiring Sgt.-At-Arms probably will be appointed boxing and wrestling instructors for the club, a movement being under way to effect that result.*

Whatever happened to the gifted Great Lakes football team? In 1918, with World War I in progress, Driscoll enlisted, and was assigned to the Great Lakes Naval Station near Chicago. Many military bases sponsored various athletic teams, but Great Lakes was something special. Driscoll quarterbacked the football team to an undefeated season against major college teams and to the 1919 Rose Bowl championship against Mare Island. Although teammate George Halas was named the MVP of the Rose Bowl, Driscoll completed four of eight passes, including one for a touchdown to Halas; dropkicked a field goal; and booted a sixty-yard punt. In total that day, Driscoll gained 236 yards through his passes, rushes, and receptions. George Halas would later say, "Few backfield men ever turned in a more perfect game than Driscoll did against Mare Island." Behind the tandem of Driscoll and Conzelman, the team just kept on playing and wound up winning the 1919 Rose Bowl over the Mare Island Marines 17-0 in the only instance in which the Rose Bowl participants were service teams. Driscoll was the star, completing a thirty-yard field goal and connecting with Halas on a thirty-two-yard touchdown pass.

With the First World War ended, football began to receive unprecedented acceptance in 1919. Teams were playing at all levels, and even the dreaded professionals were grudgingly earning respect. Walter Eckersall, a former All-American at the University of Chicago, discussed the situation in the September 29 issue of the *Chicago Tribune*:

> *With the stamp of approval placed on football by the colleges and preparatory schools and the unqualified endorsement of high military officers, who declare the game a national asset in that it teaches obedience to orders, self-sacrifice and resourcefulness, more football will be played this fall than ever before.*

*Men who left college when the United States entered the war have returned to their respective institutions, while those who had no college affiliations, and received a taste of the game in the training camps, are eager to play this fall. The non-college man has realized the benefits which can be derived from football and its close similarity with the tactics of warfare.*

*Professional football teams are being organized in all parts of the country and numbers in Chicago. These are composed of former college men and in a great many cases by service men who played in camps and cantonments . . . If professional football is to survive, and there is no reason why it should not, the players must conduct themselves like the men on the college elevens. They must be taught to abide by the officials' rulings and as soon as the public realizes the games are worth seeing the promoters of the contests can expect large crowds.*

In 1919, some confusion reigned with the discovery that there were actually two Racine Cardinals teams. One was the old standby managed by Chris O'Brien on the South Side of Chicago, while the other was an intruder from Racine, Wisconsin. This confusion would last another year or two and would even result in the Chicago version being originally labeled as being from Wisconsin when they entered the early edition of the NFL. So, when the champion Pullman Thorns, led by Donald Davidson, opened the 1919 season against the Racine Cardinals, the opponent was the Wisconsin version. O'Brien's Cardinals strolled through the field undefeated until Thanksgiving, when the Standards administered a 28-7 whipping. Along the way, the Cardinals knocked off teams like the Thorns (6-0), the Logan Squares (10-7), and the Stayms (20-13). As usual, the Cardinals remained close to home and only played neighborhood teams, while other ambitious clubs, such as the Cornell-Hamburgs and the Thorns, branched out to play the likes of the Rock Island (IL) Independents and the Detroit (MI) Heralds. The Cards did venture down to Moline, Illinois, on October 19, where they tied the locals 7-7.

The most prominent team in Chicago, however, was Hammond. With the war over, Paul Parduhn recruited an excellent team with players such as George Halas, Charlie Brickey, Frank Blocker, Johnny Barrett, and later, Paddy Driscoll. Driscoll, who was serving as Northwestern's assistant coach following his discharge from the service, joined the team after Northwestern's season ended.

## What If?

What if Paddy Driscoll and George Halas had gone away and never returned? Would pro football have survived without its earliest superstar and the man who developed one of its most successful franchises? It almost happened.

The *Great Lakes Bulletin* reported on February 2, 1919, that both Driscoll and Halas would "pass up their chances for further athletic fame at the close of the 1919 baseball season to accept opportunities in business. Both athletes have agreed to go to South America about November 1, to hold positions with Armour & Co. in a tannery and hide plant which is to be established in Buenos Aires. Driscoll at present belongs to the Chicago Cubs and Halas to the New York Americans." The 1919 baseball season did not go well for either player. Paddy spent the year with the Cubs' minor league club in Los Angeles, ending his baseball career with these bleak stats from 1917 with the Cubs: thirteen games, .107 batting average. Halas finished with similar numbers in 1919 with the Yankees: twelve games, .091 batting average. For whatever reason, neither man pursued the job opportunities in South America. Both gave up pro baseball and returned to football. Halas had a little more incentive: after being sent to St. Paul in the minor leagues later in 1919, he learned that a new man had replaced him in right field for the 1920 Yankees—a guy named Babe Ruth.

## *$20,000 Beauties*

Hammond was a solid football team with everything except a nickname. The team launched a contest to solve that dilemma, with the winner earning two free season tickets. The only problem for that contest winner was that although the team was based in Hammond, it would play the majority of its home games in baseball stadiums in nearby Chicago, finally settling at Cubs Park (now Wrigley Field) on the North Side. The team eventually became known by a variety of names including the "All Stars," the Bobcats, and the "$20,000 Beauties" (because of the hefty paychecks distributed by Parduhn). They competed with nationally known teams such as the Cleveland Tigers, the Canton Bulldogs, the Minneapolis Marines, and the Rock Island Independents. Over ten thousand people turned out to watch Hammond battle Jim Thorpe's Bulldogs to a 3-3 tie in Chicago, which the *Hammond Times* described as "the greatest grid contest that middle western fandom have ever seen."

Although Hammond became a charter member of the NFL in 1920, that team bore very little resemblance to the 1919 edition of Parduhn's collection of all-stars. The players scattered and Parduhn apparently decided to focus more time on his City Fuel and Supply Company. Team physician Alva Andrew Young was the driving force behind the Hammond Pros of 1920. The team met little success in the NFL and eventually folded following the 1926 season, when the NFL began to squeeze out the smaller, less stable franchises. Parduhn was only twenty-six years old at this time, and although his rising star as a football promoter dimmed after the 1919 season, he will always be remembered as the man who first brought a "real" professional team to Chicago, as well as the individual who provided both George Halas and Paddy Driscoll with their first jobs in pro football.

While the Cardinals did not experience any championship hopes in 1919, O'Brien's team (with a formidable 4-2-2 record) was about to make an extraordinary leap from the sandlots to national prominence in the world of professional football. The familiar opponents such as the Thorns, Stayms, and Standards would be replaced by teams from places like Detroit, Rock Island, and Decatur. For all involved, it would be an interesting adventure.

## You Mean Aikman Doesn't Have A Side Job?

For the first few decades of the NFL, the game was just a part-time job, not an occupation. In other words, the majority of the players were paid adequately, but certainly not enough to exist on for the remainder of the non-playing year. In order to survive, early players generally needed to secure gainful employment during the off-season.

Teams would attempt to attract players by assisting with job procurement. For example, in 1939, Coach E. C. "Gus" Henderson of the Detroit Lions sent out a recruitment letter to graduating prospects stating:

> You have been recommended to us by several coaches and we are defi-
> nitely interested in signing you for the Detroit Lions. We are only inter-
> ested in athletes who are ambitious and wish to make good in some busi-
> ness opportunity that we can offer you here in Detroit.

In other words, the prospect of "play for pay" was enticing, but if a team could make it worthwhile for a player year-round, it might be an attractive tool in secur-ing the exceptional player.

The Cardinals' players of the 1920s found the usual (and the unusual) means of employment. Eddie Anderson was both a medical student and the football coach at DePaul. Roger Kiley coached at Loyola of Chicago. Future sportswriter Wilfrid R. Smith was the football coach at Harrison High School and Bob Koehler held a similar position at Schurz. Will Brennan, the stocky guard, was a Chicago police officer, while Paddy Driscoll was the basketball coach at St. Mel High School and Norm Barry coached at De LaSalle High School.

On a more academic level, guard Herb Blumer, who played with the Cardinals from 1925 to 1930 and again in 1933, was a Professor of Sociology at the presti-gious University of Chicago. Big Hawaiian tackle Harry Field (from the 1935 team) spent the off-season working barefoot in a pineapple cannery in Honolulu, while his teammate Pete (Champ) Mehringer was a professional wrestler. The league's only Canadian-born player in 1938 was Earl Nolan, who was a cow puncher in the off-season. From the 1939 squad, tackle Conway Baker was a policeman in Shreveport, LA, while center Ki Aldrich was a foreman in the Texas oil fields.

In the 1940s, the players continued to sample a variety of interesting off-sea-son positions. Guard Lou Marotti was a welder, Cactus Face Duggan was a mem-ber of the Arkansas Highway Patrol, and Clint Wager played pro basketball and raised Chesapeake Bay Retrievers. Red Cochran sold sporting goods, Marshall Goldberg was involved in the sale of industrial machinery, and Mal Kutner was an oil scout.

# ♦ 3 ♦

# The Birth of the NFL:
# 1920

*"Everybody wanted to play sixty minutes.*
*If you took a guy out because he had a broken finger,*
*a fractured wrist, or a bleeding cut on his anatomy,*
*you ran the risk of not having*
*any conversation with that player . . .*
*he just wouldn't talk to you!"*

CHRIS O'BRIEN,
OWNER, CHICAGO CARDINALS, 1920

With the conclusion of World War I and with lifestyles firmly back in place, leisure activities in 1920 once again became commonplace—and acceptable. The Cardinals, along with their nearby rivals, the Thorns and the Stayms, were typical of the postgraduate teams of that era. There was emerging neighborhood fan support, a not-so-secretive effort to attract the best graduating collegiate players, and a sudden interest in what similar teams were doing in other parts of the country.

Despite the stinging opposition of college coaches and lukewarm media response, the fledgling game of professional football continued to gain a foothold in the Midwest and on the East Coast. Chicago newspapers were now listing the results of a few "pro" contests held in Ohio, Michigan, and Indiana, but this reporting remained minuscule compared to the lavish and extensive treatment of the college games. Still, coverage began to increase for the local postgraduate teams in the Chicago area. Attendance at these Sunday games now often stretched into the thousands, and excitement heightened when visiting teams arrived from other states amid the fanfare of their overblown gridiron accomplishments.

Titles and honors—such as the "Champions of Ohio," the "Champions of the West," or the "Best of the Heavyweights"—were freely claimed. Every team, it seemed, could claim to be the champion of something. Meanwhile, professional leagues had been in operation in Pennsylvania, Ohio, and other states for several years. It was not unusual for two local "champions" in different states to schedule games at the conclusion of the season to secure an extra payday, as well as to determine the overall kingpin of the Upper Midwest or something similarly grandiose.

Generally, the owners/managers/organizers of the early pro teams were entrepreneurs who loved both football as well as the local notoriety it brought to them as team spokesmen. The owners also shared another reasonable trait: they acquired a thirst for money as not only the primary support for the team, but also as the means for recruiting top-flight players. In those days, when Hammond star Paddy Driscoll was hauling down a lofty $75 a game in 1919, the owners shuddered and braced themselves for further increases that they knew would hurtle some individual game wages past the magical $100 mark.

Money, therefore, was a key consideration, and while traditional rivalries would continue to do well on the local level, it became apparent that something very special would be needed to attract patrons to contests at larger stadiums. Bigger crowds translated into more money, and that would certainly propel the expansion of the gangly game of pro football while making the owners' lives a great deal less tumultuous.

Clearly a spark was needed, a shot in the arm that would elevate interest in the game beyond the immediate local level. Dreamers might eventually hope for national acceptance, but it was considered useless and dangerous for anyone to ever place trust in that direction. At this point in time, it would be foolish to even think that pro football would ever receive the recognition and publicity garnered by the college game.

## Contracts Must Be Respected By Players

Following the 1919 season, the Racine Cardinals had firmly entrenched themselves as one of the mainstays of the Chicago Football League, although teams such as Hammond, the Thorns, and the Cornell-Hamburgs seemed more receptive to the challenge of competition outside of the Chicago area. Still, when Chris O'Brien learned of the possible organization of a nationwide football league, he was interested in finding out more about this intriguing concept.

The proposed league was being pushed primarily by members of the Ohio league, including teams such as the Canton Bulldogs, the Dayton Triangles, the Cleveland Tigers, and the Columbus Panhandles. These four clubs brought experience and a touch of prestige to the table. They provided some incentive for the Chicago area teams to consider this new pro venture.

Canton featured the great Jim Thorpe, a name known throughout the world. Thorpe's drawing power and wide celebrity status would certainly provide a boost at the gate for the Cardinals or any other Midwest team that had generally avoided competition against football teams from outside their own area. On the other hand, by joining in a league with clubs from larger cities and perhaps initiating certain rules, Canton and other teams from smaller towns hoped that the threat of another team "raiding" its players would diminish and that gate receipts would increase. While the practice of jumping from team to team existed in the Chicago area, it was not as widespread (or as costly) as it was in the Ohio League. Teams from smaller towns could not afford to engage in bidding wars in order to maintain their rosters and whatever gate appeal a certain player might bring to the team. However, teams that captured the services of the "stars" needed to pay them, and without stronger attendance, these clubs faced the real danger of folding. Pro football, especially in Ohio, was facing somewhat of a no-win situation.

So the teams needed stars to attract crowds. Once they had the stars, they needed to pay them top wages. And even if a team could pay the star player, there was little guarantee that the player would not jump ship to another competitor.

While the fans began to support the notion of pro football, the formation of the early NFL was primarily a combination of teams from two key regions, Ohio and Illinois, for the purpose of both economic survival and the development of a more viable product. The goal down the road was to provide regular schedules, promote intersectional rivalries, and establish a firm methodology for determining championships. With the foggy taste still remaining from the seemingly endless 1917-1918 season, the idea of all of the above sounded enticing to O'Brien, especially the championship criteria.

Now, instead of the usual neighborhood brawls with the Thorns and the Cornell-Hamburgs, O'Brien could only imagine the gate for a tussle between the Racine Cardinals and Jim Thorpe's Canton Bulldogs. Or, perhaps he could envision the share of the gate for a Cards' road trip to Cleveland to battle the Tigers and their masterful quarterback, Stanley Cofall out of Notre Dame. It all sounded too good to be true, and maybe it was—but O'Brien vowed to listen.

Buoyed by the efforts of Ralph Hay of the Bulldogs, a meeting was called on August 20, 1920, at Hay's Hupmobile office in Canton. This first meeting included only teams from Ohio, and it was intended to discuss not only the issues of economics in terms of escalating player salaries, the use of disguised undergraduates as players, and player "jumping," but also the looming threat of up-and-coming pro teams in other parts of the country. All of these concerns could combine to weaken the status of the pro football teams in Ohio.

It was reasonable, suggested Hay, that the Ohio teams could conceive a formal league with consistent scheduling and player policies. He hoped this structure would increase profits, subdue fears of additional player jumps, and lend some needed credibility to the professional game. Aside from his Hupmobile agency, Ralph Hay owned and managed the Canton Bulldogs. Joining him at the August 20 meeting was his star player, Jim Thorpe; Jimmy O'Donnell of Cleveland, along with his mainstay, Stanley Cofall; Carl Storck, the owner of the Dayton Triangles; and Akron representatives Art Ranney and Frank Nied. The Akron Indians actually had disbanded following the 1919 season, but Ranney and Nied had indicated that they would be forming another team in Akron for the 1920 campaign.

Out of this meeting, the early NFL was hatched. The four teams agreed to form a league and to call it the American Professional Football Conference (APFC). Ralph Hay would serve as the temporary secretary. The progress made by this handful of individuals was summarized succinctly by the *Canton Evening Repository* newspaper on August 21, 1920, as follows:

> *The purpose of the A. P. F. C. will be to raise the standard of professional football in every way possible, to eliminate bidding for players between rival clubs and to secure cooperation in the formation of schedules, at least for the bigger teams . . . members of the organization reached an agreement to refrain from offering inducements to players to jump from one team to another, which has been one of the glaring drawbacks to the game in past seasons. Contracts must be respected by players as far as possible, as well as by club managers. The move to abolish competitive bidding for star players is a matter of self protection for the magnates, as they have been facing a steady upward trend in the prices demanded by players of ability, especially those who have acquired big college reputations.*

## *Padded Their Bankrolls By Playing On Sunday*

Meanwhile, the *Dayton Journal Herald* reported that the teams had addressed the issue of collegiate players participating in games and wryly noted:

> *Last season there were quite a number of intercollegiate stars who padded their bankrolls by slipping away on a Sunday, and performing with a pro team, using every name under the sun but their own to hide their identity.*

To counteract these aspersions, the new pro conference vowed not to use undergraduates, which might have served a dual purpose of both reducing costs as well as holding out an olive branch to the infuriated college game. The loading and reloading of pro rosters with college players had often resulted in college teams losing players to both injuries and suspensions as a result of their participation in professional contests. Even teams such as Notre Dame were not immune to this practice when it was discovered that Irish players were suspended as far back as 1914 and again in 1917 for playing in local semi-pro games. The *Hammond Times* routinely noted, but did not identify, players who were participating under assumed names.

With this innovative structure in place, the professional teams faced just one remaining problem. Despite the obvious attempt at organization and specific rule making, the best-laid plans would be pulverized if only four professional teams in the state or, for that matter, the country, would observe them. Secretary Hay was asked to contact other visible professional teams around the country and invite any interested parties to attend the next meeting of the crawling, not yet walking, version of the A.P.F.C.

As the correspondence stretched around the country, it quickly became apparent that there was considerable interest in the new conference. The second meeting, held on September 17, 1920, attracted the top gridiron luminaries of the day to Canton. Chris O'Brien represented the Racine Cardinals, while George Halas was there on behalf of his new team, the Decatur (IL) Staleys. Joining these two teams from Illinois were Walter H. Flannagan of the Rock Island Independents, Doctor Alva Young from the Hammond (IN) Pros, and Earl Ball with the Muncie (IN) Flyers. The East sent just one representative, Leo Lyons of the Rochester (NY) Jeffersons.

In all, fourteen individuals represented ten teams (Massillon, Ohio, was listed as being present in the minutes, but its representatives actually were not in attendance), and the preliminary details of the new league were discussed in the showroom of Hay's Hupmobile dealership. In his autobiography, George Halas recalled the scenario:

> *The showroom, big enough for four cars—Hupmobiles and Jordans—occupied the ground floor of the three story brick Odd Fellows building. Chairs were few. I sat on a running board. We all agreed on a need for a league. In two hours, we created the American Professional Football Association. To give the Association some financial standing, we voted to issue franchises on payment of $100.*

The minutes from that historic meeting list the Racine Cardinals as being from Racine, Wisconsin. Art Ranney from Akron wrote the minutes from this meeting and apparently thought the Cards were from Wisconsin—an understandable mistake. The mistake continues to hold forth in the minutes (which apparently were never corrected), and so the initial roster of league members from that meeting looks this way:

Akron Professionals
Hammond Pros
Decatur Staleys
Racine (WI) Cardinals
Muncie Flyers
Rock Island Independents
Canton Bulldogs
Cleveland Tigers
Dayton Triangles
Massillon Tigers
Rochester Jeffersons

All of the above are considered charter members of the APFC, along with the Buffalo All-Americans (who applied for membership by letter), the Detroit Heralds, the Columbus Panhandles, and the Chicago Tigers, all of whom joined the league prior to its inaugural season. However, Massillon did not compete as a member of the league in 1920.

It was apparently a warm September day when these pro football pioneers met in Canton to give birth to the earliest version of the National Football League. Ranney's minutes indicate that the meeting was called to order at 8:15 P.M., but the benevolent host, Ralph Hay, had attempted to ease any discomfort for his guests by strategically placing several buckets of cold beer around the Hupmobile showroom. Although it was the age of prohibition, it was unlikely that any of those present would have looked upon Mr. Hay with disfavor for this unlawful act.

With Hay in firm control of the meeting, the gathered representatives hammered out several key issues regarding the status of the league. A small but pertinent change was the decision to alter the name of the organization to the American Professional Football Association. The group also struggled with the choice of the individual who would lead the league out of obscurity and into the hearts of football fans everywhere. Hay, with his considerable business acumen, would be a logical choice for this struggling endeavor. Yet Hay, and the other entrepreneurs present, moved in another, albeit logical, direction.

Instead of the seasoned Hay, the managers elected Jim Thorpe as President, assuming, of course, that Hay would be working behind the scenes to ensure the success of the league. Thorpe was an athlete, not an administrator. Yet he was probably the most recognized athletic name in the country, which alone would be a positive marketing tool for the league. Thorpe was both receptive and available. His role was ordained to be that of an icon who played football, representing the league in a positive fashion, and leaving the grunt work to Hay. It could work . . .

The minutes from that intriguing meeting were brief, to-the-point, and basically uninformative as follows:

*OLD BUSINESS*
   *Massillon withdrew from professional football for the season of 1920.*

*NEW BUSINESS*

*It was moved and seconded that a permanent organization be formed to be known as American Professional Football Association. Motion carried.*

*Moved and seconded that officers now be elected, consisting of President, Vice president, Secretary and Treasurer. Carried.*

*Mr. Jim Thorpe was unanimously elected President, Mr. Stan Cofall, Vice president, and Mr. A. F. Ranney, Secretary and Treasurer.*

*Moved and seconded that a fee of $100.00 be charged for membership in the association. Carried.*

*Moved and seconded that the President appoint a committee to work in conjunction with a lawyer to draft a constitution, bylaws and rules for the association. Carried.*

*Mr. Thorpe appointed Mr. A. A. Young of Hammond, Chairman, and Messers Cofall, Flannigan and Storch associates.*

*Moved and seconded that all Clubs mail to the secretary by January 1, 1921, a list of all players used by them this season, the secretary to furnish all Clubs with duplicate copy of same, so that each Club would have first choice in services for 1921 of his team of this season. Carried.*

*Moved and seconded that all members have printed upon their stationery, "Member of American Professional Football Association." Carried.*

*Mr. Marshall of the Brunswick Balke Collender Company, Tire Division, presented a silver loving cup to be given the team, awarded the championship by the Association. Any team winning the cup three times should be adjourned the owner.*

*It was moved and seconded that a vote of thanks be extended by the secretary to Mr. Marshall.*

*The meeting was adjourned. Next meeting to be called by the President some time in January 1921.*

So that was it! Just two neatly typed pages that would profoundly impact the world of sports in the United States throughout the rest of the century. As with most business meetings, the meat of the discussions does not appear in the minutes. Strangely, the issue on the use of collegiate players is not mentioned even though the new group so sorely needed some positive direction on that topic.

The disposition of the Brunswick Cup to the 1920 champion is also confusing. The members of the association would decide the winner, but the criteria for reaching that decision are not delineated. At this point in time it appears that there would not be an equitable schedule among the participating clubs, nor is a framework provided for competitive interaction among the member teams. Basically, the champion of the new American Professional Football Association did not necessarily need to possess the best record at the conclusion of the season.

As the league began to evolve, it would continually attempt to patch the holes in its rules and regulations. With such thin guidelines at the start, the league guaranteed itself a few years of controversy and confusion. But it was a start.

Back home, the *Chicago Daily News* attempted to explain what the new league was all about:

*Eleven clubs will be represented this fall in the association. There will be no cut-throat signing of players after the season starts. In that manner those backing the organization expect to develop their machines in the finer points of new play, exactly as is done on the college gridiron.*

Upon his return to Chicago, O'Brien immediately began the process of finalizing his roster and concluding the scheduling. It wasn't an easy task. By October 9, O'Brien was able to schedule only the first two games and he still had not contracted a place to play. Consequently, on days when Normal Park was booked, O'Brien was searching for available fields. The Cardinals eventually would play six games against APFA opponents, and O'Brien would fill any open dates against familiar local elevens and other independent squads. After a lackluster finish in 1919, O'Brien would need to fortify his team with solid, experienced players in order to compete against the professionals from the other areas. Gone were the days when neighbors could be called in so that there would be enough men to field a team or when O'Brien himself would fill in on the line. The Racine Cardinals had left the prairies and had become a business—a business whose success on the field would mirror the success in O'Brien's checkbook.

## I Would Learn How To Make Starch

O'Brien finally reserved Normal Park at 61st and Racine to serve as the home field in 1920, but the first home game would not be played there until November 14. The Cards ended up playing most of their games "away," probably because O'Brien could experience greater financial success—and fewer game-related expenses (field rental, etc.)—if he procured regular "guarantees" on the road as the visiting team. Despite the membership in the new league, O'Brien was content to schedule games primarily in his own geographical region. There would be no showdown in 1920 with big Jim Thorpe and the Canton Bulldogs, but O'Brien would initiate what has become the oldest rivalry in the NFL with the downstate Decatur Staleys. While still in Decatur, the Staleys split a pair of games with the Cardinals in 1920. Later, the Staleys moved to Chicago and an intense rivalry was initiated with the Cardinals as both teams struggled for victories, media coverage, and fans. The Staleys had not yet fielded a team, but prior to the 1920 campaign George Halas had been given free reign to develop the team that would eventually become the Chicago Bears. Halas had competed the previous year with the Hammond All-Stars and then spent the summer playing professional baseball.

Then, in March of 1920, Halas was contacted by George Chamberlain, General Superintendent of the A. E. Staley Company in Decatur, Illinois. Chamberlain offered Halas the opportunity to develop the company's football team. In his autobiography, Halas recalled the unusual circumstances surrounding the creation of the Staleys:

*Mr. Staley wanted to build it (the football team) into a football team that could compete successfully with the best semi-professional and industrial teams in the country. He was willing to put money into the enterprise. He had two objects, to stimulate employee morale and fitness and to spread the Staley name throughout the nation.*

*Mr. Chamberlain asked if I would like to move to Decatur to work for the Staley Company, play on the baseball team and manage and coach the football team as well as play on it. In between times I would learn how to make starch, putting my engineering and chemical training to use and starting a lifetime career in the fast-growing concern.*

*I don't remember how much money he offered. The magnet for me was the opportunity to build a winning football team.*

Halas was given the green light to recruit players and offer them year-round employment in the company to play and work for Mr. Staley. This was a real incentive in those days, and it gave the Decatur team a significant advantage. It was one thing for a team to recruit a player for football wages only, but that player would also need to find other work to sustain himself during the year. Halas also received permission to hold two-hour practices with the players during the regular work day, which was an additional bonus. In essence, he could hold his team "employees" captive in Decatur with the opportunity for unlimited practice in preparation for the season.

Meanwhile, O'Brien shocked the football world on Wednesday, September 8, 1920, by signing the diminutive Paddy Driscoll to an agreement that would pay the former Northwestern star a lofty $300 per game, with a guarantee of ten games. In the days when a loaf of bread cost 11¢ and an NFL franchise $100, this was truly a magnificent reward.

It could be argued that Driscoll was easily the best player in the circuit. He could run, kick, and defend. With his spectacular playing record at Northwestern (1915-1916), Hammond (1917), Great Lakes (1918), and Hammond again (1919), Driscoll had achieved a national notoriety that propelled him into the unique status of an early professional box office attraction. His punting and dropkicking were the things that created legends in his day. No one in the history of the NFL has ever exceeded his dropkicking records from his playing career, which concluded in 1929. He still holds the NFL records for most drop-kick field goals in a game (four), the longest drop-kick in a game (fifty yards, accomplished twice), and most drop-kick field goals in a career (forty-nine). He also broke loose for an eighty-yard touchdown run against Kansas City in 1925 and scored a then-league record of twenty-seven points (four touchdowns and three extra points) in one game against Rochester on October 7, 1923. But the most amazing thing about Driscoll, especially in an era when proper padding was mostly nonexistent, was his size. The graceful runner stood just 5'8" and played most of his career at about 150 pounds.

## *Following Paddy's Playing*

John Leo "Paddy" Driscoll was born on January 11, 1895, to Timothy and Elizabeth Maloney Driscoll. Nine days later, the youngster was baptized at St. Mary's Catholic Church in Evanston, Illinois. His initial football training was received at Evanston High School, where he participated in the very first game in 1913 (won by Evanston 31-13) of the ongoing Evanston-New Trier High School rivalry. At Evanston, he also played baseball and basketball, with the cagers snaring the Central States championship. Paddy was a member of the St. Mary's baseball team that captured the first National Catholic crown. It was then on to Northwestern, where he again participated in all three sports and revitalized a dismal football program beginning with the 1915 season. Behind Driscoll's leadership in 1916, Northwestern defeated the University of Chicago for the first time in fifteen years and rose to second place in the conference behind Ohio State. He was named to the All-American team and the founding father of football, Walter Camp, called him "the greatest quarterback I have ever seen."

His coach at NU, Fred W. Murphy, described Driscoll as "without a doubt the greatest football player I ever saw." In order to help support his family, Driscoll signed with the Chicago Cubs in 1917 to play professional baseball, thus essentially ending his brilliant collegiate football career. Although fully intending to continue with the Cubs, Driscoll joined the professional Hammond football team in the fall of 1917, where he delighted the local fans, especially in one game against the Cornell-Hamburgs. Hammond won that game 13-3 with Driscoll booting two long field goals, including one that astonished his teammates. After returning a punt in the first half, the *Chicago Evening Post* claimed that Driscoll was knocked out "on his feet":

> *When tackled in running back a punt, Paddy Driscoll was knocked out "on his feet." Without being aware of the fact, he drop kicked a field goal from the fifty-three yard line after calling signals for a forward pass. He had to be taken out of the game.*

Since this was not a punting or field goal situation, Driscoll was asked at half-time why he decided to go with the dropkick. "What dropkick?" he replied. "And what's the score, anyway?"

## *The First To Use The Pivot In Dodging*

In 1925, *Tribune* sportswriter Walter Eckersall delineated Driscoll's peculiar running style:

> *Driscoll was among the first to use the pivot in dodging and he ran with his knees kicking nearly as high as his chest. He was absolutely reliable in handling punts, always waiting a few yards back so that he caught the ball on the dead run.*

Despite his prowess on the gridiron, Paddy continued to play basketball and baseball during his pro football career. He starred on Paddy Carr's Big Five cage team (named after the treasurer of Cook County) and was an outfielder for several seasons with the Pyott semi-pro baseball team. He also served as the head coach at St. Mel High School in Chicago during his time in the NFL. This might be like having Dick Butkus coach at south suburban Evergreen Park High School while still playing with the Chicago Bears. But those were the days when NFL salaries still needed to be augmented by outside occupations. In the summers, Driscoll supervised the Lincoln Park beaches in Chicago and also served as Athletic Director at Camp St. George in Clearwater Lake, Wisconsin.

So in 1920, Driscoll was the man that O'Brien decided to build his team around. It was a wise choice, despite the outrageous salary for the time. With Driscoll as the foundation, O'Brien structured the Racine Cardinals with a combination of his 1919 squad along with several experienced players from other clubs in Chicago. Tackle Fred Gillies (from Cornell University), Paul LaRoss, and Willis Brennan were plucked from the Cornell-Hamburgs. Former University of Illinois standout Len Charpier moved over from the Thorns (but went back later in the season), while end Len Sachs and fullback Bernie Hallstrom were recruited from the Logan Squares.

Among the holdovers were ends Red O'Connor and Tom Whalen, tackle Joe Carey, and fullback Nick McInerney. Driscoll would also serve as player-coach, a scheme that was not uncommon in those days but one that the Cardinals would continue to embrace during O'Brien's tenure, perhaps as a monetary necessity.

How did O'Brien rise so quickly from the economic and athletic struggles on the field in 1919 to build such an impressive lineup? With $300 per game pledged to Driscoll alone, how could O'Brien afford to support a professional team along with its burgeoning expenses? How could he turn the financial aspects of the team around so quickly?

Ann Dalton, now living in Chicago's western suburbs, may hold the answers to those questions. Ms. Dalton recalls that her father, dentist Dr. Bob Price, "was part of a syndicate of business men from the neighborhood around Chicago and Damen Avenues. These men, who included doctors, lawyers, and insurance men, raised money to support the Cardinals."

O'Brien would certainly need such financial support in order to compete in the new American Professional Football Association. Later in life, O'Brien recalled the financial difficulties of those early days:

> When the league started we carried from 14 to 16 players. Of course, carrying any more would mean going farther in the hole every payday because the money didn't come in at the gate, but there was another reason . . . none of the players wanted to sit on the bench, so it cost more for utility players than some of the men who were in there playing sixty minutes.

## The Boys Were Unaccustomed To The Fragrance Of New Wool

With his roster in place, O'Brien opened up the 1920 season on Sunday, October 10, with North Side rivals, the Chicago Tigers. Organized by Rube Cook (former secretary of the Chicago Cubs) and coached by fullback Guilford "Guil" Falcon, the Tigers entertained the Cards at Cubs Park (now Wrigley Field) with a 3:00 kickoff slated. The Tigers had replaced the Hammond entry in playing its home games in Cubs Park, explained the *Chicago Daily News*:

> Professional football made a very deep impression on the fans here last Fall. Hammond occupied the Cubs Park and drew several large crowds with games against Detroit, Cleveland and Canton. This year, officials on the North Side decided to have their own club.

The Cardinals had the look—and feel—of a major league club. "Chris O'Brien gathered the Cardinals together and gave them uniforms, any of which were precisely like the others," author Rocky Wolfe wrote in 1932 in *The Chicago Visitor*. "The boys objected. They were unaccustomed to the fragrance of new wool and were fearful somebody would accuse them of using perfume!" While that comment was presumably written in jest, it did typify the evolution of the club from a prairie league contender to a member of a national professional league.

The local season had already begun the week before with a full schedule among Chicago's semi-pro entries. The familiar Pullman Thorns knocked off the Calumets 21-0 at 103rd and Corliss, while the depleted Cornell-Hamburgs were routed 33-0 by the St. Charles Legion.

In a welcome gesture, the *Chicago Tribune* heralded the Cardinals' opener against the Chicago Tigers with the headline "Strong Pro Grid Teams to Clash Next Sunday" and then commented:

*Two of the country's strongest pro football teams meet Sunday at Cub Park, where the Chicago Tigers are scheduled with the Racine Cardinals. Both elevens are composed of college stars of former years, the Cardinals being built around Paddy Driscoll, former Northwestern halfback. Shorty Des Jardien, all-America center while at the University of Chicago, will fill that position for the Tigers.*

The *Daily News* added:

*It will be the initial meeting of teams that hope to be recognized as the professional champions of the city when the season comes to a close.*

This type of pregame hype was unusual for the Cards, but the free publicity, especially focusing on the local ties of the more prominent players, was gratifying. On game day, the team garnered another mention, although in a more subtle way. The *Tribune's* sports section carried a regular question/answer column where the typical "man on the street" could contribute his insight and opinions on the sporting world. The following question of the day was asked of several bystanders at the corner of North Avenue and Dearborn Parkway:

*"Who was the greatest football player of all time?"*

While Walter Eckersall from the University of Chicago was mentioned prominently, one Alfred Friedman of 1756 North Wells stated:

*I have only seen the man that I consider the best player in football play twice, but the exhibition that I was shown was enough to convince me that he has no equal. That man is Paddy Driscoll.*

## Hammond Stars Ready For Suckers

Over in Indiana, the *Hammond Times* gurgled and then belched out this erstwhile headline: "Hammond Stars Ready For Suckers." Apparently giddy over the Hammond team's chances in its upcoming match against the Rock Island Independents, the writer explained that the Hammond Pros under Dr. Alva Young was a potent team:

*On paper, the array is formidable and those who have witnessed practice work this week say that the outfit is just as formidable on the hoof.*

There's more:

*Generally speaking, Manager Young is well satisfied with his aggregation. It is
the best that the country affords and he believes Rock Island will simply be the
first stepping stone to copping the silver loving cup offered the league champions . . .*

The next day, readers may have been surprised to learn that Rock Island had
slammed the Pros 26-0 in an easy rout that did nothing to subdue the bravado of Doc
Young, who admitted that he was pleased with the outcome:

*It was only a test game. I knew that Rock Island would be the toughest nut for
us to crack in the whole league. I could have scheduled games with teams which
I knew we could beat, but I wanted to see my men worked to the limit so that
I could pick the weak spots. I have them pegged now.*

## Alumni Who Desire To Play The Game Are In Abundance

Meanwhile, the reorganized Cardinals woke up Sunday, October 10, and trekked north
to Cubs Park. What they found was not only a worthy opponent, but also something
that was previously atypical of the Cardinals' fortunes: a huge crowd! With newspaper estimates of the fans ranging from eight thousand to ten thousand, the revamped
visitors locked horns with the Tigers and almost three hours later emerged with a 0-0
tie. The Tigers' roster was littered with names from places such as Notre Dame, Illinois,
and the Ivy League and included several members from the 1919 Hammond All-Stars,
such as Shorty Des Jardien, the 6'4" center from the University of Chicago. "Manager
Falcon this year is making a specialty of getting the best stars obtainable," wrote the
*Chicago Tribune.* "Rules of the American Professional Football Association do not permit dickering with college stars, but alumni who desire to play the game are in abundance."

Following the game, the *Tribune* noted:

*Twenty-six college alumni representing two professional football teams, scuffled
to a draw, 0-0, before 10,000 gridiron fans yesterday . . . but the opinions of the
critical rooters gave a shade decision to the Racine Cardinals, piloted by Paddy
Driscoll . . .*

Despite the lack of a victory, both teams should have been satisfied that they were
competitive in this historic first APFA league game in Chicago. With rosters limited
to thirteen players and a lack of a suitable passing element due to a more rounded
football, the game in 1920 differed in many ways from the present product. While
the field itself was one hundred yards long, the goalposts were stuck right on the goal
line. At times, the goalposts could be utilized as an extra "blocker" in goal-line rushing attempts. Yard lines were etched every five yards and the field lacked hash marks.
The next play simply began where the previous attempt ended.

The players still were not required to wear helmets, and substitutions were rare
and unwelcome, as Chris O'Brien would state later in his life:

*Everybody wanted to play sixty minutes. If you took a guy out because he had a broken finger, a fractured wrist, or a bleeding cut on his anatomy, you ran the risk of not having any conversation with that player . . . he just wouldn't talk to you!*

Needless to say, players were expected to go both ways on offense and defense and usually were removed from the game only because of significant injury.

With the bloated football difficult to grasp because of its size, passing was made even more difficult due to the rule requiring the ball to be thrown from at least five yards behind the line of scrimmage. "Passing played little part in the game," said George Halas. "We had a fat ball, hard to pass." This placed a great deal more emphasis on the running game. While not totally creative, the running game did provide some thrills and chills for the spectators in terms of watching human heads and bodies collide.

Games were often low scoring, and a team's most valuable asset was often its punter, who could keep the opposition deep in its own territory until that one lucky break might occur on a change of possession. With Paddy Driscoll's devilishly accurate toe (it was said that he could actually curve a punt!), the Cards could be a threat on both offense and defense without really generating much scoring in terms of touchdowns. Indeed, the 1920 Cardinals would score just five touchdowns in six "league" games. Defensively, Driscoll could boom punts and watch the generous rolls of the obese ball as it bounced downfield. On the other side of the line, his fabled drop-kicking ability made the Cards a threat any time they crossed the mid-field stripe. Surprisingly, he only attempted one field goal in an APFA game in 1920 and missed it.

Aside from the higher salaries earned by Driscoll and Thorpe, players generally viewed football as a part-time endeavor, and most worked their football playing around their work schedule. This provided a unique advantage to George Halas down in Decatur. Each of his players was an employee of the Staley Company, earning at least $50 per week. This was helpful in recruiting, for if Halas offered a spot on the football team to a player from another area, he could sweeten the deal with the thought of a secure, full-time job with the company.

Halas proved to be a masterful recruiter in building a professional football team from scratch in 1920. He also benefited from his own network, which included playing time with the University of Illinois, the Great Lakes team, and Hammond in 1919. Initially, he reached out to his former Great Lakes teammates, including Driscoll and Jimmy Conzelman, in an effort to launch the Staleys' program. Driscoll was also interested, but had already made a commitment to the Cardinals. Aside from Conzelman, Halas convinced Jerry Jones and Hugh Blacklock from the Great Lakes team to move to Decatur, and then snagged former Illinois stars Ross Petty and Burt Ingwersen. Dutch Sternaman also was recruited by A. E. Staley to work with Halas in organizing the team.

Also joining the Staleys were Bob Koehler (Northwestern), George Trafton, (Notre Dame), and Guy Chamberlin (Nebraska). One interesting holdover from the 1919 Staleys team was Charley Dressen, who would make his biggest impact later as a major league baseball manager. Halas, Conzelman, Trafton, and Chamberlin eventually would wind up in the Pro Football Hall of Fame.

The rest of the APFA took the field for the 1920 season, but with few binding rules, no set schedule, and no official standings. Generally, the teams in the Illinois area (Staleys, Cardinals, Rock Island, and Decatur) played each other while the teams in the Ohio region (Canton, Akron, Dayton, and Cleveland) did likewise. Among the stars that first season were, of course, player-coach Jim Thorpe of Canton and his teammate Wilbur Henry, Paddy Driscoll of Chicago, Fritz Pollard and Rip King of Akron, and Chamberlin of Decatur. Pollard later became the NFL's first black coach.

A few teams failed to measure up to the competition, most notably the Hammond Pros. The preseason euphoria wore off quickly with the loss to Rock Island and then disappeared completely following defeats by Dayton (44-0) and Decatur (28-7). The Pros did manage to knock off the Logan Squares (14-9) and the Pullman Thorns (14-13) in non-league play to finish 2-5 overall, but were 0-3 against fellow APFA members. Rochester, Muncie, and Columbus would also go winless in league play, with Muncie disbanding after its only league game, a 45-0 thrashing at the hands of Rock Island. On the top of the heap, the better teams in 1920 proved to be the Akron Pros (6-0-3), the Decatur Staleys (5-1-2), the Buffalo All-Americans (4-1-1), and the Rock Island Independents (4-2-1). Recordwise, the Cardinals were in the middle of the pack, finishing with a 3-2-1 slate in league matches and 6-2-2 overall. Late in the season, both Buffalo and Decatur battled Akron to scoreless ties, and both teams claimed the championship based on those dubious results. Although the APFA did not have championship criteria in place at the time, it is generally agreed that Akron deserved the honor based on the fact that it did not lose a game against league opponents. The Staleys, behind a marvelous defense that allowed only three touchdowns in thirteen games, finished 10-1-2 overall, with the only defeat coming at the hands of the Cardinals. The Akron Pros were even tougher on defense, allowing only seven points over eleven games.

## *Paddy Driscoll Was There With All His Cunning*

Following the opening game against the Tigers, the Cards entertained the Moline (IL) Tractors in a non-league game held at an unusual setting for O'Brien, the St. Rita High School stadium at 63rd and Oakley on the South Side. The Tractors were fresh off a big win over Clinton, Iowa, stated the *Daily News*:

> *The Moline athletes last week completely stopped the Clinton team, professional champions of the Hawkeye state and counted four touchdowns against them.*

Behind the rushing of Paddy Driscoll and Harry Curran, the Cards easily swept past the visitors 33-3 in a game that was the finale of a doubleheader with the local Amos A. A. and the Iroquois. On the following Sunday (October 24), the team traveled to Rock Island to face the Independents. Although the visitors lost 7-0, the *Rock Island Argus* newspaper documented each and every play for the most advanced game report of a Cardinals game since the trip to Michigan City back in 1902. Sports Editor Bruce Copeland did a wonderful job in covering the games of the Independents, interspersing action on the field with his own editorializing. His coverage of the Cardinals-Independents game is so thorough that for the first time, a Cardinals fan could have access to actual game statistics. This is commonplace today, but the NFL did not begin collecting statistics until 1932 and newspapers generally did not bother with this element of the game either. Although we know that Rock Island gained 398 total yards versus the Cards' 205, those totals included yards gained on punt returns, kickoffs, and penalties. The whole issue of statistics-gathering was in need of some refinement. Still, there was evidence of some sharp sports writing in Copeland's prose:

> *Paddy Driscoll was there with all his cunning at picking holes for his twisting, twirling, cut-in, dashes outside tackle. But the former Northwestern star could not gain consistently enough to score . . . All of the Independents played as never before, stung partly by the bitterness of their defeat by the Staleys. The single touchdown fails to do justice to the power of the Independents' attack or the bulwark of its defense, with the ever flashy Driscoll threatening to break away from the field and turn the tide.*

Copeland would probably admit to being a "homer" for his side, but he was brutally critical of his own team in a salvo launched following a tough 7-0 defeat to the Staleys just a week before the Cardinals game:

> *The Staleys had no valid excuse for winning, although YESTERDAY they were the best team. The Independents deserved to lose for allowing an otherwise inferior team to catch them wholly out of physical condition, rush them off their feet and precipitate them into such impotent confusion that disrupted every vestige of the incomparable teamwork of former triumphs.*

## He Wants To Have The Moniker Changed

It was about this time that O'Brien quietly changed the name of the team from the Racine Cardinals to the Chicago Cardinals. The *Hammond Times* noted the change in a brief summary of the Rock Island game:

> *The Rock Island Independents yesterday handed the Chicago Cardinals, formerly the Racine Cardinals, their first reverse of the season, 7-0.*

The *Chicago Herald Examiner* provided a more thorough report on October 20, 1920:

> *The football team formerly known as the Racine Cardinals will be known in the future as the Chicago Cardinals. Manager Chris O'Brien today announced he has applied for a new charter. The old name has been used in professional football circles this fall and as the home grounds are now on the south side he wants to have the moniker changed.*

The loss to Rock Island seemed to inspire the Cardinals, as they ran off four victories in a row over the Detroit Heralds (21-0), the Chicago Tigers (6-3), the Cincinnati Celts (20-0), and the Lansing (MI) Oldsmobiles (14-0). The first two of those games were against APFA opponents, and both had remarkable stories behind them.

The win over Detroit on October 31 was marked by a most unusual scoring surge. All three of the Cardinals' touchdowns were set up by blocked punts. Even more unusual was the fact that all three blocked punts occurred in the third quarter (in about a five-minute span). Finally, all three punts were blocked by the same man: Cardinals end Lenny Sachs.

This is believed to be a feat that has never been duplicated in the history of the NFL. Blocking three punts is certainly one achievement that would be extremely difficult to approach, even in a career. Detroit punter Steamer Horning was the victim of Sachs' efforts, and Sachs himself recovered the first block for a touchdown.

The second was recovered for a score by either end Paul Florence (credited by *Chicago Herald Examiner*) or an individual named Chapel (*Detroit Free Press*) or Chappelle (*Chicago Tribune, Hammond Times*), who was probably guard Leo Chappelle. The final block was recovered by an unknown Cardinal on the Heralds' ten-yard line, and then Paddy Driscoll ran it in from there on the very first play. Driscoll kicked all three extra points. From that point on, the game disintegrated into one huge shoving match, as witnessed by the *Tribune*:

> *After the scoring rout, the fray degenerated into a perfect prairie football, and was several times halted while the players and the officials wrangled. Three thousand fans enjoyed the disputes.*

Next up was a rematch with the Chicago Tigers, and the *Daily News* offered some insight into the weekly preparation for the early professional teams:

> *Manager Gil Falcon's Tigers have not had any mishaps and are working overtime every night this week to go under full steam for the Cardinals. Until now, professional teams have been working only three nights a week as all the men are in business, but the importance of Sunday's set-to has brought them out every night.*

On November 7, the Cardinals edged the Chicago Tigers 6-3 before a record crowd estimated at ten thousand by the *Chicago Herald Examiner*. The Tigers jumped on the board first at Cubs Park with a twenty-seven-yard dropkick in the first quarter. Driscoll scored later in the first half on a spectacular forty-yard run described by the *Chicago Tribune*:

> *Driscoll took the ball . . . and dodged back through the entire Tiger team, several of whom touched him, for the winning touchdown.*

The score had been set up moments earlier when Driscoll punted to the Tigers. Return man Milton Ghee mistakenly fell on the ball at his own one-yard line, putting the Tigers in perilous field position. Although a punt by Johnny Barrett gave the Tigers some breathing room, it wasn't far enough, as Driscoll quickly proved. Neither team was able to score again during the contest.

The win over the Tigers was pleasant for the Cardinals, but it also signaled a continued existence in the professional ranks for the team. Up until this time, Chris O'Brien had not decided if this venture would be permanent. He had made the risky jump to the new pro league rather quickly, and he was not sure if he could maintain the team and the resulting financial obligations. Perhaps the huge crowd for the Tigers' game persuaded him to completely submerge himself in pro football. As the *Daily News* stated:

*Football fans of the south side have gone wild over the Cardinals since they defeated the Tigers in a game for the professional title of Chicago at Cubs Park Sunday, and the members of the club have secured a three-year lease on Normal Park which the club will make its home stand.*

The first "home" league game was arranged for November 14 against the Cincinnati Celts in a game at Normal Park, where the *Daily News* predicted: "The south side park promises to have one of the brightest football attractions in many moons." Tickets were quickly issued and sold at Spalding's Sporting Goods Store and at the new Cardinals headquarters at 5626 South Racine.

With the easy wins over Cincinnati (20-0, in which Chappelle scored on another blocked punt) and Michigan champions Lansing (14-0), the Cardinals were coasting with a 5-1-1 record and set up another non-league game on Thanksgiving Day (November 25) at the Logan Square Athletic Club in Chicago. Meanwhile, the Decatur Staleys were back in town for a rematch with the Chicago Tigers for the "Professional Title of the Central West," according to the *Herald-Examiner*. At this point in the season, it was impossible to clarify the league standings, with the APFA teams playing anything and anyone in order to get in a weekly ball game. While the Staleys eked out a close 6-0 win over the Tigers, the Cardinals' game with the Logans was canceled. In a warm tribute to Driscoll, the game was called off when Paddy's father passed away. Out of respect to the Driscoll family, the Cardinals elected not to face the Logans.

Certainly, this was an admirable tribute to the team's greatest player. However, it could also be suggested that this was a pragmatic decision as well. Without the triple threat of Driscoll, the Cardinals might not have had such an easy time with the Logans. In addition, a loss might dissuade the Staleys from remaining in Chicago for a big home game (i.e., big money) at Normal Park with the Cardinals. The Staleys and the Cardinals had already been plotting to schedule a game, which was originally planned to have taken place on November 21, according to the *Decatur Herald*. When those plans fell through, O'Brien and Halas continued to talk and both teams scheduled separate games on Thanksgiving Day. O'Brien also may have been considering inviting one of the Ohio teams, such as Akron or Dayton, should the Staleys lose to the Tigers. If the Staleys had been defeated on Thanksgiving Day, O'Brien might have thought: "The Cardinals lost to Rock Island, but that doesn't matter since Rock Island lost to the Staleys. The Staleys beat Rock Island, but then lost to the Tigers. The Tigers, of course, lost to the Cardinals, elevating the Cardinals to the championship of the West, Midwest, North Central, or whatever!"

That scenario never came to fruition, however, since the Staleys survived their match with the Tigers. In either case (the Cards vs. the Staleys, or the Cards vs. the "world"), it would be critical for the team's hopes to ease into the big game against whomever with just the one loss on the ledger. But it is certain that O'Brien was thinking about bigger and better things, as evidenced in the *Tribune* on Thanksgiving morning when it was announced that the Logan Square game was called off:

*Owing to the death of the father of Capt. John L. (Paddy) Driscoll, the football game of the Chicago Cardinals booked this afternoon against Logan Square A.C. has been called off. Manager Chris O'Brien of the Cardinals will make an effort*

*to sign the Decatur Staley eleven for an attraction at Normal Park Sunday, pro-*
*viding the strong downstate outfit is successful in this afternoon's clash with the*
*Chicago Tigers.*

Halas finally did agree to stay over until Sunday, November 28, and play the
Cardinals at Normal Park. Although the game was important, it was not for any official title, and the teams would be competing for the attention of Chicago fans, as noted
in the *Tribune:*

*The crack Staley team from Decatur, who claim the Midwest title, will appear*
*at Normal park as the opponents of the Cardinals. The downstaters have not been*
*defeated since they were organized early in the fall, while the only black mark*
*on the record of the Cards is a setback at Rock Island.*

## The Chicago Tigers

According to Cardinal folklore, the Chicago Tigers were beaten out of existence by
the Cardinals. Prior to the second game between the Cardinals and the Chicago
Tigers in 1920, O'Brien and Guil Falcon of the Tigers were said to have agreed that
the loser of the game would disperse his team and leave Chicago. After all, it was
surmised, one city could not possibly support two professional football teams. This
presumption appears unlikely, even though the Cardinals won the game 6-3 behind
Paddy Driscoll's forty-yard touchdown gallop, and the Tigers disappeared after the
1920 season. More than likely, the Tigers suffered attendance woes by playing all
of their home games at Cubs Park in Chicago. The combination of a lofty rent at
the baseball park along with a dwindling attendance due to a losing season may
have doomed the poor Tigers. With the success of the Cardinals and the ever-present
Staleys hanging around, the Tigers simply lost their drawing power. It was a good
story, but even after the loss to the Cardinals, the Tigers hung around and completed their season. Money—not the Cardinals' victory—paved the way for the
demise of the Chicago Tigers, who scored just twenty-two points in compiling a
1-5-1 in their only APFA season.

## *Chris O'Brien's Cardinals Spring The Biggest Surprise*

Historically, this game marked the beginning of the National Football League's oldest rivalry. The Staleys would move north the next season and become the Chicago
Bears, while the Cardinals would remain in Chicago until 1960 and eventually become
the current Arizona Cardinals. The second-oldest NFL rivalry is the Cardinals-Green
Bay series, which began on November 20, 1921. The Bears-Packers tradition first com-
menced on November 27, 1921.

But on November 28, 1920, the eyes of the pro football world were on Normal
Park, and the Staleys quickly jumped out to a 6-0 lead on the opening kickoff. It wasn't
your normal score on a kickoff, like an exciting ninety-eight-yard return through a
field littered with the fallen bodies of the defense, but rather a fluke "fumble." The
opening kick nudged a Cardinal receiver and bounced towards a streaking Bob Koehler

of the Staleys. Koehler snared the pigskin and ran it in for the score. Unfortunately for the Staleys, the point after attempt by the usually accurate Hugh Blacklock was wide, but Decatur owned a 6-0 lead.

The game turned into a grudging ground battle on the cold turf, with neither team able to threaten until the Cards scrambled down to the visitors' five-yard line late in the first half. Instead of taking the easy three points, the Cards went for a touchdown but lost the ball on downs. In the end, the game was decided by another wacky play, this time on behalf of the Cardinals. Early in the third quarter, Decatur fumbled on its own twenty and none other than the irrepressible Lenny Sachs grabbed the loose ball and lunged into the end zone for the tying score. With the score knotted at 6-6, Driscoll stepped back to attempt the extra point. All the hours of practice led up to this moment when the cold, the ice, and the tough opposition would make it nearly impossible for either team to score again. Standing about ten yards behind Whalen, the center, Driscoll took the snap, quickly rotated the ball so that the laces faced out, and simultaneously began to step forward. He softly dropped the ball from slightly below his waist so that his kicking foot would make contact with the ball almost immediately after it touched the ground. As the whipping action of his kicking leg met the ball, it began to elevate instantly, cleared the reaches of the defensive line, and sailed through the uprights on the goal line for the important extra point.

The Cardinals now led 7-6, and as the game sped towards its conclusion, it became apparent that the Staleys would need something dramatic like a quick turnover or an unusual play to turn the tide in this game. Halas tried everything. First, he attempted forward passes from the shadow of his own goal line, a fairly unexpected and unusual strategy in 1920. The Staleys even unleashed a fake punt, another surprise move, which gained thirty yards but didn't help dent the Cardinals' goal line. In the end, it came down to Driscoll squirting around the ends, bouncing up the middle, and slipping off tackle, gobbling up yards, but more importantly, eating up the clock. Even the *Decatur Herald* was impressed:

> *The Staleys, on the strength of their record, claimed the professional football championship of the country, having won every game played so far by easy margins. The Cardinals not only outscored them, but also outplayed them every inch of the way, gaining almost twice as much and breaking up almost every play that was attempted.*

The *Chicago Herald American* appeared to enjoy the competition as well:

> *Chris O'Brien's Chicago Cardinals sprang the biggest surprise of the local football season yesterday when they walloped the hitherto undefeated Staleys of Decatur in a thrilling 7-6 contest at Normal Park. More than 5,000 fans saw the pastime, which was as full of football strategy and skill as three ordinary contests.*

It was about this time that players were beginning to switch back and forth between teams—an element that the newly organized league had hoped to avoid. Well-traveled Frank Rydzewski played for the Chicago Tigers against the Cardinals after playing with Hammond the week before. Now, late in this 1920 season, names like Driscoll and Halas would appear in different uniforms as well.

While the league did not have a formal process for winning championships, the Cardinals (3-1-1 in league play) and Staleys (4-1-1) initiated a meandering procedure that did indeed bring some semblance of a playoff situation to the APFA. The now vulnerable Staleys asked to meet the Cardinals once again—and quickly! The two teams agreed to battle one more time to decide "Midwestern honors." Although this would be a "home" game for Decatur, the scene of the crime would be at Cubs Park in Chicago on Sunday, December 5.

When the Cardinals and the Staleys took the field on December 5, the largest crowd (eleven thousand) to ever witness a pro game in Chicago was on hand at Cubs Park. The Cards welcomed back fullback Len Charpier from the Thorns for this outing and once again, the lineups resembled an early boarding party for the Pro Football Hall of Fame:

| CARDINALS | | STALEYS | |
|---|---|---|---|
| LE | Sachs, Larossa | RE | Halas |
| LT | Gillies | RT | Blacklock |
| LG | Zoia | RG | Jones |
| C | Clark | C | Trafton |
| RG | Chappelle | LG | May |
| RT | Carey, Brennan | LT | Ingwerson |
| RE | Florence | LE | Chamberlin |
| QB | Driscoll | QB | Pearce |
| LH | Curran, Hallstrom | RH | Lanum, Conzelman |
| RH | McInerney | LH | Sternaman |
| FB | Charpier, Egan | FB | Koehler |

Unfortunately for the Cardinals, both Driscoll and Sachs were injured early in the game. While the Staleys struggled, they still posted a 10-0 win. The only touchdown was scored in the second period on a two-yard scamper by Bob Koehler. Sternaman connected on just one of five field goal attempts for the final three points.

"We declared ourselves champions of the West," remembered Halas in his autobiography. "The Akron Indians (sic), unbeaten, proclaimed themselves champions of the East. We arranged a match for the national championship."

This title tilt would be held in Chicago at Cubs Park and was promoted as the vehicle to decide the "professional football championship." Frank Nied, the Akron manager, met with Halas in Chicago prior to the game to decide upon officials and to finalize game arrangements. Well aware of Akron's power, with the fabulous Fritz Pollard and four other collegiate All-Americans in the lineup, Halas did a little fishing of his own and snared old friend Paddy Driscoll. Driscoll would be in the Staleys' backfield for the championship game along with a new quarterback named "Fletcher," who does not appear in any roster of the Staleys from that era. The *Chicago Herald Examiner* didn't fail to notice the new recruit:

*Paddy Driscoll substituted for Lanurn at the start of the second period. It didn't take Paddy long to convince Manager George Halas of the Staleys that he hadn't made any mistake in borrowing him from the Chicago Cardinals for the afternoon.*

On the day of the game, another Chicago record crowd of twelve thousand was present as the two heavyweights battled to a scoreless draw on a slippery field. The *Tribune* reported that the Staleys' best chance of scoring arrived in the second half:

> *Only once did either threaten to score. That was in the third period, when the Staleys worked close enough to Akron's goal to permit Sternaman to attempt a place kick from the twenty-two yard line. The ball went wide of its mark, although Capt. Halas had taken the necessary precaution to have a clean, dry shoe sent in for the kicker.*

The tie didn't matter, according to Halas, who recalled: "We proclaimed ourselves World Champions!" when Akron refused his suggestion for a rematch. The Staleys then dispersed for the season, but it would be difficult not to notice Halas coveting the vast expanses of Cubs Park as he trotted off into the cold sunset in Decatur after playing five "home" games in Chicago in 1920.

There was just one game left in the weary 1920 football season. For some reason, perhaps to secure just one more paycheck, the Cardinals arranged for an away game with the local Stayms to be held on December 19. The Stayms were a good enough team, but certainly not in the class of the Cardinals. Yet the tenuous Stayms managed to tie the visitors 14-14.

Only two of the Stayms' starters from a game against the Thorns on November 22 were in the lineup for the game with the Cardinals less than a month later. In their place were Halas, Blacklock, Shoemaker, and Sternaman of the Staleys, while Dunc Annan and Guil Falcon slipped over from the Tigers. No one hid the fact that the Stayms had loaded up for this encounter, but one wonders why. The game had no bearing on any league standings, it was dreadfully cold, and it was an "away" game for the Cardinals. Maybe they just loved to play football.

Following the completion of the season, several of the local "pro" players participated in indoor football games at the Dexter Pavilion. Among the celebrity players were George Trafton of the Staleys, who played indoor ball with the Pullman Thorns, along with Guil Falcon and Donald Davidson. The Cards' Lenny Sachs joined the Roosters along with some of the original Stayms.

Meanwhile, Chris O'Brien, with a pleasant 6-2-2 record to reflect upon, began devising plans to improve the Cardinals in 1921. With the incredible talent of Driscoll to build upon, he only needed to add a player or two at key positions. If the 1920 season had concluded after the first game with the Staleys, the Cardinals would have rightfully claimed some type of Midwest championship. As it was, the team was solid and competitive, and the future was bright.

O'Brien just needed to figure out how to pay for that future!

## It Drives Us Nuts!

A true Chicago Cardinals fan has little use for any historical inaccuracies which displace any of the team's revered legacies. One such piece of lore that rears its head at least twice a year concerns the oldest team rivalry in the NFL. As explained earlier, the oldest rivalry is that of the Cardinals and Bears. The first game in this series took place on November 28, 1920, when the Cards defeated the predecessor of the Bears—the Decatur Staleys—by a score of 7-6. The next oldest rivalry would be that of the Cardinals and the Green Bay Packers, who tied a game 3-3 on November 20, 1921. The Packers then lost to the Staleys a week later (November 27) 20-0 in the first game between those two teams.

While most current examples of this inaccuracy credit the Bears and the Packers with holding the longest rivalry, the error first surfaced on September 25, 1932, in the *Chicago Tribune.* Underneath a headline which proclaimed: "Renew Oldest Rivalry in Pro Football," the *Tribune* stated:

> The Bears-Packers series is the oldest in pro football. The teams have met 23 times since 1921. Eleven times, and nine of these since 1928, the Packers have defeated the Bears. The north side Chicago team has won nine games. Three have been tied.

Although the Bears and Packers do not have the oldest NFL rivalry, the two teams found the pairing financially attractive at the time and usually met three times a year for several seasons after 1928, until more formal scheduling was implemented and a league playoff factor initiated a few years later.

Although the O'Brien brothers split from the Morgan Athletic Club in 1901, the Morgans continued to field teams such as this one, believed to be from around 1914. The Morgans and the Cardinals both shared space at Normal Park. *(Photo courtesy of the Arizona Cardinals)*

The Cardinals Athletic and Social Club football team claimed the Illinois state championship in 1902 by carefully ignoring an embarrassing loss to a team from Michigan City, Indiana.
*(Photo courtesy of the Arizona Cardinals)*

ST. JOHN    F. LANNING    W. McCARTHY    W. DALEY    W. ENSWEILER    W. HALLIGAN    P. C. SH
DANAHER    J. MALONEY    C. O'BRIEN    P. O'BRIEN    E. ROBINSON    F. BREEN    P. PETERSON
M. O'SHEA    C. CARLSON    L. BLISS    R. W. DAUER    R. ANDERSON    H. PALM
G. JOHNSON

Chris O'Brien owned a paint store at 5626 South Racine and later opened a billiard hall around 1917 at 5622 South Racine. The latter building also served as the headquarters for the Racine Cardinals. Note the signs advertising the Cardinals on the second-floor windows of the billiard hall. *(Photo courtesy of Carol Judge)*

The 1917 season extended into January when a series of tie games scrambled the local football playoffs. Although the Cardinals did not capture the Chicago title, much of the football lore from that time was saved by a 163-pound end by the name of Donald Davidson (back row, third from left). Chris O'Brien is standing in the middle of the back row.

*(Photo courtesy of Phyllis Davidson)*

Original Cardinals manager Chris O'Brien continued to play in the line until he was nearly forty. This photo is believed to be from around 1919, when O'Brien was considering plans to enter the Cardinals into the new American Professional Football Conference.

*(Photo courtesy of Carol Judge)*

In 1921, the Cards declared themselves the "Western" champions after battling the Decatur Staleys to a 0-0 tie. Paddy Driscoll (holding the football) paced the club to a 5-3-2 record. *(Photo courtesy of the Arizona Cardinals)*

While the 1925 Cardinals presented Chris O'Brien with his only league championship, the triumphant finish was marred by controversial victories over Milwaukee and Hammond. *(Photo courtesy of the Arizona Cardinals)*

Paddy Driscoll (left) was the most versatile of the early NFL stars. Signed by the Racine Cardinals on September 7, 1920, Driscoll immediately helped make Chris O'Brien's team a contender in the American Professional Football Association. Driscoll led the Cards to the 1925 championship before mounting financial woes forced O'Brien to sell his services to the Chicago Bears, where Driscoll promptly led the league in scoring in 1926. His last season was in 1929, when Driscoll was paired with the great Red Grange (right) in the Bears' backfield.

*(Corbis/UPI-Bettmann)*

Ernie Nevers still holds the single game scoring record in the NFL. On November 28, 1929, Nevers scored all of the Cardinals' points in a 40-6 rout of the Chicago Bears. He was a bruising fullback and team leader for the Cardinals who was insulted at the prospect of sitting out even a single play. He also served as player-coach in 1930 and 1931 before retiring. In 1939, owner Charles Bidwill lured him back to coach the team once again, but that experiment lasted only a single season.

*(Corbis/UPI-Bettmann)*

The Chicago Cardinals and the Chicago Bears developed an intense rivalry right from the start of the NFL. Games ended in brawls and cheap shots were common, but the Cardinals usually held their own against the more successful Bears in the early days. In 1932, the Bears won the NFL title despite being held to a tie earlier in the season by the Cardinals.

*(photo from collection of author)*

On November 5, 1989, former player Donald Davidson (right) was honored by the Arizona Cardinals as the team's oldest surviving player. He was ninety-one at the time. Current Cardinals' owner William Bidwill is on the left. *(Photo courtesy of the Arizona Cardinals)*

Phil Handler (third from right) was a mainstay for the 1934 Cardinals and later became head coach of the team. *(Photo courtesy of the Chicago Historical Society)*

This rare publicity photo of four Cardinals on a bike appeared in the *Chicago Daily News* in November of 1934. From left: Tony Schaller, Mickey Rodale, Eddie Trieste, and Jerry Rodman. *(Photo courtesy of the Chicago Historical Society)*

# ◆ 4 ◆

# Growing Pains:
# 1921 – 1924

*"Those were the days when the cure-all*
*for any injury was iodine and four fingers of bourbon!"*

JIMMY CONZELMAN,
PRO FOOTBALL PIONEER AND
LATER COACH OF THE CHICAGO CARDINALS

In an era of unkempt fields, suspicious player rosters, and frequently changing schedules, the Cardinals burst into the 1921 season with a clever marketing ploy designed to expand the team's market area. Perhaps this significant promotional effort was not originally designed to alter the course of the game. It was not the result of a lengthy brainstorming session or a tedious study to determine the possibilities for marketing the fledgling professional football league. Cardinals owner Chris O'Brien developed a simple plan in 1921 that would change the concept of professional sports in Chicago: he offered free parking!

With a plethora of professional, semi-pro, club, college, prairie, and high school teams in the greater Chicago area, the intuitive O'Brien hatched a seemingly innocent incentive for football fans. He rented enough space in a vacant, grassy area adjacent to Normal Park and publicized the fact that there was room to park "400 automobiles" for the Cardinals' home games. Simple, yet efficient.

O'Brien possibly unleashed this idea specifically for the Cards' home game against the Hammond Pros. Although Hammond is closer to Chicago proper than some of its outlying suburbs, it was still in a different state (Indiana). Noting the rise in the use of the motor car in American life—and conceivably to lure Hoosiers who might drive over from Indiana—O'Brien fashioned this early marketing gimmick based on the pragmatic logic of making the parking of a motor car convenient. What a difference this travel concept was compared to the wagons drawn by a team of horses that carried the fans of the Morgan Athletic Club to those Sunday games. O'Brien also addressed the issue of long lines by offering tickets for sale prior to the game itself and setting up ticket counters at Spalding's Sporting Goods in downtown Chicago and at "Pete's Place" just north of Normal Park at 55th and Racine. In another innovation, the Cardinals printed nifty four-page game programs with a posed photo of Paddy Driscoll aiming a pass on the cover. The back cover contained a full page advertisement from Citizens Trust and Savings Bank while the inside two pages listed the rosters, alma maters, positions, and numbers of the players.

In 1921, O'Brien elected to spend considerable time at his home field of Normal Park, and in fact played all of his games in Chicago as he continued to chase financial success for his team. After an overall 6-2-2 record in 1920 (3-2-1 against league opponents), the Cardinals were looked upon as a solid, competitive outfit. With Paddy Driscoll once again the field general, O'Brien could envision both athletic and financial success—especially now that the Cards "owned" the city of Chicago. Following the inaugural 1920 season, the Chicago Tigers folded, leaving the Cardinals as the only major pro team in town. When the Tigers cleared out their lockers, O'Brien hoped to take advantage of the situation by luring fans from the North Side down to Normal Park at 61st and Racine.

The Cardinals added Notre Dame end Norm Barry to the team as well as brothers Ralph and Arnie Horween from Harvard, who played under the name of McMahon in order to disguise their participation in the disrespectful game of pro football from their mother. Big center Frank Rydzewski was claimed from the defunct Chicago Tigers, fullback Bob Koehler switched over from Decatur, and guard Walter Voight was picked up from Hammond.

In 1921 the Cardinals would again be coached by Paddy Driscoll, but the team's schedule would be much tougher. The games against the Cornells and the Thorns were slipping into the past; local clubs would be replaced by difficult foes from Akron, Minneapolis, and Green Bay. Of the ten games played by the Cardinals in 1921, only two would be against non-league competition.

There had been other significant changes in the league structure since the conclusion of the rookie season as well. New to the league were teams from Louisville, Evansville, Cincinnati, Minneapolis, and a small town in Wisconsin called Green Bay. Just as O'Brien was about to rub his hands in delight at being the only team in the league's largest current market, a funny thing happened on the way to the bank.

## *More Interested In Football Than Starch*

Down in Decatur, Mr. Staley had apparently grown weary of supporting a football team, even if it was a successful one. Staley offered George Halas and Dutch Sternaman possession of the team, provided they would retain the name of the "Staleys" for one year for advertising purposes. Halas provided the following insight of the transaction in his autobiography:

> *Mr. Staley said: "George, I know you are more interested in football than starch. As you know, there is a slight recession in the country. Time lost practicing and playing costs a huge amount of money. I feel we can no longer underwrite the team's losses . . . George, why don't you take the team to Chicago? I think football will go over big there . . . professional teams need a big city base. Chicago is a good sports city. Look at the way the baseball games draw profitable crowds."*
>
> *I agreed with everything he said but there was still an immediate problem— ready cash. Before I could ask, Mr. Staley went on: "I'll give you $5,000 seed money to pay costs until the gate receipts start coming in. I ask only that you continue to call the team the Staleys for one season."*

Halas had also surmised that the quiet market of Decatur might not be the best place to field a profitable franchise, so he quickly made arrangements to lease Cubs

Park in Chicago through negotiations with William Veeck Sr., president of the Chicago Cubs. With the Tigers gone, the place would have been empty in the fall, so Halas and crew moved to the Windy City and set up shop. The move was an easy one, since the Staleys had used the same location for some of their "home" games in 1920. In Chicago, the Staleys found that they could attract crowds of up to twelve thousand while the gate in Decatur hovered around fifteen hundred to five thousand. With the first two home games played in Decatur to start off the 1921 season, Halas then somehow arranged to play the remaining ten games at Cubs Park, giving the Decatur-Chicago Staleys a season schedule with all twelve games at "home." In 1922, out of respect for Veeck, Halas considered renaming the team the Cubs: "But I noted football players are bigger than baseball players; so if baseball players are cubs, then certainly football players must be bears!"

Essentially, the Staleys snuck into town without a word of protest from Chris O'Brien. Theoretically, the fledgling league might have supported him had he insisted on retaining sole territorial rights in Chicago. But that wasn't his nature. "Some people said that he should have kept the Bears out of town," said O'Brien's granddaughter Patricia Needham. "But I remember him saying, 'No, this is for the sport, not the money.' Football was his love and he allowed the Bears into Chicago because he knew it would help the game that he loved."

And so it started: the Bears on the North Side and the Cardinals on the South Side. While this sudden change in direction for the Staleys might have caught O'Brien by surprise, he was smart enough to realize the economic rewards that a popular rivalry with his new neighbors might inspire. The rivalry sparked intense competition right from the start, and the Cardinals seemed to place more emphasis on the results of their games with the Bears as a barometer of their success rather than on the overall finish of the team in league play. Because of the 7-6 win over the Staleys late in the 1920 season, the Cardinals had dubbed themselves the "Western Champions," conveniently forgetting that the Staleys had defeated them 10-0 in a rematch just a week later. The teams would also massage the rules somewhat in terms of roster adjustments when playing each other—or even allowing their players to join other teams for big games.

## APFA Selects Its Second President

Following the inaugural season, the league representatives admitted that the APFA needed some policy changes in order to keep growing and operating in a sufficient manner. Although the team leaders had planned to meet in January of 1921 to review and evaluate the first year of the APFA, that meeting was postponed until April 30. League President Jim Thorpe was absent from that meeting, held at the Portage Hotel in Akron, but the agenda was addressed as scheduled.

Perhaps "Big Jim" should have been in attendance, for the league representatives decided to replace him with Joe Carr, manager of the Columbus Panhandles. Carr would oversee the league throughout its growing years and ultimately prove to be a strong, guiding force for the game for nearly two decades. Thorpe had served well in the capacity designed for him as a recognized name and personality for the league. But the time had come for the APFA to move forward and appoint a new leader with enthusiasm, knowledge of the game, and business acumen. Carr, boasting a background laced with stints in journalism, business, and sports, also displayed traits of innovation and confidence that would all be utilized by the APFA. Although his immediate responsibility to "make it happen" for the league seemed impossible, Carr relished the challenge and began to implement some significant changes.

In 1920 the league required a fee of $100 from each team for its membership in the association. However, there is no evidence that the league ever received these fees. A year later, that fee was dropped to $50 but each of the member teams was required to remit an additional $25 for league expenses. The group also voted to present Akron with the "World's Professional Football Championship" after its performance during the 1920 season. It should be noted that Akron was "voted" the championship although the league did not maintain standings during that first season. If one collected all of the games played by all of the teams that year, the Staleys (10-1-2) would have finished half a game ahead of Akron (8-0-3) and Buffalo (9-1-1).

But based on standings as the result of games played only among association members, Akron (6-0-3) would have edged the Staleys (5-1-2) and Buffalo (4-1-1). Although the Pros were voted the champions by the members, the league would not truly mature until it could synchronize schedules, determine specific rules for deciding the championship, and wring out the still-extant process of floating rosters. The league was trying, but it would take a black eye at the conclusion of the 1925 season to push the APFA up in class.

Chris O'Brien represented the Cardinals at the April meeting and reported on his own team's situation, and the other managers did likewise. The outlook was not cheerful since the problems of attracting crowds, overcoming a carnival image, and the nagging lack of definite schedules and rosters appeared to be common among all of the teams. The election of Carr was seen as a major step in overcoming these difficulties, and one of the first major changes he instituted was to establish a headquarters for the association in Columbus, Ohio. With an "address," the APFA was beginning to demonstrate some stability, as well as an intent to continue moving forward in a positive manner.

At the April 30 meeting, the league also elected the following officers to support Carr: Vice President Morgan O'Brien (Decatur Staleys) and Secretary/Treasurer Carl Storck (Dayton Triangles). In addition, the league decided to revisit the possibility of developing some bylaws, a task that former President Thorpe had not completed. President Carr selected Storck, Dr. Charles Lambert (a game official and advisor to Carr), and A. F. Ranney to a subcommittee that was charged with compiling both the constitution for the association and those tardy bylaws.

On a final note, each team was asked to provide a roster from the 1920 season to the President by May 15. Each team would then be afforded the first opportunity to include those players on its roster for the 1921 schedule or to notify the President that specific players would not be in their plans for the season. This would then allow other interested teams to negotiate with any player cast adrift by his 1920 team. The free agent was about to be created! The managers also agreed that one player could not play for more than one league team during the same week, as Paddy Driscoll had done with the Cardinals and the Staleys in 1920. But it didn't cover the likes of George Halas and George Trafton, who drifted over to the non-league Stayms roster against the Cardinals that same year.

Although the league was making some progress, it remained to be seen whether it could survive unless there were means to include all legitimate professional teams under the umbrella of the APFA. The league members agreed to abide by the rules governing rosters, team jumping, and avoiding the use of collegiate players (which was discussed on April 30, but did not appear in the minutes). However, none of these mandates would solve all mutual concerns until the majority of professional teams in the country took their place in unity with the APFA members.

President Carr hosted the next league meeting on June 18 in Cleveland, where the new constitution was unveiled and the participating teams made an effort to develop some type of organized scheduling. New memberships were also awarded to Jim Thorpe (representing interests from Toledo, including baseball Hall of Famer Roger Bresnahan) and the Detroit Tigers (replacing the Detroit Heralds). Only the Chicago Tigers failed to survive the 1920 season, while Thorpe and Toledo never did manage to field a team in 1921.

Still another meeting was held on August 27 in Chicago at the LaSalle Hotel. Because Halas was still representing the Staleys as being from Decatur, the move to Chicago—although perhaps in the planning stages—would not be accomplished until October. At the Chicago meeting, new applications were accepted from the Green Bay Packers, the Minneapolis Marines, the Tonawanda (NY) Kardex, and the Evansville (IN) Crimson Giants. As league membership began to swell (twenty-one teams would participate in one form or another during the 1921 season), the league officials still did not accept everyone—much to the chagrin of the club from Davenport, Iowa, and the Gary, Indiana Elks. In a related early gesture to attract the press, the members asked president Carr to provide season passes to selected media personnel. Chris O'Brien encouraged the addition of Green Bay, Evansville, and Minneapolis in order to give the league a more balanced geographical scheme.

The business of preparing for the upcoming season did not end there. By the start of the 1921 season, additional memberships were presented to teams from Washington, DC, and New York, thus giving the league an outlet in the nation's largest market. New York failed to make an impact, however. Going under the name "Brickey's Giants" (with former Harvard star Charley Brickey), the New Yorkers played only two league teams and failed to score in either contest.

## *The Cardinals Stumble Into The 1921 Season*

O'Brien's Cardinals embarked on their rigorous schedule by entertaining the Racine (WI) Horlicks on Sunday, September 25, at Normal Park. The visitors fell 27-0 in this exhibition game and the *Tribune* reported:

> *The local eleven, managed by Chris O'Brien, showed fairly good team work, but fumbled at critical times. The end running of Norman Barry, former Notre Dame star, was featured.*

The following week, O'Brien enlarged the seating capacity at Normal Park by thirty-five hundred for the first league game with the Minneapolis Marines on October 2. Driscoll reeled off touchdown runs of thirty and forty-five yards and then passed thirty-three yards to newcomer Rube Marquardt for another tally. With his ability to run or pass on any play, Driscoll was a threat to score any time he touched the ball.

The following week, the Cardinals faced the defending APFA Akron Professionals and their star back, Fritz Pollard. It was touted as a feature matchup gleaming with stars in both backfields. Aside from Pollard, the Pros displayed Rip King from West Virginia while Driscoll would be joined by Barry, Hallstrom, and Koehler. However, Driscoll was contained by the visitors on this day while Pollard dominated as the Pros rushed to a 17-0 first quarter lead and then smothered the Cardinals 23-0 before six thousand attendees.

Things didn't get any easier on October 16, when the Rock Island Independents visited Normal Park. Buoyed by the addition of halfback Jimmy Conzelman from the Staleys and with Notre Dame rookie tackle Frank Coughlin in the line, the Independents had barely lost in Decatur to the Chicago Staleys (14-9) the week before. Driscoll opened up the scoring with a brilliant seventy-five-yard punt return in the first quarter. The visitors then scored two quick touchdowns in the second period. That finished the scoring for the day, with Rock Island ahead 14-7.

The game was not without some controversy, however. After the Cards' only score, Conzelman engineered a drive capped by his five-yard scoring pass to Sid Nichols. On the ensuing kickoff, the Independents pulled off a successful onside kick that Conzelman recovered on the two-yard line and carried in for a touchdown. "As long as I have been playing football, it was the first time I had ever seen the play work, let alone have a part in it," Conzelman told the *Rock Island Argus*. "It was something I had dreamed of for years." The Cards and one official claimed that Conzelman was in front of the ball when it was kicked off, thus rendering the play illegal and nullifying the touchdown. The referee overruled the protest and allowed the play, thereby preserving the victory for Rock Island. The game also marked the first appearance of a mysterious "McMahon" (Horween) brother in the Cardinals backfield.

## *Keeping The Other Team From Walking On His Face*

Although Rock Island would continue to enjoy some success that season, 1921 was always remembered by future Cardinals coach Jimmy Conzelman as the year he received his coaching baptism. The hiring of young, inexperienced players/coaches was not uncommon in this era, but the method by which Conzelman learned of his promotion certainly was. After starting his pro career with the Decatur Staleys in 1920, Conzelman often recounted how he moved over to Rock Island in 1921 and became both quarterback and coach:

> *I got lucky one day in a game with Rock Island . . . went a long way for the only touchdown. That was in 1920 with the Staleys. The owner of the Rock Island club, fellow named Flanigan, asked me to play for him next year. So I did.*
>
> *Our coach was a big lineman whose name I won't mention. I was the quarterback. We're playing a game one day in 1921 and our coach is having trouble keeping the other team from walking on his face. They're going through him like he wasn't there and we're losing by 10 points in the fourth quarter.*
>
> *All of a sudden a player came running in from the bench and stuck his head in the huddle. "I got news from Mr. Flanigan," he said.*
>
> *"He said to say that he just fired the coach, that Conzelman is taking over, and that he wants you to play your hearts out for your new coach!"*

Conzelman was thus appointed as the coach of the Independents and would remain in that position until he would assume a similar role in 1923 with the Milwaukee Badgers. Without even being queried as to whether or not he wanted the job, Conzelman began his successful career as a coach, a career that would ultimately take him through the professional and collegiate ranks and back to the pros again before he would depart the game in 1948. But in 1921, the whole world was in front of him and he eagerly awaited the coaching freedom, the challenge, and the certain monetary awards to follow. He recalled his initial reaction in the book, *Pro Football's Rag Days:*

> *I was stunned. Here I was only 23 years old and the coach of a professional football team. Somehow I had the idea that my new title would bring a raise in pay. I was wrong. As a player I got $150 a game. And as player-coach I got $150 a game.*
> *I didn't know much about coaching and I discussed with Mr. Flanigan the type of formation we'd use on offense. I knew the Notre Dame box but he favored the Minnesota shift. We compromised and used the Minnesota shift.*

The appointment of Conzelman coincided with the release of Coughlin, Grover Malone, and Dave Hayes for not abiding by a new team rule requiring players to live in the Rock Island area. Supposedly, the residential mandate would ensure that all players would be available for practice on a daily basis, but may have been contrived to justify the release of Coughlin.

## Stagg Would Not Have Recognized Them

Rankled by a second straight setback, O'Brien added a couple of local legends with no college experience for the October 23 home game against the Columbus Panhandles: back Pete Steger and 235-pound lineman Garland "Gob" Buckeye, the heaviest Cardinal as well as the one with the most unique nickname. Columbus was another of the more interesting specimens from the early days of the league. Managed by Joe Carr, the Columbus roster carried only a few players with college experience. In addition, the team included six players by the name of Nesser, ranging in ages from nineteen to forty-six. The Nesser clan included five brothers (Frank, Ted, Phil, Fred, and John) along with Ted's son, Charlie Nesser. Still another brother, Al Nesser, played for Akron. The father-son combination of Ted and Charlie Nesser is the only such pair to play together in NFL history.

Although the Nessers dominated the starting lineup of the Panhandles, the visitors were no match for the Cardinals, who now included a set of brothers themselves in the McMahons (Horweens). Ralph and Arnie both saw action in the 17-6 win over Columbus, and Driscoll was removed from the game early with rib injuries. Torrential rain postponed the following game against Hammond, which was rescheduled for November 6. O'Brien had been angling for a game with Jim Thorpe and Cleveland on that date, but withdrew that plan in order to fulfill the agreement with Doc Young and the Hammond Pros.

This is the game in which O'Brien leased an adjacent lot in order to park four hundred cars and Hammond boasted that it would bring at least fifteen hundred of its own spectators to the game. O'Brien subsequently increased the seating at Normal

Park from around six thousand to seven thousand in anticipation of the strong attendance. By this time, the *Chicago Daily News* was providing almost daily, albeit brief, coverage of the Chicago Cardinals, and an article published following the rainout lent credence that O'Brien's "parking lot" might work:

> *The Hammond team, with four All-American stars on its roster, is certain to furnish high-class opposition for the Cardinals and the fact that they are certain to have a big following at the contest next week was indicated Sunday when numerous automobiles with Indiana license numbers were drawn up at Normal Park for the encounter.*

The Cards snatched the victory from the Pros when Driscoll tallied on a five-yard run and added the extra point in the first quarter for all of the scoring in a 7-0 decision. The first extensive "history" of pro football was tabulated in a 1936 publication entitled *Pro Football: Its Ups and Downs.* Authored by Dr. Henry A. March, the publication is amusing, although not totally accurate. March relates an incident from the 1921 Cardinals-Hammond game that provides a portrayal of pro football as not completely acceptable to some members of society. After all, this was the year that the Horween brothers were hiding their participation in the pro game from their mother by using alternate identities. With the "McMahon" brothers in mind, the following tale from Dr. March may contain some credibility:

> *One incident in the reign of "King" Young of Hammond should be recorded here that it may be preserved for posterity. In '21, one player engaged for a game against the "Cardinals" in Chicago was "Red" Jackson, who the fall before had captained the Chicago University team. As his name might indicate, Jackson had a flamboyant adornment of extensive, not to say luxuriant, red hair. He was in great fear that Alonzo Stagg, head coach at Chicago University, might learn that he had played professionally, even though he was out of college several months. Stagg put the fear of God in his graduates—he hated pro football with a dislike he has probably carried to his veteran's retreat in California. He dominated his players even after they graduated. So "Red" Jackson came to this game bearing a large tube of stage make-up lamp black and soused his red hair with it and covered his red eye brows. (Jack) Depler liked the effect and borrowed some of the sable stuff and soon had an appliqued mustache, which would have rendered jealous the largest sea lion in the Chicago Zoo . . . when the work was completed, the mothers of the boys, let alone Stagg would not have recognized them.*

Once the game began and the intensity of the battle warmed the players, their sweat intermingled with the masquerade, leaving Jackson and Depler dripping long messy streaks of melted black makeup. To some players, the use of false names and disguises was more important than to be "discovered" as a "college" man participating in the unacceptable game of pro football.

With the tight win over Hammond, the Cardinals enjoyed a 3-2 record and O'Brien booked an "extra" game with the Canton Bulldogs. The game was scheduled on the new Armistice Day holiday (Friday, November 11) and O'Brien was able to lease Cubs Park for the afternoon. This was another example of O'Brien's marketing vision, and it appeared that it would result in a wonderful payday for the team. Tickets were sold, plans were in place, and advance publicity stirred up interest, but the game was canceled due to Canton's travel difficulties the day of the game. As the years went by, O'Brien would face an endless array of bad luck whenever it appeared that he was finally about to savor a rich payday at the gate.

Undaunted, O'Brien invited the new Green Bay team to Normal Park on November 20 and the two teams battled to a 3-3 deadlock. This initial contest with the Packers would turn out to be the start of the second oldest rivalry in the NFL, behind the Bears and the Cardinals who first met in 1920.

The Packers were already 7-1 and had defeated the Chicago Boosters and the Cornell-Hamburgs, but all of their games had been at home in Hagemeister Park. Paced by the legendary Curly Lambeau and former Rock Island player-coach Frank Coughlin, the Packers enjoyed abundant hometown support, primarily due to the die-hard promotional efforts of George Whitney Calhoun, the sports editor of the *Green Bay Press-Gazette*. Lambeau and Calhoun founded the team in 1919 when Lambeau was working at the Indian Packing Company in Green Bay. The packing company provided jerseys and a place to practice and left the team with its nickname, which still exists today. Lambeau had earned a spot on Knute Rockne's roster as a freshman at Notre Dame in 1918, but a severe case of tonsillitis forced him back to Green Bay for treatment. That summer, Calhoun encouraged Lambeau to start a town team in Green Bay and offered to assist with the organizational elements and also provide publicity in the *Press-Gazette*. Playing primarily against town teams in Wisconsin and Michigan, such as Ishpeming and New London, the Packers fashioned a 10-1 record in 1919 and then followed that impressive slate with a 9-1-1 mark in 1920. At the conclusion of the 1920 season, Green Bay was awarded an NFL franchise and achieved a 7-2-2 finish for its maiden voyage in 1921.

The first trip to Chicago was a major event for the team and its followers. About four hundred Packers fans joined the players in Chicago after the team arranged for round trip rail transportation for any interested parties. Fans could grab the Kaukauna interurban trolley to Neenah and then board the Soo Line Special to Chicago. The round trip fare between Green Bay and Chicago was just $9.69.

Interest in the Packers was already so significant (Calhoun termed it a "bad case of footballitis") that for the first time arrangements were made with Western Union to "wire" the results of each play from Normal Park in Chicago back to Turner Hall in Green Bay on a two-second delay. After each play, a gent named Mulligan Scroogy, stationed at the front of Turner Hall, would use a megaphone to relay the results to the seven hundred fans who paid 50¢ to be in the building. While it wasn't exactly the first radio broadcast of a Cardinals game, it was the next best thing for the Packers' fans.

## *Paddy Got A Peach Of A Pass*

There was a slight Chicago twist to the 1921 Packers' roster as well. Former Ragen Athletic Club member Joe Carey started at left guard while Norm Barry joined the Packers from the Cards' five games into the season to take over the left halfback slot. In the end, it was a battle of the giants between the lines on a wet, slippery field. While the game lacked scoring, it didn't lack excitement, and the two teams pulled out with a 3-3 tie. Both Driscoll and Lambeau booted field goals to account for the scoring.

From a fan's point of view, the coverage by Calhoun and the *Green Bay Press-Gazette* was exceptional. Calhoun provided a game report, lineups, gossip, and a play-by-play of the entire game. As stellar as the coverage had been in the *Rock Island Argus*, Calhoun's efforts were superior, beginning with his lead paragraph:

> *Charlie Ray in his famous movie, "Two Minutes to Go," hasn't got anything on Paddy Driscoll, who plays quarterback for the Chicago Cardinals. The former Northwestern star took victory out of the Green Bay Packers hands in the game at Normal Park, Chicago, on Sunday by a drop kick with only four minutes to play knotting the count at 3 all.*

Although the field was in miserable shape, Calhoun brought both of the scoring scenes to life:

> *The Cardinals battled hard in the shadow of their goal posts. Three times their forward wall held tight against the onslaughts of the Packer squad. It was fourth down about 7 to go. Lambeau stepped back for a place kick with Cub Buck set to hold the ball. Buck was kneeling in about two inches of mud and water. It was a 10-1 shot that Lambeau, considering the condition of the field and the slippery ball, couldn't come through but he did. Murray shot the ball back perfectly to Buck, the line held tight giving Curly plenty of time. The Packer captain took two short steps and his trusty right foot connected squarely with the ball. The oval turned over sort of lazily in the air and it seemed as if it might fall short of the uprights. That half second seemed like an hour but finally the ball cleared the cross bar with about two feet to spare and joy ran riot in the Green Bay rooters section . . .*
>
> *Three times the giant Cardinal backs smashed up against the stone wall Packer line without a gain. Then Paddy Driscoll stepped back for a drop kick. The muck was cleared away from his kicking spot and rosin galore sprinkled all over his right shoe. Paddy got a peach of a pass from his center but it is lucky he did because Murray, Coughlin, and Buck were in on him pretty fast. Driscoll's kick sailed through the uprights with plenty to spare and the score was tied up.*

After the game, Calhoun also snared the first published postgame comment by a Cardinals player when Driscoll told him: "You've got a sweet little machine. I would like to see your backs in action on a dry field, providing you were not playing my team!"

Calhoun's nearly accurate play-by-play account allows historians some insight into the actual battle plans used by teams in the early 1920s. By carefully reviewing the results of each play and filling in the yardage to the closest plausible marker, it is possible to tally the statistics from this rainy day game from long ago:

|  | CARDINALS | PACKERS |
| --- | --- | --- |
| Rushes | 40 | 37 |
| Rushing yards | 70 | 86 |
| Passing | 3-13 | 2-4 |
| Passing yards | 38 | 46 |
| First downs | 4 | 4 |
| Total yards | 108 | 132 |
| Penalties | 1 (5 yards) | 5 (29 yards) |
| Punting | 7-247 yards (35.3) | 8-252 yards (35.3) |

Driscoll and Lambeau handled the passing for their respective teams, while Driscoll and Buck did the punting. With these statistics, one can quickly determine that the game was largely uneventful, with trudging rushing attempts, numerous punts, and not much wide-open excitement. The leading rusher for the Cards was Bob Koehler, who gained twenty-nine yards on fifteen attempts. Art Schmael did a little better for the Packers by accumulating forty yards in just ten carries, thanks to one twenty-yard run.

Following the game, the Packers' contingent departed from the Stratford Hotel at Michigan and Jackson and hopped on the 6:30 train back to Green Bay, satisfied that the team could hang in there with the big boys from Chicago. "One thing for sure," wrote Calhoun, "Chicago now knows that Green Bay has a team . . ."

The Cardinals then swept past non-league foes, the Chicago Stayms (27-0) and the Gary Elks (21-0). Now 5-2-1 overall, the Cards were ready to challenge the Staleys for the "City Professional Title," according to the *Chicago Tribune*:

> *Manager Chris O'Brien will challenge the Staleys for the local professional title. Manager O'Brien contends both teams have been beaten and a struggle for the city championship would be the proper game to close the season.*

The Staleys, meanwhile, were 8-1 but still smarting from that sole loss to Buffalo (7-6) a week earlier. After defeating Green Bay 20-0 on November 27, the Staleys opted to snub the Cardinals' direct request for a game and instead lured Buffalo back to Chicago for a grudge match. The Cards scrambled for an opponent and landed a return bout with Akron at Normal Park on December 4. The Cards dropped their tilt 7-0 while the Staleys earned some revenge with a satisfying 10-7 victory over Buffalo. It didn't matter that Buffalo had also played a game on Saturday at home (a 14-0 win over the Akron Pros). Based on the fact that both teams finished with just one loss, while Buffalo (9-1-2) experienced two ties, the Staleys (8-1) claimed the national professional championship. To help convince anyone who would listen, Halas then added a game with Canton in hopes of securing one more victory to equalize the record of Buffalo. With that victory in hand (and it was—with a 10-0 win), Halas could claim the league championship based on the better record as well as the victory over Buffalo in the second meeting of the two foes. Just to make sure, the Staleys brought the Cardinals out of winter hibernation for one last game on Sunday, December 18. A win by the Staleys would push the team a step above Buffalo for the best winning percentage in the APFA, while the Cards, with a 5-3-1 record, could claim a share of the city professional football title by conquering Chicago.

Already, in just its second year of existence, the rivalry between the Cardinals and the Staleys was attracting significant interest in the city of Chicago, as described in the *Tribune* the morning of the game (December 18, 1921):

> *Pro football fans look forward to the hardest fought game of the season this afternoon when the national champion Staleys meet the Chicago Cardinals at Cub Park.*
>   *There is intense rivalry between the teams, and this has spread to their supporters. A big crowd of south side fans is expected to invade the north side, and more rooting is looked for than usually noted at a pro game. The Staleys, having eliminated both the Buffalo All-Americans and the Canton Bulldogs for the national title, now hope to add the city championship to their laurels.*

As if a national championship were not sufficient, the Staleys needed to acquire the city honors as well, and the tough, turbulent rivalry between the two Chicago teams began to blossom. Despite the importance of this game, the two teams were still a year away from their first major riot on the field.

The adoring fans who followed these two nemeses to Cubs Park shivered through a fairly dull 0-0 tie. As a result, if the Staleys could continue to claim the national title for the year, then the Cardinals, by virtue of this 0-0 deadlock, could also reach out and declare themselves the "Western" champions with a final 5-3-2 record for 1921.

The Chicago Staleys ultimately were awarded the 1921 championship, but it would prove to be the last one for that version of the team. In 1922 Halas was awarded the franchise and renamed his team the Chicago Bears. The league itself shed the moniker of the American Professional Football Association and replaced it with the National Football League (NFL), which is still in use today. On the other hand, the Cardinals made very few changes and kept most of the roster intact. The chief additions were All-American back Johnny Mohardt from Notre Dame, Johnny Bryan from the University of Chicago, and the full-time presence of Ralph and Arnie Horween, who still played under the alias of McMahon. Gone were center Frank Rydzewski to Hammond and Pete Steger and Paul La Ross to the local Niessen's Pyotts.

In order to start stabilizing itself, beginning in 1922 the NFL required each team to post a $1,000 forfeit fee. This move forced some of the financially weaker teams to depart from the league and opened the doors for new franchises from the Toledo Maroons, the Racine (WI) Legion, the Oorang Indians, and the Milwaukee Badgers (now with Fritz Pollard). A limit of $1,200 per week for player salaries was also implemented. Teams with players such as Driscoll (at a reported $300 per game) needed to be fiscally creative to stay under that limit. In such cases, player-coaches like Driscoll could be compensated for both positions, but it is likely that many teams simply found it preferable to ignore the salary cap.

The Oorang Indians club was certainly one of the most unique teams in NFL history. Owned by dog kennel owner Walter Lingo in LaRue, Ohio, the team was formed (much like the Decatur Staleys) as an advertising vehicle for the owner's business. The team was composed entirely of Native Americans, including the legendary Jim Thorpe. Although thirty-three-year-old Thorpe was aging rather rapidly as a player by this time, he still managed to coach the team and played occasionally. With players such as Joe Little Twig, Ted Lone Wolf, Dick Deer Slayer, and Eagle Feather, Oorang played all but one of its games on the road in 1922 and finished with a 3-6 league mark.

As for the Cardinals, Chris O'Brien would continue to provide some excitement. The team would not only be highly competitive, but would unveil some interesting innovations throughout the season. The biggest change, historically, was O'Brien's decision to move the team's home games to Comiskey Park, the home of the Chicago White Sox baseball team. With this move, O'Brien expanded his seating capacity substantially over the former facility at Normal Park. The Cardinals were now much closer to downtown Chicago and O'Brien wisely promoted the easy access to the stadium by trains that stopped at 35th Street—just a short walk away from the field. O'Brien also initiated a "two for one" ticket policy for boys under sixteen who wished to attend the game. He even helped arrange for an automobile parade to honor popular players Paddy Driscoll and Johnny Mohardt at one of the games.

Two other significant factors helped boost the esteem and visibility of the Chicago Cardinals besides the winning touch and the usual promotional endeavors. In 1922, the *Chicago Tribune* assigned a sportswriter, Hugh Fullerton, to cover the Cards' games on a regular basis, and this resulted in the first in-depth coverage of their home games. The *Tribune* added photographic reporting of the Cardinals and the Bears for the first time as well. The *Daily News* and the *Herald* also increased their coverage by including more "between" games information. But the other ingredient added to the mix in 1922 was the flare-up of the infant rivalry between the Cardinals and the Bears. The cordial relationship between Halas and O'Brien escalated into off-field public squabbling and on-field pugilism as the two neighbors demonstrated that these games meant more to both of them than any other league match-up.

Perhaps this was due to the very active recruitment of Driscoll by the Bears during the previous off-season. Halas had always coveted Driscoll as a player since their days as teammates on the Great Lakes squad in 1918. He attempted to lure Driscoll to the Staleys in 1920 but was blocked by Driscoll's contract with the Cardinals. In 1922, Halas tried again, this time offering Driscoll part ownership of the team if he would play for the renamed Bears. While Driscoll was interested in this deal, Chris O'Brien was livid that the Bears would negotiate with his star attraction. He appealed to the league office, and in June of 1922 the league minutes demanded that "the management of the Chicago Bears be notified that 'Paddy' Driscoll is the property of the Chicago Cardinals and shall not be tampered with until he receives his release from the Cardinals." While the matter was closed for the moment, the inevitable hard feelings between the teams would grow and growl as the 1922 season progressed.

In 1922, the NFL limited rosters to eighteen players by October 1, so O'Brien needed a quick review of his talent and advertised for a preseason game in the *Tribune* on September 16:

> *Chris O'Brien is lining up his Cardinals in anticipation of a successful pro football season and desiring to start early wants a game for his team here September 24. He prefers to play a Midwest eleven but will meet any strong professional team. For game, phone Wentworth 2409 or write 5626 South Racine Avenue.*

Answering the challenge was a team called the Maywood Rovers, who served as cannon fodder in a 29-0 Cardinals romp at Normal Park on September 24. The veteran Cardinals then swept undefeated through their first six league games behind a fabulous defense that allowed just sixteen points over that six-game span. Driscoll again was the primary offense of the team with his field goal against Milwaukee in the opening game providing all of the points in a 3-0 thriller. But for the first time in three years, he had an abundance of talented offensive help. The backfield was loaded with big league players such as the Horweens (Harvard), Mohardt (Notre Dame), Bob Koehler (Northwestern), and Johnny "Red" Bryan (Chicago). Arnold Horween even assumed some of the kicking duties, although Driscoll drilled a league record eight field goals that season.

Up front, the Cardinals boasted some beef from end to end with veterans Willis Brennan (210 pounds) and Garland "Gob" Buckeye (235 pounds) at guard; tackles Fred Gillies (Cornell, 215 pounds), John Leonard (Indiana, 200 pounds), and Swede Rundquist (Illinois, 200 pounds); center Nick "Bull" McInerney (200 pounds); and quick ends Eddie Anderson (Notre Dame, 175 pounds), Lenny Sachs (Loyola, 175 pounds), and Dick Egan (Wilmington, 175 pounds). All were experienced on the collegiate gridiron except for Brennan, McInerney, and Buckeye, although Buckeye also played professional baseball.

## The Score Was Two Uppercuts And Three Wild Swings

This was truly the finest team that O'Brien had assembled, and it contained a unique blend of speed, power, and tenacity. While strong, the team was not particularly heavy and faced a twenty-pound average deficit per man when the Packers arrived in Chicago on October 15, 1922, to face the Cardinals in the first home game played at Comiskey Park. As usual, the *Green Bay Gazette* provided insightful copy for its readers:

> *This Sunday the Green Bay eleven travels to Chicago to give battle to Chris O'Brien's Cardinals. The game will be staged at the White Sox ball park. The Windy City pigskin organization is making great plans for this contest as it marks the reopening of the historic ball yard as a gridiron field. In (John) Mohardt and Paddy Driscoll, the Cardinals have a pair of the greatest halfbacks in professional football and their line contains many of the stars of the gridiron game.*

The Packers showed up in Chicago flinching from three straight close losses to start the season. One of the Packers' players was quoted anonymously in the *Gazette* blaming the defeats on a "jinx": "When we shake our hoodoo Green Bay is going to win a lot of games."

The game, however, was switched to Normal Park at the last minute when Comiskey Park was needed by the White Sox for its traditional season-ending City Series with the Chicago Cubs. Five straight rain postponements pushed the baseball series back to October 15 and forced the Cards to retreat to Normal Park. The Comiskey Park football debut would need to wait at least another week.

Curly Lambeau, captain of the Packers, was oozing with confidence when he told the *Gazette:* "We're going to be there fighting every minute . . . and I feel confident that we will make things more than interesting for the Cardinals. Every man on the squad is in good shape and I think we are going to break into the win column." Despite the bravado, Lambeau and company were swept aside by the Cardinals 16-3 as Driscoll and Mohardt danced around the invaders and A. McMahon tallied touchdowns from five and two yards out. But for the "McMahon" brothers, the gig was up and the *Gazette* was the first to report the name scam:

> *The Bays withered in the second half and Paddy Driscoll, Johnny Mohardt and the Horween brothers, playing under the name of McMahon, smashed through the "Blue" defense for considerable yardage. The old Harvard criss cross line buck enabled A. Horween to twice smash through for touchdowns.*

The Chicago newspapers, however, did not catch on to the Horween/McMahon illusion until three games later when the Cardinals stung the Buffalo All-Americans (who still claimed to be the 1921 league champions) by a score of 9-7 in foul weather conditions. In his review of the game, the *Chicago Tribune*'s Hugh Fullerton commented:

> *For the first half, the game was a determined and hard fought one, and the Cardinals, after Driscoll had struck to within scoring distance but had been stopped, worked a beautiful delayed pass, and A. McMahon, called by the players Horween, smashed through seven yards for the touchdown.*

Stepping up its coverage, the *Daily News* focused on the effects of the weather:

> *The tussle, despite the gummy condition of the gridiron and the handicap of a slippery oval, which was difficult to boot and flip, proved to have all the thrills and breaks which make for a good contest.*

The game was marred, or perhaps embellished, by a brawl that broke out on the field at the conclusion of the game, as described by the *Tribune*'s Fullerton:

> *In a post-game fight the score was two upper-cuts and three wild swings, ending in a tie. The boys, not having had enough fighting in an hour of desperate and at times brilliant battling, had to stage an impromptu scrap after the whistle blew . . . Buffalo objected to one penalty . . . and some were real mad at Gillies for alleged rough work, which resulted in the scrap . . . The crowd rushed on to the field, the players were separated without damage, and the Cards grabbed another hold on the national pro football league championship, while 6,000 rain soaked fans stood and cussed the street car and L service.*

By now the Chicago Cardinals were 5-0 and feeling good about the prospects for a national professional championship. The Canton Bulldogs were also undefeated, but had two ties added to four victories while the Chicago Bears owned a 5-1 mark. Another contender was the Akron Pros with an overall 4-1-1 record. Akron had lost Fritz Pollard but still retained fullback Rip King when it visited the Cardinals on November 12. The Cards widely promoted the visit of Akron, which had "been victorious in all but five of their forty-seven encounters" over the preceding three years and reminded fans that "elevated trains stop at 35th Street, only a few blocks from Comiskey Park, where the contest will be fought." This is also the game in which O'Brien first offered the "two for one" ticket deal for boys under the age of sixteen. Business was going well for O'Brien. Since the move from Normal Park, where just thirty-five hundred had witnessed the contest with Packers, attendance had risen to six thousand at Comiskey Park for the Buffalo game. The Cardinals were beginning to show a profit, both on and off the field!

## Driscoll's Periscope Was Above The Surface

A heavy rain draped Comiskey Park on November 12 as the Cardinals entertained the Akron Pros. Paddy Driscoll scored the only touchdown in a 7-0 Cardinals win. The unrelenting rain, cold, and wind put a damper on the game. Hugh Fullerton was again on the scene to describe the setting:

*The greater part of the game was played in the deep mud of the infield, because, once anchored in that mire, neither team could kick, run or pass out of it save that once, when a forward pass resulted in one of the strangest scores ever registered and gave the unbeaten Cardinals more grounds for hoping for the championship of the postgrad league.*

The lone score came about on a forty-yard pass play from Arnold Horween to Paddy Driscoll who made the most of the opportunity while dodging mud puddles, according to Fullerton:

*The score came early in the second quarter. The Cardinals gained possession of the ball near the Akron 40 yard line in the edge of the swamp, and A. McMahon dropped back and shot the soggy ball over Akron's left end to Paddy Driscoll, who was splashing along at top speed, and catching the ball, swerved suddenly past the tackler and broke for the goal line with a clear field. (Paul) Sheeks was in hot pursuit—and you know how those sheiks pursue.*

*Driscoll gained in the race when he hit an island; then came to the ford across the scalped base line, just as Sheeks leaped after him and grabbed him by both legs below the knee. Together they dived into the mud at the 5 yard line, half submerged, and still locked together, with Driscoll sliding on the side of his face and, Sheeks' non-skids refusing to hold, they slid six yards through mud and water to the goal.*

*Driscoll's periscope was above the surface and after ejecting water ballast he arose and kicked the goal for the extra point.*

The biggest game of the season was then set up for the following Sunday (November 19) between the undefeated Chicago Cardinals (6-0) and the unbeaten Canton Bulldogs (5-0-2) in Comiskey Park. The Bulldogs were paced by player-coach Guy Chamberlin, a former member of the Staleys. Although there was considerable interest in the game, O'Brien added some flavor by planning a ceremony honoring both Driscoll and the rookie Mohardt. Beginning at 1:00, an auto caravan left downtown Chicago and proceeded south to Comiskey Park for the 2:30 kickoff. Just prior to the game, the two players were presented with luggage and flowers as the largest crowd of the season (seventy-five hundred) looked on. O'Brien also arranged for a lively band to help cheer on the home club.

But on this raw, windy day, Canton managed to snap the Cardinals' winning streak by a score of 7-0 and snatched first place away as well. The Cards' championship hopes blew up quickly just seven days later when they traveled back to Canton for a quick rematch and were mobbed 20-3 by the Bulldogs. With the national championship out of reach, O'Brien looked around for whatever other title could be claimed and focused immediately on the Bears. Since the Driscoll debacle earlier in the year, the cozy relationship between the Bears and the Cardinals had chilled somewhat. The two combatants had initiated talks the previous summer for a financially rewarding Thanksgiving Day game on November 30 and O'Brien thought they had a deal. Not so, claimed the Bears: "The game was canceled because we could not agree on the park," insisted Dutch Sternaman. "Followers of our team wanted us to play on the North Side, while O'Brien was insistent about the Sox park. This happened last June, and we then drew a line through this game."

Back on the South Side, O'Brien claimed that the Bears had not backed out of the contest until November 21, when the Bears indicated that they would not play at all unless the game was moved to the North Side. O'Brien stated that the agreement had been approved by the league office and expected president Joe Carr to uphold the arrangement. Meanwhile, the Bears arranged for a home game against the Toledo Maroons, who had crept back into the title picture with a 4-0-2 league record. Finally, after a series of meetings, it was decided that it would be the Bears and the Cardinals who would meet on Thanksgiving Day. The teams came to an agreement just two days before the contest, and the event would be staged at Comiskey Park.

As usual, the game would be for the "postgraduate championship of Chicago" and the flames of the rivalry were fanned by the *Tribune* in its game day preview:

> *The arranging of the Thanksgiving day match between north and south side has stirred the rivalry between the sections, as well as between the fans of the two sections. Further, it has arrayed against each other two of the greatest football aggregations ever assembled.*
>
> *The interest in this battle has grown to the proportions of a White Sox-Cubs series, and the demand for tickets indicates that the crowd will break all records for attendance at professional football games in Chicago.*

Both teams quickly prepared for a game that was not only important locally, but also nationally. The Bears arrived with an 8-1 record and just a step behind Canton (7-0-2) and Toledo (6-0-2) while the Cardinals were still alive, albeit staggering with a 6-2 mark. In 1922, the NFL had decided the season would end on December 10, so O'Brien figured that with a little help, he could schedule at least three more games and hopefully win them all for a chance at the title. The first step would be the Bears.

## *My God, They Want to Kill Me!*

What followed resembled more of a brawl than a football game. Playing in front of a record crowd of fourteen thousand, the Cardinals upended the Bears 6-0 in a sloppy contest that took a back seat to the legendary "fight" that took place that day. Fullerton wrote:

> *Chicago's Cardinals carved the Chicago championship turkey yesterday, gobbled all the white meat, stuffing and left the Bears the neck, wing, gizzard and a bunch of black eyes.*
>
> *The struggle between the post-grad teams of north and south sides . . . ended with the score 6-0 in favor of the south siders, after a battle which included a half-riot, two fist fights, and finished peacefully enough with the clanging of patrol wagons bringing the reserves.*

The bedlam began in the third quarter with the Cardinals holding a slight 3-0 lead, thanks to a thirty-eight-yard dropkick by Driscoll. Perhaps it was some long-simmering frustration with the Cardinals that prompted Halas to help initiate the fisticuffs when Driscoll stormed around end on a sweep where he was met by Halas and Joey Sternaman. "He was picked up bodily and hurled five yards back, badly jarred . . . ," described Fullerton. The groggy Driscoll, enraged by the extra emphasis placed on the tackle by the two Bears, struggled to his feet and slugged Sternaman. This unusual display by the mild-mannered Driscoll earned him an immediate disqualification, as Fullerton noted:

> *In an instant there was prospect of a fine free for all battle, and the players rushed in, followed by the side line spectators, to join in gory battle. The officials managed to preserve peace, tore the contestants apart and banished Driscoll from the game.*

Halas remembered the incident quite well:

> *What happened was this: Paddy Driscoll made a good run around end, reaching our 20. Joe Sternaman and I thought that must not be allowed to happen again. On the next play, Driscoll set off with the ball. Joey and I brought him down with all of the force we could muster, which was considerable. Paddy was down but not out. He pulled himself to his feet, wobbled toward Joey and started pummeling him with both fists. That is when the thugs came out. So did reserve players. So did fans from both stands. The police came out, too, wielding sticks and blowing whistles and shouting. In time, in quite a time, order was restored.*

The Bears had acquired tackle Ed Healey from Rock Island just prior to this contest for $100 per game and Healey recalled his participation in his first Bears-Cardinals battle:

> *Two days later I played sixty minutes on Thanksgiving Day against the Chicago Cardinals and learned a hell of a lot about Chicago and the atmosphere that existed there.*
>
> *And then, holy cow! Out from the Cardinal bench poured a group of men with rods (guns) on! They were going out there to protect their idol, Paddy Driscoll. As you may recall, the vogue at that time was that all the gangsters in the world were functioning in Chicago. You had Ragen's Colts from back of the yards. You had the Al Capone crowd . . . So here came that bunch of South side rooters, flowing out from the bench with rods on.*
>
> *Immediately, I stopped in my tracks. I stood there in amazement. With my hands forward and looking toward heaven, I said, "Jesus, Mary and Joseph, here I am, playing on this field for a hundred bucks after joining it just two days ago, and my God, they want to kill me!"*

Halas added some insight to Healey's role as an innocent bystander: "In truth, Healey did not just stand there, hands and eyes in prayer position. No indeed. He was punching away with his teammates." In an effort to stabilize the situation, Halas offered to allow Driscoll to remain in the game, but the officials remained adamant in their decision. "My forgiveness seemed only to increase the heat," said Halas. "I found myself on my back on the ground, felled by three simultaneous blows from three directions. A disgruntled Cardinal sat astride me." His account coincides with Fullerton's description:

> *The Bears . . . offered to waive the rules and let Driscoll return to play. The officials declined, and during the argument another fight started suddenly with three*

*of the Cardinals swinging at Halas, who was knocked flat with a burly Cardinal riding him.*

The legend stretched further years later when *Tribune* writer George Strickler recounted the day and added that a policeman pressed the nose of his pistol behind the ear of Halas after he was knocked down by the Cardinals. When he was released from this grasp, Halas learned that both he and Sternaman also had been ejected and the game concluded without further incident.

When the dust settled, the boys decided that the experience was so enjoyable that they certainly needed to visit again . . . and soon! While the 6-0 defeat staggered the Bears' championship hopes, the intensity of the new rivalry loudly called out to be milked. Neither O'Brien nor Halas was ignorant of the gate receipts that a rematch could bring and it took less than twenty-four hours for the two sides to agree to another contest, this time on Sunday, December 10, at Cubs Park. Each team still had another league game three days after the Thanksgiving Day foray. The Cardinals (7-2) would entertain the Dayton Triangles (3-3-1), while the Bears (8-2) would host the Toledo Maroons (5-0-2). Canton still led the pack with an 8-0-2 slate as the league moved into its last two weekends of play for the 1922 season.

While the Bears bounced the Maroons 22-0, the sluggish Cardinals were upset by Dayton 7-3, with the loss being blamed on injuries suffered in the recent Bears game. No matter—the final game with the Bears on December 10 was the prize the Cards were seeking. Because of construction work on the expansion of Cubs Park, the game setting was changed to Comiskey Park. Out East, Canton clubbed Toledo 19-0 to claim the NFL championship with a 10-0-2 final record. This left the Bears and Cardinals to battle for the leftovers in Chicago, with the Cardinals winning once again 9-0 on the strength of three Driscoll field goals. When both teams showed up in red jerseys, the Bears pulled on some white sleeveless T-shirts over their uniforms to differentiate the teams. To the disappointment of the record fifteen thousand spectators, there were no further wrestling matches on the field, but the Bears still grabbed second place in the eighteen-team league with a 9-3 mark, with the Cardinals holding onto third place with an 8-3 record (9-3 overall). Bigger crowds, increased media coverage, an influx of talented players, and the explosion of the Bears-Cardinals rivalry earmarked the extremely competitive 1922 season.

The *Daily News* summarized the recently completed campaign:

*Postgraduate football, or the variety of the gridiron pastime that is played by former college players, has closed the most progressive season in the history of the game, both from the standpoint of class and from the standpoint of attendance, according to word from magnates of the National Football Association given out. The circuit, which includes sixteen teams, the Chicago Cardinals and Bears being the local representatives, is planning an even better season next year and the promoters are beginning to look forward to that time.*

*The Cardinals, the original Chicago representative in the league, has just finished the season with high laurels . . . since the first of November have played what probably was the heaviest schedule ever undertaken by a postgraduate football team.*

## *Turning Toward The 1923 Season*

During the offseason, O'Brien engineered some significant changes to his already imposing roster. The chief move was sending steady end and local favorite Lenny Sachs to Jimmy Conzelman's Milwaukee Badgers on September 19, 1923. This left a spot open to snare Notre Dame's gifted All-American receiver Roger Kiley, who would once again pair with his former Irish teammate, Eddie Anderson, at the ends for the Cardinals. O'Brien also managed to lasso Rip King, the great fullback from Akron. Another fine addition was that of halfback Jack Crangle from the University of Illinois. Although still playing under an assumed name (McMahon), Arnie Horween took over the coaching duties from Paddy Driscoll. Player-coaches continued to be commonplace in the league, especially since no real "coaching" was allowed during the games. Once again, the Cardinals were loaded with speed in the backfield with returnees Driscoll, the Horweens, Mohardt, and Koehler joining newcomers King, Crangle, and former Englewood High School product Art Folz.

New to the line were tackle Sully Montgomery (Centre, 213 pounds) and guard-tackle Wilfrid Smith (De Pauw, 203 pounds), who would later become an influential sportswriter in Chicago, but who spent most of the 1923 season bouncing between the Cardinals and the Hammond Pros. The team opened the season with a tune-up match with old-time local rivals, the Opals. The Opals were the reigning champs of the Midwest Football League and had not been defeated in two years, but the Cardinals managed a 13-0 win without the services of Driscoll. Art Folz quarterbacked the victors and kicked an extra point. When it came down to the business of winning the National Football League, the Cardinals tore through the early schedule with a dominating defense that chalked up four straight shutouts to open the season. Buffalo fell 3-0 on a Driscoll dropkick, Rochester was bombed 60-0, Akron was zipped 19-0, and Minneapolis was bounced 9-0 behind three more Driscoll field goals. The whopping win against the inept Rochester Jeffersons established a team point total record that would not be surpassed for another twenty-five years. It also meant the beginning of the end for the Jeffersons, who were gunned down by Rock Island 56-0 the following week and then played only two more games (both losses) before shutting down for the season. Driscoll scored twenty-seven of those points against Rochester, which still ranks third on the team's all-time list. As usual, almost all of the games were at home, with the only "away" game in 1923 being a contest at Cubs Park with the Bears.

In week five, the Dayton Triangles became the first team to score against the mighty Cardinals, but still fell in a heap 13-3 as Driscoll accounted for all of the winner's points. That victory left the Cards and the Canton Bulldogs all alone at the top of the NFL standings with perfect 5-0 records. And just as had occurred in 1922, the same two undefeated teams would meet in Comiskey Park on November 4 for a midseason showdown. Like the Cardinals, Canton fielded a superb defense that had allowed just one field goal in the first five games. The Bulldogs were so tough on defense that the team would allow just one touchdown over its twelve game schedule in 1923.

## *Debauching Of High School Boys*

Just a few days before the Cardinals-Bulldogs game, the respected football coach and athletic director at the University of Chicago, Amos Alonzo Stagg, unleashed a furious attack on the game of professional football. In a letter addressed to "All friends of college football," printed in full by the *Chicago Tribune* and other publications, Stagg vociferously ripped the professional structure:

> *. . . And now comes along another serious menace, possibly greater than all others, Sunday professional football. Under the guise of fair play but countenancing rank dishonesty in playing men under assumed names, scores of professional teams have sprung up in the last two or three years, most of them on a salary basis of some kind. These teams are bidding hard for college players in order to capitalize not only on their ability but also and mostly on the name of the college they come from . . . Cases of the debauching of high school boys infrequently have come to notice . . .*
>
> *To cooperate with Sunday professional football games is to cooperate with forces which are destructive of the finest elements of interscholastic and intercollegiate football and to add to the heavy burden of the schools and colleges in preserving it in its ennobling worth.*

From the other viewpoint, the *Tribune*'s Irving Vaughan wrote on November 4 of the growing popularity of professional and semi-professional football. He noted the increased gates of the Cardinals' games from 1920 to 1923 and observed that the "semi-pro" teams such as the Opals and Stayms attracted strong crowds and were able to pay their players small amounts:

> *Their pay roll will run from $30 to $60 per man weekly and for ex-high schoolers, graduates from the prairies and men from smaller colleges this is a very attractive stipend.*
>
> *In view of the marked growth of the semi-pro game it would be natural to suppose the big teams—the Cardinals and Bears—would suffer as a consequence. To this, Chris O'Brien, who promotes the Cardinals, says that the growth of the semi-pros means added interest and eventually the semi-pro fan creates such a high class appetite that he graduates into the ranks of the pro rooters.*
>
> *The pro league, which takes no hand in the scheduling of games, has a salary limit of $1,200 a game, but as there is no way of inflicting punishment for a violation, the promoters pay little attention to the restriction. Individual salaries, of course, are a secret, but the sum for a single game will run between $1,500 and $2,000. It is said that Paddy Driscoll, the Cards' star, has a contract that nets him in excess of $300 a battle. Other players draw as low as $75.*
>
> *Whether the pro game ever will assume the proportions of a regular league playing a regular schedule as is done in baseball is something only time will tell.*

Stagg's letter touched off a public war of words with his former player Johnny Bryan, now a quarterback with the Bears. Bryan, who toiled with the Cards in 1922, defended the pro game and even accused Stagg himself of professionalism for receiving pay while serving as a player-coach at Chicago. While Stagg's opinions were insightful and interesting, they had no bearing on the increased newspaper coverage in 1923 that made the Cardinals' 7-3 loss to Canton very big news in Chicago. The *Tribune* was now reporting on all NFL games with either a brief game summary or a more detailed description of the key scoring plays. Other Chicago-area papers were doing likewise. The expanded visibility and more extensive acceptance of pro football could not have been gratifying to Stagg.

With fifty-five hundred fans in attendance at Comiskey Park, the Cards probably owed this defeat more to the elements than to the Bulldogs. The *Tribune* speculated that the downpour "made the going hard for the fleet Cardinal eleven. The heavier Canton line was thus aided in smashing through and nailing the local backfield men before their plays were fairly started."

Paddy Driscoll dented the scoring column first with a forty-yard field goal in the opening quarter when the field was still somewhat dry. As the rain continued, the footing became even more treacherous as the runners slipped and fell on the slippery gridiron. That tenuous three-point lead finally disappeared early in the fourth stanza when Lou Smyth scored on a short plunge. While the tough loss was difficult to accept, since it dropped the Cards from both first place and the unbeaten list, it also seemed to tilt the direction of the season for the South Siders. Although the Cardinals bowled over the Hammond Pros (6-0) on November 11, the team was clearly playing below par. Driscoll was held out of the lineup against Hammond because of injuries suffered in the Canton game and only played the final quarter when it appeared that the Pros were about to overtake the Cardinals. As such, the club started with the backfield of King, C. McMahon (Ralph Horween), Crangle, and Mohardt. Regular quarterback Arnie Horween played tackle and had the unusual responsibility of barking out the signals from his line position. This caused great confusion for both teams, but was especially unsettling for the Cardinals, who seemed to lose a step in getting off each play.

The following week, the Cards met an old nemesis in ex-Bear Joey Sternaman, who was now with the Duluth Kelleys. While the Kelleys fielded a formidable team, it was not in the same class as the Cardinals. The *Daily News* warned of the line strength of the visitors prior to the game:

> *The Duluth team, which is tied with the Cardinals for the runner-up honors in the league, each squad having sustained only one defeat to date, is composed of big fellows who won fame on eastern college elevens. The line is said to be one of the greatest ever assembled . . .*

However, the Cards endured another close call and escaped with a 10-0 verdict. There was reason for optimism in the Cardinals camp following the victory, as explained by Walter Schreiber in the *Tribune*:

> *The Duluth eleven was rated as the stiffest opposition the Cardinals will have to face in their remaining games of the schedule and it now seems that Paddy Driscoll's warriors have an open path to the title of runner-up in the league. There is also a chance of the Cards winning the championship if the Canton Bulldogs, the leaders, are defeated in one of their remaining contests.*

## Whooping Things Up Merrily

Now 7-1, the Chicago Cardinals trailed only Canton (6-0-1) at this point in the season. The next date would be against the lowly Racine (WI) Legion (2-3-2). The Legion was composed almost entirely of former players from the University of Wisconsin. The large crowd would include over one thousand disabled World War I veterans invited by O'Brien. O'Brien also arranged for transportation for these guests with help from the American Legion and the Knights of Columbus. This generous gesture was reminiscent of his fundraising efforts for the families of Racine Cardinals Athletic Club members in the service during the war. The Wisconsin team brought with it something unusual for the pro circuit—fans and enthusiasm—as noted by the *Daily News* before the game:

> *There should be an abundance of the old college spirit on tap at Comiskey park tomorrow . . . A delegation of nearly 1,000 Racine rooters will be present together with the sixty-piece uniformed drum and bugle corps of the Racine post of the American Legion and a flock of trained cheer leaders, and they're bent on whooping things up merrily.*

Instead of the easy victory, the Cardinals were shocked 10-4 by the Legion and its diminutive (5'8", 205 pounds) quarterback Shorty Barr. Seeing that his club would have difficulty penetrating the tough Cardinals line with the run, Barr took to the air and surprised his opponents with a series of short but effective passes. Late in the game, with the outcome still in doubt, Barr wisely absorbed a safety to prevent the Cardinals from acquiring favorable field position. It was a risky decision, since it brought the Cardinals to within six points. Yet it proved to be the right one, much to the delight of the noisy Racine fans accompanied by their sixty piece drum and bugle corps.

The defeat was devastating to the confident Cardinals and punched out any hopes of attaining the national championship. There was still the cherished city title to capture, and with the Bears struggling somewhat with an identical 7-2 record, it appeared that the metropolitan championship was within reach. The game would once again take place on Thanksgiving morning, but this time at Cubs Park.

As usual, the *Tribune* promoted the simmering rivalry and added a touch of the neighborhood considerations in its preview of the match:

> *All the old time rivalry between north and south side partisans threatens to creep out as a result of tomorrow's struggle. The Cardinals, who up until a week ago threatened to go into the conflict as heavy favorites, found themselves backed down to little better than an even money choice yesterday and as the north side rooters continue to make much noise the Bears may be on the short end of whatever wagering takes place at game time.*

The *Daily News* countered with:

> *The south siders expect a stormy session with the lads from the north side, but, despite the crippled condition of the Cardinals, they are banking on another victory. Since the two elevens have been in action they have played five times, the Cardinals scoring three victories and the north siders one, while another battle terminated in a tie.*

The game itself proved to be an intense, hard-fought affair, with the Bears prevailing 3-0 on a first-quarter field goal by Dutch Sternaman. A huge crowd of 13,500 attended the game that also featured the return of Joey Sternaman, who rejoined the Bears after his season in Duluth had concluded four days earlier. The win pushed the Bears (8-2) up the ladder ahead of the Cardinals (7-3), but just behind the Canton Bulldogs (9-0-1) as the season began to wind down. Next up for O'Brien's crew was a visit from the legendary Oorang Indians, a team whose brief two-year span in the NFL was remembered more for the players' antics than for its victories.

## We Were All Wild Men

Football historians love to recall stories about Jim Thorpe and the Oorang Indians. As mentioned previously, the team had been created in 1922 as a promotional tool for the Oorang Kennels in LaRue, Ohio. The team was composed entirely of Native Americans who worked hard . . . and played hard. The Pro Football Researchers Association (PFRA) published a book entitled *Bulldogs on Sunday* that chronicled some of the escapades of the team during its brief existence.

As part of the halftime entertainment, the players would be required to participate in several diverse activities, according to PFRA:

> *The players found it difficult to take their football seriously because the owner was far more interested in the pre-game and halftime activities than he was in the game itself. They gave exhibitions with Airedales at work trailing and treeing a live bear. One of the players, 195 pound Nikolas Lassa, called "Long Time Sleep" by his teammates because he was so hard to wake up in the morning, even wrestled the bear. There were fancy shooting exhibitions by Indian marksmen with Airedales retrieving the targets. There were Indian dances, fancy tomahawk work, knife and lariat throwing, all done by Indians.*

The team was not quite so skillful on the field, however. It had lost all nine of its games before coming to Comiskey Park, including scary losses to Buffalo (57-0) and Canton (41-0). Perhaps the auxiliary entertainment distracted the players on the gridiron, prompting the dismal performances. But off the field, the Oorang Indians performed quite well. PFRA quoted quarterback Leon Boutwell, a Chippewa performer for Oorang:

> *White people had this misconception about Indians. They thought we were all wild men, even though almost all of us had been to college and were generally more civilized than they were. Well, it was a dandy excuse to raise hell and get away with it when the mood struck us. Since we were Indians we could get away with things the whites couldn't. Don't think we didn't take advantage of it.*

The Cardinals had only two days to prepare for the Indians following the disheartening loss to the Bears—but perhaps that would be all that was needed against a team with an 0-9 record coming into the game. True, the Indians were led by the great Jim Thorpe as player-coach and included experienced players such as Joe Guyon, Pete Calac, and Joe Little Twig, but the team had scored just one touchdown (twelve total points) in those nine losses before arriving in Chicago for the December 2 contest at Comiskey Park.

The *Daily News* delineated the Oorang roster:

> *Eight different tribes are represented on the Oorang squad. Jim Thorpe and his brother Jack are of the Sac and Fox tribe; Eagle Feather, fullback, is a Mohican, and Tomahawk, right half, and Arrow Head, left end, are Wyandottes. Red Fox at quarter and Powell, left guard, are Cherokees. Little Twig, left tackle, is a Mohawk, and Barrell, at center, hails from the Chippewas. Newosha, a Sac and Fox, plays right guard, with Long Time Sleep, at right tackle, a Flathead, and Calac, of the California tribe, at right end. Jolley, a Wyandotte, and Running Deer, Buffalo, Big Bear and Boutwell, substitutes, hail from the Chippewas, whence came Chief Bender.*

With Paddy Driscoll knocked out by an appendicitis attack and Jack Crangle sidelined by pleurisy, the Cardinals were nearly caught napping by the visitors. Oorang put forth its finest offensive showing of the year. Trailing 22-6 at the conclusion of the third period, the Indians bounced back with a score off a recovered fumble and then Guyon returned an intercepted pass ninety-six yards. The Cards held onto a 22-19 win with the little-used Art Folz at quarterback scoring one of the team's touchdowns. Attendance was a disappointing twelve hundred when word spread that both Driscoll and Thorpe would be unavailable to play.

Now 8-3, the Cardinals wrapped up the disheartening 1923 schedule with still another home game, this time against Jimmy Conzelman and the Milwaukee Badgers. Playing without Driscoll, Mohardt, and Crangle, the Cards were edged 14-12 and slumped to a final 8-4 league (9-4 overall) record. After such an inspiring start (5-0), the Cards staggered to a sixth place finish as Canton swept the title with its second straight undefeated (11-0-1) season under Guy Chamberlin. The Bears locked up second place based on a 9-2-2 record. Driscoll easily topped the league in scoring with a record seventy-eight points and broke his own mark with ten field goals on the year. He was also named to the first All-NFL team selected by various sportswriters around the country for the *Green Bay Gazette*.

## Don't Mess With Jim

Everyone seems to have a favorite Jim Thorpe story. Thorpe, who was voted as the greatest football player in history in a 1950 poll, played one game for the Cardinals in 1928 as he finished his stellar career. During his playing days, former Cardinals coach Jimmy Conzelman met up with Thorpe on the gridiron when the latter was with the Oorang Indians. Later in life, Conzelman recalled this tale:

> I grew a mustache which I was very proud of. I wore it against the Oorang Indians. I gave Jim a fake and he took it. I went 60 yards. The next time, Jim didn't take the fake. He hit me near the sidelines and I went flying. He knocked me ten feet out of bounds.
>
> Well, there I was, half senseless, sprawled out on the ground after Thorpe hit me, and he came over to me. I thought it was a nice gesture

> when he started to pick me up, but then he stared at my finely
> groomed mustache and growled: "Shave that thing off." For some rea-
> son, the mustache made him mad as hell. That night I shaved it off. I
> had enough trouble without making Jim Thorpe mad at me.

## *A Duel Of Great Field Goal Kickers*

The big news heralding the 1924 season was the partial disbanding of the two-time
champions from Canton. Despite its nearly flawless play, the team was drowning financially because of its small market and even smaller stadium. The Bulldogs moved to
Cleveland, but not all of its players decided to follow. Still, the Bulldogs, behind Guy
Chamberlin, would be tough to dethrone in 1924.

One of the league's most significant rule changes actually originated with the
Chicago Bears. The NFL managers approved Dutch Sternaman's proposal that the league
games begin on September 27 and conclude on November 30. The rule both hurt
and helped the Bears as the team compiled an unusual 6-1-4 mark in 1924. A September
21 loss to Green Bay did not count because the game was played before the "official"
start of the season. Then on December 7, the Bears claimed the championship based
on the team's 23-0 victory over Cleveland and an ensuing 13-10 win over Frankford
the following week. Those victories (and a December defeat to Rock Island) would
have given the Bears an 8-2-4 record, topping the Bulldogs' 7-2-1 mark. But President
Joe Carr reminded the members of the agreement to conclude the season by November
30, and the final league results only reflect games completed by that date. This ruling left the Bulldogs with their third straight title with a 7-1-1 record, while the Bears
were officially listed at 6-1-4 in second place.

What about the Cardinals? Despite another fast start, the Cards slipped in mid-
season and experienced a 5-4-1 finish (6-4-1 overall). Offensively, the team lost end
Roger Kiley, who began a collegiate coaching career at Loyola, while Johnny Mohardt
moved up to Racine. Newcomers joining the club were backs Johnny Hurlburt from
the University of Chicago and Bill McElwain from Northwestern, while Kiley was
replaced at end by Carl Hanke from Minnesota and the Hammond Pros. Player-coach
Arnie Horween continued to play under an alias in what must have been the worst-
kept secret in Chicago, but the fans and reporters still abided by his request for
anonymity. His brother Ralph, however, left the professional game after the 1923 season. Tackle Fred Gillies added the role of assistant coach to his duties.

Chris and Pat O'Brien opened a men's clothing and sporting goods store at 5152
South Halsted and advertised their store in the expanded game program that included
numerous ads, individual player photos, and a pledge to assist any patron who was
unable to secure a reserved seat.

*The Management of the Chicago Cardinals Football Club will zealously protect
the holders of reserve seat checks if but given the opportunity to act. Should a
holder of a coupon for any reason be unable to secure the seat called for, a visit
to the office will result in straightening out any situation, no matter how tangled. All the management asks is the prompt co-operation of patrons while at the
park, instead of complaining by letter after the "mix-up" has occurred. Under no
circumstances should holders of coupon checks surrender them to the ushers. The
coupon is for the protection of the patron, and is the most convincing evidence*

*he can invoke to support his claim.*

Cardinals fans could purchase those tickets at several locations around the city, including A. G. Spalding & Brothers (211 South State Street), Pete's Place (55th and Racine), and at the W. J. Floral Co. (5700 South Ashland). In 1924, despite another hot start, tickets for the Cardinals games were not selling as well as in the past. O'Brien continued his generosity by regularly inviting war veterans and children to be his guests at home games, but these acts of kindness also helped to fill the many vacant seats at Comiskey Park. Except for immense crowds for the Bears games, the South Siders were beginning to toil somewhat in obscurity.

The 1924 season opened early when the Cards bopped the Pullman Panthers 14-0 on September 21 with King and Koehler scoring the two touchdowns. The initial league fray was with the Milwaukee Badgers on September 28. Hanke recovered a blocked punt in the end zone and Driscoll booted a fifty-yard field goal and later tallied on a twenty-yard run to pace the winners to a 17-7 advantage. Home victories against the Packers (3-0) and the Minneapolis Marines (13-0) followed, with Hurlburt scoring from fifteen and twenty-two yards out. After just three weeks of play, the Cardinals topped the NFL with a clean 3-0 slate. Taking advantage of the possibility of another nice crowd, the Cardinals clashed with the Bears (0-1-2) on October 19 on the North Side. The *Tribune* pushed the kicking angle of the game in its preview:

> *A duel of great field goal kickers is looked for this afternoon when the Chicago Cardinals and Chicago Bears stage their football "city series" at the Cub park. All the trimmings of a college battle, with music furnished by Bramhall's band, will be in store for the rooters.*
>
> *In former years field goals have decided most of the games between these hot rivals in the National Football League. Paddy Driscoll, former Purple (Northwestern) and Great Lakes flash, is looked upon as the best drop kicker in the country since the days of Charley Brickey of Harvard. The Bears have two accurate goal shooters in Dutch Sternaman and his brother, Joe, both of Illinois. Dutch specializes at place kicks and Joe at drop kicks.*

True to the preliminary discussions, the game was decided by field goals as Joe Sternaman kicked two field goals to push the Bears to a 6-0 advantage. A huge crowd of twenty thousand viewed the defensive display. The Bears defense was especially impressive, once holding the losers on downs at the one-foot line and also blocking two of Driscoll's field goal attempts. For the Cardinals, the season went downhill from there.

The Cards' offense failed again the next week, as Hammond walked away with a 6-3 victory before thirty-five hundred attendees at Comiskey Park, many of them Boy Scouts invited to the game by O'Brien. The Cardinals attempted to open up their passing attack in an effort to loosen up the offense. In the second quarter alone, Driscoll completed a startling seven of eight passes, but Hammond stiffened near its own goal line. A third straight loss was endured when Milwaukee reversed an earlier decision and posted a 17-8 verdict.

Like manna in the desert, the Dayton Triangles visited on November 9 and the Cards grabbed a 23-0 victory to snap the losing streak at three games. The attendance dwindled to about two thousand for this game and was about the same a week later when the Cardinals knocked off Akron 13-0. However, the loss was costly for the winners.

Halfback Bill McElwain, who had just returned from a broken collarbone injury two weeks earlier, was sidelined again with a broken shoulder. With the win, the Cardinals (5-3) moved up to seventh place in the league. Since the NFL season was scheduled to end on November 30, O'Brien squeezed in two more games: a 10-10 tie with the Racine Legion and a closing 21-0 loss to the Bears in the traditional Thanksgiving Day clash.

With the conference standings based on percentages (ties did not count), the Chicago Cardinals (5-4-1) tumbled to eighth place in the eighteen-team league. The Bears (6-1-4) reluctantly accepted second place. While his team's slow finish was a concern for O'Brien, the attendance factor was equally baffling. Despite a competitive team paced by the popular Paddy Driscoll, the fans were not knocking down the doors to get into Comiskey Park. The Bears-Cardinals game at Comiskey Park on November 7 attracted an adequate six thousand attendees, but the Bears-Cleveland game on the North Side a week later drew eighteen thousand fans.

During the offseason, O'Brien vowed to himself to do whatever it would take in player transactions to push the Cardinals over the top. His boldness in acquiring new talent would be a primary factor in the success of the Cardinals in what would prove to be the wildest and wackiest season in the history of the NFL: 1925.

## The McMahon "Ruffians"

When he graduated from Harvard in 1920, little did Ralph Horween realize the impact he would have on the game of pro football. Following his graduation, when he played in Harvard's only Rose Bowl appearance (a 7-6 decision over Oregon), Horween (born Horowitz) returned home to Chicago and took a job with his family's leather tannery business. A stocky 5'10", 206-pound running back, Horween couldn't resist the urge to play football again when he and his brother Arnie joined the Cardinals in 1921. As noted previously, both brothers played their entire pro careers with the Cardinals under the name of "McMahon" because they were reluctant to let their mother know about their participation in the professional game. She apparently thought that a gentleman with a degree from Harvard should not be associated with such ruffians. Yet when Horween retired from the NFL in 1923, he never really left the league, for his company still supplies the leather used in making the league's official football. An even more incredible accomplishment for this former Cardinal is the fact that he was the first NFL alumnus to reach the age of one hundred, celebrating that birthday on August 3, 1996.

# ◆ 5 ◆

# The First Championship: 1925

*"On to Chicago, win and fight,*
*went the proud little queen of the anthracite."*

WALTER FARQUHAR,
POTTSVILLE (PA) SPORTSWRITER, 1925

One of the most bizarre chapters in Cardinals history—or for that matter, in the history of any sports team—occurred in 1925.

The year that marked the first overwhelming wave of national support for the game of professional football also left it with a dubious black eye—and all of it revolved around the city of Chicago. In a shocking two-week period during early December 1925, the Cardinals became winners who felt like losers, while their archrival the Chicago Bears fell short on the field but laughed all the way to the bank.

Throw in a championship game that wasn't for the championship, the youngest player to ever play in the NFL, a season that didn't end when the schedule did, an unlikely barnstorming tour produced solely for monetary purposes, and a questionable championship (which some folks in Pennsylvania dispute to this day), and the 1925 season remains a bewildering enigma more than seventy years later.

To set this important piece of football history in its proper place, let's reverse the gridiron time machine back to Chicago one week before Thanksgiving Day in 1925. Teams on all levels, like the Chicago Bears, the Chicago Cardinals, the University of Illinois, the Pottsville Maroons, and Chicago's Englewood High School, were involved in key contests as the 1925 season began to wane. Despite the diversity of these clubs, all the teams would eventually intermingle within the next two weeks, impacting not only the 1925 season, but also the future direction of the NFL.

Thanks to the "Four Horsemen" of Notre Dame fame, a high school sophomore who made his pro debut six days after his final high school (not college) game, a small town theater owner, and an unthinkable football carnival that turned a college senior from Wheaton, Illinois, into the richest man in his neighborhood, 1925 was about to become the wackiest year in the history of the NFL.

Let's start with the departed but not forgotten NFL teams of 1925, such as the Pottsville Maroons, Frankford Yellow Jackets, Providence Steam Roller, Buffalo Bison, Kansas City Blues, and Columbus Tigers. Minneapolis, Racine, and Kenosha had dropped out of sight from the previous season, but the NFL now included a staggering total of twenty teams with various degrees of respectability. These competitors played a ragtag, disorganized schedule from the period of September 20, 1925, through December 6, 1925. Teams could then continue to schedule games up to December 20 or opt to retire for the season after December 6.

The Duluth Kelleys played just three games and dropped them all rather easily. Meanwhile, the aforementioned Yellow Jackets took on twenty opponents, including four in one eight-day stretch, to finish in sixth place with a 13-7 record. Because of local laws, football games were not allowed in Frankford, Pennsylvania, on Sunday, so the Yellow Jackets would schedule a home game on Saturday and then hop on a train and play somewhere else on Sunday. To avoid disappointing the home fans, the Hammond Pros (1-4), the Rochester Jeffersons (0-6-1), and the Columbus Tigers (0-9) opted to play all of their games on the road.

In the end, the league champion was still determined by the best winning percentage (no matter how many games were played), not by the best record achieved by playing an equitable schedule against the same opponents (that type of radical thought had not yet occurred to the league's brain trust.) The first official championship playoff would not show up until 1933.

Who won the 1925 championship? The Chicago Cardinals. The Cardinals?

Had one picked up the newspaper on the morning of December 7, 1925, the headline in the sports pages would clearly note that the visiting Pottsville Maroons had defeated the Chicago Cardinals 21-7 for the National Football League title. With that victory, Pottsville "ended" its 1925 slate with a 10-2 record, while the runner-up Cardinals "finished" 9-2-1.

The press also reported that on the same day, the largest crowd ever to witness a professional football game showed up for a contest in New York. While only six thousand brave souls shivered in Comiskey Park in Chicago for the Cardinals' title tilt with Pottsville, some seventy-three thousand gridiron enthusiasts jammed their way into the Polo Grounds in New York to watch a pair of also-rans, the Chicago Bears and the New York Giants, grapple in a meaningless game won by the Bears 19-7.

On Saturday, November 21, the University of Illinois finished its season with a 5-3 record by defeating Ohio State 14-9. In Chicago, Englewood High School, behind all-city quarterback Charles Richardson, concluded its regular season with a 7-7 tie with Elgin High School. Now 6-1-1, and second to Lindbloom in the city school league, Englewood planned for one last challenge: a road trip to Lock Haven, Pennsylvania.

The pros were also busy on the Sunday (November 22) before Thanksgiving. The new Pottsville Maroons franchise from Pennsylvania blasted Cleveland 24-6 to up its record to 7-2 while the Bears (6-2-2) trimmed the Packers 21-0. The Cardinals (8-1) shut out Dayton 14-0 for an eighth straight victory.

In 1925, there would be no midyear swoon for Chris O'Brien's boys; the only loss had occurred in a 10-6 opening day upset to Hammond. O'Brien had made wholesale changes during the off-season. Gone were old timers like Nick McInerney, Garland Buckeye, Rip King, and Bill Whalen. Fred Gillies, Eddie Anderson, and Will Brennan continued to anchor the line, but they were joined by newcomers like end-tackle Herb Blumer (200 pounds), tackle Buck Evans (204 pounds), guard Jerry Lunz (210 pounds), and center Ralph Claypool (195 pounds). Wilfred Smith and Lenny Sachs returned to the team after sampling life elsewhere in the league. O'Brien, who always favored speed over bulk in the backfield, added more lightning with Red Dunn (Marquette) and Hal "Swede" Erickson (Washington and Jefferson), who had played for the Milwaukee Badgers in 1924. They would join holdovers Driscoll, Koehler, and Folz in a potent backfield for the 1925 Cardinals.

Although pleased with the Cardinals' sole hold on first place in the NFL, O'Brien still pointed to the Thanksgiving Day meeting with the Bears as the "make or break it" game of the season. With the Bears lurking just behind the Cardinals and Pottsville in the championship race, anything could happen with the league's season extended to December 20.

## The Galloping Ghost

After only one game, Arnie Horween left his post as coach in 1925 due to illness. O'Brien then installed ex-Notre Dame star Norm Barry as the first nonplaying coach of the Chicago Cardinals for the remainder of the season. Up until late November, the team continued to function quite well. Following the surprising opening loss to Hammond, the Cards went on a mugging spree throughout the NFL. Working behind a stingy defense, Driscoll and his counterparts brushed past the next eight straight opponents. All of these victories were home games. Included in this masterpiece of a season were three shutouts and only thirty-four points allowed over an eight-game stretch.

Meanwhile, down in Champaign, rumors were drifting about that All-American halfback Red Grange would turn professional after the close of his final football season at Illinois. Grange was the most visible player in college football at the time, a virtual superstar after a dazzling game against Michigan in 1924 when he scored five touchdowns in a 39-14 romp over the Wolverines. Four of those touchdowns arrived in the first quarter when Grange scored on three long runs and a kickoff return. This outstanding performance occurred at the dedication game of Illinois' new stadium and has always been remembered as one of the greatest running displays in the history of the Big Ten Conference. He also tossed an eighteen-yard scoring pass. In total, Grange ran 15 times for 212 yards, returned 3 kickoffs for 126 yards, and completed 6 of 8 passes for 64 more yards. His all-around abilities placed Grange (also known as the "Galloping Ghost" and the "Wheaton Iceman") on the All-American team for three straight years.

While the NFL's intent was to stay away from college players, several teams were quietly expressing their interest in Grange. Chris O'Brien's Cardinals were one of them, with O'Brien actively seeking financial support to attract Grange to the South Side. Unknown to O'Brien and other interested parties, Grange had already secretly agreed to play for another pro football team.

Early in his senior season, Grange had been approached by a gentleman named Charles C. (C. C.) Pyle. A former undertaker and entrepreneur who was overseeing a pair of theaters in Champaign, C. C. Pyle proposed an enticing business deal. In his autobiography, *The Red Grange Story*, Grange recalled that first meeting with Pyle:

> *I had heard his name mentioned a few times before, but never met him. After exchanging a few pleasantries, he got around to the real reason for wanting to see me.*
> *"How would you like to make one hundred thousand dollars, or maybe even a million?" Pyle asked. I was momentarily stunned. Regaining my composure, I*

*quickly answered the query in the affirmative. When I attempted to find out what Pyle had in mind he told me he had a plan, but wasn't at liberty to reveal the details at the time. He said he'd contact me in a few weeks and made me promise that after leaving his office I wouldn't mention our conversation to anyone.*

*I found out later that Pyle left the next day for Chicago to confer with George Halas and Ed Sternaman, co-owners of the Chicago Bears. He offered them a tentative deal whereby I would join their team immediately after my last college game against Ohio State. I was to play in the remaining league games that season and then go on tour with the Bears in a series of exhibition games that Pyle would book himself from Florida to the West Coast.*

Before Grange played his last game for Illinois, the Bears and Pyle agreed to a fifty-fifty split of the gate for the games with Pyle and Grange. Of that latter share, Grange would receive sixty percent and Pyle forty percent. By playing with the Bears, Red Grange, the quiet lad from Wheaton, would rake in thirty percent of all gate receipts. Halas later wrote that the discussions did not move easily at first with Pyle initially demanding two-thirds of the gate:

*We talked through the afternoon and the evening and the night and the next morning and on into the afternoon. After 26 hours, we did come to an agreement. We would split the earnings fifty-fifty, I would provide the Bears and pay the tour costs. Pyle would provide Red. Red would provide the crowds. It was a fair arrangement. We put it in writing. The last clause stated that if any of us were asked about a contract, we would declare none existed.*

## *You Don't Know What A Tough Place I'm In*

Rumors continued to run wild the week preceding Red's final game. His own coach, Bob Zuppke, and Illinois athletic director George Huff demanded to know if he had signed a contract. The president of the university jumped in and threatened to expel Grange from Illinois, and the leaders of Ohio State University began to growl about his presence on the field for that last game. Bewildered by all of this, Grange rushed home to the solace of his family in Wheaton on Tuesday, November 17, seeking the advice of his father, Lyle Grange, the deputy sheriff of DuPage County. Cornered by reporters at a small diner in his hometown, Grange again denied that he had signed a contract: "I'm all mixed up. And I'm worried," he told the *Chicago Tribune*. "But you can tell everybody that I'm not going to sign up for anything—pro football, selling real estate, movie contracts, anything—until I play my last football for Illinois next Saturday."

Grange was clearly perplexed as to why the pressures to resist playing pro football were so persistent, even from his own coach:

*You don't know what a tough place I'm in. Everybody's saying this and that about me turning pro and throwing down Illinois. I don't know what to do. I've tried to keep clean on this amateur stuff. I haven't taken a cent from anyone and I haven't signed a contract with anyone.*

*Folks have said I got money for playing football at Illinois. That's all the bunk. The only money I got I earned working on an ice wagon in the summer and the*

*rest my father has given me. Dad's not got much. You can see that. Now if I go
out and make a lot now it would help him out.*

*I know what the fellows down at the university will think. They'll say I'm throw-
ing the school down. But should I take advice from them? Most of the fellows
who are telling me not to earn anything on pro football will have forgotten all
about me by next year. If I'm broke, then I don't suppose they'd loan me a dollar.
Why shouldn't I get the money while I can?*

The tumult continued the next day when Zuppke kept Grange out of practice
and commented that he was not opposed to Grange playing pro football. On the other
hand, he was upset that Grange might leave school immediately (before graduation)
to do so. Zuppke also noted that the meeting between Grange and Huff was cordial
and that Huff had also advised Grange to stay in school because "turning to the pro
gridiron sport . . . might injure his chances for something more lucrative."

On Saturday, November 21, Grange completed his career at Ohio State before
over eighty-five thousand spectators. Immediately after the game, he boarded a train
for Chicago and eventually signed two contracts at the Morrison Hotel on November
22 and November 23: one with Pyle, who would serve as his manager, and the second with the Chicago Bears to play professional football. In announcing the signing,
Grange promised to return to college and stated:

*I have received many alluring offers to enter fields of enterprise in which I have
had no training or experience. I believe the public will be better satisfied with my
honesty and good motives if I turn my efforts to that field in which I have been
most useful in order to reap a reward which will keep the home fires burning.*

The signing drew incredible nationwide interest, essentially changing the visibility of pro football forever. In Red Grange, the league had a genuine American hero.
With radio popularizing the game throughout the country, he had become a household word, but there was still little opportunity for the average fan to see a star of
Grange's proportions in person. That, too, would change with his first Bears game
and the subsequent tour. The *Tribune* called Grange "the most phenomenal college
gridder of all time," and felt that just the chance for the fans to marvel at his athleticism would be memorable:

*He may not get away for one of his marathons, but that won't make much dif-
ference. The mere fact that he will be out there where the common fans can view
him will be sufficient.*

The press reaction in Chicago was substantial, as it was everywhere else around
the country. Instead of getting a few paragraphs reviewing a typical game, the practice sessions for the Bears' first game with Grange in the lineup was earning full headlines. Grange sat on the Bears bench in the game against the Green Bay Packers on
November 22. During the halftime intermission, several hundred fans jumped the walls
in an attempt to meet Grange. Only after police were called in was order restored and
the game resumed. While the Bears coasted 21-0, there was great anticipation for
Grange's first appearance on the field as a player in a Bears uniform.

And that, through no small piece of fate, would be against the Chicago Cardinals on Thanksgiving Day in Cubs Park. The Cardinals were in the right place at the right time. They took advantage of the huge influx of publicity and cash resulting from being Red Grange's first professional opponents. While the Bears were downsizing the Packers, the Cardinals knocked off the Dayton Triangles 14-0 for their eighth win in a row. The team added Ike Mahoney from Creighton to the roster, who was rumored to really be Elmer Layden of Notre Dame. The *Green Bay Press-Gazette* described Mahoney as a runner "who can skip over frozen ground like a fawn in the north woods, and he skipped several times during the encounter for big gains." The paper added:

> Now there are rumors that this young Mr. Mahoney is none other than the famous Mr. Layden of Notre Dame's 1924 Four Horsemen. His legs and body look a bit skinny to belong to Mr. Layden, but the lad sure can skip over the ground in a manner that makes one think of the former Notre Dame player . . . football rumors are quite the thing this fall, so you can take this one or leave it.

As it turned out, Ike Mahoney was indeed Ike Mahoney from Creighton. The Cardinals did attempt to persuade Layden to join them for the game with the Bears and Grange, but Layden's father advised against it.

## *Paddy Is Still A Wild Goose On The Chalk Lines*

When ticket sales were announced for the Cardinals-Bears game, it produced a frenzy among football fans anxious to see the annual Thanksgiving Day game. It had become much more than a battle for NFL or city supremacy. On Wednesday, November 25, twenty thousand tickets went on sale and were sold out almost immediately. That amount alone would have ensured the largest crowd ever to witness a pro game in Chicago. Still the rush was on for tickets for the big game as described by the *Tribune:*

> Yesterday morning fans again swarmed on the A.G. Spalding store in South State Street and . . . tickets from the previous day disappeared in less than an hour. The disappointed ones refused to disperse, however, and it was necessary to call mounted cops to break the congestion.
>
> Meanwhile, a similar scene was being enacted at the Park. In forty-five minutes four ticket sellers had unloaded the thousand or more grandstand seats that were available. Then a large flock of cops managed to bring about order until another storm broke at 1 o'clock when 3,500 bleacher seats were offered.

The Cardinals suddenly found themselves with so much media attention that Coach Barry was forced to hold a secret practice at Comiskey Park in order to prepare for the new threat in Grange. Although the Cardinals had won a previous encounter with the Bears 9-0, the Bears moved into game time as the slight favorite. The excitement was genuine; full headlines and even practice photos adorned the Chicago sports pages. Fans clamored for tickets, speculated on the impact of Grange, and wondered if the older professional players would be able to keep up with this elite runner.

Despite the glamour and the headlines, it was almost a second thought that the Cardinals were providing the opposition. Indeed, the Cards were the front runners in the NFL that week, but little notice was taken of that accomplishment. One who was not forgotten, however, was the erstwhile Paddy Driscoll. Irving Vaughan of the *Tribune* reminded the city that there would be more than one star on the field come Thanksgiving Day:

> *The Bears have their Grange for a menace but the Cards have an equally dangerous runner in Paddy Driscoll, who was waltzing on Big Ten gridirons even before "Red" hired out on the ice wagons. Paddy, who remembers that he once scored a touchdown that won for Northwestern over Chicago, is still a wild goose on the chalk lines and what's more has a toe that is dangerous anywhere inside the forty yard line.*

## How Many Thousands Could Have Been Sold?

By game day, there was still an unrelenting demand for tickets, and the *Tribune* marveled at what might have been:

> *This unheard of plea for tickets didn't abate even after the supply of reservations was exhausted. How many more thousands could have been sold is something for statisticians or mathematicians to ponder. The only certain thing is that so many could have been sold that there would be no room for the gridders to play on.*

While the official attendance was never released, it was estimated that between thirty-six thousand and forty-two thousand were in the ballpark for this game. The only one who might have been disappointed was Chris O'Brien. After playing before just three thousand fans on the South Side four days previously, the Cards were now playing before the biggest crowd to ever witness a pro football game. Usually, the visiting team (which would have been the Cardinals) received a travel guarantee and/or a share of the gate receipts. However, for this game, the fiscally conservative O'Brien had earlier agreed to a flat fee for his team's appearance. In a game where Grange alone may have pocketed as much as $12,000 to $20,000, the Cardinals probably fetched the usual visiting team share of a mere $1,200 to cover the weekly salary limitation. A split of the gate would have done wonders for O'Brien, relieving him of many of the financial difficulties that burdened his team. Instead, the greatest payday in the brief history of professional football turned out to be just another game for the Cardinals.

With tickets impossible to find, WGN radio quickly scheduled a live broadcast of the game with a brief press release outlining its plan for listeners:

> *"Red" Grange and football hold the Thanksgiving Day stage at W-G-N on the Drake Hotel. A twist of the dials to 370 meters at 10:45 A.M. today will carry listeners to the roof of the Cubs Park, where Jim Jennings is to begin the broadcasting of the game between the Chicago Bears and Chicago Cardinals. Grange is making his professional debut today as a member of the former aggregation. The customary W-G-N method is to be followed in miking the game—the announcer's story will have for a background the cheers and shouts of the spectators, brought in by other microphones situated at various points of the field and in the stands.*

In fear of a possible riot from fans scurrying for any remaining standing room tickets, the Bears asked police to cordon off the area around the park and allowed only those with tickets to enter the area. Scalpers were in a lively mood as well, although the fact that many had printed tickets in the wrong colors helped the police snatch seventeen scalpers as they attempted to sell their wares near the park.

The game itself proved to be a classic and found a place on the front pages of newspapers across the country, including the *New York Times:*

> *Red Grange today stepped from a college hero into business life as a professional football player, gained the hearty applause of a crowd of over 40,000 and some $12,000 as his share of the receipts. On the debit side there he scored one black eye. Red's team, the Chicago Bears, played a scoreless tie with the Chicago Cardinals, their bitter rivals of the South Side.*

Prior to the game, the Cardinals agreed that they would pursue a conservative game plan, sticking to a rushing game with little fanfare. More importantly, the talented Driscoll was directed to punt away from Grange, thus minimizing the impact of the flashy runner's returns. The Bears still had another deep threat in little Joey Sternaman, but the Cardinals knew his capabilities. Despite his lofty attributes as a runner, it was still worth the risk to kick to Sternaman rather than challenge the amazing repertoire of Grange.

And so the game went, back and forth, punt after punt, with neither team able to sustain any consistent offense on a muddy field that had been drenched with snow during the week. Despite the intensity of the battle, it was apparent that the crowd was there to see Grange, the biggest folk hero the city had experienced in quite some time, according to Maxwell in the *Tribune:*

> *Grange-Grange-Grange — all Grange.*
>
> *The Bears and the Cardinals are great pro teams. They have thousands of enthusiastic followers. But the more than 36,000 folk who made their turkey wait until the game was over weren't there to see their teams play. They were there to see the red head of Wheaton.*
>
> *They cheered when Grange gained ground; they cheered when he lost ground. They went into vocal hysterics when he trotted on the field, and they almost mobbed him when he left it. The Cardinals played good football. Paddy Driscoll punted away from Grange and the fans booed. They were there to see Red.*

This unusual predicament of playing before a huge crowd in a battle that meant first place did not sway the Cards from their game plan. There were some mishaps, however, when Grange was able to display his magic. On just three of Driscoll's punts, Grange ended up as the receiver and knocked off nifty returns of twenty, sixteen, and twenty yards. But that was it. The Cardinals had the best chance to score late in the game, but Driscoll's dropkick for a field goal bounced off the upright.

Offensively, Grange gathered in thirty-six yards rushing with a best attempt of seven yards. He threw six passes, but completed none. His biggest contribution may have been on defense, where he intercepted a Mahoney pass on the Bears' one-yard line to stifle a Cardinals scoring drive in the third quarter. In a game devoid of offensive activity, the Bears could manage just two first downs and the Cardinals only one.

## *Those Cardinals Are Mighty Good Players*

At the conclusion of the hard-fought contest, the on-field scene was almost surreal. The Cardinals players surrounded Grange and wished him well with handshakes and congratulatory pats on the back. (This in an era when pro games often ended in a flurry of punches, riots, or other small disorders.) The fans hurdled the walls and began to encircle the field forcing the police to quickly whisk Grange to safety in the dugout/locker room.

Once there, Grange entertained reporters and commented on his initial foray into pro ball: "It was a good game," he said, "I gave everything I had but those fellows (Cardinals) are mighty good players. It's going to be harder going in these pro games than in the university games. I only had two practices with the Bears. I hope to do better in a week or so."

The best story surviving through the years from this game involved local favorite Paddy Driscoll. Driscoll spent the entire afternoon punting away from Grange and was concerned that the unforgiving crowd was booing the rookie because he was unable to break away for any long returns. Later, he mentioned this to his wife who responded, "Paddy, they weren't booing Red. They were booing you for not giving Red a chance." That was probably the only time that the popular Driscoll was on the receiving end of the fans' dismay during his long career in Chicago. The *Chicago American* playfully called Driscoll to task:

> *Paddy Driscoll—shame on you!*
> *Forty thousand folks, including street car conductors, white wings, bootleggers, sailors, saxophone players and night watchmen went up to the Cubs Park yesterday to see "Redhead" Grange pull off eight or ten 70-yard runs. No one doubts that Red could have staged some of his pinwheeling on the chalk lines if he had the chance. But Mr. Driscoll saw to it that he had very little opportunity to get away with any of his dazzlers . . . and that's why huge flocks of the faithful dealt Paddy an undeserved buzz berry . . . Those thousands of boos would have been cheers for Driscoll if the booers knew anything about football.*

But the game quickly elevated the average person's view of football as evidenced by comments in the *Tribune:*

> *This football, exemplified by Bears and Cardinals, was cleanly played. It was more mature than the college brand. There were fewer fumbles, fewer mistakes of judgment. On defense, it was almost mechanically perfect. In fact, these pros of college experience were so proficient and so wily that even the great Red Grange could not get loose for his famous runs.*

Still, not all were sold on the pro game. Universities were still fearful that professional football would harm the college game, much the same way that professional baseball shot past college baseball in popularity. Dartmouth coach Jess Hawley was at the Thanksgiving Day game in Chicago and offered this review and visionary prediction:

> *To a college coach, it was not good football. It pleased and satisfied the public. It looked better than it was . . . I do not deny pro football its right to exist, but I feel it never will take the place of or even be a serious rival of college football.*

With this game finally out of the way, both Chicago teams set sail in different directions, although O'Brien openly lobbied for a rematch on December 20, when the Bears would return from their upcoming tour.

The Bears finalized plans with Pyle to embark on a menacing football tour that would include seven games in eleven days. The NFL title was no longer a concern for the Bears; grabbing the riches associated with showcasing Grange was—and who could blame Halas? The attendance at one game with Grange equaled the number of fans who usually showed up at seven or eight Bears home games.

Meanwhile, the Cardinals had strengthened themselves with the tie with the Bears. With a 9-1-1 record, the next game would be played against Rock Island on Sunday, November 29. Pottsville improved to 8-2 with lopsided wins over Cleveland and Green Bay and would face Frankford on the 29th. The Detroit Tigers, owned by player-coach Jimmy Conzelman, slipped to 7-2-2 after a 6-3 loss to Rock Island. Because of their deadlock with the Cardinals, the Bears failed to improve in the standings with a 6-2-3 record, but O'Brien was more than willing to give the North Siders another shot at the title with another game, anywhere, anytime.

The last stop on the Bears schedule before the start of the Grange tour would be a home date with Columbus on the 29th, while the Cards would be entertaining Rock Island with its impressive tackle Duke Slater. Realizing that a victory would solidify his claim to the championship and act as the bait to hook the Bears into a return bout (with a percentage of the gate this time), O'Brien leaked this part of the plot to the *Tribune*:

> *A victory for the Cardinals means that the south side team will own the championship of the National Professional Football league. According to manager Chris O'Brien, if the Cards beat Rock Island no other team in the league will be able to overtake Driscoll's outfit by Dec. 20, the closing date of the pro league schedule.*

While this reasoning is difficult to accept with a full three weeks left in the season and the Cardinals holding a small lead over the other contenders, it did make good copy in the newspapers. Could the Bears (with their struggling record) resist the chance to dethrone the league champions and thereby claim the title themselves?

Despite the nuisance of a sudden snowstorm, over twenty-eight thousand turned out to watch the Bears edge winless (0-9) Columbus 14-13 as Grange gained seventy-five yards in fourteen carries. On the South Side, only five thousand were on hand at Comiskey Park as the Cardinals beat Rock Island 7-0 in a muddy quagmire, helped by a penalty when thirty-five-year-old center Louis Kolis of the visitors took objection to a call and slugged the referee.

The Bears then hit the road amid glowing reports about the games arranged by C. C. Pyle, now known as "Cash and Carry" Pyle. Thirty-five thousand seats were reported to have been sold in Philadelphia.

## *I Have Always Admired Animal Acts*

The first stop was in St. Louis on December 2, where despite the presence of Jimmy Conzelman, the local All-Stars fell to the Bears 39-6 as Grange scored four touchdowns. A decent crowd of eight thousand was in session for the slaughter, with the home folks having only a Conzelman touchdown pass reception to cheer about. From there, it was on to Philadelphia. On Saturday, December 5, the Bears topped the Frankford Yellow Jackets 14-0 before forty thousand fans in the rain and then moved on to New York for another big pay day on December 6 in front of a pro record seventy-three thousand fans. The result was the same—a win for the Bears, 19-7. Grange remembered the game for another reason:

> *The Bears took a terrific physical beating against New York. Although we had won, it was one of the most bruising battles I had ever been in. I especially remember one play when Joe Alexander, the Giants' center, almost twisted my head off in making a tackle. It was clear we were all beginning to show the wear and tear of our crowded schedule. After that encounter with the Giants, the Bears were no longer able to field a team free of injuries.*

Although Grange experienced a physical beating while in New York, the pain was minimized by a series of endorsement contracts that Pyle negotiated. "Opening up our hotel room to all callers we collected about $25,000 in certified checks for endorsements of a sweater, shoe, cap, doll, and soft drink. We turned down a tie-in with a cigarette company because I didn't smoke," Grange stated. Pyle and Grange also found time to sign a movie contract and to meet probably the only other athlete in America as recognized as Grange at the time: Babe Ruth. Pegler shared Ruth's advice to Grange with an eager public:

> *As one who had heard his share of both rousing and razzing cheers, the Babe advised Red not to be thin skinned, to bank his money, and always to let the other fellows pay at least half of the dinner check . . .*

In California, a street in Glendale was named after Grange, and while he was in Washington, Grange and Halas were invited to the White House to meet President Calvin Coolidge. It was a story that Halas enjoyed recollecting:

> *The team had Monday off. We washed the uniforms. Senator McKinley of Illinois sent his limousine to take Red and me to the White House to meet President Coolidge. The senator introduced us, "Mr. President, this is George Halas and Red Grange of the Chicago Bears." President Coolidge replied, "How are you, young gentlemen? I have always admired animal acts."*

## Lining Up To Get Refunds

On Tuesday, December 8, the Bears escaped Washington with a 19-0 win over a local group of sandlot players with Grange playing little in this nonleague game. Several nagging injuries, including one to his arm that he acquired in New York, were beginning to bother him. After the game, the team left immediately for Boston, with Grange disguising himself as a train porter to avoid reporters and fans. The tour was grinding to a close, but there were still four more games to be played in the next five days as the team worked its way back to Chicago. On December 9 in Boston, the Bears encountered the Providence Steam Roller and suffered a 9-6 setback as Grange was held to eighteen yards. The next day, the Bears were crushed by a team of local players in Pittsburgh 24-0. More importantly, Grange aggravated the arm injury and was told by doctors to skip the next game in Detroit on Saturday, December 12. This, of course, was not good news for Detroit's owner Jimmy Conzelman. His team had struggled financially and hoped to reap the rewards that would be gained by the appearance of Grange and the Bears. In the book *Pro Football's Rag Days,* Conzelman explained his frustration:

> *When I heard about the crowds he (Grange) was pulling in, I booked the Bears for a game in Detroit . . . Once we broke the news, the tickets began to move like mad. I figured we would make about $20,000 clear on the game. That meant we could wipe out all our debts and have a few dollars left for the beginning of the next season.*
>
> *On the Wednesday before the game George Halas phoned and told me that Grange had been hurt and might not be able to play. I thought it only fair to tell the newspapers and I did. A few hours before the game was about to start, I looked out the window and saw a long line at the box office. I remembered thinking to myself, "What a great sports town. Grange isn't going to play but they're still lining up to buy tickets." Then I got the news from the ticket man. They were lining up to get refunds.*

Conzelman refunded nearly ten thousand tickets, but about five thousand were still on hand as Detroit thrashed the weary Bears 21-0. Following the game, the Bears quickly left by train for Chicago to complete the tour and face the Giants on December 13. Without Grange in the lineup, the Giants prevailed 9-0 in front of fifteen thousand fans. The trip was over. Eight games. Twelve days. Four wins. Four losses. All of this resulted in an immediate impact for professional football, for better or for worse. It was also an incredible experience for the players, who still went both ways throughout each game, with rarely a substitution.

## *The Cardinals Play On*

In all the hoopla surrounding the Bears' magical history tour, the Cardinals may have felt like Chicago's forgotten stepchild. With Grange in all his glory, the Cards scratched for recognition despite their first place position. The team had experienced both a winning and satisfying season with individual accomplishments assisting the club to a 9-1-1 record. In a 19-9 win over Columbus, Driscoll dropkicked four field goals, a team record until Jim Bakken arrived thirty-nine years later. One of those was a fifty-yarder, duplicating his team record from the 1924 season. These marks survived until equaled by Pat Summerall in 1954, but were not surpassed until 1964 (again by Bakken). When the Cards stuffed Kansas City 20-7, Driscoll broke away for an eighty-yard touchdown run, which remained a team best until Elmer Angsman scampered eighty-two yards for a score in 1949. Driscoll's feat is still the third best in team annals.

The team was slow in scheduling a game for December 6. The *Green Bay Gazette,* which led the league in pro football gossip, intimated that according to sources in Pottsville, "the Maroons are dickering for a game in Chicago on December 21. It is understood that Chris O'Brien is not very anxious to play, but orders from league headquarters may result in the game being staged." The newspaper probably intended the date to be Sunday, December 20, and the reluctance of O'Brien was understandable, knowing that he was determined to host the Bears on that day. The *Gazette* also reported the early demise of the Milwaukee Badgers on December 4: "The Milwaukee club has called it quits for the season without winning a single game and making a lone touchdown." The Badgers' final game under coach Johnny Bryan had been on November 22, which allowed the former Bear to rejoin his old team on its East Coast tour as a backup for Grange.

Perhaps to placate the league office, or perhaps to demonstrate that his team was simply the best, O'Brien suddenly arranged for a home game with Pottsville on Sunday, December 6. The league probably had little to do with this game being scheduled, especially with President Joe Carr hospitalized at the time due to an appendix oper- ation. It was touted as the league championship, although the league allowed games to be scheduled for two more weeks. The *Tribune*, no doubt prompted by O'Brien, heralded the upcoming battle under a championship pretense:

> *Victory for Paddy Driscoll's men will clarify any dispute as to the championship. Pottsville claims the championship of the eastern division of the league. The Cards rule the western end.*
>
> *Manager O'Brien scheduled the game as a post-season affair to settle with- out question the championship of the pro league. The Cards could hang up their moleskins and quit as champions, but Driscoll's men refuse to quit until they have had a chance at the eastern champions.*

In truth, the league at the time did not recognize geographical champions, nor did it separate the teams by divisions. An ensuing article in the *Tribune* reiterated that this would be a "post-season contest to decide the championship, as the Cards and Pottsville elevens both have closed their regular league season." Again, both claims were erroneous, since the league schedule was open until December 20 and the league did not sponsor any type of "post-season" playoff in 1925. So, while the Bears and Giants were frolicking before a huge crowd of seventy-three thousand in New York, the Cardinals and Maroons faced off before six thousand in Chicago in a battle supposedly for the league championship. In its pregame preview, the *Chicago American* noted:

> *The Coal Miners are due in town tomorrow with 200 coal busters who are ready to bet their week's wages that their boys can whack the stuffing out of our west- erners. While there will be no Red Grange on exhibition in the combat, the fans appear to have warmed to the spectacle of the two strongest pro teams in the league battling for the title and they stormed Spalding's all day yesterday for choice seats.*

The *Chicago Daily News* added:

> *The pasteboards are reported to be in greater demand than the proverbial hot cakes . . . Norm Barry, the former Notre Dame star, who has been working with Paddy Driscoll in priming the O'Briens, stated today that the south siders would be in better shape than at any time this season.*

When the game finally rolled around, the Cards came out flat and were flattened 21-7 by the visitors from Pennsylvania's coal country. The *Daily News* summarized the fate of the Cardinals:

> *Chris O'Brien's Chicago Cardinals saw the national professional football title fade from their grasp yesterday at Comiskey Park, when the powerful machine from Pottsville, Pa. romped away with the honors by a count of 21-7.*

After all of the preliminary posturing about this game being for the championship, O'Brien wasted little time in scheduling additional games prior to the December 20 deadline. O'Brien knew that his Cardinals (9-2-1) were just a step behind Pottsville (10-2) in the standings with no limit as to how many games could still be played. While O'Brien didn't anticipate a hectic eight game slate like the Bears were currently experiencing, he warily cast about for a couple of opponents who, if defeated, could help increase the Cardinals' overall winning percentage. Just one day after the unexpected loss to Pottsville on December 6, O'Brien swung into action and announced a rematch with Hammond on Saturday, December 12. The *Tribune* went along with the strategy:

> *Hammond holds a victory over the Cards, having defeated them early in the season, and Paddy Driscoll's men are anxious to even the count. Victory will not only tie up the league lead again, but will give the Cards an equal claim to Pottsville in playing the Bears here Dec. 20, according to O'Brien. Hammond, while disbanded part of the season, will recruit a list of stars for the battle Saturday.*

Again, there is no evidence that the Bears had any inkling that Pottsville would be arriving in Chicago on December 20, but the release was probably intended (by O'Brien) to plant the seed and arouse public demand for a season-ending battle between the Bears and the league champions, whichever team that might be. Although Hammond had not played a league foe since November 1 when it lost to Detroit, the team continued to play local clubs such as the Evanston Elks, the Aurora Legion, and the Whiting Friars. As such, Hammond might not prove to be the pushover O'Brien possibly anticipated, but his ultimate strategy was becoming more defined, as reported in the *Daily News:*

> *The Chicago Cardinals, who lost first place in the National Professional league to Pottsville, Pa., last week, will play the Hammond club Saturday afternoon . . . The Cards now are a half game behind the Pottsville team and a victory for Chris O'Brien's players will put them in a tie for first place. Should they win they may meet the Bears with Red Grange a week from Sunday.*

In the midst of all this, the *Daily News* published a lengthy interview with Chris O'Brien on Tuesday, December 8, that focused on the continuing drama between amateur and professional football. At issue was the persistent threat that pro football would fatally injure the college game:

> *Many verbal missiles are being cast in the general direction of professional football these days, especially since the advent of "Red" Grange on the post-graduate*

*field. College coaches and hundreds of others interested in amateur athletics and the benefits accruing for the "simon pures" have voiced disfavor and viewed with alarm the rapid growth of the game in which the players profit.*

*In the meantime the professional game has grown. This fall, especially since the close of the regular conference seasons, capacity crowds have turned out. The polo grounds at New York was crowded with 65,000 fans to see Grange. Despite the cold the Chicago Cardinals and Pottsville attracted a crowd to the White Sox park which would do credit to a baseball contest. The result, at least, is pleasing to Chris O'Brien, owner of the Cardinals, and the other men who have financed the game from its small beginnings. Let O'Brien tell his story:*

*"Most of the time I paid more than I should for the sport . . . I have often been embarrassed. On the other hand, professional football here in Chicago and other places where the college gridirons cannot accommodate thousands of sports-men who like a good clean battle, and it is on that idea that the professional league was organized five years ago . . . I may say that college football never need fear any inroads from professional sport. The college game belongs on the cam-pus and, despite the fears of some of the coaches, will always be the leading stu-dent sport. The professional game belongs in another field in the commercial world, where the workers want to get away from their daily grind just as they leave fac-tory and office to see a baseball game."*

## Mr. Grange Turned Everything Topsy-Turvy

Aside from scheduling a return bout with the disbanded Hammond team, Chris O'Brien sent a telegram to Halas on December 8, officially challenging the Bears to a game on December 20. In his wire, O'Brien tweaked Halas's pride by reminding him that the Bears had neither defeated nor scored upon the Cardinals in the two previous matches. Reporter James Crusinberry pointed to the heart of the matter in his arti-cle in the *Tribune* on December 9:

*In an ingenious way Mr. O'Brien also has arranged things so that this game (with the Bears) may be for the championship of the National Pro League. At present the Pottsville, PA team is in front by half a game, and for that reason has ten-tatively been named as the opponent for the Bears on Dec. 20.*

*But Mr. O'Brien has booked a game for Saturday of this week against the Hammond eleven and believes his team will win, thereby getting on even terms with the Pottsville outfit and making it desirable that the Bears meet the south siders for the title.*

On that same day, O'Brien also met personally with C. C. Pyle to petition his cause. While Pyle was receptive to the idea, he deferred any decision to Halas and Sternaman, the owners of the Bears. Without missing a beat, O'Brien surprisingly scheduled still another game, this one for Thursday, December 10. The opponent would be the Milwaukee Badgers, lonesome and disbanded since November 22, but Chicago-based owner Ambrose McGurk agreed to field a team to face the Cardinals on very short notice. While this type of arrangement, especially for a game on a Thursday, should have raised a few eyebrows, the astute *Tribune* explained the situation very carefully for its readers:

*The rules and regulations for scheduling games in the National League of Professional Football Clubs creates the unique possibility of winning a championship after you have been beaten out of it. These rules worked all right until Mr. Grange hopped into the league and turned everything topsy-turvy. Formerly the clubs were satisfied to perform once a week on Sundays and quit when things froze up.*

*The rule reads that each club must play at least eight games against eight different clubs to be eligible for the championship, but any club can play as many games against other league clubs as it desires up to the closing date of Dec. 20. On that date the team with the highest standing is declared the champion.*

*So, while it appeared that the Cardinals lost the title with the game last Sunday, they still can win it by grabbing a couple more victories, providing the Pottsville crowd is content to hang up its football togs and call it a season.*

In Pottsville, the team indeed did believe that its season was over. The fans celebrated the championship by decorating the town, and each of the players was presented with a gold medal honoring him for his achievements. The Maroons accepted an invitation to play an exhibition game in Miami on Christmas Day and also scheduled a highly desirable contest with the Notre Dame All-Stars in Philadelphia on Saturday, December 12.

Back in Chicago, the Cardinals dismantled Milwaukee 59-0 in a game so one-sided that it was ended early. Paddy Driscoll didn't even bother to play, but since the victory was against a league opponent (even if in name only), it boosted the Cardinals into a tie with Pottsville with a 10-2-1 record. Art Folz replaced Driscoll in the lineup, and the Cardinals even brought back old-timer Lenny Sachs for a stint at his favorite end position. Folz enjoyed a remarkable game, scoring on a thirty-yard run, a thirty-seven-yard pass reception, a forty-five-yard blocked punt return, and a fifty-five-yard run.

Yet the game was played under quizzical circumstances. O'Brien was so unsure of the caliber of the opposition that he opened the gates and didn't charge admission, surely an unusual move for a team that existed to make money and still needed to pay its players. Only a few hundred fans showed up and were undoubtedly quickly bored by the caliber of competition.

Although this maneuvering by O'Brien for the championship was perfectly legal, some whispers about the ethics involved were beginning to raise their ugly little heads. The *Tribune,* usually a loyal supporter, was the first to question the tactics:

*Down at the south side another curious angle is developing. After announcing that last Sunday's game with Pottsville would decide the league title, the Cardinals were beaten. The public took them at their word and assumed they had lost the title.*

*Now it seems that the championship game didn't mean anything. Chris O'Brien, with a natural desire to win the title—whatever that means—has scheduled two extra games for his team.*

*One was played yesterday with Milwaukee. Admission was free. But the game was a farce. The Cards won 59-0. It wasn't a football game; it was a practice. Certainly a weird game to base a championship on.*

*Saturday the Cards play again. This time they plan to walk over Hammond and grab another hold on the flag. The game will be better than yesterday's . . . but the*

*motive of the Cardinals is the same. Meanwhile Pottsville is celebrating a title vic-*
*tory . . . they think they've won the league championship. They don't know Mr. O'Brien.*

The Hammond Pros did indeed prove to be a more formidable foe, falling by a
13-0 count on December 12 in front of just twenty-five hundred fans, leaving the
Chicago Cardinals with a record of 11-2-1. On the same day in Philadelphia, the
Pottsville Maroons slipped past the Notre Dame alums 9-7. But since it was a non-
league clash, the Pottsville mark remained at 10-2 and O'Brien indicated to the media
that he would claim the league championship. Even though the season was finally ending, the fun was just beginning.

Before the Pottsville-Notre Dame game had been staged, the Frankford Yellow
Jackets (who also played a home game on December 12 in Philadelphia) complained
to Joe Carr about the intrusion of the Maroons into their area. Since the NFL provided territorial rights to its members at that time, Carr's initial reaction was to warn
Pottsville that if it did indeed play in Philadelphia without permission, the franchise
would face serious consequences. Pottsville went ahead with the game anyway, and
Carr immediately suspended the franchise. If this held true, the Cardinals would log-
ically be recognized as the 1925 league champions, whether or not they played those
two "extra" games.

On Tuesday, December 15, O'Brien and Halas met face-to-face in an attempt to
configure a third game between the two adversaries to be played on December 20.
O'Brien was desperate for the game, while Halas, now enjoying his profits, was planning for a second tour with Grange in the south and west. This encore performance
was set to begin on Friday, December 25, in Coral Gables, Florida, with the team departing from Chicago on December 21. His team, and especially his marquee player,
required rest. The last thing Halas needed at this point was still another game in the
frozen, urban tundra of Chicago. As it was, the two sides were unable to arrive at an
agreement. Perhaps it was the location, perhaps it was the division of the proceeds,
or perhaps it was apparent that Grange would not be able to play anyway, thus dam-
aging the gate potential.

So the two sides parted, Halas walking toward the warm Florida sun with his pock-
ets full. On the other hand, O'Brien's dream of capturing the national pro football
title apparently had been realized, but he had little to show monetarily for this
accomplishment.

## Sunk Into A Mire Of Scandal

Shortly after walking out of the disappointing meeting with Halas, the downtrodden
O' Brien received even more bad news. Newspapers around the country would break
the story that four players from Chicago's Englewood High School had been in the
lineup for the Milwaukee Badgers when they lost to the Cardinals on December 10.
This situation deflated the recent adulation of the pro game prompted by the appearance of Grange and the increased visibility of the NFL. But even that worthy endeavor
was struggling with the insinuations prompted by Grange's inability to play throughout the entire tour and the disintegrating performances by the Bears in its waning days
Word was also leaking out of St. Louis that the all-star team that represented that city

on the first stop of the tour included a college freshman—a frightening prospect to those in the anti-professional camp.

But the Englewood situation was worse, much worse. The scandal surrounding the use of young babes by the pros in their greedy, filthy world was appalling to the average citizen. Its final disposition would affect not only the Cardinals, but also professional football as a whole. The first question to be answered was "How in the world could this have happened?"

The *Tribune,* which had begun pecking away at the Cardinals' reputation when the extra games were scheduled, now opened up its investigation of the event full throttle:

> *Professional football, which rose to the heights of public favor less than four weeks ago with the acquisition of Red Grange to its membership, yesterday sunk into a mire of scandal with the confession of four Englewood High School boys that they had been induced to play with the Milwaukee club of the National Pro league in its farcical game against the Cardinals on Thursday of last week at the White Sox ball park.*

The four players were Bill Thompson, Jack Daniels, James Snyder, and Charles Richardson. During the game against the Cardinals, the four used the misnomers of Blood, Mooney, Mason, and Grant as they helped fill out the depleted Milwaukee roster. The only problem was that while the players could conceal their names, they were unable to hide their faces (despite being smeared with mud) and they were easily recognized by fans at the game, some of whom were graduates of Englewood. These fans contacted Englewood school officials who then turned the investigation over to E. C. Delaporte, supervisor of athletics for the Chicago public schools.

## *They Say They Got No Money*

When the four players confessed to their participation in the game, they were immediately declared ineligible for further high school athletic competition by Delaporte on December 16. Even though they apparently did not receive payment for playing, they were considered professionals by Delaporte because they violated a rule that prohibited prep players from competing in organized games with athletes over the age of twenty-one. Delaporte moved quickly and defiantly:

> *I felt the best thing to do was to clean it up at any cost. I can't understand what induced these boys to do such a thing. They say they got no money, but they are not dumb and surely know that they cannot play with professionals or even with players who are more than 21 years of age.*
>
> *I understand these boys expected to attend college and this may bar them from partaking in athletics. There was nothing for us to do but declare them professionals and make them ineligible. Their only chance for reinstatement would be by the board of control. If that body would be convinced that the boys were blameless, I might reinstate them.*

Even as the swift punishment was administered by Delaporte, too many questions remained. How did they learn about the game? Who enticed them to play? And why did they play if they were aware of the possible drastic circumstances in effect at the time? The punishment not only made them ineligible for any further high school sports, but also would follow them to the next level where no college or university would allow them to play either. The decision was devastating to all four, but especially to All-City senior players Thompson and Richardson, who were certainly collegiate-caliber players. In addition, they would be ineligible for other sports.

Now that the school system had acted, fingers began waving at the only three parties who might have been responsible for the recruitment of the players: Ambrose McGurk, owner of the Badgers; Cardinal player Art Folz, who also played at Englewood; and Chris O'Brien, who arranged the game. Suspicions also hovered around Cardinals Wilfrid Smith and Bob Koehler, who were also football coaches in the public league and who might have been able to recognize the high school players. O'Brien was the first to assert his innocence:

> *I know absolutely nothing about the make up of the Milwaukee team and supposed I was playing the best team they could assemble of their regular players. It may be that one of my players had something to do in inducing the high school boys to take part, but if so, I knew nothing about it.*

## They Seemed To Think It Would Be Quite A Stunt

Both O'Brien and Folz vowed to do whatever they could to proclaim the innocence of the "Englewood Four" and to ensure that their eligibility was restored. McGurk was nowhere to be found. In the end, Folz shouldered most of the blame and insisted that O'Brien had nothing to do with securing the high school players:

> *I am willing to take all of the blame in this prep mix-up. First I want to clear those Englewood boys of any blame and get them reinstated, and, second, I want to clear Chris O'Brien of any part in it.*
>
> *When Mr. O'Brien feared McGurk wouldn't be able to assemble a complete team for this game, I immediately thought of a lot of football players in Chicago who might fill in. Never once did I think of going to high school players. On Tuesday, two days before the game, I just happened to drop into the Englewood High School to chat with the boys. The idea came to me then of taking some of those kids into this game, because at the time I was under the impression that it was to be a game with no spectators and no admission and for that reason I thought it wouldn't affect their amateur standing.*
>
> *I mentioned it and they were eager to play. They seemed to think it would be quite a stunt, never realizing the danger I was putting them in. I promised to take them and did so. When we got to the park, I told Mr. O'Brien I had some men to give to McGurk and I took them out to the clubhouse where the players were dressing. McGurk had turned over several Milwaukee jerseys to me and I distributed them to the boys, then turned them over to McGurk, and never thought anything more about it. I was somewhat surprised to see there was quite a crowd of spectators at the game. But even then I failed to realize the danger in which I had placed the high school boys.*
>
> *Now that it has come out and these boys have been declared ineligible by the school authorities, I am heart-broken over it and would do anything in the world to get them back, because these boys were blameless in the affair. So was Chris O'Brien. I made the big mistake.*

O'Brien's statement to the *Tribune* was equally contrite:

> *No one is as sorry over what happened to those four Englewood high school boys as I am, and I want to give my story to the public and am willing to take my share of the blame, because I will admit selfishness on my part.*
>
> *I was selfish, perhaps, because I wanted another game with the Bears. I had-n't experienced a very good year (i.e. financially). I saw the chance of getting even with such a game. I expected to get it by beating Pottsville in our game with them Dec. 6. But we were beaten.*
>
> *It looked as if my chance for the Bears game was gone. But according to our rules any team can schedule games up to Dec. 20 and they count in the standing. I was only a half game behind. The Bears were scheduling of lot of extra games. I thought of McGurk, the manager of the Milwaukee team. He lived in Chicago and I hunted him up. I suggested a Thursday game and he was willing.*
>
> *We booked the game. The next day or so I remarked: "I wonder if McGurk will come through with a team all right." That remark was overheard by one of my players, Art Folz. He said perhaps he could pick up some players if extras were needed.*
>
> *I paid no more attention to it. I left matters to McGurk . . . Shortly before game time Art Folz appeared with four players. I hadn't any idea who they were. I was eager for the game. Perhaps Folz did introduce me to the boys but their names meant nothing to me. I didn't give them jerseys to wear.*
>
> *Just before time to start, I learned that there were high school amateurs on the Milwaukee team. Now I know the mistake I made was in not canceling the game right then. But there were several hundred people out there to see the game. Things were moving fast. I didn't sit down and think it out carefully. Probably I thought the best way was to go ahead and play the game, thinking that the high school boys never would be caught. Anyway, I didn't stop it.*
>
> *I have written our president, Mr. Carr, in Columbus about it. Naturally I wish to do anything I can to square these schoolboys. I have always tried to give the public square football. I am willing to do anything to save those schoolboys and put professional football in the right light.*

O'Brien made a couple of crucial statements here. He admitted that he was not in a good financial position and that his goal was to secure another game with the Bears. His other critical comment was the admission that he was aware prior to the kickoff that there were high school players on the field. Admitting this error in judgment placed him in further jeopardy with the NFL.

Following the meeting at the *Tribune* offices, Delaporte announced that he was "convinced of the sincerity of the two men." He was also satisfied that the four high school players had not been paid to play in the game, but rules had been broken on all sides: the players for participating in the game, Folz for recruiting them, and O'Brien for allowing the game to be played when he knew that the prep players were present. O'Brien still faced an NFL inquiry, as well as one by the Chicago White Sox. Team Secretary Harry Grabiner vowed that the Cardinals would never again play in Comiskey Park if O'Brien had any role in recruiting the players, while the NFL indicated that the Cardinals would be fined heavily if there was any evidence of tampering with high school athletes. As it turned out, the entire Milwaukee team was apparently made up of ringers, stated the *American:*

*It was reported that only the captain of the Milwaukee squad had come to Chicago and the rest of the men had been recruited on the South Side.*

While the meeting at the *Tribune* cleared the air, it didn't settle anything. The high school players were still ineligible and O'Brien had not been exonerated by any means. But the meeting did create a public groundswell of support for the players. Hundreds of letters were received by school authorities, reported the *Tribune:*

*The boys seem to have the universal sympathy of Chicago, especially when it has been clearly established that they received no money and thought they were simply in a practice game.*

The *Daily News* added:

*While many persons believe that the players knew what they were doing when they played in the game, the general opinion is that the sentence is far too severe.*

## Dad, I Thought I'd Learn Something About Football

Soon, the parents of the players became involved and demanded to meet directly with Chicago Public Schools Superintendent McAndrew, according to Harry Neily of the *American:*

*They allege that their sons were inveigled into a false situation by bogus promises and that they had no idea that their actions had any bearing on their amateur standing. "My son," Mr. Roy Snyder says, "was visited by Art Folz, who used to be a star football player at Englewood High School. He represented that the Cardinal football team needed practice and wished to have that kind of session behind closed gates. He assured my son that his amateur standing would be involved in no way. Consequently, he consented to play along with young Daniels, Thompson and Richardson. My son is less than 17 years old.*

*"After all the so-called scandal I asked the boy why he played. 'Why,' he replied, 'Folz asked me to and, dad, I thought I'd learn something about football from practicing with the older men. It was only a practice game and nothing ever was said about money.'*

*"However, I do not believe that my son and the three other lads involved should be sacrificed for something that was done by a promoter and without their knowledge. The boys were indiscreet—that we all admit—but they did not go out and sell their football services for so much money."*

The next step was an appearance by the players in front of the high school athletic board on Wednesday, December 23, two days after the jovial Bears, bolstered by the addition of the Cardinals Ralph Claypool and Swede Erickson, left for the team's second tour. This would be a leisurely, six-week swing through the South and then on to California. Having learned from the rigors of the first expedition, the Bears spread out their games and added players. It was agreed that if Grange was incapacitated, the tour would be canceled. The Bears would proceed to play nine games between December 25 and January 31, winning eight of them. While the crowds were not always spectacular, another record was set in Los Angeles when seventy-five thousand were on hand to watch Grange and the Bears battle the Los Angeles Tigers.

## *High School Boys Have Committed Graver Sins*

As the Bears headed south, Chris O'Brien traveled East, this time for a visit to NFL President Joe Carr in Columbus, Ohio. Once again, O'Brien explained his actions, but Carr insisted that he would not act until the high school board in Chicago had finalized its decision on December 23. After day-long deliberations, the board of control delivered a shocking decision: the Englewood players were found guilty of violating the rules of amateur sport for playing against professionals and were barred permanently from high school athletics. This decision would no doubt collapse any of their hopes for playing sports in college as well. One piece of evidence that surfaced was that the players themselves used their fake names when reporting to the officials. Neither the testimony of the players, their fathers, Folz, or O'Brien could sway the thinking of the twenty-four board members. The event was labeled as a "trial," and the board members clamored for the spotlight against the teenagers. James Crusinberry wrote of the spectacle in the *Tribune:*

> When those lads stood up before them to tell their story not one of them had half finished before he was interrupted. First one and then another of the board cross questioned the boys. They pointed the finger of guilt at the lads like a prosecuting attorney. One man even went so far as to cite the case of Leopold and Loeb in drawing a comparison, but he was quickly hushed with a remark that he was getting away from athletics.

In the *American,* Guy High complained:

> It was evident from the beginning to the spectators that the lads were in for it . . . Yards of red tape were reeled out and then in again. Objections, out of order rulings and other technicalities popped up and had to be settled. Talk of "passing the buck" almost threatened to swamp the whole business . . . Then the wheels began grinding. The four offenders, silent and uncomfortable, were brought in and lined up against the wall in the manner of men brought before a firing squad.

The verdict prompted pleas for leniency for the boys, as well for changes in the confusing world of amateur athletics. In his editorial, *Tribune* sports editor Don Maxwell wrote:

> The board was as drastic in its ruling as it might have been had the boys been paid to play and had they played with their eyes open to the consequences. It was the board's task to fix the penalty and doubtless it acted with sincerity. We do call attention to these facts:
>     The present rules of amateurism are as farcical as that game in which the Englewood boys played. Amateurs in golf make more money than pros . . . amateurs in tennis live in luxury . . .
>     In conclusion, we beg to suggest to the athletic board that leniency is sometimes a virtue. High school boys have committed graver sins than playing for nothing in what they believed was a practice game.

## *The NFL Takes A Stand*

One week later, on December 29, Joe Carr completed his investigation of the incident and was equally harsh. Although it was never proved that O'Brien played a role in the actual recruitment of the players, he was placed on probation for one year and fined $1,000, a stiff fee in 1925. O'Brien's excellent reputation and his early admission of his non-participatory role in the scandal probably spared him the fate handed out to McGurk. The Milwaukee owner was fined $500 and expelled from the league. Carr ordered McGurk to dispose of his team's assets within ninety days. Finally, Art Folz, who attempted to save the athletic careers of his former schoolmates by admitting his sins, was "barred forever from playing in the national football league" according to Carr.

The result of the game with Milwaukee was ordered to be removed from the Cardinals' record, which would have left the team with a 10-2-1 standing compared to Pottsville's 10-2 mark. However, that assignment was never carried out and the victory over the Badgers remains on the books to this day. The *Pro Football Encyclopedia* even lists the four Englewood players as members of the 1925 Milwaukee Badger roster.

Following the NFL's ruling, Chicago City Council swept into action on behalf of the prep players. On January 6, 1926, the politicos passed the following resolution:

> *WHEREAS, It has come to the attention of the City Council that the Professional Football league has strongly condemned the action of the managers of two professional football teams on permitting four Englewood High School boys, who were recently suspended from further amateur athletic competition by the High School Athletic Committee of the Chicago High Schools, to participate in a purported football contest; and*

> *WHEREAS, The City Council is in accord with the action of the Professional Football League in its protection of both amateur and professional football players; and*

> *WHEREAS, The City Council feels that professional football playing as an established project is in its infancy; and*

> *WHEREAS, The majority of amateur players have not become sufficiently imbued with the spirit of the organization and protection of both amateur and professional football players; and*

> *WHEREAS, The City Council feels that the above mentioned four boys were not cognizant of the gravity of the conduct in participating in the aforementioned professional football contest, be it*

> *RESOLVED, That the Athletic Board of Control of the Chicago High Schools be requested to grant to the four Englewood High School boys a rehearing of their case with a view of reducing the harsh penalties imposed upon them and having them reinstated to their amateur standing and permitted to participate in future athletic contests.*

> *Unanimous consent. The motion prevailed.*

There was one other announcement from Carr on December 29, 1925. The NFL president also fined Pottsville $500 and revoked the team's franchise for playing against the Notre Dame All-Stars on December 12. The game was played in Philadelphia, violating the territorial rights of the Frankford Yellow Jackets. This decision ignited another firestorm of controversy in Pottsville that has yet to subside.

It also made the Cardinals' scheduling of the Milwaukee and Hammond games moot in terms of seeking victories in order to claim the championship (which was secondary to O'Brien's quest for another game with the Bears). Pottsville surrendered its right to any title since it was no longer officially a member of the league. However, that did not sway Pottsville residents from claiming, to this day, that the Maroons were the rightful owner of the 1925 title. Beginning with local sports editor Walter S. Farquhar, who penned a lengthy ode to the alleged champions (sampled at the beginning of this chapter), Pottsville followers have sought salvation in the form of a restructuring of the final standings from the 1925 NFL season. In 1962, at the request of "the citizens of Schuylkill County," the NFL established a committee to study this issue, but recommended no changes in the final 1925 results.

The wackiness at the conclusion of the 1925 season obscured what was a great season for the Cardinals. Driscoll and Claypool were named to the first team "All-League" honor squad, and Paddy booted a record eleven field goals and scored sixty-seven points, to achieve the second-best record in the circuit.

## Championship Voted To The Chicago Cardinals

The business of the 1925 season came to a close at the NFL meetings in February of 1926 when the teams attempted to patch up the pro game's reputation by unanimously agreeing that no collegiate player could join a league team until that player's class had graduated. There would no longer be any Red Grange-type midseason disruptions. The league also upheld Carr's actions regarding the fines of O'Brien and McGurk in the Englewood High School situation and supported his ousting of Pottsville for infringing on Frankford's territorial rights. As usual, the members voted on the league champion and awarded it to the Chicago Cardinals. The *Tribune* reported that "The championship of the 1925 season was voted to the Chicago Cardinals, but Chris O'Brien, head of the club, refused to accept the title. He explained the Cardinals had been tied by the Pottsville eleven, and that the Chicago club wanted only a title won on the playing field." O'Brien apparently was referring to the twin 10-2 marks of the two teams with the Cardinals' victory over Milwaukee subtracted (which it never was). So, although the Cardinals never fully "accepted" the championship nod, they are rightly listed as the 1925 champions, both on the basis of the best record, as well as by the termination of the Pottsville franchise.

For Chris O'Brien, the extended 1925 campaign could now be put to rest. His Cardinals, whom he had guided from the early days as the Morgan Athletic Association to the Cardinal Athletic Club to the Racine Cardinals, were now toasted and recognized as the best professional football team in the United States of America. He created it, he nursed it, he fought for it. But he couldn't toast it. He couldn't afford it.

# Chris O'Brien's Pockets

Eventually Chris O'Brien's fine was rescinded when it was never proved that O'Brien had any connection whatsoever with the recruitment of the Englewood players. His only crime appeared to be that of playing the Milwaukee game when he was aware of the presence of the high school players. His excellent reputation and integrity probably led to the easing of the penalty, for O'Brien had long been regarded as a class act.

An interesting story about O'Brien's ethical nature surfaced in 1997. In his book **Pro Football in the Days of Rockne,** football historian Emil Klosinski described a road trip to Chicago by the South Bend Arrows in the pre-NFL days. A player named Paster Sobieralski related this story to Klosinski:

> "We had a game scheduled in Chicago in 1919 or 1920 in late November against the Cardinals. Whether they were called Cardinals or Normals then, I can't remember, but I do know we played on the South Side on Normal Field.
>
> We took the South Shore Line from South Bend early in the morning. It began snowing late Saturday night and continued on into Sunday. As we boarded the South Shore train, it still wasn't too bad, but while on our way, the snow storm turned into a blowing blizzard. As we arrived in Chicago, there were snow drifts piled up ten feet high in some places. Nothing was operating—we couldn't get a taxi or a street car. So we slung our uniforms over our shoulders and hiked to Normal Field, fighting the blizzard and the blustering winds. We got there about an hour before game time, but it was obvious that no game could be played that day. Our manager told us to wait by the locked gate and soon a representative of the Cardinals showed up. He said he had sent us a telegram early in the morning, but it apparently didn't arrive before we left South Bend. Without a whimper though, he said, "Well, I guess you're here to play, and the only fair thing to do is to pay you the guarantee." The guarantee was $700, and we got every penny of it. From our past experiences we didn't expect this. We were actually hoping we could get them out on the field so that we could claim a guarantee, but they paid without any fuss. This was really unusual in those days. These guys were really big time."

In 1997, Klosinski noted: "I later learned after publication, that the Cardinal official who was so generous with the guarantee was Chris O' Brien."

The money came out of his own pocket.

## ♦ 6 ♦

# The Roaring Twenties:
# 1926 – 1929

*"I believe the South Side will support winning football
and I'm going to give 'em that or bust."*

DR. DAVID JONES
OWNER, CHICAGO CARDINALS, 1929

### New Year's Day, 1926

Although Chris O'Brien had survived the Englewood escapade with his franchise intact and without being fully implicated in any recruitment of the high school players, there was still a possibility of further league ramifications at the next NFL meeting in February. It would be a long, cold January. But on these quiet winter days, when the snow and the cold combine to distract one's attention in Chicago, O'Brien was probably thinking, "Things can only get better from here on out."

The Bears continued to bask in the warmth of Florida and defeated a team called the Tampa Cardinals 17-3 on New Year's Day. The Tampa team included the aging Jim Thorpe, who was enticed down to Florida to face the Bears with a little money and a lot of sunshine. On January 2, the Bears moved over to Jacksonville and defeated the Jacksonville All-Stars 19-6 in a game that featured the professional debut of Ernie Nevers, the one player considered to be Grange's equal during the 1925 collegiate season. In a two-day period, the Bears faced Thorpe and Nevers, the two men who are now considered the best players of their generation. From there, the Bears moved to New Orleans, Los Angeles, San Francisco, Portland, and Seattle. Each stop was widely chronicled by the Chicago press, who gave the Bears front page coverage in the middle of another harsh winter. For O'Brien, it was time to lay low and begin preparing for the defense of his title.

As the Bears barnstormed across the country, they harvested the profits that went along with the newfound popularity of pro football. Yet the glamour, visibility, and dollars garnered in so short a time by Grange apparently were not enough for his manager C. C. Pyle. While carrying on negotiations for another season with the Bears, he was also quietly investigating other lucrative offers and secretly considering other options in pro football, including the creation of his own league with Grange as the headliner.

### The Iceman Has Probably Received $100,000 Cash

As soon as the Bears arrived back in Chicago on Thursday, February 4, Halas and Sternaman quickly unpacked and made plans to attend the league meetings in Detroit beginning on February 6. But during the tour, it became apparent that Grange might not even be the best player on his own team. Although Grange will always be regarded as a gifted athlete, many observers found little (5'6", 152 pounds) Joey Sternaman to be the better football player for the Bears. In referring to Grange at the conclusion of the tour, Don Maxwell of the *Tribune* commented:

> *The Iceman probably has received $100,000 cash since leaving school. This is not the half million which Pyle forecast Red would make, but it's more than the Wheaton boy could have made in any other business in the same period.*
>
> *As a football player, heralded as the greatest of all time, Grange has proved a failure. Little Joe Sternaman has out starred him in every game they've played. But as a gate attraction Red can be said to have been a winner.*
>
> *We're wondering what sort of an attraction he'll be next fall.*

In Chicago, Pyle was finalizing a lucrative movie offer for Grange, estimated to be worth another $300,000. The plethora of contracts, plans, and gimmicks clearly predicted that Pyle was headed in only one direction—to the bank—while his money tree in the person of Grange was still productive. It was also becoming obvious that the agreement with the Bears would be short lived. Pyle figured that if he had the player, why did he need the Bears?

On February 5, the *Tribune* reported on Pyle's future football plans:

> *The success of his football tour has convinced Grange and his manager that another season will be every bit as profitable. What they have in mind is a team to be known as the Grange All Stars and according to Pyle, an effort will be made to acquire a franchise in the National Pro League. To this end the pair plan on attending the league meeting at Detroit tomorrow.*
>
> *There have been stories that a pro eleven would be placed in the Yankee Stadium, New York, next fall, and there is a bare possibility that Grange and Pyle may have their eyes on that spot. If unable to acquire a park for their home, the team will be entered as a traveling organization.*

Things began to heat up as the league representatives met in Detroit during the first week of February, 1926. While the league initiated some normal business, such as increasing the team rosters from sixteen to eighteen, limiting games to two a week (except for holidays), and raising the price of a franchise to $2,500, the sting from the conclusion of the 1925 season needed to be addressed and rectified in order to maintain some public respect in the future. President Carr, never shrinking from his duty, quickly expelled the Pottsville Maroons. The *Canton Repository* stated:

> *The Pottsville Maroons, who tied with the Chicago Cardinals last Fall, were ruled out of the league for infractions of the territorial rules . . . No championship was awarded, as Chris O'Brien, head of the Cardinals, refused to accept it after Pottsville had been ousted.*

It is unclear what O'Brien refused to accept, since the league no longer presented a cup to the champion. And O'Brien could not refuse the championship itself, since he had no choice: the Cardinals were the 1925 champions despite the unusual circumstances. The league upheld Carr's earlier decision to fine both the Cardinals and the Milwaukee Badgers and to dissolve the Milwaukee franchise, which was on its way to disappearing anyway.

The league also closed its loophole concerning the potentially massive problem of teams recruiting college players immediately after they had completed their last games as amateurs. This rule was designated to forbid any repeat of the active recruitment of a player such as Red Grange, which certainly helped increase the prestige—and bank accounts—of the league members, but was perceived as an undisguised whack in the face by colleges and universities. It was time for the league to patrol itself on this sensitive issue, and again it was President Carr who pulled out the leash and went looking for strays. The new mandates were intended to leave the seniors alone until their respective classes actually graduated.

Carr also wisely perceived the need to become more harmonious with his collegiate brethren. The evil glow of the professionals still existed in the minds of many educators, and the hijacking of Grange before his graduation seemed to stagger those who strongly believed that the sole purpose of a university was to provide a quality education and not an athletic cashbox. For precisely this reason, Carr appointed George Halas as the frontman of a committee to meet with Brigadier General Palmer A. Pierce, the president of the Intercollegiate Athletic Union. This committee would seek to heal the wounds that erupted over the recent signing of college players and to agree on cooperative regulations regarding the recruitment of college players *after* their graduation. The NFL draft was still a decade away, but the NFL hoped that these initial talks between Halas and Pierce would be mutually beneficial and allow no further deterioration of the NFL's reputation.

## *There Is Room For Two Teams In New York*

Halas was beginning to feel the heat as well after basking in the warmth of financial success following the 1925 season. C. C. Pyle envisioned his window of opportunity opening wider if he could slip outside the restraints of Grange's agreement with the Bears. At the league meeting, Grange slammed the hood down on his career with the Bears by applying (along with Pyle) for his own NFL franchise in New York. The pair apparently agreed to a five-year lease of Yankee Stadium and outlined plans for a lucrative franchise in the country's largest market. However, the lease would not kick in unless the Grange All-Star team was awarded an NFL franchise.

The only problem was that the New York Giants club was already firmly in place and league officials were well aware of Joe Carr's stance on territorial rights. This proposal could work, but only if the Giants agreed to share the city with another league franchise, much as the Bears and Cardinals coexisted in Chicago. However, the Giants remained mum. Pyle argued fruitlessly for the Giants' support. "There is room for two teams in New York, just as there are two teams in Chicago," he pleaded. As Grange and Pyle watched, their dollar-coated vision of representing the league in New York became dimmer, yet this issue was far from over. Pyle managed to convince nineteen of the twenty team representatives to allow his proposed team to settle in Yankee Stadium.

The Giants were the lone dissident, but that was the vote that counted the most, and the franchise was denied. An obviously embittered Pyle vowed after the meeting that he would have a football team in New York that year even "if we have to form our own league." Pyle had done his homework, and planned immediately to organize a new pro football circuit. Within two days, Pyle hinted that he had already established solid interests from eight teams, although he would limit the conference to twelve cities. It looked like a win-win situation for Pyle and his league members. The teams would have access to the healthy gate attraction in Grange, and Pyle would have access to his own healthy franchise without needing to share the profits with another partner. Everyone would be happy.

The timing was bad for the NFL. The loss of Grange would certainly hurt, and there was a real possibility that Pyle's new venture could fly. After all, the NFL wasn't exactly stable in 1926. It was bloated with about twenty franchises, there was still no fixed means for determining the championship, and scheduling difficulties had disturbed franchises in smaller cities. As an example, from 1921 through 1925, the Cardinals played fifty-five games recognized by the league. Of those fifty-five games, only one (Canton, 1923) was played outside of Chicago. Except for an occasional venture to visit the Bears, the Cardinals usually played every single game at home. While the Cardinals usually met the visitor's guarantee, the lack of travel before the game might be deemed an advantage for O'Brien's team on the field.

It was apparent that there was a further need for stabilization well before the start of the 1926 NFL season. On paper, the owners would lose a great deal of prestige and dollars by not admitting Grange and Pyle to the league, but the establishment of such rules was one of the primary reasons for the league's existence. In order to survive, the NFL might be required to tighten its reins even further and perhaps abandon some shaky franchise loyalties in return for a more secure future.

## O'Brien's Blues

Despite the success of the 1925 team, Chris O'Brien continued to battle the one opponent that he could neither meet, nor beat, on the playing field: money.

Back in 1899, the game of football was simply that—a game. O'Brien, his brother Pat, and their friends could experience the joy of playing this strange, intriguing game. They could boast of their victories, brag about their injuries and, for a few moments, they could escape a somewhat dreary existence on the South Side of Chicago and experience the flow and joy of the simple pleasures of competition.

But now, the Cardinals were a business, a profession, and an organization that needed capital to survive. Chris O'Brien began to actively search out possible partners or buyers for the team. His tackle, Fred Gillies, was one of the first to be offered the ownership of the Cardinals by O'Brien, according to Gillies's nephew Fred Jaicks. "My uncle lived with us back then," remembered Jaicks, "and I remember him saying throughout the years that Chris O'Brien had offered the Cardinals to him. However, he was just getting started in the steel business and he didn't want the risk of owning a football team at that time." Gillies's decision was a sound one; he went on to become the President of Acme Steel on the far South Side of Chicago.

With finances already a concern and the draining events of late 1925 still occupying him, O'Brien was dealt another crunching blow when Grange and Pyle quickly proceeded with plans to form a second professional league to compete directly with the NFL. A meeting was called in Chicago on February 17 to discuss possibilities with interested parties. From this meeting, the American Football League was born, sired by the indomitable package of Grange and Pyle. Grange would be the marquee name for the league with his own franchise, the New York Yankees. In March, former Princeton standout William "Big Bill" Edwards was selected by Pyle to serve as league president. Edwards promised that his league would not touch high school or college players, and announced a league slogan of "football for all and all for football." The league then began courting members for this new endeavor, and Pyle himself personally petitioned O'Brien and the Cardinals to join as one of the Chicago franchises. No doubt Pyle promised riches and glory to the NFL champs, but O'Brien steadfastly retained his loyalty to the National Football League. In his book *Pro Football: Its Ups and Downs*, Dr. Harry March lauded O'Brien:

> *Chris O'Brien, of the Chicago Cardinals, stuck to the old league when every possible financial inducement was made to have him desert to the new outlaws. His loyalty and stability under the stress, in my opinion, have never been thoroughly appreciated by the team owners or by the public.*

## The Situation Caused Me Heartache

When it was announced that the American Football League had established a franchise in town called the Chicago Bulls, both the Bears and the Cardinals were jarred. The Bears were affected since the owner and manager of the Bulls, as well as the new league's secretary, was former Bear Joey Sternaman, brother of Halas's long-time partner Edward (Dutch) Sternaman. This cost the Bears their most valuable offensive weapon. The appearance of the Bulls seemed to instigate a rift between Halas and Dutch Sternaman. During the league meetings in July of 1926 in Philadelphia the two partners openly disagreed about scheduling, much to the chagrin of Carr. The league representatives then were forced to "elect" Halas as the Bears' spokesman so that the meetings could continue. Halas recalled the strain precipitated by the new league and Joey Sternaman's involvement with that organization:

> *The situation created considerable ill-will between Dutch and me. Dutch offered to sell me his half of the club. How I wish I had bought him out at once!*
> *The situation caused me heartache. Dutch, Joey and I had gone through hard times together. Now, when prosperity was here, we were divided. I was finding adversity more pleasant than prosperity.*

The *Chicago Tribune* provided further insight:

> *The disagreement between Halas and Sternaman over the dates is said to have centered on whether the Bears would play the Cardinals on October 17 and Thanksgiving Day as they have in the past. Halas said "Yes." Sternaman said "No."*
> *Football fans see in Sternaman's stand a desire to protect the interests of his brother, Joey. The latter is the announced owner and manager of the Chicago Bulls, the newly organized pro team in Pyle's league. And, so the fans learned, Joe is planning to play Red Grange's New York team on October 17 and Wilson's roving*

*eleven on Thanksgiving Day. In event the Bears and Cardinals were playing on the same dates the attendance at the White Sox ball park, where Joe's team will play, would be reduced materially.*

*The pro grid fans are wondering what attitude Ed Sternaman, loser in the schedule battle, will take. Some believe that he will withdraw from the part ownership in the Bears, selling his interest, in order that he may openly back his brother.*

On the other side of town, Joey Sternaman caught Chris O'Brien off guard and snagged the lease for White Sox Park, sending the Cardinals scurrying for a place to play their 1926 home schedule. O'Brien had traditionally remitted his rent for the facility to coincide with a percentage of the gate. Pyle and Sternaman negotiated a more financially appealing fixed payment for the use of the stadium that O'Brien could not match. Perhaps the White Sox were also willing to barter in an effort to distance themselves from the Englewood High School situation that occurred on their field the previous season. The only viable alternative for O'Brien was to return to the much smaller Normal Park, at 61st and Racine, which the Cardinals had abandoned earlier in the decade except for early-season games when Comiskey Park was unavailable. This move to Normal Park, with its much smaller capacity, would significantly hinder the gate receipts for the already struggling team.

## His Financial Outlook Was Dismal

With retreating financial sources and increasing expenses, O'Brien was forced to make the one move he had hoped he would never need to make. With great sorrow, he sold the contract of the popular and entertaining Paddy Driscoll to the crosstown rival Chicago Bears for $3,500. "His financial outlook was dismal," said Halas. "He had to cut expenses. The most expensive player was Paddy Driscoll, and common sense told Chris that Paddy deserved a raise, not a cut."

Joey Sternaman was also in on the bidding for Driscoll and offered a significant increase over what he was making with the Cardinals (believed to be about $500 per game) to join the Chicago Bulls. Halas intensified his efforts to ink Driscoll. After losing both Grange and Sternaman from his 1925 team, Halas needed both a gate attraction as well as a threatening offensive presence on the field. Driscoll provided both and found himself in the driver's seat during a summer of negotiations. The other very real threat to both Halas and O'Brien was that the combination of both Sternaman and Driscoll in the same backfield for the Chicago Bulls could adversely affect the box office for both of the existing NFL teams in town. On September 9, the *Tribune* updated the situation:

*Paddy Driscoll, Chicago's premier pro grid performer for the past five years, is debating today whether to sign a contract with Joe Sternaman's newly organized pro eleven in Grange's American League, or to remain with the old organization, the National League and play with the Chicago Bears, the Halas-Ed Sternaman north side combination.*

*It has been known definitely for several weeks that Driscoll would not play this season with Chris O'Brien's Cardinals, the team which he has captained for six seasons. Feeling that he could not meet Driscoll's salary demands, O'Brien sold*

> *Driscoll's contract to the Chicago Bears, and that club has been endeavoring to get Paddy's signature attached to the dotted line for the coming season.*
>
> *In the meanwhile, Joey Sternaman, player-manager of the Chicago Bulls . . . has endeavored to sign the former Northwestern luminary. It is said that the Bulls, with apparent financial abandon, have offered Driscoll a sum considerably above $5,000 for this season. The Bears also have made Driscoll a lucrative offer. And that is where the matter now rests.*

That unfortunate, albeit necessary, Driscoll transaction seemed to signify the beginning of a downward spiral for the Cardinals that unfortunately would linger for the next two decades. Driscoll had been the heart and soul of the Cardinals since the inception of the NFL; he would be missed not only for his obvious talent, but for his leadership as well. He was a team player whose patience and thoughtfulness would become his trademarks in a long career with the Bears, which continued long after the infamous trade in 1926. Driscoll played with the Bears until the 1930 season, then rejoined the club as a coach in 1941. He stayed with the team in various capacities into the 1960s.

Thus the Cardinals' ecstasy from the 1925 championship was short lived. Within a matter of months, the team had been fined heavily, lost its stadium lease and best player, and was now faced with still another rival in a city that was already tilting its favor towards the Bears. Halas also was suffering through the beginning of his bitter breakup with Dutch Sternaman that eventually would leave him groping for the means to buy out his former partner and friend.

At the July meeting, some significant work was accomplished by the NFL. The league awarded franchises to Hartford, CT; Brooklyn, NY; and, surprisingly, to Los Angeles. It also reinstated Pottsville and Racine (WI) and accepted the resignations of Cleveland, Minneapolis, and New Britain, CT. Dr. J. K. Striegel and his Pottsville club were hit with a stiff $2,500 fine as part of the reinstatement process. A tentative league schedule was developed and included the innovative technique of establishing both a beginning (September 19) and an end (December 17) to the season. This would circumvent any future controversies regarding the scheduling of games long after the prearranged schedule had concluded. The new Louisville franchise would be coached by ex-Cardinal Lenny Sachs. It would, however, enjoy only a brief existence, falling out of the league after just four games—all shutout losses.

## Driscoll Became The First To Profit From The War

Meanwhile, the AFL was quickly gearing up for its debut with nine teams scattered around the country. In addition to the franchises in Chicago and New York, Pyle lined up clubs in Boston, Brooklyn, Newark, and Philadelphia. A team also appeared in Cleveland, which looked awfully similar to the recently disbanded NFL Cleveland Bulldogs. The Rock Island Independents switched from the NFL to the AFL, and the final entry was a wandering team out of Los Angeles paced by Wildcat Wilson from the University of Washington.

Several NFL players shifted to the AFL, the most prominent being Joey Sternaman. Perhaps all were looking for the quick riches or increased notoriety that were assumed to be headed the way of anyone involved in a league that featured the irrepressible Red Grange. Most of the activity for the new league focused on the New York Yankees, who opened up their training camp in Aurora, Illinois, on September 8. Pyle began prospecting for players for the Yankees and latched on to some nuggets in All-Americans Eddie Tryon from Columbia, Pooley Hubert from Alabama, and Iowa's Wes Fry. All would join Grange in the backfield. Perhaps as an incentive to not join the new league, Art Folz received a letter on September 7 that reinstated him as an NFL player. Folz had been banished for life for his role in the recruitment of the four Englewood High School players in 1925. However, Folz never did appear in a Cardinals uniform, apparently choosing to retire from football. Along the way, O'Brien's $1,000 fine from the 1925 fiasco was also rescinded, which would have been encouraging news for the cash-strapped O' Brien.

On September 9, Driscoll finally signed to play sixteen games with the Bears for a reported $10,000. With this startling contract, Driscoll became the first—and perhaps the only—person to profit from the war between the two leagues. With Driscoll joining the Bears in training at Cubs Park, Chicago now had a total of four professional teams in session in the Chicago area. The Bulls were training at White City (63rd and South Park) on the South Side, the Yankees at Exposition Park in Aurora, and the Cardinals at the familiar confines of Normal Park on the South Side.

Without Driscoll, the Cardinals were not exactly barren. They still retained a potent backfield with Red Dunn, Ike Mahoney, Hal "Swede" Erickson, and veteran Bob Koehler. In addition, O'Brien signed Roddy Lamb, who had been the leading rusher for Rock Island in 1925, and halfback Mickey McDonnell from Duluth. Rejoining the team was Bill McElwain, the shifty back from Northwestern who missed the 1925 season with a broken collarbone. It was the intent of the team that Lamb would replace the running prowess of Driscoll. While that may have been admirable, the team would still need to fill the void of Paddy's passing, receiving, and defense as well. Most of all, who would be able to kick with the abandon of Driscoll? Who could punt on the run, drop-kick on a muddy field, and threaten to score a field goal from anywhere within the fifty-yard line? All in all, the skill of Driscoll's gifted foot was perhaps his most unique, and irreplaceable, talent. The lack of this offensive weapon would hinder the Cardinals throughout the 1926 season.

Up front, the Cardinals fielded a sturdy, but aging line. Tackle Fred Gillies and end Nick McInerney were thirty and guard Will Brennan was thirty-two. One key acquisition later in the season was that of tackle Duke Slater. Slater, a 6'1", 215-pound tackle, moved over from Rock Island after an exceptional career at the University of Iowa. He would remain with the Cardinals through the 1931 season and would eventually become a judge in the Chicago area. A key loss was that of talented end Eddie Anderson, who joined former Cardinals Gob Buckeye, Johnny Mohardt, and Jim Tays on the Chicago Bulls.

The Cardinals' first taste of life in the post-Driscoll era was against the Columbus Tigers on September 19. Even with this first home game, the Cards were forced to compete in the shadow of Grange, whose New York team continued to prepare for the season in the not-too-distant western suburb of Aurora, Illinois. Advertisements attempted to convince Chicago fans to make the trek westward by convenient train transportation:

*World famous football star and team plays Fox Valley All Stars at Exposition Grounds in Aurora. Be sure to go via fast, frequent electrically-operated trains over direct connection to field. Avoid dust, delay and crowded highways by going and returning on the Chicago Aurora and Elgin Railroad.*

While the Cardinals defeated the Tigers 14-0 before twenty-five hundred at Normal Park, Grange and his Yankees posted a 20-0 victory before eighteen thousand in a meaningless exhibition game. On the same day, Driscoll wasted no time in impressing his new Bears teammates. He drop-kicked a field goal and led the Bears to a 10-7 advantage over the reconstituted Milwaukee Badgers, now owned by former Cardinal Johnny Bryan.

## Pro Football Is Here To Stay

The second test of the new season would be another home match on September 26, this time with the wandering Los Angeles Buccaneers. The Bucs were a new entry in the league and played their entire schedule on the road. This appeared to be an exciting new concept in the league since the Duluth entry, paced by Ernie Nevers, did likewise. After playing their first game at home in Duluth, the Eskimos finished the season with thirteen straight games on the road. The team then went on to play fifteen more games on a postseason tour—all on the road.

Prior to the Los Angeles game, O'Brien traded Buck Evans to Columbus for 225-pound tackle Walter Ellis. Ellis had been an All-American tackle at the University of Detroit who split time in the 1925 pro season with Columbus and Detroit. It would turn out to be a superlative move when Ellis was named to the All-NFL team at the conclusion of the season. With Ellis on the roster, the Cards stunned Los Angeles 15-0. More importantly for O'Brien, over seventy-five hundred fans showed up to watch this early season tussle, a sight that was not lost on Don Maxwell of the *Tribune*:

> *Chicagoans skeptical of the drawing power of professional football teams would have been surprised, probably shocked, at the size of the crowd which paid its way through the turnstiles of the bandbox park where the Cardinals beat Brick Muller's eleven yesterday. The presence of 7,500 men and women at this game, played before the opening of the conference gridirons (colleges) have had a chance to whet the appetite for football, played on a day when hundreds of grid fans must have chosen to play golf, and played in a park whose chief recommendation is necessity, the presence of such a crowd seems adequate refutation of the skeptic's argument.*
>
> *Pro football is here to stay. It has something college football lacks and it lacks a lot that college football has. Pro football offers the public a chance to see gridiron stars developed in the colleges east, west, north, and south. It offers one a chance to see team positions played by experts. It offers opportunity to thousands who are shut out from college bleachers.*

The following week, the Cardinals posted still another shutout, stunning the Racine Tornadoes 20-0. Stopping the Tornadoes cold was a stifling Cardinals defense that held the visitors without a first down before three thousand in attendance. The visitors' offensive efforts were so impotent that the *Tribune's* coverage was more impressed with the halftime entertainment:

> *The Racine American Legion drum and bugle corps, national champions for four years, which paraded the gridiron, easily attracted more attention than did the Legion football team. Unfortunately, the drum corps was permitted to play only between the halves, and consequently could render no assistance to the dismal efforts of the professionals.*

On October 10, the Chicago Cardinals (4-0) moved to the top of the league standings with a 13-7 win at Green Bay. The victory tied the Cardinals with Frankford, while the Bears were a step behind at 3-0-1. This set up the most interesting weekend of the young football season in Chicago. On Sunday, October 17, not only would the Cardinals face the Bears for first place in the NFL at Cubs Park, but Red Grange and his New York Yankees (2-1) would also be in town to tangle with Joey Sternaman and the Chicago Bulls (0-3-1) at Comiskey Park. Not lost in the excitement of this initial head-to-head competition between the two pro leagues was the fact that Paddy Driscoll would be facing his former teammates for the first time as reported in the *Daily News:*

> *There has always been intense rivalry between Chris O'Brien's charges and those picked from the great field of graduating collegians by George Halas and Ed Sternaman. The competition has waxed so keen that the north side magnates recently outbid their rival in getting the services of Paddy Driscoll, who will fight against his old teammates spurred on by a $10,000 contract, the largest in professional football, unless, possibly, that of Grange, whose figures have not been made public this year.*

It would be a key weekend for the American League. Attendance had been strong, but not exceptional. Grange continued to be the calling card for financial success, but a team could not play just the Yankees week after week. For the National League, it would be a test to determine the loyalties of the Chicago fans who had supported the Bears and the Cardinals through the first several years of the league. The comparison would be easy; one would only need to look at the attendance figures in Monday's papers.

## *We Were Back To Small Gates, The Hard Grind*

Both games provided thrills, but not drama, as the Bulls shocked the Yankees 14-0 and the Bears stopped the Cardinals 16-0. Grange, hindered by an inexperienced line, was never able to shake loose against the Bulls. He was, in fact, overshadowed by the Bulls' Johnny Mohardt, who scored both touchdowns for the Bulls before sixteen thousand fans. Up north, Paddy Driscoll ambushed his old team as the Bears swept to victory. Driscoll kicked three field goals, scored the only touchdown, and booted the extra point to account for all of the scoring. While twelve thousand were in the stands, it disappointed Halas that fans were forced to choose between the two games, thus hurting the gate for both leagues:

*We were back to the small gates, the hard grind, the search for fans, the pinching of the penny. The Maras (owners of the New York Giants) learned the Red Grange euphoria had vanished. The Giants drew only 3,000 or 4,000. Mara would look through binoculars at Yankee Stadium and say "There's no one over there, either."*

The Cardinals bounced back following the defeat by the Bears to edge the Milwaukee Badgers 3-2 in a dreary game. Now 5-1, the Cardinals remained close behind Frankford (6-0-1) and the Bears (5-0-1). But on Halloween Day of 1926, the tricks began to be played on the Cardinals' title hopes. Starting with a tough 3-0 loss to Green Bay on October 31, the Cardinals would fail to win any of their remaining six games. To make matters worse, the offense of the team would completely implode, scoring just one touchdown in those six games. This huge slump resulted in a 5-6-1 record on the field along with a diminishing return at the box office.

Following the Green Bay defeat, the Cardinals' engine sputtered and stalled completely the next weekend. Because of continuing local laws in Pennsylvania prohibiting football on Sunday, the Frankford Yellow Jackets played their home games on Saturday. Visiting teams would then usually schedule another contest nearby for Sunday before returning home. This is precisely what the Cardinals did the weekend of November 6 and 7, 1926. Perhaps the travel was a factor in the opening effort of the two-game set where the Yellow Jackets stormed to a 33-7 win over the Cardinals, by far the worst defeat ever experienced by the team in league play. On the very next day, the team journeyed to New York and fell to the Giants 20-0. Certainly injuries were a factor. All pro center Ralph Claypool and fullback Gene Francis were injured in the Milwaukee game, and Red Dunn and Ike Mahoney were nursing nagging injuries as well.

Upon returning from the disastrous trip to the East, the Cardinals had only a brief time to prepare for the Armistice Day (November 11) game against the Bears in Soldier Field. With a 5-4 mark, the Cardinals had probably extinguished all of their title hopes. But, with the Bears (7-0-1) clinging to first place, the Cardinals hoped to play the role of spoiler for the North Siders' championship hopes. The game, staged for the benefit of Rosary College in River Forest, Illinois, proved to be an ugly one. A surprisingly large crowd of fifteen thousand showed up on a cold, windy day where Driscoll again provided the heroics in a 10-0 win by the Bears. The former Cardinal kicked one field goal, passed forty yards for a touchdown, and then kicked the extra point as the Bears claimed the city title once again. For the Cardinals, the injury news continued to worsen as Dunn was feared lost with a broken leg just five minutes into the game. Mahoney broke his finger a minute later.

Dismal weather plagued both leagues. The Cardinals were forced to cancel their next game with Akron on November 14 because of the sloppy condition of the Normal Park field. A week later, the proposed game with winless Louisville was canned for the same reason. The Bulls did play that day in Chicago, defeating Rock Island 3-0 before a mere fifteen hundred fans in what would prove to be the last game for the Independents. The team folded and the Cardinals brought in Duke Slater and guard Chet Widerquist for the remainder of the season.

## The Cardinals Have Been A Distinct Disappointment

By now, C. C. Pyle's American League was on the ropes. The league had lost five of its nine teams with the Philadelphia Quakers, the New York Yankees, the Los Angeles Wildcats, and the Chicago Bulls the only survivors by Thanksgiving Day. Even the Yankees were not immune to attendance woes. On November 28, after three straight losses and with Grange idled because of a hip injury, only twenty-five hundred were in Yankee Stadium to watch the home team end its losing skid with a 7-0 win over the Bulls.

In Chicago, the Bears and the Cardinals met for a third time on Turkey Day, with the *Tribune* previewing the engagement:

> The season's record of the Cardinals has been a distinct disappointment to south side fans. They won their first five games in decisive fashion, but, handicapped by injuries, they since have lost an equal number. In this loss are two defeats by the Bears, who hold the 1926 city championship.
>
> Chris O'Brien makes no secret of the fact that his turkey and trimmings will be spoiled today unless his team can defeat the Bears. Only in this manner can his team alleviate his disappointment for the Cardinals have lost more games this year than in any previous year of competition.

More rain fell before the game, leaving Cubs Park field in a muddy mess. Neither team was able to score and the game ended in a 0-0 tie. The tie did not affect the Bears' first place position in the league, but it did considerably brighten the Cardinals' season. With Slater joining Gillies at tackle, the Cardinals mounted a fierce rush that kept Driscoll in check. Dunne was also back from his leg injury. While the Cardinals-Bears game attracted eight thousand to Cubs Park, the Bulls entertained just thirty-five hundred at Comiskey Park in a scoreless tie with the Los Angeles Wildcats.

Although it appeared that the NFL was closing in on the American League, they were not exceeding the collegiate game's popularity. While the Bears were proud of the eight thousand who visited for the Cardinals game, a colossal football event just two days later at Soldier Field in Chicago stunned the entire nation with its turnout. In front of an estimated 111,000 people, the football teams representing Army and Navy played to a 21-21 tie before the largest crowd ever to watch a football game. Big-time college football was here to stay and the rush to build bigger and better stadiums began. Football was exceeding its own expectations and was showing no signs of letting up, in both the quality of play and the attendance column. The fears that pro football would injure the college game were not substantiated, so perhaps the two could continue to exist in their parallel worlds.

There was one last piece of business for the Cardinals . . .

The final game of the 1926 season was played at Soldier Field on Sunday, November 28. One day after 111,000 poured through the turnstiles to watch the epic Army-Navy battle, 14,000 (40,000 tickets were sold) watched the Cardinals lose 7-2 to the Kansas City Cowboys. In a game played for the benefit of long-gone Mercy High School, an all-girls school on the South Side, a seventy-five-yard touchdown run by Rufe DeWitz early in the game proved to be all the cushion that was needed for the Kansas City victory. The once undefeated Cardinals fell to 5-6-1 for the season, the first O'Brien NFL squad to complete its campaign with a losing record.

Frankford survived a showdown with the Bears on December 4 to win 7-6 and eventually captured the league crown with a 14-1-2 record under former Decatur Staley Guy Chamberlin. The Bears finished second with a 12-1-3 slate and Pottsville claimed third at 10-2-2. The trade for Driscoll was invaluable for the Bears. Paddy topped the league in both field goals made (twelve) and scoring (eighty-six points).

In New York, the once promising American League finished the season with just four teams and was never heard from again. Grange did lead the New York Yankees on another postseason tour to Texas and California. They were the only American Football League team to be admitted into the NFL in 1927.

## *Cleaning House*

If pro football learned anything from its mini-war in 1926, it was that the total of thirty-one professional teams operating in the two leagues was excessive. In an effort to consolidate both the number of teams and the available talent, the NFL initiated a drastic housecleaning. "In" for the 1927 season were teams from large cities and those with exciting, star players. "Out" were teams from smaller locales or with dismal attendance figures. As the gates to the 1927 season opened, out shuffled such venerable teams as the Canton Bulldogs, the Hammond Pros, the Akron Indians, and the Columbus Tigers. In all, only ten of the twenty-two teams from the 1926 season returned. In addition, Grange's New York Yankees and the Cleveland Bulldogs (previously the Kansas City Cowboys) were added to the circuit. With just twelve teams, the NFL was leaner and meaner with two huge gate attractions in Red Grange of the Yankees and Ernie Nevers, who spent the season with the touring Duluth Eskimos.

Even the Cardinals benefited from the downsizing when Chris O'Brien enticed Guy Chamberlin to Chicago as player-coach of the team. Chamberlin was a legend in the early days of the NFL. As a player-coach, he had already accumulated four league titles with the Canton Bulldogs in 1922 (10-0-2) and 1923 (11-0-1), the 1924 Cleveland Bulldogs (7-1-1), and the 1926 Frankford Yellow Jackets (14-1-2). Chamberlin moved to Chicago with a sparkling pro coaching record of 55-9-6, including his busy Frankford 1925 team (13-7). Could he continue his magic with the Cardinals?

O'Brien spent the off-season working on the business end of the club as well. On April 25, 1927, he finally incorporated the Chicago Cardinals Football Club in the state of Illinois. According to the corporate documents on file with the state, the intent of the corporation was to:

> *Own and manage the Chicago Professional team known as "Chicago Cardinals Football Club" and to promote football and athletics in general.*

The corporate headquarters was established at O'Brien's residence (5712 South Racine) with Chris O'Brien owning 3,000 of the 3,004 shares of the organization. The first directors of the corporation were Chris and his wife Frieda, along with Thomas Burian, John E. Taylor, and James P. Taylor.

O'Brien also entered into negotiations with Joey Sternaman regarding the possible merger of the Cardinals with the defunct Chicago Bulls from the old American

League. Those talks simmered throughout the summer of 1927 and the two did not agree to disagree until just prior to the start of the season. George Halas thought the merger was a done deal and wrote in his autobiography:

> *I would have welcomed Joey Sternaman back on the Bears but he became a playing partner with Chris O'Brien on the Cardinals. Chicago's two most popular players, Paddy Driscoll and Joey, would again be matched against each other although on exchanged teams.*

But on the eve of the Bears-Cardinals opening day game on Sunday, September 25, Joey Sternaman reported for duty with the Bears. Meanwhile, Chamberlin was doing his best to fortify the weak offense of the Cardinals. Its deficiencies had been uncovered in an exhibition game shutout (6-0) loss to Hammond. Chamberlin had imported several new players, including former Frankford quarterback Ben Jones, in an attempt to implement the powerful "line shift" running game that worked so well with Canton and Frankford.

It wasn't to be. Following a 9-0 opening league loss to the Bears (with Paddy Driscoll scoring all of the points), the Cardinals struggled to stay afloat in the standings. Besieged by numerous fumbles, a poor kicking game, injuries, and an inconsistent offense, the team plummeted to a 2-6-1 record prior to the annual Thanksgiving Day game with the Bears. The only real highlight was a 33-0 thumping of the Spring Valley (IL) Wildcats in a nonleague battle on October 23. Just prior to the annual Thanksgiving Day game with the Bears, O'Brien initiated a very unusual move: he fired Chamberlin and replaced him with team captain and quarterback Ben Jones. O'Brien also made several personnel decisions, including releasing starting guard Arnie Hummel and rearranging other starting positions.

## *They Had Seen The Galloping Ghost For The Last Time*

By some means, O'Brien's magic worked, and the Cardinals upset the Bears 3-0, knocking the losers out of first place contention. But a final walloping at the hands of Cleveland (32-7) left the Cardinals mired in ninth place with a 3-7-1 record, by far the team's poorest showing in the professional ranks. While the team faded on the field, bad luck continued to plague O'Brien behind the scenes. First, a game against Buffalo became lost revenue when the team folded the week it was to meet the Cards. Next, the city pinched the Cards (and all other local professional teams, except baseball) with a three percent license fee out of all gross gate receipts. Finally, the much anticipated home game against Red Grange and his New York Yankees proved to be somewhat of a bust when Grange injured his knee against the Bears two weeks before the Cardinals-New York contest. This injury was widely noted in the media and helped limit the crowd, which realized that Grange would play little, if at all. His major role that day would be to accept a crate of apples from Miss Chicago in honor of something called Presentation Day.

As it turned out, Grange never fully recovered from that injury. He didn't play at all in the Cardinals game and sat out most of the remainder of the season. "No one knew it at the time, but they had seen the Galloping Ghost gallop for the last time,"

Grange stated later. After sitting out the 1928 season to rest the knee, he signed with the Bears in 1929, but by then had lost most of the offensive cutting ability that had made him famous.

The injury was quite a blow to O'Brien. In anticipation of a huge crowd, he booked Soldier Field and even arranged for bus service from various parts of the city to the stadium. But with Grange inactive, the crowd was limited to about fifteen thousand, not in the forty thousand range O'Brien had hoped to experience. By now, he must have been wondering: "Was this all worth it?"

In 1928, the Chicago Cardinals hit bottom. And they hit with a thud.

Unable to confirm a full schedule, O'Brien was able to slate just six games, with three of those coming in the final five days of the season. With former tackle Fred Gillies as coach, the team lacked speed in the backfield and strength in the line. There were no "marquee" names in the lineup, except perhaps for the reliable tackle Fred Slater. The last two remaining Racine Cardinals, Will Brennan and Nick McInerney, left the team following the 1927 campaign (McInerney attempted a brief comeback in 1928), and Gillies was unable to do much with the many new faces reporting for practice.

## Tumbling Down Bleacher Aisles

The 1928 season began with an unusual twist in that the Cardinals played an exhibition game at Hammond. Through most of the decade, the Cardinals had rarely played an away game. Nonetheless, the visitors captured a 12-0 victory behind new quarterback Ducky Grant from St. Mary's in California. While this win was enjoyable, the first game of the regular season would be held at Normal Park on Sunday, September 23 against the Bears. The Cardinals had derailed the Bears' championship hopes in 1927 with a 3-0 upset on Thanksgiving Day. That piece of history did not go unnoticed by the local media and was well remembered by Halas, Driscoll, Sternaman, et al. The Bears easily conquered the Cards by a 15-0 count in a game that wasn't close. Driscoll's thirty-three-year-old legs were still among the best in the business as he ran back kickoffs, sprinted around the ends, and kept the Cards off balance with his kicking. It wasn't a pretty game, but the *Tribune* reported that many of the South Side fans didn't appear to notice:

> *With such an unequal match on the gridiron the tipsy punsters and cheer leaders who staggered along the side lines during the second half was a comic relief to the crowd. Those self-invited comedians mounted chairs, held forth as soap box orators, played tag with the police, and in general added most to the sport, even to crawling into box seats and tumbling down bleacher aisles.*

With an open week, O'Brien scheduled a date with the local Mills football team from the West Side. It was not a good idea. The inspired Mills players converted an extra point late in the first half to shock the Cardinals 7-6. So much for the aura of the National Football League.

After this "off" week, the Chicago Cardinals bounced back on October 7 to defeat the winless Dayton Triangles 7-0. Once again, the Cards struggled on offense and the only score was the result of a fifty-yard interception return by Swede Erickson. Unfortunately, that would prove to be the only touchdown, and the only win, registered by the Cardinals for the remainder of the 1928 season. A trip to Green Bay the following week resulted in a decisive 20-0 defeat and then, strangely, the team became inactive in league play for over a month. There is no definitive explanation for this midseason vacation, although it might be possible that O'Brien simply could not schedule any games.

Most of the previous Midwest competition, such as Rock Island, Milwaukee, Louisville, Duluth, and Racine, were defunct. The Cards had already played the Bears and Green Bay, which left Detroit and Dayton as the next closest geographical competitors in the now ten-team league. With two teams in New York, along with franchises in Pottsville, Providence, and Frankford, the Eastern clubs appeared content to slug it out with each other. Frankford and Providence even played a home and away weekend series on November 17 and 18. On the other hand, the Bears played ten straight home games from October 14 through December 9 on the way to an average 7-5-1 record. It appears that if the Eastern clubs were receptive to the possibility of a journey to Chicago it would be for a game with the Bears at the larger Cubs Park, rather than at Normal Park with the Cardinals.

O' Brien did attempt to keep his team busy against local teams. After a two-week layoff, the team was scheduled to play an outfit called the Chicago All-Stars at Normal Park on November 4, but no score was reported in the media. The Cardinals may have also tangled with the local Pullman Roseland Panthers on November 11, but that game result was ignored as well.

The Cardinals jumped back into league action with a unique road trip to Pennsylvania on November 24 and 25 to tangle with Frankford and the New York Yankees. While the crowds were nice (eight thousand in Frankford, seven thousand in New York), both games ended with identical 19-0 defeats for the Cardinals. All that remained in an attempt to salvage a dismal season was the annual Thanksgiving Day game with the Bears on November 29. O'Brien hastily attempted to pry the respected Herb Joesting away from the Minneapolis Marines for this final game, but the two sides could not come to terms.

O'Brien, ever the promoter, knew that his pet project was not going well. The man who had been with the Cardinals for nearly thirty years was approaching the sunset of his football life. Bad luck and ill winds had plagued this pro football pioneer throughout his career, but he stubbornly pushed forward. No matter what fate had in store for him, O'Brien always met it head on. He organized benefits for the families of former players during World War I; helped found the NFL in 1920; introduced innovations such as printed game programs, free parking, bus service, and mascots at his games—but he had continuously fallen short when the big pay days were within reach. He had attempted to sign Grange, and then had agreed to a flat league guarantee with the Bears before he knew that Grange would face the Cardinals in his first pro game in 1925. He withstood the persistent overtures of Pyle in 1926 to become a charter member of the new American League out of loyalty to the NFL, and he survived aspersions from the 1925 Englewood scandal. When things were looking gloomy, he refused to bend in negotiations with Joey Sternaman who was desperate to return to football after the quick demise of Pyle's American conference.

O'Brien had to realize that the end was near for his beleaguered franchise. The team continued to drain his time and his resources and was no longer functioning cohesively on the field. The better players were straying towards the more successful teams, and, while the Cardinals would be able to attract major college players, the team was no longer able to contract with the cream of the crop.

Then there was the family business. Chris and Pat O'Brien operated a popular men's clothing store on Halsted Street and added a bowling alley with eight lanes, along with a billiard hall next door. The complex at 5112-5116 South Halsted was owned by O'Brien & O'Brien Inc., which also opened a branch facility called the Windsor Park Recreation Room at 2454 East 75th Street. These businesses certainly required his attention, and it appears that the money well from investors also was drying up.

## O'Brien Thinks Thorpe Will Be Of Value

With this in mind, O'Brien did his best to pull off one more attention-grabbing promotion in the season finale against the Bears. The *Chicago Tribune* reported the following on Thanksgiving morning of 1928:

> *Chicago's professional football teams, the Bears and the Cardinals, play for the city title this morning at 11 o'clock at Wrigley Field. That both are out of the race for National league honors will have no effect on the game, for when north side battles the south side, that and nothing else counts.*
>
> *The Bears hold one victory over Chris O'Brien's team this season, even as they did at turkey time last year. And the Cardinals go into the game the underdog. But remembering last season's 3-0 victory, the Cardinals believe they again can upset their rivals.*
>
> *Manager O'Brien announced last night that Jim Thorpe, famous Indian star, may play a portion of today's contest at end . . . Despite his handicap of age, Chris thinks Thorpe will be of value in stopping the Bears' end runs. Thorpe still possesses the phenomenal kicking ability that was his a decade ago.*

Thorpe's brief appearance was little noted by the Chicago press, but to this day, those few minutes on the field have identified him forever as a member of the Chicago Cardinals. Thorpe was well past his prime when he trotted onto the field to replace end Ed Allen during the Cardinals' 34-0 loss. After a long and storied athletic career, this game with the Chicago Cardinals would prove to be the last one for Thorpe. In later years, he recalled: "I played my last game of professional football for the Chicago Cardinals against the Bears. I was then forty-one years of age, and realized it was time to quit. I played half the game. We were defeated." The *Associated Press* described Thorpe in that final game as "Now in his forties and muscle bound, he was a mere shadow of his former self."

## The Fighting Cards From Back Of The Yards

The season-ending loss (34-0) to the Bears was so one-sided that the fans found more entertainment in the stands, as reported by the *Chicago Herald*:

> *The 10,000 early holiday fans were treated to quite a spectacular battle . . . three robust and live turkeys were released for the benefit of the best tacklers in the park.*

*They soared down from the second deck between halves and quite a scramble ensued in each case before the fowl was thoroughly collared by some frantic pursuer.*

*The trio of successful pursuers were considerably better than the Cardinals who tried desperately for two hours to subdue the rampant Bears. Jack Bramhall's band played every college song from California to New York, but these Cardinals apparently had forgotten the best of their college days.*

The 1928 season was a debacle. The Chicago Cardinals finished with a 1-5 league mark and were outscored by a count of 107-7. Just as Thorpe ended his career on Thanksgiving, the game would prove to be Chris O'Brien's last outing with the Cards as well. O'Brien had been quietly seeking a buyer for the team for about three years, but it wasn't until the 1928 season when he seemed to surrender to the pressures of team ownership. Then, on Thursday, July 18, 1929, O'Brien announced that he had sold the club to wealthy Chicago physician Dr. David Jones for a reported $25,000. "He (O'Brien) sold the team so that he could pay his players," recalled his granddaughter Patricia Needham. "It broke his heart to sell the Cardinals."

George Halas claimed a role in the transfer of the Cardinals to Jones:

*It (the Cardinals team) was losing money and Chris O'Brien could not subsidize it. I was concerned the buyer might be undesirable. I induced a great Bears' fan, Dr. David Jones, to buy the club. He had served as city physician under four mayors. I promised him that if the losses continued, I would absorb 40 percent; if there were a profit, I would take none of it. That was some partnership! Heads you win; tails I lose.*

Halas and Jones had also been partners in the Chicago Bruins professional basketball franchise together, and were friends, but the agreement by Halas to support Jones in the event of fiscal danger didn't seem to include sensible financial considerations. Nevertheless, the two sides first drafted a handwritten agreement on June 14, 1929, as follows:

*I, Chris O'Brien, as owner of the Chicago Cardinals Football Club agree to sell the said club, corporation and players and all stock and assets of club to Dr. David J. Jones for the sum of twelve thousand five hundred dollars.*

*The corporation is to be turned over to Dr. David J. Jones by Chris O'Brien free of all bills, liens and liabilities.*

*Any debts that Chris O'Brien cannot settle at this time it is agreed to put money in escrow with satisfactory party to cover these amounts until settled.*

*It is understood that Dr. David J. Jones is to signify his intentions in regard to this contract within ten days.*

A second handwritten document was dated (both items are located in the Pro Football Hall of Fame) June 26, 1929:

*In consideration of the sum of five hundred dollars ($500) paid to me today by Dr. David J. Jones I hereby agree to sell, assign and transfer all the stock, franchise and corporation papers of the Chicago Cardinals Football Club, Inc. and other items as designated above to Dr. David J. Jones, said stock, corporation papers and franchise to be turned over to Dr. David J. Jones within ten days.*

*The balance of money to be turned over to George S. Halas as escrow officer within ten days.*

The document is not signed by Chris O'Brien, so it may be a draft developed by Jones and/or his attorneys. It is interesting that Halas is listed as the escrow officer and that the purchase price is listed as $12,500, much less than the $25,000 quoted by Halas and other historical sources. It could be that O'Brien needed more cash to settle related debts, or that the document above was merely an initial offer. However, when Jones passed away in 1966, his obituary indicated that he purchased the team for $12,000 which would have been close to the sum above, less the $500 down payment. In any case, Dr. David J. Jones now owned the Chicago Cardinals and quickly went to work to rebuild the team. "I believe the South Side will support winning football and I'm going to give 'em that or bust," Jones boldly predicted after his purchase.

Just two days after the deal was closed, Jones marched down to Bloomington, Illinois, and signed former Oregon quarterback Howard Maple. He then picked up ex-Illinois end Chuck Kassel, who had played the previous two seasons for Frankford. He next added giant (6'8", 233 pounds) center Teddy Scharpenter from nearby Melrose Park. While Scharpenter would not wind up on the final roster, it was clear that Jones was letting nothing stand in the way of the rebuilding of the Cardinals. When the dust settled, only three players (Duke Slater, Herb Blumer, and Mickey McDonnell) survived from the 1928 roster. Columnist Edward J. Geiger noted the changes in the *Chicago Evening American:*

> *Looks like the Chicago Bears are in for a real test this year when it comes to deciding which is to be the outstanding professional football team in Chicago. Time was, and not long ago, when the North Side team was 'way out in front, with the Chicago Cardinals just another football team, but times seemed to have changed. The Cardinals of 1929 will present a ball club that is to be feared and one that looks like championship caliber, on paper at least. Comes Dr. David J. Jones into the game. Dr. Jones has taken over the Cardinals, has scoured the country, purchased stellar players and continues to do so. Looks like George Halas and Dutch Sternaman will have something to worry about.*

Jones was brimming with ideas off the field, too. Most importantly, he leased Comiskey Park, moving the team's home games from tiny Normal Park. Next, he announced that he would call his team the "Fighting Cards from Back of the Yards" and that he would send his troops out of town to Coldwater, Michigan, for an intense preseason training camp. His next bombshell was the biggest: Jones acquired the services of multitalented fullback Ernie Nevers, who was nearly on par with Red Grange in terms of a gate attraction. As a player, he probably exceeded Grange because of his durability and kicking ability. Naturally, Jones was pleased with his preseason recruiting: "The South Side club is going to be the best in the professional game," he boasted. "The acquisition of Nevers, along with Maple, reputed to be the greatest quarter in recent years, is only a starter. We will have a team and a schedule which will be representative of what pro football really should be."

The key to gaining Nevers' services was the hiring of former Duluth Eskimo owner Ole Haugsrud as manager of the Cardinals. Jones also brought in ex-Duluth coach

Dewey Scanlon to handle that chore for the Cardinals in 1929. Although the Duluth franchise had been inactive in 1928 (and subsequently sold to a group in Orange, New Jersey), the contracts of some of the players remained the property of Haugsrud. This enabled Jones to add veteran players such as Nevers, Cobb Rooney, Walt Kiesling, and Russ Method to provide an almost instant infusion of credible talent. With such a huge turnover on the roster, Jones came up with the idea to sequester his team for the sole purpose of concentrating on the upcoming season. With the creation of the first "out of town" training camp for a professional football team, Jones demonstrated the intensity with which he was approaching the season.

## *One Of The Greatest Collections Of Football Material*

While the Cardinals' 1-5 league record and the fact that the team was outscored 107-7 in 1928 may have been startling, that was all in the past. A new coach, manager, and almost an entirely fresh roster jumped into the two-a-day drills at Waterworks Park in Coldwater, Michigan.

Tackle Duke Slater was extremely popular with the folks in Coldwater. One might surmise that this interest resulted form Slater being the only black player on the team, but the real key, according to the *Daily Reporter* was his personality and unusually large feet!

> *Much has been said relative to Duke Slater, All-American, Iowa class of '23. Duke, negro, is the comedian of the squad because of his ready answer to anything that his teammates shoot at him. To local persons interest has been centered on "Duke's" unusual understanding. The star wears no less than shoes of 13_ caliber. Grantland Rice, dean of sportswriters and critics, in a reply to an article in which it was said "Slater has yet to be knocked off his feet," looked the boy over and replied, "Why should Slater ever be knocked off his feet—look at 'em." A shoe worn by Slater is on exhibition at Iowa University field house. Slater knows his football on the field only. One never hears of his conquests from his own lips. On the gridiron he is just plain poison to his opponents.*

The Cardinals spent all day Saturday, September 21, on the road to Canton, Ohio, for what would be the first of five straight games on the road. In fact, the Cardinals would play only one home game until November 10. While the Cards dropped a 6-0 exhibition game to the Canton Bulldogs, the real setback was the season-ending injury to quarterback Howard Maple. Maple had been Jones' first big-time recruit. Would Jones, too, be a victim of the hard luck that seemed to toy with the Cardinals throughout the decade?

The regular season began at Buffalo with a satisfying 9-3 victory over the Bison. The close win was acceptable because the Cards were without the services of both Maple and Nevers, who was completing his professional baseball duties with a minor league outpost of the St. Louis team in the American League. Following a 9-2 loss at Green Bay, Nevers joined the Cardinals in time for a game on October 13 at Minneapolis. Although far from being in football shape, Nevers threw a touchdown pass for the only score in a 14-7 defeat. Next in line was the first game of the year against the Bears.

## Lineman Pushed Nevers's Nose A Trifle

In this matchup, fans would be treated to the return of both Grange and Nevers to pro football. Both had been out of action in 1928 because of injuries. Over eighteen thousand poured into Wrigley Field (formerly known as Cubs Park) and watched as the two longtime adversaries battled to a scoreless tie. Both Nevers and the ageless Paddy Driscoll missed close field goal attempts that might have been the difference for either team. Still, it was a typical Bears-Cardinals battle and the *Chicago Tribune* listed the casualties:

> *It was hard fought, broken only by breathing spaces in which the perspiring players called for the water bucket and the sopping sponges. Some unidentified Bear lineman pushed Nevers' nose a trifle with his open hand to draw first blood early in the game.*
>
> *Jake Williams, a soft spoken but exceedingly earnest southerner, kept up a drawling conversation through a split lip. And Capt. Don Murry of the Bears had first aid for a gash in his eyebrow received in a bit of hardy scrimmage. So much for the earnestness of the play.*

Two more defeats followed: a 7-6 loss to Green Bay in the first home game (October 27) before ten thousand at Soldier Field, and then an 8-0 shutout in Philadelphia to the Frankford Yellow Jackets. The Chicago Cardinals were now saddled with a surprising 1-4-1 record, but that eight-point loss at Frankford had been the largest deficit of the season. The team appeared to be competitive; the players just had not yet jelled as a unit.

The team finally turned the corner with a 16-0 win at Providence in an unusual Wednesday night game on November 6, the first night game in NFL history. The two teams battled in Kinsley Park, a field usually reserved for soccer games. The ball was painted white to help offset the poor lighting as Ernie Nevers rushed for 102 yards to pace the winners.

Returning home, the Cards, with the addition of former Pittsburgh All-American center Bill Stein, edged the Minneapolis Red Jackets 8-0 on November 10 with Nevers outshining Herb Joestling. A week later, Nevers was corralled as the Cards fell to the streaking Packers 12-0. Mired deep in the standings with a 3-5-1 record, Nevers and company then turned on the burners and collected three wins over the last four games to finish a respectable 6-6-1. Along the way, wins were recorded over Dayton (19-0 as Nevers scored all of the points), the Bears (40-6), and Orange (26-0), with the lone loss coming late in the game at the hands of the Giants 24-21. Yet if one single game will bask in glory throughout football history in Chicago, it is the annual Thanksgiving Day clash with the Bears on November 28.

## Thanksgiving Redemption

With both teams struggling on the field with subpar records for the season, the incentive of capturing the city title was still at stake. The *Chicago Tribune* reported:

> *Neither eleven has been successful in the league race and the Cardinals, for the first time since 1925, have a higher percentage in the standings than the Bears. As usual, percentages, defeats and victories are forgotten. It'll be Grange versus*

*Nevers, and north side against south side.*

While the records of both the Cardinals (4-5-1) and the Bears (4-6-1) were not glittering, the magical rivalry between the two clubs was still appealing. Throw in the meeting between Grange and Nevers, and the fan interest should have been staggering at Comiskey Park. Edgar Munzel wrote in the *Herald*:

> *That age-worn rivalry between the north and south sections of Chicago bristles with the same keenness when these two elevens take the field as is evident in the prominent "traditional" clashes of the colleges. The slowness and deliberateness that detracts in most pro games is never evident.*

Still, only about eight thousand braved the elements to watch the latest version of pro football's most competitive rivalry. Since the two teams had battled to a scoreless tie earlier in the season, the winner of this game would clearly capture local bragging rights for 1929. "The first game of the season, we played to a 0-0 score," recalled Nevers years later. "I told my players, the next time we meet the Bears, we'll beat the hell out of 'em. I knew we could. I just knew it."

As heavy, wet snow began to fall the morning of the game, Coach Scanlon realized that he would need to forego the Cardinals' usual double wing offense because of the slippery turf. Perhaps he would risk a few more passes than usual; maybe he would direct Nevers to simply blast away at the interior line. If the Cards were to prevail against Grange, Joey Sternaman, and Paddy Driscoll, the battle would need to be won in the trenches. The reliable line of Duke Slater, Herb Blumer, and future Hall of Famer, 243-pound guard Walt Kiesling would be the focal point.

And so it was. With Nevers, Gene Rose, and Mickey McDonnell blasting away at the underbelly of the Bears, Nevers was able to finally break through for a twenty-yard score early in the first quarter. Nevers missed the extra point, but the Cards scored quickly again behind the blocking of Slater.

Nevers scampered three yards for the tally and added the extra point giving the home team a 13-0 lead after the first period. The quick scores seemed to revitalize the Cards, who began to dominate on both sides of the line. McDonnell, Nevers, Cobb Rooney, and Gene Rose took turns prancing through the opposing defense. Shortly before the half, Nevers scored from six yards out and added the kick, giving the Cardinals a 20-0 halftime advantage. Former Cardinal Wilfrid Smith reported in the *Tribune* that:

> *The Cardinal line was the foundation on which these ball carriers built their successes. There was no question of its superiority. And it played no favorites. From end to end the Bear line wavered and retreated before massed interference. The guards carried on through to sweep aside the Bears' secondary defense.*

The Bears briefly challenged early in the third quarter when Walt Holmer tossed a sixty-yard scoring pass to Garland Grange (Red's brother) that cut the lead to 20-6. The Cardinals marched right back downfield with Nevers capping the drive with a one-yard plunge. His extra point left the count 27-6 after three periods of play and the partisan fans were beginning to sense a rare victory over the detested Bears.

In the fourth quarter, the Cardinals continued to dominate on both sides of the line as Nevers scored from the one and the ten, and added an extra point. The Bears were disposed of by a 40-6 count. Smith concluded his game report in the *Tribune* by summarizing the accomplishment of Nevers as he left the game:

*Then Ernie left the game and how those south siders cheered. And well they might. Forty points plus nineteen points against Dayton last Sunday gave him fifty-nine in a row which is some kind of a record but the south side didn't care. For the Cardinals had defeated the Bears.*

When the final tally was totaled, Nevers had indeed scored all forty points (six touchdowns and four extra points), an NFL record that still stands today. His six rushing touchdowns have never been surpassed either. Current Cardinals owner William Bidwill has heard stories passed down through the years about Nevers's legendary feat. "People said that as the game went on, Nevers actually would point directly at the spot in the line where he would be running," recalled Bidwill, "and even then, he couldn't be stopped." With Nevers doing the rushing, passing, and kicking against the Bears, his magical record may never be broken now that football has entered its "specialist" era. Like Joe DiMaggio's hitting streak, this might be one athletic achievement that could last for many more years. The record was Nevers's constant companion throughout his life, but he never failed to share the accomplishment. When asked about the feat, he would often say, "But what about the horses up front? They made it all possible."

Prompted by his effort against the Bears, Nevers topped the league in scoring with a record eighty-five points, despite missing two games because of baseball commitments. He was also selected as the fullback on the All-League team by the *Green Bay Gazette*. The Cardinals' late spurt moved the team up to fourth place in the final league standings (6-6-1) behind champion Green Bay's 12-0-1 mark, the New York Giants' 13-1-1 mark, and the Frankford Yellow Jackets' 10-4-5 mark.

As Dr. David Jones began to prepare for the next season and the new decade, he could look confidently at a bright future. The dismal memories of the down years since the 1925 championship were beginning to fade. He had a genuine box office attraction in Nevers, and the team itself had emerged as a contender. With the Bears stumbling (4-9-2) in 1929, the Cardinals reigned supreme in the city. If Nevers could continue to inspire, prod, and push his teammates, the Cards' return to the top of the NFL could be a realistic possibility in 1930.

# "I forgot to ask how long the season was."

While Red Grange and Ernie Nevers both signed pro contracts in late 1925, Grange would receive more of the initial publicity and adulation. By playing for the University of Illinois, Grange was within reach of most of the key Midwest and Eastern newspapers. Nevers was locked up at faraway Stanford in California where his reputation floated back in whispers and snippets to the Eastern media, whereas Grange enjoyed full-blown coverage for each of his games. When the Bears signed Grange, the team immediately embarked on an eight-game Eastern tour. By the time that tour concluded, Grange had been criticized for not playing in all of the games because of injuries. It was an unfair assessment, since Grange did play both ways, and injuries are an unavoidable part of the game.

But in 1926, Ernie Nevers played a demanding schedule of games that will never be equaled on the professional level. He played in the 1925 Rose Bowl against Notre Dame while still recovering from two broken ankles. Following his departure from Stanford, Nevers signed with Ole Haugsrud and the Duluth Eskimos. With Red Grange bolting to the new American League in 1926, Nevers was the gate attraction that the NFL so desperately needed. The only problem was that few teams were intrigued by the prospect of traveling to Duluth, Minnesota, in the middle of winter. To solve that predicament, Haugsrud agreed that the team would play most of its games on the road.

And so they did. The Eskimos opened the season at home against the Kansas City Cowboys on September 19 with a 7-0 win. The team then hit the road—and stayed there—until February 5. In all, the Eskimos played twenty-nine games (thirteen NFL contests) and meandered across the country in search of opponents. Nevers did it all for Duluth. He ran, passed, kicked, punted, and tackled throughout the tour and missed only twenty-six minutes in twenty-nine games. "You played 60 minutes," recalled Nevers, "and everybody had to go both ways." Unlike today's extended rosters, Duluth carried only fifteen players on its lengthy trip, and for most of the season, only thirteen were healthy. Since the team did not employ managers or equipment personnel, each player carried his own gear to each game. Often the team played several games in the same week, which led to some uniform problems according to Nevers: "After a rain game, the gear weighed fifty pounds. You'd get into a wet uniform that hadn't dried out from the last game."

Nevers's durability was astounding. He was on the field for nearly every minute of every game and missed only 26 minutes out of a possible 1,740 minutes played by Duluth. During the tour, he once played five full games in eight days; played offense, defense, and did all of the kicking; and disregarded an appendicitis attack to toss a long touchdown pass and kick the extra point to win at Milwaukee 7-6. Duluth finished the 1926-1927 campaign with a 19-7-3 mark (6-5-2 in the league) behind Nevers's leadership. He once admitted to only one mistake when he signed on to play pro football: "I forgot to ask how long the season would be."

# ◆ 7 ◆

## Blue Shirt Charlie's Wide World of Sports:
## 1930 – 1939

*"I may be a nut on this subject, but my idea*
*is that pro football will be*
*a helluva thing in a few more years . . ."*

CHARLIE BIDWILL,
OWNER, CHICAGO CARDINALS, 1936

Pro football's carnival-like atmosphere began to wane as the league entered its second decade in 1930. Rules were tightened, schedules finalized, and the organization began to approach big-league status.

This, however, had little effect on the success of the Chicago Cardinals, who continued struggling merely to achieve mediocrity, despite the well-intended efforts of Dr. Jones. While the marvelous presence of Ernie Nevers inspired the Cardinals to a 6-6-1 slate in 1929, the team slipped slightly to 5-6-2 in 1930 and then hit a bad streak. The 1930s were not very kind to the Chicago Cardinals as the team managed just thirty-five league wins for the entire decade.

There were some bright spots, however, as the team showcased individual stars and realized some unique experiences throughout this period. The Cards entered the decade behind aging Ernie Nevers, left it with the emergence of a young Marshall Goldberg, and picked up an intriguing new owner along the way.

Back in 1930, there was still some hope that Nevers could help the team recapture the glory of the winning seasons from just a few years earlier. His athleticism, reputation, and intensity were all assets that the club could utilize. His record-breaking scoring performance against the Bears in 1929 established him as a star in the league and a gate attraction for the Cardinals. All he needed was a strong supporting cast to draw the Cards back into the upper echelon of the league. He would also need some superior stamina since the Cards would open the 1930 season with six straight dates on the road, including four within ten days on a grueling East Coast road trip. With an unusual night game and an even more unusual indoor game, the Cardinals' 1930 season, although not totally successful, was at least a bit unique.

Up on the North Side, the Bears co-owners, George Halas and Dutch Sternaman, decided to give up coaching the team after the Bears endured a terrible 4-9-2 record in 1929. The two veterans had openly bickered for the past few years, and the performance of the team had obviously been affected. To plug the leak, Halas hired a former college coach, Ralph Jones. Jones had been the backfield coach at Illinois when Halas played there. Later, he became the head coach at Lake Forest College in Illinois. Jones was aware of the owners' feud and told them: "I'll take the job, but only if you two stay put in the front office. I want to be boss on the field. Let me do things my way and I'll win the championship in three years." The Bears did improve to 9-4-1 in 1930 and by 1932 (as Jones promised) captured the NFL title with a quizzical 7-1-6 mark.

The 1930 season would also mark the first without the inimitable Paddy Driscoll, who finally retired after serving what seemed like a lifetime in the Chicago pro ranks. Driscoll struggled to answer the call at the Bears training camp, but a leg muscle injury finally prompted the retirement of this early superstar as an active player.

Back on the South Side, with Nevers now at the coaching helm, the Cardinals opened the 1930 campaign with a 30-0 nonleague victory against the Sturgis (MI) Wildcats. The NFL season began the following week (September 21) against the defending league champions Green Bay. Behind the running of infamous back Johnny Blood, the Packers swatted the Cards 14-0. During that game Nevers was injured and his team was unable to mount much of an offensive threat.

The Packers' first score came on a ten-yard touchdown run by left halfback Verne Lewellen. Although many touchdowns were scored in the NFL that day, that was the only one attributed to a district attorney. In the days when players still held other full-time jobs, Lewellen's was one of the most visible. He was in the midst of his second term of office on the Republican side of the ticket in Wisconsin. The game also featured several future Hall of Famers including Blood, Cal Hubbard of the Packers, and Nevers and Walt Kiesling of the Cardinals.

Blood was one of the first "bad boys" in the league, a rugged individual who followed his own instincts and didn't always bow to conformity. Born John Victor McNally, Johnny borrowed his new surname from the title of the Rudolph Valentino movie "Blood and Sand." Blood was a gifted runner who could improvise both off and on the field. He was selected as a charter member of the Pro Football Hall of Fame in 1963.

Hubbard is perhaps best known for his lengthy career as a Major League Baseball umpire. With his tremendous football physique (6'5", 250 pounds), there is little question why Major League players would carefully consider whether they wanted to dispute his calls or not. As an intimidating football player, he was a cunning blocker and perhaps the league's most feared lineman at the time. Hubbard was also elected a charter member of the Football Hall of Fame in 1963.

On the Cardinals side, Kiesling was the team's largest player (6'2", 235 pounds), and was relatively quick for a guard. Walt graduated from St. Thomas College and then played two years with the Duluth Eskimos (1926-1927) and one season with Pottsville (1928). He moved to Chicago in 1929 where he was named All-Pro. Following his time with the Cardinals, Kiesling played for the Bears, Packers, and Pittsburgh before retiring in 1938. He entered the Hall of Fame in 1966.

Nevers was easily the most recognizable during his pro career, owing to the national stature he initially achieved as a collegian at Stanford. His escapades, first with Duluth and then with the Cardinals, were legendary. While he only played five seasons in the NFL, the extended "tour" campaigns pursued by Duluth—and then the Cardinals—added many more contests to his ledger. The Hall of Fame inducted Nevers as a charter member as well in 1963.

Joining Nevers and Kiesling for the 1930 Cardinals season were several other experienced players, such as veteran guard Herb Blumer, a professor of sociology at the

University of Chicago; end Charles "Chuck" Kassel, a local boy from Proviso Township High School and the University of Illinois who played with the Frankford Yellow Jackets before joining the Cards in 1929; and tackle Jess Tinsley, the former captain of Louisiana State who was back for his second season with the Cards. Among the rookie prospects was Northwestern center Mickey Erickson, a sturdy 201-pounder in the middle. The menacing Duke Slater was back at tackle to lead the way for Nevers in the Cardinals' double wing attack.

After the opening loss to the Packers, the Cardinals traveled to Minneapolis on September 28 where a fumble by the Red Jackets' star Oran Pape in the fourth quarter allowed the visitors to secure a 7-7 tie. After the visit to Minnesota, the Cards sped off to the East for a busy four away games in ten days. The four games, along with the incessant rail travel, would be a tremendous burden on the players, but when else would they be able to visit tidy outposts such as Portsmouth and Providence?

## A Full Repertoire Of Reverses, Triple Passes, And Delayed Line Bucks

The first stop was in Portsmouth, Ohio, on Sunday, October 5, where the Cardinals and the Spartans both failed to score in front of sixty-five hundred fans. Unfortunately, Nevers, who had injured his ankle in the Green Bay game, was reinjured against the Spartans, and his status for the remainder of the trip was questionable.

The journey continued just three days later (October 8), when a crowd of five thousand watched the Cardinals smother the host Newark Tornados 13-0 for their first league victory of the young season. Nevers was in street clothes for this contest in which fullback Gene Rose, subbing for Nevers, scored twice off tackle in the second quarter on runs of twenty-five and two yards, and booted the extra point following his second touchdown. Phil Handler, who later in his career would coach the Cardinals, made his first start for the team at left guard in the Newark game. Then it was on to Providence, Rhode Island, as the barnstorming Cardinals matched up with the Steam Roller. Once again Nevers was not in uniform, and the Cards were tripped by the Roller 9-7 on October 12.

The final game of the tour would be in the Polo Grounds against the New York Giants on October 15. The Cardinals had been pioneers in the first NFL night game in Providence in 1929, and the fad already had caught on during the 1930 season. The Giants scheduled this Cardinals contest as the first night game for the Polo Grounds, but the game was washed out by rain and postponed a day. When the two teams finally met on October 16, the Giants survived with a 25-12 verdict. The Cardinals were without Nevers, but initially bewildered the Giants "with a deceptive attack that included a full repertoire of reverses, triple passes and delayed line bucks," according to the *Tribune*. A surprisingly large crowd of fifteen thousand, including former New York governor Alfred E. Smith, was on hand for the night attraction. The six-game road excursion left the Cards with a disappointing 1-3-2 league record. Nevers's absence sorely hindered the Cardinals' offensive schemes.

The season's first home game against the Bears on October 19 brought little to cheer about. With Nevers still hobbled by injuries, the Bears remembered their 40-

6 thrashing from the previous season and walloped the Cardinals 32-6. The exhausted Cardinals had now played five games in just two weeks, but finally enjoyed a few days of rest before embarking on another unusual road trip. With Nevers at full strength, the Cards traveled to Philadelphia for a game with Frankford on Saturday, October 25. After a close first half, the visitors led 13-7, with Nevers scoring all of the points. Then in the fourth quarter, Charlie "Bunny" Belden scored on a seventy-eight-yard jaunt for the Cardinals, followed by a fifty-seven-yard scoring dash by Gene Rose, and the Cardinals walked away with a 34-7 victory. But there was very little time to rest.

Following the win over Frankford, the Cardinals boarded the train for the long ride back to Chicago where the team would face the Portsmouth Spartans the very next day. Portsmouth arrived well rested at Comiskey Park and enjoyed a 4-1-1 record compared to the Cardinals 2-4-2 slate. The Spartans' bruising fullback, a 235-pounder named Chief McLain, solved the Cardinals' defense early, and the visitors jumped to a 13-0 lead in the first half. Yet any time that Nevers was healthy, the Cardinals had a chance to prevail. Nevers kicked into gear late in the second quarter when he scored from three yards out and then connected with Cobb Rooney on a twenty-nine-yard scoring pass to knot the game 13-13 at the half. Despite playing an away game just a day before, followed by the long night of travel, the Cardinals appeared to grow stronger as the game went on. Nevers snapped the tie with a twenty-yard field goal in the fourth period, followed by another short Nevers touchdown run and an extra point, leaving the weary Cardinals with a satisfying 23-13 victory.

But the week wasn't over yet for the tired road warriors. Dr. Jones scheduled another away game for Wednesday, October 29, this time with the nonleague Milwaukee Night Hawks. Fortunately, the Cardinals were rarely threatened in this easy 33-6 victory. As the month of October stumbled to its conclusion, the Cardinals had squeezed in eight games in just twenty-four days. Overall, the team was 5-4-2, but the end of the season was nowhere in sight.

The Cardinals then split a pair of home games, downing Frankford 6-0 (November 2) on Nevers's fifty-yard scoring pass to Belden, before falling to Hap Moran and the New York Giants 13-7. Moran replaced the heralded Benny Friedman as the Giants' key passer in this game and completed 6 of 8 tosses for 147 yards in the first half. In the second half, with the Cardinals leading 7-0, Moran passed sixty yards for one score, then set up his own two-yard scoring run with another thirty-five-yard pass play. He also kicked the extra point for the victors.

## *His Direction Of The Cardinals Attack Showed No Fault*

What followed the next week was one of the most surprising accomplishments in the history of the Cardinals franchise. Burdened with a 4-5-2 league record and drained by a difficult thirteen game schedule (6-5-2), the Cardinals entertained the undefeated Green Bay Packers on November 16. The Packers had easily captured the league crown in 1929 with a 12-0-1 record and rolled into Chicago undefeated (8-0) once again. Counting the last two games of the 1928 season, Green Bay had not lost in twenty-three straight games dating back to 1928, with just two ties to mar the team's record over that long stretch. Meanwhile, the Cardinals had struggled to stay above water but looked forward to the game with the Packers since the team would be at full strength for one of the few times during this injury-plagued season.

Coach Nevers took advantage of the healthy status of his squad and directed a week of strenuous practices, unencumbered by midweek games or travel. Despite being heavily favored, the Packers bolstered their chances by adding three new players prior to the Cardinals game, including Oran Pape, the gifted halfback from Minneapolis. As the team prepared to head for Chicago, it was announced that two thousand die-hard Green Bay fans, along with a sixty-piece "lumberjack" band, would follow the Packers to Comiskey Park.

The high spirits of the visitors quickly soured when Nevers directed a fifty-one-yard scoring drive to provide the Cards with a 6-0 advantage in the first quarter. Although the Packers tied it up by the half, Nevers tallied on a short plunge and added the extra point that resulted in the final outcome, a 13-6 Cardinals victory. The defeat snapped Green Bay's twenty-three-game unbeaten streak and surprised just about everybody. Wilfrid Smith wrote in the *Tribune:*

> *The Packers have represented perfection in professional football so long they have become a measuring rule for the game. Thus the thousands who yesterday hoped for a victory, were stunned when it was achieved. Perhaps Green Bay did not play as in other games. Perhaps the team was stale from a succession of hard contests. No losing team ever appears to advantage in defeat.*
>
> *Explanations aside, the Packers lost to a team which excelled in all phases of attack. Nevers out kicked both Verne Lewellen and Johnny Blood. His passes were completed when the outcome rested on completion. His direction of the Cardinal attack showed no fault.*

In the *Milwaukee Journal*, Oliver Kuechle commented:

> *It's a long, long winning streak that doesn't end up somewhere. Ask the Green Bay Packers today. They know. On top of the football world with 22 straight victories since 1928, not counting the tie with Philadelphia last year, they lost to the Chicago Cardinals before 12,000 pop eyed, almost unbelieving fans at Comiskey Park . . .*

Kuechle called the Cardinals victory "amazing" and described the Packers' defeat as "catastrophic," but all was forgiven in Green Bay a few hours later when it was learned that the Bears had defeated the second-place Giants in New York, thus assuring that the Packers would remain at the top of the league standings. While the win by the Cardinals was surprising, it might not have been entirely unexpected by Nevers. With both he and his teammates free from injuries for the game, the Cardinals were able to field a fairly potent team on both sides of the attack. Slater and Blumer continued to anchor a smart, resourceful line, while the backfield was fundamentally sound and crafty. Nevers loved deception in the backfield, and the Cardinals were not shy about using reverses, laterals, and short pitches to confuse the opposition. If all else failed, Nevers would simply plow straight ahead down the field behind the unwavering blocking of Slater.

Another significant weapon provided by Nevers was his exceptional punting ability. While not in the class of Paddy Driscoll in terms of kicking field goals or extra points, Nevers was the premiere punter of his day. In the upset of the Packers, Nevers turned the game around with a booming seventy-five-yard punt near the end of the third quarter. With the Packers pinned down on their own three-yard line, the eventual exchange of punts left the Cardinals in good field position to finally engineer the winning scoring drive.

## One Of The Cardinals Swatted Joe

Nevers continued his magic a week later in a nonleague home game against the Memphis Tigers. He rushed for two touchdowns and passed for another as the Cardinals swamped the visitors 20-7. If anyone had noticed, the Cardinals had now won six of the last seven games, improving to 8-5-2 overall. While no longer a factor in the league title chase, the Cardinals were in prime shape for the final conference game of the year against the Bears on Thanksgiving Day, November 27. A significant crowd was expected at Wrigley Field for the twentieth meeting between the two clubs. Nevers would square off once again with Red Grange, who was in the Bears backfield with the rugged Bronko Nagurski. A few days before the game, the Bears added another wrinkle to the lineup by announcing that Notre Dame's excellent senior fullback, Joe Savoldi, would be joining the team. This was clearly a violation of the league rule (instituted after the Red Grange situation in 1925), which stated that no college player could play with a professional team until that player's class had graduated. Savoldi was in the Notre Dame class of 1931, but had left school following his secret marriage and subsequent annulment. So only three weeks after starting for the Irish, Savoldi jumped at the chance to become a Bear.

Nevertheless, Savoldi played a major role against the Cardinals, scoring the only touchdown in a 6-0 Bears win. The anticipated crowd of thirty thousand was limited to about eight thousand when the temperature dipped into the single digits by game time. The fans, as well as reporter Wilfrid Smith, were impressed by the rookie's performance:

> The crowd belonged to the swarthy, black haired Italian. The thousands thwarted incipient pneumonia and frost bite by stamping and yelling for Sa-Vol-Di, whether jumping Joe was engaged in play or not . . . In action against the pros, Joe played as he had against the collegians. On this jaunt, his thumping knee high stride, jerked through the clutching arms of a Cardinal tackler, who skidded on the frozen turf grabbing at nothing . . .

The Bears purposely avoided running in the direction of Slater, and the only score in the game was achieved in the second quarter after the Bears continually attacked the right side following a punt return to the Cards' twenty-four-yard line. After Savoldi plunged in for the score from less than a yard out, the extra point attempt failed. The kicking game had been in disarray for the Bears all season. Knowing that the retired Paddy Driscoll was in attendance, the Bears actually asked him at halftime to rejoin the team and take over the kicking duties. But the amused Driscoll was unable to accept the kind offer due to a prior commitment. The legendary booter was currently employed as one of the officials of this very game.

As the second half dissolved into a series of frozen punts with little offensive activity, the Bears and Cardinals managed to heat things up in the usual fashion—with a brawl. Wilfrid Smith, himself a veteran of the NFL and knowledgeable about the expected etiquette in such events, described Savoldi's induction into the rituals of the Bears-Cardinals social interaction:

> *Savoldi was replaced by Dick Nesbitt until the last six minutes. But he returned to the lineup in time to receive the accolade of professional football. On one of Grange's end runs, Joe dumped the Cardinal left end with decisive abandon. Shortly afterward, one of the Cardinals, screened by a huddle of scrambled players, swatted Joe on the mouth. Although no legal recognition was made of the assault, Savoldi didn't waste breath on promises. He retaliated right out in public with subsequent loss of 15 yards for the Bears . . .*

Two days after the game, league president Joe Carr fined the Bears $1,000 for signing Savoldi in violation of league rules. George Halas contended that the roster addition was legal since Savoldi had been forced to leave school and therefore was not a member of any certain class and thus eligible to play with the Bears. Savoldi, meanwhile, played just two more games for the Bears and then left the NFL forever. His lone touchdown in league play was the one that launched the win over the Cardinals. He turned his back on football and joined the wrestling ranks where he enjoyed a very lucrative career as a professional grappler.

With the league schedule completed, the Cardinals journeyed to Memphis for a postseason rematch with the Tigers on December 7. Playing before a record local crowd of seven thousand, the visitors squeezed past their hosts 6-0 on Bunny Belden's touchdown run. But the season was not yet complete. Responding to a Cardinals challenge from October 28 to play a game for charity, the Bears agreed to meet their city rivals one last time to close the 1930 season.

## Nevers Kicked Directly At The World's Greatest Pipe Organ

The charity selected to benefit from the contest was the governor's fund for unemployment relief, a noble cause during the economic depression. Yet one could reason that few dollars would be raised if attendance was low, a realistic assumption for a football game scheduled for December 15 in Chicago. Attendance had been severely limited a few weeks earlier by the frigid temperatures on Thanksgiving Day. With both teams still willing to play, Dr. Jones and George Halas decided to skirt the weather issue by playing the game indoors.

While Chris O'Brien's old Racine Cardinals had played several games indoors at the Dexter Park Pavilion, this would be the first game played indoors in Chicago by NFL teams. Chicago Stadium was selected as the site for this historic event and six inches of rolled earth would be installed as the playing surface. To accommodate the cozy indoor surroundings, several rules were adopted:

- *The field would be eighty yards long and kickoffs would be made from the goal line.*
- *To justify the shorter field, the offense would have twenty yards subtracted on each drive prior to crossing mid-field.*
- *A white football would be used to increase visibility for both the players and the fans.*

- *No drop or place kicks for field goals would be permitted.*
- *There would be no restrictions on punting since there would be at least ninety-four feet of open area above the playing surface.*

The response to the indoor game was surprisingly strong. Approximately ten thousand fans jammed into the stadium and witnessed a solid game won by the Bears 9-7. There were some unusual circumstances due to the indoor field, however. With cardboard side walls surrounding the field, no yard markers were visible to the fans. The fans seated on the sidelines had obstructed viewpoints due to the side walls and the players often found the temporary field to be a bit slippery. Overall, it was a nice change of pace for all involved, a successful event for charity, and a challenge for some of the stadium regulars. For example, the *Tribune* noted that the path of Ernie Nevers's extra point kick attempt in the fourth quarter would follow a path that would intersect with the stadium's magnificent pipe organ:

> *Nevers then kicked from placement directly at the world's greatest pipe organ, the bull's eye for the seventh point, and it was good, although deflected by Ralph Waldo Emmerson, the organist.*

Everyone had such a great time that there was talk of doing it again, although the most significant influence of this game would be two years later, when the Bears would play for the NFL championship in this same location. After a long and busy season, the Cardinals went home with an overall 9-7-2 (5-6-2 in league) record. They played in both an historical night game and an unusual indoor game, produced one of the greatest upsets in league history, and played the most games in one season in the team's lifetime. With Ernie Nevers and a healthy team, the Chicago Cardinals had proven that they had the ability and talent to compete with the upper crust of the NFL.

## *1931 Season Kicks Off*

Nevers paced the Cardinals to one of their best seasons in history, finishing 11-4-1 in 1931 (5-4 in league play). In an effort to ease the stress on Nevers, Dr. Jones brought in former New York Giants mentor Leroy Andrew to coach the team while Nevers would remain as field captain. Andrew was refreshing as a head coach with his honest appraisal of his talent. In a preseason interview with the *Tribune*, Andrew didn't flinch when assessing his team: "I have so many great players I don't know where to put them."

Arch Ward of the *Tribune* applauded Andrew for his insight, but cautioned:

> *But in justice to his public he feels he must tell the truth, even at the risk of losing his job if his team fails to make good.*

Following exhibition wins over the Chicago Mills (23-0) and the Pullman Panthers (31-0), quarterbacked by former Cards quarterback Art Folz, Andrew and the Cardinals marched off to Portsmouth, Ohio, for the opening NFL game of the season. The Spartans were not gracious hosts, rolling over Andrew's acclaimed charges 13-3 on Wednesday, September 23. With an injury to starting quarterback Irvin Hill, Andrew was forced to start untested rookie Hal Hilpirt. As expected, the offense struggled and was ineffective throughout the afternoon. It was only one loss, but it was enough to send the honest and optimistic Coach Andrew packing. Dr. Jones had seen enough.

With Nevers back at the coaching helm, the Cardinals dropped road games at both Green Bay (26-7) and the Bears (26-13). Now saddled with an 0-3 mark in the league, the 1931 Cardinals season appeared to be over before it really got started. With only two games scheduled between September 23 and November 1, Nevers had plenty of time to reacquaint himself with the players following the Portsmouth disaster. It would be needed.

## *South Side Snubbing*

Part of this scheduling quirk was the result of Dr. Jones's questionable decision for the Cardinals to share Wrigley Field with the Bears. The difficulty in securing the field forced the Cardinals to delay their home opener until November 15, with only three home league games scheduled during the season. It also stunned the team's loyal fans on the South Side of Chicago who couldn't believe that the team had essentially "moved." A letter that appeared in the *Tribune* was typical of the bruised feelings expressed by the Cards' fans:

> *I read with surprise that this coming season all home games of the Chicago Cardinals will be played at Wrigley Field, which leaves the south side out in the cold as far as professional football is concerned. The writer and four of his friends saw every home game of the Cardinals on the south side last season, but for reasons peculiar to true south siders we have made up our minds that if the Cardinals' games must be played up on the north side, they will have to rely on the north side for trade. I wonder how many other fans feel the same way about the snubbing.*

But there was more football news of interest as the 1931 season began. The embittered partnership between George Halas and Ed Sternaman finally ceased. Sternaman sold his interest in the Bears and Halas reorganized the corporation. While he would remain as president, wrestler Jim McMillen was elected vice president, and Charles Bidwill, president of the Bentley-Murray printing company, was named secretary. That was the end result of the reorganization; how Halas reached that point with the help of Bidwill is an entirely different saga.

With the Great Depression still hovering over all aspects of life in 1931, things were tough all over. Sternaman offered his shares of the Bears to Halas for $38,000 in an attempt to generate needed cash for his gas station and apartment building businesses. Although Halas dearly wanted to maintain command of the team, he, too, was experiencing personal financial distress. Like many other NFL clubs, the Bears were operating at a deficit. In fact, as Halas stated in his autobiography, the NFL as a whole was shaky:

> *The Depression was deadly for many league teams. Of the twenty-two clubs in the league in 1926 and eleven which had formed subsequently, only ten were operating in 1931, and four of these disappeared during or after that season.*

In reality, only Providence, Cleveland, and Frankford went away after 1931.

To raise the funds necessary to secure the shares from Sternaman, Halas tapped into some unlikely sources including Bidwill, McMillen, and even the mother of player George Trafton. Halas contracted with Sternaman for his shares of the Chicago Bears and paid him $25,000 on July 3, 1931, with two additional installments of $6,000 and $7,000 due on January 25, 1932, and July 31, 1932, respectively. While Halas had no difficulty in making that $6,000 payment, the second would prove to be more of a challenge, especially since a clause in the purchase agreement stipulated that the ownership of the Bears would automatically revert back to Sternaman if Halas failed to meet the payments as scheduled.

As economic woes continued to plague the country, Halas found himself about $5,000 short of the $7,000 needed for the final payment to Sternaman. Tapped out and with nowhere to turn, Halas appeared unable to make the final payment by the imposed deadline. It was then that Bidwill stepped in to help his old friend. Bidwill and Halas had become acquainted during their time together at the Great Lakes training base during World War I and later shared ownership in the Chicago Bruins professional basketball team. "Halas and my father were very good friends," recalled current Cardinals President William V. Bidwill. "And he did help Halas and the Bears. The financial numbers would seem insignificant in today's economy, but they were big back then." Bidwill initially invested $5,000 in the Bears and then helped arrange a loan for Halas to acquire the additional $5,000 needed to stave off the takeover efforts by Sternaman. With a noon deadline quickly approaching, Halas completed the paperwork for the loan and then delivered the $5,000 check to Sternaman's attorney with just minutes to spare. So, by the thinnest of margins, the Chicago Bears remained in the control of George Halas, while Charles W. Bidwill, a wealthy attorney/businessman/sports promoter fortified his position as one of the most influential figures on the local sporting scene.

## *Solving Green Bush And Green Bay*

The Cardinals returned to action on October 26 with a visit to the Rock Island Green Bush club. Nevers exploded for three touchdowns and the visitors waltzed through an easy 45-13 victory. If there was a weakness in the Cardinals camp, the long rest and the Green Bush victory appeared to solve a great deal of the woes. Beginning with the Rock Island game, the Cardinals knocked off six straight opponents, a streak that wasn't surpassed again until the 1948 season. During the month of November, the Cardinals swept past the Brooklyn Dodgers (14-7), the Cleveland Indians (14-6), the Green Bay Packers (21-13), and the Portsmouth Spartans (20-19). They also routed the Grand Rapids Maroons 36-0 in an exhibition game on November 11.

The game with the Packers on November 15 was a key one on the Cardinals schedule. It was the first home game of the season for the Chicagoans (albeit at Wrigley Field), and as usual, the Packers were undefeated (9-0) and in first place. In 1930, the Cardinals had managed the huge upset win over the undefeated Packers. But strapped with a 2-3 league slate, another upset seemed beyond reach, especially with the earlier 26-7 trouncing by these same Packers. Coach Nevers used the Grand Rapids game three days earlier to fine-tune his squad, but most of the regulars had experienced heavy minutes despite the rout. Would the Cardinals be able to recuperate in time?

If anything concerned Nevers, it was his offense. While his team had done well in the previous four wins, the offense never seemed to click against the staunch defenders fielded by the Packers. The two-time NFL champs were obviously strong again, and the Packers had always stymied the Cardinals' offense. The most points the Cardinals had ever scored against the Packers up until this time was in a 16-3 win way back in 1922. Nevers vowed to personally change all of that and thought that perhaps another upset victory might not be out of the question:

> *If there's one thing we Cardinals would like to do better than anything else, it is to run up the score on that Green Bay bunch. And last year we thought we had clicked when we beat them in our second game of the season. Along in the fourth quarter the score was 13-6 in our favor and we got going again toward another tally. We pushed the ball down to the one-yard line, first down, and just what do you think happened then? The gun went off and so did our touchdown. Just one more play and we would have had a new record score against the champs. Sixteen points are the most we ever made against them.*

The Cardinals, paced by Nevers's two touchdown tosses, scored early and eased themselves to a 21-13 victory. Falling along the way were the Packers' undefeated season and the Cards' scoring mark against their rivals. On a more surprising note, the Packers game drew only eight thousand fans to Wrigley Field, about one-third fewer than watched the same two teams at Comiskey Park the year before. With the marquee name of Nevers and a revitalized club playing against the best team in the league, the Cardinals management surely must have been distressed at that turnout. The switch to the North Side was viewed as a move to attract more fans, not to diminish the return. Only five thousand turned out the following week in the win over Portsmouth, compared to eight thousand between the same two teams at Comiskey Park the year before.

Now 4-3, the Cardinals rolled into the annual Thanksgiving Day bash with the Bears, but as visitors at Wrigley Field. Unswayed by the Cardinals' recent hot streak, the Bears slowed down Nevers and claimed an 18-7 victory. Just two days later (November 29), the Cards were back in Wrigley Field in what would prove to be Ernie Nevers's last game in the NFL. Playing on a Saturday to accommodate the Bears, the Cardinals knocked off the Cleveland Indians 21-0. Nevers rushed for two touchdowns, passed for a third and kicked all three extra points in a typical and fitting end to his NFL career.

However, few were there to witness it. Only fifteen hundred were in attendance, which left the Cardinals with a total of just over fourteen thousand for the three game home slate for 1931, certainly a devastating blow for Dr. Jones and his plans for financial security. In an attempt to generate some additional income, Jones scheduled three more games prior to the end of the season. On December 5, the team traveled back to Grand Rapids, Michigan, and was surprised with a 7-7 tie. A week later, the Cardinals were in St. Louis, where they defeated the Battery A Gunners 26-6. Finally, the season groaned to a close on December 20 with a 24-7 home win over the Memphis Tigers.

The hope for another title for the South Siders diminished following the 1931 season when Nevers decided to retire. His strong body had taken on incredible punishment throughout his brief pro career, although one must consider that he also played professional baseball and basketball and rarely experienced a substitution while on the football field. Nevers's decision appeared to be sudden and may have been solidified by a wrist injury. In December of 1931, while the Cardinals were playing an exhibition game in Michigan, the *Grand Rapids Herald* reported on Nevers's retirement plans:

> *Nevers says he is going to continue playing football until he is no longer able to run with a ball in his arm. That's how much he likes the game. He is also a big league baseball player, but football is his first love.*

A month later, Nevers and several other Cardinals played in a charity game in San Francisco on January 24, 1932. Aptly dubbed the "Nevers Team," the hastily collected group of players defeated a team led by Notre Dame's Frank Carideo 14-0 before forty thousand spectators in a benefit game for the Knights of Columbus. In typical fashion, Nevers scored all twenty-six points, including touchdown runs of sixty, fourteen, forty-five, and twenty yards.

But quietly, before the game, Nevers told his teammates that he was retiring. End Harry Ebding recalled hearing Nevers's surprising message: "In the dressing room before we started play Nevers told us it was his last game. He said he wanted to make a showing, and, by golly, he did." Unfortunately, Nevers suffered a broken left wrist on the last play of the game, which was originally thought to be the reason for his departure from the game. "I received the last kickoff and after being tackled, thrust out my left hand to break the fall when it happened," said Nevers. "I'm through with football and with professional baseball, too. I'm going to devote my time to private business." And just like that, the great Ernie Nevers was gone, along with the Cardinals' chances for a championship. Although the team had won twenty games overall (20-11-3) during the preceding two seasons, it had nothing to show for it.

## Not Half Of Those Men Smoke Cigarettes

Nevers eventually landed as an assistant coach at Stanford, while Dr. Jones waited until July 8, 1932, to hire Jack Chevigny as the new coach of the Chicago Cardinals. Chevigny had played three years (1926-1928) at Notre Dame as a halfback for Knute Rockne. He then spent the next three seasons (1929-1931) as backfield coach for the Irish. While Chevigny plugged the gap left by Nevers's departure as the coach, the Cardinals made little headway in replacing Nevers the player. "I'm going to develop the fastest and best balanced backfield in the circuit," predicted the new coach. In pursuit of that objective, Jones picked up veteran Walter Holmer from the Bears and signed rookie quarterback Ed Risk from Purdue. Chevigny conducted a tight training camp at Mills Stadium in Chicago and drilled his players in the use of the "Notre Dame" system involving quick passes, shifts, and cutback slants off tackle. The owner was impressed. As Dr. Jones watched his team flail Grand Rapids (13-0) and the Aurora (IL) Yellow Jackets (33-0) in exhibition play, he stated:

> *They're in excellent shape. I venture to say not half of those men out there smoke*

*cigarettes, and practically none drink. Not only that but they conduct themselves in an orderly, dignified manner, reporting on time every morning for practice and getting plenty of sleep.*

The combination of training and the new offense clicked immediately. Usually a team of slow starters, the Cardinals moved to a record of 6-1-2 (2-1-2 in the league) following a 27-7 rout of Brooklyn on October 30. Chevigny had managed to establish the theory of teamwork into his players, and it was apparently paying off with some early dividends. He explained the situation to the *Chicago Sun Times:*

*Our boys are anxious for the team to win. They don't care who scores, just so we score. When I tell an end to play a certain way against a certain team, either wide or close in, as the case may be, he plays that way—regardless. He doesn't play the way he did in college and, perhaps made all-Big Ten, or all-something.*

*The point is, the pros are eager to carry out orders. One man's plans, well carried out, are worth more in football than eleven men's ideas that conflict. Consequently, the caliber of play in the pro league is improving. In fact, the competition has gotten so tough—particularly on the defensive side—that there's no such thing as outplaying another team now. You have to outsmart them—trick them into openings.*

Part of the Cardinals' early success in 1932 was the surprise performance of halfback Joe Lillard. Armed with amazing speed, but little experience, Lillard joined the Cards prior to the Portsmouth game on October 2, 1932, and was an immediate sensation for two reasons. On one hand, Lillard had very little collegiate playing experience, which masked the usual NFL perception that most of its performers were All-Americans from large schools. This was a signal that teams would begin to sift through the talent pool available at smaller or mostly unknown colleges. On the other hand, Lillard was another rarity in the NFL at the time; he was black. This was not a signal that teams would begin to sift through the talent pool available among black athletes.

Dr. Jones swept against the tide with his comments regarding the acquisition of Lillard:

*The lowdown is that we are showing up the All-Americans of the big schools, a lot of whom get that way through the efforts of high-powered publicity departments. Look at Lillard, our colored boy. He is one of the best backs in the entire league, yet his entire college experience consists of a freshman year at Oregon State. He wanted a job and we gave him one. And he has outplayed most every back he has gone against this season.*

*I'll take the boys who have had to fight for their newspaper mention. You can have the All-Americans.*

Sadly, Lillard turned out to be the last black player in the NFL for over a decade. No one has admitted any guilt or assigned any blame for this travesty, which occurred from the time Lillard left the league in 1933 until Kenny Washington and Woody Strode were signed by the Los Angeles Rams in 1946. There is some speculation that the Depression dictated this circumstance, with the viewpoint being that NFL owners were leery of hiring a black player when so many white males were unemployed.

Or perhaps it was a strange, unwritten dogma that drifted through the league. "Strange" in that the league welcomed black players from its inception and now appeared to be shuffling away in the opposite direction.

In any event, the Cardinals enjoyed the services of Lillard while he was around. He joined the team in time for its 7-7 tie with Portsmouth following an injury to Elmer Schwartz. He immediately took over the rushing, passing, punting, and dropkicking duties . . . and even managed to find time to slug it out with Father Lumpkin of the Spartans in his first game. Newspapers around the country tabbed Lillard as the "next Fritz Pollard" and the Cardinals appeared to become instant contenders. *The Providence Sunday Journal* marveled at his "shiftiness and side-stepping, hip swinging running ability . . . the outstanding broken field running back in the league this season." In a 9-0 win over the Boston Braves, Lillard averaged 6.6 yards per carry and was just as elusive on his punt returns, knocking off 44 yards on one.

But as the team moved into the month of November with their glittering 6-1-2 record, the bottom fell out. Beginning with a 19-9 loss to Green Bay, the Cardinals dropped their last five league games, including a 34-0 rout at the hands of the Bears. Even in a dreadfully boring game, the Cardinals and the Bears managed to sneak in a few good fistfights, most notably between Bears newcomer John Doering and the Cardinals' Milan Creighton. Lillard, bothered by a bad ankle, became a nonfactor down the stretch and did not appear in the final two games.

## *They Saw A Couple Of Incipient Fights*

The concluding league game of the 1932 season on December 27 at Wrigley Field was both an athletic and a financial disaster. While the Cardinals bowed to the Boston Braves 8-6 in a lackluster effort, the "Ladies Day" crowd included only about seven hundred paying customers. Dr. Jones did not make enough revenue to meet Boston's guarantee of $4,000. The highlight of the game featured another fight, only this time it was between a pair of frustrated Cardinals as reported in the *American:*

> *They saw a couple of incipient fights, the last one between Capt. Frank McNally of the Cardinals and Walter Kiesling, Giant guard. That came just after the Cards had received a 15 yard penalty for roughness, and probably arose when the offender was bawled out by his teammates. Whatever the cause, Coach Jack Chevigny yanked McNally immediately and called Kiesling out of the game shortly thereafter, to sit beside McNally on the bench until they cooled off.*

The Cardinals avoided some hard feelings by concluding the season in St. Louis on December 4 with a 20-7 victory over the Battery A Gunners. Another game was rained out the following week in Memphis, where the Cardinals would have faced Ernie Nevers and the Tigers as part of Nevers's two-game foray out of retirement.

Back in Chicago, abusive winter weather forced the Bears (6-1-6) to defeat the Portsmouth Spartans (6-1-4) 9-0 indoors at the Chicago Stadium for the NFL championship. With the typhoon-like rain in Memphis and the blizzards in Chicago, another team solved its own weather problems. After witnessing the end of their three-year reign over the NFL (despite a 10-3-1 record), the Packers attempted to soothe their hurt feelings by boarding a ship in San Pedro, California. The Packers and their followers had the right idea: the team would play its next exhibition game in Honolulu!

## *Dr. Jones Was Losing Interest In Football*

The 1932 season would result in big changes, both for the Cardinals and the NFL. The attendance woes and inconsistent play of his team had begun to plague Dr. Jones. He wanted out.

Meanwhile, the fans seemed to like the idea of a postseason playoff, even if it was indoors, but the rules that ignored game ties and restricted passing would need some careful evaluation if the league was going to continue to grow as a spectator sport in America.

These concerns prompted some major rules changes for the 1933 season. These changes were so extraordinary that the 1933 campaign might truly be considered the birth of the "modern" NFL. For starters, the league divided itself into two divisions, with the winners in the East and the West meeting in a postseason championship game. In 1933, the NFL was divided into two divisions as follows:

| EAST | WEST |
|------|------|
| *New York Giants* | *Chicago Cardinals* |
| *Portsmouth Spartans* | *Chicago Bears* |
| *Cleveland Indians* | *Green Bay Packers* |
| *Boston Braves* | *Detroit Lions* |

Next, the goalposts were moved up to the front of the end zone. This was intended to bring back the kicking (field goal) game, which had all but disappeared in 1932. Because of the difficulty in scoring three points over goal posts placed at the rear of the end zone, a plethora of tie games emerged in 1932. Since the NFL treated tie games at the time as a washout in the standings, a team such as the Bears in 1932 could claim the league title with a 6-1-6 record while the Packers were sent home with the more impressive 10-3-1 mark. As it was, the Bears nailed down the title after winning less than half of their regular season games.

The owners of the NFL were perceptive and smart. They finally realized that their young sport was gaining popularity and confidence, but that the pros had also been guilty of persistently following the trends in college football. The landmark decisions of 1933 changed all of that, particularly with two more significant innovations. The first proposal was a very sensible one: moving the ball away from the sideline on the first play after an out-of-bounds situation. Previously, the ball had been placed adjacent to the spot where the play had gone out. The offense thus lost half of its playing field and usually needed to spend at least the first down play attempting to crawl away from this spot in order to establish a more positive field position. The ball on such plays would now be placed ten yards from the sideline.

Another pertinent change was removing a key restriction on the passing game. While the passing game was a weapon prior to 1933, it was certainly not the weapon of choice. The ball was still a bit unwieldy in size and the passer could not release his toss unless he was at least five yards behind the line of scrimmage.

This rule not only restricted the passing game, but was also difficult for the officials to enforce. In 1933, the rule that previously required the passer to observe that five-yard distance between himself and the line of scrimmage was changed. The players could now release their passes from anywhere behind the line of scrimmage, which opened up all sorts of offensive possibilities for the teams. The final significant change was not one that involved rules, but one that ultimately changed the direction of pro football. In 1933, the shape of the football itself was further refined to more closely resemble the ball that is used today. The ball had evolved from the pudgy oval used by the Morgan Athletic Association in 1899 to a sleeker sphere that could be handled easily, and thus passed much more successfully.

As the late 1930s would demonstrate, the pass would become pro football's most dangerous weapon, and a whole legion of talented, focused "receivers" would further define the image of pro football. With the Great Depression still lingering, these changes were pragmatic and resourceful. Pro football had become a contender in the entertainment field, and it needed to compete successfully for the limited entertainment dollars that were available at the time. More importantly, these changes in the rules differentiated the pros from their collegiate counterparts. The pros now possessed the ammunition to fire up a more wide-open and exciting game with more scoring, fewer tie games, and the unwrapping of exciting pass play possibilities.

The impact would be immediate with field goals increasing from six in 1932 to thirty-six in 1933, while tie games were reduced from ten to five. But bigger changes were ahead for the Cardinals as a team.

Following the 1932 season and its nightmarish conclusion with five straight league losses, coach Jack Chevigny left the team to accept a position at St. Edwards College in Austin, Texas. On May 12, 1933, the Chicago Cardinals hired veteran Oregon State coach Paul Schissler as the new mentor. Schissler had proven to be a winner during his nine seasons at OSU, and Dr. Jones was pleased with his new field boss:

> I believe we have found a man with sufficient experience and background to give the Cardinals the necessary push toward at least a first division berth in the pro league. It takes an experienced coach to handle a group of post-graduate players.

In even bigger news (although it was not announced until September 6, 1933), Dr. Jones agreed to sell the team to Charles V. Bidwill. However, Bidwill was an officer and stockholder of the Chicago Bears, so he needed time to divest himself of those assets and responsibilities before officially acquiring the Cardinals.

As usual, George Halas claimed his rightful role in the transaction:

> Dr. Jones was losing interest in football. He saw a dark financial future for football and his Cardinals. Undesirable characters again sniffed about. I looked around for another owner. I favored my old friend Charlie Bidwill. He loved the Bears. He was one of our most ardent fans. He was owner of a printing company and part owner of Sportsman's Race Track. Both were profitable . . .
> One night Dr. Jones and I were guests aboard Charlie's boat. Bidwill said he heard Dr. Jones might be willing to sell the Cardinals. "If I get my price," Dr. Jones said.
> Bidwill asked the price.
> "Fifty thousand," Dr. Jones said. That was double the sum he had paid for the club.

> *The doctor thought Bidwill was only making polite conversation but a cou-*
> *ple of nights later Bidwill called Dr. Jones and told him he'd take the club for*
> *$50,000. I rejoiced. The Cardinals remained in good hands.*

Although he agreed to stay on one more year as president of the Cardinals, the financial burden along with the time spent away from his personal life addressing football matters finally persuaded Dr. Jones to grudgingly surrender his ownership in pro football:

> *I regret to withdraw from the ranks of professional football owners. I believe it*
> *is the fastest developing sport in America. I can't do justice to two jobs and I feel*
> *at the moment that I am more valuable to the community as city physician than*
> *as a football leader.*

As an owner, Jones had nothing to be ashamed of during his four-year tenure. He developed the concept of "out-of-town" preseason training camps, brought in the great Ernie Nevers for three fun-filled seasons, and scheduled a staggering total of sixty-two games for his team in that four-year period, including several postseason exhibition contests. The Chicago Cardinals were certainly visible, if not financially successful.

## Bear With Him

Charles Bidwill was an officer and a shareholder with the Bears when he purchased the Cardinals from Dr. David Jones in 1933. His ownership of the Cardinals didn't mean that he surrendered his allegiance to the Bears. Bidwill continued to staunchly follow the Bears and in 1934, he postponed the starting time of the Cardinals Thanksgiving Day game with Green Bay from 11:00 a.m. until 2:00 p.m. "in order to permit professional fans to hear radio reports of the Bears game in Detroit," according to the *Chicago Tribune*. Later, Jimmy Conzelman recalled a critical game with the Bears during his tenure as coach of the Cardinals. The Bears needed a win over the South Siders to capture the Western Division title: "We were beating them at half," said Conzelman, "and the Bears just did manage to pull it out. Afterward, Charlie came into our dressing room shaking his head. All he could say was, 'Wow, that was close.' "

## *Bidwill Is The City's Most Active Athletic Figure*

The new owner was often bothered by the fact that big-time college and professional sports were not always accessible to the average citizen. Bidwill clearly intended to alter that pattern with the Cardinals when he purchased the team: "We hope to attract letter carriers, streetcar conductors, clerks, and above all, kids. In brief, the success of professional football depends in no small measure upon its ability to draw the workaday sport fans who either have been ignored by the colleges or who can't get away to attend Saturday games."

Bidwill had enormous experience in marketing sports events and promoting his products. Even more surprising was Bidwill's ability to experience business growth during the worst economic period of the century. To those who might have been unaware of Bidwill's burgeoning sports empire, the *Tribune's* Arch Ward provided this succinct description:

> *At a time when most persons financially interested in sport have adopted retrench-ment policies, the new boss of the Cardinals has expanded his interests until he is now perhaps the city's most active athletic figure. Bidwill is president of the Chicago Stadium Operating Company, which has exclusive rights to promote box-ing, wrestling, bicycle races and kindred events in the world's largest indoor arena. He also is a director of the American Turf Association, proprietor of a racing sta-ble, and secretary of the Chicago Business Men's Racing Association, which con-trols the Hawthorne track. In his spare moments he serves as president of the Bentley, Murray Printing Company.*

From a business point of view, Bidwill's acquisition of the Cardinals provided new hope for the team's economic success as well. "When Charlie bought the Cardinals, the team had been a vest-pocket operation," recalled Arch Wolfe, Bidwill's business manager. "He set up books, ran it as a business and in a businesslike man-ner, and yet he never got far from the game. He loved it more than anything else, and he wanted it to succeed." He also made an immediate impact upon the game as a Bears officer, even before he became officially involved as the Cardinals owner, according to Halas:

> *Charlie worked very hard to help push the three most important rules changes ever voted on at a single meeting. At the meeting early in 1933, the NFL voted to move the goal posts to the goal line, to bring the ball in from the sideline on all out-of-bounds plays, and to make the forward pass legal from any point back of the line of scrimmage instead of five yards behind. All three were significant in the advancement of professional football as a spectator sport.*

As for the 1933 season, Bidwill was cautiously optimistic:

> *We think the Cardinals will hold their own with the leading teams in the league this season. If we are proved wrong, we shall try to strengthen the club for 1934. Nothing less than a championship will be satisfactory.*

Bidwill, who prepped at St. Ignatius High School on the near South Side of Chicago, also graduated with a law degree from Loyola University. During World War I, he was an ensign in naval intelligence. Following the war, he became a corporate counsel and then gradually became involved in his many sporting activities. He earned the nickname "Blue Shirt" for his habitual preference for shirts of that color and it stuck with him throughout his career.

Bidwill might be termed a "creative genius" as a manager for such varied sport-ing activities. Besides participating in horse racing and football, Bidwill was president of the Chicago Stadium Operating Company. In this role, he touted numerous unique indoor events intended to captivate the Chicago sporting audience during the long cruel winters. He promised more indoor football, boxing, and wrestling matches, as well as an indoor lacrosse league, miniature auto racing, and six-day bike races.

Unfortunately, Bidwill's new team was about to plummet to the worst record in the franchise's history. Schissler had begun to rebuild the squad by adding noted running back Chuck Bennett from Cincinnati and acquiring the services of the gifted Gil Berry, a former MVP at the University of Illinois. But on the day that Bidwill's purchase of the team was confirmed, Berry announced that he had also signed a movie contract with Paramount Studios in Hollywood and would be leaving the team. "When I signed with the Cardinals, Dr. David Jones agreed that if I was chosen for the cast of the picture that he would cancel my contract. I don't know whether I have a future in moving pictures, but I have decided to find out." He didn't. Berry was back with the team the next season, but his poorly timed departure left Schissler with the prospect of shuffling his offense around. (Veteran Joe Lillard was not yet back with the team due to a baseball commitment.) Berry had been tabbed as the starting quarterback in Schissler's new passing attack and his loss left a huge void in the offensive scheme. His next hope was his player-assistant coach Roddy Lamb. Lamb had been an assistant with Schissler at Oregon State and had followed him to Chicago where he would also be available as a quarterback. But illness eventually shelved Lamb for most of the season.

With Berry out of the picture, Schissler could still look to other new backs such as Pete Yanuskus (Illinois), Jim Bausch (Kansas), Howie Tipton (Southern California), Les Malloy (Loyola), and Harold Moe (Oregon State). Later, Lillard would return and Don Hill would move over from Green Bay. The line would be bolstered by future Hall of Famer Walt Kiesling and Herb Blumer, who was back after spending the 1932 season studying in Europe. But Schissler would invite very few members back from the 1932 team. By signing on as coach in May, he had ample time to dissect the team's previous difficulties prior to the opening of camp at Mills Stadium in Chicago on September 1. After sweeping through four exhibition games with the Aurora Ideals (65-0), the Freeport Lions (29-6), the Indianapolis Indians (2-0), and the Princeton Tigers (20-0), the Cardinals appeared to be ready for a vastly improved season. Schissler decided upon Malloy as his starting quarterback and moved the quick but agile Bausch to fullback.

## A Right Uppercut To Lester's Prominent Chin

Despite the optimism, after leading 13-0 the Cards were stunned 14-13 by the expansion Pittsburgh Pirates in their opener on Wednesday, September 27. Four days later, the Cardinals stopped in Portsmouth, Ohio, where the Spartans prevailed 7-6. In both games, the differences in the final scores were missed extra points by Lillard, which obscured his brilliant running and passing. The club then rebounded in Cincinnati by defeating the Reds 3-0 on Lillard's seventeen-yard field goal. Lillard was stopped only once during the game by the frustrated Cincinnati defense, and that was when he was clobbered by lineman Lester Caywood, reported the *Chicago Tribune*:

> *Near the end of the game Lester Caywood, husky Cincinnati guard, and Lillard started a fight. Joe landed a right uppercut to Lester's prominent chin and Lester retaliated with a blow that sent Lillard to the turf. Both were ordered from the field by the officials.*

The Cards returned to Chicago for their first home game of the year on October 15 at Wrigley Field against the Bears. Halas (now coaching again) was wary of Lillard's elusive speed in the backfield. Wilfrid Smith predicted that this edition of the Cardinals would be much different than the club that the Bears dismantled late in 1932, 34-0:

*Joe Lillard, Negro halfback, who ran around at will last year in the first of the two game series with the Bears, is one reason for the Cards' optimism. Lillard is an exceptional runner and passer, fast as the proverbial streak, and he also can drop kick as he proved last week when his three points defeated the Cincinnati Reds.*

*Lillard wasn't of much service later in the season because of injuries. For that matter the Cardinal back field was ripped apart by injury and toward the end of the campaign Jack Chevigny, the coach, even thought it might be necessary for him to get into uniform.*

Prior to the game, the Bears hoisted their 1932 championship banner and then watched as Lillard engineered a 9-0 halftime lead for the Cardinals. Lillard sprinted forty-nine yards on a punt return for a touchdown and later kicked a thirty-yard field goal for the halftime advantage. The Bears stormed back when Luke Johnsos grabbed a short touchdown pass, followed by a Jack Manders extra point. Early in the fourth quarter, 257-pound George Musso blocked Lillard's punt from the Cards' fifteen-yard line, which rolled out of the end zone for a safety to tie the game 9-9. The Bears finally prevailed 12-9 when Manders connected on a twenty-yard field goal late in the game. And what would a Bears-Cardinals game be without the requisite brawl? Wilfrid Smith noted:

*The game was rough and frequent penalties were called to check the illegal enthu-siasm of the players. In the third period the Bears intercepted a Cardinal lateral pass and downed the ball behind the goal line, apparently for a touchdown, only to have the play recalled when Joe Kopcha, of the Bears, and Gil Bergerson, Cardinal guard, recently released by the Bears, were convicted of slugging and ejected from the game.*

The loss to the Bears essentially ended the 1933 season for the Cardinals. They were now 1-3 in the league, having lost those three games by a total of five points. Unfortunately, that pattern would continue to haunt the Cards for the remainder of the campaign; the team lost its next five games, all close ones, before salvaging a score-less tie with the lowly Boston Redskins in the final game of the season. The offense sputtered completely in those last six games, enduring three shutouts and scoring just twenty-one points over twenty-four quarters. To complete the ignominious season, some of the Cards joined the Chicago All-Stars and dropped a 20-7 contest to the St. Louis Gunners to complete the schedule. It was a truly bizarre season. The Cardinals finished 1-9-1 in the NFL (5-10-1 overall) despite a stingy defense that allowed more than fourteen points only once all season in league play. That episode occurred in the return match with the Bears, in a 22-6 loss. Rarely has a team with such a horrible record been so competitive.

Schissler vowed to return for more in 1934. Obviously, his defense was in place, but his offense was murky at best, despite embracing the attractive forward pass. In 1934, only a handful of Cardinals would return from the debacle of the 1933 season: center Frank McNally, end Milan Creighton, halfback Dick Nesbitt, fullback Hub Hinchman, back Howie Tipton, and tackle Lou Gordon. However, Joe Lillard did not return. He was next spotted playing for the Westwood Cubs in a newly organized league on the West Coast. Still, there was optimism in the Cards' camp: "I can tell you one thing about this club," said Gordon, who was elected captain, "the other teams will know we're in the league."

## *They Laughed At Chris Columbus, Too*

Before the league schedule began, football enthusiasts were treated to a spectacle that would continue to entertain fans for four more decades. In 1933, the Chicago Bears had played an exhibition game in Chicago's Soldier Field against a group of Notre Dame All-Stars. The concept proved so successful that in 1934 the *Chicago Tribune* launched the first College All-Star game, which would pit the outstanding collegians from the previous season against the defending professional champions. The Bears and the All-Stars battled to a scoreless tie in that inaugural event, but the overall game of football proved to be the ultimate winner with nearly eighty thousand in attendance and an increased national awareness of the game. For over forty years, this annual event drew huge crowds and traditionally kicked off the ensuing football season. The *Tribune* barraged its readers with insightful information on both teams in the weeks before the game, and the fans participated as well by voting for both the All-Star players and their coaches in nationwide tabulations. The program for the 1934 game proclaimed that over 165,000 people had cast votes for the players.

While this game certainly eased the tensions between the power brokers of college and professional football (and was a major contributor to local charities), it forced pro teams, such as the Cardinals, to amble into training camp without several key rookies who were members of the All-Star team. They would be forced to wait until the players completed their All-Star commitments which, in the very early days, involved more than one All-Star extravaganza. The Cardinals would also need to wait for publicity, from the *Tribune* in particular, which focused its preseason football reporting almost solely on its All-Star game activities. The Bears appeared several times in the first decade of All-Star competition due to their numerous NFL championships. Along with normal coverage of Major League Baseball and the two Chicago teams in that loop, there wasn't much space devoted to the lowly Cardinals prior to the start of the NFL regular season.

Schissler predicted a slow start for his team in 1934 when the Cards opened up training camp at Loyola University in Chicago on September 1. Those in camp were quickly joined by the seven College All-Stars: Paul Pardonner (Purdue), Mike Mikulak (Oregon), Fred Canrinus (St.Mary), Dave Cook (Illinois), Pete Mehringer (Kansas), Bill Smith (Washington), and Mike Sebastian (Pittsburgh).

Following an intrasquad game, Schissler planned for the team's first exhibition game of the season, a return to historic Normal Park to battle the Chicago Tigers. The Tigers were managed by none other than Chris O'Brien, who had sold the Cards to Dr. Jones in 1929. Now, just five years later, he intended to field a team comprised of former collegiate players with the objective of taking on any team that would play the Tigers. While it seemed odd to see the Cardinals return to Normal Park, it seemed even odder that Chris O'Brien would be on the same field with the opposing team. The *Tribune* provided rare coverage of a preseason game in what might be construed as a fitting tribute to the Cardinals of old:

> *The game and the setting recall the days of the Cardinals as National pro league contenders when Paddy Driscoll, Red Dunn, Bob Koehler, Duke Slater, Willis Brennan, Herb Blumer, Nick McInerney, Lennie Sachs, and Fred Gillies brought many victories and one national title to O'Brien, who formed the original Cardinals. Under O'Brien's ownership, the Cards played at Normal Park and in 1925 they annexed the national championship.*

The Tigers proved to be no match for the Cardinals and lost a lopsided 33-0 contest. A few days later, the Cardinals overpowered the Cleveland Panthers 52-0 at Chicago's Loyola Stadium as newcomer Homer Griffith (Southern California) and Doug Russell (Kansas) began to emerge as leaders in the talented young backfield. Following a season-opening 9-0 victory over the Cincinnati Reds in Dayton, the Cards appeared ready to emerge as a contender in 1934. During the Cincinnati game, Russell surprised everyone by returning the opening kickoff 102 yards for all the points the Cardinals would need. Still, the lack of a consistent offensive punch bothered Schissler, since that had proven to be the downfall of his club during the dismal 1933 season.

Dissatisfied with the offense, Schissler scheduled a midweek game in Bloomington, Illinois, on September 26 against a team called the Central Illinois All-Stars. The Cardinals hammered the All-Stars 32-0 as Russell and Mikulak paved the way. After winning four games and piling up 126 points in doing so (31.5 points per game), the suddenly offensive-minded Cardinals embarked on a six-game road trip to continue the NFL season. As usual, the Cards would play only three home games during the season and were beginning to resemble a barnstorming club based in Chicago, rather than a Chicago team with a solid fan support base in the city. On October 3, the Cards took part in an unusual game with the Maywood (IL) A.C. The game was played to mark the dedication of the new football field at Proviso High School in Maywood, which was built as part of a government relief project. The opposition was not expected to provide much of a test for the Chicagoans according to the *Daily News:*

> *The Cards . . . will be facing an unusual team in the Maywood eleven. Coach Golz of the A.C.'s hasn't a college graduate on his squad. Eight of the men in his starting lineup are old Proviso high school stars, toughened and experienced by a lot of semi-pro prairie football. In the last six years these players have lost only six out of sixty games and should give a good account of themselves against the Cardinals.*

The game, however, was big news in West Suburban Maywood. The local Maywood *Herald* bubbled at the prospect of over six thousand fans being in place to witness the game and the dedication:

> *Proviso High's new $80,000 stadium will be dedicated tonight under a canopy*

*of stars—it is hoped—with five kaleidoscopic hours of collegiate football and community activities plus a fitting amount of pomp and ceremony listed on the program.*

*Coach Clarence Golz of the Maywood team plans to start the game using his regulars, and should the formidable Cardinals run wild at the start he will substitute six Cardinal men to give the other Cardinals a dose of their own medicine. On the other hand, should the Maywood athletes run wild (they laughed at Chris Columbus, too), the coach of the Cardinals may ask for some Maywood boys. All of which is gratifying to all concerned.*

As the game progressed, the Maywood club declined the offer to use some of the Cardinals players and the pros from Chicago rolled to an easy 43-0 victory.

## Clear The Field Of Suspected Bear Spies

The next six league games proved to be disastrous for the Cardinals. The team lost four of those six games, and all were by shutouts. The once promising offense had disappeared except in a 16-0 win at luckless Cincinnati and in a 21-0 rout of the Brooklyn Dodgers. There was some excitement, as usual, in the first encounter of the year with the Bears, but this time, it was before the game was played. Since both squads now called Wrigley Field home, the two clubs struggled to share practice space as well. Usually, the Bears practiced in the morning while the Cardinals would take the field in the afternoon. At this point in the season (October 14), the Cardinals were still in contention with a 2-1 conference mark and the game had more importance than usual. As the *Tribune* reported the day before the big game, both sides were taking no chances with their preparations, even if the scouting was from a distance:

*Both teams practiced at Wrigley field yesterday. The Cardinals completed their drill in the afternoon after twice being interrupted to clear the field of suspected Bear spies. The Bears' drill in the morning was held up while two men in buildings opposite the park were relieved of field glasses and notebooks. These were said to have been Cardinal scouts, but the Cardinals denied they had scouts.*

Whatever information was secured by the "scouts" certainly didn't assist the Cards as the Bears won easily by a score of 20-0. The game was marked by civility, charm, and good manners as documented by the fact that only two players were tossed out of the game for fighting.

The official home opener for the Cardinals was finally played on November 11 against Detroit. The Lions escaped with a 17-13 decision before seventy-five hundred fans. The loss dropped the Cardinals to 3-5 in league competition. In the final three weeks of the season, the Cardinals continued their surprising mastery over Green Bay by knocking off the Packers twice, 9-0 and 6-0. These defeats eliminated the slim championship hopes of the Pack as the Bears captured the Western Division before losing the NFL title game to the Giants 30-13.

## Locals Badly Befuddled By Chicago's Passing Attack

The Cardinals finished the 1934 NFL campaign with a 5-6 record (9-6 overall) despite playing eight league games on the road and employing mostly rookies at a majority of the positions throughout the season. In an effort to build on the late season success of the team and to provide more training for the young club, Bidwill scheduled an extensive postseason tour immediately after the completion of the NFL season. Following the win over the Packers on November 29, the team headed West with the first game scheduled in Kansas City on December 2. The largest crowd (thirty-five hundred) to watch a pro game in Kansas that year was on hand as the Cards knocked off the Kansas City Blues 13-7, thanks to a pair of interception returns for touchdowns by Bob Neuman. On December 5, the Cardinals moved down to Oklahoma and swept the Tulsa Oilers 20-7. Heading further West, the Cards next devoured the Stanford Braves 37-2 in Los Angeles before twelve thousand fans on Sunday, December 9.

Then, on December 16, the Cardinals stifled the Southern California Maroons 41-7 behind Doug Russell's three scores before 16,000 in Los Angeles. The Cardinals remained in Los Angeles and disposed of the UCLA alumni team 17-7 on December 20 before heading North and tripping the California Giants 21-0 on December 23 in San Francisco.

The game program for the final contest in San Francisco noted the success of the Cardinals' stay in Los Angeles and marveled at the tenacity of Schissler's group:

> *There's one thing about this Chicago bunch. They don't give up or give any quarter at all during the course of the game. In this respect, they are just like a college team, in that they have plenty of spirit and lots of drive. Given sixty minutes in which to perform they do their job and do it thoroughly.*

The tour was scheduled to conclude in San Francisco but another game was set with the San Joaquin All-Stars for New Year's Day in Fresno, California. When the promoter was unable to provide the Cardinals with the requisite advance, the players voted not to participate. Instead, a lucrative game was scheduled with the formidable Chicago Bears (on their own West Coast tour), who had just been defeated for the title by the New York Giants.

The Bears were heavily favored to defeat the Giants for the title and led 10-3 at halftime on an extremely icy field. New York returned for the second half with the players wearing gym shoes instead of cleats, and the improved traction helped the Giants claim the championship with a surprising 30-13 victory. This became known as the famous "Sneakers" championship.

## Several Times The Boys Appeared Overzealous

The warm Southern California setting for another meeting between the Bears and Cardinals seemed ironic. Here were two bitter rivals, accustomed to seeing each other in cold, winter conditions, now preparing for this exhibition game as if it was for the NFL championship. Both teams also hoped to engage the touring NFL champion Giants before heading back to Chicago. The Bears-Cardinals game began drawing nationwide interest and the *Tribune's* George Shaffer reported from Los Angeles that both squads had compelling reasons for wanting to prevail in this game:

> *The Bears want to demonstrate that it was a mistake in New York last month*

*when the Giants overcame the Chicago team's commanding early lead and romped off with the National Pro Football league championship by defeating Halas' team, 30-13.*

*In the meantime, the Chicago Cardinals are looking for a little revenge of their own. Their coach, Paul Schissler, thinks the Cardinals now muster a strength considerably over their playing performances during the pro league campaign of last autumn, and what the Bears hope and fondly expect to do to the Giants, Schissler and his young, new team, hope they can do to the Bears.*

While the Bears cranked up the emotion in practice the week before the game in an attempt to recapture their midseason form, Schissler eased up on the Cardinals and reverted to light drills and plenty of pep talks. Harvey Woodruff wrote in the *Tribune*:

*Thoroughly acclimated and in good condition from nearly six weeks on the Pacific coast, where they overwhelmed all local and pro opposition, the Cardinals regard this game as their great chance to even up old scores. In fact, they remained here two weeks for just this chance.*

Prior to the game, the two teams haggled over both officials as well as recent player additions to both squads. The teams finally met on Sunday, January 13, at Gilmore Stadium in Los Angeles. With fifteen thousand in the stands and pro golfer Walter Hagen and comedian Joe E. Brown watching from the Bear's bench, the Cardinals slipped away with a 13-9 victory. Halfback Homer Griffith did the most damage with an eighty-yard run in the first quarter while quarterback Paul Pardonner drop-kicked two field goals for the Cardinals. The *Tribune* explained more about the atmosphere of the contest:

*Because of the larger number of former coast performers on the Cardinals, the crowd rooted for them and booed the officials generously, although the penalties for unnecessary roughness were divided. Several times the boys appeared overzealous, but no fisticuffs developed. Coast critics called it the roughest game of the season here.*

The shocking win over the Bears and the success of the overall tour left the young Cardinals with both confidence and experience. Although the team had just completed a rugged twenty-one-game schedule with a 15-6 record, everyone was anxious for the 1935 season to begin. The offense was running smoothly and the defense remained solid.

Pro football itself was booming. Nearly one million fans witnessed the fifty-eight NFL games in 1934 and the *Associated Press* announced that its annual poll of sports editors indicated that the growth of pro football was the most noticeable of all sports.

## *There Have Been No Profits*

The glowing future of the Chicago Cardinals dimmed just a month later when Coach Paul Schissler suddenly resigned on February 7. Citing financial considerations, Schissler explained the reasons for his decision:

*When I signed a contract with Dr. David Jones in 1933, I was hired for a rather nominal salary. However, I was supposed to receive a percentage of the profits. This arrangement was satisfactory except that there have been no profits. I can't afford to continue coaching the Cardinals for the present salary.*

Bidwill immediately named end Milan Creighton to lead the Cardinals, a surprising announcement since the trend in the league had been to move away from the dual role of player-coach. Not only would Creighton be the only player-coach, he would also be the youngest coach in the league. Creighton elected to continue the rebuilding process initiated by Schissler and added several newcomers to his already very young team. Despite the late season success of 1934 and positive prospects for success in 1935, nearly half of the squad would be newcomers with only three players (Lou Gordon, Howard Tipton, and Phil Handler) having more than two years of pro experience. Meanwhile, the Brooklyn Dodgers gobbled up the services of Schissler and hoped that he could rebuild their struggling team as he had the Cardinals.

Stressing defense and the fundamentals, Creighton began his four-year run as coach of the Chicago Cardinals by defeating Green Bay twice (7-6, 3-0) and tying the Lions 10-10 in the opening three weeks of the season. The Cards moved into first place in the West.

The Cards also squeezed in an exhibition game at La Crosse (WI) on September 22, where the host Heilmans were drubbed 41-0. The *La Crosse Tribune and Leader Press* was dismayed by the small crowd (less than one thousand) that showed up for the game, but cheerfully noted the sideline antics of owner William Bidwill:

*Owner Bidwill of the Cards paced the sidelines during the game repeating to his players, "Don't let up at all. Keep going for touchdowns. It's when a team slows up that injuries occur." And from the player bench as well as on the field the Cards were heard frequently calling, "We're going for another touchdown!" And they dove into play with a vengeance.*

Following a tough loss (17-13) at Pittsburgh, the Cardinals stunned the New York Giants 14-13 and regained first place before thirty-two thousand at the Polo Grounds, one of the largest crowds to ever witness a Cardinals game. Although the Cards would not play a home game until November, Creighton kept his team competitive and in the hunt for the league title down to the last week of the season. "That is our fight," said Creighton on his hopes for the Cardinals to capture the Western Division. "If we can reach the championship game, I think the Cardinals will decisively whip anybody the East sends out."

## A Chance For The Championship

When the Bears and the Cardinals met on December 1, the Cards (6-3-1) were tied with Detroit (6-3-2) for the league lead. While the two Chicago teams tied 7-7, the Lions roasted the Brooklyn Dodgers 28-0 to sneak ahead of the Cardinals by half a game in the standings. Since the Cards-Bears game scheduled for October 6 had been postponed because the Chicago Cubs were in the World Series and using Wrigley Field, the two teams agreed to make up that game on Sunday, December 8. By virtue of the tie with the Cardinals the previous week, the Bears (5-4-2) had been eliminated from the title chase. The Cardinals, however, needed a win over the Bears to tie the Lions and thus force a playoff for the Western Division title. For once, the Cardinals were not the underdogs in their encounter with the Bears, although they had not beaten their North Side rivals since 1929. The Cardinals' Cinderella season was summarized before the game by George Strickler of the *Tribune:*

> *While the Cardinals will consider the season a success only if they beat the Bears, with whom they played a 7-7 tie last week, non-partisan followers are ready to concede them a good year regardless of the outcome of today's contest. Starting out with a squad composed of . . . 22 youngsters only one season removed from college campuses, and a coach who had no previous experience in handling football teams, the Cardinals fought their way free from four years of cellar occupancy into the thick of the championship race and stayed there.*

The game would be sponsored by the *Chicago Daily News* for the benefit of the newspaper's "Fresh-Air Sanitarium Fund for Underprivileged Children," and the paper pushed its full support behind the event:

> *Get your tickets now and be sure of a choice seat at pro football's closing and most successful regular season spectacle . . . It will be a bitterly fought battle; no Bear-Cardinal game was ever anything else. It will be doubly bitter for two reasons: first, the Cardinals will be battling for the victory which will boost them into a tie for the western division championship of the National League with the Detroit Lions. Second, they'll be bidding for their first city championship in six years . . .*

By now, the December weather had turned raw and cold, and players on both sides took turns evaluating the frozen field itself before the big game. "It's a nice stretch of brick pavement," muttered the Bears' Bill Hewitt, while the Cards' Lou Gordon added: "If the field softens up enough for our backs to get firm footing, we're a cinch to win and tie the Lions for the Western championship."

Alas, the field didn't thaw and the Cardinals' improbable rise to the top ended when the Bears rebounded for a relatively easy 13-0 victory, denying the Cardinals a shot at the 1935 NFL title. Following the climb to almost the top of the pro football world, the Chicago Cardinals fell quickly and endured a long, hard plunge. The team would fail to exceed the .500 level for ten more years (until 1946) when the club would begin to assert itself once again as the best team in pro football.

Following the 1935 season, the NFL took another giant stride in its maturation process by holding the first draft of collegiate players. The league had been drifting towards a type of talent polarization and the draft was conceived to provide all clubs with an equal opportunity to sign the top graduating players.

The first draft pick of all-time for the Chicago Cardinals was back Jimmy Lawrence, a 5'11", 190-pound speedster out of Texas Christian. Lawrence would stick with the Cards for four years, but he was only one of three draftees who eventually played in the professional ranks.

Creighton would man the helm for the Cards for three more seasons. His 1936 squad tumbled to 3-8-1 in the league (5-9-1 overall) when injuries, particularly to

Doug Russell and end Bill Smith, decimated the squad. Russell's loss especially would hurt, since he topped the league in rushing with 499 yards in 1935.

Offensively, the team would continue to struggle. After walloping the South Bend Brewers 70-0 in an exhibition game, the Cardinals were never able to score more than two touchdowns in any NFL contest, and even struggled to stretch out a 20-0 victory over the La Crosse (WI) Heilmans in an exhibition contest on September 20. Russell missed most of the first seven league games (all defeats) before returning on November 8, as the Cardinals won their home opener 13-10 over the Eagles. Bidwill also brought back Paddy Driscoll as an assistant coach prior to this game. Although the Cardinals captured the win behind George Grosvenor's eighty-eight-yard punt return for a score, only fifteen hundred attended the game. With Russell back, the Cards knocked Pittsburgh out of the Eastern Division lead with a 14-6 win, lost a close 14-7 to defending champion Detroit, and topped the surprised Bears 14-7 for their first win over their neighbors since 1929.

It was fitting revenge for the Cardinals, who had their 1935 title hopes blindsided by the also-ran Bears at the time. The defeat knocked the Bears from contention and allowed the Packers to regain the Western title. The Cardinals' comeback season concluded a week later when they secured a scoreless tie with the champion Packers. Once again, the team finished strong, but the early woes contributed to another last-place finish.

Shortly after the Packers game, Bidwill sent his team out to California for a one-game set with the Los Angeles Bulldogs. The Cardinals received $4,000 plus expenses to play this game against a team that claimed it had a "provisional" membership in the NFL. The Bulldogs typically encouraged their visitors to overindulge in the sights and sounds of Los Angeles in the hopes of distracting their opponents. Apparently, this ploy seemed to work since the Bulldogs had previously defeated the Philadelphia Eagles and the Pittsburgh Pirates.

On the field that day (December 13), the Bulldogs reversed that hospitality and outslugged the Cardinals 13-10 in a game marked by numerous fights, penalties, and ejections. As the California sun finally set on the 1936 season, Coach Creighton could find plenty to do to improve the team's 5-9-1 record.

## *Football Didn't Pay Much Back Then*

For the 1937 season, the Cardinals added one of the most unique passing combinations in the history of the team when end Gaynell Tinsley and passer Pat Coffee joined the club as a tandem out of Louisiana State. Tinsley made a huge impression in Chicago when he led the College All-Stars to a 6-0 upset over the Green Bay Packers on September 1. Tinsley scored the only touchdown on a forty-seven-yard toss from Sammy Baugh. He then joined the Cardinals two days later at the team's training camp at Mills Stadium in Chicago. It would be the start of a bumpy, charismatic, superlative, record-setting, and disappointing three-year career for Tinsley, who caught the whole world by surprise his rookie season in 1937. Initially, Tinsley wasn't even certain that he would participate in professional football: "I thought I might just go right into coaching back at my old high school," he said. Now retired in Louisiana, Tinsley added, "Football didn't pay much back then, so teaching and coaching was much more secure.

They paid us so little that we didn't even know what a bonus was."

Joining with All-Pro Bill Smith at the ends, Tinsley provided the Cardinals with the opportunity to merge into the modern passing game. The return of oft-injured Doug Russell to the backfield along with former Bear star George Grovesnor also presented the club with a potent rushing attack. Only one key piece was missing: who would direct the offense? The answer came in the presence of the overlooked Pat Coffee, a teammate of Tinsley's at LSU.

Tinsley's impact was almost immediate. Following two unspectacular starts (a win over Green Bay and a loss at Detroit), he scored all three touchdowns in a 21-14 win over the highly touted Washington Redskins. A week later, his sixteen-yard fumble return provided the Cardinals with a 6-0 decision over the expansion Cleveland Rams. While one might define this emergence as simply the discovery of a splendid athlete, Tinsley credited it to fate. After the season opener at Green Bay, he had confided in Coach Creighton that not only was he uncomfortable playing right end (he played on the opposite side since his grade school days in Homer, LA), Tinsley was also apprehensive about not wearing the same number his Uncle Jess had worn with the Cardinals a few years earlier. Although he had never encountered this type of request, Creighton determined that he would not attempt to cheat the "fates;" he moved Tinsley to left end and changed his number to 31. Whether it was fate or innate ability, Tinsley quickly warmed up to the pro league.

Although the Cards dropped a rematch to the Packers 34-13 on October 10, Tinsley erupted for an unheard of eight catches for an incredible 148 yards. Pat Coffee earned his first extensive time in the backfield and responded by hurling passes of thirty-two and thirty-nine yards to Tinsley. Despite his team being a competitive 3-2-1 at this point of the season (with every game on the road), it was Tinsley who was grabbing the headlines: "Tinsley Newest Pro Freshman to Dazzle the Football Crowds," decried the *Chicago Tribune*:

> *Gus, as Tinsley is known to intimates, is well on his way toward breaking one league record and possibly two. He has caught 15 passes for a total gain of 358 yards. (Don) Hutson set the all-time mark last year with 34 receptions for 526 yards. Tinsley also is the leading scorer with 30 points.*

Coffee and Tinsley continued to confound the opposition with their passing repertoire. The Cardinals firmly embraced the forward pass as their main offensive weapon, but frequent breakdowns in the defense pushed the 1937 team out of playoff contention. Sensing that he was perhaps missing some of the fun, Coach Creighton returned to his former end position midway through the schedule after relinquishing his active player status earlier in the season to concentrate solely on coaching.

## *Three Bonfires In The Bleachers Added To The Carnival*

Going into the last game of the 1937 season against the Bears on December 5, Tinsley trailed only the great Don Hutson of Green Bay, who had 41 catches for 552 receiving yards, for league passing honors. The Cardinals' final game with the Bears was meaningless: the Bears had already clinched the Western Division title while the

Cardinals were mired in fourth place with a 5-4-1 mark. Before the game with the Bears, Tinsley had grabbed thirty tosses for 520 yards, so it was thought that he might have a shot at surpassing Hutson's new total reception yardage record. As a team, the Cardinals had other incentives, according to the *Tribune*:

> *In addition to Tinsley's chances for a record and the natural desire to take a fall out of the champions to spur them on, the Cardinals will be fired today by a desire to convince Creighton that they are worthy of rehire. Creighton has let it be known that he is planning wholesale changes in the team's personnel next season, and that laggards today will be spectators next year.*

The game with the Bears turned out to be one of the most entertaining in the history of the game. With both teams playing in gym shoes to help offset the impossible footing on an ice-covered field, the two clubs racked up the most total points ever scored in the pro league up to that time as the Bears prevailed 42-28. The field conditions in Wrigley Field were lamentable as reported by George Strickler:

> *A solid coating of ice covered the south end of the field extending from the 30 yard line on through the end zone. The frozen condition of the remainder of the playing surface made it impossible for linemen to get leverage or backs to drive, nullifying running plays. All the touchdowns were made on the ice over the baseball infield, where defenders, once they started could not turn or stop.*
>
> *This heightened the hilarity as backs went skidding along in undignified positions and linemen, coming out of the huddle, often arrived at the line of scrimmage on their bloomers. Three bonfires in the bleachers added a carnival touch as the game wore on into darkness.*

One aspect of the game that was successful in the murky conditions, however, was the forward pass. The two teams combined to complete thirty in sixty-four attempts for a resounding 501 yards. Tinsley dashed into the record books by snaring six passes for 155 yards, giving him a record 675 yards for his rookie season. One of Tinsley's receptions went for a team record of ninety-five yards, but it was one of the most unusual pass plays in the team's long history as described by Strickler:

> *Tinsley's . . . 95 yard run was a comical, but fitting climax to a remarkable season. The field was enveloped in complete darkness and the Cardinals were back on their own five yard line when he took a shovel pass from Coffee on an end around. He ran up the sidelines and was at midfield before the Bears realized any one was loose. Even then they had their doubts for all that was visible of the runner in the darkness was a pair of silver pants. Some Bear hero, whose identity was hidden by night, then realized pants seldom go running around without a sponsor and gave futile chase.*

The officials called the game at this point with about three minutes remaining because of darkness and even awarded the Cardinals a "free" extra point. While the Cardinals earned a fourth place finish with a 5-5-1 record, the Bears moved on to the league championship and lost 28-21 to Sammy Baugh and the Washington Redskins.

Rookies Baugh and Tinsley shattered league records, with Baugh completing eighty-one passes and Tinsley accumulating the most receiving yards (675) in history. The ninety-five-yard pass play from Coffee to Tinsley was also a league mark (upon further review, the record pass play later was adjusted to ninety-seven yards). Tinsley's thirty-six catches in 1937 broke the league record of thirty-four, but was surpassed by Hutson with forty-one. Tinsley was also named to the All-League team.

Tinsley's personal success would continue in 1938, although the team swooned and finished 2-9 in league play. He was ill during training camp, and rounded into shape slowly, but remained the bright star of the Cards' passing game. The offense itself was wildly erratic, capable of scoring points quickly and abundantly but also failing to score in four league games and scoring seven points or less in three other contests. Tinsley led the league with forty-one catches for 516 yards, but he was no longer a secret. Opposing teams tracked, hovered, and double-teamed Tinsley, and an injury to Russell stymied the running attack that would have eased the defensive pressure on Tinsley. Surprisingly, the coaching staff limited the role of Coffee, going instead with top draft choice Dwight Sloan as the team's primary passer.

Although the season started out promising with a tough 16-13 loss to the Bears at Soldier Field in which the Cardinals dominated play, it was followed by a series of uninspired defeats that quickly crushed the season. Coach Creighton warned his charges of possible drastic measures after a lackluster effort at Green Bay on September 25 (a 28-7 loss). The players seemed to respond, and showed signs of improvement three days later when the Cards fell to those same Packers 24-22 in Buffalo. However, two more flat performances, including a 14-14 tie in an exhibition game against the Los Angeles Bulldogs in Charleston, West Virginia, left the Cardinals with a dismal 1-4 ledger despite having one of the league's more talented rosters.

The tie with the Bulldogs was the breaking point for Creighton. In an unprecedented move, he fired five players on October 11 and demanded that the players match their physical talents with a renewed mental toughness:

> *This is only the beginning. We are not running a rest haven for athletes. I have no quarrel with men who play to win, but lose. But I am convinced that we have a better football team than the standing indicates and the players will prove it starting Sunday against the Bears or they will be given a chance to do their loafing in some other line of endeavor.*

The Bears grabbed a 27-7 lead in the third period before a ferocious Cardinals comeback left the Bears barely ahead 34-28 at the final gun. The second-half intensity was exactly what Coach Creighton had been seeking. However, the next three weeks were brutal as the high-powered Cardinals offense with its league-leading aerial attack was grounded in three straight shutout losses to Detroit (10-0), Philadelphia (7-0), and New York (6-0).

As the season mercifully eased to an end on November 20, the Cardinals (1-8) finally played their first home game of the year at Wrigley Field against the Lions. Prior to the game, football fans were openly questioning why the team had been such a failure in 1938. In the *Tribune,* George Strickler speculated:

> *What's wrong with the Cardinals cannot be summed up so tersely. Luck has been*

*a prominent factor in the Cardinals' campaign . . . They have the personnel . . . in fact, it is this superb personnel which makes the Cardinals' failure so mystifying. Such old Cardinals such as Paddy Driscoll and Ernie Nevers claim the present squad to be the best balanced and possessed of the greatest possibilities in the club's history.*

*Some of the trouble may be traced to Gaynell Tinsley's inability to hit his stride after a siege of illness just before reporting to training camp. The frequent use of first year men . . . may have contributed somewhat to the poor showing. And there is the complaint in some quarters that the Cardinals are pass happy, sacrificing the possibilities of a well rounded attack to concentrate on short aerials.*

Detroit knocked the Cardinals down to 1-9 with a disappointing 7-3 defeat before the Cards completed the season with a 31-17 win over the struggling Cleveland Rams. Tinsley gathered in seven passes to equal the league record of forty-one set by Don Hutson. As a team, the Cards completed 110 tosses to establish another league mark. Just as he did against the Bears the year before in the final game of the season, Tinsley broke loose for another record-shattering pass completion. This time, he teamed with Doug Russell on a ninety-eight-yard connection to break his own record for the longest pass play in league history. Ironically, it was Tinsley's only touchdown of the year.

It didn't take long for the fallout to begin following the last-place finish. Only a day after the Cleveland game, both Creighton and assistant Phil Handler turned in their resignations. Owner Bidwill announced the resignations and indirectly deflected some of the blame from Creighton (16-26-4):

*I accept his resignation reluctantly. However, I realize from the start that I put Creighton on the spot when I made him head coach of a team that was made up of players he had played with. I wish Milan the best of luck because I have the highest regard for him as a man and a coach.*

The next order of business for Bidwill was to prepare for the draft a week later. In a cornerstone event for the organization, the Cardinals selected center Ki Aldrich from Texas Christian and halfback Marshall Goldberg from Pittsburgh as the team's top two choices. Goldberg would be the first step in building the foundation for the Cardinals' championship hopes in the 1940s, while Aldrich would prove to be an immediate influence in stabilizing the Cardinals' front line.

Goldberg was nationally known after his collegiate career at Pittsburgh where he was a runner up for the Heisman Trophy and was twice picked for the All-American team. His selection was a plum for the organization, but first Goldberg needed to decide on the direction of his own future:

*When I graduated, my college coach Jock Sutherland, didn't want me to play pro football. I was offered the head coaching job at Long Island University for $3,000 and the Cardinals offered $6,000 to play for them. I figured if I only had to worry about my own production instead of 33 others, I would be much better off. The class of '39 didn't have many business opportunities, so for the first time, some of the better players looked at professional football as a chance to make some money and perhaps use it as a way to get into the business world.*

## *This Is Football, Not Tennis*

After carefully evaluating several coaching candidates, Bidwill decided on former Cardinals player-coach Ernie Nevers to head the 1939 team. If the team possessed talent, but lacked motivation, Nevers would be the one to bring it out.

Almost immediately, there were rumblings from the Cardinals training camp in Duluth, Minnesota, as the Nevers era began. With seven collegiate All-Americans on the squad (along with another seven who were "honorable mentions"), the Cardinals' preseason outlook appeared promising. Tinsley, Coffee, Smith, and Sloan, the mainstays of the 1938 team, were also expected back. However, the team was shocked when five dependable backs (Pat Coffee, Jack Robbins, John Michelosen, Vernon Huffman, and Harold Stebbins) all decided to retire from pro football. With injuries to fullback Milt Agee, Buddy Parker, and Bill Dwyer, along with Marshall Goldberg's delay because of the College All-Star game, the cupboard was bare in the Cardinals backfield. While Nevers was able to coax Robbins back into the fold, the team received another jolt when Tinsley abruptly left the team on August 16 to accept a coaching job in his hometown.

Despite the personnel losses, Nevers promised, and delivered, a punishing training camp at Duluth (MN) Teachers College. From the start, he announced that football—hard-hitting football—would be the only item on his preseason agenda. For starters, he pushed the theory of team play and individual subordination. Then, in a symbolic gesture, Nevers actually burned the team's shorts and sweatsuits, which were normally utilized for at least half of the preseason practices. The *Tribune* quoted Nevers on his lack of esteem for that particular type of apparel:

> *"Shorts!" he snorted derisively. "I've never seen anybody play in them. This is football, not tennis. We'll wear pads today, tomorrow, and every day throughout the season."*

For the first time in recent memory, the Cardinals would forego exhibition games and instead concentrate on lengthy practice sessions devoted to fundamentals. The Cardinals did break, however, to twice make the seven-mile trek over to Superior State Teachers' College in Wisconsin where the New York Giants were preparing for their test with the College All-Stars. The two pro clubs scrimmaged behind closed doors in an unprecedented move. The late league president Joe Carr had prohibited any NFL team from working with the championship club that was preparing for the All-Star game. The new NFL president Carl Storck lifted that ban, probably in the hopes that the pros could end the string of two consecutive losses to the All-Stars. The Giants did prevail 10-0 against the 1939 College All-Stars and returned the bragging rights to the pro ranks.

When Nevers broke camp in Duluth and prepared the Cards for their opener at Detroit on September 10, the *Tribune* lauded Nevers for his conditioning efforts:

> *It is doubtful whether any team ever worked harder in pre-season drill than the Cardinals, and tomorrow Nevers starts a squad of men perfectly conditioned who, from all appearances, finally have acquired a sense of responsibility to their employer.*

The high hopes for the 1939 season disappeared quickly at Detroit as the Lions jumped out to a 14-0 first-quarter lead before edging the Cardinals 21-13. While Jack Robbins rifled two late touchdown passes to Bill Smith, the rest of the offense lacked experience and the defense was continually confused by the Lions' intricate offensive patterns. Following the Detroit game, Nevers quickly dropped three players. This resulted in improved play, but still another loss, when the Packers escaped with a 14-10 victory.

The team finally tasted victory at Pittsburgh on September 23 when Goldberg scored the only touchdown in a 10-0 Cardinals win in his first extensive pro appearance following the All-Star game. It was a homecoming of sorts for Goldberg, a West Virginia native who graduated from the University of Pittsburgh. He was a two-time All-American who was versatile enough to play several positions. One critic stated that Goldberg "was an All-American fullback in 1938, but had he played tackle he would have been an All-American tackle." When Goldberg graduated, he was Pitt's all-time leading rusher, despite volunteering to play fullback his senior year for the betterment of the team. After earning All-American honors in 1937 as a halfback, Goldberg duplicated that honor as a fullback in 1938. However, the switch to fullback cost him the glamour of more carries and additional rushing yardage and probably detoured the Heisman Trophy away from his grasp.

The Cardinals opened their 1939 home season with a rare game at Soldier Field against the undefeated Lions on the night of October 1. Goldberg was allowed just two carries and the Cards were overwhelmed by the visitors 17-3. For the Cardinals, the eventual 1-3 start was painfully familiar, but things would get worse. The Cardinals managed to drop all seven remaining games. At first, the club seemed competitive, dropping a 27-20 decision to the Packers in front of a record crowd of twenty-three thousand on October 8 in Milwaukee. For the rest of the season, there would be no Gaynell Tinsley and very little Marshall Goldberg as the Chicago Cardinals scored just four touchdowns in the final six games. In truth, none of the games were close. The Cardinals got blasted by the Bears and their rookie quarterback Sid Luckman twice (44-7 and 48-7) and failed to score against Cleveland (24-0 and 14-0).

The first Bears game was the worst defeat (44-7) the Cardinals had suffered since the two teams began playing in 1920. It prompted Nevers, perhaps in an imitation of Creighton from the year before, to release two players immediately. "More releases are imminent," said the *Chicago Tribune,* "if the Cardinals do not carry out assignments any better this week than they did last Sunday against the Bears." Halas, meanwhile, was worried about the mounting cost of losing footballs (at $2.35 each) after all of those kicked extra points, and supposedly ordered his team to attempt only rushing extra points to avoid losing more footballs to the fans.

In an effort to stem the tide of defeat, Nevers held closed-door sessions with his veterans and then with his rookies. The team elected Bill Smith as its captain and vowed to improve its performance for the remainder of the year. Lost in this shuffle was the talented Goldberg. After emerging as the most touted college running back in the nation, Goldberg had been limited to just six carries in the first six games. With a pattern of falling behind early, the Cardinals had usually shifted to a heavy passing attack in order to get back into several games. Against the Bears, Goldberg had just one carry for eight yards while the Cardinals filled the air with thirty-seven passes, completing just ten. But Goldberg kept the team's welfare and intentions in the forefront. He remarked at the time:

> *We haven't had a chance to really play football yet. We've had to beat our brains out against the best clubs in the league. At no time have we been able to settle down to ball carrying, because breaks immediately made it necessary for us to open up in an attempt to come from behind. Now that we begin to tackle some teams that are nearer our class, I hope to have a chance to show it.*

While Goldberg's rushing opportunities increased slightly, more losses, continual player releases, and even a long hospital stay by owner Charles Bidwill (due to bronchial pneumonia) tarnished the remainder of the 1939 season. Even the gifted Doug Russell, formerly the league's leading rusher, was cast aside. The Cardinals wallowed in the mire of a 1-10 record surpassing the team's 1933 1-9-1 finish as the worst in the team's history. The unexpected loss of both Tinsley and Coffee before the season started had damaged the passing attack, which was further hindered when Jack Robbins, the only other qualified passer, missed extensive time because of injuries.

As the decade concluded, things had not changed much since 1930. The team was still being outdistanced by the Bears, both on the field and at the gate. The team's decision to move its home games to Wrigley Field on the North Side as well as to play the majority of its games on the road did not assist in the establishment of a strong fan base during the 1930s. In truth, the Cardinals wandered throughout the decade seemingly without purpose or definition. The team had gone through eleven head coaches since 1926, failing with a legendary player-coach, a top collegiate mentor, an unknown player-coach, and the return of that legend as the head coach. Pro football had become big business by now, with huge crowds following fan favorites such as the Bears and the Giants. It was finally time for the Cardinals to grab their fair share, but if the winds of change were to push the Cardinals to the forefront, the first soft breeze would need to come from the top.

It was then that Blue Shirt Charlie began to build himself a football team.

# The Innocence Of His Youth

More than sixty years ago, professional football players were not surrounded by agents, security guards, and personal assistants. In 1938, the Cardinals opened their training camp at Morgan Park Military Academy on 111th Street on the South Side. Longtime Cardinals fan George Houlihan of Chicago recalled the innocence of his youth when players and owners were still accessible to their young fans:

"In the late summer of 1938, myself and three friends from the old neighborhood would hitchhike each day to Morgan Park to watch our beloved Cardinals practice. Each day, Charles Bidwill, the owner of the Cardinals, and his young son Stormy would arrive at the practice about 5:00 P.M. On the last day of practice when the team was preparing to break camp, the owner and his son arrived as usual at 5:00 P.M. The coach that year was Milan Creighton, who had played end for the 1937 Cardinals. That day, Bidwill walked over to Creighton and handed him an envelope as he pointed to us sitting in the stands.

The coach came over to where we were sitting, gave us the envelope, and said Mr. Bidwill had seen us each day and wanted us to be his guests at the season opener. You can imagine how thrilled we were by Mr. Bidwill's kind gesture. From that day on we were Cardinals fans for life!

When the practice ended, players Gaynell Tinsley, Dwight Sloan, and Jack Robbins took us up to their room and gave us their shoulder pads that they had finished using. They were very happy that they had made the final cut and would be members of the 1938 Cardinals. They were all from the South and I still remember the song they had on their record player "When That Midnight Choo Choo Leaves for Alabam'.""

# Is That Why They Were So Bad?

Why were the Cardinals of 1939 so bad? A guy named Hugh "Shorty" Ray thought he could explain it.

Ray hung around the NFL for many years as the NFL's "Technical Advisor." He had a vision—a strong vision—which ultimately revolutionized the way we all evaluate an NFL game and helped push Shorty into the Pro Football Hall of Fame. Originally an official for club and prairie football games in Chicago, his vision was called "statistics." Until Shorty came along, the league and the media really didn't care for too much analysis outside of the final score, total yardage, interceptions, and attendance.

Shorty changed all of that. Armed with a crew of like-thinking individuals, Shorty set out to chart unique statistics at specific NFL games during the 1939 season. A few Cardinals games were included in this observation, and the "new" statistics uncovered by Shorty provided some insight as to why the Cardinals were lacking for victories in 1939, which Shorty explained was because of a lack of completions coupled with too many interceptions. But at 1-10, they also weren't very good.

Shorty was obsessed by the lack of actual playing time during a game. In 1939, he wrote:

> It is seen that out of the 1 hour of playing time, the teams are in action on an average of but 13 minutes, or 21.5% of playing time. On the basis of elapsed time per game, the teams are in action about 9% of the time.

His evil eye extended down to the officials, according to ref Bill Downes in a *Tribune* interview in 1948:

> Ray has it figured that there are 90 occasions in a game when the officiating crew handles the ball when time is in. The average time consumed by officials in getting the ball back into play is 7½ seconds. If the crew exceeds this by as much as 1 second, that's 90 seconds lost. Ninety seconds lost is four plays gone from the game. This could mean a defeat for a team rallying in the waning seconds.

The diminutive Shorty Ray (5'6", 136 pounds) was short in stature but a giant in the growing years of pro football. He was the NFL Supervisor of Officials from 1938 to 1952 and was enshrined in the Hall of Fame in 1966.

# ◆ 8 ◆

# The Beginning:
# 1940

*"Perhaps Aunt Minnie was right.*
*Driving a milk wagon is a nice, quiet life*
*compared with driving a football team to slaughter."*

JIMMY CONZELMAN,
COACH, CHICAGO CARDINALS

Morgan Park hasn't changed much in the past fifty years or so. And that's where the story of the Cardinals' renaissance begins.

Morgan Park is simply a neighborhood. A nice neighborhood on the far South Side of Chicago, blessed with an abundance of huge, stately shade trees. It is so far south, in fact, that its thinly disguised boundaries blend almost effortlessly with the beginnings of the south suburbs.

Morgan Park is Chicago. It reflects a combination of blue and white collar workers still stretching for their goals and scrambling to achieve their dreams. The neighborhood has always supported two secondary schools: the Morgan Park High School, a Chicago public school, and Morgan Park Academy, a private institution. In 1940, the schools shared 111th Street but little else. Morgan Park High School was literally on the other side of the tracks (commonly known as the Rock Island railroad tracks) from the Academy.

The physical separation was accentuated by the differences in the students that attended each school at the time. The public school was populated by about twenty-three hundred of the "regular" neighborhood kids, who were crammed into a school built to accommodate fourteen hundred. The academy, then known as Morgan Park Military Academy (MPMA), a boys' boarding school, hosted a privileged type of student, from points not only in the city of Chicago, but also from around the world. Parents sent their boys to MPMA to achieve learning, discipline, and responsibility, which were all readily available (especially the discipline) for the price of a handsome tuition payment.

The academy's athletic fields were also available in the summer of 1940, and so it was determined by Cardinals owner Charlie Bidwill that his club would move its preseason training camp from Duluth, Minnesota, back to the grounds of Morgan Park Military Academy. The Cards had stumbled through an NFL worst 1-10 record in 1939 under the tutelage of former playing great Ernie Nevers. Consequently, Nevers was nowhere to be found when the team regrouped for the 1940 campaign. After cautiously inquiring about the possibility of acquiring the Lions, Bidwill began to take an even more active role in the direction of the Cardinals. Previously, the well-connected sportsman had provided his coaches with a long leash in running the team. The coaches had handled personnel matters, recruited players, and even selected training camp sites.

Although he was acknowledged as a longtime Bears fan, primarily due to his lengthy friendship with George Halas, Bidwill refocused his thinking on the Cardinals as he approached the 1940 season. The rivalry between the two teams had lost some of its excitement, probably because of the Bears' overwhelming superiority in the 1930s. His decision to assume a more active role with the Cardinals would involve much more work. Although Bidwill was stretched out over several successful organizations, his work was his life, especially in the sporting arena. In order for the Cardinals to succeed, both on and off the field, the team would need a stable front office along with a dynamic, reputable coach who could work with the players in an effort to achieve mutual success. Bidwill could handle the front office with his own team of able administrators, but he would need a proven, experienced individual to handle the field chores. If that coach could add business acumen along with a favorable media-friendly persona, perhaps Bidwill could seriously begin his journey on the road to an NFL championship.

Yet teams with a mark of 1-10 and a past of similar records are usually not attractive to potential coaching candidates. In order to address this situation, Bidwill went into his sales mode and plucked out a real-life diamond to rejuvenate his floundering team. A comparatively untested professional, albeit eccentric, coach by the name of Jimmy Conzelman was hired by Bidwill to turn around the fortunes of the franchise, which had tasted only two winning seasons since the 1925 championship. Conzelman had been toiling for eight years as coach at tiny Washington University in St. Louis. He had played with George Halas and Paddy Driscoll on the 1918 Great Lakes football team, which captured the 1919 Rose Bowl. Conzelman later starred in the early pro football wars with Halas at Decatur and then with the Milwaukee Badgers and the Rock Island Independents as a player-coach. Eventually, he won the 1928 NFL title as coach of Providence. Then he elected to step away from the pro game.

Conzelman, who once was also a part owner of Detroit, appeared to be the man who could shake off the demons of defeat and twist the Cards back into the right direction. In *Pro Football's Rag Days,* Conzelman simply notes:

> *Then in 1940 Charles Bidwill asked me to come to Chicago to coach the Cardinals. I had turned the Cardinal job down twice before but this time I took it.*

Conzelman was the type of man who embraced life as if it had no boundaries or sidelines. George Strickler of the *Chicago Tribune* defined him as an "actor who writes and coaches." Conzelman prepared for the season by appearing as a coach in the St. Louis Civic Theater's performance of "Good News." Armed with a quick wit and a gift for strategic innovation, Conzelman realized the Cardinals' job would not be accomplished easily, perhaps owing in part to a defeatist attitude left over from the difficult 1939 schedule. "I became a highly disciplined person after playing for Jock Sutherland at Pittsburgh," recalled back Marshall Goldberg, a rookie in 1939. "I concentrated on winning, so I was a little depressed when I came to the Cardinals because the situation was completely disorganized."

Money might have been part of that problem, but players viewed that as part of the growing process and didn't complain. "The NFL didn't have the greatest reputation at that time," said Goldberg. "We only had three coaches and one trainer . . . Charlie Bidwill didn't make money in football, but there were people like Charlie who had money from other sources and they were able to keep the league going." The club's efforts to maintain costs were readily visible. For example, the letterhead used to contact players prior to the 1940 season had not been reprinted when Conzelman was named the coach. Instead, the name of Ernie Nevers was neatly crossed out and Conzelman's name was typed in above it!

The appointment of Conzelman as head coach proved to be a popular one with the players, noted Goldberg: "Conzelman was a personality and everyone tried to do their best for him because he was such a likable person. You'd break your neck for him!"

But could Conzelman turn things around? Would the Cardinals' management truly make the effort to mold the team into a winner? The 1940 season would turn out to be key for the Cardinals in terms of laying the foundation for future success. The team would need to reverse the complacency of losing and focus on being competitive, rather than on just being the competition. The Cardinals had undergone much change in the past few seasons, but those changes did not always result in a better football team. Therefore, this seemingly average 1940 season, although another losing one, deserves a much closer look. It holds a very important, although quiet, place in the history of the franchise.

## He'll Have To Reach Deep In His Bag Of Tricks

The draft that year had proven to be satisfactory for the Cardinals. As the team with the worst record in 1939, the Cards "earned" the top pick in the postseason draft and coach Ernie Nevers went for George Cafego, a back from Tennessee. This was somewhat of a surprise since the Cards could have picked other highly regarded talents such as Iowa's notable Nile Kinnick, Minnesota's rugged Hal Van Every, or future Bear stalwarts Bulldog Turner and George McAfee. It was rumored that the popular Kinnick might not play professional football, so perhaps that is why Nevers shied away from what was thought to be his preferred choice. If Cafego could bounce back from his knee surgery and team with Goldberg in the backfield, the Cardinals would present the potent rushing attack that had been missing in action in 1939.

As it was, the Cards selected twenty players in the draft. Eight of those picks would survive to make the final cut of thirty-three players, including Rupert Pate, a tackle from Wake Forest, the final pick in the twentieth round. The team selected ten backs, four ends, five tackles, and a center. Aside from the promising offensive threat of Cafego, the Cards also snatched back Lloyd Madden in the third round from the Colorado Mines. Although he was from a smaller school, Bidwill was impressed by the fact that Madden led the nation in scoring with 141 points his senior year. The *Chicago Daily News* asked Madden if he would continue with his scoring records in the professional ranks. "Scoring records this year?" he responded. "Gosh, no. I'm in a tougher league. I'll be thankful if they'll let me play!"

In particular, the University of Oklahoma served as a pipeline of talent with the Sooners sending ends Alton Coppage, John Shirk, and triple-threat halfback Beryl Clark to Chicago. Conzelman clearly indicated that all positions were wide open and the rookies made the most of the opportunity; several earned starting assignments during the season.

Another nice surprise was the return of Gaynell Tinsley, who had rampaged through the NFL in his 1937 rookie season. A former two-time All American from Louisiana State, Tinsley proved to be an outstanding pro receiver as well. He had set a club and league record with 675 receiving yards in 1937 and claimed a spot on the All-League honor team. Following another All-League performance in 1938, Tinsley suddenly announced his retirement during the 1939 training camp. The talented receiver had decided to return home to Louisiana and coach at Haynesville High School, where his wife also taught. When "Gus" returned in 1940, he still held NFL records at the time for most catches in a single game (eight), most receiving yards in one game (167), and most catches in a single season (tied with Green Bay's legendary Don Hutson with forty-one). "The Cardinals kept calling me after I left," said Tinsley, "so I finally decided to come back."

Still, the 1940 version of the Cardinals resembled more of a garage sale ensemble or an expansion team than an experienced franchise. Few of the players knew each other when camp opened, and even fewer had lined up next to each other in gridiron combat. Conzelman's role was immense and he knew it. Reporter James Costin noted in the *Chicago Tribune:*

> *Conzelman writes for slick magazines, he paints, he directs civic operas, he's an accomplished musician and he's a big league after dinner wit. But he'll have to reach deep into his bag of tricks if he hopes to get the Cardinals very far from their 1939 cellar position.*

Conzelman's offensive focus was to install the "Notre Dame System," which involved tricky shifts at the halfback position. However, only three of his players had any familiarity with that offense. Consequently, the coach and his key assistant, Charles "Chili" Walsh (a former Notre Dame player who also assisted Conzelman at Washington University), not only welcomed a bunch of strangers to the fold, but also introduced them to a whole new way of doing things. Certainly the acquisition of Ed Beinor and Joe Kuharich would be beneficial, but aside from those two, only fullback Mario "Motts" Tonelli (another Irish grad) was entirely familiar with the Cards' new procedures.

Tonelli was the star fullback on Notre Dame's 1938 National Championship team and had originally been drafted by the Giants in the nineteenth round of the 1939 draft. Instead of trying the pro game, Tonelli coached for a year before the Cards acquired him to team up with Goldberg prior to the 1940 season. For Tonelli, it was just another monument to his athletic success. As a child, he had been burned badly in a fire accident and had spent nearly a year recuperating. He rebounded to become an outstanding athlete both at DePaul High School in Chicago and at Notre Dame, where he helped lead the Irish to a national championship. Conzelman also assured Goldberg that he would be a more active participant in the offensive objectives of the Cardinals. That was great news for the versatile halfback, who had considered retiring following the disillusionment of his rookie season. With the Cardinals falling behind so quickly in most games, Nevers had been forced to play his passing game predominantly, thus leaving little opportunity for rookie ball carriers to shine.

When Conzelman gathered his players together in Morgan Park on Friday, August 9, there was indeed some excitement. The Cards appeared ready to initiate some deals to shore up some gaps in the system. The team moved quickly to unload high draft picks, backs George Cafego (the Cards' top choice) and eighth rounder Benny Kish of Pittsburgh. A trade was completed with the old Brooklyn Dodgers on August 24, while Cafego and Kish were still in training camp with the College All-Stars. In return, the Cards received two sturdy Notre Dame alums, Ed Beinor and Joe Kuharich. Conzelman, who admired the Notre Dame offensive schemes, was delighted to welcome the two tough linemen. Beinor, a native of nearby Harvey, Illinois, had spent the previous season coaching at Bloom High School in Chicago Heights, while Kuharich would later enjoy a successful coaching career (including stints with the Cardinals and at Notre Dame) after his playing days concluded. Both Beinor and Kuharich started at Notre Dame and were welcomed by Conzelman when they arrived from the Dodger training camp in River Head, New York. The trade of Cafego might have been a surprise, but Conzelman had already decided that he would structure his offense around Goldberg and so the trade of another back for a pair of respected linemen seemed logical to the coach.

On the same day that the swap with the Dodgers was finalized, the Cardinals also announced a deal that would send halfback Earl Crowder to Cleveland for two players to be named later. The brash movement of three backs in one day by the offensively anemic Cardinals must have certainly raised some eyebrows, but Conzelman was determined to build his own team with a solid foundation in the line before adding the frosting in the backfield. He may also have been concerned with the knee surgery Cafego endured following Tennessee's trip to the Rose Bowl earlier in the year.

## *Those Prodigal Gypsies Of The National Football League*

Another very significant change initiated for the 1940 season was Bidwill's decision to return the team back to the South Side with its home games in Comiskey Park. Previous owner Dr. David Jones had opted to share space with the Bears in Wrigley Field beginning in 1931, figuring that the reason that the Bears experienced better attendance was simply because the team played its games on the North Side.

That ruse failed to work for the Cards when their loyal fans did not eagerly follow the team up North. Consequently, the North Side fans continued to embrace the Bears but the Cardinals were never able to approach the Bears' attendance figures, even in the Bears' home park. As George Strickler noted in the *Tribune*:

> The Chicago Cardinals, those prodigal gypsies of the National Football League, will return home to the south side. Owner Charles Bidwill signed the lease that sends the Cardinals and their new coach, Jimmy Conzelman, back to Comiskey Park, where more than two decades ago they began a rise from amateur leadership to a professional championship.
> Signing of the lease yesterday successfully concluded a campaign waged by south side fans and business interests since Dr. David Jones . . . sought to stimulate attendance by moving north, where the Bears' success seemed to indicate professional football was more popular.

*Professional football was extremely popular on the north side, provided it was Bears' football. The Cardinals were unable to get the minds of north side fans off the Bears, and south side fans, considering themselves slighted by the switch, declined to follow "their team" across the city.*

*Bidwill's decision to return to Comiskey park is one of the planks in a reorganization platform that is bulwarked by a change of coaches.*

Conzelman rapidly cleaned out the debris from the 1939 season by inviting only fifteen players back to camp from that squad. The veterans would be required to compete with thirty-six newcomers as Conzelman opened up the three-week training session. The coach voiced little reason for his high expectations for the season, despite his obvious efforts to completely restructure the team. "There simply aren't any players available," he told the local media, "You either get 'em or you don't get 'em. Oh, sure, a few good men here and there, but not nearly enough to make us serious threats."

Years later, Goldberg echoed those sentiments by observing: "In 1940, we had about thirteen of the better players in the league. What we didn't have was depth—and that's what failed us. For example, the Bears (whom the Cardinals would defeat twice that season) had thirty-three good players."

As the Cardinals' players reported to the Morgan Park Military campus on 111th Street (between Bell and Western), they were assigned rooms in the "barracks" and practiced on the still-extant all-purpose field on the south end of the campus, behind the gymnasium. MPMA also maintained a nicely groomed "game" field on the north side of 111th Street (which has since been turned into condominiums), but that was strictly off-limits to the professionals in 1940.

"We stayed at the school for three weeks," remembered Goldberg, "but it wasn't much of a camp compared to today. We had one trainer, three coaches and not enough footballs to go around." What the players did have, however, was each other and that special bonding that results from experiencing common adversity. Billy Dewell, one of the top-flight receivers of the forties, joined the Cardinals late in the 1940 training camp after spending the summer winning nineteen games as a minor league pitcher in Muskogee, Oklahoma. For Dewell, the first training camp was a memorable one as the lanky end went up against one of the best in the business with the return of Gaynell "Gus" Tinsley. "Gus took me under his wing," recalled Dewell, "and taught me more moves in twenty minutes that I continued to use for the rest of my time in football."

Since Morgan Park has never been known as a vacation paradise, the players needed to be especially innovative in order to capture any sense of enjoyable nightlife. At that time, the players could walk a few blocks east of the campus, down a steep hill, cross the Rock Island railroad tracks, and experience the many wonders of the main Morgan Park shopping district—all of it concentrated into about one city block just east of the train tracks. All of that is gone now, replaced by a surprisingly noticeable vacant lot. Gone is the corner Monterey Pharmacy across from the train station, with its high counter stools and syrupy fountain drinks. Gone also is the Morgan Park Grocery at 1950 Monterey (111th Street) where the DiCola brothers or Sam Arriggo himself would personally fill your order while you waited, wrapping it up and tying it with the ever-present ball of twine hanging from the ceiling. "Junior" the butcher might demonstrate why he was the first one in the neighborhood to successfully master a Donald Duck imitation. About a block behind the shopping district, old Doc Woods welcomed patients to the first floor of his home, offered sound medical opinions, and provided lollipops to the children under his care. But that is also gone, as is Kaden's Department Store, the flagship business on Monterey Avenue (1942 Monterey), where Mr. Kaden knew the size and preferences of each customer.

Just west of the Morgan Park Military Academy entrance was the infamous Swank Roller Rink which advertised a "New Knee-Action Floor" for its patrons. Probably none of these attractions captivated the visiting Cardinals, as sleep was usually the highlight of the exhausted players' social lives during Conzelman's initial training camp. "We worked out twice each day," said fullback Mario "Motts" Tonelli. "We started at 9:30 or 10:00 in the morning and went until lunch. Then we came back out about 1:00 and practiced until 4:00 or 5:00. After dinner, we had a pep talk from Jimmy and then went over film or specific plays. At night, we were just plain tired!" Jimmy's training camp was not a fun place to be during the hot and humid August summer. During the first two weeks of the two-a-day workouts, fourteen players were injured. This made the active roster very thin, especially once the practice squad was reduced to forty men.

So that was the Morgan Park of 1940; it isn't much different now. People still struggle up the hill on 111th Street, privileged kids still attend Morgan Park Academy, and the Rock Island train still hauls workers into the city each day. Sure, the block-long shopping strip is gone. So is Doc Woods. And so are the Cardinals.

## Conzelman Was A Chain-Smoking Blur Of Movement

Yet there was a speck of optimism evident as the 1940 Cardinals moved through the muggy training camp. Perhaps it was the eagerness of management to initiate wholesale player personnel moves, but more than likely it was the charismatic and pragmatic presence of Conzelman. Here was a coach who was respected for what he had accomplished on the field at all levels of the game. He had been a pioneer in the early days of the NFL, and understood what went on inside the helmets of his players. He was stern, yet compassionate; quick with an explosive reaction, but just as quick with a kindly smile. "He had a temper and once in a while, he let it go," recalled Goldberg, "but he also was always planning some sort of a joke or innovation to keep things going."

More importantly, the coach understood the pertinent strategies needed to achieve success on the football field. Whether it be motivational, psychological, or simply expressing an understanding of a specific situation, the coach seemed at ease in dealing with his personnel. "As a coach, he expected you to do what he wanted," recalled Tonelli. "Jimmy was hard-nosed, but lenient. He told us, 'If you're not a good ball player, I'm not going to make you one overnight.'"

Conzelman was a chain smoking blur of movement, marching up and down the sidelines and never far away from a beloved bottle of Coca-Cola. His wife was always nearby with a pocketful of nickels in order to feed the nearest soda machine. He exuded confidence, which in turn inspired respect from his players.

As the 1940 training camp opened under a ceiling of eighty-two degree heat and stifling humidity, the most noticeable difference from the previous year was the overwhelming number of raw and inexperienced players. The Cards' 1940 media guide listed thirty-three players (increased by the NFL from thirty the preceding year), twenty-eight of whom were either rookies or with the club for their first or second season. The elders of the group were twenty-eight-year-old tackle Tony Blazine, who was starting his sixth year with the South Siders, and five-year veteran Conway Baker, a twenty-nine-year-old tackle. Before the season, Conzelman liked what he saw in Blazine, a 230-pounder out of tiny Illinois Wesleyan. "He is the typical example of the small time varsity player who has made good in professional football," said the coach.

From this group arose the nucleus of what would eventually become the best team in pro football. Although the coronation would be delayed by a massive world war, this was the start, the very beginning of the Cardinals' championship hopes. The 1940 edition of the Cardinals was the cornerstone—the foundation from which Charlie Bidwill would develop the NFL Champions of 1947.

Although that championship was still just a speck on the distant horizon, Conzelman's roster in 1940 was sprinkled with some familiar names such as Goldberg, Dewell, Tinsley, and Tonelli. The Cardinals' fifteenth-round draft choice that year was Joe Ziemba, a small college All-American out of St. Benedict's College in Atchison, Kansas. While a reoccurrence of a knee injury in training camp ended his football career, he ironically returned to Morgan Park Military Academy within a few years and eventually served as both football coach and athletic director.

## He's Having The Time Of His Life

Now revitalized under Conzelman's guidance, Goldberg appeared ready to claim his spot as one of the top offensive threats in the league. After one preseason practice session, the *Daily News* remarked:

> *If you watch him (Goldberg) in practice you wonder how he could get along without the game . . . As he blocks and tackles and runs with the perspiration pouring off, he looks like he's having the time of his life.*

Across town, the Chicago Bears, who would eventually stroll through the 1940 NFL schedule, began their preseason workouts near the cooler Chicago lakefront before departing on August 12 for their training camp at St. John's Military Academy in Delafield, Wisconsin. The All-Star game continued to dominate Chicago area football coverage in the *Chicago Tribune* each August. And rightly so, since sports editor Arch Ward of the *Tribune* founded the game in 1934 as a charitable fund-raiser. The *Tribune* coverage of the All-Star game was so exhaustive that the typical reader could pick up the following information on an average player of the sixty-eight-member 1940 All-Star team in Ward's column:

> *. . . Is 22 years and five months old, weighs 194.4 pounds, stands five feet 11¾ inches, and has a 44 inch chest and a 33.6 inch waist . . . his favorite food is steak, his favorite athlete is Jim Thorpe, his hobby is fishing, his favorite amusement the movies, and he's a fraternity man who worked his way through college . . . He differs little from last year's model, who preferred Joe DiMaggio and weighed three pounds less . . .*

The collegians were warmly welcomed to the city of Chicago and they went into training camp just as their rival pro team did. With such emphasis in Chicago, it was easy to see that the Cardinals—and even the Bears—would be forced to take the back seat in the city's sports pages until the game was completed.

The All-Star game continued for over three decades at Soldier Field in Chicago and served as the kickoff game for each professional season. The crowds were enormous and the games surprisingly competitive until the athletic distance between the professional champions and a collected group of former collegians became apparent in 1976, when the series was concluded. Players who were drafted by individual NFL teams but were also selected to play in the All-Star game were expected to show up for the All-Star camp, thus delaying their interaction with their professional team. The pro team likewise needed to ensure a roster spot for that player, which forced the teams to be extremely careful of their evaluations in training camp. If someone was released prior to the arrival of the All-Star player, the club might need to scramble for a replacement if the All-Star proved incapable of playing in the NFL.

In 1940, four of the Cardinals' rookies were leased to the College All-Star team, which was slated to play the Green Bay Packers on Thursday, August 29. They included Stan Anderson (Stanford), George Cafego (Tennessee), Marty Christiansen (Minnesota), and Benny Kish (Pittsburgh). Only Christiansen was on the Cards' opening day roster, and he was with the team for just one season, rushing for seventy-one yards in thirty-two attempts.

## We'll Just Congratulate The Packers

Former Cardinal Dr. Eddie Anderson, who played end on the 1925 NFL champions, was named the coach of the 1940 All-Star team and promptly offered to scrimmage the Cardinals. Previously, the collegians had never faced a professional team prior to the All-Star game itself so this suggestion was unprecedented. "While this is innovative," said Anderson, "I see no reason why the Cardinals shouldn't accept. Scrimmaging the All-Stars will help Jimmy Conzelman get his men ready for the campaign. This practice also will be ideal for the All-Stars, who will play harder against outsiders than in intra-squad games and will get more good out of the scrimmage since the Cardinals have no knowledge of our plays." The Cardinals, however, had also received an invitation to scrimmage the Packers in Green Bay for the same purpose. Just two years before, other pro teams had been prohibited from scrimmaging with the professional participant in the All-Star game.

Despite Conzelman's hesitancy, the Cardinals agreed to play both teams. The scrimmages with the Packers would be on Monday, August 19, and on Tuesday, August 20, in Green Bay, followed by practices with the All-Stars on August 22 and 24 at Dyche Stadium in Evanston, Illinois. It was also announced by all three participants that the scrimmages would be played behind closed doors, and that no exception would be made to this privacy rule. This news was greeted with some surprise, since it marked the first time that a member of the NFL would help prepare both of the combatants in an All-Star game. It would also totally disrupt Conzelman's training camp plans.

The Packers were infuriated when they learned that the Cardinals had also scheduled scrimmages against the All-Stars. Coach Curly Lambeau of the Packers immediately canceled the two practice sessions with the Cardinals and suggested that the All-Stars do likewise. The All-Stars countered with a statement that the scrimmages would still take place. Finally, Arch Ward of the *Tribune* stepped in and announced that henceforth, neither the pros nor the All-Stars would be allowed to scrimmage another pro team prior to the All-Star game. The Cardinals would now face neither opponent.

Eddie Anderson was disappointed, but amused, by all of this and deftly taunted Lambeau when asked about the possible outcome of the All-Star game:

> *In short, we haven't the faintest idea if the All-Stars are overwhelmed by the pro-*
> *fessionals. We'll just congratulate the Packers, if they should win, and call it even.*
> *Should the All-Stars surprise the Packers, we sincerely hope that they will have*
> *been able to use their best men . . . and that the Packers' failure to scrimmage*
> *against the Chicago Cardinals won't be a permanent excuse.*

Meanwhile, back in Morgan Park, Conzelman unleashed his toughest practices by initiating lengthy scrimmages during double sessions. These double dips were held in full equipment despite the heat, and it didn't take the coach long to begin trimming the roster. Satisfied that things were running smoothly, Conzelman eased up somewhat on August 16 with non-contact offensive and defensive drills. The next two practices, on Saturday, August 17, were devoted to kicking, receiving, and punt return sessions. The team worked for an hour in the morning and two hours in the afternoon, and so pleased Conzelman that he allowed the players their first day of rest on Sunday, August 18.

With this unexpected respite from the rigors of training camp, perhaps the players trekked over to the nearby air-conditioned Beverly Theater at 95th and Ashland where the movie "Lillian Russell" was playing, starring Don Ameche and Alice Faye. Or maybe they rested in the barracks and contemplated President Franklin Roosevelt's recent request for authority to order the National Guard into service for a period of one year. There was a war going on, but it was in distant Europe, far away from Morgan Park Military Academy.

No doubt Conzelman and his assistants Chile Walsh and Phil Handler spent the day on football as usual, plotting strategy, evaluating personnel, and preparing for the upcoming week of practice. The first game against Pittsburgh was looming just three weeks away (on September 8) and Conzelman's football machine still needed a great deal of attention.

## *It's Too Early To Do Any Forecasting*

Rain greeted the players when they returned for another lengthy scrimmage on Monday following the day off. Despite the slippery turf, the offensive backfield of Goldberg and Tonelli impressed the coaches with their quick gainers through the line. Conzelman was beginning to sense some possibilities for his young club, as he told the *Chicago Herald-American:*

> *From last place into the first division of the National Pro Football League would*
> *be a tremendous leap for the Chicago Cardinals, in the opinion of Coach Jimmy*

Conzelman. *"I think there will be an improvement, but I wouldn't even guar-*
*antee that we will finish with a better record than Philadelphia and Pittsburgh.*
*It's too early to do any forecasting—I've only been at this new job a little less than*
*two weeks. Changing from one system is always hard and that's our problem—*
*changing from a sort of power system into the Notre Dame style with some frills*
*and fancy stuff."*

One advantage to having so many newcomers, according to Conzelman, was that
he would not need to spend a great deal of time teaching veterans to "unlearn" past
systems.

As the days dragged by, Goldberg, Tonelli, rookie John Hall, veteran Bert Johnson,
and newcomer Hugh McCullough emerged as the standouts in the backfield.
McCullough was a shifty runner as well as an adept passer. In the days when halfbacks
were expected to handle the passing as well as the running chores, Goldberg readily
admitted that passing was not his strong point. With the addition of McCullough,
Conzelman locked in a hurler to help balance the run-orientated objectives of his "Notre
Dame" offense. The problem now rested with who would receive the football. Tinsley
and Dewell reported late to camp, so the early starting assignments at the ends went
to a pair of untested rookies from Oklahoma: John Shirk and Alton Coppage.

During the first week of September, when the students returned to Morgan Park
Military Academy, the Cardinals moved their training camp to the University of
Chicago. But things were not looking up for Conzelman. Injuries and talent problems forced the coach to continually revise his lineup and to fidget with his offense.
In addition, with the cancellation of the four scrimmages with the All-Star game participants, the Cardinals had been unable to schedule any exhibition games. The team
traveled to Pittsburgh on Sunday, September 8, with Conzelman having little indication about how his charges would perform under game conditions. Conzelman
decided to keep twenty-two rookies. Five of them found their way into the starting
lineup, the most rookies to start for any team in the league that year. The day before
the season opener, George Strickler of the *Tribune* summarized the team's plight:

> *The Chicago Cardinal football players arrived late today to open the National*
> *league championship race tomorrow against the Pittsburgh Steelers. They brought*
> *with them a new coach and a new system, but the same old prospects. The Cardinals*
> *do not expect to win the championship. In fact, they do not even expect to come*
> *close to the western division title. But they are going to start the race and promise*
> *to stick to the finish.*
>
> *The task of rebuilding has been entrusted to Jimmy Conzelman, who spent*
> *eleven years playing and coaching champions in the league before he took a highly*
> *successful whirl at college coaching. Conzelman has attacked the job in the right*
> *manner. He is rebuilding from the bottom and training his sights two years into*
> *the future.*
>
> *The Cardinals are not going to win many games this season, if any . . .*

The Steelers already had one exhibition game under their belts and had surprised
the Bears 10-9, prompting most critics to view the contest with the Cardinals as an
expected rout. Opening with Johnson at quarterback, Tonelli at fullback, and Goldberg

and Hall at halfback, the new offense sputtered at the beginning. Staying conservative, and keeping the ball on the ground, the Cardinals were down by just 7-0 at the
half. The major surprise was the mighty play of the patchwork line with Ki Aldrich
at center, Joe Kuharich and Arthur Pershing "Tarzan" White at guards, Tony Blazine
and Conway Baker at tackles, and the rookies Shirk and Coppage at ends. "Pittsburgh
found the Cardinal line stronger than even the more rabid Cardinal followers had
hoped," wrote George Strickler in the *Tribune*.

By the time the second half rolled around, the offense began to click. Behind the
fearless pounding of Tonelli, the Cards began to gobble up yardage and eventually
finished with 192 total yards compared to Pittsburgh's 129 yards. Early in the third
quarter, rookie halfback Beryl Clark connected with Hall on a forty-four-yard scoring play to tie the Steelers 7-7 and that's the way the game ended.

Surprise? Shock? Bewilderment? The tie with Pittsburgh was not expected, so it
did cause some eyebrows to lift slightly when game reports began to filter around the
country. The rookie-laden team was apparently competitive. The line was quick, strong,
and mobile. And who was this Tonelli? After playing in the 1939 All-Star team out
of Notre Dame, Tonelli had opted to become the assistant coach at Providence College
before heading back to his hometown of Chicago to play with the Cardinals. Tonelli
was virtually unstoppable against the Steelers, snatching yardage on sweeps around
the end or persistently plunging through the veteran Pittsburgh front line for consistent gains. Perhaps it was too early to elevate the Cardinals to the position of contender, but the team was showing signs that it would be more competitive than originally expected. The next week's outing against Detroit (in Buffalo) would probably
answer more of Conzelman's questions.

During the week, Conzelman added a veteran in the backfield by acquiring blocking back Herman Schneidman from Green Bay. Schneidman, a native of Quincy,
Illinois, had played six years for the Packers and was widely regarded as one of the
best pure blockers in the league.

## *The Worst Game Ever Played*

With Schneidman and Tinsley both available for the Detroit game, the team moved
on to Buffalo with cautious confidence. With another week of practice to work on
the "Notre Dame" system, as well as more mandated sessions to review the game films,
the Cards were beginning to increase their comfort level with the new offense.
Unfortunately, their arrival in Buffalo coincided with a tremendous downpour which
quickly flooded the field and resulted in a messy, scoreless tie. "It wasn't a football
game," Lions coach Potsy Clark told the *Detroit News*, "but we should have won."

The game was originally scheduled for Comiskey Park, but Bidwill, perhaps considering a move to Buffalo, met with promoter Charles Murray and agreed to move
this "home" game to New York. Although advance interest in the game was significant, Mother Nature's tremendous pregame show of thunder and lightning limited
the crowd to a little over eighteen thousand. Most had come to see the play of both
Goldberg and his Detroit counterpart Whizzer White, the future Supreme Court Justice.
White had topped the NFL in rushing with Pittsburgh in 1938 and then spent a year
as a Rhodes scholar at Oxford. His return to the league with Detroit was eagerly antic-

ipated while Goldberg's popularity from his college days at the University of Pittsburgh was still high.

With rain and mud obliterating the field, both teams splished and splashed to a scoreless tie in a game that featured virtually no offense due to the elements. The field was such a mess that the competition itself was comical. Ball carriers slipped in the mud, thrown footballs bounced harmlessly away from their destinations, and referees struggled to identify correct placements after each play. Ultimately, the tie game was rescued by the defensive play of two offensive stars: Marshall Goldberg and Gus Tinsley.

Late in the third quarter, former Cardinal Dwight "Paddlefoot" Sloan somehow completed a twenty-seven-yard pass to Lloyd Caldwell near the Cardinals' goal line. Goldberg delivered a solid hit on Caldwell and dragged him down as they both slid into the end zone. The Lions figured that they had scored, and began to celebrate. However, referee Bill Halloran determined that Caldwell's forward progress had been stopped by Goldberg on the one-yard line. On the very next play, Goldberg charged through, and nailed Sloan for a five-yard loss. The Lions lost six more on the next play before Tinsley intercepted Sloan's pass on third down to end the Detroit threat. The offensive efforts were so stagnant that both teams finally resorted to quick kicks or punts on first down in an effort to keep the ball away from their own goal lines. Football strategy had suddenly been swept back to the turn of the century! During the fourth quarter, the two teams exchanged a total of eight punts without either team running an offensive play. Strangely, there were no fumbles on any of these late punts but that was due to the receivers deciding to let the punt be downed in the mud rather than attempting to return any of the kicks.

Late in the game, the only spontaneous cheer emerged from the soaked crowd when the public address announcer informed the fans that only three minutes remained in the "contest." The lack of fan approval might be traced to the very obvious lack of offense which found the two teams combining for just one pass completion and a total of seven first downs. More astounding, according to the Pro Football Hall of Fame, is that the two teams combined for just thirty yards of total offense, easily the record for offensive non-accomplishment! Detroit Hall of Famer Alex Wojciechowiez recalled the difficulty of handling the ball in the quagmire:

> By the time the game was over, the ball felt like it weighed a ton. The ball was covered with mud as were all the players. Everything on the field looked just one way—awful!

Goldberg, who topped all rushers that day with a decent twenty-six yards in eight carries, noted:

> By halftime, the field was completely under mud and water. It seemed like we were playing water polo instead of football!

Ki Aldrich of the Cardinals and several others suffered lime burns from the combination of rain and the dirt at the stadium. When it was all over, the contest in Buffalo quickly became known as the "worst game ever played" in the NFL, and is still remembered for its improbable playing conditions and impossible offenses. But when the Cardinals toweled off after the monotonous, yet remarkable, affair, Conzelman's surprising team was still undefeated. Winless, maybe, but still undefeated, and just a half game behind Green Bay in the Western Division.

## Fiery Little Band Of Unknowns

If the 1940 Chicago Cardinals were indeed for real, the true test would arrive in the third week of the season against their old rivals, the formidable Chicago Bears. Chicago was firmly a Bears town now, but a reasonable effort against the Bears might allow the Cards to begin to chip away at their rival's lofty image. Too many years of too few home games, too few wins, and too little excitement had hindered the Cardinals' franchise. With Conzelman already catching on among the city's media as a refreshing alternative to the usual somber professional coaches, the Cardinals competitive performances on the field were helping to make a dent in the media's comprehensive coverage of the Bears. It was a true David vs. Goliath scenario as the Cardinals prepared to play their first home game in ten years back on the South Side. The Bears, with their rugged, veteran squad, had opened the season by mauling the defending champion Packers 41-10 on Sunday, September 22. Conzelman would counter this powerful machine with 22 rookies, but without mainstay Ki Aldrich, who had been hospitalized with lime burns following the Detroit game. In a pregame preview, George Strickler wrote in the *Tribune:*

> It is a confident, fiery little band of unknowns who can play good football that Conzelman will introduce to the Cardinals' south side constituency in what amounts to a homecoming in several respects for the Cardinals. The Cardinals were a south side team ten years ago before taking up their residence in Wrigley Field with the mistaken idea that more people would come to their games because more people went to see the Bears there.
>
> Whether the Cardinals, with 22 first year men, are good enough to rate high in the National League, despite all the good football they have played so far in remaining undefeated . . . should be answered tonight.

The Cardinals enjoyed a few extra days off and prepared to meet the Bears on a rare weekday night game on Wednesday, September 25, at Comiskey Park. Although not much was expected of the Cards, a large (for the Cardinals) home crowd of 23,181 curious onlookers showed up for the game. While the size of the crowd was a nice surprise, the result of the game was even more enjoyable.

Scoring early and dominating both sides of the line of scrimmage, the smaller Cardinals overpowered the Bears 21-7. The fact that the Cardinals had beaten the Bears only once in the last decade did not impress Conzelman's rookies. They had no knowledge of Chicago pro football tradition, nor did they realize that their team was expected to graciously crumble before the Bears twice each season. Behind the running of Goldberg, Tonelli, and Lloyd Madden, the Cards established an early ground gain to set up some unexpected aerial heroics. The winners tallied on their first possession of the game when Hugh McCullough connected with rookie John Hall on a thirty-six-yard pass play. Goldberg scored on a seven-yard jaunt around left end in the second quarter to push the Cardinals ahead 14-0. Goldberg's touchdown was preceded by

Madden's exciting sixty-two-yard run.

After the Bears narrowed the margin to 14-7 at the half, McCullough iced it with a ten-yard scoring toss to Tinsley early in the fourth quarter. The shocked fans also witnessed the usual non-football entanglements, this time between two unusual participants. Both lanky Cardinals end Billy Dewell and husky Bears tackle Joe Stydahar were invited to depart the premises following their second quarter confrontation. Dewell still laughs when he remembers the incident:

> *We called an off-tackle play for halfback Johnny Hall. I tried to put a body block on Joe Stydahar, but he stepped back and two of my fingers slipped into his jersey and I tried to pull them out. Then I saw something coming out of the corner of my eye and it was his fist! I ducked and he hit my helmet, but we both got thrown out for fighting. Ed Beinor ran out on the field to congratulate me and he got thrown out, too! Jimmy was really mad at both of us!*

The gratifying win over the Bears left the Cardinals atop the Western Division standings with a 1-0-2 record. However, the fairy-tale journey for the 1940 Cardinals exploded just a few days later when the Packers walloped the Chicagoans 31-6 in Milwaukee. The gifted duo of Cecil Isbell and Don Hutson picked apart the Cardinals' defense as Green Bay jumped out to a 17-0 first quarter lead. Despite the efforts of Tonelli and Hall, things got worse the following week in Detroit where the Lions blasted the Cardinals 43-14 in a rain-free zone. Tonelli's short plunge in the first quarter gave the Cardinals a 7-0 advantage, before a swarming Detroit defense blocked two of McCullough's punts and intercepted one of his passes to set up the romp. Only Hall's nifty ninety-yard return of the second-half kickoff interrupted the flow of Detroit touchdowns.

## *That Great Lynch Was Truly Great*

Maybe things could get worse. The following week, on October 13, Washington's Sammy Baugh completed twelve of seventeen passes for three touchdowns to scorch the Cardinals 28-21 after the Cards led 21-14 at the half. While the defeat was tough enough, Conzelman also lost five key players to injury: Blazine (dislocated knee); Goldberg (shoulder separation); Tinsley (injured leg and ribs); Beinor (leg injury); and, Rupert Pate (broken arm). Saddled with a downward sliding 1-3-2 mark, and with an army of players on the injured list, Conzelman signed end Frank Ivy and back Jimmy German following the Redskins game. The plummet to the bottom of the standings was complete by October 20, when the Cleveland Rams scorched the depleted Cardinals 26-14 in Cleveland.

The Cardinals struggled back to Chicago after those four straight road losses, and awaited a quick rematch on October 27 with Cleveland in just their second home game. By this time, the defeats were wearing down Conzelman as well. In an attempt to fend off additional weight loss, team doctors ordered the coach to assume a regular diet of milk shakes. While sipping away, Conzelman would doodle with new plays and formations, trying to wring out some additional hope for his wounded and decimated team. He also entertained reporters by wondering aloud how his team would fare with a player such as the extraordinary Ed Lynch. Lynch was a 5'11", 190-pound end and tackle. He enjoyed a vagabond career with Rochester (1925), Detroit and

Hartford (1926), Providence (1927), and the Orange Tornadoes (1929). His inspiration for Conzelman must have been spiritual, for in his thirty-five-game pro career, "Ace" Lynch scored just one touchdown and appeared to secure limited playing time. Lynch (a legend in Conzelman's mind) was the type of confident player whose braggadocio alone could conquer opponents, according to the coach:

> *That's all we need to make the Cardinals a winner, a couple of Ed Lynches and we'd be big people in this league. But in their absence we'll substitute a few new formations that will put a different complexion on our offense and maybe give the customers—and Cleveland—a few thrills.*
>
> *Lynch had what we miss in this league. The old gab. Lynch talked more players into defeat than any other man whoever came into professional football. Lynch turned up at end in about every game Grange played on that famous inaugural tour in 1925. Finally he turned to Grange one day and said: "Mister, I'm getting pretty tired of throwing you for a loss. Why don't you be a good boy and go around the other side once in a while. Maybe you'll be able to pick up a yard or two."*
>
> *That great Lynch was truly great. Boy, what I'd give for a dozen Lynches right now!*

Somehow, with or without Lynch, Conzelman was able to inspire his youthful squad to knock off the Rams 17-7. Rookie John Hall's fifty-yard return of an interception was the highlight of the game for the winners. Two more losses to Green Bay (28-7) and Brooklyn (14-9) followed, setting up the final game of the season in Wrigley Field against the Bears on December 1. The Bears (7-3), still smarting from the earlier loss to the Cardinals (2-6-2), needed a win to clinch the Western Division title. As usual, Conzelman would have his undermanned charges ready to play, but would they have the resources necessary to be competitive with the mighty Bears? The *Tribune* offered South Side fans little hope:

> *Whatever else one may think of the Cardinals and their chances, these facts are indisputable. The Cardinals have played sound, hard football in every start. They have come further on less than several teams which definitely have more and better balanced material. This has been due to an unconquerable spirit, born of commendable confidence. Moreover, their next assignment is a game in a series in which intense civic rivalry, begun a score of years ago, has opened the door to some unusual results, not to mention some historic occasions.*
>
> *As a matter of accuracy, however, it must be recorded that the Cardinals do not figure to beat the Bears.*

The Cardinals did not fail to deliver their usual excitement, even if they did fail to deliver a victory. After falling behind 31-0 at the half, the Cardinals rallied by scoring twenty-three points in the fourth quarter in a wacky finish. The win sent the Bears to the NFL title game against Sammy Baugh and the Washington Redskins. Washington had defeated the Bears three weeks earlier 7-3 on a controversial call that disallowed what the Bears thought would be the game-winning touchdown. The Bears' futile protest following that game prompted Redskins owner George Marshall to state: "The Bears are quitters. They're not a second half team, just a bunch of crybabies. They fold up when the going gets tough."

Tormented by anonymous letters addressed simply to "crybabies" and reviled by the Washington media, the Bears plotted a unique offensive strategy with the help of former Cardinals player-coach Fred Gillies, now a technical advisor to the Bears staff. With Gillies's assistance, the Bears unveiled some variations to the "T" formation and completely bewildered the Redskins 73-0. This game remains the most lopsided game in NFL history.

Once again in 1940, league attendance spiraled to a new record as nearly 1.6 million people attended NFL games. The Bears established a single game team record when 45,434 witnessed the Packers game on November 3. Having played the fewest games at home (three plus the Buffalo contest), the Cardinals were at the bottom of the ten-team league in overall attendance with 64,006.

# ◆ Part Two ◆

# ◆ 9 ◆

# The War Years:
# 1941 – 1942

*"You don't know what freedom is . . .*
*until you don't have it."*

MARIO "MOTTS" TONELLI,
FULLBACK, CHICAGO CARDINALS   PRISONER OF WAR, 1942-1945

Despite the late-season swoon to complete the 1940 campaign, there was reason for renewed optimism in 1941. With Marshall Goldberg blossoming as an all-around threat on both offense and defense, the Cardinals were beginning to assemble the backbone of a competitive team.

Goldberg certainly had the tools to lead the Cardinals out of the league cellar, where they had resided for three straight years. With a record slate of 5-26-2 since 1938, the team really had nowhere to go but up. Goldberg hoped to pull the Cards off the canvas with his offensive specialties: tricky open field running and his peculiar knack for breaking free on kickoff returns. Defensively, he was a rugged tackler and possessed a keen ability to blanket an opposing receiver.

As the NFL matured, it began to sense the need to further market both its products and its stars, such as Goldberg. One of the first steps taken by the league was to appoint Notre Dame athletic director Elmer Layden as Commissioner of the NFL in 1941. Layden received a five-year pact that, according to the *Associated Press,* would allow Layden to be "the final authority on all squabbles between players and clubs, levy and collect fines, govern conduct of club owners and all their employees in any activity connected with the sport, and have complete control of league finances." In other words, Layden was expected to rule with an iron fist and to use the extended powers bestowed upon him to direct and lead the NFL to the next level. In return for his startling $20,000 salary, Layden promised to move ahead, albeit cautiously: "I'll visit every league city," he said, "and study the complete picture before deciding what our future course will be. Even though this game is the fastest growing sport, we know there is room for improvement."

In 1940, the league had published the first edition of its *Official National Football League Roster & Record Manual,* which would eventually supplant the informative *Spalding's Official Guide: National Football League.* Layden encouraged the continued improvement of the NFL's manual in 1941. Both of these publications provided information on rosters, records, and schedules, although the smaller version by Spalding was the more exceptional of the two in terms of solid substance in 1940. It was started in 1935 and included pertinent information on each team, such as seasonal outlooks, draft choices, photos, and recent results. The NFL's effort to finally publish its own manual signaled an encouraging attempt to uplift the league's recognition on all fronts. Chicago fans could learn a little bit about their own teams' histories as well, since the book contained league individual records such as Paddy Driscoll's fifty-yard drop kick for a field goal in 1922 and George Halas's ninety-eight-yard run on a recovered fumble that same season.

The league also maintained weekly standings and statistics, and finally began to emphasize the personalities of the athletes via occasional mentions in regular press releases. Among the early comments were a reminder that the legendary Jim Thorpe had served as the original president of the league and that the Eagles' Alexis Thompson was the NFL's youngest owner. With the league headquarters adopting this push for publicity, Layden hoped to encourage each of the teams to follow suit locally and began to make plans for spreading his new public relations gospel.

In conjunction with the All-Star game in August of 1941, Layden hosted a "Publicity Clinic" at the league's new headquarters in Chicago (310 South Michigan). At this meeting, the commissioner laid down the law regarding the care and maintenance of the NFL's image. Each team was directed to send copies of its press releases to national wire services, and clubs were reminded that it was important to spread the good word about the league to towns and cities which did not have teams in the NFL:

*Publicity in towns in which a team does not appear and in the sections outside league territory are as important and imperative to the life of the game and the welfare of the league as the exploitation individual clubs carry on in their own neighborhoods.*

The league members were even told what to write about in their releases:

*Publicity men were urged to promote more mid-week comment of a post-mortem nature. Comment of this type is deemed more beneficial than the old method of hammering the merits of next week's opponent, a technique which quite frequently taxes the credulity and belittles the intelligence of the readers and which has become hackneyed through constant abuse.*

Layden stressed the importance of image, and the "Publicity Clinic" minutes reflected the following suggestions:

*Publicity men were instructed by the commissioner to forbid the taking of any pictures in dirty, tattered or misfit uniforms and it was especially emphasized that all players must wear stockings in publicity pictures.*
   *Publicity men were urged to be more reporter and less propagandist, fashioning releases more after news stories than out-and-out publicity blurbs. It was recommended that publicity men attempt to build tradition for National league football by delving more into the early background of the game and the exploits of some of its more prominent pioneers.*

Publicity men were also requested to make a greater effort to boost players on their respective clubs into national personalities, through the medium of feature stories.

In another unique development for the times, on July 19, 1941, Commissioner Layden announced that a new policy had been developed which would conceal the identities of game officials until those officials actually made an entrance onto the field:

> *Not even the owners and coaches of National league teams will be told who is handling their games. Officials will be notified of their assignments from week to week and will be responsible only to the commissioner's Office. Their only contact with owners and coaches will be such as is necessary on the field for the successful presentation of the game and whatever preliminary or between-the-halves program the home club devises.*

## *Sartorially Resplendent Creations*

Perhaps the NFL was determined to elevate itself above any direct or indirect grumbling about the sanctity of its officials. Layden's decree dispelled any notion that the NFL was unconcerned with the integrity of its games. In addition, all officials were now required to pass a written test and to attend a mandated rules interpretation meeting. In a final stab at respectability, the league clarified the dress code for its officials:

> *Furthermore, the officials will be obliged to appear in the new National league uniforms, sartorially resplendent creations in stripes designed to assist spectators in ascertaining more quickly whether it was the referee or the field judge who made that last decision. Referees will wear black and white striped shirts.*

The players were expected to dress professionally at all times, and Layden was always prepared to enforce his mandates. Tackle Chet Bulger was once fined by the league for violating the dress code:

> *Once we were playing in Detroit and I went down to the lobby early in the morning to get some razor blades. I guess the commissioner was standing down there but I didnt know who he was and later I got fined $50 for not having a dress coat on in public! It was true; I got fined for going to buy razor blades.*

As usual, the professional season opened in Chicago, where the Bears stomped the College All-Stars 37-13 on August 28 before more than ninety-eight thousand fans in Soldier Field. In 1941, the fans still selected the fifty-two members of the College All-Stars and the NFL claimed that there were 9,514,753 participating voters. One of the more unusual selectees for the All-Stars was unheralded back Bob Morrow from tiny Illinois Wesleyan College in Bloomington, Illinois. With fans voting for the All-Stars, the sponsoring *Chicago Tribune* was stunned when literally thousands of ballots bearing Morrow's name began arriving with a Bloomington postmark. No one had ever heard of Morrow, but with his supporters remitting hundreds of pre-printed ballots on flashy paper stock, he was a surprise addition to the team. Following the All-Star game, Morrow joined the Cardinals and began the process of proving himself all over again.

## The Word Professional Is . . . Highly Undesirable

Finally, Layden cautioned the team representatives that "the word professional is not part of the name of this league and is highly undesirable in this connection." Layden's promotional plans, instituted through the *Chicago Tribune*'s George Strickler as the league's public relations guru, did much to ensure that the league would be fan-friendly, and initiated the beginnings of increasing player profiles to the hero-type status that is evident today. Layden's progressive thinking stimulated a connection between the players and the average fan, who became aware that Marshall Goldberg enjoyed playing the piano and golfing, or that New York giant rookie Andy Marefos was a retail poultry dealer in real life. Layden had wasted little time in forging his imprint upon the league.

While the NFL was not yet ready to go global, despite its newfound marketing endeavors, the storms of war in the rest of the world were difficult to ignore as the 1941 season approached. The world war was erupting all over the planet. Europe, Russia, and North Africa were all in flames and America was drawn closer to the hostilities when Congress approved the "Lend-Lease" Act, paving the way for the United States to provide the Allies with necessary material support and supplies. Yet as the 1941 season loomed nearer, there was still hope that the United States would avoid any additional participation in the warfare. The war was still distant, but getting much closer.

As for the Chicago Cardinals, the team returned to Morgan Park Military Academy on 111th Street for its preseason training camp. Once again, Conzelman invited a staggering number of newcomers to camp in an effort to plug some obvious holes from the year before. When the final roster was determined, it included just five players who were members of the team before Conzelman's arrival just twelve short months before. If the Cardinals were expected to sport a new look in 1941, Conzelman insisted that it start with himself. The coach checked into Morgan Park Military Academy weighing just 203 pounds, his trimmest figure in years.

Conzelman's training camp was difficult, but carefully planned to harvest and solidify the talents of the individual players. Above all, Conzelman searched for consistency, as he told the press early in the season:

> In the past years the Cards have been up and down. In other words, they would play one fine game, causing high hopes which usually were dashed the next Sunday. They were flighty and unpredictable.
>
> We finally have obtained the personnel to insure a good, steady performance every time we go out on the field. Now I'm not saying we're going to win the championship, but I'm saying those hit or miss days are gone. This is the most capable looking Cardinal squad I've seen in 10 years.

## What Do You Play, Mr. Goldberg?

The Cardinals added some impressive players for the 1941 campaign, including a pair who would become two of the greatest in the team's long history: Paul Christman and Ray Mallouf. Both were instrumental in the Cards' future success. After starring in high school in Maplewood, Missouri, Christman was intent on playing for Elmer

Layden, then the head coach at Notre Dame. But Christman was on the slight side (about 185 pounds) at that time in his life (1937) and Layden told him, "Sure, I know. You've heard that I had put on a wet suit to weigh 165 pounds when I was a fullback at Notre Dame. But football has changed. It's a big man's game. You might get hurt."

Undaunted, Christman tried out at Purdue, but was dropped from that squad early in the season. "It was too late to get into another college that fall," Christman recalled, "but I made myself a couple of promises . . . that I would become a college All-American, and that someday I'd play on a team better than Notre Dame or Purdue." To pass the time, Christman went home and found employment as a lineman with a telephone company. The lack of competition and the home cooking worked wonders . . . too well! Christman had ballooned to about 230 pounds by the time he began looking for his next team. He contacted coach Don Faurot at the University of Missouri, who wasn't quite sure what to make of this project. "I walked around this plump young man. Then I poked him in the stomach, expecting to hear a vast 'hiss' like you hear when an auto tire deflates. I put him on a diet and told him to come to Missouri."

Faurot's gamble on Christman paid off well as "Pitchin' Paul" was named to the All-American teams in both 1939 and 1940. He was also known for his sly wit and affable nature. Upon joining the Cardinals in 1941 (he was a second-round draft choice), Christman immediately found himself as the target of veteran Marshall Goldberg, who enjoyed needling newcomers to the team. When Goldberg spotted Christman for the first time, he yelled, "Hey, what's your name! What do you play?"

Christman deadpanned his reply: "Poker, pitch, and pinochle. What do you play, Mr. Goldberg?"

In 1941, Christman played for the College All-Stars but left the Cardinals' training camp prior to the first game due to his commitment to the naval reserve. Because of his military commitments, Christman spent some of the 1941 season with the Kenosha (WI) Cardinals and later played with the Fleet City Bluejackets in the Navy. The *Tribune* added to the intrigue as to why Christman would not be available to the Chicago Cardinals in 1941:

> *Through no fault of his own, Christman has given the Cardinals' management some beautiful headaches, too. First, he wasn't sure if he would play professional football. Then, after he decided to join the Cardinals, the army put in a hurry-up call for him. Paul countered by joining the naval reserve. After that he was married last Monday and received a ten-day furlough. Only yesterday afternoon it was definitely learned that Christman will be too busy with his naval duties to play with the Cardinals.*

Christman eventually joined the Cardinals in 1945 following the completion of his military service.

Ray Mallouf, however, made an immediate impact as both a runner and a passer in 1941. In the first exhibition game against the Kenosha team, Mallouf completed twelve of nineteen passes on a wet field to snare the coaching staff's attention.

The military effort was already beginning to sap the strength of the NFL in 1941. Missing from the 1940 roster due to service responsibilities were back Ev "Boot" Elkins, end John Shirk, tackle Bobby Wood, and fullback Motts Tonelli. Except for Tonelli, none of these men would ever return to the NFL.

One of Conzelman's favorite players that season would turn out to be twenty-one-year-old Johnny Clement, a back from Southern Methodist who could also pass. Clement would enjoy one bright, shining season with the Cards before spending the rest of the war in the service. Clement acquired the nickname "Mr. Zero" and impressed Conzelman with his talent and courage as well as his "different" habits. He was an expert at making mud pies during practices and lectures, according to Conzelman, who would then delight in explaining this artistic process down to the details, such as what Clement would imprint on his pies. Known as a bit of a free spirit himself, Conzelman could understand the persona of "Mr. Zero" and the way his mind worked.

When asked once about his team's chances against mighty Green Bay, Conzelman commented: "Offhand, I'd say it's according to how Mr. Clement feels. There are a number of factors. If he takes the right train and gets there on time and lines up with the right team, we may do something!" On another occasion, Clement surprised his teammates by purchasing a new car, but Conzelman had the perfect explanation: "He came downtown from the south side on a street car and decided he didn't want to return the same way!"

Despite his inexperience, his side trips into daydreams on and off the field, and his apparent lack of speed ("I don't know how he gains ground. He's not fast," said Conzelman, "but we all like him."), Clement would grow into an important asset for the Cardinals as the 1941 season progressed. The Cards also added a respected end in Bill Daddio, who had been Marshall Goldberg's teammate at the University of Pittsburgh. After playing in the 1939 College All-Star game, Daddio had declined to play pro football and remained at Pittsburgh as an assistant coach during the 1939 and 1940 seasons.

The key to the 1941 squad would once again be Marshall Goldberg, although he was talking seriously about retiring to enter the business world on a full-time basis:

> After the 1940 season, Sollie Sherman, who played with the Bears, introduced me to his father-in-law who owned a machine tool business. He explained the business and offered me a six month trial job to see if I liked it and to see if he liked me. He joked that perhaps some day I might own the business and we both got a laugh out of that, but 25 years later, thats what happened. So, I played football and also worked in the machine business earning $50 per week. I'd go to work at the machine business until 1:00 and then went to football practice every day at 2:00. I was rolling in the money because a dollar went a long way back then. When my salary was raised to $65 after six months, I seriously thought about going into the business on a full-time basis.

Goldberg was the tenth-leading rusher in the league in 1940, and would move up to third in 1941, so Conzelman was delighted when he decided to return: "Goldberg is strictly a left halfback who likes to run to his right and I think he'll improve as much this year as he did last year over his 1939 form."

Although the Cardinals were vastly improved, the team failed to show much in its only exhibition game, a 21-21 tie with the Kenosha (WI) Cardinals. Despite Mallouf's pair of touchdown tosses, the team struggled in the pits and Conzelman ordered the line to be more intense during the next few practice sessions. The team would open up the regular season at home against the Cleveland Rams in a rare Tuesday night game on September 16, in what was expected to be a passing duel between the two clubs. Cleveland relied on the pitching of Parker Hall while the Cardinals could counter with Mallouf, Clement, or McCullough. Bill Dewell, a 6'4" end, was back after missing all but two games of his freshman season with a fractured ankle.

Instead of a wide-open passing game, the contest turned into a defensive struggle with the Rams finally prevailing 10-6. Mallouf suffered a slight concussion during the game and the Cards' passing attack never did take flight. After a week off from competition, the Chicagoans entertained Detroit in another night game on Saturday, September 27. Due to the usual scheduling quirks, this would be the second of only three home games for the Cardinals in 1941, with the next home game in distant December. A crowd of nearly twenty thousand showed up to watch the two teams battle to a 14-14 tie. Marshall Goldberg passed to Johnny Hall for the first score while Johnny Clement rushed two yards for the other.

## We May Decide To Go Fishing

The Cardinals then embarked on an infamous eight-game road trip, with the first stop in Milwaukee against Green Bay. Conzelman drilled his club intensively prior to the game, focusing on keeping the ball out of the hands of the Packers' superlative end, Don Hutson. With George Strickler now handling publicity for the league, Edward Prell reported on the Cardinals' pregame preparations in the *Chicago Tribune:*

> *If they are beaten by the Packers, it will not be because of lack of preparation, physically and mentally. Coach Jimmy Conzelman and his associates have held nightly squad meetings. Yesterday they continued working on ways to keep Don Hutson separated from the flying football. The peerless pass catcher of the Packers hadn't had a really big day this season and the Cards want to be sure he doesn't break out against them.*

Ultimately, Hutson did defeat the visitors, but he did it with his feet, not his hands. After Marshall Goldberg had scored on a seventy-six-yard pass play from Johnny Clement in the second stanza, the Cardinals maintained a 13-7 lead late in the game. However, Cecil Isbell's short toss to Lou Brock knotted the score on the Packers' final drive, and Hutson followed with the second of his two extra points for the day, providing the margin of victory (14-13) for the winners. Goldberg's scoring jaunt was the play of the game and established him as one of the more feared offensive threats in the league, according to Wilfrid Smith:

> *Marshall Goldberg was the hero of the Cardinal battle. This was his best game since he joined the professional ranks. Goldberg always was a threat at the flanks, he smashed into the Packer line with the force of a fullback, but his greatest contribution was a sparkling 76 yard touchdown run in the second period after receiving John Clement's pass on the line of scrimmage.*

For Conzelman, the defeat was certainly disappointing and just another stop on a long stint of personal defeats to the Packers. After quarterbacking the Rock Island Independents to a win over the Packers in 1921, none of his teams as either a player or a coach (Milwaukee, Detroit, Providence, or the Cardinals) had rewarded him with a victory over Green Bay. After two close defeats and a tie, next up for the Cardinals was a Wrigley Field date with the defending champion Bears. The Bears, rolling along with a twelve-game winning streak, may have been the best team of that particular era. Loaded with size and speed, and led by gifted quarterback Sid Luckman, the Bears were undefeated and unconcerned. "We'll decide whether to show up in Wrigley Field Sunday," said Conzelman before the game. "For all I know we may decide to go fishing—and I don't like to fish!"

The Cardinals did show up, but perhaps the fishing choice would have been more appropriate. On the day when the Bears raised their 1940 championship pennant, they wasted little time in disposing of the South Siders before 34,668, the most ever to see a Cardinals team. Scoring early and often, the Bears jumped out to a 33-0 half-time lead and breezed to a 53-7 win. A stunned Conzelman watched as his team allowed a record 613 yards and fell before the widest margin ever in the forty-two-game history of this long rivalry.

Conzelman had a quick wit and a very droll sense of humor. After the Bears drubbed the Cards, Conzelman was his usual expressive self when he was asked if this particular loss was more meddlesome than any others:

> Don't get the idea that being beaten by the Bears 53-7 bothered me a bit. Oh, not in the least. I went home after the game, had a good night's rest and a very hearty breakfast. I said good-bye to the missus and strolled down the hall to the elevator, whistling a light tune. I pushed the elevator button and took in my profile in the hall mirror. I was a picture of elegance in my hat, tweed sport jacket, and well-shined tan shoes. Then I went back to my apartment and put on my trousers.

## They Have Their Pep Back Pretty Well

If the Cardinals intended to salvage any of the 1941 season, they would need to rebound quickly and efficiently despite having to play the next six games on the road. Conzelman's ability as an innovator and a motivator would certainly be needed to offset the humiliating loss to the Bears. As the team left for its next date in Brooklyn, Conzelman was pleased with the mental resurrection of his players:

> They have their pep back pretty well. And I think we'll play some good football in the east. They were discouraged after losing that close one to the Packers. If we can win this first one against the Dodgers, it will do us a world of good.

The road was kind to the Cardinals, and the team responded with a 20-6 upset of Brooklyn on October 19. Perhaps inspired by playing against their old college coach Jock Sutherland (now coach of the Dodgers), Goldberg and Daddio paced the Cards to the victory. Goldberg was on the receiving end of a fifty-yard pass play and later scored on a three-yard run, while Daddio recovered a critical Dodger fumble which he initiated by knocking the ball out of Ace Parker's hands.

The East Coast swing continued with a close 21-14 defeat at Philadelphia, where

Clement and Dewell combined on a twenty-yard scoring strike, and then with a 10-7 win in New York before 29,289, which knocked the Giants out of first place in the Eastern Division. Daddio's sixteen-yard field goal in the third quarter provided the margin of victory, but the passing of Clement to Dewell was becoming more of a surprise every week. Due to an injury to Ray Mallouf, Clement was given the opportunity to blossom in New York. Protected by the solid line play of Joe Kuharich and Al Babartsky, Clement drilled pass after pass to Dewell as Chicago picked up two hundred yards through the air. Although the Cardinals were just 2-4-1 at this juncture of the season, their offense was ranked a lofty third in the league, and they had outgained all of their opponents except the Bears. The new passing attack was gaining momentum as noted by the *Tribune:*

> *New York writers compared Jack Clement and Bill Dewell to Cecil Isbell and Don Hutson after the Cardinals knocked the Giants out of the eastern lead Sunday. Clement completed 13-20 passes for 200 yards. This advanced the freshman from Southern Methodist to fifth among the National league passers. Dewell, also a former SMU star, caught eight of the passes for 131 yards. This fine piece of work put Dewell next to the Packers' Don Hutson in snaring passes.*

At mid-season, Goldberg had jumped to the position of the fourth leading rusher in the league and was also among the leaders in interceptions, punt returns, and kick-off returns.

## Whacks Them For Bloody Murder

Meanwhile, military preparations were beginning to affect the team's long-range planning. Clement was due to be called up by his draft board in Dallas, but received a thirty-day deferral as did Kuharich, a member of the Air Corps reserve, who had been scheduled to report for duty on November 7, 1941. Both losses would have been difficult for the Cardinals. Clement was now a bonafide offensive threat, while guard Kuharich was having an All-Pro year and also called out the offensive signals from his line position. With a week off between the New York and Green Bay (November 16) games, the Cardinals picked up Fred Vanzo from Detroit, a 230-pound blocking back out of Northwestern. The Packers had already seen Vanzo twice this season when he was with Detroit, and the Packers' weekly press release described him as "a rough and tumble blocking back who whacks them for bloody murder."

Despite the lateness of the season, Conzelman drilled the Cardinals for three hours each night in preparation for the Packers. After upsetting the supposedly invincible Bears, Green Bay had crept into first place of the Western Division by a half game. Although Bill Daddio's twenty-seven-yard field goal pushed the Cards into an early 3-0 lead, the Packers and Don Hutson quickly bounced back. Hutson snared a twenty-five-yard scoring toss from Cecil Isbell, and later scored on a short run to give the Packers a 17-9 victory.

The following week (November 23), the Cards picked up win number three by edging the Cleveland Rams 7-0. Frank "Pop" Ivy's twenty-yard return of a pass interception early in the second half provided the only points needed. Marshall Goldberg intercepted two other Cleveland passes to stymie the losers even further. The Rams (2-9) finished their season that day with the last of nine straight defeats to allow the

Cardinals to escape the Western Division cellar for the first time in four years. Meanwhile, the Cards (3-5-1) still had dates to keep with both the Lions (November 30) and the Bears (December 7).

The game at Detroit marked what turned out to be the final professional game for Whizzer White of the Lions. The former Colorado All-American and Rhodes scholar was scheduled to enter the service after this game, and the Cardinals probably agreed that this circumstance occurred a game too late. White rushed for one touchdown and passed twenty-three yards to Bill Fisk for another as the Lions jumped over the Cards into third place with a 21-3 victory. Although the Cardinals would limp into their final game against the Bears with a 3-6-1 mark, the game would be extremely important for the Bears. With Green Bay (10-1) having finished its season, the Bears (9-1) needed a victory over the Cardinals in order to force a Western Division play-off with the Packers.

Ray Mallouf, the early-season sensation, was expected back for the Cardinals after missing several weeks with a broken thumb on his throwing hand. A press release from the league office on December 6 suggested that there just might be a glimmer of hope for the out-manned Cardinals:

> *Mallouf's return, plus the stinging humiliation of a 53-7 defeat at the hands of the Bears on October 12 and the belief that Comiskey Park holds a jinx for the champions, all have combined to lift the Cardinals to eloquent confidence. It was in Comiskey Park a year ago that the Cardinals surprised the Bears 21-7, for their first victory of the season and their seventh since the series began back in 1920.*

Although the Bears were heavily favored, the team was not inclined to look past the Cardinals in anticipation of a possible playoff game with the Packers on December 14. Bears guard George Musso told the *Daily News:*

> *The very fact we beat them so hard will make them doubly anxious for revenge. And then there's that Marshall Goldberg. What a nuisance he is!*

The Cardinals were also voicing some confidence, according to guard Milt Popovich:

> *I can assure the fans of one thing: the Bears will find us a vastly different Cardinal team than the one they whipped 53-7 early in the year.*

With the entire Packes squad "scouting" the game from the cheap seats, Conzelman reminded his team of their embarrassing first encounter, and also that the Bears had already made plans for the playoff game at Wrigley Field against the Packers a week hence. Halas had announced that the upcoming Packer game had prompted the biggest surge for tickets in the history of the franchise. Such thoughts riled up the Cardinals, including injured guard Tarzan White, who bluntly stated: "I'll be in there if I have to protect my bum knee in concrete."

The inspired Cardinals took the field and immediately stunned the Bears with an overpowering drive down to the Bears' one-yard line. Goldberg was the headliner on this attack, grabbing one pass for twenty-two yards and rushing for most of the rest. But it was his fumble at the one that temporarily stalled the effort. However, on the very next play, Norm Standlee of the Bears fumbled in his own end zone and the Cards' Bill Davis recovered to put his team in front 7-0.

The Cardinals' Vanzo recovered another fumble early in the second quarter on his own thirteen. Mallouf immediately engineered a scoring drive, hitting Goldberg for fifteen yards and Dewell for another thirty-five. Goldberg scored from the six, and the scoreboard reflected the Cardinals' surprising 14-0 advantage. Sid Luckman rallied the Bears back with a seventy-yard scoring effort, and then picked off a Mallouf pass on the ensuing series to put the Bears back in business on the Cardinals' ten-yard line. Following the ejection of the Bears' Ray Bray for fighting, the Bears tied the score 14-14 on Joe Maniaci's short plunge. But the Cards weren't done yet—a fine Goldberg kickoff return, accompanied by additional roughing penalties on the Bears, left Daddio in good position to boot a twenty-two-yard field goal shortly before the end of the half. The two teams left the field with the Cardinals owning a 17-14 lead and the Bears enduring waves of boos and catcalls from the audience for both their sluggish play and their slugging hands. Edward Prell praised the officiating crew for its prompt intercession at this point in the contest:

> *It was to the credit of the fine officiating team . . . that they quickly slapped on those penalties. Their prompt and fearless action put a stop to this extracurricular activity, which was a break for the Bears, who can win football games on skill and power without resorting to roughness.*

The Bears threatened early in the third period but Goldberg recovered still another fumble on the Cards' own five-yard line. Following a Mallouf punt, the Bears were back in business on the Cards' thirty-four, and Hugh Gallarneau capped a short scoring drive by scampering the final eighteen yards for a touchdown and the Bears' first lead at 21-17. On just the third play of the fourth quarter, Mallouf pushed the Cards ahead 24-21 when he hit Bert Johnson with a touchdown pass. Now trailing 24-21, the Bears put themselves further in the hole when Luckman's pass on the next series was picked off by Johnson on his own thirty-one.

The *Daily News* described the moment:

> *A crowd of 18,879 sat in amazement as an embattled bunch of Cardinals, led by Marshall Goldberg and Ray Mallouf and featuring a hard-charging line, outplayed the Bears and threatened to knock the champions right out of the title picture. The Packers, huddled in great coats in the upper deck, were whooping lustily as they envisioned a clear claim to the western crown.*

However, the Cards were unable to capitalize on this turnover and the ensuing punt prompted Luckman to wage an eighty-three yard battle for victory, highlighted by a forty-nine-yard scoring pass to George McAfee.

The Bears would go on to win, 34-24, and then would knock off the Packers 33-14 to claim the division title. The Bears then added their second straight championship by routing the Giants 37-9 in the NFL title game. Yet the Bears hard-fought victory on December 7, 1941, soon paled with the news that invaded the locker rooms after the game. "We found out about it after the game. We never thought it would hap-

pen," said Marshall Goldberg. "We were stunned. We didn't know what to think."
The Japanese had bombed Pearl Harbor.

## Your Deal: It's In The Cards

Here is the complete and unedited version of the Cardinals' team fight song, written by Jimmy Conzelman prior to the big game with the Bears on December 7, 1941. The **Chicago Daily News** announced the arrival of this work on December 5, 1941:

"James Conzelman, noted football coach, raconteur, composer, author, wit and thespian, has dashed off a varsity song for his Chicago Cardinals. He has titled it, with his customary touch, "It's In the Cards to Win."

"The opus is designed for 1942 consumption and James does not say whether the title applies to Sunday's game with the Bears . . ."

These are the accompanying lyrics:

It's in the Cards to win
Get ready to cheer when they begin
Watch how the red team goes
Just give it a sign to break up the line of foes
Fight for the right to score
Let's roll up a lead and then go out for more
It's in the Cards to win
Get ready to cheer, let's go!

In 1946, a group of players called themselves the "Harmony Kings" and wrote a new Cardinals victory song after a mid-season thrashing of the Boston Yanks. Harry Warren of the **Chicago Tribune** referred to the "songwriters" as follows:

Mal (Stephen Foster) Kutner, Joe (Cole Porter) Parker, Tom (George M. Cohan) Kearns, Bob (George Gershwin) Zimny, Garrard (Jerome Kern) Ramsey, Vince (Johann Strauss) Banonis, Pat (Hoagy Carmichael) Harder, and Elmer (Irving Berlin) Angsman.

"It wasn't a bad song," laughed tackle Chet Bulger, "but it wasn't a good one, either!"

## *Goldberg Topped The League In Interceptions And Returns*

When the All-League team was announced on December 30, Joe Kuharich was on the first team at right guard, while Goldberg, whom the NFL designated its most improved player, joined Detroit's Whizzer White on the second team in the backfield. Billy Dewell was selected as honorable mention at end. Dewell finished the year with the third most receptions in the NFL while Goldberg topped the league in interceptions and kickoff returns and was third in rushing. Ray Mallouf finished sixth in passing (Clement was eighth) despite missing most of the year with injuries, and his eighty-yard pass to John Hall was the longest in the league that year.

Aside from the outrageous loss in the first Bears game, the Cardinals proved to be a formidable foe and a much improved team in 1941. They defeated the Eastern

Division champion Giants and lost close games to the two other top teams, Green Bay and the Bears. With the current personnel in place, Conzelman and his Cardinals appeared poised to get over the "hump" and contend for the NFL title in 1942.

But the world was changing, the league was changing, and football was changing. The war would threaten the very existence of the NFL as hundreds of players volunteered to trade in their shoulder pads and helmets for helmets of another kind. Nearly fifty individuals who had played or coached with the Cardinals would serve in the military during World War II. Among the fatalities would be former halfback Jimmy Lawrence and former coach Jack Chevigny. Yet perhaps the most intriguing story was that of Mario "Motts" Tonelli, the Chicago native who attended DePaul Academy and then starred at Notre Dame. Tonelli had volunteered for service following the 1940 season and had little idea that he would be stationed halfway around the world when the Bears edged the Cardinals on December 7, 1941.

## We Were Told To Expect War

On December 7, Motts Tonelli was getting accustomed to life at Fort Clark in the Philippines when the Bears and the Cardinals met to close out the 1941 regular season. Tonelli had entered the service in March 1941 for what he anticipated would be a one-year term in the army. "At that time, everyone was expected to serve a year in the military. I finished up the 1940 season and then talked to Jimmy Conzelman and told him that I wanted to get it (the one-year service term) over with." So Tonelli enlisted and moved on to boot camp at Camp Wallace, Texas.

From there, the trail led to Fort Bliss in Texas, and finally to San Francisco. The troops then boarded the Coolidge luxury liner for the long trip to the Philippines. Eventually, Tonelli found himself at Clark Field, where he discovered "lots of Air Corps men, but few planes or parts, so most of the pilots became infantry men." There was no war to participate in, but the troops kept busy through drilling and maneuvers. The equipment was old, scarce, and insufficient. "About ten days before the war actually started, we were on maneuvers in the field. When we came back in a few days later, all of the equipment was still out there," said Tonelli.

On the morning of December 7, 1941, the United States was the only remaining major country in the world that was not involved in the war. In Japan, a decision had been reached to conquer all of Southeast Asia, an area that would also include Pearl Harbor and the Philippines. The news of the bombing of Pearl Harbor reached Tonelli quickly: "When we found out about it, we were immediately told to expect war where we were. Since we were not officially at war our bombers were not allowed to bomb the Japanese fleet, so our planes left for Australia and left us without any air protection."

Following the attack on Pearl Harbor, Clark Field was bombed the next day, according to Tonelli: "The Japanese bombed us immediately and they knew exactly what to hit. The bombers were followed in by fighter planes which strafed the remaining planes and buildings. The Japanese were shooting down our fighter planes as soon as they took off. All we had to shoot with were our rifles since the big guns were still sitting over in the parking lot."

A land invasion by the Japanese army quickly followed and the Battle of Bataan Peninsula began on January 7, 1942. "We started our withdrawal to Subic Bay, but the heavy bombers and fighter planes attacked us like it was a regular routine. We knew they were coming since we could hear the planes reving up in Manila several miles to the east. The actual war began for us on December 8 and the battle lasted through March. We didn't have food, water, or ammunition when they finally broke through." After several months of battle, Major General Edward P. King surrendered the force on April 9, 1942, in an area known as Bataan. Approximately ten thousand American soldiers were part of that situation, and were doomed to spend the remainder of the war in captivity—if they survived. "We destroyed all of our equipment," remembered Tonelli, "and walked through the jungle to the area of the surrender. It was very chaotic. No one knew what was going on."

Perhaps the worst part of this trauma for both the prisoners and their families was that no news of the status of the captured men would reach the United States until January of 1944. For those waiting in anguish at home, the sentiment that no news is good news would need to prevail. For the American prisoners in Bataan, captivity would prove to be a nightmarish and horrible existence. In the preface to the book *Death March,* Donald Knox wrote:

> *What a prisoner did to stay alive one day might cause his death the next. There were no maps to show a prisoner how to get from sun up to sun down alive. Every emotional and physical path had to be explored afresh every day. Men who did so successfully lived; those who didn't died.*

The Japanese were not expecting the vast number of prisoners they encountered. Inadequate food, supplies, and transportation combined with inefficient management initiated one of the most bizarre and hideous episodes of the war. The prisoners needed to be moved as quickly as possible from Southern Bataan to Central Luzon. However, the prisoners were already weak from months of battle and adequate transportation was lacking. It was decided that the prisoners would be marched from Bataan to their destination of San Fernando, some sixty miles away. "They would get a group to start marching," described Tonelli, "and they marched us sixty or seventy miles in seven days. That might not seem like a lot, but we did it without food or water under a very hot sun." In *Death March's* introduction, Stanley L. Falk wrote:

> *Instead of a carefully organized military movement, the exodus from Bataan, with some notable exceptions, was a series of torturous marches, of needless exposure to a merciless sun, of crowded, filthy assembly areas stinking of disease and human refuse, and of beatings, torture and arbitrary execution.*

While estimates of the number of prisoners vary, the 10,000 Americans were probably accompanied by about 62,000 Filipinos, and all were treated miserably. Food and water were rare while beatings and unexplained executions were commonplace. Tonelli was stunned by the brutality on the march: "Soldiers who couldn't walk or keep up were shot or bayoneted, or run over by a truck. Sometimes guards would come up behind you and club their hands over both of your ears and yell 'Why are you so skinny? I think that's why I still have trouble with my ears." While these events are still denounced as barbaric and inhumane, Knox points out a cultural diversity at work:

> *To help understand Japan's point of view towards prisoners, it should be remembered that the Japanese consider anyone who surrenders a traitor to their country and worthy only of contempt and of the harshest treatment at the hand of friend and foe alike. The Western idea of surrender simply does not apply to Japanese thought. Being taken a prisoner while still able to resist was considered by the Japanese military to be a criminal act. Suicide, rather than surrender, was preferred.*

With no food or water, the captives were forced to struggle with any and all methods in order to survive, remarked Tonelli: "At night, we would sleep in a schoolyard or a church. We slept on our shirts, and in the morning, the shirts would be wet from the moisture of the dew, and we would suck out the water. We couldn't do that for too long since the shirts eventually became saturated with the salt from our own bodies."

Thousands failed to survive the forced march and the long trail finally arrived at a rail line, where further horrors awaited the men. "We never knew where we were going," said Tonelli. "After seven days, we reached the train and they loaded us into steel box cars. It was so hot. We were jammed in so tight that you couldn't sit or sleep. Guys would die standing up." After the sweltering train trip, the prisoners marched the remainder of the way to Camp O'Donnell, the first prison camp of many for Tonelli.

At Camp O'Donnell, the conditions continued to be harsh and ruthless. Food sustenance was minimal, usually consisting of tiny rice balls. Searches were a regular part of the regimen, even though the scarcely clad prisoners had little opportunity to hide something. The most revolting punishment was the immediate execution of anyone possessing Japanese money. The captors reasoned unjustly that the only way a prisoner could have received such an item was through the killing of a Japanese soldier. Thus, immediate retribution was carried out. Tonelli kept his meager possessions, including his Notre Dame class ring, in a small silver case. "They were always searching us, so I kept this buried in the dirt or under some grass and kept moving it."

## Time Didn't Mean Anything

At Camp O'Donnell, Tonelli was assigned to a burial detail. "Half of us were either sick or passing out. The commander of the camp (Captain Tsuneyoshi) told us that the Japanese were good people, and that when Japan won the war, we would be welcome in Japan since we would no longer be welcome in the United States. We were burying thirty to fifty soldiers a day. We would dig a square grave and bury twenty-five guys in a grave. If we stayed there much longer, we'd all be dead."

Tonelli began a stretch of nearly forty-two months in various Japanese prison labor camps: "Time didn't mean anything. We didn't have papers or calendars. You could tell months were going by through the changing of the seasons. We worked planting rice, harvesting rice and in factories making ingots. After a year or so, we knew things were going in our favor when we noticed U.S. planes in the sky. They flew higher than the Japanese planes and as the months went by, they kept coming lower and lower."

By late 1944, the Japanese began shipping the surviving prisoners to Japan on what are now called Hell Ships. Of all the unsavory experiences that Tonelli had the misfortune to experience, this was perhaps the greatest challenge both from a physical and mental viewpoint. The soldiers were crammed into the bottom level of the ships and embarked on the long journey, never really knowing where they were going or how long it would take to arrive there. *Death March* author Donald Knox recalled his time on one of these ships:

> *We were locked in a hold together, 500 of us. We were in there solid, wall to wall. Tight, so you couldn't put your feet between people when you tried to walk. I don't know how to describe heat, there was no way we measured temperature. It must have been 120 or 125 degrees in that hold. The Japs favorite trick was to cut off our water. It was bad enough in other places when they did this, but there, in this oven, when they cut it off, guys started going crazy.*

Tonelli recalls being transported on the *Canadian Inventor* in July of 1944 and spending about sixty days on the boat. "After going all through what we did on Bataan, the hell ships made us think that the guys who didn't make it were the lucky ones. They crammed us in the boat and all we could do was lay on a tarp covering the slat. There were no facilities. Soldiers of all nationalities were dying and praying to God together. To feed us, they lowered down buckets on ropes. We were never sure if they were the same buckets which they sent down for us to use for sanitary reasons."

Worst of all, the ships were not marked as being for medical or prisoner transport, so they were a frequent target of unknowing U.S. submarines. "It's a shame, but lots of hell ships went down," noted Tonelli. When the prisoners arrived in Japan, they were interred in various work camps, and continually threatened with death. "We were told we would be killed as soon as the Americans landed," said Tonelli. One unidentified American prisoner quoted in *Death March* felt that it was only a matter of time before the Japanese would cease to retain the prisoners in light of the escalated pressure on their country:

> *The Japanese commander called us into the compound and told us that if the war did not end by October (1945), three-quarters of the Japanese population would die. There was no doubt in any of our minds that we would be in that three-quarters.*

## Hostilities Have Ceased. See You Soon.

With so many Japanese serving in the military, the U.S. prisoners were assigned to industrial or factory work. Food was still scarce, but vitamin pills helped in more ways than one. "Once a guard was told that a vitamin pill was the equivalent of an American meal and he traded his rice for a vitamin. No one traded a real vitamin pill. The one the guard received was made out of plaster and a little bit of chocolate!"

As the months went by, Tonelli could tell that the end might be near when he noticed American reconnaissance planes, and later watched the comprehensive pattern bombing of Japan at night. Finally, on August 14, an American plane swooped over Tonelli's prison compound and dropped a large box of cigarettes with a note attached on a handkerchief. The note simply said: "Hostilities have ceased. Will see you soon." Additional planes dropped food and other supplies for the ravaged prisoners.

Japan finally surrendered on August 15, 1945, with the formal surrender accepted on September 2, 1945, on the *USS Missouri* in Tokyo Bay. Tonelli was on his way home! He was first flown by plane to a hospital ship in Yokohama Bay and then back to Clark Field in the Philippines. The final leg was a boat ride to San Francisco and then the long train ride to his beloved Chicago. Upon his release from the Japanese prison camp, the former 210-pound Chicago Cardinals fullback weighed less than 100 pounds.

## 1942: An All-Out War Effort

In the early months of 1942, the nation plunged full-time into the war effort. Change was everywhere. While the country was in a crisis, professional football realized that it needed to address its own role as well. Layden scheduled a three-day meeting in New York from March 26 to 28 to "clear the decks for an all out war effort, for the adjustment of league policies and regulations to the national emergency," according to an NFL press release " It was agreed that the league would not cease operations during the conflict, but would manage as well as it could under the circumstances. Layden indeed sounded like a commissioner as he prepared for this important meeting of the league owners:

> *From Aristotle's time on down we have been told, and it has been demonstrated, that sports and entertainment are necessary for the relaxation of the people in times of stress and worry. The National League will strive to help meet this need with the men the government has not yet called for combat service, either because of dependents, disabilities or the luck of the draw in the army draft.*

However, a suggestion to increase the number of league games by Bert Bell, president of the Pittsburgh Steelers, was not supported by Layden:

> *We feel our business, athletic entertainment, is an important factor in preserving the morale and furthering the physical well being of the people. Decreasing the number of attractions defeats these purposes. On the other hand, active participation in the war program will leave little time to experiment with an increase in the number of regular league contests.*

The NFL was still operating under archaic substitution rules prohibiting a player from returning to the game in the same quarter in which he was replaced, except in the final quarter, when two players were allowed to return once. However, with the prospect of dwindling rosters (and talent) due to the war, the attendees at the March meeting initiated a ruling which would allow two subs to reenter the game in each quarter. In addition, the thirty-three-man roster was reduced to twenty-eight for the duration of the war. "A lower limit is preferable in contests in which one team has half a dozen more replacements than its opponent," stated Layden.

## A "One Minute Interview"

As the military gobbled up the services of professional football players during the early months of the war, the NFL released a "One-Minute Interview" with Coach Conzelman on May 7, 1942, which eloquently compared the rituals of football with the realities of war:

> *Football coaches always have been apologists for their profession. For years we've been on the defensive against attacks from the reformers who regard us as muscle-bound mentalities exploiting kids for an easy living. Football has been under fire because it involved body contact and it teaches violence. It was considered useless, even dangerous.*
>
> *But that's all over now. The bleeding hearts haven't the courtesy to apologize to us, but they're coming around and asking our help in the national emergency. Why?*
>
> *Why, because the college commencement classes this month will find the customary challenge of life a pale prelude to the demands of a world at war. Instead of job seekers, or home makers, the graduates suddenly have become defenders of a familiar way of life, of an ideology, a religion and of a nation. They have been taught to build. Now they must learn to destroy.*
>
> *It may be reprehensible to inculcate a will to destroy in these amiable young men; but war is reprehensible and its basic motive is to destroy. The transition will not be an easy one. Democracy makes us a pacific people. The young man must be toughened not only physically, but mentally. He must become accustomed to violence. Football is the No. 1 medium for attuning a man to body-contact and very physical shock. It teaches that after all there isn't anything so terrifying about a punch in the puss.*

Later in May, Conzelman addressed the graduating class at the University of Dayton. This appearance marked the first time that an NFL coach had been invited on the dais at a major commencement ceremony.

## No Time For Sports To Look For Profit!

With the unpredictable 1942 season fast approaching, the legendary Curly Lambeau of the Green Bay Packers offered his predictions for the league amidst the confusion brought on by the war effort:

> *I look for the Chicago Bears to repeat in the National League this Fall. Man for man, they had the greatest team in football a year ago and since the demands of the selective service affect all teams, I don't see how you can figure the Bears will have any less of an edge this season. No matter who wins though, the important thing will be a continuance of athletic competition. Sports' main obligation to the nation now is to carry on beyond all normal duty toward an all-out war effort with what athletes are left.*
>
> *The conditioning, training and disciplining of those not yet in active service is a tremendous problem in which organized athletics must play an important part. Up to now the American system of athletics hasn't paid enough attention to youngsters. We must start training 'em younger. For professional sports the eas-*

*iest method would be to call the whole thing off. But what kind of an example would that be for the youngster who looks to the star for guidance and inspiration? Only one course is open to sports. That is—carry on without regard to the sacrifice. This is no time for sports to look for profit!*

By the time training camp rolled around in August, the Chicago Cardinals' roster was depleted of several key players. The league had vowed to continue despite the movement of so many players to military service. Conzelman was still optimistic after taking a big hit in the talent department due to the war. Among the familiar names missing in 1942 would be Johnny Clement, Ray Mallouf, Billy Dewell, Joe Kuharich, Avory Montfort, Fred Shook, Frank Balasz, Ray Rusler, Andy Chisick, Bill Davis, John Higgins, Frank Huffman, Jon Kuzman, Bill Murphy, and Tarzan White. According to *The Football Encyclopedia,* during the 1942 season, twenty-two players who had been with the Cardinals prior to the outbreak of hostilities were in the service during the 1942 season.

They embarked on various missions, from active combat, such as Tonelli experienced in the Philippines, to other needed responsibilities, as when Fred Vanzo became a physical fitness instructor for training pilots in San Diego. But all left their homes, their careers, and their families willingly and unselfishly to face the fear and the unknown of a world at war.

Joe Lokanc, a guard-linebacker out of Northwestern, spent the 1941 season with the Cardinals and then answered the call of his country. He spent what would have been his next four seasons (1942-45) in the service and thus essentially ended a promising pro football career. But to this day, he has no regrets:

*When we heard about Pearl Harbor, I wanted to enlist, although before that I was one of those guys who really didn't want us to get involved in the war. I enlisted in the Navy and went in as a chief and later became an officer, spending five years in the North Atlantic during the war. One thing that most people don't realize is that when the war ended, we didn't all get to go home. My term in the service ended in March of 1946 and then I spent five more years in the reserve. Do I regret it? Nope . . . I have no complaints. You did what you had to do.*

Several Cardinals would eventually spend at least three to five "seasons" in the service, essentially deleting the most productive athletic years of their careers. Yet none complained, none hesitated, and none refused the call.

## They Started To Run Us And Run Us And Run Us

In 1942, the Cardinals decided to move their preseason training camp out of the Chicago area once again. The destination selected was the campus of tiny Carroll College in Waukesha, Wisconsin. Wisconsin had become a popular location for pro football training camps. The Bears had been training in Delafield for several years while the Eagles were in Two Rivers, the Packers stayed at home in Green Bay, and the Giants trained at Superior. Aside from slightly cooler temperatures, these outposts offered very little else for the teams in terms of distractions. While this was not enticing for the players, it was quite acceptable for the coaches.

Conzelman and his players left Chicago for Waukesha via train on August 8 and jumped right into those familiar "two-a-day" drills on August 10. The team was welcomed by the local residents, and feted at a dinner at the Merrill Hills Country Club, where Conzelman entertained the crowd for over an hour, but "they could have sat five times that long and never even glanced at their watches," according to the local *Daily Freeman.* It was a pleasant experience for the squad, but it was probably the last enjoyable event during Conzelman's typically rugged three-week camp.

For the townspeople, however, the presence of the Cardinals was an incredible event. *The Daily Freeman* newspaper crowded its sports page with news about the Cardinals and special features on the players, coaches, and their personalities. Columnist John Aboya was quite enthralled, especially with the easy access to a personality so widely recognized as Coach Conzelman:

> *He would not have to be as gracious to his public as he is for others having attained the eminent position that he holds are, in many cases, a good deal more gruff and indifferent. He seems to feel that more friends can always be made, and he proceeds to do so all along the line. There seems to be no end to the group that he calls his intimate associates, and all those individuals are more than happy to be friends of his.*

One of the more important newcomers in 1942 was amiable tackle Chet Bulger. Bulger became not only one of the finest linemen in the league at the time but also one of its most talented narrators. Bulger was a 6'3", 235-pound tackle out of Auburn who originally went to school on a track scholarship. He was an excellent athlete at Rumford High School in Maine, but had to talk his way into a football tryout as a walk-on at Auburn. Although he preferred playing end, Bulger accepted his role in the line, and eventually evolved into a top professional prospect. He turned down an offer from Providence for $160 a game and signed with the Cardinals for $220 per outing.

He remembers his initial training camp under Conzelman with pride and enthusiasm. He recalled the dog days of the summer of 1942 in Wisconsin:

> *I remember the field at Carroll College because it was so hot because of the sun's reflection off of the limestone around the field. They fed us well and you could eat all you wanted. But then they started to run us and run us and run us. You learned not to eat too much at lunch.*
>
> *There was one lone tree beside the practice field and everyone used it for support and to throw up on it during practice. I checked on it the next year and it was about 20 feet higher!*

The energetic Conzelman immediately captivated Bulger, who remembers him mostly for his motivational techniques:

> *Jimmy was a game psychologist. He could get you so motivated and he was such a character with his mane of white hair, covered with dust from the chalkboard and his habit of continually smoking a cigarette. He wore these baggy pants and he kept his cigarettes deep down in the pockets. He'd search for his cigarettes, light one while continuing to talk, and then forget and put the pack down.*
>
> *That's when the leeches would take over. We didn't get paid in training camp,*

*and we received just $2 per day in meal money so that's why they were stealing Conzelman's cigarettes!*

The 1942 season would certainly prove to be the most challenging for Conzelman. Although the team concluded the 1941 season with high hopes and fared well in the draft, a rude ride on the roller coaster of fate would leave Conzelman with just seventeen able-bodied players by the time the last game of the season (with the Bears) would roll around on December 2. Injuries and enlistments would deplete the Cardinals' roster and leave Conzelman muttering: "It's a funny feeling to look around on the bench for a substitute and find out you haven't any."

Several newcomers were added to the preseason roster as Conzelman attempted to plug the numerous holes left by military service. His backfield was especially depleted, with Goldberg the lone returnee with any significant experience. However, Goldberg missed much of the preseason as he once again contemplated retirement. Earlier in the year, the NFL weekly press release (5/13/42) reported on Goldberg's career progression:

*Marshall Goldberg, Chicago Cardinals star and assistant superintendent of a Chicago machine manufacturing concern, has been placed in charge of the firm's Pullman, Illinois plant. Sollie Sherman, former Chicago Bear quarterback, is superintendent for the company and runs the Chicago plant. Both plants are working 24 hour shifts building machinery under government contract for defense plants in all parts of the country.*

To replace the passing arms of Mallouf and Clement, the Cardinals added Wilson "Bud" Schwenk, a nifty passer from Washington University in St. Louis. At 6'2" and 205 pounds, Schwenk was one of the first of the "big" NFL quarterbacks and enjoyed a superlative season with the Cardinals in 1942 before being called to military service. Schwenk topped the league with 295 passing attempts in 1942, completing 126 for 1,360 yards (best in the Western Division).

The numerous pass attempts reflected Conzelman's change in philosophy from favoring the rushing attack to developing an offense that would best fit the available talent. While the backfield was decimated by service duty, the line was altered significantly as well. Conzelman plugged some holes by recalling aging center Ben Scaggie Ciccone, who had broken into the league with Pittsburgh in 1934 but had been out of pro football since 1937. Ciccone played alongside tackle Ross Nagle, who somehow jumped directly to the Cardinals from high school. The draft would be of some help, particularly with the addition of top draft pick Steve Lach, a back from Duke, and lineman Vince Banonis from the University of Detroit.

The passing game, with targets such as Bill Daddio, Pop Ivy, Al Coppage, John Martin, and Lach appeared to be the safer offensive bet to Conzelman, especially after veteran tackle Al Barbartsky fractured a kneecap in training camp and was lost for the season. The running game would receive little protection, and with Schwenk quickly adapting to the professional game, the Cardinals began to take flight.

Schwenk had been essentially a "one-man" team for Washington University. In 1941, he shattered Davey O'Brien's national collegiate record of ninety-four completions by connecting on 114 of his own tosses. Those completions, good for 1,457 passing yards, helped Schwenk (1,928 total yards) snatch O'Brien's total yardage record of 1,847 yards in a season as well. He had started his collegiate career under Coach Conzelman, and Jimmy personally recruited him to help provide some offensive impetus for the Cardinals.

After three weeks of wading through the heat and humidity of Waukesha, the Chicago Cardinals embarked for Denver, Colorado, for their only exhibition game of the preseason, against the Western Army All-Stars on September 6. Columnist John Aboya and the rest of Waukesha were sorry to see the team depart:

> *The Cards were one of the best things that ever hit this town. They brought with them a lot of favorable notoriety and made the Waukesha populace football conscious. Another thing that the Cardinals did was to dispel in a lot of people's minds the thought that a lot of these pro athletes are hard to get along with, conceited and overbearing. That was proven false the minute the boys stepped off the train. The gridders were more than eager to chat with their fans. It was a pleasure to work with such men.*

Much like during the first World War, the establishment of service teams evolved during the early 1940s, and these teams began to compete against some tough competition. The Western Army All-Stars of 1942 were led by John Kimbrough, the Cardinals' top draft choice in 1941. Kimbrough, a graduate of Texas A & M, was a respected runner who was coveted by many pro teams. In his team's opener against the Redskins before fifty-five thousand in Los Angeles, Kimbrough broke loose for a long touchdown run to give the All-Stars a brief 7-0 lead before the Redskins prevailed 26-7.

Despite a sore shoulder from the Redskins' game the week before, Kimbrough scored both of his team's touchdowns as the All-Stars came from behind to edge the Cardinals 16-10. Included in Kimbrough's dazzling performance was a ninety-five-yard kickoff return in the first period. On the other side, Schwenk was impressive as Conzelman showed off his new passing game (twenty-six attempts), and the defense sparkled with four interceptions. The All-Stars proved that the win was not a fluke; they moved on to defeat the Lions 12-0 just a few days later.

Conzelman was not disturbed by the loss in Denver. He had the opportunity to watch everyone play, and he acknowledged that his team did encounter a slight handicap by playing in the high altitude without having enough time to adjust to the conditions. And the defense looked strong—very strong.

## *Bulger Did A Great Job At Tackle*

The first regularly scheduled league game was against the Cleveland Rams on Sunday, September 13, in Buffalo. Once again, the Cardinals would spend very little time in Chicago during the season. Only three home games were on the slate for 1942 and the Cards would appear in Comiskey Park only twice each season in 1943, 1944, and 1945. The team seemed content to accept its share of road games, but then spent valuable "home" dates in places like Buffalo and Milwaukee.

The 1942 season started out well enough as the Cardinals brushed aside Cleveland

(7-0) and Detroit (13-0). In the Cleveland contest, Schwenk connected on a scoring toss with rookie Steve Lach for the only score of the game. Next, Detroit was stifled when Schwenk heaved touchdown passes to Bill Daddio and Lach. Conzelman was cautious, but optimistic, after the successful start:

> *We've finally got a rugged team. When the Rams got close we really smacked 'em. Bulger and Duggan did a great job at tackle. Our offense is still rough, which isn't surprising when you make allowances for the backs who were late reporting.*

Suddenly, the undefeated and unscored upon Cardinals team was being eyed as a possible contender for the league title. While the win over the Lions was satisfying, Conzelman was leaning very heavily on the starters to camouflage a very brittle roster. "We looked a little better than we did last week," said Conzelman after the Lions' game, "but I'm not yet satisfied that we're at peak yet. I'm just a little fearful of my reserves." Another pleasant surprise was the running of Schwenk. In addition to his passing escapades, Schwenk had already rushed for sixty-six yards in the first two games, providing the offense with another needed option.

For the Lions, the loss to the Cardinals was the first since the team shifted to Detroit in 1934. The game also marked the debut of Sunday night football in Chicago as Bidwill hoped to attract fans by avoiding a head-to-head conflict with Major League Baseball that same day. It wasn't a huge success as only 15,242 were in attendance, but the turnout was satisfactory.

The Cardinals kept first place for another week when the game scheduled in Pittsburgh on September 26 was postponed until November 22 due to field conditions. During a rain storm the night before, Forbes Field had been used for a college game, leaving the playing surface in a woeful, muddy condition and giving the pros something to think about for the future when requests were received to use the same field the day before a professional game.

## For Once, The Cards Will Draw A Big Crowd To Comiskey Park

Next up for the Cardinals was another Sunday night marquee game on October 4, this time against the fearsome Green Bay Packers. The *Tribune* reported on the Cardinals' growing optimism before the game:

> *Two words describe the Chicago Cardinals, with their big test against Green Bay getting closer. The two words are "quietly confident."*
>
> *The Cardinals, leading the western division of the National Football League with two shutout victories, have prepared a double barreled passing attack for Sunday night in Comiskey Park against the Packers, foremost passing specialists of pro football. "Of course, we worked all week long on strategy to keep Don Hutson well guarded," said Coach Jimmy Conzelman. "But we haven't forgotten to make allowances for Green Bay's running plays, either. The Packers will run more against us than they did last week against the Bears, knowing our line isn't as puncture-proof. And we're going to do some running, too, don't forget that."*

A large (for the Cardinals) crowd of 24,897 turned out to view a smart, well-played game that was eventually marred by a controversial official's decision. The Packers literally "stole" the game!

The big event occurred in the fourth quarter with the Cardinals nursing a 13-10 lead. The Cards had sprinted to a 13-3 halftime advantage before allowing Don Hutson to score the first touchdown of the year against the defense. Hutson grabbed a five-yard pass from Cecil Isbell, a catch disputed by the Cards' Vince Banonis who claimed the ball hit the ground first. It was the only reception of the night for the highly touted Hutson, who was kept in check by the exemplary coverage of the Cardinals, particularly by Goldberg. Three of Isbell's passes were intercepted, including one by Goldberg in his own end zone when he stepped in front of Hutson to save a certain score. Isbell managed just five completions out of nineteen attempts for the evening.

With just a few minutes left, the Cardinals began a drive in their own territory which they hoped would be kept alive for the remainder of the game. Bob Morrow gobbled up nine yards to advance the ball to the twenty-one-yard line. After a line plunge failed, Morrow apparently picked up the first down when he barreled into a wave of Packer defenders at the twenty-three. As the players were untangled following the play, Green Bay's Charley Brock suddenly appeared with the football and scampered twenty-three yards the other way for the winning touchdown. The Cardinals players were amazed and befuddled, but referee Bobbie Cahn allowed the score.

Conzelman was livid: "When the forward progress of the ball is stopped, the play is over," he shouted. "Not one, but several seconds elapsed before Brock took the ball out of Morrow's hands and loped down the field across our goal line. No, I'm not going to protest, but I insist it was a raw decision." Tackle "Cactus Face" Duggan added: "I know the whistle blew. I heard it. Why, I could have tackled Brock." After the game, most observers, as well as several of the Packers, admitted that the play was illegal. Howard Roberts of the *Daily News* described the postgame scene:

> *The Cardinals, in their dressing room later, were frantic. So was their owner, Charlie Bidwill, who, white of face, vowed that either Cahn had officiated his last game or that he would withdraw his team from the league. Cooler heads soon calmed him, but he went away muttering.*

If anything good evolved from this difficult defeat, it was that the Cardinals were quietly earning respect around the league. Following the game, Packers coach Curly Lambeau remarked that the Cardinals of 1942 were better than the teams of 1934 and 1935, which knocked off the Packers five straight times: "They come closer to putting out the way the Bears do on every play than any other team in the league," he added. While the loss dropped the Cardinals (2-1) to second place behind the Bears, the team could quickly retrieve a share of the top slot by defeating the Bears on the following Sunday (October 11). Already, George Halas of the Bears was impressed with his longtime foes as he told the *Daily News*:

> *Am I worried, listen. Sometimes I give you the old malarkey about fearing a team, but this time its the real McCoy. Those Cardinals are the most improved team in the league. They got a great passer in Bud Schwenk and a great fullback in Marshall Goldberg.*

Bears quarterback Sid Luckman agreed, stating, "It looks as though we're in for the toughest game we've had in a long time." With Comiskey Park still unavailable during the day, the Cardinals' practice sessions were held at 83rd and Yates on the South Side. Conzelman continued to grumble about the injustice of Brock's touchdown in the previous game, and was easing the topic into his meetings as he began to motivate his club for the Bears. It was then that the infamous "spy" issue crept in to grab its rightful place in Chicago football lore.

## Two Fellows Tried To Get In

The *Chicago Tribune* dutifully reported on an unconfirmed incident which apparently disrupted the Cardinals' practice sessions:

> *A spy scare and a subsequent chase of two mysterious characters by Coach Jim Conzelman halted the Chicago Cardinals' drill yesterday where they were preparing for Sunday's game with the champion Bears.*
>
> *Conzelman's charges that the two were spying on the Cardinals and taking notes of what they saw brought a hot retort from George Halas, owner-coach of the Bears. Not even the assurance that Conzelman had absolved him of any suspicion in the affair could calm down George, who sputtered:*
>
> *"Ridiculous stuff! I haven't the slightest idea where the Cardinals practice and care less. We're too busy getting ready for Sunday's game to pay any attention to that. I guess maybe we could find some Cardinal spies around us if we looked hard enough."*

The impish Conzelman had a proud background of using events, either real or imagined, to inspire his players, but he insisted that this particular circumstance was not a part of his vivid imagination:

> *Two fellows tried to get in a couple of the gates at the front of the stadium. Then they tried to enter at a couple of other spots. Finally I noticed them outside the enclosure and one was taking notes. I strolled toward them, then started jogging. With this the two of 'em, both big, broad shouldered fellows, wearing top coats, started running, jumped into a green automobile, and drove away.*

Conzelman added further proof by stating that one of his players had recorded the license plate of the mysterious green car. The license plate was traced to an unnamed car owner who just happened to be the friend of at least two of the Chicago Bears, according to Conzelman. Despite this questionable evidence, Halas couldn't resist further comment on the "spy" incident when he intimated that coaches, such as his friend Conzelman, should have better things to do than chasing about after fictitious spies. That inspired a wry remembrance from Edward Prell in the *Tribune*, who recalled a similar situation with the Bears' owner:

> *Last fall, while the pro champions were preparing for their second battle with the Green Bay Packers, Halas suddenly exhorted trainer Andy Lotshaw to make a raid on a third story apartment in a building across the street from Wrigley Field. George was sure he had located a room from which every movement of his*

*team was being noted.*

*Lotshaw came back with the sensational report that three fellows up there were playing pinochle, looking for a fourth, and would any of the Bears care to accept the invitation?*

Whether spies were present or not quickly became a forgotten issue as the game itself began to take center stage. If Conzelman had intended to inspire his players, he certainly accomplished that: "That questionable touchdown by Charley Brock and now this spy incident really have my boys stirred up," the coach admitted. "I just hope they won't be worn out by all the excitement by Sunday." Aside from his own team, Conzelman had roped in the rest of the city as well. Both media and fan interest was at an all-time high for this longtime rivalry that had suffered in recent years due to the Bears' dominance.

## Everybody's Talking About This Game

The Bears were riding the glory of a fifteen-game winning streak, including thirty wins in their last thirty-one games, while the Cardinals were genuine challengers to the Bears' championship hopes. "Everyone's talking about this game," said Conzelman. "Elevator boys, red caps, barbers, and just fans are stopping me on the street and wishing us luck. Everyone's sore about that game with Green Bay last week. I got an order today from St. Louis for twelve tickets to the game." Warm weather and the promise of an excellent game boosted advance ticket sales at Wrigley Field.

On a sunny, pleasant day, Wrigley Field hosted 38,426 fans, as the Bears and Cardinals battled, fought, pushed, and shoved each other to the tune of an amazing 220 yards in penalties (including a league record of 150 yards assessed against the Bears). The Bears scored first when skinny Ray "Scooter" McLean returned a first-quarter punt eighty-nine yards for a touchdown. Trailing 7-0, the Cardinals took advantage of an excellent kick return by Steve Lach, two Bears penalties, and some nice running by Goldberg to move the ball to the Bears' forty-seven. From there, Schwenk tied it up at 7-7 when he connected with Lach for a touchdown.

Playing before the biggest crowd to ever see the Cardinals up to this point, with the warm sun reflecting off the team's trademark red jerseys and white helmets, the Cards were at the top of their game. Tied with the world champion Bears and pushed to the peak of their performance by a disheveled, chain-smoking, Coca-Cola-chugging creative genius of a head coach by the name of Jimmy Conzelman, the Cardinals of 1942 had achieved football respectability.

Somehow, Conzelman had patched together a club of untested rookies, including Schwenk, Banonis, Bulger, Lloyd Cheatham, and Lach, and blended them in with veterans like Goldberg, Conway Baker, Gil "Cactus Face" Duggan, Ray Apolskis, Bill Daddio, and Frank Ivy. Still, the coach knew his creation was fragile. The team was not overly big, lacked speed, and the depth chart was frightening at certain positions. That's why it is important to look back at the first quarter of that game with the Bears on October 11, 1942. With the score tied 7-7, the crowd roaring, and people hanging out of the apartment buildings across from Wrigley Field, it was a moment to treasure—a Kodak moment for the Cardinals in red.

But the hopes and dreams of that 1942 team were quickly swept away under a flood of Bears touchdowns. Working behind a solid offensive line, Bears quarterback Sid Luckman directed his team to four more first-half touchdowns as the Cardinals fell behind 34-14 at the intermission. The Cardinals' second score was set up by Bulger's fumble recovery and return to the Bears' twelve, from where Schwenk eventually scored on a four-yard run. But with five turnovers, the Cardinals were never able to recover from the first-half barrage and lost to the Bears 41-14. Still, "it was a game closer than the score would indicate," reported Howard Roberts in the *Daily News,* "and tougher than a boarding house steak."

The Cardinals were able to bounce back and win at Detroit 7-0 the following weekend, stretching their record to 3-2. But Conzelman's greatest fear was beginning to make its presence known: injuries. Already riddled by losses via military service, the Cardinals had lost Al Babartsky in training camp, then rookie guard Bob Maddock went down with a shoulder injury. In the Detroit win, Chet Bulger was lost for the season with a back injury, and in a 7-3 loss at Cleveland, rookie end Ray Elbi broke his leg. Eventually Ray Apolskis, Gil Duggan, Buddy Parker, Bill Daddio, Frank Ivy, Milt Popovich, John Martin, and Marshall Goldberg would all miss games due to injuries during the remainder of the season. The significance of these injuries cannot be minimized. Following the win at Detroit on October 18, 1942, the Cardinals would fail to win again during the rest of the league season. In fact, from that date forward until September 30, 1946—a stretch of nearly four years—the Chicago Cardinals would win just one league game.

There was little Conzelman could do during the final five games, especially with his disabled line. First Cecil Isbell shattered league passing records in leading the Packers to a 55-24 rout over the Cards on November 1. Isbell set a new mark with 333 yards passing, and his five touchdown passes tied another record. End Don Hutson hauled in three scoring passes to go along with his 204 yards in reception yardage. It was also the highest scoring game (both teams combined) in league history. Goldberg provided most of the Cardinals' highlights when he returned one of the kickoffs ninety-five yards for a score.

The Cardinals sought solace in the East, but found the Redskins just as unfriendly, and dropped a 28-0 verdict in Washington in front of 35,425. Sammy Baugh tossed three touchdown passes for the winners, giving him the league's all-time record of fifty-three at that point. Another Cardinals starter went down when guard Conway Baker suffered a concussion. Following the Washington defeat, the Cardinals took a week off from league play and played a charity game in support of the war effort. Even for the injury-riddled Cardinals, the Wichita Aero Commanders posed little threat, and the Cards enjoyed a 35-7 victory on November 15. Schwenk's passing to Frank Ivy and Bill Daddio paved the way for the welcome, albeit inconsequential, win.

## *Known Hereabouts As The Conzelmaniacs*

With three games to play, the Cardinals had little to hope for, although some players were accumulating individual achievements. Goldberg, identified by the NFL as "not one of the squad of Chicago Cardinals stretched out in a hospital or suspended between crutches," took the lead in kickoff returns, while Johnny Martin shared the top spot among defenders with pass interceptions. Quick losses to the Steelers (19-3), the Giants

(21-7), and the Bears (21-7) finally slammed the door on a 3-8 league season. It was before the Bears game that Edward Prell of the *Tribune* nominated Conzelman as the "Bravest Coach of the Year" for attempting to hold the team together despite losses to both injuries and the war effort. It was at this time, when the Cardinals were down to seventeen healthy players, that Conzelman looked around for his substitutes and found he didn't have any! Even the weekly league press release could offer little comfort:

> *As far as the games themselves are concerned, the Bears figure to have an easy time with the Cardinals. Known hereabouts as the Conzelmaniacs, the Cardinals have nothing with which to challenge the Bears except complete ignorance of the fact that no one gives them a chance. Jimmy Conzelman, the Cardinals' glib coach, best sums up his team as follows:*
> *"We opened the season with high hopes and wound up with yard rationing. At the start we had eighteen bouncing boys. Most of them are still bouncing."*

During the week prior to the Bears game on December 6, Conzelman was informed that he had been selected to receive an honorary master's degree in physical education from the University of Dayton. His correspondence from the university noted:

> *In passing the resolution the committee considered the outstanding contribution you had made to physical fitness as applied to the war effort. The committee concluded that no other individual in the country today speaks with more authority on the subject of physical education or applies that knowledge with more benefit to the common good.*

Conzelman's selection for this award had been based on the response to the commencement address he had delivered at Dayton earlier in the year. The presentation was called an "oratorical touchdown" according to Edward Prell, and the speech itself was printed twice in the *Congressional Record*. The NFL (through Charlie Bidwill) distributed over fifteen thousand copies of a booklet containing the speech, and it became mandatory reading for cadets at West Point and for physical education students at the University of Minnesota. The *Chicago Tribune* remarked that a Washington newspaper "called it the most widely commented commencement speech in 40 years." Conzelman, who was unable to complete his degree requirements at Washington University in St. Louis, primarily because of his service in World War I, pronounced himself "tickled to death" to receive the honor.

With the season completed, only a few individual honors remained. Bill Daddio led the league in field goals with five, and although Schwenk broke the mark for passing attempts (126—295, 1,350 yards), he also shattered the standard for interceptions by tossing twenty-seven. Goldberg finished sixth in rushing with 369 yards while Schwenk followed in thirteenth with 323 yards. Frank Ivy concluded the season with the second most pass receptions (twenty-seven) behind Don Hutson. Goldberg once again paced the league in kickoff returns with a total of fifteen (26.2 yard average). Johnny Martin completed a nice all-around season by finishing fourth in punting (39.3 average); fifth in interceptions with six; and sixth in receiving with twenty-two.

The promising start in 1942 had been diminished by both injuries and the war.

# ◆ 10 ◆

## The Woe Years:
## 1943 – 1945

*"What was the most hazardous experience?*
*Playing behind the Cardinals' 1945 line."*

PAUL CHRISTMAN,
QUARTERBACK, CHICAGO CARDINALS

With the war effort draining twenty-two players from the 1942 Chicago Cardinals' roster, the team's tumble to a 3-8 finish after an impressive start was disappointing, but not unexpected. In 1943, the list of Cardinals in the service would stretch to thirty-six.

Yet all teams were in the same situation, hoping to maintain their competitive nature with a patchwork player roster. It wasn't easy for any of them. The biggest advantage was to have a team loaded with family men, thus usually ensuring their exempt status. Many teams included other players whose injuries or ailments kept them out of the service, but did not keep them out of professional football. Still, the pickings were slim and the very survival of the league was in question.

In a gallant effort to keep the league in existence, the NFL developed several key changes for the 1943 season and also embraced numerous opportunities to contribute to the war effort. With nearly four hundred players now in a military uniform, the league needed to totally support the service, while at the same time determine how the circuit could continue as an entertainment vehicle with this unprecedented loss of talent.

The first tidal wave of personnel departures in 1942 had been absorbed by the teams that still somehow managed to attract a record total of 1,725,764 fans to NFL games. While that figure may be slightly misleading (it included fourteen charity games and preseason exhibitions), it did solidify the league's position as a viable sporting event during the rigors of the times. The overall attendance during the regular schedule was just six percent less than it was during the 1941 season. Part of the surprising surge in attendance could be attributed to one impressive night in August of 1942, when 101,103 turned out to watch the Bears defeat the College All-Stars 21-0 in Chicago. That attendance total was the largest to date to witness an NFL team in action.

The NFL donated the majority of the receipts from its exhibition games to service charities. In March of 1943, Commissioner Elmer Layden announced that the league had contributed the staggering amount of $680,384 to various organizations such as the Army Emergency Relief Fund, the Red Cross, the U.S.O., and the United Seamen's Service. In addition, league members actively marketed defense bonds at home games and succeeded in raising about $4 million. Pro teams also contributed by donating footballs and uniforms to service teams and by providing game passes to approximately 127,500 service men during the 1942 season. The Cardinals' main offering was a nice check of slightly over $30,000, the result of their exhibition game with the Army All-Stars in Denver.

During the off-season, the NFL was careful to quietly publicize the contributions its teams and players made to the war effort while maintaining silence about its own difficulties in terms of fielding teams with enough qualified personnel for the upcoming season. Typical of the "feel good" releases was the following document remitted to the media in March of 1943 regarding Chicagoan Chuck Gelatka, who had played with the Giants:

> *Mrs. Helen Gelatka slept pleasantly through a dream that her son, Lt. Chuck of the Army Air Corps, had come marching home.*
>
> *"He had a big grin and a new uniform," she said.*
>
> *The next morning she learned Lt. Gelatka had played a major part in the destruction of the Japanese convoy off New Guinea. Gelatka . . . who played end for the New York Giants for four years, had led a P-40 Kittyhawk attack on landing boats during the battle.*
>
> *Mrs. Gelatka, a widow with another son also in the air corps, immediately cabled the former All-American: "Good hunting! Keep it up! Get more of those Japs."*
>
> *Gelatka was one of the first National league players to enter service, joining immediately after the 1940 season, and was a member of the first contingent of American flyers assigned to Gen. Douglas MacArthur in Australia.*

While the tone of the release might be considered politically incorrect in modern times, it did capture the essence of the patriotism and pride that was evident in the NFL at the time. In an era that was unquestionably the toughest on both the NFL and the United States itself, the league, like the country, was determined to persevere.

At the league meeting on April 6, Layden was faced with an extremely sensitive—and important—issue regarding the disposition of the Cleveland Rams. With both of the Rams' owners (Dan Reeves and Fred Levy Jr.) whisked off to service, the team had requested permission to disband for the 1943 season only. While Levy quickly advanced to the position of major in the procurement department of the Army Air Corps in Dayton, his team was regretfully dismantled by the league.

Layden outlined a plan whereby other NFL clubs could "borrow" the Rams' players for the season, and developed an assignment order for the remaining nine teams to select Cleveland's personnel. The Cardinals, selecting sixth, chose halfback Leonard Janiak and tackle Boyd Clay with their two choices. In all, sixteen Cleveland players were plucked by the competition. The Rams would return, however, for the 1944 season.

Also at the April meeting, the NFL finally mandated the use of helmets by all players, reduced team rosters to twenty-eight, and allowed the use of free substitution. The latter two products were accepted largely to offset the dwindling manpower available to the league. In truth, many coaches weren't exactly receptive to the free substitution decree, but it became useful as the season wore on and teams had difficulty keeping twenty-eight healthy bodies on their rosters.

## *Bears-Cardinals Merger?*

The next meeting of the league's representatives, held on June 19 and 20, brought the manpower issue into clearer focus when the Bears and Cardinals proposed a concept that would allow the two teams to merge for the year. The available players on both the Cardinals and the Bears would be combined into one single team representing the city of Chicago. With both teams experiencing dramatic shifts in player personnel due to military service, the proposal seemed to make sense. Although the Bears lost in the 1942 title game to the Redskins after romping through the regular season undefeated, the team was without its familiar owner-coach. George Halas had entered the service during the 1942 season but only on the condition that he would not be stationed in Chicago or assigned to an athletic activity.

Over on the South Side, the Cardinals would once again lose their top passer (Bud Schwenk) and their leading receiver (Pop Ivy), along with other veterans such as Vince Banonis, Bill Daddio, Steve Lach, and Al Coppage. With the cupboard already bare, Conzelman would be forced to rebuild once again. But if anyone could patch together a team and make it competitive, it would be Conzelman.

The merger concept apparently seemed logical to both Halas and Bidwill, and it also had the possibility of paving the way for a powerhouse entry in the league. The Cardinals' gate would not suffer since the team rarely played at home anyway. On behalf of the two teams, Conzelman proposed to the league owners on June 19 that the Cardinals and the Bears be allowed to merge for the 1943 season. This suggestion was blocked by a group headed by George Marshall of the Redskins and Curly Lambeau of the Packers. Opponents of the Cardinals-Bears merger won approval for two "conditions of merger" which would effectively dilute the Chicago merger plan. The league decided that in the event of a merger of two teams, only the players from one of the teams would be eligible to be members of the "merged" team. The members of the other team would essentially become free agents. In addition, the two merged clubs would retain only one vote in league business matters, instead of one each had they remained independent.

With this new legislation in place, Conzelman withdrew his proposal on the evening of June 19 and indicated that the Cardinals would continue to operate as an individual league member. The Bears would do likewise. Yet oddly enough, at this same meeting of the NFL owners, a second request for a merger was approved for the Eagles and the Steelers under a more casual version of the new "merger" rules. The team would have no specific city designation and would play most of its games in Philadelphia. The *Associated Press* attempted to bring some sense to the whole situation following the meeting:

> *Apparently because of the power that would be concentrated should the Cardinals and the Bears consolidate, the league cut off their attempt by passing a rule forbidding the merging of player talent. Later, however, this was relaxed, allowing the Steelers and Eagles to pool their athletes but at the same time retain only a single vote in league affairs. The merger will be effective only for the 1943 season.*

With the temporary suspension of the Cleveland franchise and the merger of Pittsburgh and Philadelphia, the league was down to eight teams, its lowest total since

1932. The West would include the Bears, Cardinals, Packers, and Lions, while the East would be represented by the New York Giants, the Brooklyn Dodgers, the Washington Redskins, and the combined Pittsburgh-Philadelphia team, which became unofficially known as the "Steagles." This "combination" team surprised quite a few people by finishing with a 5-4-1 record under co-coaches Walt Kiesling (Steelers) and Greasy Neale (Eagles). However, it was well known that these two gentlemen did not belong to a mutual admiration society, so Neale stuck with the offense while Kiesling handled the defense. The players managed to get along better, and each was required to also work a full-time job in a defense plant. Frank "Bucko" Kilroy was a rookie tackle on the 1943 Steagles and later recalled his experiences for the *Philadelphia Daily News:*

> *The government thought it was important to keep the baseball and football leagues going. Those were tough times and people needed something to lift their spirits.*
> *The caliber of play wasn't topnotch because so many guys were overseas. But the games were competitive and there was an esprit de corps among the players. We only made $125 a game, we practiced at night so we could work during the day, but we loved what we were doing.*

The Steagles would become a football rarity, but the merger at least lessened the teams' difficulties in fielding a quality team. With Halas gone, the Bears were now coached by the trio of Paddy Driscoll, Luke Johnsos, and Hunk Anderson. In an effort to fortify the team, the coaches recruited the legendary Bronko Nagurski to play tackle after a nearly five-year retirement. In his book *Notre Dame, Chicago Bears, and "Hunk,"* Anderson recalls that the Cardinals were also innovative in procuring able bodies that season:

> *The manpower shortage was becoming acute in 1943. I know the Cardinals had several players on their roster who were stationed at Great Lakes Navy Center but were not members of the Navy's football squad. They played on Sunday under an assumed name because the Navy would not have permitted them to play on outside teams during the war while they were enlisted in the Navy.*

As the Cardinals prepared to stitch together another roster for the 1943 campaign, the team was jolted by the resignation of Conzelman. He had done an incredible job with limited talent for three seasons but had accumulated only eight wins during that stretch. With the failure of the Cardinals and the Bears to merge, along with the prospect of rebuilding for the fourth straight year, Jimmy decided to give Major League Baseball a try, and signed on as the assistant to Donald Barnes, president of the St. Louis Browns. Longtime assistant Phil Handler was given the head coaching job, and was immediately sent to comb through Texas, Oklahoma, and Louisiana in search of talent. With veterans Goldberg, Bulger, Baker, Duggan, Morrow, and Parker returning, there was some experience on the squad, but the roster would be extremely thin, especially in the line.

## *He Shudders When One Asks About His Line*

In an attempt to bolster the roster, Bidwill traded the rights of long-departed Gaynell

Tinsley to Brooklyn for center Bob Pierce and end Ed Rucinski, and then brought back former Cardinals Johnny Hall and Al Babartsky. By the time the 1943 training camp opened in late August in Waukesha, Wisconsin, there were several rookies around to help, including passer Ronnie Cahill (Holly Cross), end Don Currivan (Boston College), halfback Johnny Grigas (Holy Cross), and guard Garrard "Buster" Ramsey (William and Mary). Still, the prognosis from Edward Prell of the *Tribune* was not overly optimistic:

> *Phil Handler is just the type to be in charge of the Cardinals. Through 11 dreary years with Charles Bidwill's entry, Phil has learned to persevere in the face of hardships. There is no indication that the script will be changed this season, but Handler is one of those fellows who keep getting up after being knocked down.*
>
> *Several days at Waukesha have convinced Handler that there are prospects for an excellent backfield, but he shudders slightly when one asks about his line. In fact, the Cardinals are trying to arrange a few deals which will cost them spare backs for much needed linemen.*

Meanwhile, as the Cards sweltered at their Wisconsin training camp, the 1943 College All-Stars roasted the NFL champion Washington Redskins 27-7 in Chicago behind the efforts of future Cardinals Marlin "Pat" Harder (Wisconsin) and Charley Trippi (Georgia). Harder was selected as the MVP of the game after scoring two touchdowns and adding a pair of extra points. The Cards' top draft choice, Glenn Dobbs of Tulsa, was second in the MVP voting after he completed 9 of 13 passes for 116 yards. Dobbs, however, was committed to the service and would never play for the Chicago Cardinals.

With only a scrimmage against the Great Lakes Bluejackets service team to prepare them for the NFL season, the Cardinals looked somewhat rusty in an opening 35-17 loss at Detroit. The supposedly strong running attack failed to gain even a single yard, while Joe Bukant took over most of the passing chores as the Cards managed just 137 yards through the air. Since the Lions had scored only thirty-eight points during the team's entire 1942 season, the Cards' defensive play was suspect as well. "The final tabulation of 35-17 does not show the ease with which the Lions crushed an inexperienced, undermanned Cardinal eleven," wrote Edward Prell.

The following week, the Cardinals were clobbered 43-21 by the Washington Redskins in an exhibition game. Rookie Ronnie Cahill was given a chance to throw, and responded by completing a pair of touchdown passes and running for a third. But the real story was that of injuries. During the game, Handler lost rookie Floyd Rhea with a fractured vertebra as well as Marshall Goldberg, who went down with a broken leg. "I was in motion to go down the field for a pass," Goldberg said. "The ball was thrown a little behind me and I had to stop for the ball. Sammy Baugh and two other defenders reached the ball at the same time as me. I jumped up and made the catch. When I came down, my leg was under one of the defenders and it just cracked—like a gun shot. That was basically the end of my season."

During the following week, the Cardinals traded Babartsky to the Bears for back Walt Masters and end Clint Wager; signed center Vaughn Stewart from Brooklyn; and added guard Marshall Robnett and quarterback Cal Purdin. Yet these changes would be of little value unless, according to the *Tribune,* they could somehow replace the multitalented Goldberg:

> *All these fellows will have to make up for the loss of Goldberg, who was all of these: a running threat, defensive specialist, safety man and signal caller.*

## Fractured His Own Skull

In the end, the loss of Goldberg, although not necessarily deadly, would be a primary contributor to the collapse of the 1943 season. A 28-7 mauling at home against Green Bay was followed by seven more defeats as the Cardinals finished 0-10 for the season. This was the first winless slate in the history of the franchise, and the long season grew longer as the lack of depth and the usual injuries engulfed the squad. Big (6'6") end Clint Wager went down early after his arrival from the Bears by an unusual endeavor: while practicing punting, Wager fractured his own skull when he missed the ball on a punting attempt and slammed his knee into his head! Wager eventually recovered to continue his dual career as a pro football and pro basketball player.

As the season progressed, nearly all of the starters were playing both ways without a rest, including the big guys in the middle: Chet Bulger, Gil Duggan, Conway Baker, Gordon Wilson, and Marshall Robnett. Aside from injuries, the military was still looming as rookie Cal Purdin joined the Navy midway through the season.

One bright spot for the Cardinals remained the visible presence of owner Charlie Bidwill. In order to bring the game of football to the community, Bidwill served as president of the Chicago Sports Association, which provided introductory football training to over one thousand youngsters at several Chicago parks. From that initial number, ninety boys were selected to play in a six-team league, and Bidwill provided all of the uniforms for the players.

## Luckman Stuck His Cleated Shoe In His Face

In one last, valiant effort to secure a win, the Cardinals nearly put it all together in the final game of the season against the first-place Bears. The surprising Cards, in just their second home game of the season, actually held a 24-14 lead over the Bears early in the fourth quarter. At this point, Bronko Nagurski, who had seen limited action at tackle since concluding his five-year retirement, was pressed into service in the Bears' backfield. The burly thirty-five-year-old fullback smashed across the goal line early in the final period to cut the lead to 24-21 and then continued to bully the weary Cardinals defenders with his bruising line smashes. In total, Nagurski gobbled up eighty-four yards in fifteen carries as the Cardinals faltered down the stretch.

One of the highlights of the game was the sudden disappearance of veteran Cardinals guard Conway Baker in the third quarter. Baker, who worked in the off-season for the Shreveport (LA) police, was "arrested" by the officials for a play virtually unseen by anyone else in the stadium. The *Tribune* reported the real story after the game:

> *The Shreveport city jailer left yesterday's game with the Bears in such a hurry that the reason wasn't known until the contest was over . . . It's the third quarter and*

*the Cards are ahead, 17-14, rightfully thinking that an upset was in the making. Suddenly the Cards are penalized 15 yards and Capt. Baker trots off the field to be seen no more, much to his team's sorrow, because Capt. Baker, who starts at left guard, eventually plays the other guard, not to mention both tackles, as a sort of revolving lineman. He's versatile.*

*What causes Capt. Baker's departure is that an official catches him in the act of taking a swing at Sid Luckman (Bears' quarterback), and connecting so successfully that the Bears' forward passing wizard is knocked over a couple of other gladiators.*

*But Capt. Baker, who in eight seasons with the Cardinals has been known to be a champion of gentlemanly conduct on the field, reported that he swung only after Luckman had stuck his cleated shoe in his face, which is enough to roil the softest of tempers. It was the first time Capt. Baker ever was shagged from the field, and the result bore out the code of football, "get in the first punch." Capt. Baker, having got in the second one, was caught in the act and Luckman went unpunished . . . Baker, who was sorely needed to bolster up a battered Cardinal line, could only sit on the bench and bite what was left of his fingernails.*

With the heart of the Cardinals' line done for the day, Luckman and Nagurski rallied the Bears to a 35-24 triumph with Luckman tossing two fourth-quarter touchdowns. As the Cardinals sunk to their worst record in history, the team did manage to grab some individual honors. Both end Ed Rucinski and tackle Chet Bulger were named to some All-Pro teams, while the rookie Cahill finished fourth in the league in passing. Unfortunately, he also topped the circuit with twenty-one interceptions, and the Cardinals as a team combined to throw an all-time league high of thirty-nine interceptions.

As bad as things went in 1943, they became worse in 1944. Several more key Cardinals reported for military duty, including what might have been considered the entire 1943 backfield: Marshall Goldberg, Bob Morrow, Joe Bukant, and Ronnie Cahill. At least forty-two Chicago Cardinals were now in the service, with Motts Tonelli still in captivity with the Japanese and former end John Shirk being held by the German army.

## *They Suggest Legalizing Secret Signaling By Coaches*

Faced with still another year of challenges, the league owners met in Philadelphia to wrestle with their limited options for 1944. They retained the twenty-eight man roster and allowed the free substitution rule to stay for another season. The league membership returned to ten when the Cleveland Rams resumed play after their one-year hiatus, and a new franchise was awarded to the Boston Yanks. A small, but significant, coaching change was approved: coaches could now "coach" from the bench during games.

Behind the scenes, Commissioner Layden was also quietly planning for the future. Someday, he envisioned a world not at war, when players would be plentiful and fans would clamor for more sporting entertainment. The war had scarcely affected the increasing popularity of pro football, but until the advent of television, access to the games was limited to just a handful of cities.

In late August, Layden met with J. Rufus Klawans, a former Chicagoan and sports addict, who was now commissioner of the Pacific Coast Football League. Klawans was a bit of a dreamer, too. As president of the five-year-old Pacific Coast League, his dream for the future was to more formally unify a network of minor league football leagues. This system would be similar to baseball's "farm club" structure in which teams could operate within their own leagues while also developing players for the "big" leagues.

The NFL was already interacting informally with the Pacific Coast League, the American Association on the East Coast, and the Dixie League in the Southeast. "We have working agreements with all three of those leagues right now which forbids either party to raid the other's clubs," an NFL spokesman told the *Daily News.* "We can buy players and they can sell, and vice versa, but no raids. I think that's the way it will be after the war—only in a broader sense."

That final statement, "in a broader sense," might be interpreted to mean that the NFL was prepared to develop a farm system with the existing minor leagues, or it could be derived that the NFL was possibly looking to expand to other regions, particularly the South and the West Coast, to take advantage of untapped markets. Could the end of the war also signal the beginning of the NFL's new "Far West" Division?

For the present time, the NFL only needed to survive until the much-needed players returned from the service. However, another threat arrived in September of 1944: a new league, called the All-America Football Conference, was established and announced that it would begin play in 1945. Franchises had already been awarded to several cities, including Chicago, New York, Baltimore, Cleveland, Los Angeles, and San Francisco. The owners, called "men of millionaire incomes," were highly visible entities from both the business and entertainment industries, according to Arch Ward, sports editor of the *Chicago Tribune,* and the primary creator of the new conference. Among the owners were former heavyweight boxing champion Gene Tunney, actor Don Ameche, and Mrs. Lou Gehrig. The new league vowed not to tamper with the contracts of any NFL player, but the owners indicated that they were prepared to wage a war of dollars with the NFL in order to survive.

If the NFL was concerned about this forthcoming competition, it wasn't showing it. In fact, Green Bay's Curly Lambeau looked upon the All-America Conference as being good for the sport but he cautioned the newcomers about the difficulties that would lie ahead:

> *Let's be sensible about this. Every club in our circuit except the Boston Yanks has a reserve list of 60 players. When the hundreds of athletes are released from military service, each team will be three deep in every position. Now just how is any rival, starting from scratch, going to match such a setup? It's impossible. That's why it's going to be a long haul for the new ones, with a lot of headaches along the way.*

Ironically, the Cardinals were the first team to feel the threat of the new league when it was announced that former top draft choice Glenn Dobbs, now playing service football, was signed by the New York entry in the new league. It was the first shot in a different type of war that would last for several years.

## *Drink Plenty Of Beer*

The immediate future appeared dismal for the Cardinals in 1944. With most of the best players gone from a winless team, the prospects for improvement seemed distant. Following the 1943 season, the Steelers and the Eagles parted company, but the Steelers were still receptive to joining forces with another squad. In addition, with the new Boston franchise joining the league, there were now eleven teams in the circuit, a potentially difficult challenge for the schedule maker. Despite the distance between the two cities, the Steelers and the Cardinals were asked to merge for the 1944 season. Forgetting the storm of controversy which had erupted the year before when the proposed merger of the Cardinals and the Bears was tossed out, the league owners quickly approved the new merger proposal on April 21, 1944. Not everyone was happy, however. Turk Edwards, the line coach of the defending Eastern Division champion Redskins, swiftly anointed the "new" team as the favorite to win the Western Division:

> *The war has been a great equalizer among pro teams and any two teams which merge, no matter what their standing the preceding year, have a tremendous advantage.*

Edwards was wrong.

The combined team, known as the Card-Pitts, lumbered off to training camp in Waukesha, Wisconsin, with high hopes and high dreams. Under the shared head coaching partnership of the Steelers' Walt Kiesling and the Cardinals' Phil Handler, the team hoped for a solid season. The reunion of Kiesling and Handler was also seen as a positive step. The two had been the starting guards for the Chicago Cardinals from 1930 to 1933, and now as head coaches in 1944, they welcomed forty-five players to camp. This in itself was seen as an advantage. For example, the Washington Redskins were able to coax only twenty-one players to their training camp in San Diego that year. Even the *Chicago Daily News* was impressed as the Cardinals prepared for the season:

> *Kiesling and Handler will have joint control of some 45 candidates for the "varsity" and from paper indications it looks as if the new combine will have a strong voice in the NFL competition this fall.*
>
> *That bit of prophecy is gathered from a glance at the roster of veterans which the two clubs can throw on the field right now. Added to them are a batch of newcomers, most of who will be "on trial" at Waukesha.*

The *Daily News* was wrong.

When the team began training camp on August 14, the Cardinals were joined by twenty-six Steelers. The co-coaches spent plenty of time introducing everyone, but also launched a new offensive plan with the "T" formation. The "T" had been popularized by the Bears and was viewed by coaches as either a bountiful blessing or a confusing albatross. With the popular single-wing formation, the person usually doing the passing was a halfback who would take a direct snap from the center, and then have the option of either running or throwing. The quarterback was usually a blocking back.

That all changed with the "T" formation, in which the quarterback received the snap directly from the center and either handed off the ball to a runner or initiated the pass play.

The Card-Pitts' coaches were enamored with the "T" formation, but needed to find someone to run it. Walt Masters had played a little for the Cards in 1943 after being out of football for seven years, but at the age of thirty-seven, he didn't possess much speed. Johnny Grigas, the sixth-leading rusher in the league in 1943, returned, but he had completed only four of nineteen passes. The Steelers provided quick Johnny Butler, but he was limited to attempting thirteen passes the year before. For the time being, it appeared that Masters would win the job by default, but the coaches would continue to evaluate that key position. Kiesling stated: "All we need is a quarterback. Give us a quarterback and we'll make them sit up nights." Handler added: "Just give us a quarterback. There won't be any 0-10 after the Cardinals in the standings then."

The coaches were wrong. In an effort to sort things out, the team began scrimmaging heavily during the second week of practice, and the *Daily News* reported on the reaction of the co-coaches following the initial scrimmage:

> *They liked the offense, but didn't think so much of the combine's defense. That will be bolstered considerably after today, however, because 265 pounds of tackle were added to the roster in the form of giant Chet Bulger, one of the best forwards in the National Football League. Bulger, however, must get down to his playing weight of a mere 240 pounds and judging from the program that Handler and Kiesling have in store for their charges, Chet will do it before very long.*

For the effervescent Bulger, the weight gain was simply the result of following orders, perhaps a little too well:

> *After my first year in the league (1942), Coach Conzelman called me into his office. I wasn't sure what he wanted. He asked me what I weighed and I said "Maybe 225." He said 225 is too light for a tackle in professional football and he said he wanted me to do something about it.*
>
> *So I said, "Coach, what should I do?"*
>
> *He said, "I want you to go home in the off-season and eat lots of steak and drink plenty of beer."*
>
> *So what did I do? Of course I went home and followed the coach's orders!*

After two weeks in Wisconsin, the Card-Pitts continued to split things equally right down the middle and moved their training camp to Pittsburgh on September 3. The one area that would not be shared, however, was the uniform style. It was announced that Bidwill had won the approval of Steelers owner Arthur Rooney for the team to wear the traditional red and white colors of the Chicago Cardinals.

The new team finally debuted in an exhibition game against the Philadelphia Eagles on Tuesday, September 12, 1944. Still without a firm quarterback, the Card-Pitts were shut out 22-0 after the Eagles swarmed all over them early with a 20-0 advantage after the first quarter. In the *Philadelphia Record*, Red Smith appraised the season's first outing:

> *Philadelphia's 1944 football season got an appropriately moist baptism last night when the Eagles waded into the hybrid Pittsburgh Steelers-Chicago Cardinals on the quaggy turf of Shibe park.*
>
> *The autumn's first formal illustration of man's inhumanity to man involved a match between former bedfellows, now estranged from one another and bound*

*to new relationships. Last year the Eagles and Steelers operated as one team. This season the Eagles are going it alone and their divorced mates have been rewelded into partnership with the Cardinals.*

A few days later, Washington squeezed out a 3-0 win, leaving the Card-Pitts competitive, albeit offensively challenged, as the team awaited its league opener against Cleveland on September 24.

Although defeated by the Rams 30-28, the Card-Pitts found some offense in Coley McDonough, who had first surfaced with the Cardinals in 1939. From there, he was traded that same year to Pittsburgh, spent the 1942 and 1943 seasons in the service, and was now back in the NFL. McDonough triggered scoring passes of sixty-five yards to Johnny Butler and forty yards to Eddie Rucinski.

Not bad. The coaches had confidently stated that the key to the entire season rested on the discovery of an adept quarterback. Was this problem solved with McDonough? On October 1, the Card-Pitts finally grabbed a victory, although it was in another exhibition game. With McDonough at the helm and Grigas sparkling out of the backfield, the Card-Pitts edged the New York Giants 17-16.

But then, unforeseen circumstances and the injury bug showed up again. The team lost trusty tackle Gil Duggan with a separated shoulder and then the big picture was shaken when McDonough was called back into service, never to play another game of pro football. With little choice or opportunity, the coaching staff entrusted the offense to a little-used 153-pound quarterback named John Patrick McCarthy. The New Jersey native out of St. Francis College (PA) was thrown to the Green Bay Packers in the second league game on October 8. While the Packers rolled 34-7, McCarthy responded by completing seven of twenty-five passes for ninety-eight yards. In his only full season in the NFL, McCarthy would go on to complete 20 of 67 passes for 250 yards, but with 19 interceptions.

The Cardinals were not the only team with quarterback worries. With Sid Luckman unavailable, the Bears dusted off thirty-five-year-old Gene Ronzani, who had been out of the league for six years. Ronzani and McCarthy squared off in the third week of the season. The Bears breezed to a 34-7 win as McCarthy, Grigas, and Masters combined to complete just three of eighteen passes. Missing from action were the Bears' George Zorich and the Card-Pitts' Marshall Robnett, both asked to leave the premises for fighting in the first quarter. The explusion forced one very tired Vince Banonis, who wasn't prepared for such an eventuality, to play almost the entire game.

Banonis was already in the service and stationed in Wildwood, New Jersey. He managed to squeeze in only two games for the Card-Pitts in 1944 , but the Bears' game on October 15 was memorable for Banonis:

*The Card-Pitts team was something else. I remember Arch Wolfe of the Cardinals calling me to play against the Bears in Chicago. The only problem was that I was in Wildwood, New Jersey. Although I wasn't in football shape, I finally did agree to play and hitchhiked to Philadelphia Saturday morning and then took a train to New York. From there the team had arranged for a flight to Chicago but it was hard to get a seat in those days and I couldn't get a plane out of New York until midnight! We puddle-jumped across the country and didn't arrive in Chicago until 5:00 Sunday morning. I slept a couple of hours, went to Mass and then went to the field.*

*Although I didn't know the plays I told myself that I wasn't there to play much. When the other center went out, I played almost the whole game, which was tough being out of shape. After the game, I took a plane back to New York, then took a train back to Philadelphia and managed to be back on the base and ready for work at 8:00 A.M. on Monday morning. After that, someone found out and blew the whistle on me . . . we weren't supposed to play pro football while we were in the service.*

## "This is the End"

For the 0-3 Card-Pitts, the season was essentially over. In spite of the early hopes and positive prognostications, the team would stumble home again with an 0-10 record, thus proving that quantity does not necessarily overcome quality. The season progressed from bad to worse with one thunderous defeat after another. Following the loss to the Bears, Johnny Butler, Johnny Grigas, and tackle Eberle Schultz were fined $200 for indifferent play as well as for missing practice. Butler, the seventh-leading rusher in the league in 1943, was also suspended and offered for trade. These rulings infuriated the players, and the team decided to go on strike immediately, recalled Chet Bulger:

*Johnny Butler was accused of not trying and was fined a whole game's salary. So instead of showing up for practice, we'd go to a bar instead. We did that Monday, then Tuesday, then Wednesday . . . We did this all week and finally Art Rooney called us all in to a meeting and told us that Johnny would get his check. He told us to be ready to practice on Friday. So what do we do? We all get to practice early and hide like a bunch of kids from the coaches so they'd think we wouldn't be there. We played terrible on Sunday!*

By the following game, a 23-0 loss to the Giants in front of 40,734, the name of the team was beginning to shred as well. The Card-Pitts label was evolving into Car-Pits, because the team was "in the pits," or even Car-Pets, because every team in the league was walking all over them. Perhaps the *Tribune* was in the forefront of this movement when it described the Giants' game:

*The Card-Pitts played the role of a red plush rug this afternoon as the undefeated Giants paraded over and past them for a 23-0 triumph.*

Although the season spiraled into a parade of losses, almost every outing contained something of interest for everyone:

- In a 42-20 loss at Washington, police were called onto the field to stop a near riot when the opposing players encountered some disagreements. Four players were kicked out, including the newly healed "Cactus Face" Duggan and Tony Bova of the Card-Pitts.

- Although the Lions chomped on his team by the tune of 21-7, Johnny Grigas had one of the finest games in team history by rushing for 123 yards and completing 13 of 30 passes for another 177 yards. He was personally responsible for 300 of the club's 338 yards (big, big numbers in those days).

- The Card-Pitts didn't play their first home league game in Chicago until November 19. The *Tribune* didn't help drum up any business with its honest headline of "Nothing At Stake." Only thirty-five hundred showed up to watch the Rams coast to a 33-6 victory.

- Before the final game against the Bears in Pittsburgh (a "home game" for the Card-Pitts and a 49-7 loss), Grigas mysteriously disappeared from the team. His room-mate, Don Currivan, said he discovered a note in their room from Grigas which simply stated: "This is the end." Grigas finished second in the league in rushing despite missing the last game. Two teammates insisted that Grigas had indicated that he would not play if the field was frozen. By game time, the field was partly covered by snow. This game also featured a rare appearance in the Bears' back-field by 235-pound center Bulldog Turner. Turner returned one punt for nine yards and then scored on a forty-eight-yard run with six seconds left in the game. On the other side, with Grigas gone, the Cardinals finished with minus-two yards rushing as a team.

Following the Bears game, the Steelers and Cardinals broke off their engagement and never dated again. The Cardinals' losing streak had now stretched to twenty-six games over three seasons with no end in sight. Or was there?

## Merger Talks Have Merit

While the Cardinals were quietly stockpiling clever draft picks such as Paul Christman, Pat Harder, Stan Mauldin, Garrard "Buster" Ramsey, John Cochran, and Charley Trippi during these woeful years, none of these immense talents would be available until after they had completed their terms in the service. For the past three seasons, the Chicago Cardinals had managed to uncover new and creative paths to defeat. However, in 1945, the challenge to management was not only to correct the losing, but also to survive as a franchise.

The NFL owners considered several drastic measures at their league meetings in April of 1945. With the previous temporary mergers of the Eagles and Steelers in 1943 and the Cardinals and Steelers in 1944 proving to be acceptable, further mergers were considered for the 1945 campaign. Once again, the Bears and the Cardinals looked to merge, while both the Steelers and the Eagles, as well as the Brooklyn Tigers and the Boston Yanks, were also ready to pool their resources. If all three mergers had been approved, the league would field just eight teams for the 1945 season. Prior to the discussions on this topic, Commissioner Layden had stated, "It is merely a question of getting along and keeping alive until such time as we can return to a normal sta-tus." Layden, along with the individual team owners, was merely keeping all options open in consideration of the ongoing war situation.

Ultimately, only the merger of Brooklyn and Boston was approved. The two teams had finished with a combined 2-18 record in 1944 but would manage a respectable 3-6-1 mark in 1945. As for the Cardinals, another long season was certainly in store for the team. With the loyal Phil Handler still at the helm, the team attempted to tread water until the influx of returning players became a reality. One of Handler's first moves was to dump the talented but unreliable Johnny Grigas. Grigas and end

Don Currivan were dealt to the Brooklyn Tigers for tackle Bob Zimny, back Bill Reynolds, end Joe Carter, and guard Gordon Wilson. Grigas would bounce back from his "no-show" in the final game of the 1944 season but he would no longer be the featured back for Brooklyn as he had been with the Cardinals.

Handler also retained the "T" formation offense which had been installed with the Card-Pitts the year before. The "T" was the offense of the future and Handler figured that he would soon have the horses back to pull his team out of the NFL cellar with this type of attack. Meanwhile, twenty-one rookies were invited to training camp as Handler and his able assistant Buddy Parker began to construct a lineup for the upcoming season. By the time the Cardinals played their lone exhibition game on September 16 (a 7-7 tie with Washington), the war was over and the nation began to melt back to normalcy.

For the Washington game, Handler decided to place untested rookie quarterback Paul Collins in charge. Collins, a graduate of Missouri, had an auspicious debut when he completed 9 of 19 passes for 132 yards and added 52 more yards on the ground. Since Washington was coming off a 6-3-1 season in 1944, and had two of the finest quarterbacks in the league in Sammy Baugh and Frank Filchock, the deadlock was considered a successful parameter for the Cardinals. The outcome also prompted some additional wheeling and dealing from Charlie Bidwill. He purchased gifted halfback Frank Seno from the Redskins and veteran Leo Cantor from the Giants. Cantor, just out of the service, would end up leading the Cardinals in scoring that year (30 points) while Seno would conclude the season as the team's leading rusher with 355 yards.

Bidwill felt that Seno would help the most with his understanding of the "T" formation, which Washington had installed the year before. Meanwhile, rumors began to emerge about the possibility of adding some of the returning veterans as they slipped out of their military uniforms. The season began with a "home" opener against Detroit on Sunday, September 23, inexplicably held in Milwaukee. Only about sixty-five hundred fans showed up in the rain to watch the Cardinals fall for the twenty-seventh straight time, 10-0.

Collins was behind center and turned on the "T" machine, but never could get it rolling. The Cards completed just three out of twenty passes and dented the Lions for only twenty-six yards rushing. In seventeen offensive possessions, the Cardinals managed just two first downs—and one of those arrived courtesy of a penalty! The losing streak reached twenty-eight a week later when the Cleveland Rams prevailed 21-0. This time out, Handler gave Vince Oliver, a rookie from Indiana, a shot at quarterback, but the new offense sputtered once again. Only six of twenty-one passes were completed and four of those tosses were intercepted. On the ground, the Cards could collect only twenty-five yards. The good news was the return of one of the veteran stars, end Billy Dewell. Dewell played sparingly, but the addition of this tall receiver would certainly be beneficial for the young Cardinals quarterbacks.

## *I Wanted To Return To The Cardinals*

During the week, more good news floated into camp with the arrival of Paul Christman, the Cards' second pick in the 1941 draft. Christman, a 6'1", 210-pound quarterback out of Missouri, had just been discharged from the Navy. Nicknamed "Pitchin' Paul" for his All-American passing endeavors in college, his decision to join the Cardinals as a twenty-seven-year-old rookie would prove to be one of the cornerstones in the successful rebuilding of the team. Christman had struggled with the decision as to whether he should give pro football a try or enter the business world. Remembering the challenge he faced after being turned down earlier in his collegiate career by both Notre Dame and Purdue, Christman decided to tackle the pro game and to prove himself at still another level. "So from my navy base I called Phil Handler and told Phil that I wanted to return to the Cardinals," Christman said. "Handler said to fly before the ink was dry on the discharge. I got as far as Salt Lake City by plane before an army major bumped me. I reached Chicago four days later, by train!"

With Dewell and Christman both in the starting lineup on October 7 (despite little practice time), the Cardinals managed to score, but failed to detour the Philadelphia Eagles in a 21-6 defeat. Christman filled the sky with aerials but managed to complete just ten out of thirty-six passes. But the 170 yards gained through the air more than doubled the combined offense from the first two games. More importantly, none of Christman's passes were intercepted. Still it was the Cardinals' twenty-ninth straight loss and chances for avoiding a third straight winless season appeared dim.

The first pro game to be played in Chicago for the 1945 season was set for October 14 against the Bears at Wrigley Field. Although the Cardinals were 0-3, they would be facing a very unlikely Bears team. The predominant team in the early history of professional football was enduring its low ebb. Like the Cardinals, the Bears had been bruised by the endless departure of talent to the military. And like the Cardinals, the Bears of 1945 were in a very unusual situation in early October: they, too, were winless. Just before the game, the Cards welcomed back the popular Joe Kuharich from the Navy. He immediately resumed his familiar position at right guard, next to veteran tackle Chet Bulger. Kuharich would also handle the placekicking chores, provided, of course, that the Cardinals could score some touchdowns.

Kuharich, Dewell, Christman, Seno, and Cantor were all new faces added after the start of the 1945 season. The Cardinals were beginning to assemble a formidable football structure although it was not one likely to jell in the very near future. Still, the date with the Bears did present an opportunity, despite the presence of the gifted Sid Luckman at quarterback for the Bears.

It took Luckman just over two minutes to figure out the Cardinals' defense. On the Bears' second play from scrimmage, Luckman combined with end Ken Kavanaugh on a sixty-four-yard scoring play. It appeared that the usual rout was on.

But behind the rushing of Cantor, Seno, and Christman, the Cardinals fought back, and tied the game on Cantor's short touchdown run followed by Kuharich's conversion. In the third period, Cantor connected with Eddie Rucinski for sixty-two yards followed by Cantor's sixteen-yard scoring run. The Cardinals now led 14-7, and the suddenly strong Cards defense continued to shut down Luckman. A late safety added the final touch to a surprising 16-7 Cardinals win, ending the lengthy losing streak at twenty-nine games. While the first league win since the 1942 season was extremely gratifying, it was also very short-lived.

The Detroit Lions pulled the Cards back down to earth the following week with a convincing 26-0 defeat. Christman was continually harassed by the charging Detroit defense and completed just seven out of thirty-six passes for eighty-two yards. The following week (October 28) the Packers smacked the Cardinals 33-14 despite a rejuvenated Christman hitting on seventeen for thirty-one passes. The Cardinals actually piled up 363 yards in total offense but just couldn't figure out how to stop Green Bay's Don Hutson, who scored three times.

## Don't Worry, Kid!

Yet the biggest story coming out of Green Bay that day was not Don Hutson's extraordinary offensive display. Nor was it Christman's unveiling as the league's passing star of the future. No, it was the improbable appearance on the field of a frail fullback who made a brief substitution for the Cardinals. Scarcely two months out of a Japanese prison camp, Motts Tonelli was back in a Chicago Cardinals uniform.

Following his release from imprisonment in Japan, the feisty war hero began the interminable journey back to Chicago. First it was a long plane ride back to the Philippines, then a slow boat to San Francisco. His playing weight as a fullback for the Chicago Cardinals had dropped to less than one hundred pounds during his confinement.

When he arrived home in Chicago, there was little fanfare, according to Tonelli:

> When my train arrived, there wasn't a big celebration. I met my wife and my parents there at the station and that was enough for me . . . but there wasn't a celebration of any kind.

Tonelli's next stop was a hospital room for recovery and a pair of operations. During his recuperation, he was visited by Cardinals owner Charles Bidwill:

> Mr. Bidwill called me at the hospital and said that he wanted to see me. When he came up, he said, "Motts, before you left the Cardinals, you still had a three-year contract with the team. We expect you to honor that contract." Both of us knew that was nearly impossible, but I was determined to do my best for him.

So Tonelli, although obviously still weakened, began the tough trek back into playing shape and finally trotted onto the field against the Packers.

"I didn't play much," said Tonelli, "but I'll never forget Don Hutson during that game. He came over, shook my hand and said, "Don't worry, kid. I'll make you look good!" During the brief time that Tonelli shadowed Hutson from his defensive back position, the legendary Packer receiver did not have an impact on the game. Of course, he had already destroyed the Cardinals earlier.

Now 1-5, but percolating, the Cardinals next visited Sammy Baugh and the Washington Redskins. In front of thirty-five thousand fans, the Redskins prevailed 24-21, but not until after some heroics from Christman. Washington scored early and often to grab a quick 21-0 lead in the beginning of the second quarter. Christman, who completed 12 out of 20 passes for 156 yards, brought the Cards their first score with a 29-yard bullet to Jim Poole.

Early in the second half, the ground game took over as Cantor picked up twenty yards and then Seno tallied on a forty-eight-yard scoring jaunt to complete a nifty sixty-eight-yard drive. Down 21-14, Christman engineered the next scoring journey by completing four passes during an eighty-five-yard drive before Cantor equaled the score with a three-yard run. Although there were fewer than four minutes left in the game, Sammy Baugh managed to quickly position the Redskins for the winning field goal attempt by Joe Aguirre. With just twenty-five seconds remaining in the contest, Aguirre's boot was true from nineteen yards out and the hosts escaped with the 24-21 verdict.

With the season winding down, the Cardinals welcomed back two more veterans: end Pop Ivy and center Ray Apolskis. This pair arrived in time to see some action in a 23-0 loss at Pittsburgh, and then helped the Cards scare the division-leading Cleveland Rams in the Cardinals' first home game. As in the Washington game, Chicago fell behind quickly by a count of 14-0. But the suddenly "hot" Christman, who once nailed eight passes in a row, helped the Cards reduce the lead to 28-21 before falling 35-21.

The first Cards touchdown was courtesy of tackle Chet Bulger, who described how he picked up an errant Rams fumble and scored from eight yards out early in the second period:

> Linemen always dream of scoring a touchdown. The quarterback turned to look to his left and I flipped the ball out of his hands, caught it, and ran. I almost killed myself running into the wall at Comiskey Park.

While the Cardinals could get no closer than a seven-point deficit, the game marked another landmark in the rising career of Paul Christman as he finished with 19 for 44 passing for 204 yards. The Cards proved they could be trouble for any team, especially with "Pitchin' Paul" eyeing such gifted receivers as Dewell, Seno, Rucinski, and Cantor.

## I Was Lucky

More than fifty years after his historical survival, the legend of Motts Tonelli continues to grow. In late 1997, Tonelli was featured on a public television special in Chicago, and in early 1998, the entire nation met Motts Tonelli when he was the focus of an NBC News segment during the Olympic Games. Tonelli recounted how a Japanese officer, a graduate of USC, retrieved Tonelli's stolen Notre Dame class ring. A Japanese soldier had previously threatened Tonelli's life if he refused to hand over the ring. The officer had remembered Tonelli's football exploits against USC and promptly ordered the return of the ring when he learned it was Tonelli's. It became his symbol of hope, dreams, and freedom during his long, lonely months in captivity. "I was lucky," he recalled.

But Motts Tonelli fondly remembers one other act of kindness that helped change his life. "When Mr. Bidwill visited me in the hospital after my return from the war, he did something for me for which I will always be grateful. When he renewed my contract after the war, he provided me with a wonderful opportunity. Back in those days, under the rules of the NFL, you had to play both before and after the war in order to get credit for your pension for the season you missed during the war."

By appearing briefly in a game against Green Bay near the end of the 1945 season, Tonelli received "credit" for the four full seasons he missed due to his service and captivity and was thus eligible to receive an NFL players' pension. "I will always be grateful to the Bidwills," added Tonelli. "I owe them a lot."

## Conzelman Will Come To Chicago

The 1945 season would conclude with the second and final home game of the year at Comiskey Park against the Bears on Sunday, December 2. With two weeks off to prepare for the renewal of this heated rivalry, Handler used the time to fine-tune the offense and to throw in some surprises for his North Side foes. But rumors began to leak out about a possible coaching change. Handler, a longtime player and coach with the organization, was puzzled and hurt by the stories which predicted his imminent ousting as head coach. Some of the rumors even hinted at the return of Jimmy Conzelman.

Finally, Cardinals management announced on November 28 that there would indeed be a change at the top as reported by the *Chicago Tribune:*

> *Jim Conzelman will come to Chicago in mid-December to sign his 1946 contract as coach of the Cardinals, officials of the National Football league eleven said yesterday.*
>
> *Whether Phil Handler, present head coach, and his assistant, Buddy Parker, will be retained on the staff, will be for Conzelman to decide, it was indicated. Handler was Conzelman's assistant before the silver tongued Missourian resigned prior to the 1943 season to join the St. Louis Browns baseball organization.*
>
> *The Cardinals said that Conzelman will not be present for Sunday's game against the Bears in Comiskey Park. Conzelman, in Indianapolis, last night said he regretted a premature announcement of his return because of the embarrassment it had caused Handler.*

With the decision behind him, Handler returned to the work of preparing his team for the surging Bears. While the Cards would enter the game with a 1-8 slate, and the Bears were just 2-7, both teams had improved dramatically late in the season with the influx of former players. Besides, it was still the Bears versus the Cardinals. "I've never seen a Cardinal game, especially at Comiskey Park which wasn't a rough one," noted Bears coach Luke Johnsos. "Those fellows seem to save up all their best punches for us."

Despite their inauspicious records, the two teams managed to drum up some interest by corking up unique reasons to attend this latest version of their long rivalry. Bears owner George Halas, just returned from his service stint in the Pacific, declared: "We're playing for the professional football championship of Illinois!" The Cardinals, meanwhile, plunged straight ahead and vowed to bring some honor to Handler in his last game as head coach.

Once again, the Cardinals fell way behind and trailed 28-7 after three quarters. Christman and Cantor combined to complete 16 out of 29 passes for 171 yards, but it was Christman who was in control as the Cardinals waged their comeback in the final stanza. First, he connected with both Rucinski and Dewell to set up Cantor's ten-yard touchdown scamper. After Kuharich's kick, it was 28-14, and Walt Rankin quickly recovered a fumble at the Bears' twenty-nine. Christman nailed completions to Seno and Rucinski before spotting Dewell for a ten-yard score. Kuharich's extra point attempt was blocked, but the Cardinals took advantage of one more chance, trailing 28-20. Following a Sid Luckman punt, three more Christman completions brought the ball down to the Bears' four-yard line as time expired. It was a marvelous comeback effort by the Cardinals, who despite a third straight last-place finish, began to show signs of the competitive fury which would soon help them dominate the NFL.

From three straight finishes at the bottom, and thirty-two losses in their last thirty-three games, to dominance? No other team in the NFL has accomplished such a complete turnaround in so short of a time as the Chicago Cardinals. But that would come later.

Following the 1945 season, the Cardinals' Publicity Director Eddie McGuire thought he had uncovered a unique angle in promoting the experiences of the many returning war veterans. One of his questions was direct and to the point: "What was your most hazardous experience?"

Christman's answer was also direct and to the point and it had nothing to do with the war, but everything to do with a hazardous experience: "Playing behind the '45 Cardinal line!"

## The NFL's "Honor Roll"

According to the *1946 NFL Record and Roster Manual,* as of V-J Day (August 14, 1945), the NFL's roster of players in the service (limited to players who had appeared in league games) reached 638. Of these numbers, 355 were commissioned, 69 were decorated, and 19 gave their lives for their country, including 4 players who had been affiliated with the Cardinals. The following is the NFL "Honor Roll" listing those players who lost their lives in action:

- **Corporal Mike Basca (Philadelphia halfback):** Killed in France on Armistice Day in 1944 with Patton's 3rd Army.

- **Lieutenant Charles Behan (Detroit end):** Killed by Japanese machine-gun fire on Okinawa, May 18, 1945.

- **Major Keith Birlem (Chicago Cardinal and Washington end):** Killed in England, May 7, 1943, attempting to land crippled bomber after raid over Europe.

- **Lieutenant Al Blozis (New York tackle):** Killed by German machine-gun fire in Vosges Mountains of France on January 31, 1945.

- **Lieutenant Young Bussey (Chicago Bears quarterback):** Killed leading landing party on first day of Lingayen operation in Philippines.

- **Captain Smiley Johnson (Green Bay guard):** Killed on ninth day of Iwo Jima invasion.

- **Sergeant Alex Ketzko (Detroit tackle):** Killed in France on December 23, 1944, with Patch's 7th Army.

- **Lieutenant Jack Lummus (New York end):** Killed by land mine leading infantry-tank attack against last Japanese stronghold on Iwo Jima.

- **Lieutenant John O'Keefe (Philadelphia director):** Killed piloting Navy plane on patrol mission in Canal Zone.

- **Lieutenant John Supulski (Philadelphia end):** Killed in plane crash during maneuvers in Nebraska.

- **Lieutenant Don Wemple (Brooklyn end):** Killed piloting Army transport plane in India.

- **Lieutenant Chet Wetterlund (Cardinal and Detroit halfback):** Killed flying Navy Hellcat on night patrol, September 5, 1944, along New Jersey coast.

- **Captain Waddy Young (Brooklyn end):** B29 pilot killed when he dropped out of formation to cover a crippled colleague during return from first B29 raid over Tokyo, January 9, 1945.

- **Lieutenant Jack Chevigny (Chicago Cardinal coach):** Killed on second day of Iwo Jima invasion by direct shell hit on a bomb crater.

- **Captain Ed Doyle (Pottsville end):** First American officer killed in African invasion.

- **Lieutenant Eddie Kahn (Boston guard):** Died of wounds suffered in Leyete invasion, February 17, 1945.

- **Captain Lee Kizzire (Detroit halfback):** Leader of flight formation shot down December 5, 1943, over New Guinea area.

- **Private Jim Mooney (Chicago Cardinal, Brooklyn and Chicago Bears end):** Killed by sniper's bullet in France on August 12, 1944.

- **Chief Specialist Gus Sonnenberg (Providence tackle):** Died September 13, 1944, at Great Lakes Naval Training Station.

Many Chicago Cardinals served with distinction during the war. At least forty-two active players were plucked from the roster from 1940 to 1945. In addition, about twenty others served who had left the Cardinals prior to the hostilities, including former stars such as Doug Russell, Ernie Nevers, Dr. John Mohardt, and Dr. Eddie Anderson. Former coaches Paul Schissler and Jack Chevigny also served, with Chevigny losing his life on Iwo Jima. Several representatives of the Cardinals received recognition for their contributions as follows:

- **Frank Balazs** received a Presidential Unit citation.

- **Andrew Chisick** won the Silver Star and the Purple Heart for his actions in New Guinea.

- **John Shirk** was imprisoned by the Germans but eventually liberated by the Russian Army in 1945.

- **Mike Koken** was awarded the Purple Heart after being strafed by a Nazi war plane at Normandy on August 7, 1944.

# ◆ 11 ◆

## The Coach:
## Jimmy Conzelman

*"Speaking after Conzelman is like following*
*'Gone With The Wind' with a magic lantern."*

PAT O'BRIEN, ACTOR

How does one define an individual who chased his dreams, avoided typecasting, and still found time to excel at a number of professions?

Coach Jimmy Conzelman was capable of frightening rookie linemen, intimidating referees, charming theater patrons, and inspiring military aspirants. He was a poet, a boxer, an actor, and a coach. Most importantly, he was a father.

Prior to the 1946 season, Jimmy rejoined the Chicago Cardinals and his personal stock soared even higher as his team began to slowly gather national attention. He used his natural gifts both on and off the field to teach, entertain, or just shrug off the oddities of life.

Jimmy was a gifted speaker who used his own experiences (whether real or imagined) to deduce the complexities of life. His favorite target was usually himself, and he once used his experience as a parent to explain why he was usually trusted and befriended by individuals from all walks of life:

> *It must be the ease with which I am influenced. People don't like people who influence them; they like to do the influencing. Anybody can influence me. Take the case of my son. When he was a toddler, he formed the habit of sucking his thumb, and Mrs. Conzelman thought that as alleged head of the household I should do something about the thumb-sucking.*
>
> *I tried, but do you know that after I talked to my son a few evenings about it, he sold me on the idea, and there we were, both sucking our thumbs. And Mrs. Conzelman then had to get the two of us to break off the silly, but I must say, enjoyable habit.*

Ironically, the life of Jimmy Conzelman almost mirrored the history of the Chicago Cardinals, the team he would one day lead to the championship of the National Football League. James Gleason Conzelman was born March 6, 1898, the son of James Gleason Dunn and Margaret Ryan, just one year before the first version of the Morgan Athletic Association was organized. Jimmy, however, later took the name of his stepfather (a dentist), and helped raise the family after Dr. Conzelman passed away. He became an outstanding athlete at McKinley High School in St. Louis, excelling in football, basketball, and baseball, once scoring nine touchdowns in one football game.

To Jimmy, football always remained a game. And a game is something you should enjoy, and stick with as long as you can enjoy it. So, when Conzelman chose to retire from the game at times either as a player, owner, or coach, it was simply because his objectives were temporarily satisfied, or that he felt the inner need to address another challenge—whatever that challenge might be.

He weathered the painful growing years of the NFL in the 1920s and experienced the acceptance of the circuit and its ideals in the 1940s. In his case, his selection to the Pro Football Hall of Fame in 1964, only the second year of its existence, was the ultimate recognition for a life of contributions to the sport of pro football.

Along the way, he was not shy about pursuing unusual activities, especially those which might be considered "unusual" to the general football population, such as writing or acting. Nor was Conzelman afraid to use the natural gifts bestowed upon him, whether it be playing the piano, pummeling an opponent in the boxing ring, or authoring an article. He tried anything that interested him, which in the end left him with a full, satisfied life, a life that was well respected by anyone who knew him. He once described himself as "a guy afflicted with an abnormal curiosity and incapable of resisting anything new."

Because of the diversity of this man, it is worth taking a more extended look at his many accomplishments. As a member of the Pro Football Hall of Fame, his life has been well documented. However, in terms of his contributions to the Chicago Cardinals, those accomplishments vividly set the stage for future generations of players. Indeed, no coach of the Cardinals has been able to duplicate his championship since that magical year of 1947.

So what was so unusual about Jimmy Conzelman, coach of the Chicago Cardinals? Those who played for him can perhaps provide the most accurate insight:

**Vince Banonis:** "He was a great psychologist who always seemed to come up with something unusual to give us an edge in a game."

**Red Cochran:** "I thought he was extremely smart. He was a great guy, a fine motivator, and was laid-back as far as his coaching. Most importantly, he knew football and how to handle people."

**Marshall Goldberg:** "Jimmy Conzelman was a creative sort of a fellow and quite a personality. He was probably one of the more imaginative and creative coaches in the game. Jimmy was the kind of guy who you could talk to and that helped a lot."

**Mal Kutner:** "Jimmy was an organizer and a man of many arts. He was the kind of guy who could really bring a team together."

**Charlie Trippi:** "Playing for Jimmy Conzelman was like playing for your father! He had such a tremendous personality and made every player feel important."

**Gus Tinsley:** "He was so outstanding in every way, not only as a football coach, but as a man. He was always fair to the players."

**Babe Dimancheff:** "He was a wonderful man who had ways of getting the best out of you. Plus, he knew how to use the talents of his assistants."

**Chet Bulger:** "Jimmy was a great storyteller. When we'd go to New York, he'd take us to his favorite restaurant called Toots Shoor's. He'd go in there, take over the piano, and entertain the crowd. He had a great deal of charisma."

In truth, the legend of Jimmy Conzelman began quite early in his life, but accelerated as he began to distinguish himself through various athletic and cultural endeavors. Along the way, he experienced life as an advertising executive, football coach, sculptor's model, songwriter, actor, orchestra leader, construction worker, and lecturer.

Conzelman was originally captivated by the game of football in high school but began to spread his wings in other areas at Washington University in St. Louis, where he had originally hoped to become a dentist. During this time, he experimented in the music business by managing six orchestras and performing as a soloist for a local recording company, playing both the banjo and the ukulele. His songwriting credits at this ripe young age included "Lovin' Like My Kind" and "What a Baby." He also found time to handle public relations for a trucking company, and drifted to New York for a time where he served both as a model and a salesman of sculptured monuments of soldiers.

In an effort to recognize the many facets of this gifted individual, it would be best to briefly examine each of the major stops he enjoyed on his journey through life.

## *Great Lakes Naval Station (1918-1919)*

When the United States began its active participation in World War I, Conzelman, like many other young men, willingly found himself in the military service. Following his freshman year at Washington University in St. Louis, Conzelman enlisted and was assigned to the Great Lakes Naval Training Station near Chicago, where he teamed up with future greats George Halas and Paddy Driscoll on a service football team that captured the 1919 Rose Bowl. This was the only non-collegiate team ever to win that revered game and it was made possible because of the difficult schedule played by Great Lakes. The team was one of the finest ever assembled, and Conzelman was a true leader from his quarterback position as the squad played many of the leading universities in the nation during the 1919 season. On defense, he was also impressive, once returning an interception eighty yards for a touchdown in a 23-14 win over Iowa.

Because of the war, military bases organized athletic teams in many sports both to entertain the troops as well as to provide the opportunity for personnel to stay in shape through participation in some type of athletic endeavor. The Great Lakes football team jelled as a unit and quickly became a magnet for the attention of the national media. Late in the season, when the team was embroiled in a close game with Navy, Conzelman recalled:

> *The commandant told us in the dressing room before the game with the Naval Academy that if we won, we would go to the Rose Bowl. He also said we would get our discharges.*
> *We beat Navy, won the Rose Bowl, and I was out of the service about ten days later. It was the best pep talk I ever heard!*

But during this time, he also proved himself as a capable pugilist by capturing the 160-pound title at the base and then traveling with the Great Lakes boxing team to challenge other bases. Jack Kennedy, the boxing coach at Great Lakes, once pointed to Conzelman and said, "I wish every fighter, when he gets 'over there' has knees like that boy." The *Chicago Daily News* called Jimmy "the greatest all-around athlete in the U.S. Navy." He defeated William Miller for the middleweight belt at Great Lakes, according to the *Daily News:*

> *Conzelman was awarded the decision owing to his bulldog tenacity and fighting qualities. He forced the fighting and seemed to be the stronger battler at the finish . . .*

The *Chicago Evening American* remarked that:

> *Conzelman is a handy fellow. The quarterback of football, middleweight boxing champ, champion ukeleist, expert of fancy dancing. That Conzelman surely can go some.*

Conzelman was undefeated in twenty-six fights and might have pursued boxing as a profession had football not stepped in his way.

## *Decatur Staleys (1920)*

Following his discharge from the Navy, Conzelman returned to Washington University, where he played quarterback during the 1919 season and was selected to the All-Missouri Valley Conference team. With money scarce around the household, Jimmy was eager to listen when former Great Lakes teammate George Halas called to talk about his new professional football venture over in Decatur, Illinois. Conzelman became an original member of the Decatur Staleys football team (the forerunners of the current Chicago Bears). He played for Halas during the 1920 season, but then was determined to retire from the game in order to secure a full-time job to help support his mother and three younger siblings. Walter Flanagan, the owner of the Rock Island Independents, helped change Conzelman's mind when he offered him significantly more money to play than he was receiving with the Staleys.

## *Rock Island Independents (1921-1922)*

As noted in chapter four, Conzelman acquired the title of head coach three games into the 1921 season with Rock Island, and he began to mull over the possibility of making football his permanent career. Later in his life, he recalled the day at home with his family when he announced his decision:

> *We were seated around the table. "I'm going to take a coaching job, Mother," I said. She nodded in agreement.*
> *Aunt Minnie was there, big puss and all. She had to get her fin in. "Well," she said, raising one eye at me and lowering the other at the last dinner chop. "That's news, after him not working for a year."*
> *My mother interrupted. "Please, Minnie, after all, he looked for work."*
> *Aunt Minnie laughed like a rattler. "You can't tell me he couldn't find work," she chortled. "At least he could drive a milk wagon." That was her stock advice for anyone looking for a job. Drive a milk wagon! According to her, year after year there were always milk routes going a-begging.*

*Perhaps Aunt Minnie was right. Driving a milk wagon is a nice quiet life compared with driving a football team to slaughter!*

During his nearly two years as head coach, the Independents compiled a respectable 7-3-1 record. Their success caught the eye of the owners of the Milwaukee Badgers, who offered Conzelman an increase to $200 per game if he would assume the role of player-coach for the Badgers. Jimmy grabbed the offer and headed up to Wisconsin.

## *Milwaukee Badgers (1923-1924)*

The Milwaukee franchise needed refurbishing and the new coach's first job was to evaluate the current talent. One of the players released from the team was the now legendary vocalist Paul Robeson and Conzelman related this tale in *Pro Football's Rag Days:*

*One of the players I let go after several weeks was Paul Robeson. I had played against Robeson when he was at Rutgers and I was at Great Lakes. He had been a one-man team, throwing and catching passes, punting, and even playing tackle on offense at times. But he was sick of football by the time we met again in Milwaukee and wasn't going to be much use as a player. He was valuable as a member of a singing quartet we had, although the other members didn't think much of his voice.*

During his stint with Milwaukee, Conzelman recalled an unusual exhibition game down in Texas:

*My Milwaukee team played Clarendon College in Amirro, Texas. There were a lot of cowboys on horseback on the sidelines. They had booze in them, and started shooting off their pistols. Every time one of our guys was knocked out of bounds the cowboys would scare him to death by riding their horses up as close as they could get without trampling on us.*

*We were leading by a big score, and I said to our players, "The cowboys want them to score—let them." On the next play, the safety men, one of which was me, separated and gave the kids the whole center of the field. The quarterback threw a long pass and scored a touchdown. That satisfied the cowboys and they let us alone for the rest of the game.*

The team often played several games each week and tried to be prepared for anything:

*We had only about 14 players and one was needed to carry water when the field got dusty. Another drove the getaway car in case we had to leave in a hurry from some unhappy gun-toting cowboys who had bet on the wrong team.*

Following the 1923 season, Conzelman remained in Chicago. He entered the real estate business where things went so well that he dropped his coaching duties in 1924 while remaining as Milwaukee's weekend quarterback. The Milwaukee situation was not unlike other struggling professional franchises, according to Conzelman:

*You had eighteen men on the roster. One time in Milwaukee we had three play-*
*ers injured, so the owner put on a uniform and sat on the bench, just to give us*
*a look of depth!*

It was after the 1924 campaign that Jimmy received an offer "too good to be true"
from league Commissioner Joe Carr to head up a new franchise. He soon headed to
Detroit as the new owner of the Panthers. His final record with the Milwaukee Badgers
was 12-10-3.

## Detroit Panthers (1925-1926)

The Detroit experience, where he served as the player, coach, and owner of the team,
was not one of Conzelman's favorite memories. "I came here in '25, stayed two years,
blew 35 grand, gave the franchise away for nothing and have been kicking myself ever
since," he said years later. His biggest disappointment was the team's inability to cash
in on the popularity of Red Grange when Grange was scheduled to visit during the
banner year of 1925.

Conzelman figured that he had sold over twenty thousand tickets for a game with
the Bears before learning that Grange would not play due to an injury. Conzelman,
in an ethical move which was typical of his entire career, offered refunds to any fans
who were so inclined. The response staggered the coach:

*It looked like the game that would pay all the bills for the year and give us a*
*cushion to work with. I was honest, but it hurt. We still played to about 5,000.*
*But it wasn't enough.*

While that game signaled the beginning of the end for Conzelman in Detroit,
his arrival in the city was even more peculiar, as he recounted in the book, *What A*
*Game They Played,* by Richard Whittingham:

*In 1925, Joe Carr, the head of the NFL, asked me to bring pro football to Detroit.*
*He said the franchise fee was a thousand dollars, but he'd let me have Detroit for*
*fifty dollars. I said fine, and suddenly I was the owner, coach and only player for the*
*Panthers. But I got together a team and uncorked a plan to make them well known.*
*    My plan was to get Notre Dame's fabled "Four Horsemen" for the team. Not*
*only would they play football for us, but I would work out a vaudeville act and*
*the four of them and myself would take it on the road before and after the sea-*
*son. I talked to them and they were for it so I lined up some theatrical agents to*
*work out the details.*
*    I was to be the piano player. Harry Stuhldreher was a pretty good singer and*
*he was going to sing a song called "She's a Mean Job." Jim Crowley planned to*
*do a clog dance and had a routine for a comic monologue. The problem was Elmer*
*Layden and Don Miller didn't have an act, so we took some time to see if we*
*could get them to do a song or some kind of routine. Time went by and finally*
*Layden called me up and told me he had agreed to take a job with some recre-*
*ation department and to count him out. I don't think we could make it as "The*
*Three Horsemen and Conzelman," neither did the theatrical agents, and so the*
*whole deal fell apart.*

Aside from his football experience in Detroit, Conzelman also gave playing pro basketball a chance in that city, but the franchise failed. He literally gave the Detroit Panthers franchise back to the league after the financially grueling 1926 season and took over as the player-coach of the young Providence Steam Roller team. The franchise became known as the Detroit Lions, and a few years after Jimmy "gave" it back to the league, it was sold for several hundred thousand dollars. By the early 1960s, it was worth millions. "That gives you a fair measure of my business sagacity," said Conzelman. The Panthers finished 12-8-4 during those two seasons under Conzelman's leadership.

## Providence Steam Roller (1927-1930)

With Conzelman as the player-coach of the Steam Roller, the team plucked the 1928 NFL championship, and Jimmy was named the league's most valuable player. However, he suffered a knee injury during the 1928 season which essentially ended his playing career. Conzelman would remain as coach for two more years, and Providence owned a 26-16-6 record during his reign. It was at this point in his life that Jimmy decided to evaluate other career possibilities outside of pro football. After a decade in the pro game, Conzelman noted that he had nothing but "a bantam-sized bank account and a bad knee," and returned to his native St. Louis to contemplate the future.

## Washington University (1932-1939)

Growing weary of the frustrations encountered in the realm of pro football, Conzelman left the pro game and became the publisher of a weekly newspaper in Maplewood, Missouri. In 1932, he returned to football when he was named head coach at Washington University in St. Louis. It took him only two years to capture his first Missouri Valley Conference championship and he won two more before leaving the university.

During this period of time, Conzelman molded little Washington University into a big-time player on the national football scene. His clubs faced the likes of Illinois, Southern Methodist, Army, and Notre Dame. But the beginning of his collegiate coaching career was not auspicious, as Conzelman humorously recounted to the *Houston Chronicle* on September 13, 1966:

> *Our traditional game was with the University of Missouri, but Missouri didn't know it. They used to beat us by 40 or 50 points depending on the mood they were in.*
>
> *My first year there the line averaged about 179 pounds and the backfield 151. The week of the Missouri game, I went out to practice and there were all the players across the field flying kites. I yelled "Yoo-hoo!" and they all came running. "I've got some good news for you men," I told them, "We're going to beat Missouri!" They said, "Goodie!"*
>
> *We worked hard all that week and on Friday went to Columbia. On Saturday we took the field and of all things won the toss and elected to receive. Those big Missouri linemen were so eager to get their hands on our little backs, they were offside three straight plays, and were penalized 15 yards.*

*"We've got 'em on the run, coach," one of the players yelled at me.*

*We couldn't gain after that and punted on fourth down. Missouri fumbled the kick and we recovered. They found the ball under our end's back . . . Well the rest of the first half was played between our three- and four-yard lines. And just before the half, we partially blocked a pass and the ball fell into the hands of my left end, who was so busy counting the crowd he had neglected to rush. He ran 101 yards for a touchdown.*

*Well, we finally won that game 14-6 which shows what a lot of inspiration and hard work can do. Of course, a little unconsciousness doesn't hurt you either!*

Former member of the Notre Dame "Four Horsemen" and later NFL Commissioner Elmer Layden remembered the time when Conzelman brought the Washington of St. Louis team to Notre Dame when Layden was the coach there. At the press conference the night before the big game, Conzelman was asked about his team's chances against the bigger Fighting Irish squad and groaned: "Coach Layden's great big giants and monsters are gonna massacre my little boys," predicted Conzelman. Then, while he was speaking, the clouds opened outside and Jimmy smiled and added, "The deluge! Now in the mud and water, my little boys got a chance!" Layden then swaggered over to Conzelman, put his arm over his shoulder and shrugged, "I'm sorry, Jimmy. The field is covered by a tarpaulin."

During this decade, he began writing for national publications, sampled radio broadcasting, performed in stage plays, and then, in 1936, married Anne Forestal of St. Louis. His visibility provided another natural forum as a public speaker, and he was soon earning requests from around the country in that capacity.

## *Back To The Cardinals I*

Following the 1942 season, Jimmy decided that his brief tenure with the Cardinals had been enough. He, like other coaches, was handicapped by the lack of functioning football bodies and decided to accept an offer as vice president of the St. Louis Browns baseball club. After sitting out a year away from the football field, Jimmy had time to reflect and comment on his new life without the pigskin in late 1943:

*For the first time in 23 years I didn't coach a football team. All right, go ahead and yawn. At least you can't deny that 23 years is a long time. Try sitting it some time.*

*Anyway, all I have done this Fall is answer questions. They are always the same. Some guy comes up, lays a sympathetic hand on my shoulder and asks: "Don't you miss football?" Sure I do. Miss it like the devil.*

*But there are some things you don't miss. Just imagine yourself, for instance, sitting on the bench coaching a professional team playing the Chicago Bears. And just suppose, too, that the Bears are kicking your boys for 20 yards a kick, even against the wind. Those Bears do that at times . . .*

*So you're losing by 30 or 40 points with only seconds to go. The golden sun of Autumn is setting in the West, and the owner of the club is settling in his vest, as far down the bench as he can get from you. That's about the time you begin to count on your fingers the number of months your savings account will carry you without a job. About February 10th, you decide.*

*From there on each coach, according to preference, takes his own mental paths. Some like to think of suicide, a rather attractive way out of the mess. Others toy with the idea of killing the owner, although this thought is prevalent only among younger coaches. The veteran coaches know that a bankroll is a bankroll even under a camel's hair coat, and should be so regarded.*

*One coach tells me that under losing conditions late in the game, he invariably pulls for the personal heart attack. This obviously is not only unsportsman-like, but a rather nasty evasion of responsibility, designed to attract public attention from the final score to the coach's own crumpled figure in front of the bench . . .*

Obviously, Conzelman had not discarded his wit at this juncture of his career, but apparently did not miss the stress associated with coaching, either.

## Back To The Cardinals II

Charles "Stormy" Bidwill, son of the late Cardinals owner Charley Bidwill, recalled traveling with the team as a youth when Conzelman was the coach and told the *Chicago Tribune*:

*Those were the days, and Jimmy Conzelman helped make them. On those train trips he'd entertain us with his funny stories while he drank coke by the case. I was always sorry they never put pianos on the trains because you knew how Conzelman loved to play the piano all night long. Whenever Conzelman was telling a story, or playing the piano, there was always a crowd of people who loved life and good times.*

Chet Bulger remembers Conzelman's smoking habits:

*He would inhale a cigarette, with smoke coming out of his nose and mouth at the same time. We don't know if it ever came out of his ears.*

As the Cardinals became more successful, the players developed a true team camaraderie, and Jimmy was there with them. After each home game, the players, coaches, and their families would retreat to a local establishment on the South Side of Chicago. Usually it was at a favorite haunt in Hyde Park, next to the old Blackstone Hotel nicknamed the "Cardinals' Den." Vince Banonis remembers those eventful days:

*There was this Greek place we went to on the South Side and they opened the bar up to the whole team after each game on Sunday. We all went to the same place with our families and everyone got to know each other. That was one of the things that kept the Cards together. Jimmy used to show up and play the piano and we all sang songs. We all had a great time together. It was a great bunch of guys. I don't remember any two guys getting angry at each other. We stuck together on and off the field and that all stemmed from Jimmy.*

The coach was also a gifted motivator, with most players recalling their own favorite experience:

**Red Cochran:** "During the 1948 training camp, we had one day where it was extremely hot and miserable. After we finished a long, tough practice in the morning, Jimmy told us that he wanted us back for a meeting at 1:00 on the front porch after lunch. Now this was the time for us to rest before the afternoon session, so the boys were more than a little upset. But, everyone showed up growling. When we got there right at 1:00, in come three school buses up the driveway. Jimmy told us to all check out a pair of shorts and a jock. He said we were all going swimming that afternoon. He took us over to Oconomoc and we had a great time all afternoon swimming and raising hell. We came back all fired up and ready to practice . . . I still consider it a master stroke of genius for inspiring a team by a coach."

**Marshall Goldberg:** "We had a game scheduled in Los Angeles against the Rams and Jimmy called me in before the game. He told me that I had been playing well and that if I kept up that good effort and we beat the Rams, he would give me a $500 bonus, but I wasn't supposed to tell anybody. That was a significant amount of money in those days. Well, we beat the Rams and I earned the bonus. We all went out to dinner and then there was a rumor that someone had received a $500 bonus. I hadn't said anything, but as it turned out, everybody had been called in by Jimmy and he told them the same story. We all received $500 bonuses for winning that game!"

**Vince Banonis:** "Jimmy would reward you in some small, surprising way that would make you push for him when you were out there. Once we were reviewing film of a game and Jimmy said something like, 'Look at that! Did you see that? Roll it back.' I didn't know what to expect because he was pointing at me on the film. He liked what he saw on the film and said that he would give me a $5 bonus for each block on this particular play. It turns out that I had three blocks on that one play, so I made a quick bonus of $15!"

**Chet Bulger:** "After we won the 1948 All-Star game, the locker room was filled with our family and friends. We thought we'd be able to stay over and visit, but Jimmy came in and told us that we were going back immediately to our training camp in Wisconsin. Of course, there was a lot of grumbling and such. So, we got back on the bus and everyone was still moaning all the way up. But when we arrived at the camp, the bus kept right on going and took us to this very nice resort. They took us into a room at the resort and our families were waiting there! We stayed there and relaxed and visited. That was Jimmy—first class all the way."

Following the 1947 season, Conzelman was named the NFL Coach of the Year, an honor which later prompted well-deserved praise from rival coach Greasy Neale:

> *He always had a bold, imaginative attack, solid blocking and tackling. Jimmy was as good as they came.*

Bob Broeg of the *St. Louis Post-Dispatch* perhaps summarized the career of Jimmy Conzelman when he penned this simple, but accurate, description of the coach on August 27, 1969:

> *Ah, this Irishman with the Dutch surname has had the gift of the blarney, a graciousness which made him the best of fellows socially, wonderful press copy as a coach and—in that vexing capacity—a man who knew how to steam up or relax a football team.*

Conzelman's playing and coaching talents eventually landed him in the Pro Football Hall of Fame. His first tenure with the Cardinals (1940-42) had been swindled by lack of depth and the loss of personnel to the war effort. This time around, beginning in 1946, he would have some talent, but would it be enough to transcend the 1-9 inheritance from the 1945 season?

There are many stories that make up the legend of Jimmy Conzelman. While most describe his humor, wit, and nonchalance, his players remember a man who truly cared about them as human beings. Words like "class," "dignity," and "sensitive" surround the tales told by the men who played for Jimmy Conzelman. Perhaps the one player who was closest to Conzelman was the talented, triple-threat back Marshall Goldberg. Goldberg possesses many treasures from his long and varied football career. The man who was on the cover of both *Life* and *Look* magazines and is now in several halls of fame points to one small piece of paper that he will treasure forever. It's a simple, handwritten note from Jimmy Conzelman that he wrote to Goldberg more than forty years ago following a dinner honoring Goldberg and his many accomplishments. "Honestly, I don't think any group of ex-football players have more fun than we do when even a few of us get together," wrote Conzelman. "There is great warmth whenever we meet and I cherish it. You are what parents hope their sons will be—a gentleman, successful, highly regarded by everyone. I wish your Dad could have been here." According to Goldberg, he was. "Jimmy was like a father to me," he shrugged. "As great of a player or coach that he was, he was an even more outstanding person. I still miss him."

# ◆ 12 ◆

# The Resurrection:
# 1946

*"We used to be outmanned Sunday after Sunday.
Those days are over."*

JIMMY CONZELMAN,
COACH, CHICAGO CARDINALS

World War II was locked away as a very bad memory and the Chicago Cardinals were able to focus again on the game itself. With a bevy of returning servicemen, along with some delayed draft choices and a few gridders who earned some experience during the previous two seasons, the Cardinals would have plenty of hopefuls to choose from before finalizing the 1946 roster.

Bouncing back from the hideous records of 1943 (0-10), 1944 (0-10), and 1945 (1-9) would not be easy, but with the talent pool available, some improvement could almost be guaranteed. But how would the war veterans react? Would the skills still be there? Would football remain a priority after what they had experienced? With a plethora of talent returning, the 1946 Cardinals would be an older, more mature club. Now they would need to merge their available capabilities and dismiss the hodgepodge of the 1945 season, in which nearly fifty players saw action in at least one game, but just five appeared in all ten. Of that handful, only tackle Chet Bulger started more than half of the games. The mingling of war veterans returning at various points during the season had been welcomed, but any sense of continuity was lost until everyone could start off together in the 1946 training camp.

Behind the scenes, Bidwill had courted Jimmy Conzelman during the latter stages of the 1945 season to seek his return as coach of the Cardinals. When the rumors failed to disappear, the Cardinals finally announced that Conzelman would return, but the deal was not completed until March 15, 1946.

Bidwill apparently sweetened the pot by also naming Conzelman as vice president of the club as well as promising him that the team would aggressively pursue the talent necessary to contend for the NFL title. Conzelman was given more help than ever before as previous head coach Phil Handler stayed on as an assistant along with Raymond "Buddy" Parker. Both had been Jimmy's assistants during his first stint with the team. Former Bears quarterback Carl Brumbaugh was also added as an assistant (to coach the quarterbacks), as was Richard Plasman, who perhaps may best be remembered during his days with the Bears as the last NFL player to not wear a helmet during a game.

## *More Enthusiasm Than A Child With A New Toy*

Once again, Conzelman initiated sweeping changes in the roster. As the 1946 season approached, only six of the fifty-two players invited to the 1946 training camp had been on the Cardinals' roster for the opening game of the 1945 season. Conzelman himself seemed renewed as well; the 1946 team press guide described the upcoming season as follows:

> *It's a new season, new personnel with wonderful aggressive spirit, and a new coach, the latter with more enthusiasm than a child with a new toy.*

Key additions to the squad included third-round draft choice Elmer Angsman from Notre Dame, the return of versatile halfback Marshall Goldberg from the service, and other potentially tough rookies such as end Mal Kutner (Texas), tackle Stan Mauldin (Texas), guard Garrard Ramsey (William and Mary), and fullback Pat Harder (Wisconsin). The 1946 training camp roster included thirty-five "rookies," but most were rookies only in terms of NFL experience. They were older, wiser war veterans who had seen the world, and were now ready to be seen by the NFL. Only three players were under the age of twenty-four, with Angsman being the youngest at age twenty.

Kutner was obtained in a blockbuster trade with Pittsburgh, which received the rights to Johnny "Mr. Zero" Clement and Bill Daddio, along with former top draft choice Steve Lach. All three had been in the service, but each had played important roles for the Cardinals in the past. Conzelman went clearly out on a limb in order to secure an untested end for three experienced players. Kutner had been an exemplary receiver at the University of Texas before spending more than three years in the service. He would quickly prove that he had not lost a step. At first, critics smirked at the trade. While Kutner had ample skills and the god-given gifts of speed (9.7 seconds in the 100-yard dash) and sure hands, was he truly worth three players, especially in this rebuilding year? But Conzelman was confident as he noted later:

> *It's one deal I was sure of even though it looked a little one-sided at first glance. And the best part about it is that it worked out well for both sides, which doesn't always happen in such trades.*

Clement and Lach played with Pittsburgh, while Daddio eventually signed with Buffalo of the All-America League but was out of football after the 1946 season.

The Cards also traded guard Robert Dobelstein to the Giants for veteran Ward Cuff. The latter would become an anchor on the Cards' offense despite his thirty-two years, which was considered "over the hill" in those days. Cuff scoffed at such comments because he believed that a player didn't hit his prime until he was in his late twenties, as he told the *Chicago Daily News:*

> *I'm 32 now and I had one of my best years with the Giants when I was 29. Pro football is played by experts. You bruise a lot from hard contact but you don't suffer as many injuries from carelessness or inexperience as in college. Besides, you have so many good players on a team that one guy doesn't have to shoulder the load.*

Cuff had registered big numbers during his nine years with the Giants. In addition, he topped the NFL in field goals (seven out of sixteen tries) in 1939 and had the best rushing average in the league in 1943 (6.5 yard average on eighty carries).

Cuff's trade had been somewhat of a gift to the Cardinals, since Conzelman had never expected a player of his caliber to be available. But Cuff, who lived in Milwaukee with his wife and three children, and had played college ball at Marquette, wanted to finish his career at a location nearer his home. The deal was tough for the Giants to swallow, since Cuff had been both a fan favorite and a dominating player for nearly a decade. Following the trade, Giants part-owner Wellington Mara stated: "No one can ever take Cuff's place on the Giants, nor will anyone ever wear his No. 14 jersey. That number has been retired for all time." Conzelman, for one, enjoyed the enthusiasm Cuff brought with him: "He exudes optimism. Each game is a brand new adventure for him."

Also returning from previous years were more names that are now linked to some of the finest moments in Cardinals history, such as Chet Bulger, end Billy Dewell, end Frank "Pop" Ivy, center Vince Banonis, and quarterbacks Ray Mallouf and Paul Christman. Christman's outstanding performance in 1945 was just the beginning. With Conzelman's zeal for perfection and the close tutoring of new quarterback coach Brumbaugh, the difficulties in running the "T" formation were expected to be a thing of the past. At least that's what the Cardinals' 1946 *Press and Media Guide* predicted:

> *Paul arrived a bit too late to open the 1945 season, after 52 months in service, but managed to play most of the schedule, and, despite being a bit rusty and at the same time playing the "T" formation for the first time, had a very good year. This year, with Coach Conzelman and Quarterback Coach Carl Brumbaugh working with him, he may develop into the top "T" signal-caller in the National League. At least that's the berth picked for him by some pretty cute critics of the gridiron.*
>
> *His coolness under fire is something out of this world. While at Missouri he would chew a piece of lemon peel, pay no attention to a rather serious-minded opposing tackle who had visions of taking him apart, and nonchalantly pitch passes to teammates. He's still that way.*

And there would be no better target than Dewell, who many remembered as a standout for the Cardinals even before the war. Originally drafted out of Southern Methodist by the Eagles, Dewell joined the Cardinals for the 1940 season and in 1942 grabbed 28 passes good for 262 yards—third best in the league. He returned after 41 months in the Navy to play most of the 1945 season and pace the Cards with 26 receptions for 370 yards.

The pieces were beginning to fall in place. With a renewed determination and intent, Conzelman opened training camp in early August at Carroll College in Waukesha, Wisconsin. The coach plotted a rigid training encampment, with no thrills or luxuries to distract the players. He immediately installed curfew rules, with the day beginning promptly at 8:00 A.M. for breakfast. Football would then consume the day until lights were out at 11:00 P.M. Conzelman's focus was clear; he had finally been given the players with the potential to contend in the NFL. "We've really got some football players on this team," he explained at the opening of training camp. "We never had anything like this squad when I was with the Cardinals before. We've got a new type of boy—studious, serious kids who want to play winning football." Conzelman added:

> We drill twice a day, a total of four hours, and between and after practice, we have study periods and skull sessions where we study plays, make explanations and work on assignments. I'm getting a tremendous thrill out of the way our men are working and I know the rest of the staff is, too.

Training camp was never easy for the players because few worked out in the off-season. "It wasn't in our regimen," laughed Vince Banonis. Players in the 1940s rarely lifted weights and aerobics were yet to be invented. Marshall Goldberg preferred running:

> We had no pre-season training requirements. Most players worked out on their own. I liked to run uphill. I'm from West Virginia so that's how I got in shape.

Amiable tackle Chet Bulger initiated a solitary routine a week or two before training camp opened:

> In the afternoons, I'd go over to Jackson Park in Chicago. I'd tee up a football, kick it off, run after it and then walk back. Conditioning back then was for breathing and your lungs. But when you got to training camp, it was like you never ran before! It was brutal.

The 1946 season also introduced another challenge to the Cardinals when the new All-America Football Conference plunked down some big bucks for top players and dropped another team in Chicago called the Chicago Rockets. The Rockets compiled a competitive eleven, highlighted by gifted flanker Elroy "Crazy Legs" Hirsch. The core of the team was comprised of wartime veterans, including seventeen Rockets who played together for the El Toro Marines. The Rockets targeted Soldier Field as their home base and Chicagoans were faced with the task of supporting three professional football teams.

## The San Francisco Cardinals?

The league itself issued some startling news during its winter meetings when Commissioner Elmer Layden was suddenly replaced. Layden arrived at the league meetings prepared to supervise a secret draft on January 10. Instead, the league was met with the announcement that the New York Yankees of the All-America Football Conference had pirated away the Lions' Frankie Sinkwich. This was the biggest slap in the face yet by the new conference, since Sinkwich was the NFL's most valuable player in 1944. Perhaps Layden's dismissal was related to the growing threat of the new conference, but it still was a surprise to Edward Prell of the *Tribune*:

> Elmer Layden is out as commissioner of the National Football League. You never fire a gentleman and the word could have been coined for Elmer. Tonight, the ten owners, in a surprise maneuver, eased out the man . . . Bert Bell, a stocky 52-year-old native of Philadelphia, is the new chief of the 26 year old profes-

*sional football league. In half an hour's time the magnates made this drastic change . . .*

The owners then proceeded to approve legislation that would not allow the NFL to include more than ten teams, thus prohibiting any merger with teams from the new league. Players were already banned from playing in the NFL for five years if they had been employed by a team from an "unrecognized" (i.e. the All-America Conference) league.

When the formation of the All-America Football Conference was announced in 1945, the NFL worked quickly to head off the very real threat posed by the new circuit. The older league aligned itself with the Pacific Coast, Dixie, and American Association football leagues. Former Chicagoan Rufus Klawans was the President of the Pacific Coast League and an active participant in the discussions which were intended to provide a type of group therapy for the four leagues against the stress of the All-America Football Conference. The PCL had operated alone on the West Coast for several years, but its influence was threatened when the All-America group announced plans to place teams in San Francisco and Los Angeles. On the other hand, the NFL had not bothered to harvest the large market of fans on the West Coast up until that time, and the All-America group was clearly pointing in that direction.

In a somewhat surprising move, the NFL also approved the transfer of the league champion Cleveland Rams to Los Angeles. The vote was unanimous on paper, but the other owners were apparently swayed by threats of Rams owner Dan Reeves. If not allowed to move to Dallas or Los Angeles, Reeves asserted that he would be forced to pull his franchise from the NFL. In particular, the other owners were not enthralled with the difficulty—and expense—of traveling to California for games. Reeves was absolutely pleased with the decision:

> *Long before I came into pro football, back in 1937, I decided some day to have a team in Los Angeles. Such a move has been my long range program since I came into the league . . . The extra cost is incidental. When you consider we have an attendance possibility of 90,000 or more if we obtain that coliseum. We are making the shift not that we love Cleveland less, but Los Angeles more.*

As it was, the NFL would now compete face-to-face with the new circuit in the three highly visible cities of Chicago, New York, and Los Angeles. And, for the first time, the National Football League would truly be a "nationwide" organization. However, the NFL would now be directly in battle with the Pacific Coast League's Hollywood and Los Angeles entries for fan recognition and support. PCL President Klawans had journeyed to New York for these meetings in the hope of finalizing its agreements with the NFL regarding player transactions, territorial rights, and access to NFL player talent. Klawans was preparing significant plans for the PCL's future and hoped that it would eventually achieve "major league" status. To iron out these difficulties, the NFL agreed to the following considerations for its allies in the Pacific Coast League, according to the *Associated Press*, where the NFL would:

> *1. Guarantee part of any losses suffered by the coast loop's Hollywood and Los Angeles clubs if both the All-America and National have teams in Los Angeles.*

2. *Give the Coast League's San Francisco Clippers first chance to move into the National if a San Francisco franchise is opened in the future.*

3. *Not to conflict with playing dates of the Coast circuit's Los Angeles Bulldogs next season.*

*Several National League clubs immediately hooked up in working agreements with teams of the other loops. The Green Bay Packers got together with the Coast circuit's San Diego outfit; the Washington Redskins with Hollywood in California and Norfolk, VA in the Dixie League; the Boston Yanks with the American Association's Long Island Indians, which they own, and the Dixie's Portsmouth, VA club; and the New York Giants with San Francisco and Paterson, NJ.*

In a more surprising development, the Chicago Cardinals were very close to becoming the San Francisco Cardinals. With the All-America Football Conference placing a team in San Francisco, the NFL was apparently ready to ask the Chicago Cardinals to transfer its franchise to the same city. Sportswriter Lee Owen of the *San Francisco Chronicle* broke the story during the meetings of the Pacific Coast League owners on February 10, 1946:

*The Pacific Coast Professional Football League, meeting here yesterday in the first of two, probably three-day session, took no action in its initial meeting on a reported move to transfer the Chicago Cardinals, National Football league team, to this city in opposition to the invasion already made by the All-America Football Conference club which is to be coached by Lawrence T. Buck Shaw.*

*There were covert admissions from several sources, however, that the move of the Cardinals would be taken up and that action probably would be forthcoming before the session is ended. It was admitted that the NFL had been negotiating for some kind of an arrangement by which it could come to San Francisco, take over the contractual playing dates of the San Francisco Clippers in Kezar Stadium and thus give the league a firm footing in this city against the All-Americas . . .*

*Frank Ciraolo, owner of the San Francisco Clipper franchise in the Pacific Coast League, said he was not in a position to comment regarding any negotiations or any plans to move the Chicago team to this city. He refused to deny, however, that the matter was under discussion.*

Owen further speculated that the move of the Cardinals was imminent when Rufus Klawans, president of the Pacific Coast League, discussed possible expansion plans. If new franchises were granted to Salt Lake City, Honolulu, and Sacramento, these teams would join Seattle, Portland, Oakland, San Diego, and Hollywood in an eight-team circuit. Where, then, was San Francisco? Also missing was the team from Los Angeles (the Hollywood Bears), a team that had been organized in 1939 by former Cardinals coach Paul Schissler.

On February 11, another reporter from the *Chronicle*, Will Connolly, picked up on the possible journey of the Chicago Cardinals:

*J. Rufus Klawans, president and commissioner, tactfully avoided mention of the possibility of the Chicago Cardinals moving into San Francisco as the Cleveland*

*Rams did recently to Los Angeles in a gesture of combating the newly-organized All-America Football Conference. "We just concluded a working agreement with the National regarding players' contracts and territorial rights," Klawans said. "I have the future assurance that when the National decides to expand toward the coast, the Bay area will get a franchise. Of course, this doesn't necessarily mean the San Francisco Clippers. The Oakland Giants have a territorial interest, too."*

In Hawaii, the *Honolulu Advertiser* speculated that neither the Chicago Cardinals nor the San Francisco Clippers would be left out in the cold in this expansion chaos. Instead, the *Advertiser* hinted at still another interesting possibility to add to the rumor mill:

*Klawans said he "doubted that the National Football League would come into San Francisco with a team before 1947," despite persistent rumors that the San Francisco Clippers would merge shortly with the Chicago Cardinals.*

*The San Francisco News* returned with still another interpretation of the situation on February 12, 1946:

*The national league will bring a team to our town this year. It will be one of three already established concerns in the old loop; namely the Green Bay Packers, Chicago Cardinals or the Boston Yanks, probably one of the latter two. The Cardinals probably are the logical ground-breakers for San Francisco territory and they have enough players and promotional experience for a pioneering, claim-staking fight with the All-America loop.*

Despite all of the coastal posturing, the Chicago media had little or nothing to say about the proposed move. Ultimately, the *San Francisco Examiner* capped this outburst by noting the following solution to the seemingly endless speculation:

*Commissioner Rufus Klawans announced that the Bay area had ceded territorial rights to the National Football League when a franchise was open, but that the San Francisco Clippers would have major financial control of such club coming in here, with the Oakland Giants participating in a minor stock ownership.*

Obviously, the Chicago Cardinals never did make the trek westward to San Francisco and the validity of this possibility may never be known. However, William V. Bidwill, the current owner of the Arizona Cardinals, recently recalled the possible move of the Cardinals to California:

*There was a possibility of the Cardinals moving to California in 1946, but Dan Reeves received a commitment to move the Rams from cleveland to Los Angeles before he went into the service.*

As such, pro football became the first "big league" sports organization to flirt with the West Coast.

## A Guy That Tough, I Wanted

In 1946, the Chicago Cardinals would also attempt to recapture their dwindling fan base, eroded over the years because of too few home games and too few wins. Bidwill would schedule four home games at Comiskey Park, the most in several years. The team would also benefit from the return of many fans who had been in the service, but who had followed the team via letters from home. One such veteran was legendary Chicago sportswriter Bill Gleason, who kept tabs on the team through letters from his father. Despite the recent avalanche of losses, Gleason and his friends were certain that the Cardinals would be vastly improved "once the real players got back." Gleason once wrote: "We had no idea of how dramatic the change would be. While we were away, Bidwill had been hoarding draft choices and making astute trades."

Two of those important Cardinals draft choices, Marlin "Pat" Harder from Wisconsin and Elmer Angsman of Notre Dame, would begin the 1946 season in the camp of the College All-Stars. But both would quickly impress Conzelman with their skills and work ethics once they joined the Cardinals. Harder, with his trademark crew cut and tenacity on the field, would be a strong addition to the backfield. At Wisconsin, he led the Big Ten in scoring in 1941 and later was named the league's MVP. He then added the MVP title from the 1943 College All-Star game (which was open to under-grads during the war) before spending twenty-two months in the Marines. Harder would also prove to be an excellent placekicker. Angsman, on the other hand, was some-what of a question mark for the Cardinals. He wasn't huge (5'11", 190 pounds) and he was so very young (twenty) compared to the other players in the first postwar train-ing camp. But one thing that appealed to Conzelman was his determination. Former Notre Dame player Jack Connor, in his book, *Leahy's Lads,* described one unforget-table play against Navy in 1945 involving Angsman which forever established his dogged determination:

> It was a very physical game as Elmer Angsman could attest. In the middle of the first quarter, Navy's Dick Scott, a linebacker, caught Angsman with a forearm in the mouth, knocking out his four upper front teeth and causing his four lower front teeth to be jammed into his gums. He ran to the sidelines where he was met by (Coach Hugh) Devore, who was shocked by the severity of Angsman's injury. Devore said, "Elmer, you better go to the locker room."
>
> Through a mouth that was spurting blood, Angsman replied, "No, I don't want to. I want to go back in." The Notre Dame trainer stopped the flow of blood the best he could, applied some pain medication, and with gauze packing his mouth, Angsman went back in the game. He played 54 minutes that day despite his injury. No one ever doubted his toughness or his devotion to the team, and with his dis-play of courage that day, Angsman assured his place in the folklore of Notre Dame football.

Playing both halfback and fullback at Notre Dame, Angsman led his 1945 team in scoring and yardage, averaging 7.1 yards per carry. Conzelman also learned of Angsman's bravery in the Navy game and once said:

> Angsman was no heralded star at Notre Dame, but an incident in his college career really impressed me. Against Navy, he was hit so hard in the mouth that

*he spit teeth like kernels of pop corn. Yet I found out that he was back on the practice field the following Monday. A guy that tough, I wanted.*

But most important to the Cardinals' South Side followers was the fact that Angsman grew up in that end of the city (around 77th Street and May) and attended nearby Mt. Carmel High School. "He was one of our own," said Bill Gleason.

Another newcomer, albeit not from the South Side, was center Bill Blackburn. At 6'6", 225 pounds, Blackburn was twice an All-Conference pick out of Rice Institute (now University) in Texas. He spent forty-two months in the Marines and saw action in places like Guam, Saipan, and Okinawa. Conzelman was reportedly so interested in landing the services of Blackburn that he asked a friend to watch Blackburn's house in Houston so that he could sign him for the Cardinals as soon as Blackburn returned from the service. Blackburn remembers it this way:

*I knew I had been drafted by the Chicago Cardinals in 1944, but you didn't know a great deal about pro football back then. I went into the service and we were finishing up on Okinawa when the peace agreement was signed. I remained in the service until May of 1946 and flew back to Ft. Worth, Texas. When I got to Ft. Worth, I phoned my mother from the train station and told her when I would be home. I didn't make any other calls. When my train arrived, I was met by my mother, my father, my sister, and Buddy Parker, the assistant coach from the Cardinals! I still don't know how he found out, but he was there to talk to me about playing football with the Cardinals. At that time, the All-American Conference was offering large contracts in the range of $4,000-$4,5000 per year, so it was a good time for the players. My uncle helped me negotiate with the Carindals and eventually Jimmy Conzelman came down to Houston to meet with us. When we got up to $5,500 per season, my uncle said that if the Cardinals could only offer me $5,500 per year, then he could just as well hire me to work for him. I had enough sense to smile at the right time, and I did sign with the Cardinals for $5,500 per year in 1946. But I still don't know how Buddy Parker knew about my train arrival!*

One other major hole was filled when tackle Stan Mauldin was added to stabilize the line. Mauldin (6'2", 220 pounds) was another addition from the University of Texas. After being named the university's "Outstanding Athlete" in 1942, Mauldin spent three years in the Air Corps and piloted thirty-five bombing missions. At guard, the Cardinals could count on Garrard "Buster" Ramsey, who had originally signed with the team in 1943 before spending three years in the Navy. Ramsey (6'1", 210 pounds) was an All-American at William and Mary and was also a member of the College All-Stars squad in 1946.

All in all, Bidwill and Conzelman had assembled an extraordinary array of talent. It was a confident, mature group that embarked for Conzelman's training camp in August of 1946. This was the largest such gathering of Cardinals players in the team's history. It compared overwhelmingly with the twelve players who started things off at the 1945 camp before reinforcements arrived.

Conzelman worked the squad through three weeks of arduous training before meeting the Newark (NJ) Bombers of the American League at Newark on September 7.

Conzelman studied his options for the Cardinals, already being hailed as the most improved team in the league, and decided that the best way to utilize this immense amount of talent would be to break from the usual football paradigm. Instead of using just eleven players and having them play both offense and defense, Conzelman announced that he would use the exhibition game against Newark to test a radical new concept. He decided to scrap the usual process and utilized two "starting" lines, one for offense and one for defense, without labeling either of them as the "starters."

He further astonished the football world by declaring that the Cardinals possessed three talented quarterbacks (Paul Christman, Ray Mallouf, and Jim Reynolds) and that each quarterback would work with his own separate backfield. Against Newark, it took only three plays for the formidable Cardinals to score as returnee Frank Seno blasted seventy yards for the initial tally. Then (in order), Angsman, Kutner, Dewell, Wilford Garnaas, and James Strausbaugh scored in the first half as the Chicagoans rolled up a 42-0 advantage. Three other touchdowns of fifty-eight yards (Strausbaugh), fifty-five yards (Reynolds), and sixty-four yards (Harder) were called back because of penalties. The Cardinals settled for a 48-6 victory when Cuff added a pair of second-half field goals. On September 13, the team closed out its exhibition season with a 47-0 rout of Greensboro (NC) of the Dixie League and remained in North Carolina to prepare for the league opener at Pittsburgh on Friday, September 20.

## *Greater Crowds Are Seeing Better Football*

Meanwhile, pro football was booming. On September 13, 1946, 92,800 watched the Bears face the Eagles in Philadelphia in an exhibition game, while back in Chicago, 51,962 showed up in Soldier Field to watch the upstart Chicago Rockets face the Cleveland Browns in an All-America Football Conference contest. This huge crowd shattered the record for professional attendance at a pro game in Chicago and proved that the new league was for real. With its solid financial backing, along with the editorial resources of the *Chicago Tribune* behind it, the new conference was poised to make its own indelible impact.

The Cardinals were concerned about their own impact on the NFL in 1946, and Conzelman anxiously awaited the match with Pittsburgh, which would provide insight as to how well his team would fare against big-league competition. While the two exhibitions were successful in terms of victories, they were actually little more than scrimmages against outmatched minor league opposition. The Steelers, just two seasons away from their inglorious partnership with the Cardinals in 1944, had some questions of their own to answer for new head coach Dr. John Bain "Jock" Sutherland. "I have a fair ball club but I won't know how good it is until tomorrow night," Sutherland commented the day before the game. "The Cardinals—like all other league entries—are much stronger this year."

Sutherland was taking over a team that finished 2-8 in 1945, but had opened up the 1946 campaign with four straight exhibition wins. In addition, Sutherland (Goldberg's college coach at Pittsburgh) was making a homecoming trek back to Pittsburgh in his first league game with his new professional team. The idea of watching two decent teams and observing the return of a popular local hero who had left town eight years earlier was enough to prompt the Pittsburgh fans to gobble up every ticket for this game. It was an unusual occurrence in recent Cardinals competition—a sell-out. "The pros are back from war and business is picking up on all fronts in the National Football League," gushed the weekly league press release. "Greater crowds are seeing better football in which the emphasis is on offense."

For the opener, Conzelman decided to start Mallouf at quarterback and went with four rookies in the lineup: Ramsey at guard, Harder at fullback, Al Hust (Tennessee) at end, and Loyd Arms (Oklahoma A & M) at the other guard. Goldberg and Seno would complete the backfield, Frank Ivy would return at the other end, Bob Zimny (Indiana) and Ralph Foster (Oklahoma A & M) would man the tackles, and Vince Banonis would handle the center spot.

Pittsburgh came out firing behind former Cardinals Johnny Clement and Steve Lach in front of the rain-soaked capacity crowd of 33,700. Following a Harder fumble on the Cardinals' forty-five-yard line, Lach led the Steelers down to the eight where Bill Dudley found Charles Seabright open for the first score. Pittsburgh increased that lead to 14-0 after Mallouf's punt was blocked and recovered on the Cards' thirty-three. Clement hit Val Jansante with a sixteen-yard pass that set up a one-yard scoring run by Tony Compagno. The Cardinals garnered their only tally late in the third quarter when Loyd Arms recovered a fumble at the Steelers' thirty-six. Goldberg then picked his way through the defense for a twenty-yard gain, and finally scored on a thirteen-yard pass from Mallouf.

Despite the 14-7 setback, Conzelman continued to work the club strenuously in practice, making adjustments to the "T" and attempting to eliminate the turnovers which proved to be so costly in the Pittsburgh battle. Bidwill brought Chicago its first taste of "Monday Night Football" when the Cardinals regrouped for their earliest home game in years on Monday night, September 29. It was the league opener for the Lions, a 7-3 club in 1945. Because of injuries, Conzelman restructured the left side of his line and inserted Dewell at end, Mauldin at tackle, J. C. "Jake" Colhouer at guard, and big Bill Blackburn in the middle. Colhouer (6'1", 210 pounds) had been a ninth-round draft choice out of Oklahoma A & M, and was a veteran of two College All-Star games.

Conzelman unveiled his "new" Cardinals for the first time in Chicago and stunned the crowd of 26,842 at Comiskey Park with an easy 34-14 win over the Lions. The evening started calmly enough when the Joliet (IL) VFW honored Detroit back Tippy Madarik, a Joliet native, before the game. Once the festivities concluded, the Cardinals blasted off to a surprising 28-0 halftime lead behind the running of rookie backs Elmer Angsman, Pat Harder, and Jim Strausbaugh. Harder scored on the twelfth play of the game from one yard out to earn a 7-0 advantage for the Cards after one period.

In the second period, Strausbaugh swept around right end for a six-yard score; Mallouf connected with Kutner on a long scoring pass; and then Christman found Dewell for a fifteen-yard touchdown toss. Suddenly it was 28-0, and the Cardinals of old were no more. The final score of 34-14 (Cuff added two second-half field goals) resulted in the most points scored against the Lions since 1934. But with only a "short" week remaining before the Cards' next game, Conzelman immediately jumped into preparations for the next adversary, due the following Sunday: George Halas and the Chicago Bears.

In particular, Conzelman drilled his defense in anticipation of the threat from George "One Play" McAfee. Conzelman's theme for the week was "Stop McAfee," a deceptive runner who could hurt you with his running or his kick returns. In very limited action in 1945, McAfee had averaged an astounding 8.6 yards per carry. Following practice each day, the Cardinals met with their coaches at the Hyde Park Hotel to confer on both offensive and defensive alignments. On the North Side, Halas was attempting to unlock the key to the Cardinals' potent offense, which comfortably interchanged several players without losing a step. Defensively, the Cardinals had restricted Detroit to minus-seventeen yards rushing, so Halas was aware of that threat as well.

For the first time in many years, a Cardinals game was enjoying widespread interest. Harry Warren wrote in the *Tribune*:

> *Chicago's Bears and Cardinals, representing the oldest rivalry in professional football, will renew the civil gridiron war, started back in 1920, at Comiskey Park today before what promises to be the largest gathering ever to see one of the series on the South Side.*
>
> *Only a few reserved seats were obtainable last night and at 9 A.M. this morning 20,000 grandstand seats will go on sale at Comiskey Park, which means that possibly the capacity of the park—some 49,500 spectators—will watch today's battle.*
>
> *Today will be the first meeting of teams coached by George Halas and Jimmy Conzelman since Pearl Harbor day, December 7, 1941. That battle, too, was in Comiskey Park. The Bears, taking advantage of an interference penalty called against the Cardinals, swept to a victory in the final periods of the game, 34-24. That interference penalty was responsible for a remark by Conzelman after the game to the effect that he "could build a defense to stop 11 men, but he had never gotten around to mold a defense capable of coping with 12 men."*

As it turned out, nearly 40,000 (39,263) were on hand in Comiskey Park to witness the duel. At that point in time, it was the largest home crowd in the Cardinals' long history. The fans on the South Side had finally built up some momentum for their club and showed up in throngs to cheer on their heroes. Although it was early in the season, the winner of this game would grab the lead in the Western Division.

With the temperature soaring past the eighty-degree mark, the two sturdy lines battled furiously throughout the opening quarter. The Cardinals finally nudged across a score late in the period when Jimmy Strausbaugh ran one in from the twelve. This score had been set up by a nifty thirty-six-yard run by Angsman and two critical passes from Christman to Goldberg and Dewell. Early in the second period, Ward Cuff succeeded on a seventeen-yard field goal attempt, and the feisty Cardinals owned a 10-0 lead.

The Bears retaliated with Hugh Gallarneau's seven-yard touchdown and it remained 10-7 at the break. Early in the second half, Christman and Dewell connected again. With the ball on the Cards' own eighteen, Christman dropped back and hurled a bomb that was grabbed by Dewell on the Bears' thirty-five. The tall Cardinals end faked out the final defender, Dick Schwelder, and raced in for the score as the advantage swelled to 17-7. It was the third longest touchdown pass (eighty-two yards) in Cardinals history at the time, surpassed only by the two Gaynell Tinsley gems in the late 1930s. The Bears were stopped on the ensuing drive, but a costly turnover by the Cards on their own nineteen enabled Sid Luckman to narrow the gap to 17-14 at the end of the third quarter.

But the smaller Cardinals line finally wore down in the heat and surrendered an unlikely three touchdowns in the final period as the Bears prevailed 34-17. Three lost fumbles proved to be deadly for the South Siders.

Despite the loss, the NFL was now fully aware of the Cardinals and the team's potent attack. If this was indeed the year of the "offense," then the Cards typified the new breed of team. An NFL weekly press release accurately depicted the Cardinals' assault forces:

> *The Cardinals are blending the speed of their star rookies, Elmer Angsman of Notre Dame, and Pat Harder of Wisconsin and Jim Strausbaugh of Ohio State, with the capable passing of Paul Christman and Ray Mallouf to achieve a balance of attack. They have picked up 467 yards on the ground and 413 in the air for a total of 880 yards in three starts, an average of 293 yards a game.*

Elmer Angsman had emerged as the leading rusher in the league after only three games and proved to be an immense surprise to a team which was virtually top-heavy with talented running backs. The Cards also unveiled a surprising new punter in center Bill Blackburn, who averaged forty-nine yards per kick against the Bears. Conzelman explained the selection of Blackburn for this duty:

> *It was just a hunch. I remembered Blackie had kicked a couple of good ones in practice and decided to try him out. He was standing 12 yards back, because he's a little slow getting the ball away. But it's the first time I've ever had a center who can boom that ball 70 yards.*

## There Was No Way He Could Catch That

Hoping to bounce back from the fourth-quarter collapse against the Bears, the Cardinals arrived in Detroit on Saturday, October 12, for a meeting with the Lions. Under the tutelage of Coach Gus Dorais, the Lions looked to rebound from the earlier 34-14 pasting at the hands of the Chicago Cardinals. Detroit had picked up one of the Cards' excess backs, Paul Sarringhaus, the week before the game. Conzelman made some changes as well. Dick Plasman, who had originally joined the squad strictly as a coach, was activated as a player. In addition, Ray Mallouf, who had missed the Bears game with injuries, was back in place, as was veteran Chet Bulger, who had missed several games at tackle. His return was expected to bolster the defense.

Against Detroit, in old Briggs Stadium, the Cardinals came out roaring and sprinted to a 27-0 halftime lead before finishing with an easy 36-14 win. Christman was on fire, completing 20 of 34 passes for 263 yards, including 4 touchdown passes. Billy Dewell was the primary target, leaping high to grab pass after pass. He scored two touchdowns, and then capped off his day with a stunning one-handed reception for thirty-eight yards that amazed both friends and foes. "There was no way he could catch that," remembers Chet Bulger. "Billy jumped as high as the goal posts, tapped the ball over their heads and caught the ball in the end zone. It was amazing." With Bulger back in the lineup, the Lions were held to a minus-twenty-four yards rushing and only six total first downs for the day.

The impressive destruction of the Lions, when held in comparison to the fourth quarter collapse against the Bears, was prompting some observers to suggest that the

Cardinals were either the best team in the NFL or one of the worst, depending on the day. Certainly Conzelman would strive to achieve a higher level of consistency throughout the season, especially in the second half of games. Yet, the campaign was young, and the Cardinals had already won two contests. This in itself was an achievement since the team had savored just one victory in the three previous seasons.

Christman's performance in Detroit vaulted him to the top of the league's passing ranks. Angsman, Harder, Seno, and Goldberg continued to saturate the opposition with hard-charging rushing out of the backfield. The next stop for Conzelman's crew was a date with the New York Giants (2-1) in the Polo Grounds on October 20.

The Cardinals' exciting reputation had already reached the East Coast and a Giants' home opener record crowd of 50,681 jammed into the stadium. The fans turned out to watch two strong teams in action, but they were also there to welcome back local legend Ward Cuff, who now lined up with the visiting team. Once again, the Cardinals swarmed out to an early lead with Cuff doing most of the damage. Following Goldberg's touchdown (which knotted the score at 7-7), Cuff scored on a short plunge, and then added the extra point and a forty-two-yard field goal to stretch the Cardinals' lead to 17-7 at the half.

The Giants fought back to grab a 21-17 advantage early in the fourth quarter right before one of the most exciting plays in the history of the game occurred. Following the Giants' scoring drive, Frank Seno was sent out to await the kickoff. The long, arching kick drove him back five yards into the end zone, where he calmly viewed the protection his teammates were setting up in front of him. Never hesitating, Seno scrambled right up the middle, picking his way through the Giants' defense behind his blockers. Around midfield, he suddenly swept to his left and with a burst of speed managed to outdistance the remaining defenders. When he crossed the goal line, Seno had traveled an amazing105 yards, which was good enough for a new NFL record for longest kickoff return. His merry jaunt surpassed the mark of 102 yards set in 1934 by former Cardinal Doug Russell.

Now leading 24-21 in the fourth quarter, the Cardinals only needed to hold off the Giants for a few more minutes.  But the Giants, who would go on to capture the Eastern Division title, were not finished. With time running out, quarterback Frank Filchock found Frank Liebel with a pass play that Ward Cuff apparently stopped with a fine tackle on the Cards' five-yard line. But while heading down, the inventive Liebel lateraled to a wide-open Howie Livingston, who strolled in for the winning touchdown. It was the second bad break administered by Livingston on this day. Earlier, he had scored on a fumble recovery for the Giants' first touchdown. The early and late scores by Livingston helped the Giants grab a 28-24 victory.

## This Is The Finest Squad I've Ever Coached

The defeat was a tough one for the Cardinals, but it failed to diminish the zeal of Conzelman: "This is the finest squad I've ever coached," he remarked after the New York loss. "It hasn't deserved to lose. It has spirit and ability. We led both the Bears and Giants for three quarters and got beat in the final period." The team's confidence and personality was beginning to catch on as well. For a club that had prevailed in just three games in four years, it was starting to acquire more than just passing interest from the press. Christman remained the league's top passer, Cuff had become the circuit's leading scorer, and the defense under Phil Handler had suddenly become very frugal, especially for opposing runners. All of these parts were combining to push the once lowly Cards to the edge of greatness. Added to this mixture was a healthy dose of spirit, which *Chicago Daily News* columnist John P. Carmichael noted following the New York game:

> *Pat Harder, the Cardinal fullback, was squirming along the ground with a couple of Giants trying to stop that "inching" for extra yardage. An official, waiting for him to get up, said: "If you keep on doing that, you'll have to take the consequences . . ." meaning that Pat was asking for piling on by such tactics.*
> *"Never mind," snapped the former Wisconsin star, "you just tend to your job!"*
> *This happened only last Sunday in New York. Even a year ago, not to go back further, the Cards weren't big enough to talk back to anybody. You don't annoy officials when you're down.*

The rapid development of Angsman and Harder was paying immediate dividends for the Cardinals both on offense and defense. With an abundance of skillful players, Conzelman was able to pick and choose the right situations for the right type of player. While both were able to contribute offensively, Conzelman began to use them both in concert with Goldberg in the defensive backfield as well. The sixth game of the season would showcase the Los Angeles Rams and their great quarterback, Bob Waterfield. Waterfield, who was married to film star Jane Russell, looked most often to receiver Jim Benton in the Rams' offensive attack. Benton was the league's top receiver in 1945 and was now joined by two other luminaries from the Rams' backfield, Tom Harmon and Kenny Washington. Washington and teammate Woody Strode were the first black athletes to play in the league since Joe Lillard had departed the Cardinals over a decade before. As the defending NFL champions (when the team was in Cleveland), the Rams would be a good measuring device in determining how far the Cardinals had progressed as a team.

Another huge crowd approaching the forty thousand mark showed up at Comiskey Park and found out that the Cardinals were indeed "for real." Buoyed by the electrifying passing of Christman and the staunch defense of Goldberg, the Cardinals scored early and often to swamp the Rams 34-10 as reported by Bill Fay in the *Tribune*:

> *The crowd of 38,180 which visited Comiskey Park yesterday afternoon to watch Bob Waterfield and Jim Benton—the famed passing combination of the champion Rams—went home talking about Paul Christman and Bill Dewell. Paul pitched and Bill caught. The aerial act spearheaded a five touchdown attack which gave the Cardinals a 34-10 triumph.*
> *Gone were the second half jitters which caused their downfall at the hands of the Bears and Giants. The Cards were a 60 minute ball club. They bottled up Benton. They stopped Waterfield with vital interceptions—two by Marshall Goldberg, who also started the first touchdown drive with a fumble recovery. They turned loose a pair of slashing backs in Pat Harder and Frank Seno, and whenever they needed yardage in chunks—Christman threw to Dewell.*

On that day, Christman succeeded on 16 out of 30 passes for 226 yards. Dewell claimed 5 of those tosses for 101 yards and a touchdown. Once again, the lanky receiver had them gasping with his leaping acrobatic receptions, including a pair inside the five which set up two Cardinals touchdowns. Christman was pitchin' all over the place, hitting receivers near and far such as Dewell, Seno, Goldberg, Harder, Strausbaugh, and Kutner. No defense was safe from Christman and his talented arsenal of receivers as the quarterback continued to lead the league in passing over Sammy Baugh of the Redskins and Sid Luckman of the Bears.

The victory briefly revived the Cards' hopes of contending for the Western Division title since the team (3-3) was just a step behind the Bears (3-1-1) in the race. Moving into the backstretch of the league season, the Cardinals traveled to Boston for a date with the winless Yanks. For once, the Cardinals were heavily favored in this game, which would feature former teammate Johnny Grigas and future teammate Babe Dimancheff. In the Boston game, won by the Cardinals 28-14, the team finally demonstrated some consistency. The Cards scored in each quarter, and were never really threatened. Christman and Mallouf shared the passing duties, with Christman collecting 13 out of 21 for 191 yards. As usual, Dewell was quite visible, adding 6 catches for 109 yards.

Mallouf and Kutner collaborated on another unusual touchdown as part of an eighty-three-yard score in the third quarter. Mallouf completed a toss to Kutner for what looked to be a nice thirty-one-yard gain. But Kutner spotted his cohort Bill Blackburn nearby and tossed the ball to him as Kutner was being tackled. Blackburn then lumbered the remaining fifty-two yards for the score.

The Cardinals' offense was now difficult to ignore and the weekly NFL press release on November 11 confirmed what the rest of the league was beginning to fear:

> Any lingering doubt over the right of Jimmy Conzelman's young Chicago Cardinals to be classed as championship contenders in the National Football League is dispelled by the latest official statistics.
>
> Cardinals hold the No. 1 position in passing, scoring, kickoff returns and field goal kicking and are represented among the leaders in every department of individual effort except punt returns.
>
> The up and coming Chicago Cardinals continue to be the National Football League's offensive leader, setting the pace on the basis of yards gained as well as points scored . . . Official statistics released today show the Cardinals gaining ground at the rate of 345.2 yards per game over a span of seven contests . . .

Now 4-3 and generally feared by every team in the league, the Cardinals of 1946 prompted their coach to reflect a little on the recent past before the next contest at Green Bay (3-3):

> This certainly is not like the old daze, and I do mean d-a-z-e. My biggest trouble is to keep the team free from overconfidence. I think we have learned our lesson, however, in that respect. We lost to the Bears and the Giants because of overconfidence, but hereafter we will wait until the final whistle before we start counting up a victory. The boys realize we still have a chance of winning the western division title and they are ready to give anybody a helluva debate on the subject.

The game between the two old rivals was critical for both squads. Both teams were still in the division title chase, but a loss would drop either out of contention. The meeting would also provide an intriguing sidelight; the Cardinals' offense was the best in the league while the Packers' defense was at the top of that category.

In the end, the defense didn't rest. Forcing Paul Christman to set a team record with five fumbles, the Packers' swarming defenders were all over the Cardinals' quarterback, and the visitors churned out a 19-7 upset before a Comiskey Park crowd of 30,691. The two teams combined for eleven fumbles (eight turnovers) in a sloppy game impeded by the cold, damp weather. A Christman to Seno pass for thirty-four yards in the third quarter was all the scoring the Cards could muster.

With three games left and no chance for any championship recognition, the Cardinals embarked on a three-day train ride to Los Angeles. The next game against the Rams on November 17 would mark the team's first foray out to California for a league game. The team still frowned upon air travel, so the players piled on for the long, numbing ride west. However, the long train rides were experiences that are still remembered fondly by the players. "One time we got off of the train in Nevada and worked out," recalled Marshall Goldberg. "It really wasn't too bad for our conditioning. We would usually arrive on a Saturday and work out in Los Angeles right away, then play the game on Sunday." Chet Bulger outlined some of the mischief that always seemed to accompany the Cardinals:

> *One year they tried to put big blocking dummies in the baggage car. We were supposed to go down there and hit the dummies. That didn't go over too well because there were no showers on the train. We did that once or twice and smelled like a bunch of goats.*

## Stay Away From The Sand Boxes And Swings

Upon arriving in Los Angeles, the Cardinals discovered that their arrival at the Alexandria Hotel had coincided with the tail end of a three-day rain deluge. While the rain had stopped, most local fields were still very wet and no one was very anxious for the Cardinals to use their facilities for a much-needed practice. The innovative Conzelman finally convinced the manager of a city playground in downtown Los Angeles to allow his team to practice at that location. He then explained the ground rules to his bemused players in the hotel lobby in front of some confused bellhops and other assorted guests:

> *I want to make one thing very plain before we go out to practice. I want you guys to stay away from the sand boxes and the swings. And stay off the merry-go-round. It would just be our luck for Christman to fall off the giraffe and break his arm— Paul's—not the giraffe's. Let's go!*

The defending champion Rams (3-3-1) had crawled back into a third-place tie with the Cardinals (4-4) and were still smarting from the mugging absorbed earlier in the season at the hands of the Cardinals. Once again, it would be the passing combinations of Christman and Dewell versus Bob Waterfield and Jim Benton which were expected to decide the outcome of this game. "We'll be all right if it doesn't rain," explained Conzelman. "A wet field spoils our passing offense and we haven't enough big backs to shift to a slugging ground game. Also, we have the smallest line in the league. It needs dry footing for traction to develop charging speed."

The rain moved away in time for the game on November 17 in front of 38,271 in the Los Angeles Coliseum. As Conzelman predicted, the dry field encouraged an aerial duel between Christman and Waterfield, and that is exactly what ensued. Christman, however, was a little shaky. Four of his passes were intercepted, including one in the first quarter by Waterfield that led to the game's first score: a forty-yard field goal by Waterfield.

The Rams' quarterback was back at it again early in the second period when his short passes to Tom Harmon and Fred Gehrke set up Gehrke's nine-yard scoring dash. Down 10-0, Christman and Dewell then connected on a fifty-two-yard scoring pass to narrow the gap to 10-7. Starting from his own forty-eight, Christman found Dewell on the Rams' forty where the receiver headed for the right side in an attempt to elude the Rams' defenders. Fred Naumetz lunged at Dewell at the twenty and knocked his helmet off in the process. But it wasn't enough to stop the Cards' top receiver and he sprinted bare headed into the end zone.

In the very next offensive series, Mallouf completed his only pass of the day, but it was a thirty-one-yard scoring effort to Mal Kutner. Kutner displayed some of his 9.7 speed which had garnered him some 100-yard dash championships at the University of Texas. Ward Cuff added the extra point and suddenly the Cardinals were up 14-10 at the half. The two teams battled throughout the third quarter with no further scoring, and the visitors retained their four-point lead entering the final period. But in true Hollywood style, Waterfield rode to the Rams' rescue late in the game. Taking advantage of a Cardinals fumble on the Rams' thirty-nine, Waterfield reversed the direction of the game with his pinpoint passing and leadership. With just two minutes remaining, he spotted Steve Pritko in the end zone and mailed a twenty-eight-yard touchdown pass, enabling the Rams to escape with a 17-14 victory. Waterfield demonstrated why he was the best in the league that day. In addition to passing for 162 yards, he kicked a field goal, intercepted 3 passes, and kept the Cards in the hole by averaging 47 yards per punt.

Following the long train ride back to the cold environs of Chicago, the Cardinals would finish the season with games against the top two teams in the league: the Green Bay Packers and the Chicago Bears. The league did not provide the Cards with any favors, either, by sending the team immediately up to Green Bay after the journey from Southern California. Conzelman attempted to squeeze in a couple of practices in Comiskey Park as soon as the team arrived back in Chicago, but the club's equipment was delayed, forcing the coach to alter his plans. The Cardinals did manage to practice on the Friday and Saturday mornings prior to the game before catching a train to Green Bay on Saturday afternoon.

Since the Packers (5-3) were still in the Western Division title race behind the Bears (6-1-1), their match with the Cardinals (4-5) was extremely important. With a more leisurely week of practice, the Packers were able to concentrate on solving the Cardinals' passing attack. Impressed by Mallouf's performance in Los Angeles, Conzelman added to the Packers' worries by announcing that Mallouf would probably share time with Christman in the upcoming game. This would mean that the Packers would need to prepare for the styles of both quarterbacks, or it could be just another

Conzelman ruse to force his opponents to burn up practice time on devising the means to stop two quarterbacks instead of just one.

Fans in Green Bay were excited not only by the game, but also by a widely publicized "homecoming" for Packers stars of the past. During halftime, Dr. D. W. Kelly, the second president of the team, was scheduled to introduce the All-Time Packers All-Stars as selected by the Green Bay fans. A cold, dark drizzle limited the crowd to 16,150, who watched as the teams sloshed to a 3-3 halftime tie behind field goals from Ward Cuff and Ted Fritsch. The Packers gained the lead (6-3) after three periods when Fritsch nailed a kick from thirty-six yards out. With the skies darkening, the lights were finally turned on in the fourth quarter, and the Cardinals' outlook also brightened.

Beginning from his own twenty, Christman scattered tosses to Kutner, Goldberg, and Harder to set up his own one-yard quarterback sneak for the Cards' first touchdown. Moments later, the offense was back in business when Kutner picked off an Irv Comp pass at the Packers' thirty-three-yard line. This time, Christman aimed for Dewell, and found his favorite target for a twenty-three-yard gain. Following a shifty run by Angsman, Goldberg picked up the touchdown from the one. The Cardinals moved ahead 17-6 and completed the convincing 24-6 win when Angsman broke away for a sixty-one-yard score off right tackle. Green Bay's loss, coupled with the Bears' 42-6 trouncing of Detroit, clinched the Western Division title for the Bears.

## Ivy Is The Best Defensive End In The League

The lightning-quick fourth-quarter offensive barrage against Green Bay pleased Conzelman, and he looked forward to the final, although meaningless, game against the Bears. He eased back on practices and urged his players to relax:

> *No use overdoing a good thing. Our offense has worked well all year. We were ahead of the Bears, 17-7, the first time we played them—then our defense cracked. We think we have the answer to that sitting over there.*

Conzelman was referring to his decision to "platoon" offensive stars Christman and Dewell with fullback Walt Rankin and end Frank Ivy when the team was on defense. This would allow Christman and Dewell to earn some needed rest during the game while positioning the tough defensive abilities of Rankin and Ivy right where the team needed them. Conzelman had also shuffled end Mal Kutner to the defensive backfield following the earlier loss to the Bears. Conzelman added:

> *That Rankin has become a great line backer-upper in the last few months. And Ivy is the best defensive end in the league. If they play the game they can play, the Bears won't score 34 points against us this time.*

In an era when players still played both offense and defense during the game, Conzelman's strategy helped sustain morale and encouraged a mode of "team" contributions rather than individual accolades. For example, Ivy and Rankin had both been with the team for five years, and had demonstrated that they were capable of making solid offensive contributions. Yet with the dominating backfield of Christman, Goldberg, Harder, and Angsman, along with Dewell and Kutner at the ends, the opportunities for other players to frolic on offense were limited. It was a nice problem for a coach to have, and Conzelman admitted as much:

> *We'd like to give them the chance. Naturally Pat Harder's been our offensive full back. The only time I remember Rankin carrying the ball was in Boston. He went 60 yards for a touchdown—and the play was called back by an offside penalty.*

Since the team was finally enjoying some success, the players seemed to accept their roles and appeared to have some fun with the situation. William Fay told this locker room tale in the *Chicago Tribune:*

> *After practice yesterday, Christman was dressing near Rankin. Walter pointed to the quarterback and said to Ivy: "I've seen that fellow somewhere—his face looks familiar."*
> *"It should," Ivy said. "We pass him about 12 times every Sunday—on the way to the bench."*
> *"So we do," Rankin agreed. "You know, I'd like to meet him in a huddle some time. He's probably a very nice fellow."*

## *The Bears Scarcely Knew What Hit Them*

Thus, the relaxed Cardinals moved up to Wrigley Field on December 1 to finish the 1946 season against the Bears. This time, the game between the two intense rivals attracted a huge crowd of 47,511. In return, they were treated to one of the most wildly exciting games in the history of professional football in Chicago. It all started out looking like a rout; surprisingly the 21-7 advantage in the second quarter was held by the upstart Cardinals. The Bears grabbed a 7-0 first-quarter lead before the Cards answered with a three-touchdown barrage in less than three minutes of the second quarter.

First, Christman and Angsman combined on a forty-two-yard pass play which led to Christman's thirty-three-yard scoring toss to Kutner.

Next, Garrard Ramsey recovered a Sid Luckman fumble on the Bears' twenty-six. An offside penalty moved the ball back to the thirty-one from where Pat Harder took it in on a delay play up the middle.

Finally, the Cards kicked off again and on the first play from scrimmage, Bill Blackburn recovered a Hugh Gallarneau fumble on the Bears' thirty-two. This time, Marshall Goldberg completed a second consecutive "one-play" drive while duplicating Harder's delay play and scrambling the thirty-two yards for the score.

It took the Cardinals just two minutes and fourteen seconds to hoist a 21-7 lead and stun the division champion Bears. Much to their credit, the Bears rebounded early in the second half with Luckman reducing the margin to 21-14 after a five-yard scoring pass to Dante Magnani. Pat Harder pushed the lead back up to two touchdowns when he followed his own forty-two-yard run with a three-yard touchdown dash to close out the third quarter with the Cardinals apparently safely ahead 28-14.

The Cards were still out in front 28-21 with less than four minutes to go when the Bears took over for the final time on the Cards' forty-one-yard line. Taking advantage of a roughing penalty on the Cardinals, Luckman guided his team down to the one, where Joe Osmanski tied the game at 28-28 with just fifty-five seconds remaining. As many satisfied football fans began to leave after witnessing the thrilling, high-scoring game, Christman decided that the game was not yet over. Surprisingly, the Bears were not willing to settle for the hard-fought tie and attempted to catch the Cardinals off-guard with an onside kick. Frank Maznicki's looping kick precipitated a huge pile-up of players, and the officials were challenged with the task of trying to unclog the field. When the usual pushing, shoving, grappling, and gouging concluded, the Cardinals were awarded the ball at midfield. This decision so incensed the Bears that Halas's team was penalized fifteen yards for disputing the call too vociferously. With precious few seconds remaining, and the ball on the Bears' thirty-five, Christman quickly found Mal Kutner for a thirty-yard gain. Down to just a few seconds, but with the ball on the five, Christman returned to Kutner across the middle for the winning touchdown with just fourteen seconds remaining on the clock. As William Fay wrote: "It all happened so fast that the Bears scarcely knew what hit them."

What the Cardinals did know was that they finished the 1946 season with a 6-5 record, the first time in eleven years that the team finished above the .500 mark. This record was good for third place in the Western Division, but more importantly, positioned the Chicago Cardinals for a definite run at the championship in 1947. But could a team that had finished 1-9 just the year before accumulate enough ammunition to fight for the top prize so quickly? With most key players in place and the strong finish to the 1946 season, John Carmichael wrote an early prediction for 1947 in the *Daily News*:

> *Now, for the first time in years, the Cards "belong" in the pro grid upper strata. They have a chance to beat anybody whenever they walk on to the field.*

The pieces were beginning to fall into place for the Chicago Cardinals. With a solid duo at quarterback (Paul Christman, Ray Mallouf), a pair of sure-handed receivers (Billy Dewell, Mal Kutner), three hungry running backs (Marshall Goldberg, Pat Harder, Elmer Angsman), and a rugged group of aggressive linemen, the Cardinals could hardly wait for the 1947 season to begin.

The wait would be worth it.

## If I Lived Seven Years, I'd Be OK

One of the "unknown" tales of courage and heroism which evolved from the World War II years involved Cardinals great Marshall Goldberg. The All-American back out of the University of Pittsburgh had joined the Cardinals in 1939 and then entered the service when called by his country.

Goldberg was as happy as anyone when the hostilities ceased and his tenure in the service was completed. But something was wrong . . . and he couldn't explain it at the time:

"We were mustered out in San Diego and we took a train ride to the Great Lakes base near Chicago. When I came back from the service, I was sick and my weight had been dropping. I stayed in a lower bunk almost the entire time on the train ride back.

"When I got back in Chicago, I immediately went to see my doctor and they found testicular cancer—the same illness that Brian Piccolo had. I had an operation in March of 1946 and after the operation, I bought an exercycle and stayed on that to get in shape. The Cardinals were scared to death and they kept the whole thing out of the papers, but I was able to play in August. The doctors said that if I lived seven years, I'd be OK."

New coach Jimmy Conzelman opened up the 1940 training camp at Morgan Park Military Academy in Chicago. Among the players in attendance were: (kneeling) Andy Sabados, Tony Blazine, and Willie Phillips; (standing, from left) Tony Ippolito, Motts Tonelli, Joe Ziemba, and Ed Norris. *(Photo from collection of author)*

Mario "Motts" Tonelli was a 210-pound standout when he started at fullback for the Cardinals in 1940. *(Photo courtesy of Motts Tonelli)*

By the time Tonelli was liberated from Japanese internment near the end of World War II in 1945, he weighed less than 100 pounds. *(Photo courtesy of Motts Tonelli)*

In this photo from the 1942 training camp, quarterback Lloyd Cheatham (No. 33) blocks for halfback Marshall Goldberg (No. 73). *(Photo from collection of author)*

While the 1945 team struggled on the field, returning war veterans, such as Motts Tonelli (bottom, third from right) sparked some hope for the future. *(Photo courtesy of Motts Tonelli)*

Coach Jimmy Conzelman was a favorite of players, fans, and writers. The multi-talented coach was comfortable either behind the sidelines or behind a piano. His rebuilding of the Cardinals led to the 1947 championship and then another title game in 1948. Shortly after the 1948 season, he abruptly walked away from pro football, never to return again. *(Corbis/UPI-Bettmann)*

The "Dream Backfield" breaks out in this 1947 training camp photo. In 1947, the Chicago Cardinals were the first professional squad to sign four former first-team collegiate All-Americans to start in the same backfield. From left: quarterback Paul Christman (Missouri, No. 44), fullback Pat Harder (Wisconsin, No. 34), halfback Marshall Goldberg (Pittsburgh, No. 99), and halfback Charley Trippi (Georgia, No. 62). *(Photo from collection of author)*

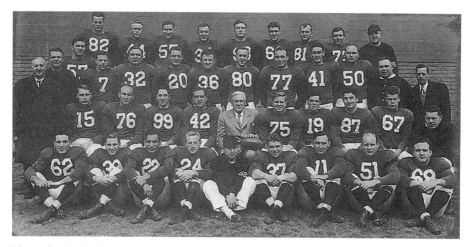

The 1947 Cardinals won the NFL championship with a 10-3 overall record. They bettered the Philadelphia Eagles 28-21 in the title contest at Comiskey Park in Chicago.

*(Photo courtesy of Vic Schwall)*

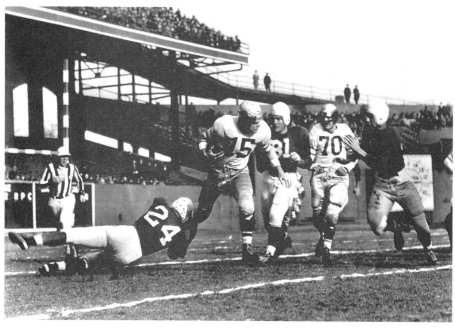

Defensive back John "Red" Cochran (No. 24) tackles Eagles' running back Steve Van Buren (No. 15) in the 1947 championship game in Comiskey Park. Moving in to help out are end Joe Parker (No. 81) and Bill Campbell. Bringing up the rear is Philadelphia's tough tackle Al Wistert (No. 70). Note that Cochran and the other Cardinals are playing in gym shoes on the frozen turf. The Cardinals swept to a 28-21 win to grab the title on December 28, 1947.

*(Corbis/UPI-Bettmann)*

Cardinals coach Jimmy Conzelman puts his arms around bashful Elmer Angsman (left) and Charley Trippi, who split the four touchdowns in the 28-21 victory over the Eagles. *(Corbis/UPI-Bettmann)*

Coach Jimmy Conzelman is surrounded by his happy players following the victory in the championship game in 1947. This remains the only time a Cardinals' team has won a championship. *(Photo courtesy of Vic Schwall)*

Cardinals back Marshall Goldberg (No. 99) and end Sam Goldman (No. 70) come up from the rear on Bears back Don Kindt (No. 6) in the Western Division Championship of the NFL in 1948. The Cardinals and the Bears have the oldest rivalry in professional football.

*(Corbis/UPI-Bettmann)*

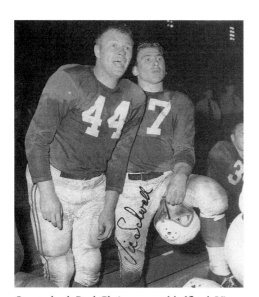

Quarterback Paul Christman and halfback Vic Schwall await the call to action in a 1948 game. Schwall was a native Chicagoan who became an All-American at Northwestern before starring with the Chicago Cardinals.

*(Photo courtesy of Vic Schwall)*

End Don Stonesifer paced the Cardinals in receiving for five straight years, from 1952 to 1956. The All-American receiver from Northwestern was difficult to defend due to his size (6'0", 220 pounds) and uncanny leaping ability.

*(Photo courtesy of Don Stonesifer)*

# ◆ 13 ◆

## The Year:
## 1947

*"In many respects, they were the strongest team we played
all last year. They had a great backfield with Paul Christman,
Pat Harder and Marshall Goldberg. With Charley Trippi
added to those three, it is no wonder that the Cardinal quartet
has been labeled the 'Dream Backfield.' "*

STEVE OWEN,
COACH, NEW YORK GIANTS, SEPTEMBER 8, 1947

It was beginning to look a lot like Christmas! For the first time in their history, the Cards acknowledged their depth and potential by opening up the ticket windows well before the beginning of the 1947 season in the first all-out effort to solicit season-ticket packages. The response was immediate and rewarding; the team sold over $25,000 worth of tickets in the first ten days of the sale and additional direct mail promotions were expected to garner final sales totaling $250,000. Staff member Margaret X. Olson was inundated with orders, including an atmospheric total of $3,000 worth of season-ticket applications which were received in just one day.

Long the stepchild in Chicago sports, the Cardinals were simply not accustomed to this type of monetary success. "It's got us completely flabbergasted . . . though it's a nice kind of flabbergast!" gushed owner Charles W. Bidwill in an interview with the *Chicago Daily News*. The orders kept piling in throughout the spring, surprising both Bidwill and his diligent staff. "Here I am, just back from Florida, and look at my mail," added Bidwill as he gestured towards bulging sacks of mail—all brimming with cold, hard cash.

The front office anticipated advance sales of perhaps $5,000, but the windfall failed to abate as fans anticipated the upcoming campaign. The effort was aided in no small way by a suddenly friendly media. In July, veteran *Daily News* columnist Harry Sheer exhorted his readers to plan ahead for the Cards' opening date of September 10, 1947, with the New York Giants:

> *On that night, at Comiskey Park, you will get a preview of the two clubs which can make or break the 1947 National Football League title race . . . And if your ticket is not already earmarked, do that tomorrow . . . fair warning. The game will baptize the '47 pro grid campaign here . . . but every scout and every expert in the NFL will be jammed into Sox park that night . . . wondering what Jimmy Conzelman will do with Charley Trippi, Pat Harder, Marshall Goldberg, Elmer Angsman, Paul Christman, Bill De Correvont and the rest of his 'golden boys.'*

With such welcome (and free) promotional support, the legend of the Cardinals began to grow, reach out, and grab sports fans all over the country. "Look at these letters," noted an astounded Bidwill. "One guy moved to California and you see in his letter that he almost cried. Wait'll Halas sees this!"

Bidwill estimated that the average request was for four season tickets, with most other fans requesting seats for that opening brawl on September 10 with the Giants. "There are 46,886 permanent seats in Sox Park and we expect to add about 7,000 temporary chairs so we'll be able to take care of the fans who don't get season books," added Bidwill.

As for George Halas, the friendly—if not tenacious—competitor from the North Side, he did notice the surge in the Cardinals' financial fortunes. Halas sent Bidwill the following wry note: "Just send the overflow on to our new office on Madison Street . . . it couldn't happen to a nicer . . . and richer . . . guy!"

Chances are that Charlie would have sent part of his good fortune on to others . . . he was that much of a philanthropist. Behind the scenes, he might sponsor a girls' softball team, repair a roof on a church, or quietly "lend" a player some extra cash during tough times. "He was a wonderful person," said backfield star Marshall Goldberg, "and a man who was extremely loyal to his players."

Despite his dramatic capabilities, his well-fortified fields of influence, and his generous nature, Mr. Bidwill could not have assisted Mr. Halas—even if he was receptive to the latter's tongue-in-cheek suggestion for revenue sharing.

In an unfair swipe at life, Charles Bidwill lost his after an heroic fight with pneumonia on April 19, 1947, at St. George Hospital in Chicago. He had entered the hospital four days earlier for treatment of a severe cold and pulmonary congestion. At just fifty-one years of age, Bidwill was too young to depart, too young to be deprived of the many opportunities which would have presented themselves in the future. Gone too suddenly and too swiftly, he left his many friends, acquaintances, and business associates the chance to publicly honor the man who had quietly touched so many. Benjamin Lindheimer, executive director of the Arlington Park racetrack at the time, told the *Tribune:*

> *Charles Bidwill's death is a distinct loss to the sports world to which I had the opportunity of knowing of his helpful activities. In football, racing and softball, his personality and effort were well known to countless fans. He always took a keen and deep personal interest in those who were a part of his sports enterprises. I hope that great consolation will come to his family from the knowledge that his many friends and associates will always cherish his memory as a fine sportsman.*

He had remained a common man who enjoyed each day of his life. "He liked whatever he was doing," recalled his son William Bidwill. "He enjoyed being around the football team and being around the racetrack." During the funeral at St. Catherine of Sienna Church, the Reverend Joseph C. Billstein, Professor of Christian Doctrine at Bidwill's alma mater of St. Ignatius High School in Chicago, perhaps described Bidwill and his influence the best:

> *From every section of not merely this great city but from literally all parts of this beloved land of ours and from every grade and walk of life you have come here*

*this morning to pay your final tribute, to give your parting salute to a man whom you have loved and who indeed was a character in his own inimitable manner.*

In one of the largest funeral processions ever seen in the city, hundreds of mourners paid tribute to Bidwill as he was laid to rest in Calvary Cemetery on the North Side of Chicago. Among the mourners were NFL Commissioner Bert Bell, ex-Chicago Mayor Edward Kelly, and former heavyweight boxing champion Jack Dempsey. George Halas was one of the pallbearers.

As for the Chicago Cardinals, it was decided that for the time being, it would be business as usual, according to Bidwill's chief aid, Ray Benningsen:

*All of Mr. Bidwill's enterprises will be carried on by his present organization. All of us who have been working with him will continue without any change.*

Aside from his printing business, Bentley, Murray & Company, Bidwill was also involved in the following organizations, according to the *Chicago Tribune:*

*Known more for his football and horse racing activities in Chicago, Bidwill also had sports interests in the south. He was president of the Chicago Cardinals, a major stockholder in Sportsman's Park race track, and managing director of Hawthorne (Chicago), sponsor of big time girls' softball, owner of four Florida dog tracks, and had stock in Lincoln Fields at suburban Crete (IL) and in Churchill Downs, home of the Kentucky Derby.*

## His Football Future Is Assured

Prior to his death, Bidwill had wisely gambled some of the Cardinals' dollars with the intent, the sole intent, of winning an NFL championship. Like a wily gambler, he spent money with the expectation and confidence that he would receive a return on his investment. With just about everyone returning from the promising 1946 squad, just a few more pieces were needed to complete the championship roster. Never reneging on his promise to provide Conzelman with the horses needed to win it all, Bidwill decided to personally mine for one of the greatest jewels in NFL history to complete his dream team. It revolved around a former draft choice (in 1945) and fledgling baseball player named Charley Trippi. Trippi had been an astounding athlete at the University of Georgia, who now found himself in the right place at the right time: smack dab in the middle of a bidding war for his services between Bidwill and the New York Yankees of the All-America Football Conference. Bidwill had little love for the new league, especially when the Chicago Rockets franchise landed in Soldier Field, giving the city three professional football teams in what was becoming a very crowded market. Bidwill also flinched when *Tribune* sports editor (and the spirit behind the new circuit) Arch Ward hinted that the Cardinals should seek another location and leave the Bears and the Rockets to battle it out in Chicago for fan support. The new team also stung Bidwill when it lured a couple of his players, Bob Morrow and Lloyd Cheatham, away from the Cardinals when the bidding wars first started in January of 1946. Both leagues were zealously pursuing the incoming draftees, going as far as not publicizing their draft choices in order to minimize the working knowledge of the other side.

Upon his release from the service, Trippi was at the top of the most wanted list for both leagues. The Cardinals had selected Trippi with their first choice in the 1945 draft (when his original college class would have graduated) while the Yankees had snared the rights to him in the AAFC draft. His value was not only significant as a gifted player, but his marquee-type notoriety was sorely needed by both leagues.

Trippi had enjoyed a phenomenal collegiate football career at Georgia. A native of Pittston, Pennsylvania, he had dreamed of playing at Fordham University. But Coach Jim Crowley had deemed him as too little (at 160 pounds) to play at this level. Trippi eventually found his way to Georgia in 1941 and within a year had gained twenty pounds and a spot in the Bulldogs' backfield. At Georgia in 1942, Trippi teamed with All-American back Frankie Sinkwich and the two of them paced the team to a victory over UCLA in the Rose Bowl and a number two national ranking.

By the time the 1943 season rolled around, Trippi found himself with the Third Air Force football team and even made the All-Service team in 1944. Because of relaxed rules for participation in the annual College All-Star game, he also played in that annual event in 1943, 1944, 1945, and 1947. Following the war, he resumed his collegiate career at Georgia, playing left halfback in Coach Wally Butts's "T" formation for the final six games of 1945. Trippi was virtually a one-man team in 1946 as Georgia cruised through the regular season undefeated and then knocked off North Carolina 20-10 in the Sugar Bowl. Trippi was the leading scorer in the SEC, won the Maxwell Award, and was runner-up for the Heisman trophy. Coach Butts was duly impressed:

> *Trippi was the finest boy and the greatest athlete I have had the privilege of coaching. He also was the finest defensive player I've seen and was always a team player. Everything Trippi did was with one thought in mind, to win. He never did anything with the thought of "promoting Trippi."*

Following the 1947 Sugar Bowl, both pro football leagues presented substantial offers to the speedy halfback, and the efforts of both teams to land this valuable athlete were highly publicized. Although the Yankees' offer was said to be higher, Trippi eventually agreed to terms with the Cardinals, as reported by the *Associated Press*:

> *Charley Trippi slipped past the clutching arms of the New York Yankees' football team today, stiff armed the Yankees' baseball secondary, and wound up with the Chicago Cardinals for what is known in the gridiron parlance as pay dirt.*

The four-year deal was in the $100,000 range and was probably the result of Bidwill's personal effort to persuade Trippi to join the Cards. After all, he had performed some legal work in the past for the young player and had been receptive to Trippi's request that he also be allowed to pursue his professional baseball career. "I'm playing both sports as long as I can," Trippi told the *Washington Post* before he signed on January 17, 1947. "Whatever pro football team I go with must understand that; and the same goes for the ball club I join."

Bidwill recommended that Trippi accept a baseball offer from the Chicago Cubs, where he would be assigned to the Pacific Coast League. Other teams, such as the Braves and the Red Sox, were also chasing after Trippi's baseball talents. As usual, Bidwill had already constructed a long-range plan for the dual athletic career of Trippi:

> *I told them (the Cubs) we would want him to report for football early the first year, in mid-August, but that after that they could count on his finishing out the baseball season. Actually, I don't know how good a baseball player he is, and neither does Charley. I think, though, that his heart is in football.*

For Trippi, the generous contract was just the tip of the financial iceberg, according to the *Washington Post:*

> *He was, and to some extent remains, in the wonderful position of having rich and eager promoters bidding for him. His football future is assured, but four big league (baseball) clubs still want him. And there will be moving pictures, endorsements of sports equipment and radio programs.*
>
> *That the baseball offers have been ready can be seen from the fact that he turned down a $30,000 bonus with the Boston Red Sox, who would have given him a considerable salary to boot.*

Cardinals president Ray Benningsen marveled at Bidwill's tenacity following the signing of Trippi:

> *Nobody in the Cardinals organization had any contacts with Trippi outside of Charlie. It was his greatest victory. Yet, I knew every move in advance. During the time when he was carrying on his cross-country dickering with Trippi, I'd hear from him five or six times a day. He'd call from New York or Florida or New Orleans.*

## *He Ran Over Opposition With Reckless Abandon*

Bidwill, ever the promoter, managed to create some additional publicity out of the Trippi negotiations. While the agreement with the Cardinals momentarily was kept a secret, Bidwill suggested that Trippi spill the news that he planned to move on to New York to participate in further discussions about his future athletic possibilities. "Mr. Bidwill asked me in good faith to go to New York and see what the Yanks had to offer," recalled Trippi. "Whatever the offer was, he said he would match or beat it." This news "leak" was devoured by the New York press and brightened the day of the Yankees' front office. However, on the day that Trippi was expected to be joining the Yankees, he announced his decision at a huge press conference in New York and grabbed a train for Chicago, where he inked his contract with Bidwill at the Blackstone Hotel. "Bidwill already had bagged Trippi," commented Jimmy Conzelman, "while Dan Topping (New York owner) was putting on his hunting jacket and practicing bird calls." Trippi explained that, "I had to find out, of course, what the All-America Conference had to offer. But basically, my heart was set on playing for Mr. Bidwill."

Bidwill was delighted with his new acquisition:

> *I would like to say this means a championship for the Cardinals, but you know that's going too far. They'll know we're in the league anyway!*

Conzelman added:

*We aren't winning any championships yet, but getting Trippi sure will make great strides toward that goal.*

The NFL was also pleased, since the signing of Trippi was a convincing victory in the ongoing battle with the All-America Conference. George Halas remarked:

*It's a great thing for Chicago and the National Football League. I wouldn't be surprised if the Bears found their toughest competition right on the South Side next fall.*

Curly Lambeau of the Packers sent Bidwill a telegram which simply stated: "Congratulations on signing Trippi. Great victory for our league." Dan Reeves of the Rams wired: "Congratulations on your signing of Trippi. Was a wonderful thing for our league."

The signing of Trippi left the already formidable Cardinals with four bonafide All-Americans in the backfield: Marshall Goldberg, Paul Christman, Pat Harder, and Trippi. It was the start of what became known as the "Million Dollar" or "Dream" backfield, possibly the finest collection of backs in the same lineup in the history of pro football. The Cardinals' 1947 media guide glowed at the prospect:

*1947 will be noted for the debut in professional ball, and with the Chicago Cardinals, we're happy to say, of Charlie Trippi, the "Golden Boy from Georgia," most publicized football player in the nation. His yardage in the newspapers and on the air lanes has been exceeded only on the football field, where he ran over opposition with reckless abandon. Coaches who have played against him say, "You can figure right now he'll be a sixty-minute player for you. You don't have to worry about him making good," all of which is great news to Mr. Conzelman.*

*The late Charlie Bidwill's "Dream Backfield" finally comes into being with Paul Christman at quarter, Marshall Goldberg and Trippi at the halves, and the one and only Pat Harder at fullback. Those four gentlemen were Bidwill's dream the past couple of years—it's just too bad he couldn't wait to see them in action.*

Yet Conzelman scoffed at the "dream" idea:

*The idea sounds good on paper, but it won't work with sufficient results. All are power runners. In every successful backfield there must be speed and that's why somebody else must be in the backfield. Power is all right but if we can add some speed with the power, we will be happy about the situation.*

In addition to the aforementioned stars, the team still included holdovers Ward Cuff, Ray Mallouf, Walt Rankin, and Elmer Angsman in the backfield along with new-comers Vic Schwall, Rabbit Smith, "Red" Cochran, Jeff Burkett, and former Chicago high school phenom Bill De Correvont (purchased from the Lions). From an offensive standpoint, the Cardinals would be loaded.

In what would prove to be an exciting off-season, Conzelman and Benningsen began to whittle away at the log jam in the backfield by selling veteran Ward Cuff to the Packers on April 19. Cuff had been the third-leading scorer in the NFL in 1946 with fifty-five points and a ten-year career average per carry of 5.4 yards, but the wealth of new talent made him expendable, especially with Harder performing the kicking chores with deadly accuracy. On June 10, De Correvont was brought over from Detroit while Red Cochran, a veteran of fifty-four months in the Air Corps, was signed on July 20. Another end-halfback, Jack Doolan, was picked up from the Giants.

These signings, along with the return of so many veterans, prompted Conzelman to be cautiously optimistic when queried about the upcoming season: "The Cards will be improved with Trippi in the backfield, and we have a fast, young club, but we showed lack of seasoning at this last year." Conzelman groused that his team would be weak at defensive end with dependable Frank Ivy as the only sure bet. As such, he predicted that both the Bears and the Rams would eclipse his Cardinals in the Western Division of the NFL. He was also a little concerned over the condition of Trippi, who had suffered an injury while playing minor league baseball with the Atlanta Crackers.

While attempting to make a catch in an early June game against Birmingham, Trippi endured a shoulder injury that sidelined him along with his .364 batting average. Trippi was also named the outstanding Italian-American athlete in the United States that month, which fit nicely in the family trophy case along with the prestigious Maxwell Award and the Washington Touchdown Club honors he had received following the 1946 collegiate season.

## I'd Rather Play In An All-Star Game Than Eat

Trippi recovered well enough to agree to participate in the 1947 College All-Star Game, which would be his record fourth appearance. Because of the easing of qualifications during war time which had previously limited this game to graduating seniors, Trippi had personally made this summer classic a regular habit. The 1947 All-Stars, coached by Frank Leahy of Notre Dame, surprised the Chicago Bears 16-0, and the game once again thrilled Trippi: "I'd rather play in an All-Star game than eat. It is great training in learning how to keep your nerves steady in front of a big crowd."

Joining Trippi on the College All-Stars were future Cardinals Vic Schwall, Rabbit Smith, and Clarence Esser, none of whom would be on board when Conzelman loaded the train in Chicago's North Western station for training camp in Waukesha (WI) on Monday, August 4. However, the coach did gather forty-eight players for the trip to Carroll College along with assistant coaches Phil Handler, Buddy Parker, and Dick Plasman. Of that player roster of forty-eight, ten were from Texas and five from Oklahoma . . . fully one-third of the team. "If you are from some place besides Texas or Oklahoma," observed Marshall Goldberg, "you have to have a passport to get into camp."

In fact, members of the media observed that perhaps the intense heat had already affected the Cardinals, since some of the players mumbled something about Waukesha being the "first stop on the trip to Soldier Field." Not so, explained the teams' Business manager Arch Wolfe, who stated:

> *What they really mean is that the trip they just completed from Chicago is expected to have as its eventual destination Soldier's Field in August of next year. These boys have a pretty good chance of winning the National Football League title during the coming season. As champions of the league they will oppose the College All-*

*Stars next August in Soldier's Field. So, they really have Soldier's Field in mind,*
*although such things as getting in shape for a rough season and winning more games*
*than any other team in the league are involved before they realize their goal.*

With the Bears distracted by the College All-Stars, the Cardinals finally found themselves to be at the center of the watchful eye of the media and all sorts of unusual information poured out of Waukesha and its one-hundred-degree heat.

For example, it was learned that big tackle Stan Mauldin was attempting to bulk up by drinking three quarts of milk per day . . . and that linemen Vince Banonis and Ray Apolskis were confusing teammates during scrimmages by speaking to each other in Lithuanian . . . and that quarterback Paul Christman was actually "gun shy" until he suffered a hit in each game. "He even told me to get a weak line in front of him the other day, just so the defense could get through and smear him," explained Conzelman.

The long weeks in Wisconsin were heightened by intense practice sessions and stiff competition for roster spots. The players realized that this team was special and asserted their talents in order to fly above the roster cuts. "The biggest thing about that camp was the number of talented players with all of the war veterans and older college players returning," said Red Cochran, who was attempting pro football after completing his war-interrupted career at Wake Forest. "Even then, it was a close-knit group; guys were kidding each other about getting cut from the team and people kept telling me I was being sent to Bloomfield, New Jersey (the Cards' farm club)."

Surprisingly, the early days of camp were injury free, except for some minor leg discomfort experienced by star end Billy Dewell. Conzelman kept away from any contact drills until Saturday, August 9, and amused himself by holding speed races between members of his line. One of the "biggest" race surprises was the unveiling of the quickness of Joe Coomer, a 6'6", 280-pound tackle. Coomer had been obtained in a trade with Pittsburgh and was another key piece in Conzelman's search for a weakness-free roster. Coomer would be battling for a roster spot and time at tackle with athletes such as Chet Bulger (248 pounds), Kevin Jacobs (250 pounds), Caleb Martin (250 pounds), LaVerne Lauffer (271 pounds), Ed Schneider (250 pounds), Tom Kearns (250 pounds), Stan Mauldin, (215 pounds) Walter Szot (225 pounds), and Bob Zimny (230 pounds). "At that time, we were considered a big line, but not really huge outside of me and Coomer," said Bulger. "I went about 284 and Coomer was really around 310. Everyone lied about their weight!" The Cardinals' tackles were not only large, but resourceful. All were experienced veterans and most had been in the service, adding a dose of experience to their impressive size. Bulger and Szot served in the Marines, Coomer spent forty-six months in the Army, Mauldin was a pilot in the Air Corps and flew thirty-five missions over Europe, and Zimny was a sergeant in the Army.

After nearly a week of conditioning, Conzelman unleashed his forces in an intrasquad exhibition between the "Blues" and the "Reds" on Sunday, August 10. Conzelman hoped to learn more about the several rookies and newcomers in camp. To achieve this, he teamed De Correvont, Goldberg, Christman, and Harder in the "Red" backfield with Cochran, Boris "Babe" Dimancheff, Rankin, and rookie Jeff Burkett starting for the "Blues." The backfield talent was so immense that players like Mallouf and Angsman were afforded the designation as "extras" for the outing. As it turned out, the initial scrimmage proved anything but pleasant. A total of nine Cardinals were injured with rookie guard Plato Andros and end Joe Parker suffering cuts, while Dimancheff injured his shoulder. Several others, including Dewell, Kutner, and De Correvont, experienced pulled muscles.

## They Burned The Machine Down

The line continued working on its strategy and blocking techniques, usually with the help of some makeshift blocking sleds, according to Chet Bulger:

> *We didn't have regular sleds, so Phil Handler built a seven man sled out of wood and canvas, with no padding. It was tough on your shoulders, so we gave some kids $5 apiece to do something about it. About midnight they came back and burned the machine down. We were so happy, but two days later, sure enough, it was back. It killed me.*

Over the next week, the injuries—as well as the temperature—increased in Waukesha. By Monday, August 18, Dimancheff (shoulder), Banonis (strained back), and Szot (broken toe) were all in the hospital as the rest of the team strained to escape the heat as it soared past one hundred degrees. "It was so bad," remembers Bulger. "The college itself was built out of limestone, so the football field was down where the limestone had been taken out. We had this big field down there with the sun baking down off the limestone walls. It was like an oven." While it was still too early to firmly define the team's possibilities, Conzelman was concerned over depth in the line. He was also pleased with the play of three rookies: huge (6'5", 230 pounds) end Barney Barnett from Northeastern A & M, tackle Caleb Martin (6'4", 245 pounds) from Louisiana Tech, and guard Plato Andros, a solid 225 pounds, who had been drafted by the Cards in 1944. Surprisingly, Conzelman was perplexed by his starting backfield of Christman, Goldberg, Trippi, and Harder which had already been dubbed the "Dream Backfield" by the media. Once again, the coach pointed out that all four were power runners and he preferred to have at least one starter with breakaway speed. He contemplated the imminent arrival of All-Stars Rabbit Smith or Vic Schwall to perhaps test this situation.

On Friday, August 22, the College All-Stars stunned the Chicago Bears 16-0 in the postgraduate baptism for Trippi, Esser, Schwall, and Rabbit Smith. The quartet immediately headed north to join the Cardinals, while the current squad members journeyed over to Green Bay to scout the exhibition game between the Packers and the New York Giants. Up to this time, Conzelman had been reluctant to trim the roster and pointed to a full-blown team outing on Monday, August 25, to help determine the final cuts. In a benefit game for the Carroll College athletic fund, he divided the squad into two units, the "Cardinals" and the "Giants." The backfield for the "Cardinals" would consist of Mallouf, Trippi, Angsman, and Harder, while the runners for the "Giants" would be Christman, Dimancheff, Goldberg, and Rankin. These players evoked considerable interest among the locals who were attuned to recent college football history. In addition to the well-known exploits of Trippi, the crowd could witness former Big Ten (then the Big Nine) scoring champs Harder (Wisconsin), Schwall (Northwestern), and Dimancheff (Purdue), along with Notre Dame's former leading scorer (Angsman) and Pittsburgh's renowned All-American Marshall Goldberg.

When the festivities began before six thousand on the Waukesha High School field, the intensity of the battle was evident. With thirty-five roster spots at stake, the teammates-turned-combatants fearlessly blasted away at each other. The luckless Dimancheff, just recovered from a shoulder injury, went out first with a broken nose. Angsman broke a finger while Coomer and Mauldin departed with cuts. Later, Walt Rankin twisted his ankle. The "Giants" tallied the first score on Rankin's twenty-two-yard scamper with Alex Lukachik adding the extra point. Late in the game, the "Cardinals" evened it up when Rabbit Smith scored on an old-fashioned Statue of Liberty play from nine yards away. Harder kicked the extra point. Trippi failed to see any action until just thirty seconds remained in the game, when he was inserted on defense. While all of the backs ran well, the passing of Christman (4-21) and Mallouf (6-20) was rusty. One of the big surprises was the punting of rookie Jeff Burkett, who boomed one kick for seventy-four yards.

There was one last piece of business before the team broke camp: the annual "Rookies' Night." The job of the rookies was "to put on a show for the veterans, the coaches and sundry interlopers," according to the *Daily News:*

> *The results had even the most frozen faced guy in the crowd rolling in the aisles. Chief victims of unrehearsed satires were Coaches Jimmy Conzelman and Phil Handler. With Northwestern's Vic Schwall doing up Conzelman-powdered hair, chain smoking cigarettes and pockets full of cokes.*
>
> *It took two rookie linemen, guard Plato Andros and tackle Caleb Martin, to impersonate Handler . . . And there was a rumor today that two certain freshmen were going to have a long, hard week. Charley Trippi even smoked his first cigar, two puffs anyway, satirizing Marshall Goldberg and his clippings.*
>
> *Then Charley sat down and roared as his teammates did a job on him as "Charley Clippi, who needs plenty of rest, no practice and a $300,000 contract."*

The team was coming together, both on and off the field.

## *The Team Looks Pretty Good On Paper*

As promised, Conzelman began the tough job of trimming the roster. Tackle Marvin Jacobs and back Roy Anderson were sent to the Cardinals' farm club in Bloomfield, New Jersey, while end Emil Lussow and backs John Stojak and Morton Lowy were released. More cuts would follow as the team continued its two-per-day drills until just before breaking camp in Waukesha on Wednesday, September 3. By then, the squad was reduced to thirty-five players as it headed to Buffalo, New York, for an exhibition with the Eagles on September 5.

Although the talent was there, it was difficult for Conzelman to assess the club until it faced live competition:

> *The team looks pretty good on paper, but these new men have not been under fire in professional competition. The veterans, of course, know what they will be up against and I am as anxious as anybody else to see what our freshmen can do when the going gets rough.*

It was, however, impossible to harness the growing media acclaim. The array of talent in the "Dream Backfield," the recent loss of Charlie Bidwill, and the sudden elevation of the Cardinals to superstars was almost too much for the local media to handle. When the Cardinals broke camp to begin their long journey in quest of the NFL crown, Harry Sheer of the *Daily News* reminisced about Bidwill's vision:

> *This is the day that was just a pipe dream to the late Charlie Bidwill three years ago.*
>
> *Charlie was dreaming up a backfield for his 1947 Chicago Cardinals. he knew what he wanted . . . if things went right. They had to be real football players first, All-Americans second.*
>
> *Last January, "Blue Shirt Charlie's" dream had jelled . . . he signed Georgia's Charlie Trippi to go with the legendary Mad Marshall Goldberg, Pitchin' Paul Christman and the Mule, powerful Pat Harder.*
>
> *In brief, here is what the Eagles and Giants must contend with the next seven days, as far as the "Dream Backfield" is concerned.*
>
> *Christman, Missouri All-American quarterback, best passer in Cardinals' history and pitching with deadly precision this year.*
>
> *Goldberg, Pittsburgh All-American, in the best condition of his pro career, running brilliantly and just as hard as he ever did under Jock Sutherland.*
>
> *Harder, Wisconsin All-American, faster even at 205 pounds and headed towards a rating as the best fullback in the National Football League.*
>
> *Trippi, Georgia All-American, called by coaches the finest football player in the country today.*
>
> *But there is one point the "Dream Backfield" would like to make, and its spokesperson is its patriarch, Marshall Goldberg: "Dream Backfield or not, you've got to have a dream line to go with it. As for me, I'll take Kutner and Dewell at ends; Bulger, Zimny and Mauldin at tackles; Banonis, Blackburn and Campbell at center; and Apolskis, Andros and Ramsey at guards. It's a dream running behind those guys, believe me."*

No one knows why the game was scheduled for Buffalo, but the Cardinals traveled from Wisconsin while the Eagles came in from their training camp in Saranac Lake in New York. Perhaps it was out of consideration to Trippi, whose parents were now residents of Buffalo.

Trippi's professional debut in front of a sparse crowd of 16,282 was inconsequential. He toted the ball just four times for nine yards, although he did break away for a sixty-one-yard kickoff return as the Cards breezed past the Eagles 38-21. Nevertheless, the *Daily News* was impressed:

> *If anyone is trying to tell you that Charlie Trippi, Pat Harder, Marshall Goldberg and Paul Christman do not form a "Dream Backfield" then the Philadelphia Eagles would like to meet that guy. The "Dream Backfield" and the Cardinals were all everyone said they would be last night. Actually, they were a "Dream Team."*

Ironically, these same two clubs which opened the 1947 season would provide a memorable closing to the season as well.

The Cardinals returned home to prepare for the next exhibition game against the

New York Giants at Comiskey Park. Giants coach Steve Owen was understandably wary of the Cards' offensive potential, which first surfaced the previous season:

*In many respects, they were the strongest team we played all last year. They had a great backfield with Paul Christman, Pat Harder, and Marshall Goldberg. With Charlie Trippi added to those three, it is no wonder that the Cardinal quartet has been labeled the "Dream Backfield." They're rightly named. I don't know of any coach in the country who wouldn't trade his entire roster of backs for the four of 'em.*

Since the White Sox were still using their stadium, the Cardinals made arrangements to practice during the week at abandoned Stagg Field on the University of Chicago campus. After he pushed his team through one final practice, Conzelman groaned:

*We'll be in the ball game, but with that Giant line . . . two lines, to be exact, I can't tell how long.*

## If They Don't Score First, They Still Can Score Last

While the game with the Giants was sponsored by the *Chicago Daily News* for that newspaper's Veteran's fund, there was some added significance when it was decided that the contest would also serve as a formal memorial to the late Charlie Bidwill. This would also be Chicago's first look at the 1947 Cardinals.

John Carmichael of the *Daily News* promoted the game by wisely tapping into the excitement of the Cardinals:

*The Cardinals are ready to roll. They're finally feeling the surge of strength which comes from the knowledge that if they don't score first, they still can score last, a vital thing in pro football where the emphasis is on going all the way, all the time.*

Despite the fact that the game was held on a Wednesday (September 11) night, even the Cardinals had to be shocked when 39,850 fans showed up for an exhibition game. A light rain swept through the area about an hour before the game but failed to hold down the crowd or its enthusiasm. The Giants were optimistic prior to the contest after previously defeating the vaunted Eastern College All-Stars 21-0. As the kickoff drew near, South Side fans continued to pour through the Comiskey Park gates, boisterous in their yearning to see the "new look" Cards as well as catch a glimpse of the wondrous Trippi and his cohorts.

The crowd, the excitement, and the passion were all new to the Cardinals and their followers. Following a brief remembrance for Bidwill preceding the game, the Cardinals jumped all over the visitors and rolled to a startling 52-21 victory. Trippi was given just three chances to prove himself versus the Giants. In that brief time, he left little doubt that he would be an immediate force to reckon with in the professional ranks. Harry Warren described the magical display in the *Chicago Tribune*:

*The game, offering the professional debut of Trippi and the unveiling of the 1947 Cardinal team, surpassed the expectations of the most devout Cardinal fans. The crowd of 39,850 saw more fireworks than a Fourth of July display could offer and left the field almost as awe struck as the Giants, who had suffered their sec-*

*ond worst defeat in history.*

    *Trippi carried the ball only three times, but that was enough to convince every-body he will get along all right in professional football. He picked up 138 yards in those three tries, one of 71 yards to set up a touchdown, another of 65 to score, and a mere two in his final attempt.*

To this day, Trippi remembers that game more fondly than any other in his long pro career: "In that exhibition game against the Giants, I was able to get off to a good start in Chicago with those two long runs. It was our first game in Chicago that year and I wanted to prove to the fans that I could play football and wasn't some overnight sensation." It was one of those games in which everyone joined in the fun. Bill De Correvont raced seventy-two yards for a touchdown, Pat Harder booted a field goal, and Jeff Burkett added his first pro touchdown. To top things off, Cards center Bill Blackburn returned two interceptions for touchdowns.

Following the game, Conzelman hinted that his club could be competitive, but moaned that the team still needed a few more players, as reported in the *Daily News:*

*He was empty-handed and he was smiling, but regardless of these discrepancies, Jimmy Conzelman was the personification of a fellow crying with a loaf of bread under his arm. "We could use four more good football players," moaned the coach of the more-than somewhat terrific Cardinals. But regardless of the protestations of the gray-thatched coach, the Cardinals are the hottest thing the South Side has experienced since the Stockyards' fire.*

Goldberg, who had been with the Cardinals through too few good times was found grinning in the locker room after the game: "What a difference! What a pleasure to be with a club like this!" The *Daily News* quoted an anonymous former player describing the squad as "The best Cardinals team in history . . . and it may easily be the greatest club in football history."

Basking in the confidence that they could score from anywhere at any time, the Cards closed out their exhibition season on Friday, September 19, at the Cotton Bowl in Dallas. The opposition would be furnished by the lowly Boston Yanks, winless and nearly scoreless in their first four exhibition outings. Conzelman had witnessed enough upsets throughout his lengthy career, so even though this was merely an "exhibition" game, he warned his team to approach the Yanks cautiously: "They'll be plenty tough," Conzelman warned. "I know the caliber of men we're going against. They'll be clicking tomorrow night."

Boston offered some familiar faces in its backfield, beginning with recent Cardinals Frank Seno and the unpredictable Johnny Grigas. Grigas was still remembered by assistant coach Phil Handler for failing to show up for the final game of the 1944 season, despite the fact that Grigas needed only a handful of yards to capture the league rushing title. To counter the Boston defense, Conzelman experimented with still another starting lineup in the backfield, going with Mallouf at quarterback, Goldberg and Dimancheff at the halfback slots, and Rankin at fullback.

In a game played for the benefit of underprivileged children in the Dallas area, the Yanks showed up with some defensive intensity of their own. The highly touted Cardinals offensive attack was stymied time and again as the two teams dueled through a scoreless first half. Only a late seven-yard scoring pass from Christman to Goldberg enabled the Cards to capture a 7-3 victory to conclude the exhibition season with an undefeated slate of 3-0. The win was not secured easily, especially with Trippi on the sidelines with an injured ankle in the final period.

The injury proved to be minor and the Cardinals remained in Dallas for a few days to rest and prepare for the season opener against Detroit on Sunday, September 28, in Chicago. On Wednesday (September 24), the Cardinals embarked for St. Louis where the team was honored at a luncheon and then drilled briefly at Washington University. The Cards returned to Chicago on the 25th and then continued preparations at the University of Chicago for the Lions' game.

## *A Flock Of Nightmares*

Along the way, the Cards announced the signing of Walter "Dub" Laws (formerly the Bears' property) and also confirmed that retiring halfback Marshall Goldberg would be honored on October 5 as the team and its fans would celebrate "Marshall Goldberg Day." The eloquent Goldberg had decided that the many years of playing both ways had been enough, and he looked forward to expanding his business interests. "Football was not going to be my livelihood. I was doing well in the machinery business and I didn't want to risk that."

While the Cardinals' backfield prowess was already infamous, the work of the guys up front was being noticed as well. In the *Tribune*, Harry Warren wrote about a conversation he overheard in the press box during the exhibition season opener:

> *Following the Cardinals' 38-21 triumph over the Philadelphia Eagles in Buffalo, a group of the scouts were comparing notes. One seemed to voice the general opinion when he said: "I'll admit they have a good backfield, but that Cardinal line is going to cause National league coaches a flock of nightmares this season."*
>
> *The scout saw his prophecy come true on the night of September 10 when the Cardinals turned in a 52 to 21 triumph over the New York Giants, who were regarded as having the best forward walls in the National league.*
>
> *Members of the so-called Cardinal dream backfield—Paul Christman, Pat Harder, Marshall Goldberg and Charlie Trippi—realize the yardage they pick up this season will depend upon the line that operates in front of them.*

From end to end, the Cardinals fielded a solid line. Billy Dewell and Mal Kutner served as the bookends, and the pair had no peers as a deadly receiving combination in the NFL. In 1946, the two combined to snare 54 passes for 1,277 yards and 12 touchdowns, averaging an amazing 23.6 yards per catch.

Both Dewell (6'4", 210 pounds) and Kutner (6'2", 197 pounds) possessed height and good hands. While Dewell was known for his acrobatic catches and his unique faking ability, Kutner simply turned on the burners when needed as one of the fastest men in the league. "Few realize how valuable Kutner is to us," praised Conzelman. "Because of his great speed and quick reactions, we use him at defensive halfback. As a result, he plays 50 to 55 minutes in every game. That's remarkable for anyone these days and almost unbelievable for a man of his physique." For Kutner, it was a dream come true to be paired with the lanky Dewell:

*Billy was my hero when I was growing up in Dallas and he was playing for SMU. I used to worship him as my college hero when I was playing in high school. He was such a great athlete and I never thought that I would ever meet him. Then, after the war, here we were as teammates!*

Rookie Clarence Esser was a smallish (6', 190 pounds) tackle at Wisconsin where he was the team MVP in 1944 and 1946. Conzelman moved him to end as he did Jack Doolan, the former halfback with the Giants, who eventually claimed a defensive end slot for the Cards.

Joe Parker and Frank "Pop" Ivy also impressed the coaches with their work on the defensive side. Parker (6'1", 220 pounds), a rancher in the off season, was an All-American at Texas before spending thirty-two months in the service. Ivy (6'3", 210 pounds) had been an All-American at Oklahoma and was the second-leading receiver in the NFL for the Cards in 1942. His career was disrupted by twenty-six months with the infantry in Europe, but he returned and played the defensive end position with a passion. Another halfback who landed on his feet with the Cards was Boris Stephen "Babe" Dimancheff, the former Purdue All-American. Babe spent two seasons with the Boston Yanks before the Cards acquired him in a trade for center Bill Godwin prior to the 1947 season. "I was delighted to join the Cardinals," said Dimancheff. "I really didn't like Boston or the organization. I told them that if they didn't trade me, I'd take an offer to join New York in the new league, so I was very happy to go to Chicago."

At tackle, Chet Bulger (a slimmed down 238 pounds) and Stan Mauldin (215 pounds) were rather light but quick. Bulger (Auburn) and Mauldin (Texas) were expected to swing the gates open for the horses in the Cardinals' backfield. Bob Zimny (230 pounds), a native Chicagoan and a graduate of St. Rita High School, and Walt Szot (215 pounds) earned praise for their work at defensive tackle. Big Joe Coomer (280 pounds) took over as nose tackle on the defensive line, while Tom Kearns and rookie Caleb Martin filled out the tackle positions.

The guard spots were handled by a group of gentlemen who might be branded "unique" as a group. Buoyed by the fiery Garrard "Buster" Ramsey (6'1", 210 pounds) and Ray Apolskis (5'11", 210 pounds), the guards were comprised of savvy veterans and promising rookies. Apolskis was another South Sider who graduated from Fenger High School and was an All-American at Marquette University. He switched from center to guard in 1946 and was now entering his fifth season with the team. Ramsey was back for his second season of what would ultimately prove to be an All-Pro career for the Tennessee native who won All-American honors at William and Mary College. Ramsey was an invigorating leader who played through pain and was respected throughout the league. "He really was a player-coach on the field," recalled Vince Banonis. "He was very enthusiastic and played both ways every game." Babe Dimancheff remembered: "He had this whiskey voice, and he was quite talkative on the field, but he was a heck of a football player who could back it up all the way." Red Cochran takes the praise of Ramsey one step further: "He's the most deserving player to be in the Hall of Fame that's not in there in the whole history of football."

## *Greek Children Ought To Honor Their Ancestors*

Loyd Arms (6'1", 215 pounds) fought off illness for much of the 1946 season but still debuted as one of the more promising guards in the league. His strength and stature could be misleading, for he was also a war veteran who could boast of being a national wrestling champion while at Oklahoma A & M. Also contributing at the guard position were second-year man J. C. "Jake" Colhouer (6'1", 210 pounds), and rookies Plato Andros (6'0", 225 pounds) and Hamilton Nichols, Jr. (5'11", 210 pounds). Plato became the immediate darling of Chicago's Greek community when they learned of his proud ancestry. Plato and his brother Demosthenes were both football players at Oklahoma, but inquiring minds wanted to learn more about the origins of their names. Plato was accustomed to the question and always had the reply ready:

> *Maybe you're wondering about our names. Well, our godfather is a great student himself. And he thought two Greek children ought to honor their ancestors. Besides, he figured both Dee and I would be great students, too. Ergo . . . Plato and Demosthenes Andros. The boys used to rib both of us, but they quit a couple of years ago. They think twice when you grow up to be our size, you know!*

Andros's strength was legendary, remarked Bulger:

> *One time we were in this little tavern after practice and the owner was complaining about this big, old jerk organ. He was saying that he wished he could move it. The Greek (Plato) just went over there and moved it by himself, fixtures and all.*

The team was well fortified at center with two of the best in Bill Blackburn (6'6", 225 pounds) and Vince Banonis (6'1", 230 pounds). Both were war veterans and both had the ability to move quickly on the field. Blackburn was slow to grow as a youth and actually played in the backfield in his early years at Rice before spending forty-two months in the service. He also became the Cards' punter in 1946. Banonis, who was originally drafted by the Cards in 1942, experienced forty-one months in the Navy following his All-American career at Detroit. Both Banonis and Blackburn shared time at linebacker on the defensive side of the ball. But the best part about this unusual partnership between Banonis and Blackburn was their friendship, both on and off the field. The two centers, along with Elmer Angsman and Buster Ramsey, were known as "the Gang." The four spent many a happy hour together off the field, but on the field, they were all business. The combination of Banonis and Blackburn was so unique that, "Jimmy ignored us," according to Banonis. "It wasn't widely known, but Jimmy told me to take care of our position. Both Bill and I played both ways, so we substituted on our own. If I was tired, I would call him in. If Bill needed a rest, I would go back in for him. Jimmy never told us who should or should not play."

Another Oklahoma grad, Bill Campbell (6'0", 195 pounds), could help out at center or play anywhere else on the team. Conzelman described him as a gridder with "more natural ability than any player I've ever seen." Campbell was hardened by thirty-one months in the Air Corps, including thirty-four missions over Europe.

With the line set and the dream backfield in place, the Cardinals awaited the opener with the visiting Lions and their dynamic halfback, Bill Dudley. Dudley had recently been acquired from the Pittsburgh Steelers and was the league's leading ground gainer in 1946 as well as its MVP. Conzelman devoted the final two practice sessions to devising strategies to stop Dudley, and the Lions were probably planning for Trippi in a similar vein.

Trippi enjoyed an adequate day by picking up thirty yards in just five carries, but the Lions forgot about the deadly passing of Christman until it was all too late. Following an unproductive preseason and the emergence of the spectacular ground game, the Cardinals' passing attack had been slighted, but not forgotten. Christman's competitive nature took over as he rifled 16 out of 24 completions for 320 yards in just 3 quarters to pace the Cardinals to an easy 45-21 rout of the Lions. Dudley did manage to gain sixty-five yards in eleven carries, but his output was eclipsed by that of Harder, who scored twenty-one points on a pair of touchdowns, six extra points, and a field goal. And he pretty much matched Dudley's rushing performance by picking up fifty-eight yards in eleven attempts.

Christman was simply incredible. He added scoring tosses to Kutner (eight yards), and Dimancheff (forty-four yards), while Mallouf added a seventeen-yard strike to Burkett in the fourth quarter. Even more impressive was the work of the Cardinals' defense, especially Trippi and Ramsey. The fleet Trippi had no trouble deploying against the enemy's runners and receivers while Buster Ramsey sunk the hopes of the Lions with both a fumble recovery and an interception to thrill the crowd of 22,739 in Comiskey Park. When the offensive barrage ended, the Cardinals had racked up 576 total yards, the third best in league annals. If the 1947 Cardinals were truly "for real," they would quickly get the opportunity to prove themselves the following week.

Next up was an early season encounter with the defending champion Bears, fresh from a 29-20 upset at the hands of the Green Bay Packers. The Bears had dominated the Cardinals in recent history by capturing fifteen of the last eighteen meetings, but something was different this time, according to George Halas:

> *I think we're going to improve each day, but I don't think we'll be good enough to beat the Cardinals Sunday. As I've said since last winter, this is a potent outfit.*

For the first time in years, the Cardinals were the favorites in a game with the Bears. But Conzelman wasn't so sure as he reviewed the scouting report with his team:

> *The Cardinals will have to show great improvement over the games played against the Lions last Sunday and in some of their exhibitions, or the Bears will run them right out of Comiskey Park next Sunday!*
> *The Bears should have beaten the Packers last Sunday. The Packers were able to win only through interceptions. The Bears really out-played the Packers throughout the afternoon and they will really be up for that game next Sunday. That's a team that you can't afford to let down a minute against. A letdown, only momentarily, will mean a Bear touchdown.*

Unbelievably, all reserved seats at Comiskey Park were sold out a week before the game, and some predicted that an unheard of total of over fifty thousand could show up for the date on October 5. "It was unbelievable," said Bulger about the crowd. "There wasn't an empty seat and the income tax people were standing by the gate, counting everyone as they went in." The Cardinals also announced the signing of talented end Jack Karwales, a former standout at the University of Michigan who most recently was with the Bears.

On game day, the Cardinals opened up the ticket windows and offered ten thousand general admission tickets and twenty-five hundred bleacher seats. All were gobbled up quickly, and as a result, the largest crowd to watch an NFL game in Chicago (51,123) was in place. Before the game, veteran Marshall Goldberg was honored for his many contributions to the Cardinals' organization. He was presented with a new car by Cardinals fans and with a "motion picture" kit by his teammates on the team. "It was nice of the team to do that," remembered Goldberg, "because at that time I was set to leave the game and concentrate on my business career at the end of the season."

The motion picture gear was the last thing the Cardinals gave away that day. Bouncing back from an early 7-0 deficit, Conzelman's boys broke down the Bears in a variety of ways and breezed to a 31-7 victory. Christman connected on 12 out of 26 passes for 151 yards and 2 touchdowns. Christman, who wasn't fond of carrying the ball, also snuck in for another touchdown. Dewell (six yards) and Dimancheff (thirty-five yards) were responsible for the touchdown receptions while Trippi delighted the crowd with the best gainer of his young career: a forty-one-yard run in the first quarter. The many weapons of the Cardinals' offense were on display, from Trippi's speed, to Christman's passing, to Harder's kicking. Although Jeff Burkett needed to punt only once, it was a fifty-yard boomer that buried the Bears deep in their own territory.

As usual, some extracurricular activity was evident as Trippi was introduced to the Bears-Cardinals rivalry. In the fourth quarter, Mike Jarmoluk of the Bears was tossed out after he was found guilty of kicking Trippi. After the game, the Cardinals celebrated their victory by "going to one of the local bars," said Red Cochran, "and Buster Ramsey would take over the microphone and we would sing and drink all night!" Trippi added: "The chemistry between us was very good. We all enjoyed being together and we all wanted to win very badly. After the games, we'd party together, have a few beers and sing. That's the only way to play a team sport. You work hard together and then have fun together!"

## If You Don't Have Tickets, Please Stay Away

The joy ride continued the following week (October 12) when the Cardinals visited the undefeated Packers. All tickets for the game had sold out early, leaving the city in a bit of an unusual situation, as noted the night before the game by the *Tribune*.

> *Green Bay, a town that takes pride in its spirit of hospitality, tonight presented a picture of chagrin. The capacity of City Stadium is placed at 24,800 and all seats for tomorrow's game have been sold for more than two weeks. For the last several days, Packer and town officials have broadcast warnings to the effect: "If you don't have tickets for Sunday's game, please stay away."*
>
> *The Northland Hotel, which for years has tried to take care of the same guests*

*year after year, tonight admitted the situation had gotten out of hand. The hotel lobby, usually an orderly center of attraction, tonight presented a scene of near confusion in a last minute rush for rooms that were not available.*

Packers Coach Curly Lambeau, although pleased with his team's opening wins against the Bears and the Rams, was not brimming with confidence at the prospect of facing the Cardinals:

*We're a little tired now after those games with the Bears and Rams. I'm just afraid the Cardinals may prove to be a little bit too good for us. I'm sure they'll have a faster backfield and faster ends than the Rams. We'll need a little luck against the Cards.*

Lady Luck did frown upon Christman's passing in the game as he completed just 7 of 26 for 125 yards. Unfortunately for the Packers, their quarterback Jack Jacobs encountered the same type of bad luck (four for nineteen passes, seventy-two yards). This left the outcome up to the opposing defenses and the rushers, and the Cardinals prevailed on both accounts to grab a 14-10 victory.

The Cardinals attracted the largest crowd (25,502) ever to see a football game in Green Bay and left town with the only unblemished record (3-0) in the NFL. With Harder limited by an injury, John "Red" Cochran was thrust into the limelight, both on offense and defense. Cochran responded by scoring the winning touchdown on a two-yard run, then intercepting a fourth quarter pass to nullify the Packers' final drive. Chet Bulger had derailed an earlier fourth-quarter series by Green Bay when he recovered a fumble. Burkett's punts were once again a blessing as he averaged 47.2 yards on six kicks.

## Shakespeare Never Had Much Traffic With Football

However, several key players, including Harder, Andros, Smith, and Kutner, limped out of the Green Bay game with injuries. Their availability for the next game was in question as the team boarded the City of Los Angeles train at Northwestern station on Wednesday, October 15, for the long trip to visit the Rams. The Cardinals were flying high and the expectations among the fans were not only for the team to win, but to win decisively. Conzelman found all of the sudden attention and adulation amusing:

*You know, that fellow Bill Shakespeare never had much traffic with football, but when he said: "Uneasy lies the head that wears the crown," he knew whereof he was speaking.*

Dr. Irving Wellin joined the team on the trip to look after the injured and to remove stitches from recent injuries incurred by Angsman and Mallouf. There was also some concern over stomach discomfort experienced by punter Jeff Burkett, but he decided to evaluate that situation further when the team arrived in Los Angeles. Conzelman used the lengthy ride to develop game plans and hammer out issues at team meetings. With the players "imprisoned" on the train, they were forced to concentrate on the upcoming game and to mentally prepare themselves for their individual responsibilities. There was no escaping Coach Conzelman—"Jimmy would never fly, so we were always faced with those long train rides," remarked Dimancheff.

If there were stops along the way, it wasn't unusual for Conzelman to haul the players out of the train and have them run through plays while still in their business suits. Red Cochran remembered a typical West Coast trip: "At various stops, if there was time, we'd get out on the train platform and do calisthenics or even jog around the train if we could. But basically, those rides were hell." Charlie Trippi remembers "playing a lot of gin rummy and pinochle. That was our diversion. You had to do something or you'd go crazy!"

"It was awful," added Kutner, "but one thing about the Chicago Cardinals, we always went first class. We all had bedrooms, and the team had its own diner and baggage car. We played cards and had meetings, but the trip was a lot more fun coming home if you had won." Chet Bulger revealed that "Billy Dewell always read books. He always had three or four with him and we could borrow them if we wanted. Arch Wolfe preferred comic books. Everything was always the 'Lone Ranger.' He liked that stuff."

On this particular trip, Conzelman broke his team out into four separate study groups for team meetings: the quarterbacks, the ends, the linemen, and the halfbacks/fullbacks. His message was intended to instill an awareness of the Rams' potent offense behind dangerous quarterback Bob Waterfield and shifty halfbacks such as Tom Harmon and Kenny Washington. The time was also used to review offensive formations and to implement any strategy changes for the upcoming battle.

Meanwhile, in Los Angeles, the newspapers were filled with the tales and exploits of the Cardinals' "Dream Backfield" and advance ticket sales were soaring. Rams coach Bob Snyder was hospitalized with influenza and was expected to miss the game. Snyder spent his down time devising a reliable defensive scheme to slow down the Cardinals' offense, but after careful consideration, he scrapped that plan on the eve of the game and sent his assistants George Trafton and Joe Stydahar a simple message: "Outscore them."

When the Cardinals arrived in Los Angeles, Burkett's discomfort had not abated so he was rushed to Cedars of Lebanon Hospital in Hollywood where he underwent an emergency appendectomy on Saturday, October 18. Burkett sailed through the procedure but his participation in the game would be limited to listening to the encounter on the radio from his hospital bed. Burkett's presence would be missed, however. His surprising ability as a punter had not been expected by Conzelman who now was using the rookie as another defensive weapon. Burkett's punts would often leave the opposition deep in their own territory, and in any exchange of punts, the Cardinals usually walked away with an advantage in yardage. After the first three weeks of the 1947 season, Burkett topped the NFL with a 47.4 punting average and had developed into an all-around offensive threat as well.

For the third straight week, the Cardinals established some type of attendance record. The crowd in Los Angeles on October 20 was 69,631, the largest audience in the history of the league. If Coach Snyder had figured out the best way to defeat the Cardinals was simply to outscore them, he was right. But it was the Rams' defense which rose to the occasion on that warm afternoon to stifle the Cards and pave the way for a stunning 27-7 win. The highly vaunted Chicago offense sputtered and stumbled, with both the passing and rushing games shut down by the Rams. Defensively, the Cardinals could not solve the running of Harmon, Washington, Pat West, and Dante Magnani, who plundered the defense for 260 yards on the ground. The Cardinals could manage just eighty rushing yards with Trippi held to thirty-six in nine attempts. Conzelman was terse, and to the point, in his analysis of the game:

> *We got the hell kicked out of us. We were down after two hard games. We'll be ready for the Rams when we meet again in two weeks.*

The loss dropped the Cards (3-1) back into a three-way tie with the Rams and the Packers for first place in the division, while the rapidly improving Bears were just a step behind at 2-2. It would be a miserable three-day train ride back to Chicago following the unexpected pummeling by the Rams. Conzelman's motivational abilities would be keenly tested during the dreary return trip. Burkett attempted to escape the hospital in order to return with the team on the Monday train, but the doctors advised against such an arduous trip so soon after the operation. The rookie standout reluctantly agreed to rest in Los Angeles for a few more days before flying back to Chicago.

Along the way, the team was soon missing another player when Paul Christman hopped off the train during a brief stop in Kansas City on Wednesday, October 22, to phone his family. The call took a little longer than expected, and when Christman returned to the platform, the Cardinals' train had departed, leaving the quarterback to seek another means of transportation back to Chicago. The quick phone call ended up costing the quarterback $50 in team fines.

Practices began anew on Thursday, October 23, in Comiskey Park, when the coach unleashed a five-hour session on the team. Conzelman planned extensive drills for his team with only three days of work available before the Boston Yanks (1-2-1) arrived in town. Following the regular practice, there was a mandatory film session during which the coaches broke down the individual performances from the Rams debacle. Assistant coach Phil Handler also awaited news from the league office in New York on possible penalties for his animated protest of what he considered questionable officiating by the back judge in the Los Angeles game. When the news finally rolled in, it wasn't good: Handler was fined $50 and suspended indefinitely. Pop Ivy also received word that he was on the receiving end of an automatic $50 fine for his part in a fracas during the Rams game.

In an attempt to drive home his point regarding lackadaisical play, Conzelman forced the team to watch a two-hour epic motion picture starring the Cardinals in their embarrassing loss to the Rams, as well as their careless performance in the scary preseason win over Boston. The team still had a hold on its claim to the league championship, and the coach was not about to allow his team to lose that grip. The usually loose Cardinals were sober and subdued during practice; Conzelman had apparently made his point.

On Friday, Conzelman pushed the team through three hours of meetings and drills, a heavy menu for a team to absorb in midseason. He also announced that Pat Harder would be doubtful for Sunday's game and would be replaced by either Cochran or Angsman. Mallouf would handle Burkett's punting duties.

## *The Chicago Cardinals Forgot Their Grief For Two Hours*

On Saturday morning, the players awoke to learn the horrifying news that Burkett was one of fifty-two victims of a plane crash in Utah. Burkett had attempted to join his teammates on the train ride home from Los Angeles, but remained in that city to recuperate until Friday morning. He was a passenger on a United Airlines DC-6 which left Los Angeles at 11:23 A.M. (Chicago time) for the nonstop, six-hour flight. At 1:21, pilot Scotty MacMillan reported the presence of a fire in the baggage compartment and deployed an automatic extinguishing system. By 1:26, he indicated that the fire was going out and that he would be attempting an emergency landing at the Bryce Canyon (UT) field. However, witnesses on the ground reported that the plane was indeed on fire, and the flames may have destroyed the tail control lines.

MacMillan's valiant efforts to save his passengers ended when the plane went down less than thirty seconds from the air strip. The time was 1:32. Burkett, a war veteran and the NFL's leading punter, was dead at the age of twenty-six. The team—and the city—-was stunned. "There hasn't been a punter in recent NFL history like Burkett," wrote Harry Sheer in the *Daily News*. "He was developing into a dangerous end, a hard-playing deadeye defensive halfback . . . obviously into future stardom . . . There will be no replacement for Jeff Burkett at Comiskey Park tomorrow." Center Vince Banonis concurred: "Jeff was one of the greatest punters I've ever seen. He would definitely have set some records in the NFL." As a person, Burkett was even more of a star. "He was a wonderful person," added Marshall Goldberg. "It was a shame he was unable to reach his great potential."

Jefferson Davis Burkett was a native of Hattiesburg, Mississippi, who resided in Chicago at 5514 South Blackstone. He won letters in football, basketball, and track at LSU while also serving as president of the student body. During the war, he was a first lieutenant in the infantry, and spent three years in the military. His loss would be a tough one for the Cardinals, a team still reeling from the unexpected passing of owner Charlie Bidwill a few months earlier as well as that of team physician Dr. William Meacham.

Suddenly, the loss to the Rams seemed insignificant. The bright sunshine of this happy season had been forever dimmed. "It was pretty hard for us to regroup for the game after this because it was such a sad situation," noted Goldberg. "As players we knew we had to focus on the game and go on—but it wasn't easy."

Perhaps the toughest job fell on the shoulders of Coach Conzelman. He not only needed to prepare his team for a big game on Sunday, but when word reached him about the air disaster, he rushed to Municipal (now Midway) Airport to comfort Burkett's wife, who had been awaiting the arrival of the plane.

One day later, the Cardinals joined together as a team, dropped their personal problems, and took the field, still numbed by the recent events. Following the national anthem, players and fans observed a moment of silence in memory of Burkett. And then the game went on as scheduled, stated Harry Warren in the *Tribune*:

> The Chicago Cardinals forgot their grief for two hours and a half yesterday. They had a job to do.

> *Mourning the loss of their teammate, Jeff Burkett, who was killed in the plane crash last Friday, the Cardinals went out in Comiskey Park and defeated the Boston Yanks 27-7, for their fourth National Football League victory in five games.*
>
> *In the Cardinal dressing room before the kick-off the usual friendly bantering was replaced by a grim silence. The Cardinals not only were grieving over the loss of Burkett, the punter, but Burkett the man.*
>
> *If Burkett had been present, he would have liked the work of his teammates in yesterday's game, played before 22,286. He would have commended the punting of Ray Mallouf, who now has taken over the kicking duties of the late Louisiana State star.*

To defeat the Yanks, Christman took to the air again, and was successful on 20 out of 32 tosses for 249 yards. Trippi scored his first touchdown as a Cardinal early in the first quarter on a two-yard plunge. Following a Yanks touchdown to tie the score, Loyd Arms recovered a fumble for the Cards on Boston's twenty-seven. Runs by Goldberg, Angsman, and Trippi brought the ball down to the eight, where Dewell made a diving catch to put the Cards ahead 14-7. In the third quarter, Cochran scored on a seven-yard run and Dewell gathered in a fifteen-yard pass from Christman in the final period. The win left the Chicago Cardinals at the top of the division with Green Bay, both with identical 4-1 records. The Rams and Bears were just a game behind with 3-2 marks.

Just two weeks after the shellacking in Los Angeles, the Rams paid a visit to Comiskey Park for the repeat match on November 2. Coach Bob Snyder, well recovered from his bout with the flu, was surprisingly candid in his assessment of the game:

> *We are in good shape for the Cardinals. We beat 'em rather handily in Los Angeles, and while we may not come up with another 27 to 7 score, I see no reason why we can't do it again.*

The wily Conzelman was much more pragmatic, sticking to his usual rhetoric which habitually cast the Cardinals as the underdogs:

> *We are in worse shape today than we were a week ago. These kids might surprise me—and I hope they do—but as I said before we do not appear to be in physical shape to meet those Rams so soon.*

There was some truth to Conzelman's complaints. Harder, Kutner, and Trippi had all been nursing injuries in recent weeks. However, with the seemingly limitless talent pool in the backfield, Conzelman knew that the abilities of Cochran, Angsman, Dimancheff, Rankin, and De Correvont were within easy reach. Against the Rams, he started Christman, Goldberg, Harder, and De Correvont in the backfield when Trippi's ankle injury limited him to just two plays. De Correvont responded with a team-high sixty-three yards in nine carries to push the Cardinals to a 17-10 victory. This win, coupled with Green Bay's 18-17 loss to Pittsburgh, moved the Cardinals (5-1) to sole possession of first place at the midpoint in the season.

In front of a crowd of 40,575, the win over the Rams was sweet revenge for the Cardinals. Like most of the Cards' success stories, it was also a true team effort.

Christman was on target again (13 for 26, 238 yards) but the defense was the real story. Cochran and Bill Blackburn each intercepted two passes, while Vince Banonis and Jake Colhouer both recovered enemy fumbles. The one puzzle the defense was unable to solve was the running of Rams halfback Kenny Washington. The former UCLA star blitzed the Cardinals for a ninety-two-yard scoring run in the first period and nearly tied the game in the fourth period when he was stopped after a thirty-one-yard gainer. Another hometown hero was Mallouf, who twice dropped punts within the Rams' one-yard line. Offensively, Angsman scored both of the team's touchdowns on a two-yard run and on a nineteen-yard reception from Christman. It was also becoming apparent that Christman was firmly in grasp of the team on the field. Although he didn't possess the strongest arm, he picked up the Cardinals through his leadership and perseverance. "He was exceptional," said Kutner. "Paul was a pressure quarterback and a great field general. There was no doubt who was the boss in the huddle."

The second half of the season opened with a quick trip to Detroit. The Lions had been pushed around by the Cardinals 45-21 in the first game of the season, and there was little indication that this contest would be more than a scrimmage for the Chicagoans. While the Cards would be without Trippi again, the Lions would do without the services of Bill Dudley, the 1946 league MVP and the league's current leading scorer. Although the Cardinals coasted to a 17-7 win, neither team seemed inspired after the Cardinals punched out an early 10-0 lead in the first quarter. De Correvont, starting in place of Trippi, scored from the two and Harder later added a fifteen-yard field goal. Harder (sixty-one yards), De Correvont (thirty-six yards), and Goldberg (twenty-five yards) paced a Cardinals offense that was plagued by a subpar day from Christman (four for seventeen, seventy-four yards). With this "breather" out of the way, the Cardinals returned to Chicago for the final home game of the year against Green Bay on November 16.

While the powerful Cardinal offense was well documented, the defense was quietly asserting itself as well. Through seven games, the Cardinals (6-1) had allowed the fewest points (eighty-nine) and the fewest first downs (ninety-nine) in the league. Green Bay (5-3) was nearly as stingy on defense, especially against the pass. The Packers had suffered their three defeats by a total of just eight points, but still figured to be in the championship race with a victory over the Cardinals. Meanwhile, on the North Side, the Bears (5-2) had been nearly unstoppable over the past month and were quietly lurking in the Cards' shadow, waiting for the opportunity to overtake the season-long division leaders.

By the end of the third period of the Green Bay game, it seemed that the Bears' wait was nearly over. The Packers had carved out a 20-7 lead after three quarters and were ready to waltz in with the upset victory. But then a little luck—and a great deal of determination—brought the Cards off the canvas. Early in the fourth quarter, Christman led a nine-play drive which culminated with Pat Harder's one-yard plunge. His extra point narrowed the gap to 20-14. On their next possession, the Cards started on their own thirty-four before a Christman pass was grabbed by Kutner at the Green Bay twenty-three . . . and fumbled.

Some luck? Dewell was prowling in the area and pounced on the loose ball to retain possession. From there, Christman and Kutner combined again for a scoring toss to tie the score at 20-20. Harder came on and was perfect with the extra-point try, giving the Cardinals a 21-20 advantage.

But the Packers weren't ready to surrender. They moved from their own twenty-seven to the Cardinals' fifteen before being stopped. With just thirty-five seconds remaining, former Cardinal Ward Cuff lined up for the game-winning field goal attempt. This fifteen-yard chip shot was no big deal for the veteran Cuff . . . a gimme . . . a sure thing . . .

Some luck? As Cuff moved into his kick, the crowd of 40,086 grew silent, then roared with excitement as the ball somehow veered away from the goal posts, ensuring the Cardinals' breathtaking 21-20 victory. Cuff slumped at his misfortune, again. A week earlier, his last-ditch field goal attempt against the Bears had been blocked, and the Packers were jabbed with another close loss.

While the Cardinals (7-1) continued to win, the sharpness seen in the earlier games seemed to be lacking. Conzelman looked at his calendar and noted that the team had been at it almost nonstop for over three months. He decided that some rest might be a proper remedy and gave the players two days off. Due to a quirk in the schedule, the Cards would conclude their season with four straight road games, including the next three Sundays in Washington, New York, and Philadelphia, before meeting the Bears in the season finale.

He hoped the rest would help heal some of those nagging injuries, the latest a knee injury suffered by guard Buster Ramsey in the Green Bay game. Trippi played briefly against the Packers but still was not at full strength. The team did welcome the return of center Bill Campbell, who had been out the entire regular season from an injury suffered in the exhibition game with the Giants.

## It Was A Good Sneeze

Still, the Cardinals were enjoying the limelight and the prestige of being the front runners in the NFL, from national press coverage to free dress shirts from a local clothier for any player who scored a Cardinals touchdown. Conzelman continued to spin yarns, although many were in comparing the team of 1947 with the "have-nots" from earlier in the decade when fan support was not quite where it was during the current campaign:

> *The Cardinals were losing 28-0 when our halfback was knocked out. Four Cardinals went over to carry him to the bench on a stretcher but on the way, they tipped it over. A disgusted fan yelled out: "Didn't they learn you bums nothin' in colliatch? You ain't even good pallbearers!"*

Prior to the Washington game, the coach addressed the Football Writers Association luncheon and was asked about his own coaching job with the team:

> *As for my Cardinals, I like to say we're not very deep. That way I can show what a terrific coaching job I've done. No one appreciates the endless hours I've put in with Charlie Trippi, teaching him to be a great football player!*

In the *Washington Times-Herald*, Bob Addie summarized the Cardinals' banner season:

*The Cardinals, of course, have been the sensation of the league. From the orphans of the league, they've suddenly developed into the greatest drawing card and they've already played to over 180,000 in five home games.*

On the road, the Cardinals were treated like contenders by management, perhaps because for one of the few times in the history of the franchise up to that point, there was ample funding to support the entourage on the road. According to an article in *Football Digest,* the players deserved the best and earned it for both their abilities on the field and their personae off the field:

*Another reason for the Cardinals gentlemanly bearing is that they are in fact, gentlemen. There is no formal bed check when the club goes traveling; no training table; no "don't smoke" or "don't drink" pronouncements. The Cards travel in style and live up to their surroundings.*

*The club helps. On a typical Cardinal road trip, a couple of Pullman cars are requisitioned by the team. Everybody gets a lower berth. Meal allowance is $5.50 a day, equal to tops for the league. The players stay at the best hotels in cities throughout the circuit.*

*"Figuring everything," president (Ray) Benningsen said recently in a harrowed voice, "our traveling expenses are horrendous. For just railroad fare, hotel expenses and meals—nothing else—we spent $75,000 on the road in 1947!"*

The first stop on the season-ending road show would be in Washington (2-6) on November 23. The Cards' league-leading pass defense would surely be tested by the NFL's top passer, Sammy Baugh of the Redskins. The determined Chicago defense still ruled the charts in terms of allowing the fewest points, the lowest total yardage, and the least passing yards. If the Cardinals could stop Baugh, there would be little else for the Redskins to offer.

Offensively, the Cards lost one of their weapons in one of the most unusual injuries in football history. While riding the overnight Baltimore & Ohio train to Washington with his teammates, star end Billy Dewell sneezed. It was a good sneeze.

So good that Dewell suffered a sacroiliac strain and was out for the game. He still remembers the specifics of that unusual "injury":

*I was waiting for Paul Christman to go to breakfast on the train. I was all slouched down and then got this sudden sneeze. It took me about five minutes to get out of the chair because the sneeze kicked a vertebrae right out of place. They tried to get me ready to play, but there was no way I could play. But our trainer Mush Eshler was incredible and I was able to play the whole game the next week.*

As it turned out, Dewell didn't miss much. Although the Redskins correctly took advantage of Dewell's absence by double-teaming Kutner throughout the afternoon, it was Sammy Baugh and the Washington offense which was nothing to sneeze at.

The Redskins celebrated the eleven-year NFL reign of Sammy Baugh by holding a "Sammy Baugh Day" ceremony before the Cardinals' game. The Washington Touchdown Club gave Baugh a shiny new station wagon, and he gave them the performance of his career. Before it was all over, Baugh had completed 25 out of 33 passes for 355 yards and an incredible 6 touchdowns, still tied for the most ever thrown against the Cardinals in one game. Baugh's torrid achievement resurrected the slumping Redskins and buried the Cardinals 45-21. The Cards were obviously surprised by this touchdown deluge and were powerless to stop it. "Conzelman chain-smoked and fidgeted in high water flannel slacks and a zoot sport jacket," during the game, observed the *Washington News*.

Baugh's barrage also shattered his own single-season records for most passes completed and most passing yardage, the former also being an NFL record. To add to the woe, both Goldberg and Rabbit Smith were injured while Baugh's luminous role was balanced in the book of pass completions by Christman's difficulties. The Cards' magical quarterback could pull only eight completions (twenty attempts) out of his hat for a mere ninety-two yards and three interceptions. Conzelman put out the call for a relief pitcher, and Ray Mallouf responded by completing thirteen out of twenty-four for ninety-nine yards in his first extended appearance of the year. Things were so bad that Trippi's brilliant eighty-two-yard punt return was called back early in the fourth quarter because of a penalty, setting up still another Washington touchdown.

After a game like that, there was little one could say to break the somber mood, but the effusive Christman found a way. Looking around at his silent teammates, he quipped:

> How about that Sammy Baugh? Before the game, he gets a new car. During the game, he completes six touchdown passes. After the game, he hasn't even got his pants dirty. And this is the first time I've been off my back all afternoon!

Certainly, the cannon arm of Baugh fired the shot heard around the NFL, and no one was more delighted than George Halas. Suddenly, after a season of trailing the Cards, the Bears were now tied for first place with their city rivals:

> I don't know whether the Bears can win the western division race, but at least the matter now is in our own hands. Before the Cards lost we just had to hope for a break. Now it's up to us and I think we've got a good chance.

As the NFL season moved towards its conclusion, the league office summoned representatives of the Bears and Cardinals to meet in Philadelphia on Monday, November 24, to determine the site of a divisional playoff game if one was needed. Although three games remained, the two clubs were tied with 7-2 marks, and there was a distinct possibility that there could be a deadlock after the final game. A coin flip was held between Cardinals president Ray Benningsen and Rudy Custer, the Bears' business manager. Custer won the toss and selected Wrigley Field as the site for a possible December 21 playoff game. If no playoffs were necessary, the league championship would be held on that date.

It didn't take the Bears long to ease ahead of the deadlock when they defeated Detroit on Thanksgiving Day, November 27. The idle Cardinals prepared for their November 30 date in New York where they fully expected to keep pace with the Bears against the winless Giants (0-7-2). The Cards had pummeled New York 52-21 in preseason play and there was nothing to indicate that a similar result would not be imminent. Yet the smiles were gone and the team was all business as it departed for New York on November 28. Harry Warren of the *Tribune* provided this observation:

*The usual wise-cracking that has marked the departure of the Chicago Cardinals for earlier games this season was absent yesterday as the team boarded a train for New York for tomorrow's game in the Polo Grounds with the Giants.*

*The loss to the Washington Redskins last Sunday has placed the Giants contest, as well as the one with the Philadelphia Eagles next week, in the category of serious business. The Cardinals realize that if they are to remain in the running for the western division championship of the National Football League, the Giants and Eagles must be defeated . . .*

*Not that the Giants entertain any particular friendship for the Chicago Bears, who will be something like a 100-1 shot to win the western division title if New York wins tomorrow, but Coach Steve Owen's players would like nothing better than to whip the Cardinals. It was the Cardinals who started the Giants off on a disastrous season by beating the New York eleven, 52-21, in an exhibition game.*

In the *Chicago Herald American,* syndicated columnist Roger Treat predicted that the Cardinals were simply "unpredictable" and that the team's performance was likely to vary widely in this pivotal encounter:

*Panic hits the fluttering Cardinals and they blow wide apart—or they pull themselves out of the mud pile where Sam Baugh pitched them and come back to win like a champion.*

## The Jekyll And Hyde Of Football

However, in the biggest upset of the pro season, the Giants emerged with a wild 35-31 victory over the Cardinals. This loss, coupled with the Bears' win in Detroit, knocked the Cardinals out of first place, and seemed to shut the door on any championship hopes for 1947. The struggling Giants captured their first game of the year behind Paul Governali, who scored two touchdowns and passed for another pair. The bewildered Cardinals had no answer on defense for the second week in a row as the Giants countered every Chicago surge with one of their own.

The Giants led 7-3 after the first quarter before the Cards captured the lead midway through the second period. Stan Mauldin blasted New York halfback George Franck and forced a fumble on the Cardinals' own seventeen. Vince Banonis grabbed the loose ball and immediately looked to initiate a lateral. With no one to toss the ball to, Banonis tucked the ball away and began to run . . . and run . . . and run. "I looked around for someone to lateral to, but no one was there. Since no one was there I just started to run!" Banonis recalled.

After a journey of eighty-three yards, Banonis was in the end zone and the Cardinals owned a 10-7 lead. The fumble return by Banonis was the longest in Cardinals history at that time and is still the third best in team annals. Offensively, the Cardinals were superb—Christman regained his marksmanship (13 for 34, 275 yards) with Harder (11 carries, 85 yards) and Angsman (3 carries, 80 yards) gobbling up the turf. The lead sailed back and forth throughout the game before the Giants escaped with the surprising victory.

The road wouldn't get any easier for the Cardinals, either. The next contest would be at Philadelphia against the Eastern Division leaders. It would be a "must" game for both teams; the Eagles needed to maintain their slight lead over Pittsburgh to avoid a playoff, while a Cardinals victory was necessary in order to keep pace behind the Bears and possibly force a playoff with a win on the last day of the season. Once again, the Cardinals would be facing a team that they had defeated handily (38-21) in the preseason. A loss to the Eagles in this game, and the season would be essentially over—with nothing to show for it despite the lofty preseason expectations. "Although the Cardinals already may have lost the western title, the players can salvage respect," surmised veteran sportswriter Wilfrid Smith.

The season had suddenly turned sour for the team that had been coasting toward the title game and was now stumbling right out of the playoffs. The *Daily News* called the Cardinals the "Jekyll and Hyde" of pro football and added:

> *Just how the Chicago Cardinals have disintegrated from the most powerful team in the National Football league to a literal "pushover" . . . is the puzzler of the year.*

The two losses were shocking to the Cardinals, and more than fifty years later, it is still difficult for the players to explain them. "That's the psychology of football," suggested Marshall Goldberg. "Some days you can't do anything right, and if all of your teammates are all in the same state, anything can happen. You either win or lose with the same people." Charlie Trippi noted: "You won't win all of your games in the NFL. Sometimes your best effort isn't enough, and you have a tendency to have off days. That's football."

After a listless first half, the Eagles led 7-3. Superb running back Steve Van Buren scored the only touchdown when he skirted the right side on Philadelphia's first possession before Harder nailed a fourteen-yard field goal from a difficult right angle placement. The Cards struggled into the halftime break with just one rushing first down and little else to brag about for their efforts.

In the hushed locker room, Conzelman looked over his listless players. If ever a team needed a "pep" talk, this was the team. Yet Conzelman decided not to say a word. Later, Paul Christman asked him why he didn't say a thing to the players. Conzelman replied:

> *I didn't have to. I could see on your faces what you were thinking—there goes the championship right out the window.*

The second half was another story . . .

After taking the opening kickoff, the Cardinals marched seventy-nine yards in eleven plays for the go-ahead touchdown. With the ball on the Eagles' five-yard line, Goldberg hit the right side for two yards. Operating out of the "T" formation, Christman gave a straight handoff to left halfback Trippi, who skipped into the end zone behind a monster block from left tackle Chet Bulger. As Bulger pinched his man to the inside, Trippi squeezed into the end zone between Bulger and the goal post (which was still positioned exactly on the goal line). Harder's kick pushed the Cardinals ahead 10-7, but this was just the beginning of the second-half fireworks.

On the next possession, Christman lofted a pass from his own thirty-four to Trippi in the left flat. Despite being surrounded by three defenders and being hit almost immediately by two of them, Trippi eluded the trio and scampered sixty-two yards before being hauled down at the Philadelphia fourteen. Another Christman pass, this time to Dewell, brought the ball down to the one. From there, Vince Banonis stood up the middle of the defense from his center position, and Christman merely stepped into the end zone behind Banonis.

Mal Kutner added to the scoring barrage a few minutes later when he intercepted a deflected pass, and with the blocking help of Blackburn and Mauldin, raced fifty-six yards down the right sideline for a touchdown. It was plays such as this that prompted teammate Marshall Goldberg to comment about Kutner:

> *He's such a brilliant defensive player that the Cardinals play him at defensive halfback when the other team has the ball and he blankets everything that comes his way.*

Kutner snared another score from the offensive side when Christman found him from twenty-one yards out. The play was made possible by the staunch blocking of both Banonis and Ray Apolskis and then finished when Kutner dragged two defenders into the end zone with him after he made the catch. From a 7-3 halftime deficit, the Chicago Cardinals were now safely ahead 31-7 and ready for a rematch with the Bears.

To complete the 45-21 rout, Harder took a pitch from Mallouf to score from five yards out, and Trippi picked off another pass and took it in from fifty-nine yards. In one lovely half of football, it appeared that both the offense and the defense of the Cardinals had finally answered the call at the same time. John Carmichael reported on the impressive victory in the *Daily News:*

> *It was a bitter, bruising battle, full of elbows, sly fists, twisting hands and nervous knees as the Cards won their first National League game from Philadelphia in 12 years. The distraught officials handed out 214 yards in penalties, piling up more yardage with the ball than most of the carriers . . .*

But the news got even better. When the Cardinals were preparing to depart from Philadelphia, they learned that the Los Angeles Rams had upset the Bears in Chicago 17-14. This left the Bears and the Cardinals tied for the division lead with identical 8-3 records. The final game of the season in Wrigley Field now loomed as the most important episode in the NFL's longest running rivalry. It would be "winner-take-all" for either the Cardinals or the Bears. In the Eastern Division, Philadelphia would need to defeat Green Bay the following week to qualify for a possible playoff with Pittsburgh.

## *Sleeping In A Chair Every Night*

As the South Side prepared to meet the North Side on Sunday, December 14, the local media began to churn out reports, predictions, and prognostications. Harry Warren wrote in the *Tribune:*

> *Chicago's Cardinals and Bears, without the benefit of such weapons of war as blackjacks, brass knucks and six ounce boxing gloves will meet in Wrigley Field*

*Sunday to decide the western division championship of the National Football League.*

Both camps were confident of a victory. Tickets for the NFL Championship game to be played on December 21 were sold at both Comiskey Park and Wrigley Field. Now it was up to the two Chicago football teams to decide where that championship game would be played.

With just a few games left to prepare for the division championship honors, Conzelman held a Monday practice for the first time during the season. Typically, this was an off day for the players to rest and for the coaches to begin developing their game plan for the next opponent. The usually open Conzelman also closed off his practice sessions to visitors and the press, apparently for the purpose of installing new offensive and defensive maneuvers specifically for the Bears game. Edgar C. Greene delineated this tactical situation in the *Herald:*

> *The South side armory that houses the Cardinals' secrets is patrolled by police-men keeping newspapermen, casual interlopers and Bear spies from previewing the weapons in store for George Halas and company.*

But what could Conzelman possibly dream up for an opponent this late in the season? In the September 18, 1961, issue of *Sports Illustrated,* Conzelman explained his strategy:

> *We were scheduled to meet the Chicago Bears for the Western Division championship and the right to play Philadelphia for the national championship. They were stronger than we were. So we thought we'd have to score first to have a chance. The game was played at Wrigley Field, home of the Bears, and we always figured that the score was 7-0 against us before we took the field against the home team.*
>
> *So we studied our scouting reports, and they showed that one of the Bears line-backers was not as fast as the others. We decided to devise a play that would run our fastest halfback—Babe Dimancheff—at such an angle that this particular linebacker on the Bears would have to cover him. So we designed a pass play, taking into account the defense our scouts said the Bears would use deep in our territory. Now, ideally, we would use this play right at the start—and that meant we were hoping to win the toss and elect to receive.*
>
> *Well, we had the play worked out Tuesday afternoon for the big game on the following Sunday. But at practice Babe Dimancheff didn't show up. I asked where he was, and somebody said, "He's at the hospital. His wife is having a baby." That was all right. One day's delay in rehearsing the play wouldn't make the dif-ference. But next day Babe failed to show again. But he did telephone. He said the doctor said the baby might not arrive for two or three days. I asked him if it might be possible for him to drop in at practice and just run through the all-important play that we had built around him. Babe said, "Oh, Coach, I could-n't leave my wife for a minute at a time like this."*
>
> *So I said, "Babe, are you staying at the hospital around the clock?" He said he was and he promised that he would come to practice when the baby was born and he was absolutely sure that mother and child were doing well. I said, "Have you got a room out there at the hospital, Babe?" He said he didn't exactly have*

*a room. I asked him if he had a bed in the waiting room or the corridor or what.*
*The Babe said, "No, Coach, I'm sleeping in a chair."*

*I couldn't help saying that this game Sunday was pretty important to all of us*
*and although I understood his feelings perfectly it was rather awkward to have*
*the key man in our key play getting into condition by sleeping in a chair every*
*night. He agreed that it was a shame.*

By mid-week, all reserved and bleacher seats at Wrigley Field had been sold out,
and a crowd of over fifty thousand was now expected. Both teams would be at near
full-strength, although the Cardinals announced that rising rookie tackle Caleb Martin
would be out of action due to internal injuries suffered in the Eagles' game. Guard
Buster Ramsey was also doubtful. As the week progressed and the weather report diminished, Conzelman kept his team indoors for additional private indoor practices at 5200
South Cottage Grove. The Bears did likewise, noted the *Tribune*:

*The Cardinals also abandoned Comiskey Park this week and have been drilling*
*at the 124th field artillery armory on 52nd street. Coach Jimmy Conzelman*
*announced flatly that the Cardinal practice sessions of Thursday and Friday would*
*be secret . . . While the Bears were not so insistent on the strict secrecy sessions,*
*those fellows doing sentry duty outside the Chicago avenue armory were not walk-*
*ing up and down just to keep warm.*

Also on Thursday (December 11), Conzelman awaited the return of Dimancheff:

*Thursday came along. No Babe. But he called up with another cheerful bulletin*
*from the doctor and added that he himself was resting well in his chair.*

Both the Bears and the Cardinals held their final full practice sessions on Friday,
and the Bears assured the media that the Wrigley Field turf would be dry for the big
game. Eleven tons of hay and a canvas tarp would remain on the field until just prior
to the game on Sunday, and the Bears began to sell standing-room-only tickets. Both
teams were exuding confidence, albeit with respect for their opponents. Conzelman
told the *Daily News*:

*The Bears look like the best offensive team in history. Our scout who saw the Rams*
*beat the Bears reported Los Angeles was outplayed all the way, but managed to*
*hold in the right spots. That's what we'll have to do Sunday—hold in the right*
*spots.*

Conzelman was still itching to practice his new "trick" play and finally received
some good news from Dimancheff:

*But late Friday afternoon there was a call from Dimancheff. He said, "Great*
*news, Coach. It's a girl, and we're naming her Victoria for the big victory we're*
*going to win Sunday." I congratulated Babe and asked him if he could come to*
*a meeting that evening so we could diagram the play for him on the blackboard.*
*He said he'd be there and would have a cigar for me. I had the feeling by this*
*time that the cigar would be all I'd have to show for the game with the Bears.*

*That evening we had our meeting and explained the play to Babe. I was get-*
*ting a little dubious about our chances, but Babe—after five nights sleeping in*

*that chair—was bubbling over with confidence as he passed out the cigars.*

Dimancheff, now living in California, still recalls that unusual week:

*My wife did go into the hospital at the beginning of the week and I stayed with her and didn't practice all week. When the baby was born (Judith Ann, not Victoria as Conzelman remembered), I attended the team meeting and handed out cigars. We went over the play and we all felt it would work, but we never did actually practice it.*

On Sunday, December 14, the Cardinals and the Bears met for the 52nd time since 1920. Despite all the thrills, chills, and personal grudge matches experienced during those many years, this final game of 1947 was the first with such lofty objectives. Chicago's growling newspapers fired out lyrical messages passionately and persistently.

### Chicago Tribune:
*Explosive football produced in the laboratories of the Bears and Cardinals, will provide entertainment today for 48,000 fans who will jam Wrigley Field . . . To appropriate a well-worn phrase—"This is it!"*

### Chicago Daily News:
*It's the game all Chicago has been waiting for, the greatest climax pro football has known locally. It has caught the popular fancy so completely that all seats were sold weeks ago, and the park will be jammed with close to 50,000 fans. The Bears rate a slight favorite, probably largely from force of habit. Off the statistics, it figures to be as close as the proverbial rich uncle.*

### Chicago Herald American:
*They'll be scalping seats in the corner saloon . . . that bistro with the television set pointed at Wrigley Field. Get yours early and watch a bevy of transplanted Chicagoans cut up the Western Division championship.*

## No One Could Catch The "Babe"

Conzelman was probably elated when the Cardinals won the coin toss and elected to receive. Despite Dimancheff's lack of practice with the recently conceived play, the coach still hoped that it worked as an early, quick strike for the offense:

*We won the toss . . . and the Bears kicked over the goal line. The ball was brought out to the 20, and Paul Christman called for the key play. The defensive left halfback of the Bears was pulled toward the center of the field on a fake by our right end, Mal Kutner. Babe Dimancheff swung to the outside, followed by the slower linebacker of the Bears. Babe gradually pulled away from him, and then at the 40-yard line he turned, and Christman threw the long pass. It worked perfectly. Babe grabbed it and streaked for a touchdown. We kicked the point and we were off to the 7 to 0 lead we figured we needed.*

Harry Sheer captured the moment in his report for the *Daily News:*

*To make it a complete sleeper, they moved Boris "Babe" Dimancheff, their clutch receiver and left half, to right . . . for the first and only time this season. The first play . . . sure enough, Dimancheff is at right half. Dimancheff moves off to the flat, to his right. End Mal Kutner dips to his left and, just as Handler and Parker figured . . . Holovak (Bears' linebacker) faded with him.*

*That sent Dimancheff rocketing down the west sideline, with Holovak caught flatfooted on the decoy. No one could catch the "Babe" now. Christman hung the ball on a string, perfect, and Dimancheff dragged it in with a brilliant try on the Bear 49. He was off and away, 80 yards for a touchdown, 16 seconds after the opening whistle.*

Dimancheff remembers "the play" this way:

*The play was concocted for me as the right halfback instead of me being at left half as usual. Mal Kutner, the right end, came across to his left and when I came out of the backfield, the linebacker had to cover me. I acted like I was going outside, but then went in, and Christman hit me with a perfect pass.*

Perhaps lost in the glow of the success of "The Play" was the contribution of assistant coaches Phil Handler, Buddy Parker, and Bill Plasman. "Much of the credit for the success of the team should go to the assistant coaches," stated Red Cochran. "Jimmy let these guys do what they wanted to do. They had a lot to do with designing that play." Chet Bulger added: "Buddy Parker was like a computer. He would analyze every play at every game. He knew what would work."

The Cardinals' lead swelled to 27-7 at the half and they cruised to a surprisingly easy 30-21 victory. Wilfrid Smith's analysis correctly identified Dimancheff's touchdown as the key point in the game:

*The Bears never completely recovered from the shock of Paul Christman's 80 yard touchdown pass to Babe Dimancheff on the first scrimmage. And when they did exhibit intermittent flashes of their famed power, they shackled those efforts by penalty and by errors of judgment and execution.*

"We knew it would work," stated Conzelman. "Every guy on the team played it perfectly . . . the most vital play of the game."

The Cardinals intercepted 4 of Sid Luckman's passes and limited the Bears' passing ace to 10 out of 27 completions for 212 yards. Meanwhile Christman connected on 10 out of 22 for 329 yards. Also on offense, Elmer Angsman recovered from a bout with the flu to score a pair of touchdowns and Mal Kutner added another. Pat Harder contributed a field goal and four extra points.

## *Those Valiant, Scrappy, Ingenious Cardinals*

Interceptions by Vince Banonis and Hamilton Nichols, along with fumble recoveries by Jack Doolan and Bill Blackburn, helped keep the Bears at a disadvantage in front of 48,632. Roger Treat summed up the victory party in the *Herald American:*

*They murdered the Bears yesterday, these valiant, scrappy, ingenious Cardinals who had to come up from two serious knockdowns late in the season and win under terrific pressure, two games in a row.*

Out East, the Eagles surprised Green Bay 28-14 to move into a first-place tie with Pittsburgh (8-4) for the division title. Steve Van Buren paced the Eagles with 3 touchdowns and 96 yards which enabled him to establish a new NFL season rushing record with 1,008 yards. The Philadelphia victory, however, would necessitate a playoff between the Eagles and the Steelers on December 21, thus pushing the NFL championship game in Chicago back to December 28.

The Cardinals would host the title game in Comiskey Park, but the Eastern Division playoff left the Cards with a two-week wait before their next competition. Conzelman countered that dilemma by awarding his team three days off while warning them that the holiday season would be short. "This holiday season—don't interpret it too literally," he told his players. "Holidays don't mean us."

Still, that didn't prohibit the coach from allowing his team some R&R immediately following the division title victory over the Bears:

*After playing and wining two games that we had to win, there was an inevitable letdown emotionally. It was a tough two weeks, and I think the team was "up" even more against Philadelphia than it was against the Bears. The players wouldn't say a word to each other in the dressing room before the game. It was a different sort of readiness than I've ever seen before, and I've played in some big games. And when the game started, they hit the line, they gave everything they had until the last whistle.*

With the regular season completed, the Cardinals learned that Pat Harder was the leading scorer in the league based on his 102 points (7 touchdowns, 7 field goals, and 39 extra points), despite missing 2 games because of injuries.

Harder's courageous all-around play and the Cardinals' return to the top of the league inspired Wilfrid Smith of the *Tribune* to reminisce about his own days with the 1925 championship team and to pay tribute to Cardinals founder Chris O'Brien on December 16:

*When the Chicago Cardinals play Pittsburgh or Philadelphia for the National Football League title December 28 in Comiskey Park, the gangling gray haired gent pacing the lower deck aisles will be Chris O'Brien. Twenty-two years ago Chris was the owner, manager and part time coach of the last Cardinal eleven to win this professional title.*

*Chris has waited these years for this day . . . O'Brien will have company in Comiskey Park December 28. If he looks around he'll find Nick McInerney, Willis Brennan, or even Gob Buckeye . . . The Cards have two weeks to prepare for the final battle. It will not surprise us if O'Brien will report for some of the practice sessions. Twenty-two years is a mighty long time to wait for your team to again reach the top.*

Without knowing which team they would be facing, the Cardinals returned to practice on Thursday, December 18, with a light workout, and then a film review of the Bears' game and the previous two games with the Eagles. The Cards had already defeated the Eagles during the exhibition season (38-21) and on the regular schedule (45-21) but had not met the Steelers. Still, Conzelman voiced no preference for which team he would be most comfortable facing on December 28:

> *Both have good clubs and I don't know which we would rather play against. Philadelphia has the finest and fastest backs in the country, and Pittsburgh uses the single wing back formation, which we are not used to playing against.*

As the week concluded, Conzelman and Phil Handler departed for Pittsburgh to participate both in the NFL draft as well as to scout the Pittsburgh-Philadelphia game. Writers spotted the Cardinals' coaching staff in the stands and Conzelman was asked why he was scouting so late in the season. He told the *Pittsburgh Gazette:*

> *We can't leave a stone unturned. After all, the Cardinals waited nearly a quarter of a century to play in a title game!*

Back in Chicago, the team also turned its attention to the Eagles-Steelers game on Sunday, December 21. The *New York Times* tabbed the Eagles as three-point favorites, but Philadelphia easily flew past Pittsburgh 21-0 to set up the NFL Championship bout with the Cardinals.

After the game, the Eagles' locker room echoed with cries of "Bring on the Cardinals," and each player on the team vowed his dedication to defeating the Cards by promising to drink no more than two bottles of beer while celebrating the win over Pittsburgh. In Chicago, the Cardinals were anxious to return to action, but first, the players met to divide the shares of the proceeds from the upcoming NFL Championship game. In a generous, but not unexpected, gesture from such a class group of individuals, the first full share was voted to the widow of Jeff Burkett.

## Media Guide Player Highlights

The 1947 Cardinals were one of the most beloved teams in the history of football, full of superb athletes, individual personalities, and memorable characters. Professional football players were just beginning to become celebrated as public figures at the time, but little "inside" information was available to the fans. One of the few sources providing personal insight about the players was found in the individual team media guides. Here are some of the innocent glimpses of each player, provided by the 1947 Chicago Cardinals press guide.

- **Roy Anderson:** won letters in football, boxing, basketball, and track at Nevada.
- **Elmer Angsman:** former Notre Dame star broke two ribs and lost eight teeth in games against Navy.
- **Russell Bradford:** held javelin toss record while at Iowa Teachers College.
- **Jeff Burkett:** claimed Southeastern Conference record in high jump during career at LSU.
- **Paul Christman:** hobby is collecting counterfeit coins.

- **John Cochran:** father played professional baseball from 1911 to 1935.

- **Jack Crain:** sold cowboy boots while in college at Texas.

- **Bill De Correvont:** led Austin High School to Chicago city championship.

- **Harold Fredricks:** in off-season is a farmer and baker specializing in muffins.

- **Marshall Goldberg:** invented gadgets and secret pizza pie recipe.

- **Gerald Griffin:** played in Cigar Bowl with Rollins College.

- **Pat Harder:** mother was born in Hales Corner, Wisconsin.

- **Jack MacKenzie:** father was a member of Notre Dame swim team.

- **Ray Mallouf:** both parents were born in Syria.

- **Walt Rankin:** collects Victrola records and ropes calves in off-season.

- **Vic Schwall:** was an ice skater at Schurz High School in Chicago.

- **Rabbit Smith:** hobbies are fishing and hunting.

- **John Stojak:** never played college football but fought in the Battle of the Bulge.

- **Charlie Trippi:** started high school career as a center and likes gin rummy.

- **Bill Blackburn:** born in Welutka (OK), but fought at Okinawa.

- **Vince Banonis:** won two letters in baseball at University of Detroit.

- **Bill Campbell:** mother born in Illinois, father born in Arkansas.

- **Plato Andros:** was eighth-grade record holder in shot put and discus.

- **Ray Apolskis:** works at Marshall Field's store in Chicago.

- **Loyd Arms:** was NCAA wrestling champion while at Oklahoma A & M.

- **Ed Cameron:** MVP of 1946 Orange Bowl and blossoming heavyweight boxer.

- **Jake Colhouer:** was class president at Oklahoma.

- **Bill Conoly:** hobby is golf.

- **Hamilton Nichols:** also participates in midget auto racing.

- **Buster Ramsey:** brother was All-Southern tackle at William and Mary in 1946.

- **Fred Roval:** nicknamed "Rover" and makes ice cream in off-season.

- **Chet Bulger:** held high school record in Maine for both longest field goal and shot put.

- **Joe Coomer:** won ten letters at Austin College; nicknamed "Smokey."

- **Tom Kearns:** majored in Finance at University of Miami.

- **LaVerne Lauffer:** owns a dairy in Mokena, Illinois.

- **Stan Mauldin:** hobbies are flying, hunting, and fishing.
- **Walt Szot:** brothers Steve (Fordham) and Al (Rutgers) also played college football.
- **Bob Zimny:** enjoys drawing home designs, woodworking, and building scale models of homes.
- **Barney Barnett:** played minor league baseball in Western League.
- **George Cotton:** was Pharmacist's Mate in Navy.
- **Billy Dewell:** was captain of basketball team at Texas.
- **Pop Ivy:** won four letters at Skiatook (OK) High School.
- **Mal Kutner:** captain of first Dallas team to win a Texas state basketball title.
- **Babe Dimancheff:** both parents born in Bulgaria; hobbies are gold and music.
- **Jack Doolan:** played previously with Redskins and Giants.
- **Clarence Esser:** captain of 1946 Wisconsin football team.
- **Emil Lussow:** highest scoring end in nation in 1942.
- **Joe Parker:** is a rancher in off-season.
- **Ed Rucinski:** majored in English and Speech at Indiana.

# ◆ 14 ◆

## The Championship: 1947

*"It's just too bad that Charlie couldn't see this."*

MRS. VIOLET BIDWILL,
DECEMBER 28, 1947

So it was settled. The Cardinals would meet the Eagles for the 1947 NFL Championship at Comiskey Park in Chicago on December 28. Up to this time, the Cardinals could boast of just the beleaguered 1925 title while the Eagles had never won an NFL crown. Both clubs would be hungry, determined, and spirited for the big game.

For the championship game in Chicago, the Eagles left the North Philadelphia Station on Train No. 49 (The General) at 6:09 P.M. on Friday, December 26, with arrival scheduled in Chicago at 8:20 A.M. the next morning. While the Eagles usually stayed at the Edgewater Beach Hotel in Chicago, for some reason, a switch was made to the Hotel Sherman for the championship game, which may have contributed in some small part to the Cardinals' victory. When the team issued its new travel rules in April 1948, the following comment was included (perhaps authored by General Manager Al Ennis):

> For the 1947 Championship game at Chicago, we elected to stay at the Hotel Sherman, in downtown Chicago, and had a most unpleasant experience there. At no time did any member of the management contact any of our party to see if things were going satisfactorily, or in any way evince the slightest interest in our behalf. We shall not stop at the Sherman again.

In reviewing the travel policies of the Eagles, it is interesting to note that this team, like the rest of the members of the NFL at the time, kept a keen eye on each and every expense. For example, the Eagles players were still required to provide their own shoes and there were strict rules as to the use of taxis as well as for meal money allotment:

> Buses will meet the train upon arrival in Chicago to transfer the team to the hotel. All players must use this method of transportation. DO NOT TAKE TAXICABS.
>     The Club will not be responsible for any of your expenses except room and meals. Any other expenses which you may incur will be charged to your account and will be deducted from your next pay check . . . Your time is your own after the game, and the Road Secretary will give each of you $2.00 for your evening meal.

Although the Eagles didn't arrive in Chicago until the day before the game, predictions surrounding the contest had been surfacing in newspapers across the country. If it had not already done so, the nation was in the process of discovering Jimmy Conzelman and his Chicago Cardinals. The *New York Mirror* established the Cardinals as an early twelve-point favorite in the title tilt and critics jousted over whether the Cards' two-week layoff would be an advantage or a disadvantage. Giants coach Steve Owens told the *New York Daily News* that the Cardinals might be ripe for a case of overconfidence:

> *The Cardinals hold two decisions over the Eagles this year, but they're liable to act chesty and think the game is a cinch. I'm sure the Eagles will be up for the game.*

The Cardinals' injury list expanded after the Bears game with Pop Ivy suffering a separated shoulder and Mal Kutner receiving attention after an unfortunate collision with a Wrigley Field dugout. Both Buster Ramsey and Clarence Esser would be questionable for the championship game.

Once again, the Cardinals moved their practice sessions indoors, and the Comiskey Park field was buried by eighteen tons of hay and canvas the week before the championship game. The league also announced that the contest could not end in a tie; in the event of a draw at the conclusion of the regulation time, there would be a sudden-death rule in effect. Ticket sales were brisk, with fans having their choice of ducats ranging in price from $2.50 (bleachers) to $5.00 (box).

For the Cardinals, there would be no rest during this holiday season. As promised, Conzelman drilled the team every day of the week, including Christmas Day. The coach would take nothing for granted despite the two previous victories:

> *No doubt about it, the Eagles are the class of the East. They're a rough, tough ball club and now that they've ended their jinx of never reaching the title game they'll be hard to stop. I'm sure we'll be up for this one and don't think we're not giving a little thought to playing in the 1948 All-Star game.*

Conzelman was primarily concerned with stopping the running attack of the Eagles, which featured record-breaking Steve Van Buren and quick Bosh Pritchard. Van Buren would bring his record 1,008 rushing yards (217 attempts) to Chicago, while Pritchard, who did not earn as many carries, was equally dangerous as exemplified by his 79-yard touchdown run against the Steelers in the playoff. Balancing the running attack was the passing of quarterback Tommy Thompson (106 for 211, 1,680 yards), and his favorite target, a Chicago native by the name of Pete Pihos, who topped the Eagles with 23 receptions for 382 yards during the season. It was a potent offense, and one that could explode for huge numbers against the Cardinals. Conzelman was aware of it:

> *There's no doubt about our job—we've got to play our best to win. A letdown against guys like Van Buren and Thompson would be fatal. They'll murder you.*

## Dimancheff Did A Brilliant Job

On the other side of the field, Conzelman could counter with the passing of Christman

(138 for 301, 2,191 yards), the receiving of Kutner (43 receptions for 944 yards, 22-yard average) and Dewell (42 catches for 576 yards, 14-yard average), and of course, his "Dream Backfield." As the season wore on, the "Dream Backfield" had taken on a new personality, wrote the *New York Times*:

> *The Chicago Cardinals hope to get going "fastest with the mostest" in a counter offensive against the running of Philadelphia's champion ball carrier, Steve Van Buren.*
>
> *But Coach Jimmy Conzelman's real galloping threats are Elmer Angsman the ex-Notre Dame blaster, and Boris Dimancheff, former Purdue scat-back, who have been an unheralded nightmare to Cardinal opponents while the so-called "Dream Backfield" of Charlie Trippi, Marshall Goldberg, Paul Christman and Pat Harder basked in the limelight.*
>
> *Angsman, despite constant battering, never missed a game all season . . . and piled up 412 yards in 110 attempts to pace the club's ball-carrying department. Dimancheff did a brilliant job of spelling Trippi at left halfback all season and his romp with a game-opening pass from Christman covering 80 yards for a touchdown, unquestionably broke the back of the Bears in the Western Division showdown.*

With the abundance of running backs available, the cagey Goldberg was playing defense almost exclusively, where he was developing into a pioneer at what is now known as the safety position. "Goldberg," said Conzelman, "is the best man on pass defense that I have ever seen."

By Christmas Day, 1947, Conzelman had figured out what the championship game would entail:

> *Sunday's game with the Philadelphia Eagles boils down to the proposition of shooting the works. We certainly are going to and I'm sure that's what the Eagles also have in mind . . . we can't hold back on anything this time. We won't have to think about scouts taking picks on us for a game the following week and I know Coach Greasy Neale of the Eagles will come up with some stuff that hasn't been displayed this season.*

Coach Neale, despite the two previous losses to the Cards, was surprisingly optimistic: "The way we are going, we're likely to beat anybody." Conzelman would be well prepared as usual, but he worried about two things prior to the game:

> *Greasy Neale and his defenses are one of them, and the contrasting mental attitudes of the two clubs is the other. Greasy threw an eight man line against the Rams and they never had time to adjust to it. That's the way it goes. If you meet a confusing defense, you've only got 60 minutes to figure it out, change your offense and in the meantime, keep them from scoring.*

As with any team sport, it would be difficult to defeat the same opponent three times in the same season. With the advent of comprehensive scouting and the heavy use of game film, the enemy could be studied and dissected. Previous weaknesses could be evaluated and corrected, while new moves to counter the typical strategies of the opponent could be developed. With these tools within reach, the veteran Greasy Neale could surprise the Cardinals with a totally new look. If Neale tipped his hand with the eight-man front against Los Angeles, Conzelman had no choice but to prepare for its possible return in the championship game.

The old coach also understood emotions. It would be tough for him to suppress any overconfidence in his players after they had routed the Eagles just three weeks earlier. As a player himself, he realized that the best friend of any team could be self-motivation. Not the type that a brief pregame fiery pep talk can inspire, in which you growl, snarl, and blast the nearest locker with your helmet before you charge onto the field. No, he feared the type of inner emotion that you can't control; the feeling that swells up inside you when you've been wounded by defeat, and your own pride stubbornly forces you to move faster and harder without hesitation. It gives you that intangible push to sacrifice everything in order to achieve satisfaction, and calm that beast raging within you. The Eagles would have that internal frenzy, Conzelman knew, and he wondered if his talented group would be able to withstand the initial surge of the Eastern champions.

## *Write Something Grim And Frightening*

Two days before the game, Conzelman had an unusual request for reporter Edgar C. Greene of the *Herald:*

> *Do me a favor, will you? Write something grim and frightening about that game Sunday. The boys are working good. They feel fine. But they're not grim enough. Shucks, we felt fine before we played Washington. We were happy as clams before New York and got beat both times!*

Physically, the team would be in good shape after a season-long string of injuries. Only tackles Caleb Martin, Clarence Esser, and defensive end Frank Ivy would be out of the game for sure. Martin suffered internal injuries which required surgery following the previous game with the Eagles, and some of the Cardinals were questioning the legitimacy of the hit/kick which sidelined Martin. Ivy, a stone wall at right defensive end, was gone with a separated shoulder from the Bears' game, and would be toughest to replace. Conzelman had been successful in patching up the backfield earlier in the season when injuries to Harder and Trippi had surfaced. Now he needed to perform some more magic with the line. To help deflect the nuisance of Ivy's loss, Conzelman switched a pair of Rice University graduates to defensive end. Center Bill Campbell and guard Hamilton Nichols were the chosen ones. The team also hoped to regain the services of guard Buster Ramsey, who had been named to one All-Pro team despite playing just a few games. If Ramsey could return to action, it would please his teammates in more ways than one. On one hand, he was a valuable contributor in the middle, and would relieve some of the pressure on the battered line. On the other, his presence on the field would relieve some injured egos and a few wounded eardrums. During his tenure on the sidelines, Ramsey had evolved into something more than a cheerleader for the team, according to Edgar C. Greene in the *Herald:*

> *Buster Ramsey has taken over the job as chief heckler for the Cardinals' linemen,*

*a job that keeps half the Cards infuriated at Buster but taking it out on the opposition.*

*Ramsey makes a point to personally criticize his own linemen every time a gain is made, a block or tackle missed, when the player returns to the bench. The habit doesn't create popularity . . . but the fury incited by Ramsey's invective becomes viciousness when transplanted to the active line . . . but no one has as yet figured a way to silence the voluble guard.*

"He was a little loud, but we put up with him!" explained his friend Vic Banonis. Tackle Chet Bulger was even more direct: "He irritated the hell out of you, but he was a great, great football player!"

The Philadelphia Eagles' train arrived in Chicago at 11:10 on Saturday morning, December 27. Following the Cardinals' final workout at Comiskey Park, the Eagles took the field that afternoon, focusing mostly on loosening up after the long train ride that had been delayed almost three hours by a snowstorm. The team had held a light workout the day before in an armory in Philadelphia where Coach Neale had divided his club into four teams for a brief touch-football session. Coach Neale was pleased to be in Chicago, and happy with the way the season had evolved for his team:

*This is the chance our players have been looking for; ever since the squad assembled at Saranac Lake early in August, they had their gun sights focused on getting into the title game.*

During their busy two-hour final practice stint, the Cardinals concentrated on defending against the passing of Thompson and the running of Van Buren. "Greasy Neale has a fine team," Conzelman told the *New York Times.* "It's a lot stronger than most folks around here credit it with being. The Philadelphia line rates as one of the best in the league." Indeed, the Eagles topped the NFL in allowing the fewest yards by opposing offenses during the regular season. But the ever-cautious Conzelman evaded questions regarding a prediction on the outcome of the game:

*How could any one predict the result? It's like a game of chance. You roll the dice and then hope for the best. Sure, we beat the Eagles 45-21 in the regular season and 38-21 in an exhibition game, but you have to throw out the exhibition and then recall that two of our touchdowns in the other contest were the result of interceptions and another resulted from a recovered fumble.*

Columnist Arthur Daley of the *New York Times* shared Conzelman's reasoning:

*When Conzelman and Neale get together, it's wise to throw away the crystal ball because forecasts are useless.*

## *This Is Another Ball Game Entirely*

The issue of the two previous drubbings of the Eagles was perceived as almost a detriment for the Cardinals by some writers, including Harry Sheer in the *Daily News:*

*They have all the offensive and defensive weapons necessary . . . they have done*

*it twice already: 38-21 and 45-21 . . . and they're on the home grounds at Comiskey
Park. This is another ball game entirely. Complacency on the part of the Cardinals
is just the first stage of an upset and the second stage is the Cards kicking themselves up and down Michigan Avenue on Sunday night. Speaking bluntly, the
Big Red will have to play the best football of the year to win.*

John Carmichael, also of the *Daily News,* chose to reflect on the historical significance of the Cardinals' berth in the title game after such a difficult history and a
roller-coaster ride of a season:

*The last time the Cardinals won a championship, such teams as Portsmouth, Ohio
and Pottsville, Pennsylvania were playing pro ball and that's well over 20 years
ago. As far as the present generation is concerned, this will be the Cardinals' first
crown, if nothing happens.*
 *This isn't a particularly smooth-working Cardinals squad. Even in some of
its winningest performances, it has looked uncertain on occasions. But it has had
the happy faculty of getting "hot" when it had to and it has enough high-class
talent to carry it over the rougher spots.*

With the final practices completed, the Cardinals and Eagles went over last-minute
details and hoped for some much-needed rest. It was difficult for some to sleep that
night with dreams of the championship floating about. "You try and sleep, but you
fantasize about what you're going to do the next day," stated Trippi. "You don't sleep
much because the anxiety is always there." To counter his tension, end Mal Kutner
would take a long walk the night before the game: "The closer you got to the game,
the more tense you became. I was hell in the morning!"
 In 1947, the Cardinals were not required to be sequestered in a downtown hotel
the night before a home game, so the players stayed in their own homes or apartments
with orders to report to Comiskey Park a few hours before the game.
 The Eagles were encamped at the Hotel Sherman at Randolph and Clark (now
the State of Illinois Building). If curfew wasn't a problem, there were plenty of attractions within walking distance of the hotel, or perhaps the players could enjoy the Hotel
Sherman's own night club, "The College Inn." At that time, downtown Chicago was
a mecca for the movie industry, with plush theaters seemingly on every corner. Some
of the blockbusters in town were Errol Flynn in "Escape Me Never" at the United
Artists (Randolph and Dearborn); George Raft in "Intrigue" at the Oriental (Randolph
and State); Fred MacMurray in "Singapore" at the Clark (Clark and Madison); Bing
Crosby and Bob Hope in "Road to Rio" at the State-Lake (State and Lake); Gregory
Peck in "Gentleman's Agreement" at the Apollo (Randolph and Clark); James Cagney
in "Great Guy" at the LaSalle (Madison and Clark); Ronald Reagan in "That Hagen
Girl" at the McVickers (Madison and State): and, Rex Harrison in "The Foxes of
Harrow" at the Monroe (Dearborn and Monroe).
 The City of Chicago awoke to a clear day on Sunday, December 28. It would be
a cold, but not unreasonable, day for late December in Chicago. Temperatures were
expected to hover slightly below the freezing mark (about twenty-eight degrees) by
the 1:05 P.M. kickoff time. In the Cardinals' camp, the news was spreading that this
indeed would be Goldberg's last game. He had finally reached the pinnacle of his pro-

fession after treading patiently through the lean years. It was now possible for him to leave the game while on top and devote himself full time to his business endeavors. If this occurred, stated the *New York Times,* "The Cardinals would be hard pressed to replace him."

The players usually arrived at the field between 10:00 and 10:30 for taping and pregame meetings. As usual, Goldberg taped his own ankles, and took the opportunity to contemplate his role in the game. He had waited nearly a decade for the chance to perform in the NFL Championship game. "We took our time getting ready," he said. "You just concentrated on the game and your own obligations over and over again in your mind."

Those who ventured out onto the field noted that the condition of the field was not conducive to good footing. "The field was hard as cement," recalled Vince Banonis. "Jimmy Conzelman had the foresight to make sneakers available and that really helped. That gave us a lot of traction." "It was bitter cold," added tackle Chet Bulger. "When you play in Chicago that late in the year, it's a penetrating type of cold. The good thing was that in those days, you always had one wool jersey. They were uncomfortable at the beginning of the season, but at the end of the year it was pretty good."

The crowd began to arrive early, but it would fall short of a sellout. Perhaps this was due to the frigid weather, or perhaps the feeling that the game would not be competitive since the Cards had been anointed as the heavy favorite and had already routed the Eagles twice. There was also the availability of local media for the fans. The game would be broadcast on WENR and WJJD radio, and, after some earlier reports denying the possibility, it was announced that WBKB would televise the game locally. Still, an audience of 30,759 was on hand to watch the Chicago Cardinals and the Philadelphia Eagles battle it out for league supremacy as well as for the winners' shares of approximately $1,200 per player. The prevailing team would also land a berth in pro football's summer marquee event, the 1948 College All-Star game.

## *Filed Their Shoes To Razor Sharpness*

Due to the frozen field conditions, the Cardinals appeared for the game in their gym shoes while the Eagles opted for modified football shoes, which were actually sharply honed cleats attached to regular football boots. "They had filed the cleats on their shoes to razor sharpness," reported the *Green Bay Gazette.*

The Cardinals apparently learned of the illegal work on the Eagles' shoes from a clubhouse boy who had peeked in on the Philadelphia locker room before the game. No mention of the shoes was made until the game started when the Cardinals pointed out the handiwork, and the Eagles were assessed a pair of early penalties by referee Tom Dowd for "illegal equipment." Philadelphia trainer Freddie Schubach later claimed that umpire Harry Robb had inspected the shoes thirty minutes before the game and commented "there's nothing wrong with them." Dowd replied, "The cleats were too sharp and they cut a Cardinal's face in the first five minutes."

Philadelphia coach Neale was still livid about the rulings after the game:

> *It won't show in the final score, but at the start of the game we were penalized five yards for illegal equipment when we could have made a first down, and that*

*cost us plenty.*

Former Eagles end Jack Ferrante recalled the situation years later in the *1979 NFC Championship Game Program:*

> *Comiskey was like a skating rink. I hadn't seen anything like it before, but we had taken the weather into account as we got ready in the pre-game. We had on regular football shoes, but the cleats were filed to pretty sharp points. That gave us the traction we needed. I thought they'd work better than the tennis shoes the Cards were wearing. Everything was great until early in the game, when one of their guys got cut by one of our filed cleats and raised hell with the officials. They made us change into basketball shoes right on the spot . . . We just couldn't get any traction. You'd think we were wearing leather-soled shoes on a hockey rink they way we were slipping and sliding.*

It also cost the Eagles the services of their quarterback for four plays when Thompson retreated to the sidelines to change shoes. With both teams now in gym shoes, the footing was treacherous early in the game and the players slipped all over the field. "During this period, they staggered around like 22 drunken men in a dark alley," explained Art Daley in the *Green Bay Gazette.* On just the Cardinals' second play from scrimmage, Christman hit a patch of ice and tumbled freely behind the line of scrimmage.

With the great shoe controversy behind them, the two teams settled down to measure one another. As Conzelman had hoped, the Eagles lined up in their unusual eight-man defensive line (five linemen and three linebackers), one that George Halas did not admire fondly:

> *Eight man line? Bah! All ya gotta do is pinch a back through there and he's practically alone—in the clear.*

And that's exactly the way Conzelman planned to attack it. With just over six minutes gone in the game, Trippi burst through the line and swept past defender Russ Craft for a forty-four-yard touchdown. Pat Harder added the extra point and the Cards delighted the home crowd with a quick 7-0 lead. Conzelman's strategy was apparent. With eight Eagles crowding the line, the Cards usually put one man in motion to draw the attention of one of the three defensive backs, while another could be idled by the threat of a pass receiver coming out of the backfield. This left just one deep defender available should a Cardinals runner crack through the rigid Philadelphia front wall. With the punishing blocking of Banonis, Blackburn, Andros, and Bulger up front, the Cardinals had discovered the Achilles' heel of their opponents. Much of the credit was due to assistant coach Phil Handler, who was particularly adept at breaking down opponents' formations. "We did our homework on the eight-man line," said Banonis. "The blockers attacked at the point where the play was going to take place."

According to Bulger, the blocking strategy was simple: "We considered the end not even in the blocking scheme. We ignored him. What we ran was like a dive play. The backs were taught to run close to the guard and the guard would then need to move his man to make the opening. Even though we were successful against it, the

Eagles stayed with that defense."

"We had a lot of success against the Eagles' eight-man front," added Trippi. "There were really no linebackers, so if you could elude the defensive backs, the defense was very vulnerable."

Before the game, most sportswriters figured that the Cards would succeed via the passing lanes, while the Eagles needed to profit from the expected ground game, fronted by Van Buren, the league's leading rusher. As the game wore on, it appeared that just the opposite would be true. Conzelman had counteracted the Eagles' rushing attack by inserting his three agile centers into the defensive alignment. Banonis remained at center while Blackburn started at defensive end and Bill Campbell moved to defensive halfback. "We usually used a six-man line with a middle linebacker and four defensive backs," explained Red Cochran.

Trippi's touchdown run followed two spectacular individual efforts by his teammates. On the previous Eagles possession, tackle Stan Mauldin sacked Thompson for a huge loss, thus forcing the Eagles to punt. On the punt return, Red Cochran brought it all the way back to the Philadelphia twenty-one. Unfortunately, the Cards were called for clipping and the ball was returned to the Eagles' forty-four. From there, Trippi blasted through the big hole provided by Banonis on a quick opener and dashed in for the score.

As the first quarter slipped past, the Cardinals continued to lead 7-0. The anticipated passing attack generated by Christman was thus far absent. Pitchin' Paul missed on his first six attempts, with most of those fluttering above the heads of his tall receivers. On the other side, Van Buren was going nowhere against the Cards' defense, with Banonis consistently clogging up the middle. Thompson began to test the Cards' secondary with some short passes as an alternative method for moving the ball.

The Eagles mounted their first serious threat early in the second period, following Ernie Steele's punt return to the Cards' thirty-eight. Once again, the running game was flattened, but Thompson completed three passes to bring the ball down to the Cardinals' fourteen-yard line, where the defense held. Three plays later, Christman was sacked on the four, and Chicago was pinned deep in its own territory. Mallouf was forced to punt from the rear of his end zone, and responded with a booming punt to near mid-field. The ball appeared to glance off the leg of one of the Eagles, and was recovered by Coomer, but the officials unpiled the players and awarded the ball to the visitors on the Chicago forty-seven.

Three plays netted just a pair of yards and the Eagles launched a squib kick to the Cards' nineteen. Three runs totaled twelve yards and left the Cardinals with a first down on the thirty. From there, Angsman punched through left guard on a quick opener and was off to the races for the Cardinals' second score. Pat McHugh grabbed Angsman from behind around the five-yard line, and Angsman simply carried him, along with the ball, into the end zone.

Once again, Harder added the extra point and the Eagles trailed 14-0 at the 6:54 mark of the second quarter. "The play was called the '42 Double Trap,'" remembered Angsman. "Since they had eight men on the line, if I got through, all I had to do was beat their halfback and Pat McHugh, the safety."

"We surprised them with our cross blocking," recalled Goldberg. "When Trippi and Angsman went through the line, it was so wide open that you could drive a truck through it. Once they got through, there was no one there to stop them." The Cardinals threatened again moments later when Banonis blocked a punt by Joe Muha and the Cards took over on the Eagles' thirty-five. However, Craft intercepted a Christman pass in the end zone to close that window of opportunity.

After the Eagles and the Cardinals both failed on their next possessions, the visitors took over, and Thompson needed just two plays to bring the Eagles back into contention with less than two minutes left in the half. After succeeding on one short pass to Ferrante for nine yards, Thompson then found McHugh wide open for a fifty-three-yard payoff. The kick by Cliff Patton narrowed the gap to 14-7.

Dimancheff then returned the ensuing kickoff thirty-four yards to the Cards' forty-six before Dewell snatched a pass on the Eagles' twenty-one. A final Christman toss to Dimancheff in the end zone failed, and the teams broke for the half with the Cardinals still ahead by a touchdown.

## *Ran Like Some Kid Being Chased By A Cop*

During the halftime break, the bumps and bruises were beginning to show. The Cardinals players were particularly aware of the rugged play of Eagles guard Frank "Bucko" Kilroy and tackle Al Wistert. After the game, someone asked Paul Christman if it was indeed true that Kilroy had punched him during the game:

> *Yeah, that dumb soandso. Even his teammates were telling him to cut it out. He hit me once, knocked me down, then brought both his fists down on the back of my head.*

The jarring falls to the frozen earth and the violent collisions of elbows, arms, and hands contributed to a series of minor injuries suffered by Cards. Still, they were ahead by a touchdown, and confident that they could continue to contain Van Buren. The two quick touchdowns by the Cards had masked the fact that the offense had been unable to sustain any long drives in the first half. If the game wandered into the fourth quarter with the Cards still holding a slim lead, Christman would need to direct some tactics intended to chew up a bit of the clock.

To start the second half, both teams squandered a pair of possessions, although Thompson was beginning to connect with his targets more easily. With the Eagles moving down to the Cardinals' twenty-seven, Buster Ramsey intercepted a Thompson pass and brought it back forty-two yards to Philadelphia's thirty-four. The Cards failed to convert on this turnover and the Eagles failed as well on their next attempt. Midway through the period, Joe Muha lofted a punt which bounced four times before Trippi gathered it in on his own twenty-five. With no blockers, and three Eagles in front of him, Trippi moved to his left and immediately evaded three defenders, fell down once himself, and then skirted seventy-five yards into the end zone. It may have been the finest punt return in the long history of the Chicago Cardinals. Frank O'Gara described Trippi's triumph in the *Philadelphia Inquirer*:

> *He picked it up as it bounced around on the Cards' 25, and when he battered the first cordon of off-balanced tacklers, there were not many green jerseys in his path. He was hit three more times as he wheeled down the field, but nobody could smack him solidly. Once in the clear, Charlie himself slipped on the Eagles' 25*

*as he tried to cut back behind the final block, but scrambled up and raced across. It was now 21-7 and everyone expected the Eagles to give up gracefully.*

The *Green Bay Gazette* marveled at the now infamous punt return:

*Trippi's longest chase, on a punt return, was strictly a solo since he got no blocking. He didn't need it, what with his odd shoulder motion steering him around would-be tacklers.*

As Trippi zigzagged across the field eluding fallen tacklers, Greasy Neale was said to have yelled at one of his players: "Get up and be ready. He'll be coming back this way any second now!" By the time Trippi finally neared the goal line, he found himself with an unexpected escort, burly tackle Chet Bulger: "We had a set play on punts where I would bump two guys, start down field and keep going. In that game, I was waiting for another guy on the Eagles to come over after Charley, but he never came over. That's how I got in that play."

Harder's kick increased the lead to 21-7, but the ingenious Thompson was hardly through for the day. He immediately guided the Eagles on a seventy-three-yard scoring drive which consumed fifteen plays. With the Eagles apparently discarding the running attack, Thompson surprised the Cards by opening up the drive out of the spread formation (called the "Z-wide style" by the Eagles), which looked like the current "shotgun" approach with backfield blocking forsaken for more receivers. With Thompson all alone deep in his own backfield, he hit on a quick twenty-yard gain to Ferrante to move the Eagles to mid-field. Thompson was a master of deception and utilized fakes and trickery to open up some holes in the Cardinals' secondary. With the ball on the Chicago six, Philadelphia returned to the ground attack and failed three times to cross the end line. Van Buren finally smashed in from the one, and the Eagles cut the gap to 21-14 at the end of the third quarter.

The Cardinals began the fourth quarter on their own twenty-one and survived two big scares in the opening drive of the quarter. First, Trippi lost control of a handoff and appeared to have lost the ball in the backfield, which would have put the Eagles in excellent field position inside the Cardinals' twenty. But not only did the Cards retain possession, the Eagles were also assessed a penalty on the play. This gave Christman some breathing room, but two plays later his long pass was intercepted and returned to the Chicago forty-two. Once again, the hand of fate appeared, and the Eagles were called for clipping. The ball was moved back to the Philadelphia thirty-one. Although the Cards did lose possession, the exchange was probably equal to that of a punt. Thompson failed to move the Eagles for a first down, and Philadelphia was forced to punt from its own thirty-nine.

The punt angled away miserably and Chicago took over on its own forty-seven. Then, for the first time all day, the running game kicked into gear and Angsman in particular helped push the ball down to the Eagles' seventeen, where a Trippi fumble turned the ball back over to Philadelphia. Thompson struck quickly, finding Pete Pihos with a thirty-five-yard pass to the Cards' twenty-three-yard line. However, the spirits of success were once again abandoning the Eagles. A holding infraction was spotted and the big play was brought back to the Eagles' own twenty-one. Again.

Joe Muha surprised the defense with a spectacular sixty-nine-yard quick kick that put the Cardinals deep into their own corner at the ten-yard line. Christman, who was enduring probably his worst day ever as a passer, then returned the favor by combining with Trippi for a twenty-yard gain and some much-savored operating territory. With the passing weapon back in the Cardinals' arsenal, the Eagles slipped again when Angsman burst through the middle once more and galloped seventy yards for another touchdown. According to the *Inquirer,* Angsman "didn't experience the indignity of an alien hand during his 70-yard scoring scamper." Angsman's personal rampage against the Eagles enabled him to break the NFL record for rushing yards in a title game at that time. He finished with 159 yards in just ten carries to shatter the mark of the Bears' Bill Osmanski of 109 yards established in 1940. Conzelman's offensive strategy was working perfectly, with the three long touchdown runs shredding the vaunted eight-man line: "They were delayed smashes that caught Philadelphia entirely off guard and left their secondary badly faked out of position," the coach would state later. Greasy Neale still wasn't convinced as he pointed to the condition of the field: "We had our defensive men all set, but they just couldn't recover on the slippery field when Angsman and Trippi set sail."

Angsman's sudden eruption boosted the Chicago lead to 28-14, just about what the odds makers thought it would be, with a little over seven minutes left. Thompson returned to the air, completing passes of twenty-one and fifteen yards to bring the Eagles into Chicago territory. A questionable pass-interference call on Trippi in the end zone provided the Eagles with a nice placement on the one-yard line, where plunges by Van Buren and Russ Craft were unable to dent the Cardinals' defensive wall. Craft finally managed to squeeze in from a few inches out following the blocking of Frank Kilroy and Jay McDowell, and the Cardinals' lead was trimmed to 28-21.

As the game wore on, the competition became even more intense. Since the two teams shared the same sideline, some peculiar bantering was going on between the two benches, while the diligence on the field did not go unnoticed by the *Green Bay Press-Gazette:*

> As the game wore on, the belligerents got rougher and rougher and the Cardinals' threats at some of the Eagles, including tackles Wistert and Kilroy who were having a big time with their fists and elbows. Pat Harder and Loyd Arms came out with bloody faces from deep cuts.

There was still more than four minutes left to play when Dimancheff staggered the Eagles with a forty-six-yard kickoff return to the Cardinals' forty-seven. From there, Conzelman's plan was simple and pragmatic: keep the ball on the ground. Christman rolled out twelve straight running plays and earned a critical first down on a quarterback sneak as the Cardinals slowly moved down field. With the final moments melting away, the Eagles were frustrated in their attempts to retrieve the ball for one final fling. Twice they refused penalty yardage in order to keep the ball in play, but Christman deviously squeezed the last few seconds out of the clock on three keeper plays to secure the NFL Championship with a 28-21 victory.

As the two teams filed off the field there were the usual handshakes and polite congratulations, but no tumultuous celebrations. No high fives. No jumping into the stands. No Gatorade baths. No trips to Disneyland. No jeering of the losers.

The Chicago Cardinals had accomplished their mission, and they quietly walked off the field like businessmen who had just completed a successful business luncheon meeting. Once inside the warmer confines of the Comiskey Park locker room, it was an entirely different story.

The players, coaches, and staff let loose, as described by Robert Cromie in the *Chicago Tribune:*

> *The dressing room sounded like New Year's Eve at State and Randolph when the Cardinals ran in after tumbling the Philadelphia Eagles . . . "That's the way to go! That's the way to go!" Someone kept shouting over and over, and the great Marshall Goldberg, for whom yesterday's game was his last, struck a mock-heroic pose with his teammates and yelled at the score of photographers: "Just a minute, boys! Don't take any pictures unless I'm in 'em."*
>
> *Flashbulbs went off like Roman candles, the Cardinals grinned at each other and pounded each other on the back, then began stripping off uniforms with one hand as they greeted admirers with the other, meanwhile telling newsmen how such and such a play went, or how hard so and so hit the line.*

Conzelman raced around the locker room, hugging players and shaking hands. Phil Handler was simply in awe after waiting so many years for the Cardinals to return to the top. "How did you like what we did to that line?" Handler asked to no one in particular. "We put in special blocking last week. Just wanted to show those guys we could run through their eight-man line." Conzelman added:

> *The defense of the Eagles was great and they sure rushed the passer. We would look bad time after time trying to run against it, but then suddenly we'd pop a man into the open and he was off to the races. Once a back breaks through the eight-man line there is not much to stop him.*

The *Green Bay Press-Gazette* touted Conzelman's success while partially blaming the Eagles for giving the Cards a most welcome boost:

> *Funny thing, though, the Cardinal job was simplified somewhat by the Eagles screwy eight-man line. Coach Greasy Neale installed it during the Ram game and it produced the first upset of the season . . . and later a victory over the Packers to clinch a tie for the Eastern title. But against the Cardinals, the eight-block wall was so much foolishness with scat men like Trippi and Angsman.*

Meanwhile, Harry Sheer of the *Chicago Daily News* gushed over the new champions and their two new heroes, who presented the South Side with its first championship in over two decades:

> *No crown ever nestled so firmly or as appropriately as the National Football League crown nestles on the Chicago Cardinals today. Twenty-two long, humiliating years then, makes for December 28, 1947. When it came, Sunday at Comiskey Park, the legion of red-shirted battlers did what most everyone said they'd do way back last September.*
>
> *Twice, Chicago's twenty-two year old Elmer Angsman ran like some kid being chased by a cop for a touchdown . . . 70 yards apiece.*

*Twice, the Big Red $100,000 baby, Charlie Trippi, ran with the zeal of a man chasing $100,000, for 44 yards from scrimmage for the Cardinals' opening touchdown, again 75 yards with a punt in the most spectacular run of the longest season in NFL history.*

*That was all the Cardinals needed . . . four plays, four touchdowns, a dead bunch of Eagles . . . a championship their first since 1925.*

While most of the team joined in the celebration, a few, particularly Pat Harder, delayed their participation in order to seek medical attention. Harder's left eye was swollen shut, while Christman, Coomer, Andros, and Arms all had cut and bruised faces. Except for Harder, all of those injuries were claimed to have been the courtesy of the Eagles' Frank Kilroy. Boxer Tony Zale was in the stands for the game and was asked by the *Herald* if he would prefer to get in the ring with Kilroy or Rocky Graziano. Zale indicated that Graziano would be his choice because, "That Kilroy seems to punch pretty good!" The artistry on Harder's face wasn't from Kilroy, however. "Nah, that blank, blank Wistert done mine," said the Cardinals fullback.

In the other locker room, Eagles coach Greasy Neale was disappointed, but not unhappy with his team's performance:

*The boys played the grittiest game of any team I ever coached. It was heart-warming, the way they fought their way back after disappointments that would have taken the starch out of many so-called great teams. Did you ever see a greater individual performance than that of Thompson's? I'm not in the habit of glossing over any failures of our team or individuals, but today we made very few. We knew we'd have to stop Christman's passes and the catching of Dewell and Kutner.*

With the great Steve Van Buren limited to only twenty-six yards on eighteen rushing attempts, Thompson took to the air with record-breaking results. The Philadelphia hurler completed 27 of 44 passes for 297 yards, shattering Sammy Baugh's 1937 championship-game completion record of 18 for 33. Christman suffered through a long day (three for fourteen, fifty-four yards) but was brilliant in masterminding his team's final drive. After the game, he was far from downcast: "I don't care how I played as long as the team won."

Statistically, the game was about even. The Cardinals collected 336 total yards, while the Eagles accumulated 357. Both teams were forced to punt eight times, but the Eagles held a commanding lead in first downs: twenty-two to ten. Obviously, the four "big" plays turned the tide for the winners, but an unsung part of the offense was that of the kicking game. The Cardinals piled up 220 yards on punt (150) and kickoff (70) returns while Philadelphia could manage just 73 in total. "We did everything but beat them," groaned Neale. For Conzelman, the championship marked his second journey to the top of the heap as an NFL coach. His 1928 team at Providence had also captured the crown, but he was too weary to enjoy his personal repeat: "It feels pretty good, but the season was too long for me to have too many emotions left," he stated after the game.

Neale, who was completing his 31st season as a football coach, was already looking forward to the future:

*More power to them . . . I hope they win the Western title next year so that we can have the pleasure of knocking them off in Philadelphia next year. Nobody will beat us in '48 if the boys play like they did today.*

One player who did not expect to be around for the 1948 season was Marshall Goldberg, the pioneer of the team. Goldberg alone had experienced the bewildering coaching regime of Ernie Nevers, played with broken bones, survived a world war, defeated cancer, and sacrificed himself continuously for the good of the team. Now, amid the chaos of the joyful championship celebration, he admitted: "I'm too old for this. I hit Steve van Buren once and it hurt so much it made me sick."

However, Goldberg would return for one more try, as would this talented cadre of Chicago Cardinals. What would be missing in 1948 were the same links that were lost in 1947: Charlie Bidwill and Jeff Burkett. Conzelman acknowledged that he didn't invoke the memory of either man during his inspirational pregame commentary: "These boys were plenty grim without trying to inject a maudlin note."

After the game, the *Associated Press* reported that Violet Bidwill, the widow of the late owner, fought back the tears—both for the joy of the team's victory and for the memory of her husband. "It's just too bad that Charlie couldn't see this," she whispered through a veil of tears.

# Chicago Cardinals: Football Champions Of The World

Although the Chicago Cardinals were now the football champions of the world, it wasn't possible to please everyone on the South Side. As the happy team was trotting off the field, a fan leaned over the rail and shouted to Elmer Angsman: "You're a honey, kid! You're a honey, boy! Even though I lost, I'm for you, kid." "Lost?" Angsman was startled. "Yeah," the fan said a bit sadly. "I gave twelve points.'"

Apparently, winning the NFL title by a mere seven points had not been good enough for this fan, perhaps noting that the Cardinals had been twelve-point favorites, and he had placed his bets in the "office pool" accordingly!

For their efforts, the Cardinals were awarded the winning shares of $1,132 each. That evening, the Chicago Cardinals celebrated their NFL Championship in the Marine Dining Room at the now departed Edgewater Beach Hotel (5300 Sheridan Road). During the evening, Violet Bidwill presented each player with a miniature gold football as a reminder of their championship success. "We each received an envelope to open later," added Chet Bulger. "Each contained a $1,000 bill!" The team enjoyed its last night together and took the time to autograph the menu in the restaurant. The menu is now housed in the Chicago Historical Society as a tribute to the 1947 World Champions.

The off-season work for the Cardinals began immediately. On December 29, Conzelman left on a scouting trip while Phil Handler departed for the Sugar Bowl game. Buddy Parker embarked for the Cotton Bowl while Dick Plasman went to scout the Orange Bowl. The team received some welcome news when Charlie Trippi informed the Atlanta Crackers that he would no longer play professional baseball. "That's a decision he has to make," said Earl Mann, president of the Crackers. "In all fairness, I think we got our money's worth."

Back in Chicago, Ray Benningsen, the Cardinals' president, was asked by a reporter how it felt for the team to finally be the champions. "I can tell you in two words," he replied.

"Wonderful!"

# ◆ 15 ◆

## The Aftermath:
## 1948 – 1959

*"The game (1948 NFL Championship)*
*should never have been played."*

MARSHALL GOLDBERG, 1999

It was a scene like something out of a dream. Bright lights, a warm night, and 101,220 fans in the stands, all to see the Chicago Cardinals.

It had finally all come together: Chris O'Brien's stubbornness; Dr. David Jones's unrestricted optimism; and Charlie Bidwill's dream. The Chicago Cardinals were the football champions of the world and stood ready on the evening of August 20, 1948, to meet the College All-Stars in this popular preseason classic.

While the All-Star game had consistently grown in popularity since its inception in 1934 by Arch Ward and the *Chicago Tribune,* the 1948 game provided a little more drama than usual.

For one, it was the first (and only) appearance by the hometown Cardinals in this long-running event. Next, the pros had endured defeat in both the 1946 and 1947 All-Star games, and therefore the pride of the league was at stake, even though this was intended to be a meaningless exhibition game. In fact, the two previous professional representatives, the Los Angeles Rams (1946) and the Chicago Bears (1947), had both been shut out by the All-Stars by identical 16-0 scores. Finally, the impetus behind the game continued to be the *Tribune's* Mr. Arch Ward, who was also the brain-trust behind the All America Conference, the evil twin of the NFL. Ward had planted the Rockets of the All America league in Chicago, much to the chagrin of both the Bears and the Cardinals. Both leagues continued to wage a bitter battle over players, fans, and media support.

With this in mind, and perhaps because of his own competitive nature, Conzelman treated this contest as if it were a regular league game and brought the Cardinals into training camp much earlier than usual. This overly long year would eventually contribute to the exhaustion Conzelman experienced at the season's conclusion. There was also a concern that putting too much emphasis on this early game might hinder the Cards' performances later in the season when the games really counted.

With the *Tribune's* extensive pregame coverage bolstering the speed, power, and individual talents of the All-Stars, the Cardinals found themselves identified as the underdogs entering the game. The All-Stars, under the tutelage of Frank Leahy of Notre Dame, included three very versatile quarterbacks in Johnny Lujack (Notre Dame), Bobby Layne (Texas), and Bob Chappuis (Michigan), who were expected to shred the Cardinals' defense.

Conzelman himself was taciturn in his approach to the big game. Despite his extensive preparation, the avalanche of *Tribune* publicity heralded "the greatest collegiate all-star squad ever assembled," and Conzelman had to be concerned about the potential of his opposition. Because of his depth of talent, Frank Leahy would elect to utilize both a "T" formation as well as a single-wing offensive set. This, he reasoned, would be the best way to take advantage of the individual quarterbacking talents of his players. He could also continually refresh his players on this typical summer night with his hefty seventy-man roster, compared to the Cardinals' thirty-nine players.

During the pregame preparations, Conzelman continued to fret. There was a certain amount of pressure present from the NFL, which wasn't receptive to the prospect of another loss in this series. With Ward gloriously promoting the wonders of the All-Stars, another NFL defeat could certainly tarnish its capabilities as well as open the door for further marketing jabs from Ward and the All America Conference. But the players were excited about the possibility of playing in front of what was expected to be a huge crowd. "Playing in front of our home town meant the interest would be there," said Red Cochran. "We kidded Bill De Correvont (a former Chicago prep phenom) about playing in front of a crowd like he was used to in high school." De Correvont's Austin High School team had captured the city title in front of more than 100,000 in 1937.

## The Most Perfectly Coached Team

Ultimately, Jimmy did what he does best: prepare and inspire his players to compete in every single game. The All-Star Game of 1948 was no exception. A humorous story which appeared in the press (found in an unidentified article at the Pro Football Hall of Fame) following the game noted that Conzelman was more fired up than usual as he prepared to send his team out on the field to face this unknown quantity:

> *Conzelman . . . had worked himself up into a lather of volcanic oratory. He feared the Cardinals would be knocked off by the College All-Stars. He ranted at his players and impressed them with the fact a hundred thousand human beings would be watching them in Soldier Field.*
>
> *Conzelman paced up and down the dressing room with a rolled-up newspaper in his hand. He pounded the newsprint club into the palm of one hand for emphasis, and he used the paper as a pointer as he singled out this player and that. He told his guys if they didn't snap out of it the College stars would beat them by 40 points.*
>
> *Just then, a drunk staggered into the Cardinals' dressing room hollering: 'Where's that great coach Jimmy Conzelman? Gimme a look at the old so-and-so!'*
>
> *Conzelman whirled in his tracks and threw the newspaper at the drunk so hard that he (Conzelman) fell down. The entire Cardinal squad broke out with hilarious laughter at the sight of their coach. Conzelman got up, dusted himself off and walked out of the dressing room—his grinning players following him. That night they played one of the greatest games in Cardinal history.*

The *Washington Post* reported that the 101,220 fans were "flabbergasted" that night. The *Birmingham News* stated: "The Cards looked like what you would expect from the champions of the National Football League. They were out to win, but they were unmerciful. They were cool and masterful . . . " Matty Bell, coach of Southern Methodist added, "That (the Cardinals) was the most perfectly coached team as a whole I ever saw in action. The line play was out of this world."

The Cardinals surged to a 14-0 halftime lead behind the rushing scores of Elmer Angsman (two yards) and Vic Schwall (fourteen yards). The team then held off an All-Star threat midway through the third quarter, when Marshall Goldberg, "the old war horse from Pitt, perhaps playing his final game," stopped Notre Dame's Floyd Simmons at the one.

In the final period, Vince Banonis returned an intercepted pass twenty-seven yards for a score and Ray Mallouf capped the scoring with an eleven-yard toss to Charley Trippi. The final score was 28-0 and Trippi paced the rushers with eighty yards in fourteen carries. It was the largest margin of victory in the series up to that time. It also reversed the 16-0 defeat the Chicago Bears endured the year before. Zipp Newman wrote in the *Birmingham News:*

> *The Cards were a far different looking professional team than the ponderous Chicago Bears a year ago. They were keyed to just the right pitch. They were sure of themselves from the start.*

"I knew we would win," said halfback Vic Schwall. "We could turn it on offensively whenever we wanted." When it was all over, the Chicago Cardinals, playing in front of their largest crowd in history, walloped the College All-Stars 28-0 and looked nearly invincible moving into the 1948 regular season.

The Cards defeated the Eagles 21-14 in the season opener on September 24. However, the joy of that victory was dimmed by a locker room tragedy following the game. Big Stan Mauldin, the sturdy tackle of the Cardinals, had complained of headaches before the game. "I was the only guy who knew he was in trouble during the game," recalled Schwall. "Stan sat down next to me on the bench and said that he didn't feel good."

"He was the last guy in the shower," said Chet Bulger. "He took a really long cold shower and then came out and just dropped over. It was a big loss because he was such a leader." Shortly thereafter, Mauldin died, apparently of a heart attack. His teammates were crushed by the loss.

"It was tough to play the next game after Stan's death," recalled Red Cochran. Regarding Mauldin, Jimmy Conzelman once said:

> *Mauldin had tremendous speed and instinct. We didn't use the expression "pursuit" then, as they do now in football, but he pursued aggressively, either across the line following the play or by pulling out to meet it on the other side, and he had the knack of knowing when to go easy because the play would be coming back to his side.*

The following week, the stunned and mournful Cardinals dropped their only game of the season, a 21-14 loss to the Bears. Even Conzelman found that he couldn't inspire his team after the devastating loss of Mauldin: "I couldn't be sentimental and I couldn't be irreverent, so I said nothing."

After that game, the Chicago Cardinals smoked the NFL by winning eleven straight games and edging the Bears 24-21 in the final game of the season to once again claim the Western Conference title. Because of the team's depth, the loss of Paul Christman with a broken hand for most of the season didn't slow the team down a bit. "Ray Mallouf came along and we won eleven straight," remarked end Billy Dewell. "He was one of the best forward passers I ever saw."

The once-beaten Chicago Cardinals were scheduled to meet the Eagles in a championship game rematch in Philadelphia's Shibe Park on December 19. "The ironic part of it," noted Cardinals center Vince Banonis, "was that the day before, it was very warm in Philadelphia. We practiced in our T-shirts. The next day, we get up and there's a foot of snow on the windowsill. The bad part about the field was that it was never shoveled during the night when it began snowing hard, so the tarp had all of this snow on it. Both teams had to help get the tarp off the field. During the game, it was tough to center the ball since the ball would get sucked in by the mud."

"If it wasn't for an unbelievable weather day, we could have beaten anyone," recalled team captain Billy Dewell. "I remember Paul Christman looking out the window that morning at the hotel and then telling me, 'Don't look outside.' "

With the blinding snow continuing to fall at kickoff time, the game began under extremely adverse conditions. "You couldn't even see the yard markers," recalled Goldberg. "The game never should have been played." Both teams struggled ineffectively until late in the third quarter, when a Cardinals fumble was recovered by Frank Kilroy at the Cards' seventeen-yard line. "It was nobody's fault," said Conzelman, "just a mix-up on the handoff."

Then, early in the fourth quarter, Steve Van Buren rambled in from five yards out for the only score of the game. The Eagles grabbed a 7-0 victory for the team's first NFL championship.

"It was a crime that we lost that game," stated Cochran. "We had a much better ball club in '48 than in '47. We had beaten the Eagles twice going into that game. We were averaging thirty-three points per game and we were shut out, so you know something was wrong."

After the game, Conzelman remembered a small, kind gesture extended by Eagles coach Greasy Neale. As Neale shook Conzelman's hand he said, "I never beat you, Jim, when you had Mauldin. He was the greatest tackle I ever saw." Conzelman added: "I'll never forget that. A fellow coach, at the moment of his own greatest triumph, paying such a warm and sincere tribute to another team's player."

Conzelman dropped football for good following the 1948 season, which concluded with the finest record in Cardinals history (11-1). The game, it seems, had burned him out. Following the conclusion of the season, he told reporters, "I am very tired . . . this is a helluva grind."

"Jimmy was tired," noted Chet Bulger. "Coaching had become more of a chore for him."

The Cardinals' management was shocked by the resignation, which was described by a member of the front office to the *Associated Press* as "coming like a bolt from the blue . . . We haven't any idea as to his successor."

In truth, the coach was concerned about the future. Pro football did not have a pension program at the time nor did head coaches' contracts last forever. On January 6, 1949, Conzelman resigned from his $25,000 a year job with the Chicago Cardinals with the following letter to Mrs. Charles Bidwill, Chairman of the Board of Directors:

> *My Dear Vi—*
>      *It has been increasingly difficult the past few years to take my family back and forth between St. Louis and Chicago. The situation has not been helped by having a school-age son a part of that twice-a-year change. Because I think that it is about time I take root in one locality, I have decided to tender my resignation as coach of the Chicago Cardinals, effective January 12, 1949, and to take a job with the D'Arcy Advertising Company.*

The resignation was accepted with regret by Cardinals President Ray C. Benningsen, who commented: "Jim's resignation was accepted reluctantly, accepted only out of respect to his desire to retire to a life which will not make such great demands on him physically."

Later Benningsen added, "Football has been rough on Jimmy and he absolutely means what he says about settling down. He's absolutely crazy about his son Jimmy Jr. But I wonder if he'll be happy out of football?"

Conzelman insisted that he had not lost his love of football, but was concerned with his family's future. "I was still looking for more personal security than I could find in football," he said in *Pro Football's Rag Days*. "Remember, we had no pension plans back then. That winter I went back to St. Louis to work for an advertising agency." He also turned down a lucrative offer to coach the Redskins and never returned to the game of football.

## *Reading Football Magazines*

The end of the 1948 season also marked the end of the line for the Chicago Cardinals as contenders in the National Football League. At first, there was no apparent reason for this quick slide back into the pack, although the departure of the inspirational Conzelman was certainly a factor. Marshall Goldberg was the first of the stars from the great teams of 1947-48 to leave when he finally retired after threatening to do so since before the war. "I gave up football when I received enough salary in the machinery business to compensate for the money I made from football," he said. However, Goldberg elected to remain with the team as an assistant coach and chief scout. Part of that new job was somewhat difficult for the former All-American: "We didn't really travel to scout college players back then," recalled Goldberg, "so I set up sort of a network with coaches I knew in various parts of the country who would contact us regarding a good player. Believe it or not, a lot of the scouting before that was done by reading the national football magazines that were printed before the season. The Cardinals often relied on that information when selecting draft choices after the season. One thing did surprise me though, was that it was not tough to coach your former teammates. It's all part of the game."

With Conzelman gone, the management of the Cardinals faced the important decision of who to anoint as the new head coach of the club. In the end, the decision was not a decision, according to the announcement by Cardinals President Ray C. Benningsen when Phil Handler and Buddy Parker were selected as co-coaches for the 1949 season. "Handler and Parker are capable football fundamentalists and each enjoys the confidence and friendship of the entire Chicago Cardinals' personnel," stated Benningsen in the Cards' *Media Guide*. "The two men have been pals since Buddy joined the Cardinals in 1937 and there isn't any question in my mind that this is one situation where two head men will work in harmony all the time." Reporters apparently snickered that this unusual arrangement was necessary simply because Violet Bidwill could not decide on one candidate over the other.

Although Goldberg was one key missing ingredient, the new co-coaches welcomed back most of the stalwarts from the previous two campaigns. The latest version of the "Dream Backfield" was already firmly entrenched with Paul Christman, Pat Harder, Elmer Angsman, and Charley Trippi behind a solid line. One other missing person of note was quarterback Ray Mallouf, who was moved to the New York Giants on September 19. To compensate for the vacancy behind Christman (who was still struggling with lingering injuries and rumored to be retiring), the Cards grabbed quarterback Jim Hardy from the Los Angeles Rams. Although largely unknown in Chicago, Hardy was available once it became apparent that he would ride the bench in Los Angeles behind Bob Waterfield and Norm Van Brocklin. This was despite the fact that Hardy was 1948's leading passer in the Western Division with 1,390 yards, including a whopping 406 in one game against the Cardinals.

Babe Dimancheff was one of the first players to welcome Hardy to the Cardinals' camp, according to the *Tribune*:

> Babe went over to lend a helping hand and the newcomer was appreciative. "That boy can really throw the ball," Babe said to Coach Buddy Parker. "I think he's really got it."
> "No doubt about it, Babe," said Parker, "If you haven't been introduced, he's Jim Hardy, the top passer in the Western Division last year."

The Cards opened the season strongly with a convincing 38-7 win over Washington, but then struggled over the next five games. They managed just a 2-3 record following a tough 24-7 loss at home to Detroit on October 23. It was difficult for both the fans and the media to understand how the mighty Cardinals could drop three games so early in the season with virtually the same personnel that had ransacked the league for the past two seasons.

## It Wasn't That The Coaches Didn't Get Along

Apparently, this was painfully obvious to the club's management as well. After the Detroit loss, Benningsen stepped in and moved Handler upstairs to the dubious position of vice president in charge of "signing talent." Parker would remain as the team's sole head coach with Goldberg and Dick Plasman to assist him. In addition, veteran tackle Chet Bulger was named as a player-assistant coach. To Benningsen, the decision was logical:

> In professional football, you have to be looking ahead. If we're going to have a bad year, next year becomes that much more important. In our discussions, we decided that Buddy Parker can carry along by himself while Phil goes searching for the eight to ten new players we plan to bring up for next season.

Parker accepted his new solo assignment with dignity and class and explained his version of the season to the *Tribune:*

> *It was a combination of things. I don't like to bring up injuries but it is true we have had more than our share. It certainly wasn't that the coaches didn't get along. We did.*

The coaching change had little effect on the team's performance as the Cards fell to the Giants 41-38 the following week. Then Parker reeled off four victories and a tie over the next five games, including a team-scoring record in a 65-20 rampage over the New York Bulldogs. Now 6-4-1, Parker prepared his club for the season-ender against the Bears, and the Cardinals began to resemble the squads of the recent glory years. But the 8-3 Bears would not be fazed by the Cards' recent surge. They bombed the South Siders 52-21 in the season finale. Bears quarterback Johnny Lujack completed 24 of 40 passes for an NFL record 465 yards. The loss so shocked Parker that he resigned the day after that debacle and stated:

> *I'm tired of being a head coach. The duties are too demanding and it's tough for a young coach to beat the old pro hands.*

Parker's decision was surprising, especially since he was popular with the players. Soon, rumors began circulating that Parker had been growing increasingly frustrated with apparent interference by the front office, an allegation that would continue to haunt the club in similar situations for several more years.

On the same day that Parker decided to depart, Paul Christman stated his intentions to retire: "If I had to do it all over again, I still would go with no other team. Everyone has been wonderful, from the coaches on down."

Although Christman would later rescind his thoughts on retirement, he had played his last game with the Chicago Cardinals, as had team captain Billy Dewell and tackle Chet Bulger. Dewell eased into retirement soon after the conclusion of the 1949 season, while Bulger signed on with the Lions. Dewell remained with the team as the ends coach. The one obvious bright spot for the management of the 1949 Cardinals was the fact that the team was one of only six teams in the NFL to demonstrate a profit for the year.

In December of 1949, the NFL ended its annoying four-year rivalry with the All America Conference by announcing that it would absorb the San Francisco Forty-Niners, the Baltimore Colts, and the Cleveland Browns. The league would split into two divisions, the National and the American, which would unfortunately split up the Bears (National) and the Cardinals (American), but would allow for a season-ending playoff game for the league championship.

In another interesting development, the league approved a sweeping change that would now allow "free substitution." The new rule would pave the way for the game as it is known today, with liberal substitutions and the assigning of players to offense or defense based on their individual abilities. The era of the two-way player was gasping and wheezing in the wake of this historical decision.

## *Fiery Ex-Packers Coach*

Meanwhile, the Cardinals waited until February 1, 1950, before signing former Green Bay Packers coach Curly Lambeau as the team's newest coach. Lambeau had resigned from the Packers on September 30, 1949, after thirty-one years with the team, in an apparent dispute with the Packers' management. He arrived hale and hearty in Chicago and told the *New York Times* that, "I am confident that I can do a better coaching job for the Chicago Cardinals than I did in Green Bay." Lambeau had captured six NFL titles with the Packers and it was assumed that he could equal that success in Chicago. Violet Bidwill was pleased with this development and said: "I am extremely happy over this acquisition of the fiery ex-Packer coach." Lambeau promptly added former Green Bay ace Cecil Isbell as an assistant coach and was assured by Benningsen that he would have full control over the team's strategies and objectives: "Lambeau will have a free hand on the field and that's no idle statement. I gave my word I would drawup no sure-fire plays for him."

Lambeau's most immediate impact was to trade the recently un-resigned Paul Christman to the Packers and insert Jim Hardy as the starting quarterback. Lambeau favored the passing game, which altered the landscape of the Cardinals' usual rushing offense, as noted by the Brown's chief scout Tim Temerario in the *Cleveland Plain-Dealer:*

> *They look different than they did last year. Last year, Elmer Angsman, Charlie Trippi, and Pat Harder really piled up the yardage running. Now they throw more. They're a solid football team, capable of giving us a big afternoon.*

As the season opener with Philadelphia on September 24, 1950, loomed, Lambeau oozed confidence and told the *Tribune:* "There isn't a team in the league that has better personnel than the Cardinals and I know we will prove it tomorrow."

What followed was perhaps the most remarkable two-game swing for a quarterback in Cardinals history. With Lambeau brimming with confidence and Hardy firmly in place at quarterback, the Cards eagerly anticipated the season opener at Comiskey Park with their heated rivals from Philadelphia.

Against the Eagles, perhaps the term "nightmare" might be too positive a word to describe what Hardy endured that afternoon. In the harrowing 45-7 loss to Philadelphia, Hardy was forced into a league-record eight interceptions and also lost a pair of fumbles for a total of ten individual turnovers! With substitute quarterback Frank Tripucka injured, Hardy gallantly played the entire game and never was left off the hook by the swarming Eagles defenders. "They (the Eagles) rolled over an impotent and inept Cardinal eleven," stated writer Harry Warren of the *Tribune.*

Yet just one week later, Hardy utilized the other half of his Jekyll and Hyde playing personality to scorch the Colts 55-13. Hardy broke the team's touchdown passing record by tossing six, including a league record of five to end Bob Shaw. Shaw grabbed a total of 8 passes for 165 yards, while Hardy clicked on 13 out of 30 tosses for 281 yards. The team's dormant rushing attack also jumped to life, paced by Trippi's sixteen carries for eighty yards and rugged Vic Schwall's seventy-two markers in just four attempts.

By November 12, the Cardinals accumulated a disappointing 3-4 record, but confidently expected to even that slate in a game at New York against the Giants. The Cards had socked the team 17-3 just two weeks before. After easily whipping the Giants the first time, Lambeau drilled his team prior to the next game by focusing on the Giants' familiar "T" formation. It turned out to be one of the biggest mistakes of Lambeau's coaching career.

Wily New York coach Steve Owens, himself embroiled in a tidy but uneventful 5-2 season, suddenly decided to switch from his usual offense to the single wing at the start of the Cardinals' game. He then went with the unpredictable "A" formation for the rest of the way. Lambeau—and the Cardinals—were unable to react to Owens's cunning game plan and the Cards were flattened 51-21. Owens was almost giddy in his assessment of the game, in which the losers failed to mount any defensive opposition to his surprise offense:

*We worked secretly with the A-formation all week. Our plan was to use it to give us a quick start against the Cardinals. But it worked so well against Chicago's defense, which concentrated on an 8-man line, that we stayed with it all game.*

## Stadiums May Have To Be Turned Into Studios

While in New York, Lambeau was queried on the latest threat to the league—television. Lambeau blamed both the televising of some games, as well as the new platooning of players, as the primary reasons for declining attendance around the league in the following interview with the *New York Times*:

*As regards television, continued small attendance may compel us to seek revenue from that medium, which will result in even smaller turnouts. Our stadiums may have to be turned into studios.*

Following the embarrassment to the Giants, the Jekyll and Hyde format showed up in Philadelphia on November 19. The Eagles had opened the season by slaughtering the Cardinals 45-7 in Chicago. However, on the return visit to Philadelphia, the Cards snuck in and snatched a surprising 14-10 upset, based primarily on Don Paul's sensational eighty-two-yard punt return and the rushing advances of Harder, Trippi, and Angsman. As the season swayed back and forth in terms of wins and losses, Lambeau's crew settled for a disappointing 5-7 record and chants of "Goodbye, Curly" could be heard echoing through Comiskey Park.

A major highlight proved to be a late-season upset of the Bears (20-10) in a game that probably cost the Bears the Western Division Championship (they lost in a playoff to the Rams). Pat Harder, playing with a heavily damaged knee, energized his club with sixty-four yards in twelve carries and also grabbed three passes for fifty-six yards. "Maybe it sounds like I'm popping off," Harder shouted in the noisy locker room, "but I guess we showed them who the best fullback in the league is. I can thank the whole bunch around here for what I did today." Less than two months later, Harder announced his retirement:

*Professional football has given me my house and some of the good things in life, but the future means a lot more than the few more years of football which I suppose I could play.*

During the off-season, the Cardinals and the NFL faced another challenge when players began jumping to play pro ball in Canada. The lure was simple: the players would play in small markets, but garner big paychecks. Center Bill Blackburn, another holdover from the glory days, was one of the first to depart when he inked a five-year pact at about $9,000 per year with a team in Calgary. Then nifty end Bob Shaw and tackle Jim Lipinski announced they were heading north as well. The only problem with Shaw's intention was that he remained under contract with the Chicago Cardinals, and President Benningsen quickly indicated that he would initiate immediate legal proceedings to protect his team's property: "I don't know whether we'll sue Shaw or whether we'll sue the Canadian club that signed him."

Ironically, Shaw reversed his decision on June 15, 1951, but surprisingly still showed up for training camp with the Calgary Stampeders on June 22 after openly admitting that he had signed a contract with the Cardinals: "But my intention all along was to come to the Stampeders and I made sure by seeing my lawyer, that the club couldn't take legal action against me."

The Canadian issue worsened when quarterback Jim Hardy headed to Canada as well. With the opening of training camp nearing, the depleted 1951 Cardinals would be without the services of Blackburn, Harder, Shaw, Lipinski, Hardy, and veteran Vince Banonis (to Detroit), or as Cardinals' scout Wally Cruice told the *Green Bay Gazette:* "Outside of that, we haven't got any tackles, no ends, and one or two backs."

Harder eventually was coaxed into un-retiring but was traded to the Lions on September 19 for fellow fullback Jack Panelli. A week later, another old hand was lost when Buster Ramsey was waived, although he remained affiliated with the organization as an assistant coach. With the Canadian legalities swirling in lawyers' offices, Lambeau evaluated his offensive options and decided to go with Trippi as the Cardinals' quarterback in 1951. Trippi had earned acclaim in just about every position possible during his service with the team, so the move seemed logical to Lambeau. In his first full game as the team's quarterback in an exhibition against the New York Yanks, Trippi was unstoppable. He launched a twenty-eight-yard touchdown pass to Don Paul, and then ran a perfect bootleg for a score in the Cards' 28-7 win over the Yanks. Writer Gene Kessler of the *Chicago Sun-Times* was in awe following this performance:

*Chicago professional football fans discovered . . . that so long as Charlie Trippi is able to play quarterback, the Cardinals won't field the worst squad in the National Football league . . . Once his deception was so blinding that he drew the entire Yank squad into the middle while he ran around his left end by himself for a touchdown.*

Off the field, the front office had also been restructured prior to the 1951 season. Benningsen left the Cardinals while Violet Bidwill's new husband Walter Wolfner became managing director. The two Bidwill sons, Charles "Stormy" Bidwill and William V. Bidwill, were named president and vice president, respectively.

The season opener on September 30, 1951, found the Cards on the short end of a 17-14 result with the Eagles, although rookie end Don Stonesifer made an immediate impact when he grabbed three passes for sixty-nine yards. Stonesifer was already emerging as one of the premier receivers in the NFL, with sure hands and quick reflexes. Los Angeles coach Joe Stydahar once said: "Stonesifer was great against us . . . He's quick and almost impossible to cover."

The Cards then bounced back to stun the Bears 28-14 before embarking on a five-game losing streak that seemed to crush the team both physically and spiritually.

## *It Was Awfully Attractive Financially*

Following an anemic offensive effort in a 7-3 loss to the Redskins on October 21, and with Tripucka knocked out of action, the Cardinals forgave prodigal son Jim Hardy and added him to the roster. Hardy had been appointed Director of Athletics for the Hoffman Television Corporation in Los Angeles after the Canadian football vision burst and told the *Los Angeles Times* that he was delighted with the opportunity to join the Cardinals: "I couldn't afford to pass up the offer to go back to football. It was awfully attractive financially."

On the same day (October 24) that Hardy was welcomed back into the fold, Cardinals General Manager Walter Wolfner stated that, despite the team's ugly 1-3 record, "I have no intentions of changing coaches at this time." Wolfner, not widely regarded as a "football" person around the league, probably didn't do much for Lambeau—or the team—by that pronouncement so early in the season. But then things turned nasty. There were rumors that Wolfner was feuding with Lambeau, that Lambeau was feuding with assistant coach Phil Handler, and that very few members of the Cardinals' management were even on speaking terms.

This internal fracas erupted when Lambeau publicly criticized the struggling Cardinals' offense as well as Trippi for his failure to call the right plays as the Cardinals threatened the Redskins' goal line the previous Sunday. The proud Trippi was incensed and accused Lambeau of "passing the buck" when referring to the play-calling for the Cardinals. Lambeau had stated that Trippi was "on his own" when calling the plays and hinted that this situation was responsible for the close loss to Washington. The obviously riled Trippi responded quickly in the heat of battle, according to the *New York American:*

> *That's a lie. The Cardinals' coaching staff called 90% of the plays against Washington . . . I was pretty much on my own until the Cardinals reached the Washington 10 or 15 yard-line. And then I got my instructions from the bench. All the players know who's calling the plays, and they're behind me 100%. I intend to coach after finishing with pro football and I have a reputation to maintain. I don't like to be blamed for somebody else's doing.*

Following this exchange of verbal missiles, Wolfner called a meeting of the Cardinals' brass including himself, Lambeau, Handler, Isbell, and Violet Bidwill. After some tense and honest discussions, the coaching staff was instructed to take full responsibility for the selection of all plays, as Wolfner explained to the *Tribune:* "At the meeting today, I told Curly that it would be the coaches' responsibility to call all plays. In baseball, the manager dictates the strategy, so why not in football?"

Lambeau responded well to the meeting and indicated that the result would be beneficial to all concerned. On October 26, Lambeau and Trippi publicly made up with Lambeau stating: "It was only a misunderstanding. I feel better now. All we want to do now, Charley, is win!"

All the Cards could do was lose three more games to embrace a woeful 1-6 mark as the season faded into its final stretch. While the *Chicago Tribune* asked "What's Wrong With the Cardinals" on October 31, Coach Joe Stydahar of the Los Angeles Rams confided in the *Los Angeles Times* on the recently powerful Chicago Cardinals: "It beats me how a team with their personnel has won only one game."

## *My Ole Lady Sure Can Take It On The Chin*

By early December, after a gloomy 49-28 loss at Cleveland, the Cardinals were saddled with a woeful 2-8 mark and Wolfner took the opportunity in the *Tribune* to level both barrels at Lambeau again:

> *Lambeau's made mistakes . . . we're not going to take any hasty action . . . There's no harmony among the coaches. They're still at loggerheads most of the time, not speaking to each other most of the time. They've had the material. Why, with the players we've got on this team, they ought to be fighting for the championship.*

Wolfner then responded to a query regarding the possible move, or sale, of the club, since the Cardinals were not exactly successful at the gate:

> *You can say 100% that the Cardinals are not for sale, and won't be. My ole lady sure can take it on the chin!*

With that said, on December 7, 1951, the legendary Curly Lambeau resigned as the head coach of the Chicago Cardinals, but agreed to remain with the team for its two final games. Inevitably, Wolfner was the first to share his opinion on this difficult situation and did not do so in a diplomatic fashion:

> *Lambeau lost control of his assistant coaches and his players as well. Lambeau hasn't even spoken to one of his assistants for the last three weeks. This feeling can be attributed to Lambeau's alibing after losing games. He always blamed his assistants for the defeats.*

Lambeau quickly responded in the *New York Tribune*:

> *I've never blamed my assistants in my life. I've always shouldered full responsibility for any losses. There is hardly a coaching set-up in which there is complete agreement. But club owners certainly don't air this kind of thing in public. I felt I just didn't fit into the Cardinals' organization.*

Later, Lambeau told the *Green Bay Gazette* that he had been contemplating resigning ever since Ray Benningsen had left the club: "No man can do a satisfactory job if he constantly is harassed by front office second-guessing."

In the *Tribune,* Curly further explored his respect for the departed Benningsen:

*I liked Ray. He knew where a coach's authority began and where it ended. That situation has not prevailed since his resignation and I simply can't work under the current set-up and retain my self respect.*

The *San Francisco Examiner* found more to talk about with Lambeau and he obliged, stating:

*A gridiron leader has little chance to build morale when management interferes with the normal relationship between a player and a coach. This is true particularly when the office manager, through inexperience, has little knowledge of the problems that beset a coach.*

By this time, there was little doubt that Lambeau was targeting Wolfner. Wolfner, on the other hand, may have had little experience in the world of professional football, but he knew enough about management to reject Curly's offer to coach the last two games for the Cardinals. Curly left the Cardinals for good on December 8, 1951.

The following day, the Cardinals, now under the leadership of Handler, dropped a 20-17 decision to the Redskins before a paltry crowd of just 9,459 at Comiskey Park. The team completed a 3-9 campaign by once again surprising the Bears 24-14 as the ever-effective Trippi collected 145 yards on just 13 carries.

With the sluggish season behind them, the Cardinals immediately focused on the search for a new coach and tabbed former Cards player Joe Kuharich as that man on January 8, 1952. He signed a two-year contract for $15,000 per year and at the age of thirty-four became the NFL's youngest head coach.

The naming of Kuharich was welcomed by members of the extended Cardinals family, including former coach Jimmy Conzelman:

*He played for me in 1941 and was a smart, shrewd player. He played guard, but I had him call my offensive signals for me. With Joe calling the shots, we went out and won a couple of games we didn't figure to win.*

Kuharich's former coach at Notre Dame, Elmer Layden, previewed his personal traits as a player and coach:

*If hard work will do the job, then the Cardinals are on the way back. Joe played for me at Notre Dame and he was one of the best and smartest players it has been my opportunity to coach. Kuharich loved to play football and he played for keeps. A hard worker, hustler and as smart as they come. The Cardinals under Kuharich, will be tough to handle next season and don't be surprised if they land on top of the heap in 1953.*

Kuharich, who had last played for the Cards in 1945, was a Notre Dame grad and an up-and-coming college coach at the University of San Francisco. The Dons had just completed an undefeated (9-0) season under Kuharich with the help of a budding superstar named Ollie Matson. Kuharich was so impressed with his All-American back at San Francisco that he once said, "If Ollie played for California or Notre Dame, he'd be another Thorpe or Grange." So, it was no surprise that Matson joined Kuharich in Chicago for the 1952 season.

Matson possessed blazing speed and the breakaway ability that the Cardinals sorely needed, but how long would he be around? Because of the Korean conflict, NFL Commissioner Bert Bell warned that the rosters around the league could be diminished during the 1952 season: "Due to the increasing conflict in the world situation today, it becomes apparent that the draft lists of the individual clubs will be effected to a higher degree than last season."

Bell estimated that up to twenty-five percent of the league's draftees might end up in the military, and that might include the Cardinals' top choices, such as Matson, Johnny Karras (halfback, Illinois), Don Coleman (guard, Michigan State), Darrell Crawford (quarterback, Georgia Tech), and Darrell Brewster (end, Purdue).

## *We're Here To Stay In Chicago*

Meanwhile, on the business side of the organization, the Cardinals agreed to a three-year contract to continue to play their home games at Comiskey Park. Wolfner hoped that this agreement would squelch budding rumors that the team was on the sale block and would be moved from Chicago: "We're here to stay in Chicago and we're out to give the Cardinal fans a national league title as well as being Chicago champs."

As Kuharich moved towards the opening of his training camp at Lake Forest (IL) College, he promised that the Cardinals' offense would be the "T" formation with various splits and spreads," which would suit the skills of Matson just fine. However, Matson (who grabbed a bronze medal in the four-hundred-meter dash in the 1952 Olympics at Helsinki) never seemed to mesh with the offense during his rookie season, scrambling for 344 yards on just 96 carries. As a team, the Cards rolled early in the season under Kuharich by winning three of their first four games before sliding to a 4-8 finish. In truth, opposing defenses eventually learned to confine Matson and to take away his intimidating open-field threat.

Charley Trippi returned to quarterback after Jim Hardy was traded to Detroit and completed 84 for 181 (890 yards). Fifty-four of those catches (617 yards, fourth-best in the league) went to talented end Don Stonesifer. For Stonesifer, the reason for this was simple: "Back then, I called the plays for Charley and so I just happened to call our plays for myself more often!" Trippi also topped the rushing column with 72 carries for 350 yards.

In reality, the Cardinals' offense lacked real firepower and things got worse during the off-season when Matson was called into military service and Kuharich was surprised by a curious demand from Wolfner. As reported in the *Pittsburgh Sun-Telegraph,* it seems that the managing director was concerned that assistant coach Bill Daddio was too tough on the players and that assistant Mike Nixon wasn't qualified enough in the inner workings of the "T" formation. Apparently, Wolfner directed Kuharich to fire the two coaches, and when the astounded Kuharich refused, all three coaches were out of a job!

This scenario set the stage for a dismal 1953 season and the hiring of new coach Joe Stydahar. Wolfner plucked Stydahar from the Los Angeles Rams, where he had captured the 1951 NFL title. Wolfner was obviously pleased with himself:

*In Joe Stydahar, the Cardinals have obtained a great coach and a fine gentleman who has proven himself in the world's toughest football league. I am sure he will attend meticulously to each detail of the vast chore which comprises the organization of a professional football team.*

Stydahar, apparently ignoring—or not believing—the recent internal difficulties experienced by his predecessors Lambeau and Kuharich, explained his position in a column written for *The Big Red* team newsletter in June of 1953:

*I am very pleased with the excellent support I have received from the Cardinal management. The Cardinals have given me their 100% cooperation in formulating my plans to bring the Cardinals a championship for the great sports fans of Chicago. In my estimation, to be successful in any endeavor whether it be professional football or business, management and employees must work together. Especially in pro football where there is a tremendous investment involved, close cooperation is a must to protect such an investment.*

The Cards chose an unprecedented six quarterbacks in the 1953 draft, including one that would have an immediate impact as a starter: James Root from Miami of Ohio. The club also picked up veteran Steve Romanik from the Bears, as well as former UCLA quarterback Ray Nagel in order to relieve Trippi of the ballhandling chores. But the lack of depth was apparent early on to Stydahar, who noted that the club needed immediate help at quarterback and guard, and also to fill the gaps left by departures for military service. "Einstein couldn't have done it any better," said Stydahar in reference to patching a team together without really knowing what personnel would be available. "No matter how you figure it, until the season starts, there is no way to tell what 'X' equals in those factors."

Although Trippi paced all Cardinals rushers in 1953 with 433 yards in 97 carries, it was to no avail as his team lost its first 7 games enroute to a perplexing 1-10-1 season. Root did pass for 1,149 yards (80 for 192) and fellow rookie Johnny Olszewski, a fullback out of California, contributed 386 yards (106 carries), second best behind Trippi's totals. In defensive end Pat Summerall, acquired in a purchase from the Lions, the Cardinals finally had a placekicker to equal the great Pat Harder from the late 1940s. Summerall was perfect on all twenty-three extra points during the long season. Once again, the Cardinals caught the Bears napping in the final game of the season for the lone victory of the season.

The season was frustrating for Stydahar, who was not familiar with defeat in these quantities. At first he blamed himself. After the lone tie with the Rams snapped the seven-game losing streak, he commented, "If it's in a football team—and we now know for certain that it is in the Cardinals—only the coach is to blame for not bringing it out. That's his job."

But just three weeks later, when a 21-17 loss to the Steelers dropped the Cards to 0-10-1, the enraged coach fined every player on the team $100 (later rescinded) and publicly flailed the team's effort: "I don't know what's the matter with this team. The boys don't seem to have any pride in their work. They play just well enough to lose."

## *Brings The Sandman Almost Immediately*

Meanwhile, Ollie Matson was in the service and posting big numbers for the Fort Ord (CA) football team. The conclusion of military service for several players was the primary hope for the 1954 Cardinals as players such as Matson, Chuck Ulrich, Leo Sugar, Louis Stephens, Glenn Lippman, Don Coleman, John Feltch, and Don Kasperan were all expected to return. For Stydahar, the prognosis for the next season was obvious, according to the *Green Bay Gazette:*

> *The first thing we need is speed. And we've got to get a come-through guy who can get you all the way in the clutch. Like Ollie Matson. We need an offensive line. We need everything.*

David Condon, the witty columnist of the *Chicago Tribune,* speculated on the stress level of Stydahar after the harrowing 1953 season, when he learned what the coach would do to combat job-related insomnia:

> *(Stydahar) leaps from bed and does calisthenics when he can't sleep . . . says it releases the tension and brings the sandman almost immediately . . . an associate of Joe's has suggested that with the season the Cardinals enjoyed, he must have had to resort to the calisthenics almost every evening!*

During the off-season, Wolfner engineered a trade with Los Angeles that brought in Dick "Night Train" Lane, an invaluable defensive addition to the Chicago Cardinals, and welcomed back eleven military personnel. Ollie Matson was one of them, although he would miss the first game of the season because of his service commitments. Finally, the Cards' low standing in 1953 earned them the top pick in the draft, quarterback Lamar McHan of Arkansas, and the team selected twenty-nine other players as well. By June of 1954, Wolfner was feeling pretty good about himself and the team's prospects during the upcoming season, according to the *San Francisco Examiner:*

> *We drafted to our weaknesses of last season and everybody agrees that we came up with one of the best draft lists in the league. The deal we made with the Los Angeles Rams at the league meeting last Winter, in which we got Dick Lane . . . will prove to be one of the best deals ever made in National Football League history.*
>
> *We feel we have improved to the point where we will be in the fight for the league title this year!*

Wolfner's optimism crashed rather quickly when the Cardinals dropped five straight to open the 1954 season, and soon the losses and slight crowds helped prompt more rumors that Wolfner would move the team to another city. Specifically, there were noises that he had already been plotting to move the club to St. Louis, his hometown. This time around, he did not categorically deny the possibility:

> *I believe St. Louis would support big-league football, but there would have to be tangible evidence of a guaranteed interest before I'd even consider moving. Therefore, the Cardinals are not for sale and we are seeking no partners. If we moved the team, it would only be because of a more profitable market.*

Wolfner indicated that despite probable financial losses for the team, there would be no concern that money would force the team to move, primarily because the losses would be absorbed by the nearby Hawthorne Race Track that Wolfner also managed for the organization.

As the season progressed, it was apparent that the team was going nowhere in the standings. Lane topped the league with ten interceptions and teamed with Trippi and Matson to form a fierce defensive secondary. Matson returned to pace the team in rushing with 506 yards in 101 carries, backed by Olszewski's 352 yards in 106 attempts. The aging Trippi was still a threat as demonstrated by his sparkling 8.4 rushing average (18 carries, 152 yards). Once again Stonesifer was the leading receiver, grabbing 44 passes for 607 yards, with Matson snaring 34 for 611 yards. The erratic McHan struggled through his rookie season, but still managed to complete 105 passes in 255 attempts for 1,475 yards.

## *It Would Raise Hob With A Lot Of Clubs*

The Cardinals were unable to shake loose from the holds of mediocrity, despite the midseason appointment of veteran coach Earle "Greasy" Neale as advisory coach for the team. No one was quite sure what this meant, but Neale did the job for about a week as the Cardinals continued to spiral downwards and finished with a mediocre 2-10 record. Sensing that the club would need more than just talent to return to its winning ways of years gone by, Wolfner devised an unusual motivational plan that delighted players, but dismayed fellow owners.

Near the conclusion of the 1954 season, Wolfner announced plans for the team to distribute fifty percent of its net profits in 1955 to the players and coaches. Wolfner explained the plan further to Harry Warren in the *Tribune:*

> *This incentive program will in no way affect the players or coaches salaries. The distribution of profits will be in addition to their regular contract figures. All players will share alike in the distribution. A player's salary will have no effect on the amount he receives.*
>
> *Naturally, we believe this program will give the players and coaches added incentive to win and we know that a winning team will bring more fans, more gate receipts, and result in more money for the players and coaches.*

Other owners weren't too keen on the idea, such as Green Bay's president Russell W. Bogda, who noted:

> *An incentive plan is a good thing, but I don't believe this one will work. You'll have a good year, then a bad one, and then player trouble.*
>
> *It would, I am afraid, raise hob with a lot of clubs. Some of us are not in that high profit bracket . . . As far as incentive is concerned, it seems to me the players have enough now with the playoff for the championship and the All-Star game.*

The two key words in Wolfner's proposal were "net profits." Those items caught the attention of the Bears' George Halas, who stated:

> *If Mr. Wolfner included his race track profits in the deal, I think he would have*

*something tangible to offer. If more money is the answer to better player perfor-*
*mance, I think he should double every player's salary immediately.*

Despite the woeful season, three Cardinals were named to the Pro Bowl: defensive halfbacks Lane and Matson and defensive tackle Jerry Groom. As the Cardinals said hello to a new incentive plan and a new season, they said goodbye to veteran coach Stydahar. Wolfner replaced him with assistant Ray Richards, a knowledgeable leader with more than thirty years of experience as a player and coach.

The club also formed an alliance with the Chicago White Sox before the 1955 season that seemingly united the two organizations in terms of scouting operations, facilities, and ticket outlets. In addition, Charles A. Comiskey II was named to the Cardinals' Board of Directors. "Chuck Comiskey's entrance into the Cardinals' organization is just the first step to perpetuate the Cards in Chicago," announced Wolfner.

## Halas Is Becoming A Mean Old Man

The team was also strengthened in the draft by adding Oklahoma end Max Boydston and USC halfback Lindon Crow. With an added year of experience, McHan was expected to lead a talented backfield of Matson, Trippi, and Olszewski, while the experienced line included veterans such as Groom, Stonesifer, Jack Simmons, Leo Sanford, Jack Jennings, and Len Teeuws. Under Richards's tutelage, the Cards showed early promise—and hope—by jumping out to a 2-1 mark by defeating the Giants (28-17) and the Redskins (24-10) after dropping the opener to Pittsburgh 14-7 on a last-minute touchdown pass from Steelers quarterback Jim Finks. As the season drew to a close, the Cards (3-5-1) prepared for their annual battle with the division-leading Bears (6-3).

As usual, there was some sort of controversy affiliated with this game between rivals. Unlike previous battles, where fistfights or accusations of spies were prevalent, the theme of the 1955 bout was the condition of the Comiskey Park field. George Halas bitterly complained about the prospect of a muddy field for the game, in which the Bears had much more to lose than the Cardinals: "We sent a scout out there this morning. He reported back that the condition of the field was disgraceful. Chicago fans are deserving of a better break."

The Cards' crafty publicity chief Eddie McGuire retorted:

*What is he beefing about? We are more anxious about a dry field than he is. We got more speed than he has and it is to our advantage to have fast going. Halas is just becoming a mean old man.*

Halas was evidently fearful that the upset-minded Cards would knock off his Bears and thus derail any immediate plans for adding a title in 1955:

*In my 36 years of professional football, I have never encountered a team in a better position for staging an upset than the Cardinals. They're lying in the weeds for us.*

Halas's premonitions were eerily accurate as the Cardinals salvaged another mediocre season with a stunning 53-14 rout of the North Siders in a snowstorm, best described by George Strickler in the *Tribune:*

> *Being of sound and disposing mind and memory, I hereby make, publish and declare the following to be the truth, the whole truth and nothing if not astounding:*
> *The Chicago Cardinals, who a week ago could not get out of their own way against the Washington Redskins, yesterday whipped, humbled, and humiliated the mighty Chicago Bears, 53-14!*

At the end of the game, the victorious Cardinals were both jubilant and cocky, simultaneously challenging the Bears to a fight while carrying Coach Richards off on their shoulders. The Cardinals scored the most points ever scored against the Bears. Matson scored twice from one on a run and on a seventy-seven-yard punt return, while rookie standout Dave Mann tallied from nineteen and fifty-one yards away. Stonesifer was sensational, grabbing two touchdown passes from McHan, and Summerall nailed field goals from twelve and forty yards. In the locker room, McHan praised his teammates by saying, "The boys really gave me protection today. What great catches they made! The ball wasn't wet, but it was slippery, and I threw some wobbly ones."

Unfortunately, the luster of the victory was diminished in season-ending losses to the Eagles (27-3) and the Rams (35-24) that relegated the Cards to another sub-.500 finish at 4-7-1. Coach Richards had brought stability and unity to the team, and it appeared that he was being allowed to coach the players in his own way as well. Matson (475 yards rushing) and Stonesifer (28 catches, 330 yards) topped the team offensively again. Summerall paced the team in scoring with fifty-three points.

## *He'll Have To Make Peace With The Rest Of The Players*

With almost everyone back in 1956 except Trippi, the Cardinals emerged as one of the biggest surprises of the early season by marching through their first four games undefeated as the offense focused more and more on the running of Ollie Matson. The team then stumbled slightly but was still 5-2 and in the hunt when it traveled to Pittsburgh on November 18 as a solid favorite over the downtrodden Steelers. On the morning of the game, Coach Richards suffered a gallstone attack, but somehow managed to drag himself to the stadium (he was hospitalized after the contest). But he felt worse when his starting quarterback Lamar McHan apparently asked to be relieved of his playing duties because of nervousness right before the game. Richards was in pain and enraged, but he still sent McHan out with the starting lineup where he failed to complete a pass in the first half.

The Steelers, coming in with a modest 2-5 slate, took advantage of an inept Cardinals offense to register a rather easy 14-7 victory. The Cards' only score came late in the fourth quarter when McHan connected with Matson on a forty-five-yard scoring toss.

What happened next is somewhat unclear, but the end result was that McHan was tagged with the largest player fine ($3,000) in NFL history up to that time and briefly banned for life from the Chicago Cardinals. While details are murky, the real damage did not come from the pregame situation but at practice the following Monday, when

"McHan walked off the practice field in a huff yesterday as a climax to his weird performance on Sunday . . ." according to the *Tribune*. The article by Edward Prell added:

> *The $3,000 fine was levied by Richards' four assistant coaches against McHan for insubordination in the Pittsburgh game. They said the 23 year old former University of Arkansas star had refused to "take orders and suggestions."*
>
> *Wolfner said that, in addition to his failure to cooperate in Pittsburgh, McHan walked off the field without permission . . . "He'll have to make peace with the players," an official of the club said. "He must learn that there are 32 other members of the club."*

McHan quickly met with Coach Richards and apologized. His suspension was lifted, his fine eventually returned, and he played for the Cardinals the following week. "I'll just have to try and make this team all over again," said McHan. Richards was accommodating, noting:

> *Lamar has shown a willingness to make good again. The other players have accepted him back on the team. They have told me that, if Lamar is 100 percent with them, they'll go all the way with him.*

Jim Root, a starter for the Cards in 1953, opened at quarterback the following week when the Cards defeated the Steelers 38-27 in snowy Comiskey Park. Root completed 11 out of 16 passes for 153 yards in the first half as the Cardinals built a 24-7 lead. McHan joined the fracas in the second half and the Cardinals held on for the win. Ollie Matson scampered for 159 yards in 16 carries in the easy win that brought the Cardinals (6-3) to within half a game of the Giants. However, consecutive close losses to the Packers (24-21) and the Bears (10-3) emptied any hopes for a title run. Still, a 24-7 win at Cleveland on December 9 allowed Richards to finish with his only winning record (7-5) with the team and the only winning season of the decade for the Chicago Cardinals.

Matson exploded for 924 yards (192 attempts) in 1956 for his best season yet, while the dependable Olszewski picked up 598 on 157 carries. McHan's passing percentage was up to 47 percent, but his hurling was way down as he connected on only 72 out of 152 for 1,159 yards, with Stonesifer topping the receivers with 22 catches for 320 yards. Summerall was once again the leading scorer with sixty points and was perfect on all thirty of his extra points.

With most hands back for the 1957 season, much was expected of the Chicago Cardinals, especially after the team's second-place finish behind the Giants just a year before. After a 44-14 blasting of the Redskins on October 20, the Cards were still contenders with a 2-2 mark. But the rest of the season proved to be a disaster with the team losing seven of its last eight games to conclude the schedule with a 3-9 slate. Needless to say, Wolfner lost patience quickly with Coach Richards and sacked him. With three years of service (14-21-1), Richards had the longest tenure of any Cardinals coach in the 1950s.

To stem the tide, Wolfner next brought in former Cardinals lineman Frank "Pop" Ivy to coach the club in 1958. Ivy favored a passing attack, but still had Ollie Matson (577 yards, 134 carries in 1957) and talented rookie John David Crow to lug the ball.

Ivy's luck was no better than his predecessor's as the Cardinals avoided the cellar in 1958, but still slid to a mediocre 2-9-1, with the last six losses coming in a row to end the season. More distressing for Wolfner, however, was the attendance. In three out of the five games, there were fewer than twenty thousand paid in the stands.

In hopes of evading another disaster on the field in 1959, the Cardinals shocked the professional football field on February 29, 1959, by trading Ollie Matson to the Rams for a huge bounty. In return for Matson the Cardinals would receive four starting linemen, three backs, a draft choice in 1959, and a player to be named later . . . a total of nine players. The Pro Football Hall of Fame holds the telegram from the Rams' Pete Rozelle that announced the trade to a disbelieving audience:

> *Los Angeles Rams trade to Chicago Cardinals tackle Ken Panfil, tackle Frank Fuller, tackle Art Hauser, tackle Glen Holtzman, end John Tracey, fullback Larry Hickman, halfback Don Brown, the Rams' second draft choice in the 1959 selection meeting, plus a player to be delivered during the 1959 training camp, in exchange for halfback Ollie Matson.*

At the time, the immensity of the trade and his obvious value must have impressed Matson, but originally he was not excited about the trade, stating: "I wanted to finish my career with the Cardinals." His career had been impeccable with the Cardinals. In just six seasons in Chicago, Matson picked up 3,331 rushing yards in 761 attempts, grabbed 130 passes for 2,150 yards, terrorized opponents on kick returns, and made 5 Pro Bowl appearances. The curious trade made sense for the Cardinals, who figured that they could bolster a squad that had won just two games the previous season. To others, including the fans, it was foolishness. Even George Halas checked in with his opinion:

> *I don't know how the Cardinals could have traded him. He's a "wonder" player. There are too few of them in the league . . . There isn't any value really great enough to make you give them up.*

With Matson gone, the 1959 season started earlier than usual with an August 5 exhibition against the Toronto Argonauts of the Canadian Football League. The Cards moved north of the border to stagger Toronto 55-27 in the first of seven preseason exhibitions. One of the highlights of the preseason was the nationally televised game with the Pittsburgh Steelers. It was broadcast by Chuck Thompson and Howard Cosell on ABC from Austin, Texas, on August 22. The Cards won 21-0. The Cardinals later played their annual exhibition in St. Louis, dropping a 21-13 decision to Bobby Layne and the Steelers on September 12. With Lamar McHan moving on to Green Bay, Ivy experimented with both King Hill and M. C. Reynolds at quarterback before settling on Hill for the season opener. Hill had managed to complete just five out of fifteen passes in the final preseason tune-up, a surprising 31-17 win over the defending champion Colts, with Johnny Unitas connecting on twenty-four for forty-six passes for the losers.

Coach Ivy admitted concern with his offensive leader:

> *It's ironic, I know. Here we just beat the world champs, and I'm tremendously disappointed. Our offense just isn't going the way it should. It's absolutely imper-*

*ative that we start hitting our receivers.*

As the Cardinals prepared for the 1959 season opener on September 27 at home against Washington, the city was embracing the "Go-Go" Chicago White Sox, who had just clinched the first American League pennant for the club in forty years. There wasn't a whole lot of interest in the Cardinals, but with two games in a row to start off the campaign, Ivy looked for a quick getaway for his team in the NFL East. With a roster that had almost completely turned over in the year since Ivy took over (only nine remained from the last Ray Richards squad in 1957), the coach faced a tough initial foe in the Washington Redskins with its diminutive quarterback, 5'7" Eddie LeBaron.

For the 1959 season, the Cardinals moved from their traditional home field of Comiskey Park to mammoth Soldier Field in Chicago. Wolfner scheduled just four home games in Chicago and elected to play two of his home games in Minneapolis. The new house on the lakefront apparently appealed to the Cardinals, especially half-back Bobby Joe Conrad. In leading the Cards to a convincing 49-21 win over the Redskins, Conrad tallied three touchdowns and booted seven extra points to collect twenty-five of the Cardinals' points on the day. It was the most devastating individual scoring performance since end Bob Shaw caught those five touchdown passes for thirty points against Baltimore in 1950. Conrad's performance still rates as the fourth-best individual scoring effort in the history of the Cardinals behind Ernie Nevers (forty points), Shaw (thirty points), and Paddy Driscoll (twenty-seven points). As a team, the Cards gobbled up 569 yards, second best in team annals at the time. Ivy had unveiled an intriguing new offense that impressed both the crowd and the *Tribune's* Cooper Rollow:

> *The Cards' colorful double winged T attack drew repeated cheers from the Soldiers' Field assemblage as a succession of intricate handoffs, double reverses, and delayed pitch backs were employed with remarkable success. Downfield blocking in many instances was responsible for long gains.*

Conrad was aided by the speedy John David Crow, while tackle Ken Panfil, full-back Mal Hammack, and guard Ken Gray were superlative in blocking roles. Quarterback King Hill sparkled in the opener by canning 14 out of 23 passes for 229 yards and perfectly balanced the fleet Cardinals' running attack. Slightly giddy after the resounding win, the Cards next awaited the always tough Cleveland Browns and their marvelous young fullback Jim Brown. Cleveland coach Paul Brown was an admirer of both Ivy and the dazzling offensive style he brought to the game: "Ivy has brought a breath of fresh air into the league. His innovations have inspired other coaches to try new ideas."

The confident Cards quickly faded against the invaders and fell 34-7 in muddy Soldier Field. The game initiated a four-game losing streak, with the first two games at home being duplicated in away losses to Washington and Cleveland. In the fifth game of the season, the Cards hosted the Eagles in Minneapolis. Before the game, Ivy grumbled about the recent lack of offensive production, but he was pleased as his club jumped out to a 24-0 lead early in the second half. The smile quickly turned into a frown, then a rage, as the Cards completely collapsed in the second half and dropped a 28-24 decision. The "home" game in Minnesota's Metropolitan Stadium drew only 20,112 fans, but the Cardinals would return for one more game in November.

## *The Most Spectacular, Daredevil Offense In Football*

A week later, Ivy personally snapped the slump by calling all of the offensive plays in a real home game at Soldier Field as the Cards slammed the Steelers and their talented quarterbacks Bobby Layne and Len Dawson 45-24. Ivy kept the ball on the ground and Crow and Conrad responded with superlative rushing efforts as the team picked up 266 rushing yards.

Now 2-4, but with obvious potential, the Cards flew off to New York to face the league-leading (5-1) Giants. The talented backfield of quarterback Charley Connerly and halfback Frank Gifford awaited the Chicagoans, although Gifford was still hobbled by an injury: "I feel fine," said Gifford. "I guarantee I'll play." And play he did, as two of his catches (twenty-four and thirty-two yards) set up two of the three field goals by ex-Card Pat Summerall as the Giants survived 9-3. It was, unfortunately, the closest the Cards would come to winning a game the remainder of the year.

Summerall, who had been an extremely accurate kicker for the Cardinals, later explained the background of his trade to the Giants in the book *Iron Men*:

> *"Pop" Ivy was named head coach of the Cardinals in 1958. I called him up and asked him where I was going to fit in his plans . . . I wasn't having a very good time playing in Chicago and was thinking seriously of not playing anymore and getting involved full-time in the farming business . . . so I wanted to hear what Ivy had to say. He told me, "Pat, you're one of our key guys and I want you to come back because we're going to do this and that." It was all very encouraging, so I decided I would play another year. A short time later I went down to the post office in Lake City (FL) to pick something up and bought the afternoon paper. There was a story in the sports section that said I had been traded to the Giants. Some "key guy"!*

As the last five weeks of the season dragged on, the Cardinals managed to uncover a different way to lose each time. None of the games were particularly close as the Cardinals dropped their last six games to complete the 1959 schedule with a 2-10 record. Leo Sugar, Mal Hammack, Carl Brettschneider, Woodley Lewis, and others played well, but turnovers continued to plague the club. Cooper Rollow of the *Tribune* summarized the trademarks of the season following a 27-17 loss to the Eagles in which the losers fumbled the ball away six times:

> *That the Cards are the fumblingest team in the league is a matter of statistical record. They are also, it is suspected, one of the unluckiest. The Chicagoans did a lot of things the right way Sunday. As usual, they thrilled the crowd with the most intricate, spectacular, and daredevil offense in football.*

The Cardinals played one more "home" game in Minneapolis on November 22 before a sellout crowd of 26,625. This time, the mighty New York Giants provided the opposition and scored early and often to defeat the Cardinals 30-20. The game was apparently played in Minneapolis to showcase the NFL, as a local group was hopeful of entering the NFL in 1960. But the Cardinals may have also been testing the waters to determine if the team could draw attendees in another city. After all, rumors had been circulating in the city about a possible move to another locale ever since Wolfner had accessed a position of power in the organization.

The last home game, and the final game ever played in Chicago by the Cardinals, took place on November 29, 1959. Fittingly, the opposition was furnished by the Chicago Bears, a team that Chris O'Brien had allowed to share geographical football space in the city nearly forty years previously. Coach Ivy approached the game from a pragmatic viewpoint:

> *We're such an unpredictable team we're liable to do anything. The fellows have appeared to be intense and serious in practice this week. But a coach is the last person in the world to know how his team is going to play. I won't know whether the Cards are "up" for this game until kickoff time.*

It would be the 70th game between these two ancient rivals, but the last one played in Chicago. Tickets for the Soldier Field adventure were going fast at $2.50 for reserved seats and $1.75 for bleacher sections. The Bears, rebounding after a slow start, would feature Johnny Morris, Willie Galimore, Rick Casares, Jim Dooley, Harlon Hill, and Ed Brown, while the Cardinals would counter with Crow, Hill, Conrad, Joe Childress, and Ken Hall.

On an icy field, the Bears managed to storm past the Cardinals 31-7 to remain in title contention, while the losers slipped further and further into oblivion. The crowd was nice, at nearly forty-nine thousand, but wasn't there to help on the road as the Chicago Cardinals dropped their last two games of their final season to Detroit (45-21) and Pittsburgh (35-20).

And then, just like that, the Chicago Cardinals were gone.

# Epilogue

*"The Chicago Cardinals Football Club is a Chicago institution and will remain that way!"*

WALTER WOLFNER,
MANAGING DIRECTOR, CHICAGO CARDINALS, 1955

Somehow the headline didn't fit, it didn't seem right. But there it was, stunning a city and shaking generations of Chicago fans:

### *Cardinals Move To St. Louis!*

While "The Move" was certainly not a surprise to NFL insiders, it was quite a jolt to Chicago Cardinals football fans who opened up the *Tribune* on March 14, 1960. After more than sixty years on the gritty South Side of Chicago, the Cardinals would abandon the city in a deal that remains controversial to this day. The *Tribune* offered no solace to its bewildered readers:

> *The Chicago Cardinals, one of the founding clubs of the National Football League, Sunday night requested and received permission to transfer their franchise to St. Louis for the 1960 season.*
> *Walter Wolfner, managing director of the team and husband of the former Violet M. Bidwill, chairman of the club's Board of Directors, made the request after the league agreed to pay the Cardinals $500,000 in equal annual payments over a ten year period.*

The payment of the $500,000 apparently was earmarked for moving expenses, as well as to reimburse the Chicago Park District for $125,000 for improvements made to the aging Soldier Field stadium prior to the Cardinals' move there for the 1959 season.

However, the two main ingredients in "The Move" were the dwindling fan base and the tenacious struggle for television revenue between the Cardinals and the Bears, as noted in the *Tribune:*

> *The move not only will leave the Bears as the only professional team in the nation's third largest market, but it opens up that territory to television. In the past, when either the Cardinals or the Bears were at home, the Chicago area was blacked out. The Bears will now be able to televise their road games back to Chicago . . .*
> *"There has been long, constant pressure from within the league to have us move,"*

*Wolfner said. "Mrs. Wolfner and I have been reluctant to make a move, but when we could not receive sufficient fan support to warrant our staying, we named our terms and to our surprise they (the NFL) accepted them."*

*Wolfner contended the purpose of the pressure "was to open up Chicago for TV." He made no mention of the visiting owners who resented accepting checks only for the flat guarantee in Chicago in exchange for checks well over the guarantee figure when the Cardinals played on the road.*

The news of the departure followed by just one day Wolfner's sale of ten percent of the team's stock to Joseph Griesedieck, president of the Falstaff Brewing Company of St. Louis. Griesedieck had been eyeing a franchise for St. Louis and had already headed a committee that had plunked down $50,000 with the NFL in hopes of capturing one of the NFL's two new expansion teams slated for play in 1961. In this latest maneuver, Wolfner asserted that the sale of the stock had "nothing whatever to do with any contemplated move we might make." The *Tribune* added:

*Wolfner said at the present time and under current circumstances it would hurt the Cardinals too much to move the franchise.*

A day later, the Chicago Cardinals were only a memory.

## *The Madison Street Agreement*

In the years since, speculation has continued about the move, including the role George Halas and the Bears might have assumed behind the scenes. In the book, *The League: The Rise and Decline of the NFL,* author David Harris speaks of the possible involvement of the Bears:

*The move took the Cardinals out of Chicago and into St. Louis. At the time, it had been considered the solution to a long standing NFL problem—how to share what was then the nation's second largest market with George Halas' Bears. The two franchises had split the territory since the 1930s under the terms of what was called "the Madison Street agreement." The Bears would play all their games on the north side of Madison, the Cardinals on the south. The problem developed in the late 1950s, when the Cardinals wanted to move north of Madison to play their games in (Northwestern University's) Dyche Stadium. Halas called on Bert Bell to arbitrate and Bell upheld the earlier agreement and prevented the Cardinals from leaving Madison's south side. The ruling heightened the Cardinals' stadium frustrations and . . . a move was a definite possibility.*

*The pressure that put the move over the top came from CBS. Chicago was then the League's only shared market and, since TV sets in cities where a home game was taking place were then completely blacked out from football programming, it meant that the nation's number two market was largely inaccessible. Shortly after Pete Rozelle began his commissionership, a deal for moving the Cardinals to St. Louis was finally worked out. According to Rozelle, $500,000 was paid to the Cardinals' franchise for "improvements" it had made to Chicago's Soldier Field and then the Cardinals left town for St. Louis. The money came from "several sources." Among them were the rest of the League's owners and CBS.*

Wolfner could not completely finalize the deal until he could definitely secure a lease to play at Busch Stadium as well as secure a television agreement. These arrangements were quickly made, and on March 29, Wolfner stated: "We have a favorable lease now and this move is permanent."

So, after flirting with possible moves to Atlanta and Houston, the Cardinals finally announced that the team would depart for St. Louis. It was a crushing blow to long-time fans such as Tom Bresnahan and Art Klawans. Current Cardinals President William V. Bidwill remembers the move more concisely:

> *Basically, it was because of television. It wasn't necessarily a move to anywhere, but a move out of Chicago because of the television problems.*

Like jilted lovers, the longtime fans of the club tried to forget about the team, while still dearly missing it. Former fan Tom Breshnahan is still stung by the abrupt departure of his favorite team, even after nearly forty years:

> *We felt somewhat betrayed by the team, probably because as a youngster grow-ing up you could always get into Comiskey Park on a Sunday and watch the Cardinals play . . . and then . . . suddenly, there's no pro football on the South Side and Comiskey Park is empty. That's what hurt the most. People really loved the Chicago Cardinals.*

Season-ticket holder Art Klawans thought the move could have been avoided:

> *After the 1959 season, the Chicago Cardinals wanted to move their home games out of Soldier Field and into Dyche Stadium at Northwestern University in Evanston, just north of the city of Chicago. They wanted to play in Dyche but George Halas of the Bears apparently invoked an old agreement between the two teams that prohibited the Cards from playing any home games north of Madison Street, the dividing line between the North and South Sides. Likewise, the Bears couldn't play south of Madison Street.*
>
> *So, in effect, the Chicago Cardinals were forced out of Chicago by Halas and we (the fans) were all disappointed. There were still a lot of die-hard fans and our team abandoned us. We loved the Cardinals so we blamed Halas!*

In January of 1962, Violet Bidwill passed away and ownership of the club was absorbed by her sons William V. Bidwill and Charles W. "Stormy" Bidwill. By 1972, William Bidwill and his family acquired sole ownership of the team. The corporation originally formed by Chris O'Brien back in 1927 as the "Chicago Cardinals Football Club" was ultimately dissolved on February 26, 1973.

In St. Louis, the Cardinals were greeted with enthusiasm and affection, but the team was crippled at the box office initially by being forced to play in tiny Busch Stadium. "It's the only place I know," Bill Bidwill noted at the time, "where there are 34,000 seats, and 24,000 of them are bad." Eventually, the new Busch Stadium was built, and the Cardinals did enjoy some success, winning division titles in 1974 and 1975. But by 1987, the club was averaging less than twenty-eight thousand attendees per home game and the love affair between the team and the city was fizzling.

Eventually, the club pulled up stakes again in 1988 when it headed West and became known as the Phoenix Cardinals. In 1994, the name of the team was changed to the

Arizona Cardinals. Then, in January of 1999, the Arizona Cardinals accomplished something that no other Cardinals team had achieved since the championship season of 1947. The Cardinals ended a half-century drought by finally winning an NFL playoff game.

◆ ◆ ◆

The latest chapter in the ongoing saga of the Chicago Cardinals was written in August of 1997, when Elmer Angsman and former equipment manager Phil Bouzeous hammered out a plan to honor the 1947 NFL champions. With the active support of the Bidwill family, a four-day reunion was held August 15-18 which was attended by twenty-one of the surviving twenty-two players from that team.

Angsman served as the master of ceremonies. As each player was introduced, he was presented with a championship ring to commemorate the illustrious 1947 season. A loving crowd of longtime Chicago Cardinals fans packed the banquet room at Sportsman's Park in suburban Chicago to embrace their heroes and watch as the Cardinals were finally honored for their remarkable achievements of fifty years earlier. "Look at this, look at this," Babe Dimancheff repeated to no one in particular as he cradled his championship ring. For the fans who clamored for autographs and for the players who verbally jabbed at each other and tearfully hugged their former teammates, it was as if the many years of distance and change had never existed.

It was then that Billy Dewell, still recovering from hip surgery, pulled himself to his feet and delivered another emotional jolt to an unforgettable evening that inspired thousands of memories. Dewell, the proud captain of the 1947 Chicago Cardinals, champions of the National Football League, spoke softly, yet firmly. His message was short, sweet, and moving. "I have always felt fortunate to have been chosen to be a member of the Chicago Cardinals football team," he said. "The owners, coaches, trainers and assistants, teammates and fans provided an environment that many players never experience. It was great! So I wrote a poem."

Perhaps there is no better way to conclude this one-hundred-year history of the Chicago Cardinals than to share Billy's brief poem, which takes us back to a different time and place, a time *when football was football:*

### The Prize
*The game is played.*
*The race is won.*
*The bout is fought.*
*What is it that is won?*
*The pain is endured.*
*The victories are fun.*
*Defeats are . . . accepted.*
*What is it that is won?*
*The fame is—fleeting.*
*The prize is—competing!*

The Cardinals, at least for one night, were back in Chicago.

## And Then What Happened?

Here are a few of the more important—or interesting—summaries of the many individuals connected with the Cardinals:

- **Elmer Angsman:** The South Side native with poor eyesight but a determined will to succeed romped through the NFL for seven seasons with the Cardinals. He still looms large in the team's all-time records, including the second-longest (eighty-two yards) run, the most consecutive games with a touchdown (five), the third best rushing average for a season (1948: 5.4), and the fourth-most career rushing touchdowns (twenty-seven). He remained in Chicago following his career and became a successful businessman, but he will always be remembered for those two long scoring runs in the 1947 championship game as well as his intensity to succeed on the field. As such, he was always a favorite of coach Jimmy Conzelman, who once recalled his favorite memory of Angsman, the football player:

  *I'll never forget the sight of Elmer getting ready for combat. He'd put in his contact lenses, take out his false teeth, put in a rubber mouthpiece, then get a shot in an ankle that was always bothering him.*

- **Vince Banonis:** Vince Banonis was an All-American at the University of Detroit and was with the Cardinals until 1951 when he was traded to his hometown of Detroit. Banonis retired after the 1953 season and entered the automotive supply business. He retired from that career in 1984 and still resides in the Detroit area. He is one of those rare football players who was on an NFL championship team on three different occasions. He is still remembered as one of the players who turned around both the perception and the visibility of the Cardinals.

- **Charles Bidwill Sr.:** The life of Charlie Bidwill has been documented earlier in this book, but the results of his perseverance during the dark days of the NFL are still evident today. The Arizona Cardinals of the National Football League remain the most visible monument to him. Although Bidwill passed away on April 19, 1947, before witnessing the Cardinals' world championship he so coveted, his efforts were immortalized forever when he was elected to the Pro Football Hall of Fame in 1967. He is perhaps most revered for his pragmatic thinking and his vision for the future, especially when the early days of his ownership coincided with the Great Depression. Arthur Rooney of the Pittsburgh Steelers once said: "Having a man like Charlie Bidwill during those tenuous times of the NFL was very important. He backed every piece of progressive legislation and his presence among the league owners helped the league gain respect from outside sources. He was a dominant force for many years."

  Longtime friend and rival George Halas noted: "Charlie always knew the NFL would reach the place where it is now. He was a man of great vision where the league was concerned and he was always willing to put the good of the league before his own team or personal feelings." His death at the age of fifty-one after a very brief illness was a shock to sports fans in Chicago. Until the end, he remained true to his own ideals.

- **Bill Blackburn:** Blackburn was a Cardinals mainstay for five seasons before finishing his career with two years in the Canadian league with Calgary. After his playing career ended in Canada, Blackburn went into business with his mother and eventually became involved with both the grocery and insurance businesses, rising to the position of vice president with a large insurance company and serving on the boards of twenty-one different insurance companies. Today, he resides in Texas, keeps active in the insurance business, and still holds the NFL record for the most touchdowns scored on interceptions in a game, with two in 1948. "I didn't realize I had the record until one night when someone called me and asked if I was the same guy that Howard Cosell was talking about on 'Monday Night Football' when someone tied the record. It's nice to still have the record after over fifty years!"

- **Chet Bulger:** The veteran tackle played with the Cardinals through 1949 and then completed his pro career with a year in Detroit with the Lions. Although he was a native of Maine, Chet returned to Chicago and began a long coaching career at De LaSalle High School. After Bulger subbed for an ill teacher at De La Salle, one of the administrators told him: "You belong in the classroom." He eventually became the athletic director as well as the football and track coach. He is a member of several Halls of Fame, including the Maine Sports Hall of Fame, the Chicago Sports Hall of Fame, and the Catholic League Hall of Fame. In his native Maine, the annual "Chet Bulger Award" is presented to the state's finest high school lineman. Today, Bulger still works part-time for De LaSalle's development office and he hosts a yearly golf outing to raise funds for the school. His feelings for the Cardinals and their glory years still run deep: "There is no such thing as luck, but you're lucky to be at a certain place at a certain time. It was such a group of characters and they're still loyal to each other."

- **Paul Christman:** "Pitchin' " Paul remained with the Cardinals until the 1950 season when he was sold to the Green Bay Packers. During his brief five-year (1945-49) career with the Cardinals, Christman captured all of the team's passing records and is still the fourth-leading passer in team history in terms of passing yardage. Modern fans remember Christman for his outstanding skills as a broadcaster for ABC, NBC, and CBS. Following his playing career, Christman began broadcasting Cardinals games in 1958. Later, he did other pro games as well as college contests and was behind the microphone for the first Super Bowl game. He had a simple philosophy during his prominent broadcasting career: "Never insult the intelligence of the listener. If you have nothing to say, shut up." Christman passed away from a heart attack on March 2, 1970, in Lake Forest, Illinois. He was fifty-one.

- **Jimmy Conzelman:** Following his resignation from the Cardinals in early 1949, Jimmy Conzelman became the vice president of the D'Arcy Advertising Agency in St. Louis and a director of the St. Louis professional baseball team. He still kept close to the game as an observer and pushed for the NFL to expand into the South well before that situation occurred.

  Jimmy's final play was on July 31, 1970, when he passed away in St. Louis. Ironically, his passing was on the same day as the annual College All-Star game, the start of another football season which the old coach so thoroughly enjoyed. While tributes and plaudits rolled in, it was a chance for the football world to once again remember one of its own:

*George Halas: "You ask how good Conzelman was for football? Well, he's enshrined in both the college and pro football halls of fame!"*

Perhaps columnist David Condon of the *Chicago Tribune* noted it best in his final tribute to the coach. Brushing aside pure facts for emotion, Condon wrote:

*Sometimes a guy with a heavy heart has to get it off his chest. (Tribune writer George) Strickler and I were nuts about Jimmy Conzelman, and I had to tell you about him in this morning's essay. And right now we'll bet Jimmy's saying to St. Pete: "Stop me if you've heard this one . . ."*

Or, as Conzelman said in 1970 just prior to his passing: "I've done almost anything and everything I've wanted to." According to his former players, to this day, he is still missed.

- **Bill De Correvont:** Although De Correvont was a member of the 1947 championship team and enjoyed modest success as a pro, he is perhaps best known as the most celebrated high school player ever to come out of Chicago. The halfback led the nation's prep players in scoring that year with 210 points and finished his high school career by leading Austin over Tennessee champion Jackson High School in Memphis by a score of 13-0 on December 11, 1937. He later played at Northwestern and in the pro ranks with the Cardinals, Redskins, Lions, and Bears. He passed away on September 6, 1995, at the age of seventy-six.

- **Billy Dewell:** Another wartime hero of the Cardinals was Billy Dewell, the three-sport star who courageously gave up his football career to represent his country in the military. Billy served as the Cards' captain from 1946 to 1949 after originally joining the team in 1940 following the minor league baseball season. After rejoining the team in 1946 following World War II, Dewell found the 1947 championship to be especially gratifying:

*After joining the Cardinals in 1940 when they were just starting to build the ball club, and we weren't winning—the championship was really sweet and very satisfying!*

Dewell stayed with the Cardinals until after the 1949 season and began a career in sales. Now retired and living in Texas, he fondly remembers his years with the Cardinals:

*It was great to play with the Cardinals as we began to improve by assembling a really great bunch of players who were able to work as a team, while using their personal talents . . . which were very, very good.*

- **Babe Dimancheff:** Most Cardinals felt that Dimancheff was the quickest man on the 1947 team, if not in all of football. When his playing career ended,

Dimancheff moved into the coaching ranks, beginning with stints at a Michigan high school and at Butler University. He then moved into the pro ranks and served as an assistant with such teams as the Steelers, Cowboys, and Bears. He was part of a group which was unsuccessful in its attempt to purchase an NFL team, but he later worked with teams in the World Football League and the Continental Football League, serving as both a general manager and a head coach. If there is a sad side to his tenure with the Chicago Cardinals, it was the loss of his daughter, Judith Ann. The little girl, whose birth so mesmerized Coach Jimmy Conzelman as the Cards prepared to tackle the Bears in 1947, lost a valiant battle to leukemia on December 13, 1950. "It was just after her third birthday," said Dimancheff. "We didn't know much about it back then, but all of the Cardinals gave blood." To the "Babe," those kind gestures were typical of his teammates: "We had togetherness. Each one did his job and cared about each other. That was the key."

- **Paddy Driscoll:** Following the conclusion of his playing career with the Bears in 1929, Driscoll remained in football in a variety of positions. He continued coaching sports at St. Mel High School in Chicago (his 1925 basketball team won the National Catholic High School Championship) and was head football coach at Marquette University from 1937 to 1940. He then rejoined the Bears as an assistant coach and later served two years as head coach (1956-57) when George Halas temporarily retired. Under Paddy's direction, the 1956 Bears won the Western Division title but fell to the New York Giants in the NFL title game. Upon the return of Halas, Driscoll moved into the front office as a vice president and director of research and planning. He was still working with the Bears at the time of his death on June 28, 1968, at the age of seventy-three. A favorite story about Driscoll has survived from his head coaching stint at Marquette. During this time, Marquette was a twenty-seven-point underdog in an upcoming game against Boston University and practices were not going well. When the team arrived for practice two days before the game, they found that Driscoll had started a bonfire on the practice field. "No practice today," he told his players. "You can't play football anyhow, so we might as well toast marshmallows." The inspired and insulted Marquette team turned around and won that game although Paddy burned the marshmallows! Today, Driscoll is remembered as the greatest player of his era and the last of the great dropkickers. He was elected to the Pro Football Hall of Fame in 1965.

- **Marshall Goldberg:** Marshall Goldberg always pursued excellence and achieved it both on the football field and in his business career. Goldberg announced his retirement after the 1947 season to pursue his blossoming position with a Chicago company that rebuilt and constructed special machines. The Cardinals approached the owner of the company in an effort to secure Goldberg for one more season. He did rejoin the Cardinals for the 1948 season, but with the stipulation that he play only defense. Goldberg continued to work even during the football season and his dual career paid off; he eventually became president and owner of the company. While he is respected as the patriarch of the "Dream Backfield," Goldberg revolutionized the defensive safety position as it is known today. He was one of the most versatile players in the history of the NFL, as acknowledged by Coach Jimmy

Conzelman in the book *Pro Football's Rag Days:* "He might well have been the first defensive specialist in pro football. And he was a great one . . . Marshall Goldberg may be one of the most underrated players ever to play in the pros. At one time in one season he led the league in five different departments. Imagine what a player with those statistics could command in today's market!"

Goldberg was briefly a television star after his playing career was over, teaming with none other than Mike Wallace on Chicago Cardinals sports shows. "It was fun . . . a nice, easy pregame show. We met for about an hour before our show started and went over the plays and the traits of the other team," recalls Goldberg.

At the time of his retirement following the 1948 season, Goldberg held the all-time team records for yards gained, attempts, touchdowns, and interceptions. He is a member of the Jewish Sports Hall of Fame, the Citizen Savings Hall of Fame, the National Football Foundation Hall of Fame, and is one of only four Cardinals to have had their jersey numbers retired.

- **Pat Harder:** Marlin "Pat" Harder overcame knee injuries to become the leading rusher in the Big Ten and to top the NFL in scoring three times. In the 1943 College All-Star game, Harder was selected as the MVP after pacing the Collegians to a 27-7 win over the Washington Redskins. Former college teammate Elroy "Crazy Legs" Hirsch once said, "Pat was one of the toughest competitors I've ever met. When it was third and one, he was the guy you could count on." Harder played for the Cards from 1946 to 1950 and then finished his career with the Detroit Lions from 1951 to 1953. Following the conclusion of his playing days, Harder became a respected NFL official. "You didn't argue with him when he made a decision," recalled Hirsch. "This was one tough man." Pat Harder passed away in 1992 at the age of seventy.

- **Walt Kiesling:** Kiesling survived a rugged thirteen-year pro career (1926-1939), including five years (1929-1933) with the Chicago Cardinals. After his playing career with six different teams concluded, Kiesling embarked on a coaching career, taking over the Steelers three games into the 1939 season. He coached the Steelers through 1942 and then shared coaching duties when Pittsburgh merged with Philadelphia (1943) and the Caridnals (1944). He was also an assistant with the Packers and the Steelers before becoming Pittsburgh's head coach once again from 1954 to 1956. In total, Kiesling spent thirty-four years in pro football before he passed away on March 2, 1962, at the age of fifty-eight. He was elected to the Pro Football Hall of Fame in 1966.

- **Mal Kutner:** How good was Kutner? Marshall Goldberg, perhaps the greatest defensive player of his era, once said: "I covered Don Hutson for six years in games and I've tried to cover Kutner in practice." Kutner was brilliant on both sides of the ball and rarely sat out a play during his career. His career basically ended when he suffered a knee injury during training camp in 1949. "We had finished our scrimmage and I was called back by one of the assistant coaches for some more drills. Sure enough, I got hurt. It was a fluke accident—no one hit me. I just came down and felt it. It definitely cut my career short." Kutner left the team following the 1950 season and returned to the oil business in Texas, eventually becoming vice president of an independent oil company. "To me, he's a Hall of Fame candidate," said former teammate Babe Dimancheff.

- **Stan Mauldin:** One of the saddest days in the history of the Chicago Cardinals occurred on September 25, 1948, when tackle Stan Mauldin collapsed and died in the locker room following the opening game of the season in Chicago. The twenty-seven-year-old from the University of Texas was just beginning his third season in the pros after an illustrious service career during the war. As an aggressive, agile lineman, the whole pro football world lay before him. Then tragedy struck.

  Coroner A. L. Brodie stated that Mauldin died of an "acute heart attack." Widely respected by friends and foes alike, Mauldin received the ultimate tribute when his family was voted a share of any playoff receipts by both the Cardinals and the Eagles. Today, he is one of only four Cardinals players who have had their jersey number retired by the team in its century-old history. The proud number seventy-seven will never be worn again.

- **Ernie Nevers:** As player-coach of the Cardinals, Nevers was one of the NFL's early superstars. Although his pro playing career lasted just five seasons, Nevers was selected to the inaugural class of the Pro Football Hall of Fame in 1963. Born June 11, 1903, in Willow River, Minnesota, Nevers graduated from Stanford and played professional baseball, basketball, and football. Following his playing career, Nevers coached the Cardinals again in 1939 and was head coach at Lafayette and an assistant at both Stanford and Iowa. Eventually, he became involved in business ventures in the San Francisco area, was a broadcaster for 49ers games, and was a director for the Seattle Rangers of the Continental Football League. He passed away in San Rafael, California, on May 3, 1976, at the age of seventy-two.

- **Chris O'Brien:** The enterprising "Father of Professional Football in Chicago" led a full and happy life after selling his beloved Cardinals to Dr. David Jones in 1929. He even made a brief return to the game in 1934 when he organized the Chicago Tigers, a short-lived team which managed to snare exhibition contests with both the Bears and Cardinals that year. O'Brien continued to live on Racine Avenue and managed many of the activities at nearby Normal Park. The entire O'Brien family worked the concession stands for numerous events at the park, including the "Combined Irish Alliance of Cook County Athletic Carnival," which featured a middleweight championship fight. He continued to follow the Cardinals and was at the game when his former team won the NFL title in 1947. O'Brien never experienced much financial serenity from his many business ventures and eventually worked in the office of the clerk of the Circuit Court in Chicago. He passed away on June 3, 1951, at the age of sixty-nine. True to the Cardinals until the end, his death certificate noted his occupation as being a "football team owner/promoter."

- **Garrard Ramsey:** Garrard Sliger "Buster" Ramsey was a fourteenth-round draft choice of the Cardinals in 1943, but he didn't join the club until 1946. Despite his smallish stature (6'1", 219 pounds) and his college (William and Mary) experience, Ramsey quickly became one of the most feared guard-linebackers in the league. He also became one of the team's favorites for his fierce intensity, unshakeable honesty, and neverending chatter. Ramsey played just five years in the NFL, but earned several All-Pro mentions. "He could drive you nuts with his comments," laughs former center Vince Banonis, "but he was always there when you needed him." Today, Ramsey resides in Tennessee and enjoys entertaining former teammates as they travel through his state.

- **Fred "Duke" Slater:** Slater is perhaps the most underrated tackle in the history of the game. While he received many honors in college and with the Cards, legendary coach Glen "Pop" Warner also selected Duke as his starting tackle on his selection of the eleven best players in history (prior to 1950). Frederick Wayman Slater was an All-American at Iowa before embarking on a ten-year pro career, the last six with the Cardinals. He retired after the 1931 season, but moved quickly into a legal career. During the off-seasons, Slater attended law school and earned his law degree in 1928. Slater was elected to the Municipal Court in 1948 and achieved the status of Superior Court judge in 1960. In 1964, he became a Circuit Court judge. Slater, who lived at 4800 Chicago Beach Drive, passed away on August 15, 1966, at the age of sixty-seven. Upon learning of Slater's death, Chicago Mayor Richard J. Daley said, "The passing of Judge Fred Slater is saddening news to me and to thousands of his Chicago fellow citizens. He was a real leader of men and a model for youngsters, and he will be greatly missed." Duke Slater is a member of the College Football Hall of Fame.

- **Gaynell Tinsley:** "Gus" Tinsley's spectacular NFL career was shortened by a knee injury in 1940. He returned home to Louisiana to teach and coach at his local high school and eventually became the head coach at LSU from 1948 to 1954. Despite his brief pro career, Tinsley was named by one 1969 poll to "The Best Eleven of the Thirties," where he was paired with Don Hutson at the ends. Today, he is retired, but still enjoys working with his several champion walking horses.

- **Mario "Motts" Tonelli:** Tonelli, the hero of World War II, somehow easily slid back into a normal lifestyle following forty-two months as a Japanese prisoner-of-war. Shortly after his return and a brief stint with the Cardinals and the Chicago Rockets, Tonelli became the first Republican (and the youngest) to capture the office of Cook County Commissioner in Chicago. After serving eight years, he eventually became Cook County's foremost official in the environmental protection unit. Today, he is unable to forget the memories of Bataan but still considers himself a very lucky person. He remains in demand as a speaker and his story continues to be told in publications across the country, primarily due to his visibility on both local and national television segments. In 1998, two more prestigious honors were added when he was selected to receive the Gene Autry Award in Arizona and the Frank Leahy Award in Florida.

- **Charley Trippi:** Trippi ended his nine-year playing career with the Cardinals following the 1955 season, excelling as a halfback, quarterback, punter, and defensive back. He averaged a whopping 5.1 yards per carry during his stint in Chicago —which is still the best in Cardinals history—along with his 13.7 yard average for career punt returns. When he retired, he held fifteen team records, including most rushing yardage, most punts, and most punt returns. Coach Jimmy Conzelman was one of Trippi's biggest boosters, as evidenced by this comment:

*Trippi was one of the greatest backs I ever had or ever seen, for that matter, during my 28 years in professional football. His attitude, his ability and competitive spirit, the combination which made him one of football's all-time greats, also made him an easy player to coach. I think my feelings in regards to Charley Trippi may be summed up by saying he is a "Coach's Dream."*

Even the legendary Jim Thorpe was amazed by Trippi, calling him "the greatest football player I ever saw." Following his playing career, he was an assistant coach with the Cardinals as well as with the University of Georgia. Mr. Trippi is now a retired real estate broker and living in Athens, Georgia. He was elected to the Pro Football Hall of Fame in 1968 and is also a member of the College Football Hall of Fame, the Georgia Sports Hall of Fame, and the Rose Bowl Hall of Fame.

# Cardinals Greats

### Hall of Fame

The Cardinals are well represented in the Pro Football Hall of Fame in Canton, Ohio. Beginning with the selection of Ernie Nevers as a charter member in 1963, the Cardinals have witnessed fourteen of their own as entrants into the Hall of Fame.

Here's the list:

Charles Bidwill, Guy Chamberlin, Jimmy Conzelman, Paddy Driscoll, Walt Kiesling, Curly Lambeau, Dick "Night Train" Lane, Ollie Mattson, Ernie Nevers, Jim Thorpe, Charley Trippi, Larry Wilson, and Dan Dierdorf.

Some of these selections are a little bit of a stretch, such as Thorpe, who played one game with the Cards in 1928, while the infamous Lambeau (who has a stadium named for him in Wisconsin) coached the Cards in 1950-51 after earning legendary laurels as the founding father of the Green Bay Packers.

### Retired Numbers

In the long history of the Cardinals, it is interesting to note that in nearly one hundred years, only four team uniform numbers have been retired.

The retired numbers are those of Marshall Goldberg (No. 99), J. V. Cain (No. 88), Stan Mauldin (No. 77), and Larry Wilson (No. 8). Only Wilson is a member of the Hall of Fame, but each made a unique contribution to pro football's oldest team.

Goldberg is an icon, a true team leader who witnessed the highs and the lows of the Cards' resurgence in the 1940s. He was a solid two-way player who unselfishly concentrated on defense to help the Cards catapult to the championship in 1947.

Wilson entered the Hall of Fame in 1978 after a stellar thirteen-year career in which he was probably the most feared free safety in the NFL. The early Cards would have welcomed a "tough as nails" type of player like Wilson, who once intercepted a pass and returned it for a touchdown with two broken wrists.

Cain was an unsung hero during his brief stint with the Cards (1974-77), and exemplified his versatility at both tight end and wide receiver. Unfortunately, his career was struck down prematurely when he collapsed and died from a heart attack during training camp in 1979.

The final notable was Stan Mauldin, a burly tackle out of Texas who toiled in the trenches from 1946 to 1948. Mauldin was an integral part of the Cards' front line during the championship season in 1947. When he returned home from the war he played as a champion for the team he loved. Sadly, Mauldin passed away in the locker room following the opening game of the 1948 season. It was a cruel, unforgiving loss for his teammates—especially to Goldberg, who was there with him.

# APPENDIX C

## All-Time Results, 1899-1959

Team records for all seasons were compiled from various newspaper accounts of individual games from 1899 to 1948. Non-league games not included after 1948. Source for team records for 1949 to 1959: *Arizona Cardinals Media Guide*. Attendance figures are given when known.

\* = Non-league game.

### MORGAN ATHLETIC ASSOCIATION
**1899 (6-1-1)  Captain Thomas Clancy**

| Oct. 15 | Shermans | 29-0 |
|---|---|---|
| Oct. 29 | Dearborn A. A. | 5-11 |
| Nov. 2 | Palmetto A. C. | 6-0 |
| Nov. 9 | Garfield Juniors | 5-0 |
| Nov. 16 | Dearborn A. A. | 6-0 |
| Nov. 16 | Kensingtons | 11-0 |
| Nov. 23 | Englewoods | 37-0 |
| Nov. 30 | Kensingtons | 0-0 |

### MORGAN ATHLETIC CLUB
**1900 (6-2-1)  Captain Chris O'Brien**

| Sept. 30 | Maplewoods | 23-0 |
|---|---|---|
| Oct. 7 | Hyde Park Columbias | 0-5 |
| Oct. 14 | Lakewoods | 10-0 |
| Oct. 21 | Wabash | 15-10 |
| Oct. 28 | Dearborns | 22-5 |
| Nov. 4 | Lyceums | 0-0 |
| Nov. 11 | Pullman Kensingtons | 6-0 |
| Nov. 30 | Grand Crossing Eagles | Won |
| Dec. 2 | Delawares | 0-8 |

### CARDINALS ATHLETIC AND SOCIAL CLUB
**1901 (4-0-1)  Captain J. P. O'Brien**

| Oct. 6 | Garfields | 0-0 |
|---|---|---|
| Oct. 20 | Dearborns | 11-0 |
| Oct. 27 | Grand Crossing Eagles | 23-5 |
| Nov. 10 | Maplewoods | 28-0 |
| Nov. 17 | Columbias | 14-5 |

NOTE: Claimed City Championship

**1902 (5-1)  Captain Chris O'Brien**

| Oct. 26 | Cornells | 6-0 |
|---|---|---|
| Nov. 2 | At Elgin | 10-0 |
| Nov. 16 | At Michigan City (IN), | 5-15 |
| Nov. 23 | Columbias | 6-0 |
| Nov. 27 | At Woodstock Olivers | 5-0 |
| Dec. 7 | Kensingtons | Won |

NOTE: Claimed Cook County, IL Championship

NOTE: Records from 1903-1915 unavailable.

### RACINE CARDINALS
**1916 (0-4)  Manager Chris O'Brien**

| Oct. 15 | Cornell A. C. | 0-6 |
|---|---|---|
| Oct. 29 | Iroquois A. C. | 0-28 |
| Nov. 5 | Standards | 0-41 |
| Nov. 19 | Alpines | 0-20 |

**1917 (3-3-5)  Manager Chris O'Brien**

| Oct. 14 | Mohawks | 0-0 |
|---|---|---|
| Oct. 21 | Hamlins | 0-20 |
| Oct. 28 | Tornadoes | 6-25 |
| Nov. 4 | United States Giants | 0-0 |
| Nov. 11 | Standards | Won |
| Nov. 18 | Opals | Won |
| Nov. 25 | Pullman Thorns | 0-0 |
| Nov. 29 | Standards | 19-6 |
| Dec. 2 | Logan Squares | 0-0 |
| Jan. 6 | Tornadoes | 3-3 |
| Jan. 20 | Tornadoes | 7-21 |

**1918 (3-2-1)  Manager Chris O'Brien**

| Oct. 6 | Gary Techs | 0-0 |
|---|---|---|
| Nov. 10 | Pullman Thorns | 0-6 |
| Nov. 28 | E. Chicago Gophers | Won |
| Dec. 1 | Pullman Thorns | 0-20 |
| Dec. 8 | Igorrotes | 6-0 |
| Dec. 15 | E. Chicago Gophers | 13-0 |

**1919 (4-2-2)  Manager Chris O'Brien**

| Oct. 5 | Pullman Thorns | 7-0 |
|---|---|---|
| Oct. 19 | Moline | 7-7 |
| Oct. 26 | Pullman Thorns | 6-0 |
| Nov. 2 | Logan Squares | 10-7 |
| Nov. 9 | Calerton A. C. | 6-7 |
| Nov. 23 | Chicago Stayms | 20-13 |
| Nov. 27 | Standards | 7-28 |
| Dec. 19 | Chicago Stayms | 14-14 |

### RACINE/CHICAGO CARDINALS
**1920 (6-2-2; league 3-2-1)  Head Coach John "Paddy" Driscoll**

| Oct. 10 | At Chicago Tigers | 0-0 | 8,000 |
|---|---|---|---|
| Oct. 17 | Moline Athletics* | 33-3 | — — |
| Oct. 24 | At Rock Island Independents | 0-7 | — — |
| Oct. 31 | Detroit Lions/Heralds | 21-0 | — — |
| Nov. 7 | At Chicago Tigers | 6-3 | — — |

| Nov. 14 | Cincinnati Celts* | 20-0 | — — |
| Nov. 21 | Lansing (MI) | | |
| | Oldsmobiles* | 14-0 | — — |
| Nov. 28 | Decatur Staleys | 7-6 | — — |
| Dec. 5 | At Decatur Staleys | 0-10 | — — |
| Dec. 19 | At Chicago Stayms* | 14-14 | — — |

Home: 5-0. Away: 1-2-2.
NOTE: Team became known as Chicago Cardinals on October 20, 1920.

## CHICAGO CARDINALS (until 1960)
### 1921 (6-3-2; league 3-3-2) Head Coach John "Paddy" Driscoll

| Sept. 25 | Racine Horlicks* | 27-0 | — — |
| Oct. 2 | Minneapolis | | |
| | Marines | 20-0 | 4,000 |
| Oct. 9 | Akron Pros | 0-23 | 6,000 |
| Oct. 16 | Rock Island | | |
| | Independents | 7-14 | 4,000 |
| Oct. 23 | Columbus Panhandles | 17-6 | 6,000 |
| Nov. 6 | Hammond Pros | 7-0 | — — |
| Nov. 20 | Green Bay Packers | 3-3 | 2,000 |
| Nov. 24 | At Chicago Stayms* | 27-0 | — — |
| Nov. 27 | Gary Elks* | 21-0 | 2,000 |
| Dec. 4 | Akron Pros | 0-7 | 3,500 |
| Dec. 18 | At Chicago Staleys | 0-0 | 2,000 |

Home: 5-3-1. Away: 1-0-1

### 1922 (9-3; league 7-2-1) Head Coach John "Paddy" Driscoll

| Sept. 24 | Maplewood Rovers* | 29-0 | 1,000 |
| Oct. 1 | Milwaukee Badgers | 3-0 | 3,500 |
| Oct. 15 | Green Bay Packers | 16-3 | 3,500 |
| Oct. 22 | Minneapolis Marines | 3-0 | 4,000 |
| Oct. 29 | Columbus Panhandles | 37-6 | 5,000 |
| Nov. 5 | Buffalo All-Americans | 9-7 | — — |
| Nov. 12 | Akron Pros | 7-0 | 2,000 |
| Nov. 19 | Canton Bulldogs | 0-7 | 7,500 |
| Nov. 26 | At Canton Bulldogs | 3-20 | 2,500 |
| Nov. 30 | Chicago Bears | 6-0 | 14,000 |
| Dec. 3 | Dayton Triangles | 3-7 | 3,000 |
| Dec. 10 | Chicago Bears | 9-0 | 15,000 |

Home: 9-2. Away: 0-1

### 1923 (9-4, league 8-4) Head Coach Arnie Horween

| Sept. 23 | Opal A. C.* | 13-0 | — — |
| Sept. 30 | Buffalo All-Americans | 3-0 | — — |
| Oct. 7 | Rochester Jeffersons | 60-0 | 5,000 |
| Oct. 14 | Akron Pros | 19-0 | — — |
| Oct. 21 | Minneapolis Marines | 9-0 | 4,000 |
| Oct. 28 | Dayton Triangles | 13-3 | 5,000 |
| Nov. 4 | Canton Bulldogs | 3-7 | 5,500 |
| Nov. 11 | Hammond Pros | 6-0 | 3,500 |
| Nov. 18 | Duluth Kelleys | 10-0 | 5,500 |
| Nov. 25 | Racine Legion | 4-10 | 7,000 |

| Nov. 29 | At Chicago Bears | 0-3 | 13,500 |
| Dec. 2 | Oorang Indians | 22-19 | 1,200 |
| Dec. 9 | Milwaukee Badgers | 12-14 | 6,000 |

Home: 9-3. Away: 0-1

### 1924 (6-4-1; league 5-4-1) Head Coach Arnie Horween

| Sept. 21 | Pullman Panthers* | 14-0 | — — |
| Sept. 28 | Milwaukee Badgers | 17-7 | 4,000 |
| Oct. 5 | Green Bay Packers | 3-0 | 2,800 |
| Oct. 12 | Minneapolis Marines | 13-0 | 8,060 |
| Oct. 19 | At Chicago Bears | 0-6 | 20,000 |
| Oct. 26 | Hammond Pros | 3-6 | 3,500 |
| Nov. 2 | Milwaukee Badgers | 8-17 | 3,000 |
| Nov. 9 | Dayton Triangles | 23-0 | 2,500 |
| Nov. 16 | Akron Pros | 13-0 | 2,500 |
| Nov. 23 | Racine Legion | 10-10 | — — |
| Nov. 27 | Chicago Bears | 0-21 | 6,000 |

Home: 6-3-1. Away: 0-1

### 1925 (11-2-1) Head Coach Norm Barry

| Sept. 27 | Hammond Pros | 6-10 | — — |
| Oct. 4 | Milwaukee Badgers | 34-0 | 2,500 |
| Oct. 11 | Columbus Tigers | 19-9 | — — |
| Oct. 18 | Kansas City Cowboys | 20-7 | — — |
| Oct. 25 | Chicago Bears | 9-0 | 13,000 |
| Nov. 1 | Duluth Kelleys | 10-6 | — — |
| Nov. 8 | Green Bay Packers | 9-6 | 4,000 |
| Nov. 15 | Buffalo Bisons | 23-6 | 4,000 |
| Nov. 22 | Dayton Triangles | 14-0 | 3,000 |
| Nov. 26 | At Chicago Bears | 0-0 | 39,000 |
| Nov. 29 | Rock Island Independents | 7-0 | 3,000 |
| Dec. 6 | Pottsville Maroons | 7-21 | 6,000 |
| Dec. 10 | Milwaukee Badgers | 59-0 | 500 |
| Dec. 12 | Hammond Pros | 13-0 | — — |

Home: 11-2. Away: 0-0-1
NOTE: NFL Champions

### 1926 (5-6-1) Co-Coaches Norm Barry (Backfield), Fred Gillies (Line)

| Sept. 19 | Columbus Tigers | 14-0 | 2,500 |
| Sept. 26 | LA Buccaneers | 15-0 | 7,500 |
| Oct. 3 | Racine Tornadoes | 20-0 | 3,000 |
| Oct. 10 | At Green Bay Packers | 13-7 | 5,000 |
| Oct. 17 | At Chicago Bears | 0-16 | 12,000 |
| Oct. 24 | At Milwaukee Badgers | 3-2 | — — |
| Oct. 31 | Green Bay Packers | 0-3 | 3,000 |
| Nov. 6 | At Frankford Yellow | | |
| | Jackets | 7-33 | 8,000 |
| Nov. 7 | At NY Giants | 0-20 | 10,000 |
| Nov. 11 | Chicago Bears* | 0-10 | 15,000 |
| Nov. 25 | At Chicago Bears | 0-0 | 8,000 |
| Nov. 28 | Kansas City Cowboys | 2-7 | 14,000 |

Home: 3-3. Away: 2-3-1

### 1927 (4-8-1; league 3-7-1) Head Coach Guy Chamberlin (9 games); Head Coach

## Ben Jones (2 games)

| | | | |
|---|---|---|---|
| Sept. 18 | Hammond* | 0-6 | — — |
| Sept. 25 | Chicago Bears | 0-9 | 4,000 |
| Oct. 2 | Maroons Pottsville | 19-7 | 2,000 |
| Oct. 9 | Dayton Triangles | 7-0 | 2,500 |
| Oct. 16 | At Green Bay Packers | 0-13 | 6,000 |
| Oct. 23 | At Spring Valley (IL) Wildcats* | 33-0 | 3,000 |
| Oct. 30 | NY Yankees | 6-7 | 15,000 |
| Nov. 6 | Green Bay | 6-6 | 3,500 |
| Nov. 13 | At NY Yankees | 6-20 | 10,000 |
| Nov. 19 | At Frankford Yellow Jackets | 8-12 | — — |
| Nov. 20 | At NY Giants | 7-28 | 10,000 |
| Nov. 24 | At Chicago Bears | 3-0 | 6,000 |
| Nov. 27 | Cleveland Browns Bulldogs | 7-32 | 5,000 |

Home: 2-3-1. Away: 2-5

NOTE: Ben Jones coached the final two games of the season after Chamberlin was released.

## 1928 (2-6; league 1-5) Head Coach Fred Gillies

| | | | |
|---|---|---|---|
| Sept. 16 | At Hammond* | 12-0 | — — |
| Sept. 23 | Chicago Bears | 0-15 | 5,000 |
| Sept. 30 | Chicago Mills* | 6-7 | — — |
| Oct. 7 | Dayton Triangles | 7-0 | — — |
| Oct. 14 | At Green Bay Packers | 0-20 | 4,200 |
| Nov. 4 | Chicago All-Stars | — | — — |
| Nov. 11 | Pullman Panthers | — | — — |
| Nov. 24 | At Frankford Yellow Jackets | 0-19 | 8,000 |
| Nov. 25 | At NY Yankees | 0-19 | 7,000 |
| Nov. 29 | At Chicago Bears | 0-34 | 10,000 |

Home: 1-2. Away: 1-4

## 1929 (6-7-1; league 6-6-1) Head Coach Dewey Scanlon

| | | | |
|---|---|---|---|
| Sept. 22 | At Canton Bulldogs* | 0-6 | — — |
| Sept. 29 | At Buffalo Bisons | 9-3 | 4,000 |
| Oct. 6 | At Green Bay Packers | 2-9 | 7,000 |
| Oct. 13 | At Minneapolis Redjackets | 7-14 | — — |
| Oct. 20 | At Chicago Bears | 0-0 | 18,000 |
| Oct. 27 | Green Bay Packers | 6-7 | 10,000 |
| Nov. 2 | At Frankford Yellow Jackets | 0-8 | 6,000 |
| Nov. 6 | At Providence Steam Roller | 16-0 | 6,000 |
| Nov. 10 | Minneapolis Red Jackets | 8-0 | 6,000 |
| Nov. 17 | Green Bay | 0-12 | 15,000 |
| Nov. 24 | Dayton Triangles | 19-0 | 3,000 |
| Nov. 28 | Chicago Bears | 40-6 | 7,000 |
| Dec. 1 | At NY. Giants | 21-24 | 5,000 |
| Dec. 8 | At Orange Tornadoes | 26-0 | — — |

Home: 3-2. Away: 3-5-1

## 1930 (9-7-2; league 5-6-2) Head Coach Ernie Nevers

| | | | |
|---|---|---|---|
| Sept. 14 | At Sturgis (MI)* | 30-0 | — — |
| Sept. 21 | At Green Bay Packers | 0-14 | 8,000 |
| Sept 28 | At Minneapolis Redjackets | 7-7 | — — |
| Oct. 5 | At Portsmouth Spartans | 0-0 | 6,500 |
| Oct. 8 | At Newark Tornadoes | 13-0 | 5,000 |
| Oct. 12 | At Providence Steam Roller | 7-9 | 6,500 |
| Oct. 16 | At NY Giants | 12-25 | 15,000 |
| Oct. 19 | Chicago Bears | 6-32 | 10,000 |
| Oct. 25 | At Frankford Yellow Jackets | 34-7 | — — |
| Oct. 26 | Portsmouth Spartans | 23-13 | 8,000 |
| Oct. 29 | At Milwaukee Badgers* | 33-6 | 1,500 |
| Nov. 2 | Frankford Yellow Jackets | 6-0 | 3,000 |
| Nov. 9 | NY Giants | 7-13 | 4,000 |
| Nov. 16 | Green Bay Packers | 13-6 | 17,000 |
| Nov. 23 | Memphis Tigers* | 20-7 | 5,000 |
| Nov. 27 | At Chicago Bears | 0-6 | 8,175 |
| Dec. 7 | At Memphis Tigers* | 6-0 | 7,000 |
| Dec. 15 | At Chicago Bears* | 7-9 | 10,000 |

Home: 4-2. Away 5-5-2

## 1931 (12-4-1; league 5-4) Head Coach Roy Andrews (3 games); Head Coach Ernie Nevers (14 games)

| | | | |
|---|---|---|---|
| Sept. 16 | At Chicago Harley-Mills* | 25-0 | — — |
| Sept. 20 | Pullman Panthers* | 31-0 | — — |
| Sept. 23 | At Portsmouth Spartans | 3-13 | 8,000 |
| Oct. 11 | At Green Bay | 7-26 | 8,000 |
| Oct. 18 | At Chicago Bears | 13-26 | 9,000 |
| Oct. 25 | At Rock Island Green Bush* | 45-13 | — — |
| Nov. 1 | At Brooklyn Dodgers | 14-7 | 15,000 |
| Nov. 8 | At Cleveland Indians | 14-6 | 10,000 |
| Nov. 11 | At Grand Rapids* | 36-0 | — — |
| Nov. 15 | Green Bay Packers | 21-13 | 9,000 |
| Nov. 22 | Portsmouth Spartans | 20-19 | 5,000 |
| Nov. 26 | At Chicago Bears | 7-18 | 14,000 |
| Nov. 28 | Cleveland Indians | 21-0 | 1,500 |
| Dec. 5 | At Grand Rapids* | 7-7 | 4,000 |
| Dec. 13 | At St. Louis Gunners* | 26-6 | 12,000 |
| Dec. 20 | Memphis Tigers* | 24-7 | 3,000 |
| Jan. 17 | At Southern CA All-Stars* | 14-0 | 10,000 |

Home: 5-0. Away: 7-4-1

NOTE: Roy Andrews resigned after Portsmouth game

## 1932 (7-6-2; league 2-6-2) Head Coach Jack Chevigny

| | | | |
|---|---|---|---|
| Sept. 7 | At Grand Rapids* | 13-0 | — — |
| Sept. 14 | At Aurora Yellow Jackets* | 33-0 | 1,500 |
| Sept. 18 | At Green Bay Packers | 7-15 | 3,000 |
| Sept. 25 | Battle Creek Maroons* | 19-0 | 2,000 |

| | | | |
|---|---|---|---|
| Oct. 2 | At Portsmouth Spartans | 7-7 | — — |
| Oct. 9 | Chicago Bears | 0-0 | 8,000 |
| Oct. 16 | At Boston Braves | 9-0 | 18,000 |
| Oct. 23 | At Providence Steam Roller | 7-0 | — — |
| Oct. 30 | Brooklyn Dodgers | 27-7 | 5,000 |
| Nov. 6 | Green Bay Packers | 9-19 | 8,323 |
| Nov. 13 | At Brooklyn Dodgers | 0-3 | 17,000 |
| Nov. 20 | At Staten Island Stapletons | 7-21 | 5,000 |
| Nov. 24 | At Chicago Bears | 0-34 | 6,800 |
| Nov. 27 | Boston Braves | 6-8 | 12,700 |
| Dec. 4 | At St. Louis Gunners* | 20-7 | 4,000 |

Home: 2-2-1. Away: 5-4-1.

### 1933 (5-9-1; league 1-9-1)  Head Coach Paul Schissler

| | | | |
|---|---|---|---|
| Sept. 10 | At Aurora Ideals* | 65-0 | — — |
| Sept. 17 | Freeport Lions* | 29-6 | — — |
| Sept. 20 | Indianapolis Indians* | 2-0 | — — |
| Sept. 24 | At Princeton (IL) Tigers* | 20-0 | — — |
| Sept. 27 | At Pittsburgh Pirates | 13-14 | 5,000 |
| Oct. 1 | At Portsmouth Spartans | 6-7 | — — |
| Oct. 8 | At Cincinnati Reds | 3-0 | 1,500 |
| Oct. 15 | Chicago Bears | 9-12 | 12,000 |
| Oct. 22 | At Boston Redskins | 0-10 | 16,000 |
| Oct. 29 | At Brooklyn Dodgers | 0-7 | 18,000 |
| Nov. 5 | Green Bay Packers | 6-14 | 5,000 |
| Nov. 12 | Cincinnati Reds | 9-12 | 7,000 |
| Nov. 19 | Brooklyn Dodgers | 0-3 | 4,000 |
| Nov. 30 | At Chicago Bears | 6-22 | 8,000 |
| Dec. 3 | Boston Redskins | 0-0 | 7,000 |

Home: 2-4-1. Away: 3-5.

### 1934 (16-6; league 5-6)  Head Coach Paul Schissler

| | | | |
|---|---|---|---|
| Sept. 16 | At Chicago Tigers* | 33-0 | — — |
| Sept. 19 | Cleveland Panthers* | 52-0 | — — |
| Sept. 23 | At Cincinnati Reds | 9-0 | 5,400 |
| Sept. 26 | Central Illinois All-Stars* | 32-0 | 2,500 |
| Sept. 30 | At Detroit Lions | 0-6 | 18,000 |
| Oct. 3 | At Maywood (IL) A. C.* | 43-0 | 6,000 |
| Oct. 7 | At Cincinnati Reds | 16-0 | 2,500 |
| Oct. 14 | At Chicago Bears | 0-20 | 17,500 |
| Oct. 21 | At Green Bay Packers | 0-15 | 3,750 |
| Oct. 28 | At Boston Redskins | 0-9 | 10,000 |
| Nov. 6 | At Brooklyn Dodgers | 21-0 | 7,000 |
| Nov. 11 | Detroit Lions | 13-17 | 7,500 |
| Nov. 18 | At Green Bay Packers | 9-0 | 3,500 |
| Nov. 25 | At Chicago Bears | 6-17 | 13,800 |
| Nov. 29 | Green Bay Packers | 6-0 | 3,500 |
| Dec. 2 | At Kansas City Blues* | 13-7 | 3,500 |
| Dec. 5 | At Tulsa Oilers* | 20-7 | 1,200 |
| Dec. 9 | At Stanford Braves* | 37-2 | 12,000 |
| Dec. 16 | At. S. California Maroons* | 41-7 | 16,000 |

| | | | |
|---|---|---|---|
| Dec. 20 | UCLA Alumni* | 17-7 | — — |
| Dec. 23 | At California Giants* | 21-0 | 5,000 |
| Jan. 13 | Chicago Bears* (Los Angeles, CA) | 13-9 | 15,000 |

Home: 3-1. Away: 13-5

### 1935 (8-4-2; league 6-4-2)  Head Coach Milan Creighton

| | | | |
|---|---|---|---|
| Sept. 1 | At Calumet (IN) All-Stars* | 20-0 | — — |
| Sept. 15 | At Green Bay Packers | 7-6 | — — |
| Sept. 22 | At La Crosse (WI) Heilemans* | 41-0 | 1,000 |
| Sept. 29 | At Detroit Lions | 10-10 | 10,000 |
| Oct. 13 | At Green Bay Packers | 3-0 | 18,000 |
| Oct. 20 | At Pittsburgh Pirates | 13-17 | 6,000 |
| Oct. 27 | At NY Giants | 14-13 | 32,000 |
| Nov. 3 | Detroit Lions | 6-7 | 5,000 |
| Nov. 10 | Philadelphia Eagles | 12-3 | 5,000 |
| Nov. 19 | At Brooklyn Dodgers | 12-14 | 12,000 |
| Nov. 24 | At Boston Redskins | 6-0 | 5,000 |
| Nov. 28 | Green Bay Packers | 9-7 | 7,500 |
| Dec. 1 | At Chicago Bears | 7-7 | 12,167 |
| Dec. 8 | Chicago Bears | 0-13 | 17,373 |

Home: 2-2. Away: 6-2-2.

### 1936 (5-8-2; league 3-8-1)  Head Coach Milan Creighton

| | | | |
|---|---|---|---|
| Aug. 31 | At South Bend (IN) Brewers* | 70-0 | — — |
| Sept. 13 | At Green Bay Packers | 7-10 | 11,000 |
| Sept. 20 | At La Crosse (WI) Heilemans* | 20-0 | 4,000 |
| Sept. 28 | At Detroit Lions | 0-39 | 25,800 |
| Oct. 4 | At Green Bay Packers | 0-24 | 11,500 |
| Oct. 11 | At Chicago Bears | 3-7 | 16,288 |
| Oct. 18 | At NY Giants | 6-14 | 17,000 |
| Oct. 25 | At Brooklyn Dodgers | 0-9 | 17,000 |
| Nov. 1 | At Boston Redskins | 10-13 | 7,000 |
| Nov. 8 | Philadelphia Eagles | 13-0 | 1,500 |
| Nov. 15 | Pittsburgh Pirates | 14-6 | 3,856 |
| Nov. 22 | Detroit Lions | 7-14 | 7,579 |
| Nov. 29 | Chicago Bears | 14-7 | 13,704 |
| Dec. 6 | Green Bay Packers | 0-0 | 5,000 |
| Dec. 13 | At LA Bulldogs* | 10-10 | 14,000 |

Home: 3-1-1. Away: 2-8-0.

### 1937 (6-5-1; league 5-5-1)  Head Coach Milan Creighton

| | | | |
|---|---|---|---|
| Sept. 12 | At Green Bay Packers | 14-7 | 10,000 |
| Sept. 19 | At Detroit Lions | 7-16 | 18,000 |
| Sept. 24 | At Washington Redskins | 21-14 | 22,000 |
| Sept. 26 | At Philadelphia Eagles | 6-6 | 10,000 |
| Oct. 3 | At Cleveland Rams | 6-0 | 10,400 |
| Oct. 10 | At Green Bay Packers | 13-34 | 16,181 |
| Oct. 17 | At Chicago Bears | 7-16 | 22,978 |
| Oct. 24 | At Pittsburgh Pirates | 13-7 | 10,000 |

| | | | |
|---|---|---|---|
| Oct. 31 | Cleveland Rams | 13-7 | 9,923 |
| Nov. 10 | At Chicago Gunners* | 19-3 | 5,800 |
| Nov. 21 | Detroit Lions | 7-16 | 8,576 |
| Dec. 5 | Chicago Bears | 28-42 | 7,313 |

Home: 1-2. Away: 5-3-1.

### 1938 (3-9-2; league 2-9) Head Coach Milan Creighton

| | | | |
|---|---|---|---|
| Sept. 1 | At College All-Stars* (St. Louis, MO) | 32-0 | 8,724 |
| Sept. 11 | Chicago Bears | 13-16 | 20,000 |
| Sept. 17 | At Cleveland Rams | 7-6 | 7,448 |
| Sept. 25 | At Green Bay Packers | 7-28 | 22,000 |
| Sept. 28 | At Green Bay (Buffalo) | 22-24 | 17,000 |
| Oct. 2 | At Brooklyn Dodgers | 0-13 | 17,129 |
| Oct. 11 | At LA Bulldogs* (WV) | 14-14 | 6,500 |
| Oct. 16 | At Chicago Bears | 28-34 | 21,614 |
| Oct. 23 | At Detroit Lions | 0-10 | 17,500 |
| Oct. 26 | At Philadelphia Eagles (Erie, PA) | 0-7 | 15,000 |
| Nov. 6 | At NY Giants | 0-6 | 22,184 |
| Nov. 13 | At Cincinnati Bengals* | 14-14 | 5,000 |
| Nov. 20 | Detroit Lions | 3-7 | 8,279 |
| Nov. 27 | Cleveland Rams | 31-17 | 2,200 |

Home: 1-2. Away: 2-7-2.

### 1939 (1-10) Head Coach Ernie Nevers

| | | | |
|---|---|---|---|
| Sept. 10 | At Detroit Lions | 13-21 | 15,075 |
| Sept. 17 | At Green Bay Packers | 10-24 | 11,792 |
| Sept. 24 | At Pittsburgh Pirates | 10-0 | 19,008 |
| Oct. 1 | Detroit Lions | 3-17 | 10,000 |
| Oct. 8 | At Green Bay | 20-27 | 23,000 |
| Oct. 15 | At Chicago Bears | 7-44 | 29,592 |
| Oct. 22 | Cleveland Rams | 0-24 | 10,043 |
| Nov. 5 | At Cleveland Rams | 0-14 | 8,378 |
| Nov. 12 | At NY Giants | 7-17 | 28,217 |
| Nov. 19 | At Washington Redskins | 7-28 | 26,667 |
| Nov. 26 | Chicago Bears | 7-48 | 16,055 |

Home: 0-3. Away: 1-7.

### 1940 (2-7-2) Head Coach Jimmy Conzelman

| | | | |
|---|---|---|---|
| Sept. 8 | At Pittsburgh Steelers | 7-7 | 22,383 |
| Sept. 15 | At Detroit Lions (Buffalo, NY) | 0-0 | 18,048 |
| Sept. 25 | Chicago Bears | 21-7 | 23,181 |
| Sept. 29 | At Green Bay Packers | 6-31 | 20,234 |
| Oct. 5 | At Detroit Lions | 14-43 | 20,619 |
| Oct. 13 | At Washington Redskins | 21-28 | 33,694 |
| Oct. 20 | At Cleveland Rams | 14-26 | 13,683 |
| Oct. 27 | Cleveland Rams | 17-7 | 10,313 |
| Nov. 1 | Green Bay Packers | 7-28 | 11,364 |
| Nov. 24 | At Brooklyn Dodgers | 9-14 | 16,619 |
| Dec. 1 | At Chicago Bears | 23-31 | 13,092 |

Home: 2-1. Away: 0-6-2.

### 1941 (3-7-2; league 3-7-1) Head Coach Jimmy Conzelman

| | | | |
|---|---|---|---|
| Sept. 9 | At Kenosha Cardinals* | 21-21 | 3,000 |
| Sept. 16 | Cleveland Rams | 6-10 | 15,000 |
| Sept. 27 | Detroit Lions | 14-14 | 20,000 |
| Oct. 5 | At Green Bay Packers | 13-14 | 10,000 |
| Oct. 12 | At Chicago Bears | 7-53 | 34,688 |
| Oct. 19 | At Brooklyn Dodgers | 20-6 | 12,054 |
| Oct. 26 | At Philadelphia Eagles | 14-21 | 12,683 |
| Nov. 2 | At NY Giants | 10-7 | 29,289 |
| Nov. 16 | At Green Bay Packers | 9-17 | 15,495 |
| Nov. 23 | At Cleveland Rams | 7-0 | 5,000 |
| Nov. 30 | At Detroit Lions | 3-21 | 17,051 |
| Dec. 7 | Chicago Bears | 24-34 | 18,879 |

Home: 0-2-1. Away: 3-5-1.

### 1942 (4-9; league 3-8) Head Coach Jimmy Conzelman

| | | | |
|---|---|---|---|
| Sept. 6 | At Western Army All-Stars* (Denver, CO) | 10-16 | 20,000 |
| Sept. 13 | At Cleveland Rams (Buffalo, NY) | 7-0 | 18,698 |
| Sept. 20 | Detroit Lions | 13-0 | 16,242 |
| Oct. 4 | Green Bay Packers | 13-17 | 24,897 |
| Oct. 11 | At Chicago Bears | 14-41 | 38,426 |
| Oct. 18 | At Detroit Lions | 7-0 | 14,000 |
| Oct. 25 | At Cleveland Rams | 3-7 | 7,896 |
| Nov. 1 | At Green Bay Packers | 24-55 | 14,782 |
| Nov. 8 | At Washington Redskins | 0-28 | 35,425 |
| Nov. 15 | At Wichita Aero Commandos* | 35-7 | — — |
| Nov. 22 | At Pittsburgh Steelers | 3-19 | 20,711 |
| Nov. 29 | At NY Giants | 7-21 | 20,354 |
| Dec. 6 | Chicago Bears | 7-21 | 8,251 |

Home: 1-2. Away: 3-7.

### 1943 (0-11; league 0-10) Head Coach Phil Handler

| | | | |
|---|---|---|---|
| Sept. 19 | At Detroit Lions | 14-35 | 23,402 |
| Sept. 26 | Washington Redskins (Buffalo, NY)* | 21-43 | 20,707 |
| Oct. 3 | Green Bay Packers | 7-28 | 18,063 |
| Oct. 10 | Chicago Bears | 0-20 | 24,658 |
| Oct. 17 | Detroit Lions (Buffalo, NY) | 0-7 | 15,072 |
| Oct. 24 | At Washington Redskins | 7-13 | 35,540 |
| Oct. 31 | At Phila.-Pitt. Steagles | 13-34 | 16,351 |
| Nov. 7 | At Brooklyn Dodgers | 0-7 | 13,340 |
| Nov. 14 | At Green Bay Packers | 14-35 | 10,831 |
| Nov. 21 | At NY Giants | 13-24 | 19,804 |
| Nov. 28 | Chicago Bears | 24-35 | 17,219 |

Home: 0-5. Away: 0-6.

### 1944 (1-12; league 1-10)—Cardinals combined with Pittsburgh Steelers for 1944 season
### Head Coach Phil Handler (Cardinals);

### Head Coach Walt Kiesling (Steelers)

| | | | |
|---|---|---|---|
| Sept. 12 | Philadelphia Eagles* | 0-22 | 20,000 |
| Sept. 18 | Washington Redskins* | | |
| | (Pittsburgh, PA) | 0-3 | 17,085 |
| Sept. 24 | Cleveland Rams | | |
| | (Pittsburgh, PA) | 28-30 | 20,968 |
| Oct. 1 | NY Giants* | | |
| | (Pittsburgh, PA) | 17-16 | 20,428 |
| Oct. 8 | At Green Bay Packers | 7-34 | 16,525 |
| Oct. 15 | At Chicago Bears | 7-34 | 20,940 |
| Oct. 22 | At NY Giants | 0-23 | 40,734 |
| Oct. 29 | At Washington Redskins | 20-42 | 35,000 |
| Nov. 5 | Detroit Lions | | |
| | (Pittsburgh, PA) | 6-27 | 17,743 |
| Nov. 12 | At Detroit Lions | 7-21 | 13,329 |
| Nov. 19 | Cleveland Rams | 6-33 | 3,500 |
| Nov. 26 | Green Bay Packers | 20-35 | 6,000 |
| Dec. 3 | Chicago Bears | | |
| | (Pittsburgh, PA) | 7-49 | 9,069 |

Home: 1-7. Away: 0-5.

### 1945 (1-9-1; league 1-9) Head Coach Phil Handler

| | | | |
|---|---|---|---|
| Sept. 17 | Washington Redskins* | | |
| | (Buffalo, NY) | 7-7 | 11,936 |
| Sept. 23 | Detroit Lions | | |
| | (Milwaukee, WI) | 0-10 | 6,500 |
| Sept. 30 | At Cleveland Rams | 0-21 | 10,872 |
| Oct. 7 | At Philadelphia Eagles | 6-26 | 25,581 |
| Oct. 14 | At Chicago Bears | 16-7 | 20,784 |
| Oct. 21 | At Detroit Lions | 0-26 | 32,644 |
| Oct. 28 | At Green Bay Packers | 14-33 | 19,221 |
| Nov. 4 | At Washington Redskins | 21-24 | 35,000 |
| Nov. 11 | At Pittsburgh Steelers | 0-23 | 13,153 |
| Nov. 18 | Cleveland Rams | 21-35 | 17,023 |
| Dec. 2 | Chicago Bears | 20-28 | 13,925 |

Home: 0-3-1. Away: 1-6.

### 1946 (8-5; league 6-5) Head Coach Jimmy Conzelman

| | | | |
|---|---|---|---|
| Sept. 8 | At Newark Bombers* | 48-6 | — — |
| Sept. 13 | At Greensboro Generals* | 47-0 | — — |
| Sept. 20 | At Pittsburgh Steelers | 7-14 | 33,700 |
| Sept. 30 | Detroit Lions | 34-14 | 26,842 |
| Oct. 6 | Chicago Bears | 17-34 | 39,263 |
| Oct. 13 | At Detroit Lions | 36-14 | 23,987 |
| Oct. 20 | At NY Giants | 24-28 | 50,681 |
| Oct. 27 | LA Rams | 34-10 | 38,180 |
| Nov. 3 | At Boston Yankees | 28-14 | 10,556 |
| Nov. 10 | Green Bay Packers | 7-19 | 30,691 |
| Nov. 17 | At LA Rams | 14-17 | 38,271 |
| Nov. 24 | At Green Bay Packers | 24-6 | 16,150 |
| Dec. 1 | At Chicago Bears | 35-28 | 47,511 |

Home: 2-2. Away: 6-3.      260-198

### 1947 (13-3; league 9-3) Head Coach Jimmy

### Conzelman

| | | | |
|---|---|---|---|
| Sept. 5 | Philadelphia Eagles | | |
| | (Buffalo, NY)* | 38-21 | 16,282 |
| Sept. 10 | NY Giants* | 52-21 | 39,850 |
| Sept. 19 | Boston Yankees | | |
| | (Dallas, TX)* | 7-3 | 18,000 |
| Sept. 28 | Detroit Lions | 45-21 | 22,739 |
| Oct. 5 | Chicago Bears | 31-7 | 51,123 |
| Oct. 12 | At Green Bay Packers | 14-10 | 25,502 |
| Oct. 19 | At LA Rams | 7-27 | 69,631 |
| Oct. 26 | Boston Yankees | 27-7 | 22,286 |
| Nov. 2 | LA Rams | 17-10 | 40,575 |
| Nov. 9 | At Detroit Lions | 17-7 | 27,513 |
| Nov. 16 | Green Bay Packers | 21-20 | 40,086 |
| Nov. 23 | At Washington Redskins | 21-45 | 35,362 |
| Nov. 30 | At NY Giants | 31-35 | 28,744 |
| Dec. 7 | At Philadelphia Eagles | 45-21 | 34,432 |
| Dec. 14 | At Chicago Bears | 30-21 | 48,632 |
| Dec. 28 | Philadelphia Eagles* | 28-21 | 30,759 |
| | (NFL Championship Game) | | |

Home: 7-0. Away: 6-3.

### 1948 (15-2; league 11-2) Head Coach Jimmy Conzelman

| | | | |
|---|---|---|---|
| Aug. 20 | At College All-Stars* | | |
| | (Chicago, IL) | 28-0 | 101,220 |
| Sept. 6 | Washington Redskins | | |
| | (Denver, CO)* | 46-20 | 17,782 |
| Sept. 10 | At Philadelphia Eagles* | 23-9 | 65,000 |
| Sept. 19 | Pittsburgh Steelers* | 35-14 | 16,834 |
| Sept. 24 | Philadelphia Eagles | 21-14 | 25,875 |
| Oct. 4 | Chicago Bears | 17-28 | 52,765 |
| Oct. 10 | At Green Bay Packers | 17-7 | 34,369 |
| Oct. 17 | At NY Giants | 63-35 | 35,342 |
| Oct. 24 | Boston Yankees | 49-27 | 23,433 |
| Oct. 31 | At LA Rams | 27-22 | 32,149 |
| Nov. 7 | Detroit Lions | 56-20 | 24,051 |
| Nov. 14 | At Pittsburgh Steelers | 24-7 | 33,364 |
| Nov. 21 | LA Rams | 27-24 | 29,031 |
| Nov. 25 | At Detroit Lions | 28-14 | 22,957 |
| Dec. 5 | Green Bay Packers | 42-7 | 26,072 |
| Dec. 12 | At Chicago Bears | 24-21 | 51,283 |
| Dec. 28 | At Philadelphia Eagles* | 0-7 | 36,309 |
| | (NFL Championship Game) | | |

Home: 6-1. Away: 9-1.

### 1949 (5-5-1) Head Coach Buddy Parker (5 games); Head Coach Phil Handler (7 games)

| | | | |
|---|---|---|---|
| Sept. 26 | Washington Redskins | 38-7 | 24,136 |
| Oct. 2 | Chicago Bears | 7-17 | 52,867 |
| Oct. 8 | At Philadelphia Eagles | 3-28 | 34,576 |
| Oct. 16 | At Green Bay Packers | 39-17 | 18,164 |
| Oct. 23 | Detroit Lions | 7-24 | 23,215 |
| Oct. 30 | NY Giants | 38-41 | 21,339 |
| Nov. 6 | At Detroit Lions | 42-19 | 22,479 |
| Nov. 20 | LA Rams | 28-28 | 34,100 |

Nov. 27    Green Bay Packers        41-21    16,787
Dec. 4     At LA Rams               31-27    74,673
Dec. 11    At Chicago Bears         21-52    50,101
Home: 2-3-1. Away: 4-2.

## 1950 (5-7)  Head Coach Earl "Curly" Lambeau

Sept. 24   Philadelphia Eagles       7-45    24,914
Oct. 2     Baltimore Colts          53-13    14,439
Oct. 8     At Chicago Bears          6-27    48,025
Oct. 15    At Cleveland Browns      24-34    33,774
Oct. 22    At Washington Redskins   38-28    27,856
Oct. 29    NY Giants                17-3     23,964
Nov. 5     Cleveland Browns          7-10    38,456
Nov. 12    At NY Giants             21-51    22,380
Nov. 19    At Philadelphia Eagles   14-10    28,368
Nov. 23    Pittsburgh Steelers      17-28    11,622
Dec. 3     Chicago Bears            20-10    31,919
Dec. 10    At Pittsburgh Steelers    7-28    18,301
Home: 3-3 Away: 2-4

## 1951 (3-9)  Head Coach Earl "Curly" Lambeau

Sept. 30   Philadelphia Eagles      14-17    16,129
Oct. 7     Chicago Bears            28-14    33,781
Oct. 14    At NY Giants             17-28    28,095
Oct. 21    At Washington Redskins    3-7     22,960
Oct. 28    Pittsburgh Steelers      14-28    14,773
Nov. 4     Cleveland Browns         17-34    19,742
Nov. 11    At LA Rams               21-45    29,996
Nov. 18    At San Francisco 49ers   27-21    19,658
Nov. 25    NY Giants                 0-10    11,892
Dec. 2     At Cleveland Browns      28-49    30,550
Dec. 9     Washington Redskins      17-20     9,459
Dec. 16    At Chicago Bears         24-14    15,085
Home: 1-5. Away: 2-4.

## 1952 (4-8)  Head Coach Joe Kuharich

Sept. 29   Washington Redskins       7-23    17,837
Oct. 5     Chicago Bears            21-10    34,697
Oct. 12    At Washington Redskins   17-6     24,600
Oct. 19    At NY Giants             24-23    41,182
Oct. 26    Pittsburgh Steelers      28-34    20,395
Nov. 2     NY Giants                 6-28    27,195
Nov. 9     At Cleveland Browns      13-28    34,097
Nov. 16    At Philadelphia Eagles    7-10    18,908
Nov. 23    At Pittsburgh Steelers   14-17    — —
Nov. 30    Philadelphia Eagles      28-22    13,577
Dec. 7     Cleveland Browns          0-10    24,541
Dec. 14    At Chicago Bears          7-10    32,578
Home: 2-4. Away: 2-4.

## 1953 (1-10-1)  Head Coach Joe Stydahar

Sept. 27   Washington Redskins      13-24    16,055
Oct. 4     Cleveland Browns          7-27    24,374
Oct. 11    At Pittsburgh Steelers   28-31    25,935
Oct. 18    At NY Giants              7-21    30,301

Oct. 25    Philadelphia Eagles      17-56    22,064
Nov. 1     NY Giants                20-23    17,499
Nov. 8     At Washington Redskins   17-28    — —
Nov. 15    LA Rams                  24-24    26,674
Nov. 21    At Philadelphia Eagles    0-38    19,402
Nov. 29    At Cleveland Browns      16-27    24,499
Dec. 6     Pittsburgh Steelers      17-21    — —
Dec. 13    At Chicago Bears         24-17    38,059
Home: 0-5-1. Away: 1-5.

## 1954 (2-10)  Head Coach Joe Stydahar

Sept. 26   NY Giants                10-41    16,780
Oct. 3     Philadelphia Eagles      16-35    17,084
Oct. 10    At Cleveland Browns       7-31    24,101
Oct. 17    At NY Giants             17-31    31,256
Oct. 24    Cleveland Browns          3-35    23,823
Oct. 31    Pittsburgh Steelers      17-14    18,765
Nov. 7     At Philadelphia Eagles   14-30    21,963
Nov. 14    At LA Rams               17-28    40,739
Nov. 21    Washington Redskins      38-16    15,619
Nov. 28    At Pittsburgh Steelers   17-20    14,460
Dec. 5     Chicago Bears             7-29    33,594
Dec. 12    At Washington Redskins   20-37    18,107
Home: 2-4. Away: 0-6.

## 1955 (4-7-1)  Head Coach Ray Richards

Sept. 26   At Pittsburgh Steelers    7-14    26,359
Oct. 2     NY Giants                28-17     9,555
Oct. 9     At Washington Redskins   24-10    26,337
Oct. 16    At NY Giants              0-10     7,000
Oct. 23    Philadelphia Eagles      24-24    24,620
Oct. 30    Cleveland Browns         20-26    29,471
Nov. 5     Pittsburgh Steelers      27-13    23,310
Nov. 13    At Green Bay             14-31    20,104
Nov. 20    Washington Redskins       0-31    16,901
Nov. 27    Chicago Bears            53-14    47,314
Dec. 4     At Philadelphia Eagles    3-27    19,378
Dec. 11    At Cleveland Browns      24-35    25,914
Home: 3-2-1. Away: 1-5.

## 1956 (7-5)  Head Coach Ray Richards

Sept. 30   Cleveland Browns          9-7     20,966
Oct. 7     NY Giants                35-27    21,799
Oct. 14    At Washington Redskins   31-3     25,794
Oct. 21    At Philadelphia Eagles   20-6     36,545
Oct. 28    Washington Redskins      14-17    30,533
Nov. 4     Philadelphia Eagles      28-17    27,609
Nov. 11    At NY Giants             10-23    62,410
Nov. 18    At Pittsburgh Steelers    7-14    24,086
Nov. 25    Pittsburgh Steelers      38-27    17,724
Dec. 2     Green Bay                21-24    22,620
Dec. 9     At Chicago Bears          3-10    48,606
Dec. 16    At Cleveland Browns      24-7     25,312
Home: 4-2. Away: 3-3.

## 1957 (3-9)  Head Coach Ray Richards

Sept. 29   At San Francisco 49ers   20-10    35,743

| Oct. 6 | Washington Redskins | 14-37 | 18,278 |
| Oct. 13 | At Pittsburgh Steelers | 20-29 | 29,446 |
| Oct. 20 | At Washington Redskins | 44-14 | 23,159 |
| Oct. 27 | Cleveland Browns | 7-17 | 26,341 |
| Nov. 3 | Philadelphia Eagles | 21-38 | 18,718 |
| Nov. 10 | At NY Giants | 14-27 | 46,402 |
| Nov. 24 | NY Giants | 21-28 | 19,200 |
| Dec. 1 | At Cleveland Browns | 0-31 | 40,525 |
| Dec. 8 | Chicago Bears | 6-14 | 43,735 |
| Dec. 15 | At Philadelphia Eagles | 31-27 | 12,555 |
| Dec. 22 | Pittsburgh Steelers | 2-27 | 10,084 |

Home: 0-6. Away: 3-3

### 1958 (2-9-1) Head Coach Frank "Pop" Ivy

| Sept. 28 | At NY Giants | | |
| | (Buffalo, NY) | 7-37 | —— |
| Oct. 4 | Washington Redskins | 37-10 | 21,824 |
| Oct. 12 | At Cleveland Browns | 28-35 | 65,403 |
| Oct. 19 | At NY Giants | 23-6 | 52,684 |
| Oct. 26 | Cleveland Browns | 24-38 | 30,933 |
| Nov. 2 | Philadelphia Eagles | 21-21 | 17,486 |
| Nov. 9 | At Washington Redskins | 31-45 | 26,196 |
| Nov. 16 | At Philadelphia Eagles | 21-49 | 18,315 |
| Nov. 23 | Pittsburgh Steelers | 20-27 | 15,946 |
| Nov. 30 | LA Rams | 14-20 | 13,014 |
| Dec. 7 | At Chicago Bears | 14-30 | 41,617 |
| Dec. 13 | At Pittsburgh Steelers | 21-38 | 16,660 |

Home: 1-3-1. Away: 1-6

### 1959 (2-10) Head Coach Frank "Pop" Ivy

| Sept. 27 | Washington Redskins | 49-21 | 21,892 |
| Oct. 4 | Cleveland Browns | 7-34 | 19,935 |
| Oct. 11 | At Washington Redskins | 14-23 | 25,937 |
| Oct. 18 | At Cleveland Browns | 7-17 | 46,422 |
| Oct. 25 | Philadelphia Eagles | | |
| | (Minneapolis, MN) | 24-48 | 20,112 |
| Nov. 1 | Pittsburgh Steelers | 45-24 | 23,187 |
| Nov. 8 | At NY Giants | 3-9 | 56,779 |
| Nov. 15 | At Philadelphia Eagles | 17-27 | 28,887 |
| Nov. 22 | NY Giants | | |
| | (Minneapolis, MN) | 20-30 | 26,625 |
| Nov. 29 | Chicago Bears | 7-31 | 48,687 |
| Dec. 6 | At Detroit Lions | 21-45 | 45,811 |
| Dec. 13 | At Pittsburgh Steelers | 20-35 | 19,011 |

Home: 2-2. Home (Neutral),: 0-2. Away: 0-6
NOTE: Four Cardinal home games played at
Chicago's Soldier Field, two at Metropolitan
Stadium in Minneapolis

# Bibliography

## BOOKS/MAGAZINES

Anderson, Heartley with Emil Klosinski. *Notre Dame, Chicago Bears, and "Hunk": Football Memoirs in Highlight.* Oviedo, Florida: Sun-Gator Publishing Co., 1976.

*Arizona Cardinals 1998 Media Guide,* edited by Paul Jensen and Greg Gladysiewski.

Claassen, Harold. *The History of Professional Football.* Englewood Cliffs, New Jersey: Prentice-Hall, 1963.

Connor, Jack. *Leahy's Lads: The Story of the Famous Notre Dame Football Teams of the 1940s.* South Bend: Diamond Communications, Inc., 1994.

Cope, Myron. *The Game That Was: The Early Days of Pro Football.* Cleveland: World Publishing Co., 1970.

Curran, Bob. *Pro Football's Rag Days.* Englewood Cliffs, New Jersey: Prentice-Hall, 1969.

Danzig, Allison. *Oh, How They Played the Game: The Early Days of Football and the Heroes Who Made It Great.* New York: Macmillan, 1971.

Einstein, Charles. "Jolly Good Fellows." *Football Digest,* November, 1948.

Grange, Harold "Red". *The Red Grange Story.* Urbana: University of Illinois Press, 1993.

Halas, George S. Halas. *An Autobiography.* Chicago: Bonus Books, 1986.

Harris, David. *The League: The Rise and Decline of the NFL.* New York: Bantam Books, 1986.

Hirshberg, Al. *Glory Runners.* New York: G. P. Putnam, 1968.

Jablonsky, Thomas J. *Pride in the Jungle. Community and Everyday Life in Back of Yards Chicago.* Baltimore: John Hopkins University Press, 1993.

Klosinski, Emil. *Pro Football in the Days of Rockne.* New York: Carlton Press, 1970.

Knox, Donald. *Death March: The Survivors of Bataan.* New York: Harcourt Brace Jovanovich, 1981.

Kobler, John. *Capone. The Life and World of Al Capone.* New York: G. P. Putnam's Sons, 1971.

Lester, Robin. *Stagg's University.* Urbana: University of Illinois Press, 1995.

Leuthner, Stuart. *Iron Men: Bronko, Crazylegs, and the Boys Recall the Golden Days of Professional Football.* Garden City, New York: Doubleday, 1988.

MacNamara, Harry. "The Chicago Cardinals." *Sport Magazine,* January, 1955.

March, Harry A. *Pro Football: Its "Ups" and "Downs".* Albany: Lyon, 1939.

Neft, David S. and Richard Cohen. *The Football Encyclopedia.* New York: St. Martin's Press, 1991.

*1979 NFC Championship Game Program*

*1946 NFL Record and Roster Manual*

Oriard, Michael. *Reading Football.* Chapel Hill: The University of North Carolina Press, 1993.

Perrin, Tom. *Football, A College History.* Jefferson, North Carolina: McFarland & Company, Inc., 1987.

Pruter, Robert. "Yesterday's City. Glory on the Gridiron." *Chicago History,* Fall, 1995.

Riess, Steven A. *The Evolution of an Urban Society and the Rise of Sports.* Urbana: University of Illinois Press, 1989.

Riess, Steven A. "A Social Profile of the Professional Football Player, 1920-82." *The Business of Professional Sports,* edited by Paul D. Staudohar and James A. Mangan. Urbana: University of Illinois Press, 1991.

Roberts, Howard. *The Story of Pro Football.* New York: Rand McNally & Company, 1953.

Roosevelt, Theodore. "The Value of Athletic Training." *Harper's Weekly,* December 23, 1893.

Sinclair, Upton. *The Jungle.* Urbana: University of Illinois Press, 1988.

"Spalding's Official Football Guide." Several issues of this annual publication were reviewed.

Todd, Arthur et al. *The Chicago Recreation Survey 1937.* Chicago: Chicago Recreation Commission and Northwestern University, 1938.

Treat, Roger. *The Encyclopedia of Football.* New York: A. S. Barnes and Company, 1977.

Utley, Robert M. *Frontier Regulars: The United States Army and the Indian,* 1866-1891. Lincoln: University of Nebraska Press, 1973.

Whitman, John W. *Bataan: Our Last Ditch.* New York: Hippocrene Books, Inc., 1990.

Whittingham, Richard. *What a Game They Played: Stories of the Early Days of Pro Football By Those Who Were There.* New York: Harper & Row, 1984.

## NEWSPAPERS

*Akron Beacon*

*Boston Daily Record*

*Boston Post*

*Canton (OH) Evening Depository*

*Chicago Daily News*

*Chicago Evening American*

*Chicago Evening Post*

*Chicago Herald Examiner*

*Chicago Journal*

*Chicago South Side Daily Sun*

*Chicago Tribune*

*Detroit News*

*Elgin (IL) Courier News*

*Elgin (IL) Daily News*

*Grand Rapids (MI) Herald*

*Green Bay (WI) Gazette*

*Green Valley (AZ) News and Sun*

*Hammond (IN) Times*

*Honolulu Advertiser*

*Houston Chronicle*

*La Crosse (WI) Tribune and Leader-Press*

*Maywood (IL) Herald*

*Memphis Evening Appeal*

*Michigan City (IN) Evening Dispatch*

*Michigan City (IN) Evening News*

*Milwaukee Journal*

*New York Daily Mirror*

*New York Daily News*

*New York Journal*

*New York Times*

*New York World Telegram and Sun*

*Philadelphia Daily News*

*Philadelphia Evening Bulletin*

*Philadelphia Record*

*Phoenix Gazette*

*Pittsburgh Gazette*

*Providence Sunday Journal*

*Rock Island (IL) Argus*

*San Francisco Chronicle*

*San Francisco Examiner*

*San Francisco News*

*Southtown Economist (Chicago)*

*St. Louis Post-Dispatch*

*Washington News*

*Washington Post*

*Washington Times-Herald*

*Waukesha (WI) Daily Freeman*

*Woodstock (IL) Sentinel*